The Poetry of the Americas

Modernist Literature & Culture

Kevin J. H. Dettmar & Mark Wollaeger, Series Editors

The Poetry of the Americas

*From Good Neighbors
to Countercultures*

Harris Feinsod

OXFORD
UNIVERSITY PRESS

OXFORD
UNIVERSITY PRESS

Oxford University Press is a department of the University of Oxford. It furthers
the University's objective of excellence in research, scholarship, and education
by publishing worldwide. Oxford is a registered trade mark of Oxford University
Press in the UK and certain other countries.

Published in the United States of America by Oxford University Press
198 Madison Avenue, New York, NY 10016, United States of America.

© Oxford University Press 2017

Library of Congress Cataloging-in-Publication Data
Names: Feinsod, Harris, author.
Title: The poetry of the Americas : from good neighbors to countercultures /
Harris Feinsod.
Description: New York : Oxford University Press, 2017. |
Series: Modernist literature and culture | Includes bibliographical references and index.
Identifiers: LCCN 2017006327 (print) | LCCN 2017025178 (ebook) |
ISBN 9780190682019 (updf) | ISBN 9780190682026 (epub) |
ISBN 9780190682002 (hardback)
Subjects: LCSH: American poetry—20th century—History and criticism. |
Latin American poetry—20th century—History and criticism. |
Comparative literature—American and Latin American. |
Comparative literature—Latin American and American. |
American literature—Appreciation—Latin America. |
Latin American literature—Appreciation—United States. |
United States—Foreign relations—Latin America. |
Latin America—Foreign relations—United States. |
BISAC: LITERARY CRITICISM / Poetry.
Classification: LCC PS323.5 (ebook) | LCC PS323.5 .F45 2017 (print) |
DDC 811/.509—dc23
LC record available at https://lccn.loc.gov/2017006327

9 8 7 6 5 4 3 2 1
Printed by Sheridan Books, Inc., United States of America

To the memory of Marlene JaRo (1953–2012)

Contents

Illustrations

Series Editors' Foreword

Harris Feinsod's *The Poetry of the Americas* offers a deft and dauntingly comprehensive study of the public life of poems that contributes to multiple fields: comparative modernisms, Latin American studies, twentieth-century American literature, comparative literature, literary relations along the global axis of North and South, the history of poetic forms, cultural diplomacy and the cultural Cold War, and intersections between historicism and formalism. That this list is not exhaustive indicates the ambition of Feinsod's book, which takes in a larger and more diverse selection of poets and poems than one might expect to see even in a project devoted to the recovery of hitherto occluded patterns of literary affinity. Feinsod marshals this multitude within an overarching narrative of an emergent ideal of hemispheric poetic interrelation grounded not only in supporting institutions (state-sponsored, private, and collaborative), literary conferences, anthologies, and friendships, but also (and crucially) in poetic form. Efforts to achieve a "poetry of the Americas"—as well as various forms of resistance to such a thing— is the master story that holds together the many stories that Feinsod tells here.

For *The Poetry of the Americas* is essentially an achievement of storytelling. Isis-like, Feinsod has combed through scattered archives, gathering from "unpublished author's files, biographical anecdotes and ephemeral correspondence, visual poems traced on the backs of postcards, degraded tape reels, bureaucratic dossiers, samizdat pamphlets, faded or microfilmed newsprint, and 'minor' poems in the small runs of the poetry collections," in order to piece together the lost body of a history of Pan-American imaginings. This is not to say that Feinsod's historical reconstruction presupposes an organic wholeness; there's a coherence to the *idea* of overcoming the historical divide of "two Americas," but it assumes literary and social form unevenly, intermittently, diversely. Feinsod sketches three broad phases in this history. Antifascist struggles in World War II produced a kind of hemispheric solidarity in which poets looked up to different flags even as they participated in forms of diplomatic rapprochement; but the Cold War encouraged forms of insularity that turned poets back to largely symbolic expressions designed to sustain the creative diplomatic energies of the Good Neighbor era; in the sixties, countercultural poets regathered in renewed efforts of hemispheric integration.

With these broad historical contours, Feinsod pays close attention to the ways in which poetic form helps turn poems into acts of diplomacy. Emphasis thus falls on the worldliness of poems, but more specifically on formal techniques that enmesh poems in shifting crosscurrents of hemispheric power. Exemplary here are Feinsod's virtuoso close readings of how sound patterns in Elizabeth Bishop's *Questions of Travel* reveal the dispersed presence of anticommunist tendencies within what are typically considered the progressive coordinates of her poetry. With bold claims buttressed by subtle readings, this discussion also highlights Feinsod's refusal of what has been called the "fetishism of the covert" in studies of cultural diplomacy: organizations such as the Office of the Coordinator of Inter-American Affairs sponsored many writers and artists at the dawn of the Cold War, as has been well documented in recent years, but sponsorship did not necessarily determine the views and practices of the sponsored. Feinsod carefully historicizes the interplay of individual agency and institutional influence as it is expressed in the wide range of instances he considers.

And, again, that range: Bishop of course shares space in Chapter 5 with Robert Lowell, whose well-known misadventures in cultural diplomacy (drunk, naked, and seated on an equestrian statue in Buenos Aires) are subordinated here to his complicated textual engagements with Latin America in *For the Union Dead*, but the chapter also takes in Derek Walcott, whose trope of the gulf reproduces some of the anticommunism found in Bishop, and Heberto Padilla, who was imprisoned in 1971 by the Castro government. This comparative dimension structures every chapter. Feinsod largely follows the interpretive protocol that says poems are best studied in relation to one another, and for this book these relations are always hemispheric, bringing together poems by, among others, Jorge Carrera Andrade and Hart Crane and by Pablo Neruda and Julia de Burgos (Chapter 1), by Wallace Stevens and José Lezama Lima (Chapter 2), by Allen Ginsberg, Lawrence Ferlinghetti, Philip Lamantia, and Ernesto Cardenal (Chapter 3) ... you get the idea. This heady mixture of familiar and unfamiliar, canonical and non-, is organized both by the unfolding story of hemispheric interrelation and by fresh matters of form pertinent to each poetic constellation, from culturally specific repurposings of lyric subjectivity and strategic use of multilingual writing to collaborative writing, hoax translations, and figural and auditory modes of intercultural address. Breadth of coverage is thus doubled by analytic depth, the moving panorama (or pantoscope) by granular detail in moments of analytic arrest.

We have told here a mini-story about the complex weave of stories Feinsod brings together in *The Poetry of the Americas*. We expect that a diverse range of readers will seize on an equally diverse array of insights offered in this book. So rather than highlight one more, such as the revelation that Ginsberg's "Howl" draws on what Feinsod describes as the midcentury genre of the meditation on ruins, we'll end here, admiring how Rockland looks through the lens of Chichén Itzá.

Mark Wollaeger and
Kevin J. H. Dettmar

Acknowledgments

I first conceived the idea of a book about the poetry of the hemispheric Americas at Stanford University under the guidance of Roland Greene, and his many years of patient mentorship and warm friendship have left the largest marks on it. Nick Jenkins has been a likewise imaginative interlocutor, encouraging and challenging in just the right combination. At Stanford, I was also fortunate to learn from Robert Harrison, Ursula Heise, Héctor Hoyos, Seth Lerer, Michael Predmore, Ramón Saldívar, and Hayden White. The brilliant camaraderie of Mike Benveniste, Allison Carruth, Marisa Galvez, Heather Houser, Ju Yon Kim, David Marno, and Claire Seiler has extended long past our time together in the Bay Area. Joe Shapiro in particular has inspired my thinking at every turn since 2001.

At Northwestern University, Susannah Gottlieb has offered her support in too many ways to name. For an uncommonly hospitable scholarly atmosphere, I thank the English Department as a whole. I've been especially grateful for accommodation from chairpersons in English and Comparative Literary Studies: Christopher Bush, Susannah Gottlieb, Christopher Herbert, Susan Manning, and Laurie Shannon. Nick Davis, Brian Edwards, Reg Gibbons, and Susan Manning have each been exceptionally encouraging at many junctures. For their distinct forms of amity as readers or in conversation, I also thank Kate Baldwin, César Braga-Pinto, Katy Breen, Jorge Coronado, Jay Grossman, Kasey Evans, Hannah Feldman, Jim Hodge, John Keene, Jules Law, Jeff Masten, Shaundra Myers, Susie Philips, Ed Roberson, Carl Smith, Julia Stern, Wendy Wall, Will West, Ivy Wilson, and Kelly Wisecup. For additional dimensions of friendship and sustenance I thank Nathalie Bouzaglo, Corey Byrnes, Emily Maguire, Patrick Noonan, Emily Rohrbach, and Tristram Wolff. Andrew

Leong and Nasser Mufti commented on large sections of the manuscript and spent hours in generous and ongoing conversations that I cherish. Alejandra Uslenghi's unfalteringly good advice is a wonder. Rebecca Johnson's range of insights, energies, and understanding has buoyed me. And John Alba Cutler's collaboration, criticism, and good cheer under every conceivable circumstance deserve special mention. The book likewise benefited from countless talks with Rachel Galvin, from the resourceful response of the Chicagoland Junior Faculty Writing Group, and from the feedback of Adrienne Brown, Leah Feldman, Edgar Garcia, Julie Orlemanski, David C. Simon, Chris Taylor, Zach Samalin, and Sonali Thakkar.

As I wrote, Northwestern graduate students in the Poetry and Poetics Colloquium created a terrific climate for poetry scholarship. I thank in particular Ira Murfin, Alanna Hickey, Toby Altman, Todd Nordgren, and Patricia Anzini. My research assistants over the years—Ezra Olson, Bryce O'Tierney, Sofía Rivera Sojo, and Elissa Rothman—have all become trusted interlocutors. Andrew Hungate and Maria Dikcis each made key contributions at a late stage. Jennifer Britton, Kathy Daniels, Dave Kuzel, and Nathan Mead made logistics easy.

Audiences at ACLA, MLA, MSA, Post45, Johns Hopkins University, Wake Forest University, and University of Illinois at Chicago all responded to work in progress. I am grateful for invitations to share work from Sunil Agnani, Patricia Dixon, Loren Glass, Christopher Nealon, and Yopie Prins, and for encouraging conversations in the wings with Jeremy Braddock, Natalia Cecire, Deborah Cohn, Pete Coviello, Claire Fox, Andrew Goldstone, Omaar Hena, Virginia Jackson, Peter Kalliney, Tom McEnaney, Urayoán Noel, Siobhan Phillips, Sonya Posmentier, Lytle Shaw, Harry Stecopoulos, and Irene Yoon. I owe special thanks to Michelle Clayton and María del Pilar Blanco for their diverse forms of support.

Writing fellowships gave me crucial time to work, and the nourishment of diverse communities. Thanks to Michael Schafer for the Ric Weiland Graduate Fellowship, and to Frances and Theodore Geballe for the Geballe Prize Dissertation Fellowship at The Stanford Humanities Center. At the SHC I benefited from conversations with Gavin Jones, Heather Love, Karen Sánchez-Eppler, and Scott Saul. I completed the manuscript under the auspices of the Early Career Fellowship at the University of Pittsburgh Humanities Center, where Jonathan Arac has given shape to a terrific intellectual community. Also in Pittsburgh, Gayle Rogers made me at home and read portions of the book with uncommon depth of insight, and Greg Barnhisel offered crucial suggestions. I enjoyed especially wide-ranging conversations with Jennifer Josten, as well as Dan Balderston,

Khalil Chaar-Pérez, Brad Fest, Racheal Forlow, Dan Kubis, Joshua Lund, and Imani Owens.

A project of this nature is not possible without the work of librarians, archivists, and technologists. Adán Griego, Annette Keogh, and Bill O'Hanlon of Stanford pointed me to crucial boxes of papers or digitized key reels of tape. Molly Schwartzburg's attentiveness enhanced a Mellon Foundation Research Fellowship at the Harry Ransom Center. Through Northwestern's Arthur Vining Davis Workshop in the Digital Humanities, Curt Bozif, Josh Honn, Sergei Kalugin, and Matt Taylor enabled the creation of the Open Door Archive. Darío Oses, Adriana Valenzuela, Elena Marfull, Javier Ormeño, and Carolina Briones plied me with information and hospitality at the Fundación Pablo Neruda at La Chascona in Santiago de Chile, and I received especially gracious attention from Kristen Nitray of Stony Brook University, Melissa Watterworth Batt of UConn, Dean Rogers of Vassar, and Rob Melton at UCSD's Archive for New Poetry.

Cotten Seiler and Lena Burgos La Fuente gave some of the ideas here early audiences. A few pages of the introduction spring from "The Era of Inter-American Cultural Diplomacy," *American Quarterly* 66.4 (2014): 1129–1141, and a small section of Chapter One has been revised from "Between Dissidence and Good Neighbor Diplomacy: Reading Julia de Burgos with the FBI," *Centro: Journal of the Center for Puerto Rican Studies* 26.2 (2014): 98–127. Two reviewers for Oxford University Press offered suggestions that greatly improved the manuscript. The impact of Mark Wollaeger's editorial interest in the book cannot be overstated, nor can his role, alongside Kevin Dettmar, in forging a vibrant forum for argument on the legacies and futures of modernist literature and culture. Thanks equally to my able editor, Sarah Pirovitz, and to Stephen Dodson, who brought surplus erudition to his work as copyeditor. Northwestern University's Alice Kaplan Institute for the Humanities made available a generous permissions subvention.

At Brown University in 2003, the late Robert Creeley first opened a line of inquiry that led to this book, as did a course taught by Susan Bernstein and Forrest Gander. Susan Stewart and Marjorie Perloff offered warmhearted and challenging advice at early stages. Later, Clayton Eshleman, Linda Oppen, Nathaniel Tarn, and Cecilia Vicuña graciously shared their memories or their personal archives. Shortly before his death, Hilary Putnam went out of his way to ply me with information about his father Samuel Putnam. Carlos T. Blackburn first introduced me to *The New American Poetry* two decades ago and spent hours on the phone talking about Paul Blackburn. Margaret Randall has been a remarkably patient storehouse of memories, a committed correspondent, and a kind friend. Her six decades of underacknowledged commitment to forging a hemispheric literary culture lends this book a tutelary spirit.

Finally, I owe everything to the support of family: Bernard Feinsod and Joseph Feinsod, Walter and Lois Licht, and (adoptively) Eliot Ballard, Dane Cho, Sean Hallowell, Michal Kapitulnick, Lizzy Klein, Mike Metzger, Gabe Milner, and Lealah Pollock. Thanks most of all to Emily Licht for more than a dozen years of unqualified and bottomless love, her endless patience for the strum of ideas, her company across the Americas, and her clutch reminder that a Martin 16 Series was the wrong instrument on which to compose the book's final chapter.

Abbreviations

CUL	Butler Rare Book and Manuscript Library, Columbia University Library
EU	Stuart A. Rose Manuscript, Archives, and Rare Book Library, Emory University
FPN	Archivo Fundación Pablo Neruda, Santiago de Chile
HRC	Harry Ransom Center, University of Texas at Austin
HU	Houghton Library, Harvard University
IACF	International Association for Cultural Freedom Records, University of Chicago Special Collections
NLC	Newberry Library, Chicago
PENN	Kislak Center for Special Collections, Rare Books and Manuscripts, Penn Libraries
PUL	Princeton University Library Department of Rare Books and Special Collections
RUL	Special Collections and University Archives, Rutgers University Libraries
SIUC	Special Collections Research Center, Southern Illinois University Carbondale
SBUL	Stony Brook University Libraries
SUL	Department of Special Collections, Stanford University Libraries
TLOU	Taylorian Library, Oxford University
UCB	The Bancroft Library, University of California Berkeley

UCSD	Mandeville Special Collections Library, University of California San Diego
UCON	University of Connecticut Special Collections
VUL	Vassar University Library
YALE	Yale Collection of American Literature, Beinecke Rare Book and Manuscript Library

A Note on the Text

Except where otherwise noted, all translations are my own. I have elected not to italicize non-English-language text, unless it appears italicized in quoted text.

Introduction

Hazarding the Poetry of the Americas

In 1891, when exiled Cuban revolutionary José Martí published *Versos Sencillos* in New York, he prefaced his modernista poetry collection with an origin story. According to this story, his "simple verses" consoled his disappointment at the rise of a coercive hemispheric political system, which he had witnessed first-hand as a diplomat and journalist at the Pan-American Congress in 1889–1890.[1] As he wrote: "My friends know how these verses came from my heart. It was in that winter of despair, when [out of] ignorance, or fanatical faith, or fear, or courtesy, the Latin American nations met in Washington, under the terrible eagle."[2] Agonized by the likely futures of nations that, to his eyes, had rushed blindly into a hemispheric system newly defined by the exercise of US hegemony, Martí linked the writing of his poems to a convalescence in the Catskills in the summer of 1890: "The doctor sent me off to the mountains: there streams ran, the clouds closed in, and I wrote poetry." Martí's lyric posture as the "hombre sincero" (honest man) from the land of the palm, who casts into the world the truth of his "alma" (soul), doubled as a condemnation of what he saw as the false, transitory idealism of Washington's new Pan-Americanism. In his most famous essay, "Nuestra América," published the same year, Martí in passing clarified a vision for a poetry of the Americas, advocating for "la unión tácita y urgente del alma continental" (unsaid, urgent union of the continental soul) and a new "himno unánime" (unanimous hymn).[3] In one respect, Martí's poetry occupies a deeply conventional lyric stance that has been assumed by many poets, one that is defined by a retreat from the sociopolitical organization of the world into an untrammeled landscape and language of spiritual value.[4] But in another respect, Martí invests this stance with a new and particular tension between an incipient poetry of the Americas and the inequities of the inter-American political system.

This book argues that the idea of a poetry of the Americas subsequently motivated a great many poems and poets of both the United States and Latin America, cohering resiliently across the twentieth century, despite how frequently efforts toward a robust cultural hemispherism were scuttled by patterns of US intervention and imperial expansion after the Spanish-American War of 1898.[5] Often, forms of hemispheric identification overrode understandings of poetry's monolingual and national characteristics that were common then and remain so now.[6] I propose that the poetry of the Americas coevolved with the modern inter-American political system, driven in many instances by networks and institutions of hemispheric exchange, and in others by structural forces that link isolated poetic activities through the retrospective gaze of transnational literary history. We hear versions and inversions of Martí's continental hymn in the hemispheric desire that Pablo Neruda called "amor americano" in his vast chronicle *Canto General* (1950), and in the sonorous "fluent mundo"—a symbolic world of American globalization—that Wallace Stevens named in "Notes Toward a Supreme Fiction" (1942).[7] Each of these epithets is at once an expression of geopolitical desire, a vision of an alternate world order, and the manifestation of a network of writers and institutions that stand behind poems like these. They are bound together in no small measure by practices that, in the late 1930s, came to be known as "creative diplomacy" or "cultural diplomacy."[8] *The Poetry of the Americas: From Good Neighbors to Countercultures* is about the poems of this era, the documentary history that envelops them, and the hemispheric perspectives developed between these two corpora.

Of course, at least as early as the Bolivarian national independence movements, writers had posited varieties of relation between the politics and poetry of the Americas. A tradition of Latin American scholarship highlights the ongoing role of "letrados" (men of letters) in the political work of urban planning and nation building, but also international commerce and modern geopolitics.[9] Relatedly, scholars of hemispheric American studies variously define a nineteenth-century hemispheric literary public sphere comprised of lettered creole elites, as well as a Pan-American cultural era with accordion-like period boundaries from 1890 to World War I, from 1910 to 1941, or from 1898 onward.[10]

This book maintains that the poetry of the Americas, as a self-conscious literary-political project, unmistakably structures many forms of poetic art in the period from 1938 to 1973. From the intensification of the Roosevelt-era Good Neighbor Policy (1938–1945) through the inter-American "drought" of the early Cold War (1945–1959) and into the long decade of countercultural promise following the Cuban revolution (1959–1973), a distinct corpus of poems created new languages of hemispheric cultural membership that often struck writers and readers as more nimble than the cross-national strategies of representation available to other media of cultural interchange, such as the nascent products of the culture industry.[11] Throughout this era of inter-American cultural diplomacy, a significant company of expressive artists and critics, in tandem with politicians and international institutions, took seriously the claim that literary culture formed a basis for inter-American political understanding.

In sundry and sometimes surprising ways, the relation named by Martí touched many of the major modern poets of Spanish America, including Martín Adán (Peru), Julia de Burgos (Puerto Rico), Jorge Luis Borges (Argentina), Jorge Carrera Andrade (Ecuador), Ernesto Cardenal (Nicaragua), Nicolás Guillén (Cuba), José Lezama Lima (Cuba), Gabriela Mistral (Chile), Pablo Neruda (Chile), Heberto Padilla (Cuba), and Octavio Paz (Mexico), as well as the Anglophone Americas, including Elizabeth Bishop, Allen Ginsberg, Langston Hughes, Charles Olson, Wallace Stevens, William Carlos Williams, and Derek Walcott. Even such a partial list encompasses multiple hierarchies of literary prestige and political power. With the exception of Walcott, the Anglophone poets are all of the United States, and all loom large in its canon, while the Spanish-language poets hail from many nations, and include writers that have scarcely been translated as well as figures long assimilated to a "world literature" canon, such as Borges, Neruda, and Paz. Such asymmetries may seem symptomatic of a hemispheric political system characterized by US hegemony, a world literary sphere centered in Paris, or the differential "cosmopolitan desires" of US and Latin American writers, but this book argues that all these writers can be otherwise comprehended by a multidirectional, inter-American history of poetry, alongside scores of poets whose places in national canons are still less secure, and whose achievements gain enhanced legibility within a hemispheric frame.[12] These include figures such as World War II–era soldier-poet Lysander Kemp and the anthologist Dudley Fitts; young poet-translators Paul Blackburn, Clayton Eshleman, Margaret Randall, and Sergio Mondragón (Mexico); and revolutionary guerillero poets such as Javier Heraud (Peru) and Roque Dalton (El Salvador). For many, the activities of writing, reciting, translating, and publishing poetry were imagined as specific acts of cultural diplomacy, in a complex push and pull with coercive apparatuses of state power.

Not many of these names are recorded in the organizational archives of inter-American institutions, or in official histories of inter-American political congresses such as the one published in 1965 by Samuel Guy Inman, a missionary educator and key formulator of Good Neighbor diplomacy's anti-interventionist cultural aims in the Roosevelt era.[13] And yet, like Martí in Washington, DC in 1890, poets often attended inter-American conferences as diplomats or journalists, or else wrote at a distance, contributing to a large archive of poems and commentaries that hoped to shape attitudes toward inter-American statecraft. To formulate a minimal outline, one might think of the Puerto Rican nationalist poet Julia de Burgos's unlikely stretch as an audit clerk at Nelson Rockefeller's Office of the Coordinator of Inter-American Affairs in 1944–1945, of the young liberal Octavio Paz at the founding United Nations proceedings in San Francisco in 1945 as he wrote the poems collected in *Libertad bajo palabra* (1948), of the communist Pablo Neruda aghast at the new wave of authoritarians populating the meeting of the Organization of American States (OAS) in Bogotá in 1948 as he wrote *Canto General* in hiding, and of a distinctly anticommunist Elizabeth Bishop repulsed by Brazil's role in the OAS's Punta del Este conference in 1962 while she continued working on the poems collected in *Questions of Travel* (1965). In their poems, the geopolitical feeling these occasions aroused can take the diverse forms of apostrophic aversion, defiant vituperation, or elaborate acoustical pattern, but these poets share in an effort to make poetic forms into cultural-diplomatic bulwarks against the perceived blunders of political inter-Americanism.

This book gathers together the dispersed archive of literary commentary on the meetings of political inter-Americanism, and overlays it with several related histories, including an elusive history of inter-American literary congresses. This history is best understood as an amnesiac sequence of false "firsts." In 1941, while working as a cultural affairs officer for the US State Department, poet-translator Muna Lee organized the "First Inter-American Writers Congress" in Puerto Rico, which was attended by William Carlos Williams, Luis Palés Matos, Archibald MacLeish, and others.[14] Allen Ginsberg, Lawrence Ferlinghetti, Fernando Alegría, Nicanor Parra, and Gonzalo Rojas likewise thought the "First Encounter of American Writers" that Rojas convened at Concepción de Chile in 1960 was an attempt to break the chilling effects of the Cold War through cultural diplomacy.[15] Just four years later, after Ernesto Cardenal declared the young countercultural poets Randall and Mondragón to represent "la verdadera Unión Panamericana" (the true Pan-American Union) in the pages of their little magazine *El Corno Emplumado,* dozens of young poets flocking to Mexico City also thought they were assembling the "First Gathering of American Poets" as an alternative to the Alliance for Progress.[16] These meetings all prelude the heyday of international poetry congresses in the 1960s, such as Poetry International '67 in London. The amnesiac quality of these "firsts" helps to explain why they have not been read back into collections as varied as Williams's *Paterson* (1946), Ferlinghetti's *Starting from San Francisco* (1961), Ginsberg's *Reality Sandwiches* (1963), Adán's *La mano desasida* (1964), and the collaboratively authored poem *Renga* (1971), orchestrated by Octavio Paz. From the standpoint of literary history, these "firsts" re-emerge forever in their infancy, as if coming to "the new world naked," in Williams's phrase.[17] In thrall to modernism's ideologies of innovation, and sometimes eager to disavow the influence of sponsoring institutions, inheritors of cultural inter-Americanism tended to pulverize older models in the very moments they called new ones to order. Perhaps the resiliency and exuberance of the inter-American conception has been proportional to its fugacity.

If previous literary histories do not render visible the dimensions of a supranational poetry of the Americas, this is partly because canonical poems like Stevens's "Notes Toward a Supreme Fiction" or Neruda's "Alturas de Macchu Picchu" do not tell the whole story. As often, this story is scattered in archives on three continents, tucked in unpublished author's files, biographical anecdotes and ephemeral correspondence, visual poems traced on the backs of postcards, degraded tape reels, bureaucratic dossiers, samizdat pamphlets, faded or microfilmed newsprint, and "minor" poems in the small runs of the poetry collections I began to name above. It crosses conventional period boundaries such as 1945, it lingers in the dazed postwar phase between late and Cold War modernisms, and it reconvenes in successive literary formations, such as the formalist US "middle generation" and its reciprocal tendencies in Latin America and the Caribbean, and the countercultural, neo-avant-garde, and revolutionary works of the 1960s. Assembling this ephemeral, multilingual, aesthetically diverse, trans-generational archive, this book traces cross-national connections that knit poets together in a complex pattern of institutional contexts and anti-institutional formations. The primary institutional context is an era of state sponsorship, from new cultural diplomacy practices in the late 1930s to the "cultural Cold War" of the 1960s. The formations that commingle with it include a growing noncommercial print sphere of small avant-garde magazines, a counterpublic of private correspondents, and a newly viable market for literary translation.

Much of this intercultural traffic was motivated by a century-old idea that there exist "two Americas" (and, among Lusophone, Francophone, creole, and indigenous observers, often three or more). In particular, the dual conception invented by the Colombian letrado José María Torres Caicedo's 1856 poem "Las dos Américas" conditions the very possibility of inter-American literary praxis.[18] The nature of the partition may be conceived as a differentiation of language, race, and other cultural factors; as a fragmentary legacy of colonial violence and racial slavery; as a history of conflicts over political sovereignty and imperial suzerainty; as a problem of geographical and climatological variation, and so on.[19] Each conception raises distinct challenges for what historian Richard Morse calls "the hazards of mending or transcending the north-south breach in 'American' historiography," in order to arrive at a provisional determination of "what America, *latu sensu*, is all about."[20] In this complex terrain of hemispheric imaginings, poets of the Americas have long mustered their available cultural resources in the service of hazarding an inter-American community by adopting social roles central to their concepts of poetic art. Doubling as diplomats, cultural ambassadors, translators, propagandists, scholars, editors, correspondents, amateur archaeologists, tourists, anti-imperialist dissidents, and provocateurs, poets of the Americas authored the protocols of an "inter-American poetics." This aesthetic outcome of geopolitical experience often complicates our understandings of these poets' simultaneous belongings to national literary formations.[21]

But the material recovery of these hemispheric circulations also tells a partial story, for the structure of relations between poets of the Americas and inter-American politics exceeds circulatory and translational routes, textual co-presences, personal friendships, or institutions of cultural diplomacy. Just as often, it is revealed in the very form of verbal art, where it arises as a matter of polygenesis, or proliferates along ambiguous lines of causation, structured by the hemispheric situation in which poetic language transforms imaginings of the Americas from a scene of uneven modernization into a supranational venue of verbal creativity. The chapters of this book each underline a different formal tendency, including cross-cultural uses of poetic address, or how poems call out to others (Chapter 1); artificial strategies of multilingual writing, or "xenoglossia" (Chapter 2); appeals to indigenous heritages through the genre of the "meditation on ruins" (Chapter 3); practices of anthologization and contests over the role of translation (Chapters 1 and 4); an array of figural devices and auditory schemes (Chapter 5); and collaborative writing practices and hoax translations (Chapter 6). Such forms are bound up with the geopolitical horizons of their day, and we miss much if we believe, as did the lion's share of midcentury academic literary criticism, that the lyric utterances of poetic speakers are aesthetically and trans-historically autonomous from a poet's stance toward state boundaries or intercultural belongings. Working to undo a false but persistent opposition between "historicism" and "formalism" as mutually exclusive methodological orientations, this book affirms the consubstantiality of form and history, and it offers reading strategies for braiding the history of form with the form of history.[22] That is, I expose the inter-animations of poetic form and political history—showing, for example, how Neruda's and Olson's poetic figures of pre-Columbian ruins came to allegorize the situation of political inter-Americanism at the start of the Cold War (Chapter 3), or how Bishop's ostensibly ludic sound schemes, in her Brazil poems, serve as vessels for her anticommunist attitudes after the Cuban Revolution (Chapter 5).

I therefore emphasize material and institutional facts of hemispheric commerce, diplomacy, and technological communication, as well as biographical and textual dimensions of literary circulation, while revealing what I describe as a "tropological history" of inter-American relations. I do so through comparative analyses of formal tendencies that link writers who sometimes ignored or even disavowed one another—writers who, in Édouard Glissant's analysis, "at the moment [their language] entered into the poetics of worldwide Relation . . . chose to cover up its expressive relationship with the other."[23] There are determinate reasons for paying linked attention to both historical "institutions" and more nebulous comparative "formations."[24] Inter-American institutional projects such as the Office of the Coordinator for Inter-American Affairs in the early 1940s and the Pan American Union in the early 1960s often sponsored—as well as impelled the critique of—hemispheric poetry. But between these interludes, the cultural insularism and legal regimes of nation-states in the early Cold War twisted transnational literary formations into being that were in several respects consolations for the "drought" itself. In this light, Chapter 2 discusses the use of foreign words in poems by the mutually disavowing Stevens, Lezama, and Borges, to name only one such constellation. To do so, I draw on a quiet tradition of comparative scholarship that understands inter-American poetic formations across periods in non-causal and unlinked ways—what Rachel Price follows the Brazilian poet Augusto de Campos in naming a "*discordia concors*," drawing on Samuel Johnson's metaphysical poetic device.[25] By turns, the poetry of the Americas generates many such tropes of relation and disarticulation for diverse historical occasions.

Put differently, the historical rhythm of inter-Americanism's political and poetic coevolution is neither linear nor progressive: it is full of flashpoints and lacunae, peaks and gullies, false promises and shallow fulfillments. Consider one early moment of false promise. In 1918, Salomón de la Selva, a Nicaraguan poet living in Manhattan, published an issue of a bilingual magazine entitled *Pan American Poetry* as well as a volume of poems in English titled *Tropical Town, and Other Poems*. In "The Dreamer's Heart Knows Its Own Bitterness (A Pan-American Poem on the Entrance of the United States Into the War)," de la Selva postulates "And North and South would hear me sing," offering a conditional *ars poetica* linking the spirit of Pan-American fellowship to demo-cratic solidarities occasioned by global war.[26] For him, lyric address did not particularize the many US modernists (such as Robert Frost, Muna Lee, Vachel Lindsay, Edna St. Vincent Millay, Carl Sandburg, and Sara Teasdale) with whom he associated in and around New York, nor did it isolate Latin American read-ers, including modernistas such as Leopoldo Lugones and José Santos Chocano. Rather, de la Selva imagined a cross-lingual verse for multiple publics joined in diplomatic "fellowship," distributed widely across the geographical expanse of the American hemisphere.[27] Of course, de la Selva could not realize his ambi-tion, for he wrote at a time when the predominantly political and economic determinations of inter-Americanism made little room for the cultural claims he sought to put to their service. After his lack of US citizenship prevented him from enlisting in the American Expeditionary Forces and drove him to fight for the British instead, he returned to Mexico and Nicaragua with a growing conviction in anti-imperialist Latin Americanism, in contrast with his former Pan-American ethos. US military intervention in 1920s Nicaragua strongly colored his conversion. When dozens of poets unknowingly reinvented de la Selva's inter-American rhetoric during World War II (the topic of Chapter 1), his example was wholly forgotten.

Notwithstanding the neglect of de la Selva's conditional inter-Americanism, by the early 1970s the Mexican poet and diplomat Octavio Paz could see so many versions of it on offer that he definitely affirmed something near to de la Selva's position: "despite languages and cultural differences, the Western World has only one modern poetry."[28] From de la Selva's promise to Paz's retrospective certainty, taking seriously the hemispherism of modern poets attenuates the utility of cat-egories such as US, Mexican, or Nicaraguan poetry. It redraws the horizons—of reception and mutual influence, but also of historical and political possibility—against which we read some of the most canonical works of poetic art, even as it valorizes other, noncanonical works. Indeed, it alters our categories of regional differentiation between "American" and "Latin American" poetry, and manifests instead their sustained interrelation in a hemispheric configuration called *the poetry of the Americas*.

The Poetry of the Americas: A Genealogy

As a phrase, *the poetry of the Americas* hardly strains the ear. Its ease carries with it, perhaps, a self-antiquing quality, as if it were already a literary formation with a grand career, and its genitive structure implies, perhaps wrongly, that there might be a natural poetry in the grandness of the hemispheric conception. The history of the phrase, which is linked to 1940s cultural diplomacy initiatives, is in fact more productively contradictory, and requires some denaturing and rescaling of expectations. Certainly, we can suspect contradiction from a phrase that locates a singular yet amorphous literary formation (*poetry*) in a plural cultural-political matrix (*the Americas*). Elites whirring fluidly around increasingly well-connected sea-lanes and skyways sometimes figure this matrix in their poetry as neighborly, navigable, and knowable. Conversely, writers seeking hemispheric solidarity from below may configure it as polycentric and politically fractious. The career of the term *poetry of the Americas* therefore deserves some philological scrutiny, and a considered distinction from nearly cognate terms like *poetry of América* and *inter-American poetics*.

The idea that there exists a poetry and poetics of "América" (to use the accented Spanish word for the unity of hemispheric geography) is an old one. Juan María Gutiérrez's 1846 anthology *América poética* offers an early collection of poets with this continental purchase. Martí wrote that José María Heredia (1803–1839), with his anticolonial leanings and sublime romantic odes encompassing the weave of American nature and culture from Niagara Falls to the Teocalli de Cholula, was "el primer poeta de América."[29] Martí was also the first of countless Latin American poets for whom Walt Whitman's democratic expansiveness evoked hemispheric unity. In the historiography of inter-American poetic influence, surely Whitman cuts the most well-worn pathways, which often go by the names of "Whitmanism" and the "Whitman question."[30] Such Whitmanian pathways struck the Dominican communist Pedro Mir as excessively focused on the manifestation of the poet's own lyric presence, and his "Contracanto a Walt Whitman" (Countersong to Walt Whitman, 1952) rewrote "Song of Myself" in the plural "we" of a laborite collectivity.[31] In another respect, Octavio Paz found Whitmanism too easy a way of conceptualizing the inter-American theme. "The ocean is grand, but it is also monotonous," he wrote of Whitman. "I venerate the ocean but I converse with the rivers, especially the underground rivers" (amongst which he singled out Ezra Pound, Stevens, and Williams).[32] Still, in 1975, Gordon Brotherston wrote briefly but elegantly about a tradition he called "the great song of America," evoking a range of epic texts since the age of revolutions—from

Andrés Bello to Pablo Neruda and from Joel Barlow to Whitman and Charles Olson—that seek moral, geographical, and historical identity in America, and thus respond to "the challenge of writing on a continental scale, of creating a 'poem of America.' "[33] Kirsten Silva Gruesz details a thick nineteenth-century literary history replete with these sublime scalar gestures, and she shifts critical emphasis to forms of encounter and modes of cultural ambassadorship among lettered intellectuals traversing and imagining the hemisphere.[34] In the mid-twentieth century, I argue in Chapter 3, inheritors of the "great song" tradition like Neruda, Cardenal, Olson, and Adán sought to squarely face the disgraces of colonial possession at the root of this discourse.

While Martí's sense of a poetic unity in the phrase "el primer poeta de América" is commonly translated as "first poet of the Americas," the English-language epithet *poet of the Americas* is in fact much newer. Without the fragile acute accent on the *é*, it has rarely been possible and remains difficult to write or speak of a singular *America* in a way that suggests more than the US nation.[35] And so, in place of the unachieved unity of *América*, the pluricultural *Americas* suggest a multifaceted stage for literary history. Together, the translational friction between *América* and *Americas* defines a dialectical relation between unity and differentiation: both an engine and a paradox for a comparative poetics. Yet only the hemispheric democracy movements of World War II, where this book's first chapter begins, gave rise to the designation *poet of the Americas*, just when Good Neighbor diplomacy's multilateral rhetoric took special pains to make vivid the plural sovereignties of the American republics. In those years, as US scholars began to write the first English-language histories of Latin American literature, Rubén Darío was described not only as the "father of modernism" (modernismo), but also as "the poet of the Americas," "recognized in three continents." Unfortunately, the coiners of this sobriquet demeaned the very plurality they sought to evoke when they continued: "Darío was too big to be monopolized by any single country. However, it is probable that the unimportance of his country of origin made it easier for all the Americas to claim—and acclaim—him."[36] This remark is a cautionary reminder that to claim or acclaim the poetry of the Americas could also be a way of extending cultural imperialism, erasing cultural particularity, or overprivileging reception. Nonetheless, if Darío was the definite article (*the* poet of the Americas), others were granted indefinite designations in this new configuration. Archibald MacLeish dedicated a collection of his inter-American radio broadcasts to Muna Lee, bestowing on her the title "A Poet of the Americas," concatenating in this term both her role as poet-translator and her work as a cultural affairs officer for the State Department.[37] Activist and performer Paul Robeson, in 1958, called his friend Pablo Neruda "a great poet of the Americas in our own day," implicitly lending the phrase a new meaning as a term of racial amelioration and geopolitical integration fit to combat the twin impasses of Jim Crow and the global Cold War.[38]

The poetry of the Americas—like contiguous categories such as "the novel of the Americas" or "the literature of the Americas"—is also of Good Neighbor-era vintage. In subsequent years, it appeared in poetry journals of New World surrealism like *Tiger's Eye* (1947), in the 1950s in *Masses and Mainstream*, and in anthologies such as Hortensia Ruiz del Vizo's *Black Poetry of the Americas* (1972) and the Pan American Union's *Young Poetry of the Americas* (1965)—the agency's attempt to draft behind the spirit of countercultural hemispherism promoted by small magazines like *El Corno Emplumado*.[39] Academics studying Latin American literature in the 1960s and 1970s brought the phrase into marginally wider circulation. These dates index a new kind of hemispheric literary thinking particular to the midcentury era of inter-American cultural diplomacy, but let us register here another amnesia around the midcentury idea of the poetry of the Americas. In 2002, Gruesz wrote that hemispheric literary history remained bereft of significant critical works: "the traditional disciplinary model of Goethean *Weltliteratur* . . . has yielded remarkably little fruit in this context."[40] And despite a groundswell in the late 1980s, a pattern of equivocation emerged in titles like Gustavo Pérez Firmat's *Do the Americas Have a Common Literature?* (1990), which alluded to Edmundo O'Gorman's 1939 essay "Do the Americas Have a Common History?" (as it was known in Flores's 1941 translation and Lewis Hanke's 1965 exploration of the theme).[41] Furthermore, serious inter-American accounts of modern poetry mostly lagged behind the post-1990 outpouring in hemispheric and circum-Atlantic literary and cultural studies, as if confirming T.S. Eliot's fleeting claim in 1945 that poetry is the most "stubbornly national" art in the cultural hierarchies of modernity.[42] This book charts an alternative genealogy for a far less stubbornly national poetry of the Americas with clear origins in the debates of World War II's hemispheric democracy campaigns.

In order to stress intra-hemispheric reciprocities in the poetry of the Americas and to signal the variety of forms and discourses through which poets articulate a relation to statecraft, I often refer to an *inter-American poetics*. The prefix *inter-* favors common political designations of the era over a *trans-*American imaginary whose utopian allure may too readily promise to override the residual power of nation-states.[43] *Inter-American poetics* can also be distinguished from frameworks employed by scholars who have previously taken an interest in the hemispherism of modern poetry. Such scholars describe pronounced lines of translational exchange; a "New World poetics" defined by the critical reinvention of shared colonial histories; the "hemispheric poetics" of a vanguard who, triangulated with Paris, burst into a New World Pleiades of experimental canons; and a "transnational poetics" of modernist compression and synthesis that emerged as an ethnonational response to globalization.[44] In these instances, the preference for *poetics* over *poetry* signals a literary-theoretical orientation toward an incomplete, processive, constructivist cultural assemblage. As Charles Bernstein puts it: "I would proclaim, like a Dada Edgar Poe dreaming of Nicolás Guillén doing Google searches, that the poem of the Americas does not exist. For the Americas is an imaginary cultural space whose mutant and multiform manifestations are as evanescent as the last breaths of a dying tongue."[45] Bernstein's caution is more serious than the pose he strikes as a provocateur, but his preference for "poetics" over "poems" or "poetry" might be regarded as a work-around for the messy business of recomposing literary history after a post-national redisciplining of humanistic inquiry. By writing of the *poetry* of the Americas I do not propose to identify a completed process, but to provide a literary-historical purchase on transnational assemblages of writers that sought precisely to fashion imaginings of "the poem of the Americas." Such a purchase shows us how often—and in how many more terms than we commonly concede—modern poets participated in constructive inter-American projects, as well as how disaffiliations from these projects can be read in hemispheric terms.

Thus, even if the poetry of the Americas remains a contested critical category, its retrojection onto a noteworthy corpus of mid-twentieth-century poetic works courts anachronism less than one might suppose. Variations on it inform the criticism of many poet-theorists, editors, and anthologists. Octavio Paz, more than most writers of his era, spent his working career giving critical shape, aesthetic form, and diplomatic commitment to his belief in a singular international modernism. A brief synopsis of this career, highlighting its inter-American inflections, illuminates the stakes of the topic. To Paz's way of thinking, the comparative histories of Anglo-American and Spanish-American poetry were among the most significant tributaries of a global ecumene. His early career was impressed by French cosmopolitanism and then by the expansive internationalism of Spanish loyalism, but a little later, in 1943, he won a Guggenheim grant to study for a year at the University of California, Berkeley on the proposed topic "América and its Poetic Expression."[46] Paz's proposal joined a range of state-funded World War II–era texts that supplied heuristic models of hemispheric literary history, and although he did not complete it, his year in the United States at the war's end reveals his rich sense of relations between the poetry of the Americas and inter-American politics. Paz has been rightly critiqued for his shortsighted analysis of Los Angeles Chicanos in this period, an element of his theory of Mexican national identity, *The Labyrinth of Solitude*. Yet, cumulatively, poems from his time in the United States, such as oneiric descriptions of Latino GIs in California, reflections on comparative lyric nativism in his account of visiting Robert Frost in Vermont, and his several weeks of journalism covering the foundational United Nations conference in San Francisco, reveal a Martí-like preoccupation with the relation between the poet's lyric stance and the problem of geopolitical unity.[47]

Paz's subsequent essays on poetry and poetics—in works such as *El arco y la lira* (The Bow and the Lyre, 1956), *Corriente alterna* (Alternating Current, 1967), *Los hijos del limo* (Children of the Mire, 1974), and the multivolume miscellanies of his *Obras completas*—all present a remarkably broad outline of international modernism in the West. Defined by Paz according to the intensity of its exaggerated, accelerated radical attitudes and programs, it radiates from a francophone center to a "widening of literary space" that came to include Eastern Europe and the Americas and, increasingly, Paz's own encounters with East Asian and South Asian cultural forms.[48] Crucially, in Paz's account this global radiance does not consolidate as a system of Europhilic centers and colonial peripheries. Rather, it creates an ongoing situation of symmetries, resemblances, and oppositions. In particular, Paz was struck by the possibility of reading Anglo-American and Spanish-American replies to European modernism in tandem, as the transmission of European trends awakened drowsy literary scenes in London and Madrid (through William Butler Yeats and Juan Ramón Jiménez) and then in Buenos Aires, Santiago, Lima, Mexico City, Havana, greater New York, and Chicago. For Paz, the cosmopolitanisms of Ezra Pound and Vicente Huidobro in the 1910s could thus be understood as inverse responses to the French avant-garde, while the New World Americanisms emerging with William Carlos Williams and César Vallejo in the 1920s were structured as cognate negations of European influence. None of Paz's proliferating comparisons were meant to be exhaustive. As he wrote in his Charles Eliot Norton Lectures at Harvard University, "I have given these examples not to propose a linear idea of literary history but rather to emphasize its complexity and its transnational character. A literature is a language existing not in isolation but in constant relation with other languages, other literatures."[49]

It is worth emphasizing how much Paz's Norton Lectures took pains to decenter an Anglocentric narrative of the rise of modern poetry. His dazzling contrapuntal readings of the international avant-gardes unambiguously declare that diverse traditions ultimately comprise a singular poetry of the Western world, and they predate any serious institutional rearrangement of a "global modernist" canon by thirty years. Paz's *Los hijos del limo* therefore offers a striking alternative to other Eurocentric theorizations of international modernism, from Hugo Friedrich's *The Structure of Modern Poetry* (1974) to Fredric Jameson's *A Singular Modernity* (2002). Mark Wollaeger's introduction to "global modernism" goes some of the way to validating the sequence of resemblances Paz illuminates. He writes: "what is needed . . . is . . . something more like . . . Wittgenstein's family resemblance, a polythetic form of classification in which the aim is to specify a set of criteria, subsets of which are enough to constitute a sense of decentered resemblance."[50] This impulse might in fact return us to the poet-theorists of Paz's generation, who offer significant programs for conceptualizing international modernisms in their own right.

Indeed, Paz was probably the most far-reaching of a generation of poet-theorists especially active in the 1950s–1990s, including the Franco-Caribbean poets Aimé Césaire and Édouard Glissant, the Brazilian concrete poet Haroldo de Campos, the Anglo-Caribbean poet and historian Edward Kamau Brathwaite, the Jewish-American anthologist and ethnopoet Jerome Rothenberg, and the Franco-British anthropologist, poet, translator, and editor Nathaniel Tarn. Such writers offered strong models of what Robert Duncan called "the symposium of the whole" or of what has more recently been called a transnational poetics: an expanded spatiotemporal configuration, modernist in its enthusiasms, which challenges the romantic theory that the poet incarnates, in George Steiner's phrase, "the quiddity of his native speech."[51] Through creative anthologization and ethnopoetic attention (Rothenberg); new conceptions of relation (Glissant); theories of anti-colonial aesthetic "devoration," "cannibalism," and "transcreation" (de Campos); anthropological defenses of lyric responsibility (Tarn); and theories of "nation language" (Brathwaite), such poet-theorists laid the groundwork for an expansive new idea of a poetry and a poetics of the Americas.[52] Yet, their lack of identity as a clear school, their degrees of separation in the cultural networks of the era, and the ongoing predominance of national literary history, prevented them and others from cohering as a group of commentators on the poetry of the Americas.

Inheriting these programs, Bernstein calls for "a syncretic poetics of ingenuity and invention," one that is "averse to the accumulative and developmental model of literature still reigning in the U.S. literary academy (and elsewhere in the Americas)."[53] These disruptive, vanguard values, seen as coincidental rather than filial in their articulations across the hemisphere, are certainly promising.

However, Bernstein suggests too neatly that "the poetics of the Americas that I am imagining is not about comparisons: it is about encounter, and change through encounter." On this point, I part company with Bernstein, for we miss much if we abandon comparison in order to assume that co-presence, contact, and encounter—however imaginative—are the engines of literary change. The generations of poets I discuss had their own working figurations of a category proximate to "the poetry of the Americas" premised on contact *as well as* a strong validation of non-Eurocentric, non-affiliative models of comparison: analogies, symmetries, resemblances, oppositions, and irreducible formulae. This book seeks to expand the critical vocabulary of attention to such models through its discussions of the generic modes, structures of address, figures, devices, schemes, multilingual idioms, circulatory patterns, gnomic distillations, and strategic aversions that pattern the comparative formation of the poetry of the Americas. But I do not simply advocate for an enlarged vocabulary so much as an enlarged geohistorical horizon—the Americas, and their structures of political feeling and experience—against which the activity of poetry has been practiced.

Integrationist Literary History

How to envisage the enlarged collection of poets who pertain to the poetry of the Americas? Describing my topic in conversation, I am inevitably asked: "so which poets do you write about?" This natural question causes me more consternation than it should, for I often want to give the quick answer "lots of them," an answer I know my conversation partner will find unsatisfactory. The invocation of breadth is not an evasion but a desire to attenuate authorial status in the structure of literary history, a desire that drove poets as diverse as Paz, Kenneth Koch, and Roque Dalton in the 1960s to write collaborative and heteronymic poetry that critiqued the claims of cultural cosmopolitanism (Chapter 6). In this study, instead of four or six poets, several dozen enter and fade from an evolving succession of formations. "Each poet is a stanza in that poem of poems," writes Paz, "and each poem is a version, a metaphor of this plural text."[54] Nor is the answer "lots of them" the result of a misplaced conviction in the book's "coverage" so much as it is an attempt to structure a study that does not wall off the potential for integrating larger circuits of evidence. This gesture verifies a challenge issued nearly thirty years ago by Earl Miner, a forerunner in the field of comparative poetics: "we have yet to awaken, and perhaps never will, from the dream of a pantascopic poetics, even while our theories have come to be based on ever smaller selections of the increasingly available evidence."[55]

A pantascopic outlook, or an effort to take in the "whole view," poses a problem for the way in which one understands *poem* as a comparative unit of critical discourse, and for how one imagines the relations of poems to other poems. I discuss a great deal of poetry definable as *lyric*, in the now-common Hegelian sense of an achievement of subjectivity, or in Reuben Brower's model of "the mind in *solitary* speech." However, I stress *poem* instead of *lyric* because, while the relation of lyric subjectivity's expressive dynamics to the problems of imagining an inter-American system inform many poets I discuss (e.g., Jorge Carrera Andrade, Jorge Luis Borges, Elizabeth Bishop, Derek Walcott, and Heberto Padilla), many other vanguard poetic tendencies (e.g., material poetry and modern epic) consciously reject lyric models to amplify the textures of linguistic and historical materialism. To my mind, the deceptively ordinary term *poem* always requires the formal, generic, and contextual specification that scholars of "historical poetics" such as Virginia Jackson and Yopie Prins call for in their attention to the "enormous variety of verse genres in active circulation."[56]

The chapters that follow therefore offer an array of theoretical orientations to the status of poems as a form of verbal art, and an allowance for a variety of post–New Critical reading practices, all in the interest of exposing the intersections of geopolitical history with evolving assemblages of poems. Such poems are artifacts of the geopolitical histories to which they allude in their semantic and acoustical dimensions, but they are also images of alternative histories, which they suggest in their rhetorical desires and in their stance toward other poems of the era.[57] By turns, identifying poetry *in and of history* entails attention to the book-historical practice of anthologization, to the use of a particular kind of multilingual diction or lexical texture, to the emergence of a genre, to the theory and practice of translation, or to the politics of rhyme and homophony. That is, some poems gain interest as aesthetic or artifactual wholes susceptible to stock-in-trade hermeneutic operations, while others gain interest in so far as their stance divulges a relation to other poems. By highlighting the way poems relate to other poems, I aim in particular to find terms that allow us to compare diverging poetries, as well as to record the twinned histories of translation and anthologization, which evolve in this period from vindicating inter-American friendship in the 1940s to creating rivalries in the literary marketplace of the 1960s.

Here, my readings hew most closely to one of four lines of thought— *artifactualism, integrationism, assimilationism,* and *irreducibilism*—that Roland Greene outlines in an unassuming but significant encyclopedia entry defining the term *poem*. I find particularly helpful what Greene calls the "integration-ist" school of thinking about poems, which takes seriously "the notion that poems rarely exist in isolation from other poems."[58] An integrationist view could posit many nesting scales of affiliation—the sequence, anthology, career narra-tive, coterie, or canon—as the arrangement by which a diversified collection of poems gains collective integrity.[59] Writers, critics, and editors who tacitly hold integrationist views of poetry, such as participants in coteries or consecrators of national anthologies, might therefore constrain or delimit an understanding of poetry's hemispheric or global purchase. Others, such as the composers of more experimental anthologies, editors of little magazines, authors of correspondence networks, and translators, might rescale the integrationist view of poetry to translingual and pluralistic dimensions conducive to the thought of an inter-American poetics. Integrationism also offers a lens for understanding poetry's diverse roles in formations, institutions, or historical conjunctures without sac-rificing attention to its aesthetic phenomena.

But integrationism as Greene describes it (along with *assimilationism*, a standpoint defined by the relations between poetry and the other arts) largely neglects the midcentury sociological connotations that readers will reflexively call to mind when confronted with such terms, especially in the context of the crescendo of civil rights discourses and the integration of postcolonial states into the postwar geopolitical system.[60] In fact, many poets and theorists nurtured an integrationist view of poetry that meshed social and geopolitical integration with the logics of sequencing, collecting, and forming literary communities. Metaphors between "regional integration" as a metageographical discourse and intranational racial integration already struck some poets as crucial by the time of Langston Hughes's World War II–era commentaries on racial democracy as a key challenge to Good Neighbor diplomacy, discussed in Chapter 1. In the post-war world, poet-statesmen like Aimé Césaire likewise argued for a radical form of integration of Caribbean postcolonial subjects within the French nation-state.[61]

Latin American poets of the early Cold War disclose an integrationist tendency by transforming iconic figures of US racial amelioration such as Abraham Lincoln into poetic figures of hemispheric unity. In a retort to US Cold War policy, they revivified Lincoln's spirit for a degraded era of what Neruda called the "Marshall cocktail" recipe for foreign relations in his paean to Lincoln, "Que despierte el leñador" ("Let the Railsplitter Awaken," 1948). Neruda sought an addressee to triangulate the competing geopolitical claims of a US-led First World, a Communist Second World, and a developing Third World in the early Cold War, finding this addressee in the American GIs returning from the scattered theaters of World War II, closing "como una corola/de innumerables pétalos anónimos/ para renacer y olvidar" (like a corolla/of innumerable anonymous petals/to be reborn and to forget).[62] To the GI, Neruda addresses an emphatic poetry of epi-deictic praise, as in the poem's famous incitation "Pensemos en toda la tierra,/ golpeando con amor en la mesa" (Let us think of the whole world,/pounding the table with love). But he also addresses him with a didactic poetry, alerting him to caudillos cynically supported by the OAS, and a premonitory poetry that threat-ens retaliation for a renewed policy of US interventionism. With the Spanish Civil War's Abraham Lincoln Brigades fresh in his mind as what Perry Anderson calls "an internationalism perfected and perverted as never before," he summons in the icon of Lincoln an ameliorative, unifying figural power.[63]

Ernesto Cardenal's small press in Managua, El Hilo Azul, likewise published, among a series of chapbooks, a 1951 anthological primer on Lincoln by assem-bling the poems of Whitman, Benét, Masters, Markham, Bynner, Sandburg, and Lindsay.[64] Cardenal's casebook takes inspiration from Lindsay: "Would I might rouse the Lincoln in you all." Lincoln's cult was widely enough diffused in mid-century Latin America that Charles Olson's "Anecdotes of the Late War" (1954) characterized the Hispanized word "link-/cone" as one of the "broken/elegances" littering the Lee Highway (US 29) that crossed the Potomac into Washington, DC, from the south:

> Reverse of
> sic transit gloria, the
> Latin American whom the cab driver told me
> he picked up at Union Station had
> one word of english—link-
> cone. And drove him
> straight to the monument, the man
> went up the stairs and fell down on his knees
> where he could see the statue and stayed there
> in the attitude of prayer.[65]

For Olson, as for Cardenal and Neruda, "link-/cone" serves as a romantic icon of hemispheric idealism around which a strain of early Cold War poetry countered twin segregationist feelings: nationalist retrenchment and ongoing racial inequality. His disarticulation of the word "link-/cone" homophonically describes hemispheric integration. A decade later, El Corno Emplumado's stance toward the myriad literary schools of the early 1960s, at the high-water mark of the Civil Rights Movement, adopted the same impulse, to the point that Randall and Mondragón were privately labeled "integrationists" by poets who felt they sacrificed editorial standards for a wider range of national and ethnic inclusions.

Thus, national canon-formation might be seen to follow a segregationist disposition that points toward the artifactual autonomy of individual poetic expressions, while the poetry of the Americas often emphasized the integrationism of poets, anthologists, comparatists, and others concerned with establishing literary institutions and formations that allowed for widening relations between expressive artists from racially, linguistically, and geographically diverse arenas.[66] These transnational dynamics of integration could inflect the ethos of even those poets who wrote or fought on behalf of political projects of national self-determination in Puerto Rico, Cuba, Nicaragua, El Salvador, and elsewhere—poets who by my logic might seem to bear out a "segregationist" political impulse. Anti-imperialist and decolonial nationalisms could coexist with integrationist aesthetic politics, a fact that poses a challenge to our tendency to write the literary history of the Americas as a top-down story of superpower hegemony or a bottom-up tale of postcolonial resistance. In this spirit, I historicize rather than reenact the era's obstinate protocols for inclusion based on racially coded aesthetic taste profiles, established group dynamics, or national belongings. In so doing, I hope to strategically unsettle major historiographical and aesthetic distinctions between "the raw and the cooked," the academy and the countercultural avant-garde, established white poets and minoritized ethnic poets, the left and the right, and above all the North and the South.

Cultural Diplomacy from Good Neighbors to Countercultures

Integrationism names one nexus of relations between the literary-historical structure of the poetry of the Americas and a defining midcentury social formation, but such factors emerged in dialogue with—and were often overwritten by—the cultural ideologies of statecraft. The cultural-political ethos of Good Neighbor diplomacy, followed quickly by the varied hemispheric fronts of the global Cold War, could occupy the spaces of poetic enunciation and determine the material pathways of poems and poets through the Americas. This is true of poems that are declaratively political as well as many that are aversively expressive or obstreperously experimental. In short, from 1938 until the shine wore off around the year 1973, the large network of poets described in this book conceived several of their works—though by no means all of them—as creative acts of diplomacy or as aesthetic alternatives to cultural diplomacy's mandates.

Here, I join a recent wave of scholars giving new visibility to an era of inter-American cultural diplomacy, resituating writers in the enormous "state-private network" of foreign policy collaborations between private cultural institutions and government agencies of the United States, Cuba, Chile, and elsewhere.[67] The poets I discuss jostle among an eclectic array of cultural actors who circulated through traveling art exhibitions, mobile film units, cultural ambassadorships, radio broadcasts, literary translations, and intellectual congresses. Their names include filmmakers and entertainers such as Orson Welles, Walt Disney, Carmen Miranda, and John Huston; cultural brokers like Lincoln Kirstein, Blanche Knopf, Rafael Squirru, and Emir Rodríguez Monegal; policymakers such as Muna Lee; and artists from Diego Rivera to Gordon Parks and José Luis Cuevas. A misapprehended era in hemispheric histories of cultural assemblage comes into view: a midcentury era of state-sponsored cultural diplomacy, aligning expressive culture across the arts in relation to a multifocal history of Cold War inter-American institutions.

Recent accounts of the origins and itineraries of the cultural Cold War in the Americas amend some long-held tenets of cultural diplomacy scholarship. When Christopher Lasch, in a 1967 exposé in the *Nation*, coined the term "the cultural cold war," he argued that midcentury liberal intellectuals often served as amanuenses to state power, a view solidified by landmark "revisionist" studies of abstract expressionism, literary intellectuals, jazz, middlebrow culture, and other domains.[68] These studies document the quixotic attempts to "weaponize" culture by cold warriors at the Department of State and at the CIA in consort with the Congress for Cultural Freedom, accumulating an image of a Cold War "unpopular front," as Louis Menand cheekily dubs it, or a pernicious "archive of authority," in Andrew Rubin's term.[69] The institutionalization of aesthetic modernism is a crucial story of these years, but I follow critics of the revisionist paradigm who now de-emphasize what Claire Fox calls "fetishism of the covert," or the act of exposing state support for art worlds and literary scenes that self-identified as apolitical and autonomous. Partnerships between government agencies and foundations, museums, and presses was often overt, asking us to rethink the school of Cold War cultural history that saw the flow of state power through art in "top-down or diffusionist" terms, whereby governments instrumentalized artists and artworks for strategic outcomes.[70] Similarly, Deborah Cohn helpfully admonishes us to understand "the skewed lines of cause and effect that allowed Cold War operations to be turned to other uses by those who organized and participated in them," such as "writers who had their own literary and political agendas, and who rightly viewed themselves as agents of their own cause, rather than vehicles for transmitting official U.S. policy."[71] To push back against the "revisionist" thesis of cultural weaponization is also to parse the distinct kinds of work that diverse agencies enacted (for example, what Greg Barnhisel calls the "culturalism" of the Department of State and the Library of Congress versus the "informationalism" of agencies and foundations associated with Nelson Rockefeller, such as the Office of the Coordinator for Inter-American Affairs, institutions that all figure prominently in Chapter 1).[72]

Given this emphasis, many scholars understandably tend to organize their studies around one or more institutional apparatuses, despite the tangled inter-relationships of agencies and foundations promoting inter-American culture from the Good Neighbor period through the Alliance for Progress. In *Americans All: Good Neighbor Cultural Diplomacy in World War II*, Darlene Sadlier covers the Office of the Coordinator of Inter-American Affairs (CIAA), modeling her institutional history on the institution's divisions into "separate units devoted to [the] specific media" of film, radio, and print.[73] Others such as Fox excavate the doings of the State Department's Division of Intellectual Cooperation, the Visual Arts Section of the Pan American Union (PAU), and the umbrella political entity of the Organization of American States (OAS), while Cohn tracks legal and cultural institutions such as the McCarran-Walter Act of 1952, the Congress for Cultural Freedom (CCF), the US University, the International PEN Center; and the Center for Inter-American Relations (CIAR), now called the Americas Society. In addition to these institutions, the pages below consider in passing the work of such diverse organizations as the National Translation Center (NTC), the United States Information Service (USIS), the Centro Mexicano de Escritores, the Unión de Escritores y Artistas de Cuba (UNEAC), and Casa de las Américas.

This book shares an acknowledgement with the aforementioned studies that anyone hoping to understand midcentury hemispheric cultural circulation must weather a blizzard of acronyms—and rehumanize the policymakers who whipped them up. For example, I endeavor to recover the crucial 1940s cultural policy roles played by Archibald MacLeish at CIAA and Muna Lee at the Department of State, and the 1960s work of Argentine curator Rafael Squirru at PAU. In Chapters 4 and 5, the little-known Keith Botsford haunts the doings of poets who took an interest in inter-Americanism to a surprising degree. Botsford took a 1950 bachelor's degree from Iowa University and a 1952 master's degree from the cloak-and-dagger staging ground of Yale before working as a translator in Paris and as a comparative literature professor in Puerto Rico. In 1962, his

Iowa friend John Hunt conscripted him into the CCF, and he served as its "South American liaison" between 1962 and 1965 in Brazil and Mexico City, bringing Bishop, Lowell, and Walcott into the CIA-sponsored anticommunist cultural diplomacy orbit and exhibiting and containing Borges during the CCF's 1964 International Conference of Poets in Berlin. Moving to PEN in 1965, he similarly managed Neruda during the organization's Bled Round Tables, and as the director of the NTC in Austin in the late 1960s he meted out small CIA-funded translation grants sought after by the likes of Blackburn, Randall, Eshleman, and many others.

Yet, while this book embraces such details regarding the personalities and the institutional mechanics fostering cultural diplomacy, it differs markedly from most recent studies by adopting a multi-archival approach based on authors' personal records, thereby demoting institutional repositories as the motor forces of literary history. Coercive state power did flow through cultural-diplomatic institutions and their functionaries, but I decline to mute considerations of aesthetic and expressive practices in order to recover institutional history. Poems, I argue, were so often written and received as complex expressions of diplomatic culture in their own right that literary scholars interested in how poets traverse the Americas and imagine the poetics of the hemisphere from their national and partial situations should be expected to investigate how a poet's formal choices and figurative language can be read in relation to the widespread institutions of cultural diplomacy that Cold War cultural historians have revealed. In covertly funded wartime anthology projects like Dudley Fitts's *Anthology of Contemporary Latin American Poetry* (1942); in the great works of diplomat-poets like Carrera Andrade, Paz, and Neruda; and in the underhistoricized activities of Blackburn, Eshleman, Bishop, Lowell, Walcott, and Padilla in the 1960s, the soft-power mechanisms of hemispheric cultural diplomacy saturate poetic art. To overprivilege the policy documents of institutional archives reveals a background apparatus that shaped literary history in some ways, but forecloses the period's ongoing conviction in the *semi-autonomous* workings of expressive culture.[74] By putting the relation between poetic form and institutional history at the center of my study, I hope to break a narrative impasse that leads scholars to alternately ignore, vilify, or valorize institutional cultural policy. We do not face the choice between willing away, critiquing, or pining nostalgically for the heady days of state arts sponsorship. To begin, we ought to ask how and when such sponsorship might productively alter our readings of significant literary works. In the cases of William Carlos Williams and Elizabeth Bishop, I will argue that rethinking the relation between formally interesting poems and irksome inter-American politics challenges a tendency to declare such writers the champions of a hemispheric biculturalism.

Finally, a word about periodization bears mention here. Several chapters of this book carefully historicize Cold War cultural dynamics, but the title elides mention of the Cold War in favor of the interval "from Good Neighbors to Countercultures," because notions of hemispheric idealism in poetry predate what Lasch, in 1967, retrospectively dubbed "the cultural Cold War." When a robust cultural diplomacy project developed in the 1930s and 1940s, its inter-American rhetoric strategically promoted a broad antifascist coalition that included expressions of transnational communism, as in the Council for Pan-American Democracy, as well as corporate liberalism, as in CIAA. These formulations certainly shaped the United States' anticommunist cultural diplomacy of the Cold War, but they did not guarantee its advent. Therefore, I suggest how inter-American ideologemes moved into and out of Cold War discourses, without granting the Cold War a teleological role in the periodization of literary culture's relation to inter-American statecraft.

From a different standpoint, David Luis-Brown and Stephen M. Park define an earlier "Pan-American era" notable principally as an "institutional and ideological project defined by U.S. efforts to gain economic and political control over Latin America."[75] This was true of the Pan-Americanism observed by Martí, but by the late 1930s agency staffers varied in their ideological positions, running the gamut from liberals to anti-imperialist leftists. Likewise, in key texts of the era, writers who sought to mark aesthetic period boundaries such as *modernism* and *postmodernism* confronted the deceptive cognates *modernismo* and *posmodernismo*, terms whose diverse usages and cross-cultural transmissions this book clarifies. In the transformation of the poetry of the Americas "from Good Neighbors to countercultures," an interval of swerving transformations and amnesiac repetitions coincided with the historical period of the Cold War and the aesthetic frame of modernism in no small measure, but not entirely. A reader of this book may experience a form of the non-coincidence I'm marking here, whatever her predetermined framework for comprehending the period. Whether a reader comes to these pages with a national frame of reference for a given poet or poetic tradition, from the precincts of US Cold War cultural history, or from a postcolonial Latin American perspective, some familiar material ought to appear freshly contextualized. What is at stake is a synthetic account of midcentury hemispherism itself, one that imbricates the comparative study of modern poetry with hemispheric American cultural studies on the one hand and with Cold War institutional history on the other.

Six Chapters in the Poetry of the Americas

The six chapters that follow each tell their own story, stories that are inflected by distinct methodological and formal concerns, distinct political affiliations and alignments, and distinct groups of poets. Each chapter therefore asks for its own patient absorption. However, as will become clear from the number of poets and concerns that reappear from chapter to chapter, the book cumulatively narrates an evolving, networked history of the midcentury poetry of the Americas. This history cuts a jagged path: it careens from the exuberant inter-American projects of World War II (Chapter 1) to the ways poets used diverse elements of poetic form and genre to negotiate the abandonment of these projects in the early Cold War (Chapters 2 and 3), and then to the reconfigurations and renewals of inter-Americanism in the 1960s (Chapters 4 through 6).

Chapter 1, "Hemispheric Solidarities: Wartime Poetry and the Limits of the Good Neighbor," models the book's literary-historical orientation by introducing the unlikely roles poets played at the center of hemispheric cultural diplomacy initiatives between 1938 and 1945, the years when Good Neighbor diplomacy was motivated by a broad antifascist coalition. Comparing diplomat-poets like Williams, Neruda, Archibald MacLeish, and Langston Hughes, I unearth new works and new details (such as a visual poem composed by Neruda for Bishop). Moreover, I compare these writers to Puerto Rican poet Julia de Burgos, Ecuadorian Consul General Jorge Carrera Andrade, soldier-poet Lysander Kemp, and others who coalesced around the anthologies, translations, and congresses of Good Neighbor initiatives. Borrowing metaphors of bridging and broadcasting from new infrastructures of hemispheric modernization and invoking strategies of apostrophic address to an impossibly large hemispheric public, Good Neighbor poetry promoted Popular Front antifascism, but also enabled advocates of decolonial politics, racial democracy, and international feminism.

By contrast, Chapter 2, entitled "A Xenoglossary for the Americas," advances a "tropological history" of inter-Americanism by showing how foreign words (xenoglossia) became a key poetic device for Wallace Stevens, José Lezama Lima, and Jorge Luis Borges after World War II, at the low ebb of political inter-Americanism. In one of the book's revisionary gestures, I show how Stevens's monumental "Notes Toward a Supreme Fiction" used this device in climactic verses like "at last I call you by name, my green, my fluent mundo" in order to reimagine the poetic identity of the Americas—a gesture resonant with the US

Congress's contemporaneous debates about globalization. While Stevens's "lingua franca et jocundissima" (his self-designated attempt to fashion a playful, sonorous global language) was rebuked in the United States by nationalistic postwar critics, I show how it belongs to a rich vein of postwar poetry by Borges and Lezama, who respond to national and insular literary formations with similar turns toward international language norms.

Chapter 3, "The Ruins of Inter-Americanism," develops a second "tropological history" of inter-Americanism during the early Cold War by describing a major genre of postwar writing: the postromantic meditation on pre-Columbian ruins. Individually, ruin poems of the Americas—by Neruda, Ginsberg, Adán, Olson, Robert Barlow, Lawrence Ferlinghetti, Philip Lamantia, and Ernesto Cardenal—are usually understood as expressions of universal humanism, exercises in postmodern tourism, or symptoms of neo-imperial fortune hunting. At best, they prelude the ethnopoetic praxis of the 1970s. By contrast, I argue that ruin poems galvanized by Neruda's *Alturas de Macchu Picchu* (1947) respond to the rapid demise of the movement for hemispheric democracy. Through their identifications with indigenous civic histories, poets critiqued the collapse of political and cultural inter-Americanism. Moving beyond poets like Neruda and Olson who had previously maintained a formal relation to Good Neighbor diplomacy, I show how even Allen Ginsberg's poetic theories developed during sojourns in Mayan Mexico, and the tropes of ruin poetry subtend his conception of a "destroyed" generation in "Howl" (1956), as well as poems by many writers in his cohort.

The book's final three chapters track dramatic expansions of inter-American poetic relations after 1959. Chapter 4, "The New Inter-American Poetry," shows how revolutionary enthusiasms, experimental magazines, and translation fueled this expansion. Plenty of previous critics note the boom, but most US accounts of the period's poetry center on intranational polarities ("margin versus mainstream" or "raw versus cooked") inflamed by Donald Allen's *The New American Poetry* (1960). I instead describe a larger formation I call "the new inter-American poetry," recovering dialogues best emblematized by the hemispheric little magazine *El Corno Emplumado*, as well as the reciprocations engendered between the works of rebellious Beats and revolutionary Cuban barbudos, Paul Blackburn and Julio Cortázar, Clayton Eshleman and Javier Heraud, and others. Of course, these exchanges were not without their blind spots. To that end, I suggest the limits of the oft-praised communities imagined by Frank O'Hara's *Lunch Poems* (1964), when read alongside poems by contemporaneous visitors to Manhattan such as Mario Benedetti (Uruguay) and Alcides Iznaga (Cuba).

Chapter 5, "Questions of Anticommunism: Hemispheric Lyric in the 1960s," reveals exchanges among better-established poets, especially Bishop and Robert Lowell of the United States, Derek Walcott of Saint Lucia, and Heberto Padilla of Cuba, who curried favor with Kennedy-era cultural diplomacy projects designed to mitigate the revolutionary fidelismo animating many of the poems discussed in Chapter 4. Bishop's turn as a CCF-affiliated cultural diplomat inflects her Brazil poems, which I describe not as self-conscious critiques of travel literature (as they are so commonly understood) but as negotiations of liberal ideas about international class politics and poverty, revealed in elaborate sound patterns. Transfiguring middle-generation formalism, Walcott created a flexible phenomenological, racial, and geographic figure in his central conceit of "the gulf" in order to lyricize his increasingly vexed relation to the hemispheric tours he attended with support from the CCF and the Farfield and Rockefeller Foundations. Actively influenced by Lowell's psycho-political stance, Padilla's critiques of revolutionary Cuba aggravated a crisis of cultural permissiveness in the state bureaucracy known as "the Padilla Affair" after the poet was imprisoned and forced to recite a coerced confession as a condition of his release. In all, lyric sequences by Bishop, Lowell, and Walcott sought new strategies of hemispheric cultural diplomacy by enacting crises of confessional lyric formalism as an aesthetic ideology in service to anticommunist policy. Meanwhile, the Padilla affair showed how these same strategies of liberal poetic subjectivity, when practiced by poets in the orbit of Second World cultural policy, posed challenges to a revolutionary imagination.

Last, Chapter 6, "Renga and Heteronymy: Cosmopolitan Poetics after 1967," uses the backdrop of the myriad international poetry conferences of the 1960s to analyze poetic performances of cosmopolitanism and the discourse of translation. The ethical role of convening poets to perform and translate one another's works was mainstreamed as a literary idea in service to the maintenance of a peaceful world, so much so that Paz, in the multilingual, collaboratively authored *Renga* (1971), announced he was living in "the century of translation." I juxtapose *Renga* and Kenneth Koch's collection of hoax translations "Some South American Poets" in order to elucidate how these antithetical authorial modes endorse and critique the tenor of cultural diplomacy under the Pax Americana. Through new forms of critical cosmopolitanism, these works alternately memorialize and parody the midcentury groundswell of poetic inter-Americanism that the book recounts.

If the publication of works like Paz's *Los hijos del limo* is any indication, the year 1973 engenders some strong new conceptions of the poetry of the Americas as a critical standpoint and literary practice. But it also marks a violent terminus. After Neruda's diplomatic efforts to navigate a Cold War thaw in the mid-1960s, his return to an anti-American politics in his final poem "Incitación a Nixoncidio" (Incitation to Nixoncide) indexes the depths of the crisis in hemispheric cultural reciprocity at the moment of the US-backed Chilean coup and Neruda's own death. The failure of cultural permissiveness that roiled Cuba in 1971 during the Padilla affair and led to the cosmopolitan intellectual abandonment of the Cuban Revolution marks another endpoint.[76] Indeed, one of the defining statements of that "disenchantment"—Chilean diplomat Jorge Edwards's testimonial novel *Persona Non Grata* (1973)—suggests how Chile's coup and Cuba's "quinquenio gris" (five gray years) were linked faces of the desertion of "a long tradition of diplomat/writers in Latin America, a tradition that was broken by the military coup of September 1973."[77] Yet another ending is marked by the disavowals of many intellectuals after the 1967 exposés of covert CIA influence of state-funded cultural diplomacy. The intensive rise of Chicano/a, Nuyorican, Native American, Black Nationalist, and other ethnonational literary formations shifts the terms of hemispherism in crucial ways, even as the generation of poet-theorists I earlier compared to Paz begins to productively characterize the poetics of the Americas.[78] By crisscrossing the generational, linguistic, and geographical boundaries of the midcentury, prior to these termini and new beginnings, I define a literary-historical moment in which the poetry of the Americas, even if it rarely held a seat at the OAS, invested heavily in the project of critiquing and organizing American states.

1. Hemispheric Solidarities

Wartime Poetry and the Limits of the Good Neighbor

As new, increasingly insistent "principles of inter-American solidarity and cooperation" alloyed in the antifascist crucible of World War II, Mexican historian
Edmundo O'Gorman argued that a shared culture of the Americas remained little more than a "geographical hallucination."[1] "It is remotely possible," O'Gorman
wrote, "that at some future time América may be the perpetuator of culture—the
burning torch [. . .]. But in the name of all that is common sense, let no one try
to create it gratuitously just because a road may cross the continent from pole to
pole."[2] Yet the transformation of the slogan "hemispheric solidarity" from what
Hubert C. Herring called a "pleasant elective" of 1930s Good Neighbor diplomacy
to an "imperious necessity" of the war intensified inter-American cultural ideals
sooner than O'Gorman forecast, and in the very terms he rejected.[3] The United
States invested heavily in agencies charged with inventing techniques of "cultural diplomacy," such as Nelson Rockefeller's Office of the Coordinator of Inter-
American Affairs (CIAA, 1940–1945), and it enhanced a network of hemispheric
transportation and communication infrastructures that came to include shortwave radio, Pan American World Airways, a "Good Neighbor Fleet" of cargo and
passenger ships, and the completion of the Pan American Highway (O'Gorman's
"road from pole to pole").[4] Emergent concepts of inter-American cultural relations were inextricable from this stock imaginary of networked "organization

spaces" wrought by infrastructural modernization.[5] For example, Dudley Fitts's enormous *Anthology of Contemporary Latin American Poetry*, silently funded by CIAA and published by New Directions in December 1942, compiled 95 Latin American poets from 21 nations and 17 US translators in 667 pages. Fitts's anthology plainly sought to symbolically repair the schisms O'Gorman identified. As a review in *The Nation* quipped, "The man-hours of labor that have gone into it, if laid end to end, would bridge the gap in the pan-American highway."[6]

This chapter narrates the hemispheric solidarities that poets sought to forge in the seven years from 1938 to 1945, following the establishment of a Cultural Relations Division at the US Department of State. In those years, the Good Neighbor policy's infrastructure of inter-American cultural diplomacy grew into a porously connected network of state agencies including CIAA, the Office of War Information (OWI), Voice of America (VOA), the Hispanic Foundation at the Library of Congress, and the Pan American Union (PAU), as well as non-governmental organizations such as the Committee on Cultural Relations with Latin America (CCRLA) and the Council for Pan-American Democracy (CPAD). Promoting inter-American culture with both elite and popular dimensions, these agencies collaborated with an honor roll of Hollywood studios, universities, libraries, presses, broadcast companies, and museums to create state-private partnerships. Such partnerships were not unprecedented, but their instigators felt them to be new and makeshift. Designating them in 1940 as "The Art of the Good Neighbor," Archibald MacLeish remarked, "there are phrases which can be pronounced only in quotation marks. 'Cultural relations' is one of them."[7] However, he continued, "the awkward phrase" stood for "serious things," namely a shift past US commercial interests as inter-Americanism's unilateral beneficiary, as it had been since the founding of the Pan American Union in 1890. MacLeish promised to consolidate the new "realization of informed persons that the present struggle of the propagandas in Latin America is a struggle for something more than markets." His phrase anticipates the great Cold War shibboleth "winning hearts and minds."

While "The Art of the Good Neighbor" encompassed many kinds of expressive media, poetry played a notable role. Recent scholars of Good Neighbor cultural relations tend to deemphasize the poetic quantum beyond markets evoked by MacLeish, tracking instead the relations between government sponsorship and the highly publicized, profitable careers of Walt Disney, Orson Welles, Carmen Miranda, and Blanche and Alfred Knopf, or exploring metaphors of good neighborliness in the fast-expanding international culture industries and literary marketplaces for which names such as Disney and Knopf function as meton-ymies.[8] But MacLeish, who spearheaded an array of programs in his employ-ments at OWI, the Library of Congress, and the Literature Committee of CIAA's Cultural Relations Division, joined a large ensemble of US, Latin American, and displaced European poets in the swirl of efforts at hemispheric cultural diplo-macy. Poetry became a paragon of conscientious inter-Americanism, even as it vied with radio, film, prose, and the plastic arts in the media ecology of cultural exchange. As Fitts wrote to Peruvian poet Xavier Abril, poetry was the "creá-tor spiritus of our common cause."[9] In this way, poetry's distinctive idioms of transnational solidarity struck many writers of the late 1930s and early 1940s as immune to charges of cultural imperialism dogging newer communication tech-nologies.[10] Accordingly, speculations on a supranational poetry of the Americas flourished with a new intensity. Paz devoted his Guggenheim Fellowship in Berkeley, California, in 1943 to a proposal on the hemispheric question of "América and its Poetic Expression."[11] By war's end in 1945, Spanish exile Ramón J. Sender wrote: "May it not be that America, the whole of America, north and south, is living in the very age of the rhapsodists?"[12]

The impressive roster of poets whose careers, for better or for worse, inter-sected with wartime inter-American cultural diplomacy initiatives includes Jorge Carrera Andrade (Ecuador), Jorge Luis Borges (Argentina), Fitts (US), Langston Hughes (US), Lysander Kemp (US), MacLeish (US), Ezequiel Martínez Estrada (Argentina), Gabriela Mistral (Chile), Vinicius de Moraes (Brazil), Pablo Neruda (Chile), Emilio Oribe (Uruguay), Paz (Mexico), John Peale Bishop (US), Muriel Rukeyser (US), and William Carlos Williams (US). Prominent inter-American intellectuals, publishers, translators, and other networkers also underlay this story, such as Waldo Frank (US), Muna Lee (US/Puerto Rico), Victoria Ocampo (Argentina), Jorge Mañach (Cuba), and Samuel Putnam (US). This chapter recov-ers their network of intersecting dialogues and debates, alongside those of lesser-known Puerto Rican writers Julia de Burgos, Juan Antonio Corretjer, Ángel Flores, and Luis Palés Matos, for Puerto Rico proved to be one of the limit cases for official wartime conceptions of hemispheric solidarity and mutual defense. The grandiosity of an anti-interventionist, affluent, racially harmonious, dem-ocratic vision of the hemisphere naturally led some critics to reconceive Good Neighbor diplomacy from the standpoint of Puerto Rico, one of the hemisphere's militarized, poor, still-colonial, racially complex societies.

The poetic traffic of these writers moved across the radio waves, highways, skyways, and postal routes of a new inter-American infrastructure whose technoscapes had long been central to modernist discourses, although they remain largely absent from terminologies of hemispheric comparison. A fresh corpus of poetry and translation emerged in pamphlets, broadcasts, books, anthologies, and special "Pan-American" numbers of journals, often despite wartime paper shortages, and not without hostilities emerging among competitive coteries of translators.[13] Poets increasingly emulated one another across a newly imagined cisatlantic canon, and poems whose histories I recount in the following pages— such as Carrera Andrade's imitation of Hart Crane *To the Bay Bridge* (Canto al Puente de Oakland, 1941), Hughes's "Broadcast to the West Indies" (1943), and Williams's flirtation with Afro-Caribbean poetic models in *The Wedge* (1944) and *Paterson* (1946)—each disputed the new inter-American infrastructures in surprising ways. Taken together, these works point toward a dispersive yet coherent archive of poems arrayed across wartime discourses of hemispheric linkage. A wave of essay collections, including Frank's *South American Journey* (1943) and Alfonso Reyes's *Norte y sur* (1942), preluded volumes of poetry drenched in the inter-American theme, including Kemp's *Northern Stranger* (1946), Elizabeth Bishop's *North & South* (1946), Wallace Stevens's *Transport to Summer* (1947), PAU director Angel Flores's translation of Neruda's *Residence on Earth* (1946), Bishop's emulations of Neruda, Muna Lee's translation of Carrera Andrade's *A Secret Country* (1946), de Moraes's *Nossa Senhora do Los Angeles* (1946), Hughes and Ben Carruthers's translations of Nicolás Guillén's *Cuba Libre* (1948), and Muriel Rukeyser's *The Green Wave* (1948). Finally, a profuse rhetoric of wartime solidarity buttressed the infrastructure of hemispheric connection in this burgeoning inter-American poetry. As exiled Hispanist Américo Castro made clear, war fueled most speculation about "what kind of fertile contacts might be established among the nations of this continent, the last refuge of hope and peace."[14] Chilean scholar Fernando Alegría later recalled: "when I came to the US to continue my university studies in 1940, I came to the US of Whitman. These were the years of Franklin D. Roosevelt, the heroic years of the war against fascism, the years in which the Pan-Americanist doctrine for the first time assumed a true social significance."[15]

Of course, coalitional politics did not equate to aesthetic conformity, and the poetry of wartime hemispheric solidarity thus ranged from diplomatic to dissident, sometimes in the same breath. Jorge Carrera Andrade's poems make explicit inter-American appeals in the spirit of Whitmanian fellowship, cultivating apostrophic terms of shared hemispheric experience through the poetics of address. Others employ the transfigurative power of metaphor in the service of hemispheric thought, or transliterate forms, rhythms, and icons on the North/South bias to voice terms for cross-cultural exchange. Still others take Good Neighbor rhetoric as a mask for the articulation of dissident perspectives. For example, poems by Puerto Rican nationalists in New York such as Julia de Burgos, as well as GIs in the Caribbean Defense Command such as Lysander Kemp, expose imperial blind spots in the anti-interventionist rhetoric of the Good Neighbor policy. Hughes and de Moraes stage the promise of racial democracy as a moral corollary to inter-American fellowship. Communists and their sympathizers such as Neruda used the common terrain of Popular Front antifascism to forge inter-American solidarities on terms they hoped would preserve democratic solidarity from Fifth Column incursions into Argentina or Mexico, but also from cooptation by the corporate liberal state. Their positions responded to the war's rapid transformation of the Good Neighbor policy from a toothless public relations campaign into a dramatic propaganda blitz, and its tendency to mask the demolition of multilateralism in a democratic rhetoric of "hemispheric alliance."[16]

This chapter reassembles the dizzying network of interconnected poems, anthologies, poets, and literary-diplomatic careers that participated in these processes. The authors of these works usually did so with a crucial awareness of their status as ideological tools in hemispheric patterns of influence, and sometimes staged openhanded critiques of their own complicity. Although diverse concerns motivate each of the many poems in this corpus, the chapter endeavors to highlight two interlocking features of poetry's role in inter-American cultural diplomacy that cohere throughout. First, it documents how poems of wartime hemispheric solidarity consistently troped technologies of hemispheric linkage, from roads, bridges, postcards, and maps to the nascent products of the culture industry such as radio, newspapers, film, and popular music. Second, it shows how writers imagined literary practices of anthologization, translation, and figuration as technologies of hemispheric linkage by their own lights. In this sense, poets reoriented the stock tropes of technological interconnectivity, bending them in partisan ways to comment on pressing sociopolitical problems in the rhetoric of hemispheric solidarity. To demonstrate the range of positions that broached the rhetoric of hemispheric solidarity, the following pages braid together six stories of wartime poetry: Fitts's anthology project, Carrera Andrade's accounts of the bridgework of poetic diplomacy, Hughes and de Moraes's poems of racial democracy, Burgos and Neruda's poetics of Puerto Rican nationhood, William's peculiar poetics of bicultural identity, and Kemp's lyric critique of hemispheric militarization.

The Office of the Coordinator of Inter-American Poetry

MacLeish's call for a new poetic art of "cultural relations" drew on a normative premise of *coordination*, which structured much of cultural inter-Americanism in the early 1940s. The title of Rockefeller's agency—the Office of the Coordinator of Inter-American Affairs (CIAA)—indicates the premise's novelty. Formed in 1940 in order to consolidate the scattered "Latin-American programs" conducted by the US Departments of State, Agriculture, Treasury, and Commerce, CIAA harmonized a peculiar mixture of defense interests with developmental humanitarianism, and sweetened economic liberalism with cultural diplomacy.[17] The office coordinated new transportation, commercial, cultural, and educational interests: Bolivian tungsten for US arms manufactures and crude oil pipelines; health care, capital loans, and regional planning initiatives; bracero workers and academic exchanges; radio and poetry. In all cases, the office strategically emphasized hemispheric linkage systems once a program to combat Axis influences was articulated, as it was when journalist and self-described Latin America expert Carleton Beals presaged *The Coming Struggle for Latin America* (1938). Coordination involved data collection, as political, educational, natural, and cultural resources were catalogued and filed, down to typescript bibliographies of the Latin American literature translated into English. The very title of *coordinator* was a new word at the intersection of corporate liberalism and government bureaucracy, defined by Rockefeller as someone who lost none of his entrepreneurial virility while clownishly juggling state affairs: "A coordinator is someone who can keep all the balls in the air without losing his own."[18]

The *coordinator* label aptly suits the editorial and translational roles of the poets employed by CIAA to produce the *Anthology of Contemporary Latin American Poetry*, published by New Directions in December 1942 with no mention of CIAA support, a practice later standardized by Cold War cultural diplomacy (Figure 1.1).[19] Here, *coordination* names how these wartime editors and translators understood a range of functions most often described by sociologists of culture using terms such as brokerage, gatekeeping, and intermediation.[20] Jeremy Braddock, in his sociological study of the art of modernist collecting as a form of intervention into the cultural marketplace, shows how anthologization was a key modernist aesthetic practice.[21] The ideology of literary coordination describes the moment that anthologization abutted the protocols of the state-sponsored, transnational cultural project stewarded by cultural relations officers

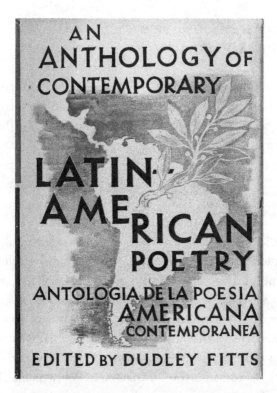

Fig 1.1 *Anthology of Contemporary Latin American Poetry*, by Dudley Fitts.
© 1947 by New Directions Publishing Corp. Reprinted by permission of New
Directions Publishing Corp.

such as MacLeish at the CIAA (who critics described as a cultural "coordinator"
in the period), Lewis Hanke at the Library of Congress, and Concha Romero
James at the State Department.

One of inter-American poetry's primary "coordinators" was John Peale
Bishop, best remembered as the model for the Princetonian poet Tom D'Invilliers
in F. Scott Fitzgerald's *This Side of Paradise*. Bishop headed the small publications
division at CIAA during the first few years of its existence, before the agency
subordinated its literary initiatives to other disciplines and mass-market magazines. The most substantial effort produced under his leadership was *Anthology
of Contemporary Latin American Poetry*, edited by his friend Dudley Fitts, a
poet, translator, classicist, and schoolmaster at Phillips Academy Andover. Fitts
worked in haste with an obstinately literalistic theory of translation, infuriat-
ing several of his translators over the course of the eighteen-month production
cycle with his preferences for "precisionists of the Semantic School" and the

"pedant-plodder" over the "poet-paraphraser."[22] He likened his coordinating role to Harriet Beecher Stowe's cruel slave master Simon Legree.[23] During this time, his publisher and former student James Laughlin, cartoonishly casting himself in private correspondence as the initiative's "Xavier Ambiguyan, Human Comic," addressed Fitts with a rotating series of multilingual, punning epithets such as "Bolivar of the Bards" and the "Revered Edi TORO."[24] Many cultural relations workers were enlisted in the cause of the anthology as translators and consultants, such as Donald Walsh, Langston Hughes, Rolfe Humphries, Muna Lee and Angel Flores. While Flores went on to helm the publications division after it moved to PAU in 1943, the most industrious among the anthology contributors was Lee, the prolific Pan-Americanist, feminist, translator, and cultural programmer whose groundbreaking work led to a position at the State Department as a cultural affairs specialist in 1941.[25] Lee began translating Latin American poetry in the late 1910s in a circle of poets that included William Carlos Williams, Vachel Lindsay, Sarah Teasdale, Salomón de la Selva, and Luis Muñoz Marín, to whom she was married from 1919 to 1946, a period in which he rose from his youthful status as a bohemian socialist poet of works such as "God's Pamphleteer" to the first democratically elected governor of Puerto Rico.[26] As poetry's coordinators on behalf of wartime solidarity, Bishop, Fitts, Lee, MacLeish, and Flores gained major reputations as US brokers of Latin American literature. Fitts's anthology was so influential that postwar poets such as Octavio Paz and José Lezama Lima long continued writing him in the mistaken belief that he could offer them an entryway to the US literary marketplace. As late as 1951, Fitts opined to Flores: "scarcely a day goes by that someone in Latin America doesn't send me a book."[27]

Anthology of Contemporary Latin American Poetry copiously surveyed the "poets of our own day writing in our own idiom" in the quarter-century following the 1916 death of Rubén Darío, a date representing the end of modernismo. The epigrammatic Enrique González Martínez sonnet "Tuércele el cuello al cisne de engañoso plumaje" (Then twist the neck of that delusive swan) served as a program for the volume, following in the wake of Paul Verlaine's call to "Prends l'éloquence et tords-lui son cou!" (Take eloquence and wring its neck!), and now proposing a figural assault on the Parnassian outlook Darío had praised in his poem "Los cisnes." In a biographical note, H. R. Hays labeled "Tuercele el cuello" "the manifesto of post-Modernism,"[28] by which he meant *posmodernismo*, a school of poetry characterized by an anti-ornamental valorization of ordinary speech rhythms and mundane subjects. Fitts labeled the entire anthology of "tougher, more intellectualized" new poetry "post-Modernism." Thus, the first literary reference to *postmodernism* in the United States characterized diverse vanguard threads of Latin American poetry assembled in wartime for popular consumption. In the CIAA anthology, "post-Modernism" also signified the revaluation and promotion of poetry translation as an infrastructure of cultural diplomacy, and a rescaling of this ethic on the hemispheric order.

Fitts's anthology remained in print throughout the 1940s, but garnered few accolades at first. The self-incriminating anthologist professed his "gloomy foreknowledge" that he would be "damned all over Latin America" for impolitic exclusions and inclusions, and sat back "in this bleak terrain, trying to avoid the brickbats as they fly."[29] Spurned translator Lloyd Mallan and his coterie orchestrated critiques in the *New York Times Book Review* and *The Nation*.[30] Mallan had transformed his Abraham Lincoln Brigade credentials from the Spanish Civil War into a lively translation program that included exclusive rights to Rafael Alberti before his reputation for inaccuracy caught up to him. While attempting to convince small press publisher Harry Duncan to bring out one of his wartime anthology projects, he confessed, "my personal theory has always been that poetry, particularly Spanish poetry, should be approximated rather than translated."[31] Muna Lee recalls warning Pablo Neruda of Mallan's ineptitude:

> Several evenings ago, I saw Francisco Aguilera and as usual we began talking about translations. He volunteered the information that Lloyd Mallam* had been writing to him asking for manuscript copies by Pablo Neruda, Aguilera's personal friend. Aguilera's response was to tell L. M. that he had none available to send, and to get an airmail letter off to Neruda warning him that under no circumstances should he permit L. M. to translate. We then proceeded to indulge in the usual cordial comments on Mallam* himself, and to give him full credit for whatever he did for the Republican cause in the Spanish war, and to express the heart-felt hope that he might some day learn Spanish so that he may implement his earnest ambitions (to employ a verb popular in Departmental handouts).
> *Or is it Mallan? I feel disinclined to look it up.[32]

In contrast to Neruda, Jorge Luis Borges received no such fair warning. He granted his earliest US translation rights to Mallan's amateurish friends C. V. and Mary Wickers of Pittsburgh, which may be one practical reason for the delay in seeing his works into English. Bound by contractual obligation, he declined Waldo Frank's offer to translate *Ficciones* (1944) in 1946.[33]

Borges's affiliation with Mallan's cohort also explains why Borges harshly censured Fitts's anthology in the pages of *Sur*, Victoria Ocampo's prominent Buenos Aires journal:

> Fuera de una visible predilección por el verso caótico y por las metáforas incoherentes, el método seguido por el editor se confunde con el azar. Creo percibir en él esa resignación peculiar de los historiadores de la literatura y los filólogos, que admiten y clasifican todos los libros como la astronomía clasifica todos los astros, y la paciente y generosa dermatología todos los males de la piel.[34]

> (Aside from a noticeable predilection for chaotic verse and incoherent metaphors, the method followed by the editor gets mixed up with chance. I think I perceive in it that peculiar resignation of the literary historians and the philologists, who accept and classify every book just as astronomy classifies every star, and dermatology, patiently and generously, every kind of skin disease.)

Borges could not have been aware that Fitts's taxonomic fervor—to the ostensible detriment of his literary judgment—came from the stipulation in his government contract requiring him to include poets from each of the twenty-one independent nations of Latin America.[35] As Bishop explained to Fitts, integrationist inclusiveness trampled taste and discernment: "it will be necessary to bring in the Bill Benet of Honduras and the Millay of Uruguay."[36] On the other hand, Borges's suspiciousness suggestively echoed Argentina's obstructionist response to US-led hemispheric cooperation efforts, for Argentina was the only Latin American nation to remain neutral through the war. In spite of such suspicions, *Sur* became an important inter-American promoter, largely due to the mediations of Waldo Frank, who had even suggested the journal's name over a decade earlier. *Sur* published an issue on US literature in 1944 that hewed closely to *American Harvest* (1942), a CIAA-funded anthology edited by John Peale Bishop and Allen Tate.[37]

In all, the CIAA anthologies sharpened literature's cutting edge as a form of cultural diplomacy by recontextualizing the Latin American vanguard alongside US modernism in a new hemispheric canon of "contemporary" poetry, while promoting literature as a vehicle for geopolitical integration. The capacious network of poets across the hemisphere who were thrust into dialogues with one another—including nearly every poet discussed in this chapter—would not be rivaled until *El Corno Emplumado* came along in the 1960s. Of course, certain figures emerged as the most prominent and representative nodes in the Fitts network. Chief among them was Jorge Carrera Andrade.

Bridging the Hemisphere: Carrera Andrade's Hart Crane

Ecuadorian poet-diplomat Jorge Carrera Andrade (Figure 1.2) offers the clear-est example of how coordinators of inter-American poetry recast the Latin American vanguard from a regional response to Eurocentric modernism into a form of Good Neighbor diplomacy. Fitts, Bishop, and Lee worked to certify Carrera Andrade as the official hemispheric poetic subject, although their cer-tification did not entirely rely on Carrera Andrade's own imagination of inter-Americanism. In his forgotten ode *To the Bay Bridge*, Carrera Andrade construed inter-Americanism as homage to US modernism through his emulations and cri-tiques of Hart Crane, and his poems offered soaring praise toward the bridging actions of hemispheric infrastructural modernization. But Carrera Andrade's readers principally saw in his poetry a dazzling use of metaphor, the choice device of the ultraist avant-garde movement that influenced him as a young poet. In the translation of his collection *A Secret Country* (1946), this device made available

Fig 1.2 Jorge Carrera Andrade, portrait by "du Charme Studio," San Francisco, 1943.

the translation of surrealistic revolutionary consciousness into a Disneyfied geographical exoticism.

With the exception of Neruda, Carrera Andrade was the most widely read Latin American poet in the United States of the early 1940s. George Dillon of *Poetry* in Chicago claimed to break the magazine's editorial policy of "almost never" printing translations in order to showcase Carrera Andrade's "rare and unusual poems," and his position at the head of Fitts's massive anthology was another sign of his prominence.[38] Writing in schoolteacher's Spanish, Fitts placed Carrera Andrade in the company of Vallejo, Neruda, Nicolás Guillén, "y unos tres o cuatro más—: poetas, es decir, de una estatura comparable al Eliot y Pound de mi tradición" (and three or four others—: poets, that is, of a comparable stature to Eliot and Pound in my tradition).[39] Carl Sandburg, Stevens, and Williams were soon numbered among his US admirers. Sandburg, in thrall to Carrera Andrade's regionalism, called him "brother in the poetry quest a little more than any other in this hemisphere."[40] Williams saw in his "clear images" a nostalgic lane-end to an "aboriginal" primitivism.[41] Stevens was captured by novelty, writing to him "This is my first contact with South American poetry, and it is really a very great event for me."[42] Simultaneously, others allied Carrera Andrade's flights of metaphoric abstraction with those of Stevens himself.[43]

After the fear of a Japanese attack on the Americas forced Carrera Andrade from a diplomatic post in Tokyo, in December of 1940 he arrived in San Francisco, where he served as Ecuadorian consul general until 1945. An effective self-promoter, within months of his arrival in San Francisco he was speaking regularly at Pan-American cultural events across California, assisting Fitts's anthology, and advocating for "un más intenso interconocimiento" (a more intensely connected awareness) uniting North and South American countries.[44] In *Poetry* he published a well-regarded survey of tendencies in Latin American poetics entitled "The New American and His Point of View Towards Poetry," which gave an important literary-historical snapshot of Latin American poetry even as it boosted for CIAA objectives. In it, he argued that aesthetic trends from negrismo to Nerudismo amounted to a "second discovery" of América—a wartime, "spiritual" discovery stimulating the "wearied forces of humanity" with the spontaneous "feeling for democracy."[45] For Carrera Andrade, the "more or less" peaceful, interracial coexistence of the Americas amounted to a "universal poetry" in itself.[46]

Carrera Andrade also found a unique publishing venue for his latest poetry in service to the war effort: a three-canto ode entitled *To the Bay Bridge* (Canto al Puente de Oakland, 1941), brought out in a bilingual edition by the short-lived

Office of Pan-American Relations at Stanford University's Hoover Library on War, Revolution and Peace (Figure 1.3).[47] The San Francisco–Oakland Bay Bridge was opened to traffic in late 1936, six months before the Golden Gate Bridge ("the bridge that couldn't be built"). The two bridges exemplified the engineering feats that David E. Nye calls the emblems of the "American technological sublime."[48] Carrera Andrade championed a spirit of infrastructural optimism that looked west to the Pacific Rim and south to Latin America. His poem is notable as the most openhanded lyric expression of wartime hemispheric solidarity. To that end, he mailed an inscribed copy to Rockefeller.[49]

In three cantos, *To the Bay Bridge* examines the bridge's architectural features and reimagines them in ultraist metaphors, apostrophizing a peaceful icon of hemispheric unity. It therefore joins a lineage of inter-American praise poems and chronicles, from José Maria Heredia's ambassadorial ode "Niagara" (1827) to José Martí's essay on the Brooklyn Bridge (1883), which figure as distant but

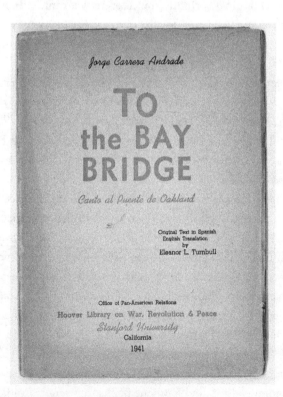

Figure 1.3 Jorge Carrera Andrade, *To the Bay Bridge/Canto al Puente de Oakland*, trans. Eleanor L. Turnbull (Stanford, CA: Office of Pan-American Relations, Hoover Library on War, Revolution & Peace, 1941).

distinct aspects of the poem's cultural memory.⁵⁰ Its more immediate frame of reference is Diego Rivera's *Pan-American Unity: Marriage of the Artistic Expression of the North and of the South on This Continent* (1940) (Figure 1.4), a mural painted for the Golden Gate International Exhibition on Treasure Island, a man-made island constructed using the earth excavated from the Yerba Buena tunnel connecting the two spans of the bridge celebrated by Carrera Andrade.⁵¹ In the mural, the Bay Bridge forms a principle of compositional symmetry. In the central panel, the Bridge's West Span reaches out from behind a totemic, Mexica-machine hybrid toward the indigenous theme of the mural's "South American" left, while the East Span links an industrialized "North America" at the viewer's right. The mural's representation of the Bay Bridge metaphorizes the connectivity between Mexican folkways and US industrial progress.

Yet another intertextual allusion informs Carrera Andrade's metaphors and diction, although its presence is less readily marked: Hart Crane's symphonic epic to national unity *The Bridge* (1930)—and especially its trans-borough proem, "To Brooklyn Bridge." Crane suggests that the Brooklyn Bridge's "choiring strings" offer a nostalgic symbol of innovation, looking backward to the bridge's completion in 1883. Even Joseph Stella's 1941 futurist painting of it is titled *Old Brooklyn Bridge*. Crane poeticizes what he calls a "mystical synthesis" of the nation, inaugurating an era of modernization from 1880 to 1930 defined by a massive acceleration of spatiotemporal connectedness.⁵² Often, Crane's epic measures out this infrastructure of national space in the idioms and instruments of a populist musical fantasia, as if the transcontinental roadways churned from the barrel on the chest of an organ grinder:

> Macadam, gun-grey as the tunny's belt,
> Leaps from Far Rockaway to Golden Gate:
> Listen: the miles a hurdy-gurdy grinds—
> Down gold arpeggios mile on mile unwinds⁵³

We see here an example of what Crane famously described to Harriet Monroe as the "logic of metaphor," with its emphasis on the poet's right to arrogate to his poem condensed lyrical language that strains rational intellection.⁵⁴ A roadway, whose steely color Crane likens to the underbelly of a tuna, "leaps" (again like a fish) from the continental nation's easternmost to westernmost point. This action is at once bridge-like, through an implied visual metaphor between the fish's dorsal and the suspension cables of the bridge, as well as musical, through the hurdy-gurdy's movement, which produces an aureate popular music out of a purely mechanistic "grinding" action.

Fig 1.4 Diego Rivera, *Pan-American Unity: Marriage of the Artistic Expression of the North and of the South of this Continent* (1940). © 2016 Banco de México Diego Rivera Frida Kahlo Museums Trust, Mexico, D.F./Artists Rights Society (ARS), New York.

Carrera Andrade's ultraist metaphors are not perfectly matched to Crane's logic of metaphor, yet they do relay Crane's music from the Golden Gate, in borrowings that seem intentional and explicit. Carrera Andrade's Bay Bridge is made of "Millas de hierro y cielo entretejidos—/medir se puede sólo con la musica" (Miles of interwoven iron and sky—/measured only in music). Thus, if Crane's "To Brooklyn Bridge" is the site of what Brian Reed calls a national "theophany," Carrera Andrade's *To the Bay Bridge* loosely rewrites it into a more capacious New World prophecy.[55] Carrera Andrade calques Crane's blazon-like rhythms of disclosure and his musical metaphors, threading Crane's rhetorical question "How could mere toil align thy choiring strings?" through his bellicose declaration "Tus tuberías de órgano celeste/una música soplan de hierro victorioso" (Your pipes of celestial organ/sound a music of victorious iron). In Crane's proem, the path of a gull "Over the chained bay waters Liberty" signals the bridge's status as a form of freedom from marine fetters. Carrera Andrade "recasts" this image as oxymoron: "Tus lanzas son de paz,/tus cadenas marítimas a los hombres libertan" (Your lances are for peace,/your maritime chains liberate men). Further, Carrera Andrade borrows Crane's propensity for archaic syntactic constructions, as when "por tus ángeles férreos escoltado" (by your iron angels escorted) evokes Crane's "Implicitly thy freedom staying thee!"[56] As Carrera Andrade's poem careens between emulation, misprision, and critique, it imbues Crane's unmarked terms such as "victory" and "freedom" with new resonances in the atmosphere of the war. In all, Carrera Andrade's poem emphatically styles episodes and idioms of celebration after Crane's poem, even if his homage neglects the dedicatory conventions that would otherwise reveal his panegyric allusions and borrowings.

These close formal observations suggest more promiscuous genetic textual relations among the poetries of the Americas in the 1940s than many scholars admit. Yet, even as they point toward a record of cross-cultural borrowings, they signal ruptures in the shared access to a mythography of the hemisphere across New World modernisms. Carrera Andrade builds a literary-historical bridge toward Crane only to signal the limits of Crane's connective imagination. Crane tenders the Brooklyn Bridge's central span as a vaulting, orchestral symbol of New World coherence in contrast to the fragmentary metropolis of Eliot's *The Waste Land*, burnishing Eliot's Old World alienation with New World optimism through the theurgic potential of industrial modernity. To put it schematically, the exuberant bedlamite on Crane's parapets does not share a fatalistic imaginary with the Dantesque commuters on Eliot's London Bridge. By contrast, Carrera Andrade asks readers to reexamine Crane's exuberance, pointing out the limits of his New World coherence. Crane sought to extend his vision during his 1931 Guggenheim to Mexico, where he planned a Montezuma tragedy entitled "Cortez: An Enactment." Yet his symbolic extensions make few gestures beyond the imperial consolidation of the United States (accordingly, Crane himself was largely ignored by major 1930s Mexican interpreters of US literature, such as Salvador Novo).[57] Among early 1930s historical works, Crane's epic raptures of North American history evoke Herbert Bolton's famous 1932 address, "The Epic of Greater America," which O'Gorman critiqued as the "impetuous sketch" of an imperial hemisphere.[58]

To the Bay Bridge indulges a techno-sublimity of its own, but it avoids Crane's romance of connectivity in order to make sense of its object through cautious exercises in hemispheric comparison and measurement. The brief second canto of the three-canto poem tacitly analogizes the Bay Bridge and the Equator, apostrophizing the bridge while animating its structural features. Its physical weight strikes the Ecuadorian speaker as intelligible because he regards his native equator as a planetary "fiel de balanza" (needle on the scales) that provides him with a natural dispensation to comprehend "form" at the magnitude of the hemisphere. He is "hombre de una tierra sin vocación de nube,/donde la luz exacta ninguna forma olvida" (man from a land without vocation of cloud,/where the exacting light/never forgets a form). Carrera Andrade's speaker exhibits a native genius for deriving evenhanded, diplomatic meanings from technological and poetic forms.

To the speaker, the meanings of the bridge's form reside in its covert promise of peace: "tu secreta misión de paz y enlace/en un complot de mares apresados/y rescatadas islas" (your secret mission for peace and junction/in a conspiracy of captured seas/and recovered islands). Such elated fixation on peace requires clarification, as does its status as an ode, as opposed to the elegies, hymns, nocturnes, and vituperations so common to late-1930s Spanish-language war poetry. Carrera Andrade would later describe the San Francisco Bay Area as a flashpoint for inter-Americanism, but also as a huge war machine.[59] His poem celebrates Latino producers of the wartime food economy, whose "huertas" (victory gardens) transport food across the bridge. Yet he later recalled that the Bay Bridge bisected the naval installations at Yerba Buena and Treasure Island launching "fuerzas pacíficas," that shipyards in Richmond churned out a battleship per day, and that physicist Ernest Lawrence's cyclotron particle accelerator was installed in the service of the Manhattan Project in the Berkeley labs. In short, his diplomatic mission left him with the impression that San Francisco's Rivera-like "spirit of Pan-American Unity" was choked out by an emerging military superpower.

Amid infrastructures of total war, the bridge's metaphoric meanings matter to the poet precisely in so far as they are hard to stabilize:

> Tu armazón de alegría
> a la tarde se cambia en osamenta
> o metálico fósil
> de un animal de nubes,
>
> o senda de pacíficas espadas
> o red colgada, en pesca de luceros
> —encendida langosta de la altura—,
> o salto de la tierra sobre el límite.
>
> Tu profecía inmensa restablece
> la paz segura de los años próximos
>
> (Your framework of joy
> turns skeletal at evening
> or metallic fossil
> of an animal of clouds,
>
> or path of peaceable swords
> or a suspended purse seine, fishing for stars
> —illuminated lobster of the heights—
> or a leap of the earth over a limit.
>
> Your immense prophecy restores
> the certain peace of the coming years)

Here, an indecisive repetition of the vowel *o* insists long enough that it gains the status of a device. As the poem's primary unit of conjunction, *o* links the metaphoric transformations of the bridge, which "turns skeletal . . ./or metallic fossil/. . . or path of peaceable swords." As these transformations accrete, the *o* doubles as an apostrophe, a coupling that has been announced by the first stanza of the poem, in which apostrophe and metaphor reinforce one another: "¡oh atleta mineral y zócalo del cielo!" (oh mineral athlete and plinth for the heavens!)."[60] As an anaphoric skeleton, the *o* signals both accretion and apostrophe. The structure of the poem is the poet's autotelic address to his imaginative facility to change the meanings of the bridge's steelwork through exacting perceptions. Other Carrera Andrade poems employ the same anaphoric *o*. "Zona Minada" (Mined Zone) apostrophizes an eroticized hemispheric geography, each new metaphor wounding the enumeration of the landscape like the mines from which it takes its title. In both poems, the renovating impulse of poetic praise solaces a landscape of industrial damage.

To the Bay Bridge reduplicates this procedure in smaller, semantic units of the poem, layering discrete vertebrae on the anaphoric skeleton. The oxymoronic "pacíficas espadas" exemplify "peacefulness" despite the fact that they are named for the martial character of their form, and in repetitions of the word "pacífica" they augment the polysemy of the Pacific Ocean itself, anchoring a front of the war on an etymological foundation, as the calm sea that Magellan observed as he rounded Cape Horn. Like an "encendida langosta" (illuminated lobster)—an image recalling Crane's comparison of roadways to leaping tuna—or like the net that catches the lobster, the bridge externalizes structural purposes of connection, extension and linkage, rendering them with the material integrity that was fast becoming a reigning orthodoxy of architectural modernism. These transmutations all propose the bridge as a structurally honest guarantor of a postwar peace. Shooting through the vagaries of its metaphors, *To the Bay Bridge* triangulates the rhetoric of democratic humanitarianism, inter-American modernization, and subaltern nativism (the Ecuadorian point of view), propagandizing through that admixture on behalf of the "peaceful" apotheosis of the New World.

Writing in San Francisco soon after, Muriel Rukeyser echoed Carrera Andrade's paean to peace: "In a time of long war, surrounded by the images of war, we imagine peace. Among the resistances, we imagine poetry. And what city makes the welcome, in what soil do these roots flourish?"[61] The "Chapultepec Park" poems in Rukeyser's *Beast in View* (1944) reciprocate Carrera Andrade's poem by taking inter-American symbols as occasions to imagine peace amid war, and foreshadow the 1945 Act of Chapultepec, the hemispheric security treaty laying groundwork for the United Nations meeting that same year.

Virtuosic use of metaphor in the mode of Neruda had been Carrera Andrade's distinguishing characteristic since his very first collection in 1926. As Bishop remarked in his introduction to *A Secret Country*, "his comparisons constantly astonish us." Hays, who called Carrera Andrade "Magician of Metaphors," describes an exemplary ultraist technique, a quasi-Futurist penchant for jarring analogy that Borges, Ramón Gómez de la Serna, Guillermo de Torre, and Oliverio Girondo had developed in the early 1920s, and disseminated in the *Índice de la nueva poesía americana* (1927) edited by Borges, Alberto Hidalgo, and Vicente Huidobro.[62] Yet to a former ultraist such as Borges, Carrera Andrade's subject matter impoverished his pyrotechnics: "La culpa de los Huidobro, de los Peralta, de los Carrera Andrade, no es el abuso de metáforas deslumbrantes: es la circunstancia banal de que infatigablemente las buscan y de que infatigablemente no las encuentran" (The fault of the Huidobros, the Peraltas, and the Carrera Andrades is not the abuse of dazzling metaphors: it is the banal circumstance from which they tirelessly search them out and in which they tirelessly do not find them).[63] Reviewing Fitts's anthology, Borges scorned Carrera Andrade: "sospecho que para inaugurar una antología de todo el continente hubiera sido posible exhumar un ejercicio menos insípido que *Primavera & Compañia* del ecuatoriano Jorge Carrera Andrade" (I suspect it would have been possible to inaugurate an anthology of the entire continent by exhuming a less insipid exercise than "Spring & Company" by the Ecuadorian Jorge Carrera Andrade).[64] Although Carrera Andrade had written this early poem when he was in the "revolutionary" phase of his twenties, Borges drew consternation from verses such as "y sólo se ocupa de llevar hoy día/soplos de propaganda por todos los rincones" (And today is only concerned with puffing/Propaganda into every corner). Easy as it might be to disregard *To the Bay Bridge* as more propaganda, it also enacts a generative inter-American ideal. Carrera Andrade's United Nations poetry voices national claims on universal humanity in the service of wartime antifascism and post-war peace. Paz, who befriended Carrera Andrade in wartime Berkeley, would similarly endorse the inter-American system when he worked as a correspondent for *Mañana* during the UN founding proceedings in San Francisco in 1945. His columns rebuked critics who saw inter-Americanism as a US "wolf's costume."[65]

In a routine irony of transnational reception history, the source of Carrera Andrade's appeal to US readers was not his valorization of inter-Americanism in *To the Bay Bridge*. His appeal relied instead on the exotic qualities of *Un país secreto* (A Secret Country, 1940), self-published in Tokyo, translated by Muna Lee with an introduction by Bishop in 1942–1943, but delayed because of turmoil in CIAA's publication division until 1946, after Carrera Andrade was restationed in Venezuela.[66] While *To the Bay Bridge* offers a Crane-inspired poetry of technological linkage in a realist hemispheric geography, US readers preferred *A Secret Country*'s poems in which "No hay norte ni sur, este ni oeste" (There is neither North nor South, neither East nor West), only a metaphoric ship of inter-American unity with cargo for exotica mongers: "En la nave de veinte cornetas/embarqué mi baúl de papagayos/hacia otro extremo de la tierra" (On the ship with twenty pennants/I embarked my trunk of parrots/toward the other end of earth)."[67] Bishop's introduction aligns Carrera Andrade's aesthetic value with the puerile global freedoms of imperial geography lessons:

When I was a child and first went to school, I was taught that the Equator was an imaginary line encircling the globe midway between the poles. Later, in that book from which I first learned how the sensation of distance can be evoked by the strange names of far places, I was told of a country called Ecuador. Its name had been given it because it lay athwart that line which, first and last, is a convenience of the imagination. [...] More than once, in reading the poems of Jorge Carrera Andrade, I have recalled that ignorant time when, with a child's possessiveness, I collected in my mind the names of far countries. His *Secret Country* has something of that remote and romantic attraction that a first book of geography has.[68]

Darlene Sadlier describes such cartographic apperceptions as a "magic geography" popularized by propaganda films such as Walt Disney's *Saludos Amigos* (1942).[69] Readers of Elizabeth Bishop may think first of her poem "The Map" for an index of the astounding popularity of such exercises in Disneyfied magic geographies in the poems of the mid-1940s. No poet lampoons the vogue for US understandings of ultraist metaphor as cartoon geography better than Lysander Kemp, who titled a poem "Landscapes by Lorca and Disney" while stationed as a GI in Ecuador.

Reviewing *A Secret Country* in 1947, Babette Deutsch noted that Carrera Andrade followed a trajectory from revolutionary to aesthete, proletarian to diplomat, but that his poems transcended such polarities. They are "not political or programmatic, but they are, what is more important, profoundly humane."[70] We ought to ask why their appeals to humaneness court suspicion. How did discourses of humanitarian commitment, so essential to the experience of the 1930s literary left, feed so effortlessly into US wartime politics and programs toward Latin America? To understand how wartime cultural diplomacy could mummify left radicalism, we need to look at inter-Americanism's dissenting leftist practitioners: in particular, Langston Hughes and the poets encircling Waldo Frank.

Minority Islands: Hughes, Frank, de Moraes, and the Poem of Racial Democracy

Langston Hughes enjoyed a readership in Latin America that outstripped Carrera Andrade and Neruda's reciprocal popularity in the United States. As Vera Kutzinski demonstrates, the many late-1920s translations of "I, Too" (by José Fernandez de Castro in Cuba, Xavier Villaurrutia in Mexico, and Jorge Luis Borges in Argentina) and his early 1930s visits to Havana made Hughes the best-loved and most-read US poet throughout the Spanish language world, second only to Whitman, whose hemispheric amplitude he strategically echoed.[71] Hughes also assumed a brief role as an inter-American cultural diplomat, which is notable for its divergences from Carrera Andrade. One of several African-American Good Neighbors at the edge of CIAA activities, Hughes wrote several poems underscoring the imperative expressed by the African-American philosopher and literary patron Alain Locke in a 1944 lecture tour of Haiti: "democratic race equality and fraternity," too often ignored, was the Good Neighbor policy's "morally inescapable" corollary.[72] Like Locke, Hughes observed the new cultural relations apparatus firsthand, only to be frustrated by the limited potential of popular music and cinema exchanges among "the Xavier Cugats, the Elsa Houstons, and the Carmen Mirandas." In the salon run by Frances Grant's Pan American Women's Association, Hughes advocated instead for "a more comprehensive exchange of cultural values."[73] He proposed an Afrocentric inter-American culture that might include intellectuals like W. E. B. Du Bois, Richard Wright, and Arna Bontemps heading south, while Afro-Cuban performer Eusebia Cosme and poet Nicolás Guillén might come north. Unfortunately, championing Guillén at times proved difficult. In 1941, Guillén wrote Hughes in confusion after the US government denied his visa to attend the fourth meeting of the League of American Writers.[74]

In the August 14, 1943, edition of the American Labor Party's Harlem weekly *People's Voice*, Hughes published a poem entitled "Broadcast to the West Indies," a lightly musicalized circum-Caribbean address that went uncollected during his lifetime. Preceded by a mock station identification, the first two of its eleven stanzas read as follows:

> Radio Station: Harlem
> Wave Length: The Human Heart
>
> Hello, Jamaica!
> Hello, Haiti!
> Hello, Cuba!
> Hello, Panama!
> Hello, St. Kitts!
> Hello, Bahamas!
> All you islands and all you lands
> That rim the sun-warmed Caribbean!
> Hello! Hello! Hello! Hello!
> I, Harlem,
> Speak to you!

I, Harlem,
Island, too.
In the great sea of this day's turmoil.
I, Harlem,
Little land, too,
Bordered by the sea that washes
    and mingles
With all the other waters of the
    world.[75]

Behind its apparent simplicity—that over-extended watchword of Hughes criticism—the poem shrewdly parodies the inter-American war propaganda produced by CIAA. Hughes himself was among the many cultural workers CIAA enlisted in its efforts through the translations Dudley Fitts asked him to produce for his anthology, and between 1942 and 1944, Hughes occasionally read poems on goodwill broadcasts to the Caribbean and Latin America, subject to the approval of sponsoring organizations such as the Office of War Information.[76] Such broadcasts fed the expansion of shortwave radio as an avenue for inter-American propaganda, with ambitious programs hosted by Orson Welles, Archibald MacLeish, and Juan Ramón Jiménez filling airtime for the CIAA's Division of Radio (Figure 1.5).[77]

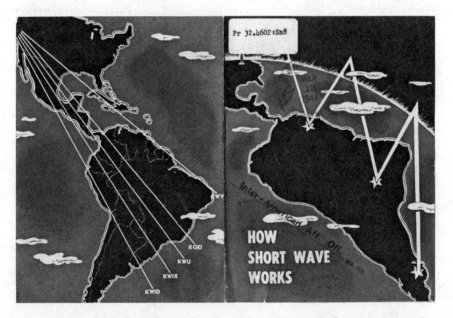

Fig 1.5 US Inter-American Affairs Office, "How Short Wave Works," 1943. Courtesy of Stanford University Libraries.

Hughes's poem therefore speaks to both dissident and liberal models of inter-American cultural relations. On one hand, Hughes's description of Harlem reidentifying with the islands of the West Indies keys in to the demography of East Harlem's El Barrio community, often called Puerto Rico's New York colonia, although Puerto Rico, as a US colonial protectorate rather than an independent nation, is notably absent from Hughes's catalog. On the other hand, Hughes's comparisons evoke a common analogy of the period. CIAA pamphlets regularly parceled out geographical comparisons between Maryland and El Salvador, or between Texas and Venezuela, gesturing to the emergent paradiplomatic practice of twinning towns and declaring sister cities.[78] Hughes reorients the analogy between the Southern United States and South America in terms of a poetics of extranational racial allegiance. Harlem, marooned within the island metropolis of Manhattan, bottles and casts messages of solidarity to the archipelagoes a Gulf Stream away.

Nor is the poem's novelty found in its collectivized ego "I, Harlem." This self-identification evoked his signature 1926 revision of Walt Whitman in his "Epilogue" to *The Weary Blues*, with its famous refrain "I, too, sing America," now reimagined as a translocal Caribbean identification "I, Harlem/Island too." Perhaps one can also hear in its repetitions a translingual homophone for Federico García Lorca's plaint "¡Ay, Harlem! ¡Ay, Harlem! ¡Ay, Harlem!," which punctures Lorca's celebration of African-American experience "El rey de Harlem" (The King of Harlem).[79] Rolfe Humphries's English-language edition of Lorca's posthumous *Poet in New York* had just appeared in 1940, and Hughes himself translated Lorca's *Boda de sangre* in 1938, as well as several other writers associated with what Barry Carr calls the "webs of radical internationalism in the Red circum-Caribbean."[80] Already by the mid-1940s, such writers included Guillén, Jacques Roumain (Haiti), Afro-Chinese poet Regino Pedroso (Cuba), and folk dancer and writer Nellie Campobello (Mexico).[81]

Only as "Broadcast to the West Indies" progresses does its abrasive racial critique of Good Neighbor diplomacy clarify why Hughes never read it on the radio nor collected it in a volume such as *Jim Crow's Last Stand* (1943). Midway through the poem, the tone—at once naively salutatory and sharply parodic—veers toward a revolutionary voice of hemispheric racial solidarity with new candor. Hughes permits a speculative moment of Axis sympathy on the grounds that the Axis has made anti–Jim Crow appeals to the Afro-Antilles:

> They say—the Axis—
> That the U.S.A. is bad:

It lynches Negroes,
Starves them, pushes them aside.
In some states the vote is dead.
Those things are partly true.
They say—the enemy—
Via short wave every day,
That there is now no way
For you to put any faith at all
In what the Yankees say—
They have no love for you
Or any colored people anywhere.
That's also partly true.

Hughes of course rejects this tentative, scandalous identification with the Axis, but not before articulating his own "axis" of West-Indian solidarity premised on shared oppression:

Certain things we know in common:
Suffering,
Domination,
Segregation—
Locally called
Jim Crow.

Here, war occasions a new kind of inter-American turn—both as a figure of address and as a poetic "coordination" of Caribbean geography. With racial democracy now a rhetorical battlefield in the propaganda of the Axis and the allied "United Nations," the poem suggests new terms for transnational literary relations among black political actors who, as Vaughn Rasberry argues, saw a latent kinship between democratic liberalism and European fascism when it came to the status of racial minorities, and who saw in wartime antifascism "a discursive field ripe for strategic manipulation."[82] Therefore, "Broadcast to the West Indies" mimics US inter-Americanism even as it seeks to counter it with deeper commonalities and routes of intrahemispheric communication. The poem beams its messages at the Caribbean with diction as narrow as the short-wave bandwidth, cutting through the geolinguistic differences (French, Creole, Spanish, and English) dividing the nations and protectorates to which it extends fraternal greetings. Memorializing the event of the broadcast—a word that etymologically evokes an agricultural dissemination—the radio poem announces its independence from print circulation. Its metaphoric emotional "wavelength" ("a direct line/From your heart to mine") stands in open wonder at the long-range instantaneity of radio technologies, rehumanizing the bandwidth through a sentimental universalism. Although Hughes plays up instantaneity as a radiophonic fiction, the printing of the poem in a New York proletarian newspaper makes the Caribbean an apostrophic or absent addressee, allowing African-American laboring classes to imagine translocal solidarity.

Cumulatively, these features make "Broadcast to the West Indies" a representative specimen for a recent generation of comparative poetry scholarship wont to quarrel with T. S. Eliot's and W. H. Auden's midcentury claims that poetry refuses participation in transnational cultural life more obstinately than other expressive arts such as novels, films, and artworks. Jahan Ramazani, a principal exponent of this view, understands poems by Hughes as part of a "traveling poetry" founded upon the poetic compression of geographical distance.[83] For Kutzinski, likewise, Hughes figures the "connections" of a "fringe modernism" stitched together by "travel and personal contacts and by way of translation."[84] Yet the poem's archipelagic inventory, with its pathos of isolation, belies its evocations of connectivity. The island motif and the apostrophic address enumerate a paradox of disconnectivity even as the radiophonic element clamors to connect. The poem asks us to bear in mind William J. Maxwell's contention that the mobile identities of transnational modernity did not often travel freely, but were shaped by patterns of state sponsorship and censure.[85] We might call this the "double voice" of wartime Good Neighbor culture, typified by poems like "Broadcast to the West Indies," which do not easily slice along grains of aesthetic or political partisanship. While employed as a propagandist and goodwill ambassador, Hughes doubled as a transnational dissident.

This "double-voiced" inter-Americanism, equal parts dissidence and diplomacy, was quite common during the war. Crucially, it extended to hemispheric latitudes such as Argentina, where Axis inroads made US influence weakest, as well as locations where US influence reigned, such as Puerto Rico. In the next few pages, I'll show how Waldo Frank pioneered a double-voiced inter-Americanism in his cultural diplomatic work in unaligned Argentina and the Southern Cone. In the remaining sections of the chapter, I'll turn to the mechanics of this double voice in works by poets concerned with the cause of Puerto Rican independence.

One of the key ligatures in the United States' wartime campaign for cultural credibility among intellectuals in the Southern Cone was the novelist and critic Waldo Frank. After rejecting the Department of State's 1941 entreaties, in 1942 Frank agreed to undertake a CIAA-funded lecture junket in Brazil, Argentina,

Chile, and Peru, which he subsequently recounted in the travel narrative *South American Journey* (1943).[86] He intimated publicly that he traveled owing to the spontaneous invitations of Latin American intellectuals, but letters to Nelson Rockefeller reveal that CIAA allotted Frank $6,500 over the course of his six-month excursion.[87] It was a pittance compared to the enormous monies CIAA invested in Disney and Welles, but still significant for an avowed radical with a huge FBI file.[88] Frank was too valuable to the CIAA not to send south, for in the previous decade he had become an inter-American cultural infrastructure unto himself. *America Hispana* (1929), his portrait of Spanish-American regeneration, was wildly successful, and the hemispheric tour that he took before writing it galvanized connections between vanguard little magazines such as Juan Marinello's *Revista de Avance* (Cuba), José Mariátegui's *Amauta* (Lima), and Victoria Ocampo's *Sur* (Buenos Aires). Across the 1930s, he maintained a lively place in anti-imperialist and inter-American leftist networks.

The 1942 tour married Frank's leftist bona fides to the antifascism of wartime hemispheric solidarity. On his well-publicized circuit, he boldly voiced positions that strayed from US foreign policy platforms. He called for Latin American nations to embrace socialist production models and to expropriate and nationalize US-owned natural resources; for the United States to make progress toward racial democracy; for American states to denounce neighbor dictatorships wherever they arose; and for a new model of intercultural exchange based on hemispheric educational curricula, which might rectify the "frothy failure" of the "benevolent committees."[89] Frank displayed a talent for giving vent to Latin American anti-US sentiment while still promoting a "religion of democracy" chiming with US rhetoric.[90] This "common *democratic* destiny" of the "American hemisphere" was a peculiarly creative figure for Frank, blending the "old story" of Bolívar's continental ambition with the poetic formulae of Emerson, Whitman, and Thoreau. Frank sought to renew this story, "to tell it again, in the new terms," although his close friend Lewis Mumford gently lampooned these new terms as Frank's mystical egoism.[91] Nonetheless, the literary elite struggling to combat German influence in neutral Argentina greeted his formulations with high seriousness. At a welcome dinner sponsored by the Sociedad Argentina de Escritores (SADE), Nobel laureate Carlos Saavedra Lamas claimed that Frank emblematized a new kind of "creative diplomat," a term that should be flagged, like MacLeish's usage of "cultural relations," for the novelty with which Saavedra uttered it.

Frank styled himself an apolitical "creative diplomat" particularly when confronting and critiquing prominent politicians. When he held an audience with

President Castillo at the Casa Rosada in Buenos Aires, he pitched his "sense of the hemisphere" and his attendant "anxiety" for unallied Argentina. But, as he continued, "the remark about the hemisphere [Castillo] takes indulgently, as if I had recited a line from a familiar sonnet."[92] This passing remark deserves emphasis. It underscores how "hemispheric democracy" was conceived as poesis as much as realpolitik. Indeed, wherever he went, Frank evaded official diplomatic status, describing himself as a "symbol": "a safe and eloquent means of keeping before the public the cause which everybody knows I stand for."[93] Cultural diplomacy metonymically substitutes the values of the artist's cultural freedom and creative expression for political speech. Frank speaks only "as the free and independent artist, as the personal friend."[94] While such formulations later become familiar to what Frank Ninkovich calls the cultural Cold War's "liberal ecumene," Frank's exploratory notions of cultural freedom in 1942 have an incipient force all their own.[95] A hemispheric network of belle-lettrists and literary vanguards activated the idea of creative autonomy for the use of wartime cultural diplomacy.

Frank's Argentine literary hosts received him with occasional poems that figure him as just such a symbolic, open secret. In his remarks at the SADE welcome dinner, broadcast on national radio and widely republished in the press, poet Vicente Barbieri offered a "Salutación a Waldo Frank" that affirmed his status as symbol:

> Llega con tu equipaje sumario y sin afán.
> Conocemos tu avío, sereno Waldo Frank.
>
> Sólo queremos verte tan pequeño y tenaz,
> con una mano al pecho y a un lado el antifaz.[96]
>
> (You arrive, your luggage light and lank,
> we recognize your readiness, serene Waldo Frank.
>
> We only want to see you, so slight and steadfast,
> hand to your chest and at one side the mask.)

These couplets hinge on a pun in the word *antifaz*, which refers to Frank's diplomatic "disguise," but also to his acute role as an "antifascist" agitator. The newspaper *Argentina Libre* published the poem beneath vanguard artist Toño Salazar's caricature of Frank delicately holding aloft an olive branch against an industrial skyline (Figure 1.6).

Likewise, SADE president Ezequiel Martínez Estrada returned to poetry after nearly a decade of cultural criticism in order to write "A Waldo Frank" (To Waldo

Fig 1.6   Toño Salazar, "Waldo Frank," *Argentina Libre* (May 7, 1942): 6. Waldo Frank Papers, Series VIII, Box 127, Folder 3532, PENN. Used by permission of the Heirs of Toño Salazar's Artistic Heritage: Nuria Sagrera Gallardo and Maria Elisa Guirola Sagrera.

Frank). He feted Frank's arrival with a parody of Whitman's Lincoln elegy ("Oh capitán, mi capitán!"), inscribing Frank in a Whitmanian world brotherhood by calling him "camarada." But soon the poem turns away from Frank's figure of Lincolnesque unity to address young Argentine poet-recruits:

> ¡Poetas!: él es nuestro camarada que llega,
> es un cantor de América —es un alma, y no más.
> Aquel que esté dispuesto a dar lo que posee
> —riqueza, juventud, amor, renombre, paz—
> aquel que sea rápido, y ágil, y esté resuelto;
> aquel que sea intrépido, viril y alto y audaz;
> aquel que se halle sano y sea generoso;
> aquel que tenga anhelos de ser mejor y más;
> aquel que ame en América la tierra del futuro,
> del cuerpo y del espíritu, material e ideal;

que abandone las aulas, si estudia; que abandone
su taller, si trabaja —deje amigos y hogar—
pues a todos nosotros, uno a uno (uno a uno
él nos conoce a todos) a todos nombrará,
y es preciso estar prontos y responder: "¡Presente,
mi capitán!"[97]

(Poets! Our comrade arrives,
a singer of América—a soul, and nothing more.
He who is willing to give what he has
—wealth, youth, love, renown, peace—
he who is quick, and agile, and determined;
he who is undaunted, virile, tall, and audacious;
he who discovers his goodness and is generous;
he who longs to be more and better;
he who loves, in América, the land of the future,
body and soul, matter and ideal;
who abandons the classrooms if he studies; abandons
his workshop if he works—leaves his friends and his home—
so all of us, one by one (one by one
he makes us known to all), he names us all,
and it is right to be ready to respond: "Here,
my captain!")

Martínez Estrada calls for Argentine writers to martial spiritually virile attentions to the cause of a hemispheric solidarity, to bear out its Hegelian potential as a "land of the future," in a popular slogan of the day.

The poem's plea for spiritual virility may be understood as a rejoinder to Frank's diagnosis of Argentina's moral lassitude with respect to "the inter-American imperative." Frank saw this lassitude all over Argentine literary culture: in the recent suicides of Leopoldo Lugones, Horacio Quiroga, and Alfonsina Storni; in the "subtler resignations" of Samuel Glusberg's self-exile to Chile; in Eduardo Mallea's "wraiths of spiritual, actionless limbo"; and in Martínez Estrada himself, who had set aside the "lyre for the scalpel" in order to "excoriate the moral bankruptcy" of the Argentines in *Radiografía de la pampa* (X-Ray of the Pampas).[98] Borges too became a mere literature of escape; when Frank offered to translate *Ficciones* in 1946, Borges wrote self-effacingly to Frank that his entire body of short fiction was "fantastic, symbolical, or merely fanciful stuff."[99] Frank's incitation is one reason that despite Argentina's wartime neutrality, *Sur* promoted inter-Americanism over and against government censure. Following Frank's visit, Martínez Estrada, Maria Rosa Oliva, and Victoria Ocampo each conducted a cultural diplomacy tour of the United States.[100] Although his indictment of *Sur*'s literature of dismay raised few hackles, Frank's stay in Argentina took an infamous turn when he impugned the moral indolence of the neutral Argentine government in a farewell editorial. The government declared him persona non grata, and, in an appalling event that made international headlines, a group of fascist sympathizers disguised as police officers broke into his apartment to pistol-whip him.

This shocking dust-up tends to efface the broader record of Frank's poeticized brand of cultural diplomacy. More often, Latin American poets furnished shelter for the cultural diplomat outside the swirl of political confrontation.[101] In Brazil, he avoided making official comment altogether, first by decamping for Petrópolis to stay with Gabriela Mistral, who plied him with the poems she was composing for *Lagar* (1954). But he spent most of his time in Brazil with the young poet Vinicius de Moraes, a low-level functionary in Getulio Vargas's dictatorship who was assigned as Frank's personal aide. They accompanied the vanguard poet Oswald de Andrade on visits to the enormous set in São Cristóvão where Orson Welles was filming a documentary on samba for the failed film *It's All True*, and they slummed around the louche brothels of the La Mangue neighborhood, which Frank expurgated from his accounts. While these detours probably focused on sexual tourism, de Moraes later credited them with his conversions to the political left and to the poetry of Brazilian folkways that culminated in his screenplay for the popular international film *Black Orpheus* (1959). In commemoration of their exploits, de Moraes wrote "Balada do Mangue," his famously ribald redondilha (or seven-syllable meter) about the "pobres flores gonocócicas" (poor gonorrheal flowers) of the brothel, "Que à noite despetalais/As vossas pétalas tóxicas!" (Who at night undress your toxic petals!). He dedicated the poem to Frank, mailing him a copy with a sequence of glosses on the poem's vernacular turns of phrase.[102] According to Vinicius, reciprocal inter-American books had gestated from their friendship: "um de Waldo Frank sobre o Brasil. Outro de um jovem poeta brasileiro, amigo do grande poeta americano, sobre Waldo Frank através o Brasil" (One by Waldo Frank about Brazil. Another by a young Brazilian poet, friend of the great American poet, about Waldo Frank traversing Brazil).[103] Shortly after the war, Vinicius became a diplomatic consul in Los Angeles, California, and Frank's *South American Journey* (1943) and Vinicius's *Nossa Senhora do Los Angeles* (1946) approximate these long-separated books.

Returning to the United States in 1943, Frank reformulated his tropes of hemispheric solidarity in an article for *Foreign Affairs*. Observing a map of the world covered by anti-democratic regimes, Frank referred to the Americas as a democratic "island in this over whelming land-mass; a minority island surrounded by the far greater lands and populations of the other hemisphere."[104] The "minority island" is a curious and evocative term, with its scalar shift between the world-region and the insular unit, its inscription of "isolationist" principles in a new global picture, and its shaky equation of democracy as a minority politics on the world scale with the causes of poor nations on regional scales and minorities isolated in racist states. Frank argued that the "the American hemisphere must become an island dedicated to the democratic will of creating persons." The "island hemisphere" would overcome "the strong need not to know the weak neighbor," and thus improve minority conditions caused by Jim Crow in the United States and by its imperial effects abroad.[105] "The minority island" therefore flexibly sought to resolve intra-national and intra-hemispheric conflicts in the same figure, and it provides a heuristic for evaluating the hemispheric cultural work that wartime poets of the Americas sought to achieve. The figure calls attention to the impacts of crisis rhetoric, racial democracy, and humanitarianism on poetry. It warrants an attention to minor literary artifacts and local, often insular literary contexts, rescaled in terms of hemispheric frames of reference and horizons of experience. However else they differ, Vinicius's poetry of the Brazilian Mangue, with its local appeals to racialized populism, the Whitmanian occasional poems of the *Sur* group, and the wartime elegies that wind their way into Mistral's *Lagar* (1954) all gather around Frank as a symbolic shorthand for wartime hemispheric democracy. Like Hughes's figure of the shortwave radio, Frank's own egoistic "creative diplomat" persona became an inter-American cultural infrastructure. Each offered mechanisms for imagining the hemisphere as a minority island "in the great sea of this day's turmoil."

Between Dissidence and Diplomacy: Neruda, Bishop, Burgos

Still more than Frank's Argentina trip, Pablo Neruda's February 1943 visit to New York City occasioned the war's most finely modulated performance of double-voiced cultural diplomacy. When his biographers report this visit, they mistake it as a CIAA or Voice of America–funded cultural ambassadorship to headline the "Night of the Americas" gala at the Martin Beck Theater on Broadway.[106] In reality, Neruda traveled at his own expense without CIAA input, most likely at the invitation of the Council for Pan American Democracy (a communist-led organization utilizing CIAA rhetoric), whose secretary later noted that Good Neighbor policymakers underestimated Neruda's utility given his "amplias vinculaciones continentales" (extensive hemispheric linkages).[107] These linkages invite us to loosen critical assumptions about his career narrative, placing him among a surprising collection of wartime poets that includes Julia de Burgos and Elizabeth Bishop. Arresting the inevitable progress of Burgos's, Bishop's, and Neruda's biographical narratives at a glancing moment of their unobserved cross-affiliations in 1942 and 1943, fresh relations around matters of Puerto Rican independence and decolonial politics emerge in a clutch of poems which have been alternately forgotten or comprehended only by parochial literary histories.

One ephemeral artifact expediently evokes these linkages: a pair of luxury postcards, penned in December 1942 by Neruda, then serving as Chilean consul general in Mexico City, and mailed to Elizabeth Bishop and her companion Marjorie Carr Stevens in Key West, Florida. One card is illustrated with a powdered and rouged Lady Liberty allegory, wearing a Panamanian flag fashioned into a "mermaid-style" dress (Figure 1.7). On the back, Neruda has traced an epistolary calligramme (visual poem) in the mermaid's embossed outline. Although his gesture feels practiced, it is also exceptional, for it is the only example of visual poetry in his extant corpus. Written in easy, diplomatic English, it reads: "Dear Marjorie, keep eating and drinking rye or bourbon until you take this shape. We are seeing you soon again. Pablo [&] Delia."[108] A playful, avant-garde poetic gesture, the card is also punctured by politics. An arrow identified in shorthand as the Trotskyite "4th Int" (Fourth International) runs through the mermaid's heart, drawing drops of whiskey-blood into a small cup. This dart of Trotskyite cupidity, piercing the mythically liquored figure of Elizabeth Bishop's lover, suggests how literary and political inter-Americanism operate as transecting systems. It is especially strange given that Neruda was divisively committed to the Stalinist Third International, a commitment that informed his contentious activities in Mexico, including his asylum request for David Siqueiros, who stood accused of conspiring against Trotsky's life. These commitments ultimately led to Neruda's self-described "diplomatic suicide."[109]

The intimacy presumed in the card points backward in time to an extensive, albeit poorly documented, friendship between Bishop, Carr Stevens, Neruda, and his second wife Delia del Carril, which lasted from late April through October of

1942 and ranged from Mérida to the capital to Cuernavaca.[110] In Mexico, Bishop was like the Cuban émigré of her poem "Jeronymo's House," seeking refuge from a metaphorical hurricane. In her case, the storm was the wartime naval mobilization sweeping through Key West, leveling blocks of housing for poor, black, and Hispanic communities. Bishop sympathetically registers these communities in poems such as "Jeronymo's House" and through her patronage of the unschooled painter Gregorio Valdes, who she later eulogized in the Havana literary journal *Orígenes*.[111] Mexico was a land of refugees to Bishop. She traveled as a tourist, but her most lasting personal associations in her six-month sojourn were with Neruda's circle of political émigré friends from Spain and Russia, such as Loyalist poet José Herrera Petere, for whom Neruda sought to provide work in the United States through Archibald MacLeish. Bishop studied Spanish through Neruda's poetry, and later emulated his Spanish Civil War–era elegy "Alberto Rojas Jiménez viene volando" in her poem "Invitation to Miss Marianne Moore" (1948). Early drafts bear the asterisk "With Apologies to Pablo Neruda."[112] However, at first she wrote to Moore that Neruda's poetry was "not the kind I—nor you—like, very very loose, surrealist imagery."[113]

Reciprocally, the postcard points forward to Neruda's interest in alerting his US literary and political contacts of his visit to New York City. As one journalist told it, the reason for his visit was an official diplomatic junket for a "debut" on the Broadway stage at the gala Noche de las Americas (Night of the Americas) at Broadway's Martin Beck Theatre on February 14, 1943 (Figure 1.8).[114] The event promised a rapprochement between two unaligned groups. The first of these included CIAA's favored culture industry stars and starlets, such as Carmen Miranda, the band leader Xavier Cugat, and Walt Disney, who attended in the capacity of an FBI informant, having been conscripted by the bureau as a Latin American affairs expert after his Rockefeller-sponsored goodwill mission.[115] The second group included radical Latin American diplomats, intellectuals, and labor leaders, such as Peru's indigenista Marxist senator José Uriel García, Haitian poet-diplomat Jacques Roumain, Puerto Rican politician (and former bohemian poet) Luis Muñoz Marín, and the other guest of honor, Mexican labor leader Vicente Lombardo Toledano, who trumpeted Philip Murray's notion that the Good Neighbor policy deserved a "good labor policy."[116] Writing in the *New Masses*, Putnam declared the combination of Neruda and Lombardo Toledano "perhaps the most important single event to take place in connection with our inter-American cultural relations program."[117] By emphasizing "our" cultural relations program, Putnam expressly opposed the Rockefeller committee, stressing instead CPAD's intersectional alliances of inter-American labor and culture

Fig 1.7 One of two postcards sent by Pablo Neruda to Marjorie Carr Stevens and Elizabeth Bishop, December 1942. Elizabeth Bishop Papers, Box 16, Folder 14, VUL. © 1942 Pablo Neruda and Fundación Pablo Neruda.

(b)

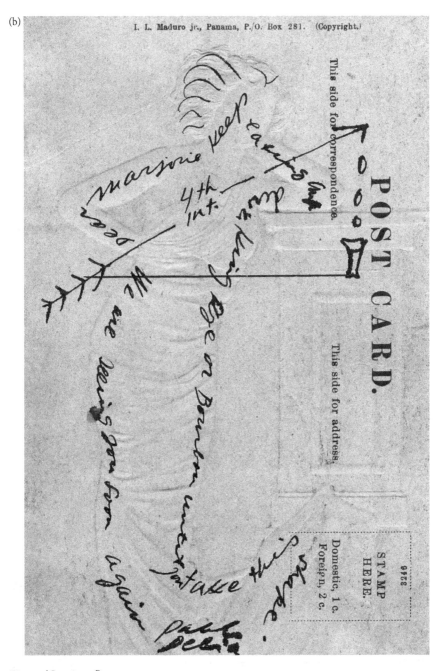

Fig 1.7 (*Continued*)

Fig 1.8 Council for Pan-American Democracy, "Night of the Americas" flyer, 1943.
Document 21029 from the FBI file of Walt Disney. Courtesy of Marc Eliot.

through the Congress of Industrial Organizations (CIO) and the Confederation
of Latin American Workers (CTAL).

Putnam's pronouncement reflects the double voice of his own inter-American
cultural work. His biweekly "Good Neighbors" column in the *Daily Worker* toed
the line carefully between commitments to the Communist Party of the United
States of America (CPUSA) and liberal inter-American affiliations. When the
Library of Congress Hispanic Foundation's Lewis Hanke landed him a CIAA-
funded job translating Euclides da Cunha's novel *Os Sertões* (Rebellion in the
Backlands) for the University of Chicago Press, Putnam wrote to comrade Juan

Antonio Corretjer to clarify whether CPUSA Latinos would smile on the project.[118] Corretjer, too, was an important contact for Neruda in New York. Just released from the United States Penitentiary, Atlanta, he had served time since 1937 alongside Pedro Albizu Campos and other Puerto Rican nationalists on charges of sedition. In Harlem, Neruda attended the inauguration of *Pueblos Hispanos*, the new Spanish-language Nationalist weekly edited by Corretjer and Consuelo Lee Tapia.

The outright antagonism of *Pueblos Hispanos* toward CIAA requires some emphasis, for CIAA policy toward Puerto Rico aggravatingly blended colonial administration with general neglect and the occasional diplomatic salvo. *Pueblos Hispanos* therefore agitated against precisely the rhetorical gestures of hemispheric solidarity and mutual understanding that comprised CIAA protocol. The newspaper's mission statement promoted solidarity among the colonias of minority Hispanics in the United States; immediate independence for Puerto Rico and the liberation of the Philippines; the end of racial, religious, and gender discrimination; organized labor through the hemisphere; and the antifascist legacy of Spanish Republicanism. As *Pueblos Hispanos* agitated on behalf of a Nationalist counter-imaginary to CIAA's Good Neighbor diplomacy, Neruda became an important ally. They published Neruda's "Canto de amor a Stalingrado" as a broadside in the paper.[119] Later, Corretjer's difficult epic poem of Puerto Rico, *Yerba bruja* (1954), would come to owe great debts to Neruda's *Canto General* (1950).

Possibly, Neruda first contacted Corretjer through Julia de Burgos. When Burgos and Neruda crossed paths in Cuba in March 1942 (just a few weeks before Neruda met Bishop), her poetry impressed him so much that he offered to write an introduction to her next book. Burgos also exemplified the double voice of Good Neighbor diplomacy. Soon after Cuba, she moved to New York, where she worked with Corretjer on *Pueblos Hispanos* as editor of the cultural page, contributing poems and articles that spoke to the newspaper's CPUSA-endorsed, interethnic, laborite, feminist agenda for Puerto Rican independence. Yet by 1944 she had moved to an ideologically incompatible position in Washington, DC, as clerical staff at the CIAA offices, even as she continued to harbor Nationalist leanings.[120] The principal record of this interlude in Burgos's career is a revealing FBI file that includes a messy dossier of her poems translated by bureau "ghost-translators" and a Hatch Act Interview that prosecuted her "poesía comprometida" (committed poetry) for its role in stoking revolutionary nationalism, which led to Attorney General Frances Biddle's recommendation to terminate her employment at CIAA.[121]

Here, for example, is Burgos's poem "Campo" (Countryside), first as it appeared in *Pueblos Hispanos* on July 3, 1943, followed by the bureau's revelatory July 1944 translation:

¡Ese camino real abandonado!
¡Esa niña que va descalza tumbando mariposas!
¡Esa mañana amarga que se lava la cara en el arroyo!

Campo . . .
Jíbara atolondrada igual que la inocencia que te llena los párpados . . .
Semilla taciturna que quieres no nacer en desvelada tierra de preguntas . . .
Potro que ensillas manso horizonte armado de llanto campesino . . .

¡La tradición está ardiendo en el campo!
¡La esperanza está ardiendo en el campo!
¡El hombre está ardiendo en el campo!

Es la tierra que se abre, quemada de injusticias.
No la apagan los ríos;
no la apagan los charcos;
ni el apetito de las nubes;
ni el apetito de los pájaros.

La brasa está en el pecho robusto de raíces,
pecho de tierra adulta madura para el salto,
y para desemboquen en sus ojos las estrellas ignoradas,
y para recibir a Dios en sus barrios,
y para secarse las tormentas del cuerpo entumecido,
y para ponerle guardarraya a los amos.

Tiene pasos de luz la tierra blanca.
Tiene brazos de fe la tierra negra.
Tiene pulmón de viento la tierra enrojecida.

Hay mucho monte erguido desalojando cerros para la gran fogata,
para el desquite de los surcos,
para el sepulcro de las zafras.

¡Madura . . .
recogerá la tierra su cosecha de hombres libertados!

¡La tiniebla hay que echarla del campo!
¡Con los riscos, si falta los brazos![122]

(That abandoned main road,

that barefoot boy chasing butterflies,

that bitter morning which washes its face in the stream.

Countryside . . .

Native as stupefied as the innocence which fills your eyes . . .

Taciturn seed which does not wish to develop in the wakeful land
filled with

[questions . . .]

colt, which you ride under the horizon filled with the cries of the
countryside . . .

Treason is burning in the countryside,

Hope is burning in the countryside,

Man is burning in the countryside.

It is the land which is opened up, enflamed by injustices.

The rivers do not extinguish it.

The lakes do not extinguish it.

Nor the appetite of the clouds,

nor the thirst of the birds.

The ember glows in the strong breast filled with roots,

breast of the adult earth, all ready for the plunder,

ready to have unknown stars fill its eyes,

ready to receive God in its districts,

ready to shake pain from its swollen body,

ready to put a check on its masters.

The white soil has feet of light,

the black soil has arms of faith,

the red soil has the breath of the wind.

There are many steep mountains which thrust aside hills to receive the
big light,

to retrieve furrows,

to bury the saffre.

Ripe . . .

The soil will gather its harvest of freed men.

Darkness must be chased from the countryside.

With rocks, if we lack arms!)[123]

I quote at such length because there are more than a few notable imputations here, choices odd enough to suggest FBI ghost-translation could be a selectively paranoid enterprise. In the most egregious imputations, the translator translates *tradición* as *treason* rather than *tradition*, and *salto* as *plunder* rather than *leap*. Simultaneously, he misses charged social lexicons of race and class, reducing *jíbara* to *native*, and he mistakenly regenders the poem's surprising revolutionary subject, a *niña*, as a young boy. Moreover, *zafras*, or *sugar harvest*, is ascribed the false cognate *saffre* (an obsolete spelling of *sapphire*), suggesting the translator's insensitivity to the poem's specific socioagrarian topography. Finally, he mutes other instances of class-based grievance, rendering *desalojando* as *thrust aside*, instead of, say, *evicting*, and "Para el desquite de los surcos" as "to retrieve furrows" rather than something like "for the furrows' retribution" or "for the ruts' revenge."

Cumulatively, the translation's jumble of errata reveal a pattern: the translator unsystematically but insistently overrides the poem's central conceit, which locates a blazing language of revolt in a pantheon of social and natural agencies (female peasants, their traditions, the natural landscape that surrounds them, and the agricultural wounds they inflict on the earth). Meanwhile, the translator imputes an alternative lexicon of seditions and crimes of property (treason, plunder) that is nowhere in evidence. The ghost-translator exhibits a variety of reading that is deaf to regionalism, ideologically motivated, and selectively paranoid. His readings reject the basic premises of Burgos's most openly revolutionary poems, while imputing revolutionary crimes to her most harmless phrasings. Building on a file full of tendentious misreadings and interpretations of her activities, a Hatch Act investigation led to Burgos's quick termination as a federal employee.

In this way, Puerto Rican nationalism was the tripwire on which Burgos's expressions of state-sponsored Good Neighbor diplomacy foundered. For Neruda, however, Good Neighbor diplomacy was an effective front for alternative inter-American configurations, stressing Puerto Rican sovereignty at the junctures of ethnonationalism, aesthetic modernism, and international socialism. A week after meeting with *Pueblos Hispanos*, Neruda recited his poems for New York's Pan-American Women's Association, a vibrant feminist organization founded by Frances R. Grant.[124] From there, he spent time in Washington, DC, in the company of Puerto Rican writer and editor Angel Flores, director of the Committee on Intellectual Affairs at the Pan American Union, and soon to be Neruda's principal US translator for the next fifteen years.[125]

The predominance of Puerto Rican hosts on Neruda's trip should not be understated, for few places mattered more than Puerto Rico to leftist critics of Good Neighbor diplomacy. Earl Browder, secretary general of the CPUSA and an ex-cellmate of Corretjer's in Atlanta, published a political platform entitled *Victory—and After* (1942), translated into Spanish by Corretjer, that identified Puerto Rico as a particular lacuna in the civic education of US citizens, and a festering hypocrisy in the practice of wartime hemispheric solidarity.[126] According to Browder, the "United States public and most of its leading circles" remained "blissfully unaware that our government since 1898 has been holding in imperialistic subjection a Latin American nation, one of the most developed culturally." He continued: "This blank in the public and official mind so far as Puerto Rico is concerned is interpreted by Latin Americans generally as meaning that we do not really consider them human beings, and that our official pronouncements of human brotherhood are but diplomatic fictions."[127] Browder's proof included the US failure to provide civilian defense on Puerto Rico (viewed as a military outpost and not as a "nation of close to two million men, women, and children"). Indeed, the Communist Party's anti-imperial defense of Puerto Rican nationalism was seconded only by a few public US figures, such as American Labor Party congressman Vito Marcantonio, who represented multiethnic Harlem. Thirty years later, when Neruda wrote a *New York Times* editorial protesting CIA intervention in Chile, he reminisced about the same "blank" in the "diplomatic fiction" of the Good Neighbor:

> I happened once to be sitting next to a leading socialite at a New York dinner table. Picking a topic that might interest us both, I got onto Puerto Rico. She didn't know what it was all about. She didn't know they spoke Spanish. She didn't know that Puerto Rico was an American colony. And still less of course, did she know that the Puerto Ricans want to be, and could be, an independent republic like the other nations of Latin America. This lady of good faith cried out aloud and declared then and there to all the other guests that she had just discovered an embarrassing fact. "We should liberate that country immediately," she said, "it's unthinkable that the United States should have colonies!" What a very nice lady![128]

Such recollections suggest that Neruda's support of Puerto Rican nationalists was the principal aim of his Good Neighbor mission. They also suggest how he modulated inter-American rhetoric among distinct communities. His private avant-garde epistolary with Bishop offsets the propagandistic poetry he circulates through the transnational counter-public of *Pueblos Hispanos*. Earlier, he sought to subvert Dudley Fitts's certified images of Latin American poetry in his anthology by trying to swap a communist pamphlet-poem entitled "7 de noviembre: Oda a un día de victorias" for the love poems Fitts chose to print instead.[129]

Why did Neruda's support for Puerto Rican nationalism remain so subterranean? Triangulating Neruda with Burgos and Bishop, the two emerging female poets he befriended and championed in 1942, shows how hard it was for decolonial politics to enter into the discursive terrain of Good Neighbor diplomacy. For example, CIAA fired Burgos for the radical Latin Americanist solidarity she expressed in her poetry, yet her poetry would have served the agency's cultural diplomacy initiatives far better than her skill as an audit clerk. Consider, as a nominee for cultural ambassadorship, a stanza from her poem "Canción a los Pueblos Hispanos de América y del mundo" (Song to the Hispanic People of America and the World), a poem the FBI noticed because Burgos dedicated it to Corretjer on the newspaper's anniversary:

> Pueblos Hispanos, pueblos que lívidos contemplan
> desde el sueño hecho sangre de la bondad martiana,
> en Puerto Rico, un amo golpeando libertades.[130]

A literal translation might read: "Hispanic People, people who, in Puerto Rico, furiously contemplate—from the dream made blood by the goodness of Martí—a possessor striking down freedoms." Contra CIAA, Burgos offers a vision of hemispheric solidarity that acknowledges colonial and imperial mechanisms of injustice, and the popular unrest they engender. She suggests, therefore, that a "contemplative" legacy of Latin American political thought ("bondad martiana") might be the terms of restorative justice. When Hughes or Frank spoke in like idioms during their state-sponsored goodwill lectures and broadcasts, they gained credibility with Latin American audiences far more than the culture industry mavens and bureaucrats who otherwise flooded Rockefeller's agency.

Now here is how Burgos's FBI ghost-translator renders these lines:

> Hispanic Peoples, who with their pale faces
> contemplate from their sleep made bloody with Martian kindness,
> a master fighting liberties in Puerto Rico.[131]

Pale faces, not *angry thinkers*. *Martian*, not *pertaining to José Martí*. During World War II, Martí's identity, to say nothing of his thought, was so alien to the majority of Anglophone readers that the errant ghost-translator literalizes his status as extraterrestrial.

This can be explained away as a humorous mistake, but it can also be held up as exemplary of an Anglophone regime of innocent naiveté toward traditions of Latin American anticolonialism.[132] Compare Elizabeth Bishop's 1942 "Jeronymo's

House," a picturesque persona poem in which a Cuban émigré on the island of Key West describes the contents of his neat but fragile vernacular house in fastidious two-beat lines:

> Also I have
>> hung on a hook
> an old French horn
>> repainted with
> aluminum paint.
>> I play each year
> in the parade
>> for José Marti [sic].*¹³³

The asterisk leads to a footnote explaining that José Martí is "A Cuban patriot," a didactic expedient for Bishop's Anglophone readership in the Trotskyite *Partisan Review* where it was first published. Later editions of Bishop's poem do not preserve the paratext.

Both "Jeronymo's House" and "Canción a los Pueblos Hispanos de América y del mundo" are written in the voices of diasporic Caribbean subjects isolated in the United States, but this commonality should not obscure their crucial differences. Bishop's persona individualizes and ventriloquizes the "pueblo hispano" through Jeronymo's tidy observations. She confines his social consciousness to the walls of a feminized, domestic interior, and gives him a bit part tooting in a patriotic parade. By contrast, Burgos assumes Martí's bardic posture, so often reserved for the male political poem of the 1930s, openly inciting a collective to the fever pitch of revolt. Yet, at the moment they pass before the eyes of Anglophone readers, the two poems converge, through their circumscription of the anticolonial, hemispheric function that goes by the name "Martí." To Bishop, Martí is a figure of didactic exposition, precisely the gloss that Burgos's translator, fumblingly mistaking Martí for an alien being, so dreadfully needs. In these ways, wartime poems of hemispheric scope checked their references to "nuestra América" at the gates of Anglophony.

William Carlos Williams and the Ardor of Puerto Rico

If Puerto Rico was an egregious "blank" in Anglo-American civic education, few poets were better positioned to fill it in than William Carlos Williams. Because

Williams's poems frequently celebrate his Puerto Rican heritage, his bicultural identity has come to suture a biographical narrative to his place in the widening multiethnic and transnational purview of US poetry canons.[134] Indeed, as scholars since the late 1980s sought to expand these canons, Williams's bicultural, Antillean origin story and his vigorous presence in 1930s cultural front periodicals paradoxically confirmed his status as a sacred cow of US poetry more than ever. Yet when the US Department of State engaged Williams in April 1941 to visit the island for the first time in his life, they hardly shared the Browderite goal of furnishing US citizens with an intercultural understanding of Puerto Rican desires for political self-determination (Figure 1.9). To the contrary, they hoped to mitigate the nationalist political climate on the island inflamed by Albizu Campos, Corretjer, Burgos, and the independence movement. Thus, Williams's bicultural self-commemoration structured his attitude toward an assimilationist and imperial cultural diplomacy mechanism.

Fig 1.9 William Carlos Williams in Puerto Rico, April 1941. Photographer unknown. William Carlos Williams Papers, YALE. © 2017 by William Carlos Williams. Used by permission of the William Carlos Williams Estate in care of the Jean V. Naggar Literary Agency, Inc.

The following pages reconstruct Williams's participation, during his 1941 Caribbean excursion, in the "First Inter-American Writers Conference" at the University of Puerto Rico in Rio Piedras. Subsequently, I demonstrate how several threads of his poetry in the period uneasily aligned Williams's flare for genealogical self-commemoration of his bicultural, hemispheric origins with remarkably undemocratic and annexationist political leanings toward the Caribbean, and with his fitful attempt to write and translate an appropriative Afro-Caribbean or "negrista" poetry. I will therefore read outward from his work as a cultural ambassador in the Good Neighbor era to his translations of Luis Palés Matos's poems, motifs in *Paterson* (1946), and especially the poems of his wartime collection *The Wedge* (1944). In these poems, William's inter-Americanism emerges as a convulsive geopolitical and racial motif, placing his bicultural self-fashioning in a scene of historical complexity that previously has gone misunderstood.

To attend his short goodwill ambassadorship in Puerto Rico, Williams and his wife Florence took their first flight in an airplane, skipping "by enormous leaps" across Caribbean harbors in a Pan American Clipper, a seaplane popularly known as a "flying boat."[135] When Williams later narrated his flight to Puerto Rico in a three-stanza section of *Paterson* Book I, he used the seaplane's perspective and its rhythm of descent to link together the diverse discourses of Afro-Caribbean identity, counterrevolutionary politics, and nostalgic self-commemorations of his Antillean origins. Here is the aerial view of the Haitian bay water that Williams reconnoitered during his flight to Puerto Rico:

> While at 10,000 feet, coming in over
> the sombre mountains of Haiti, the land-locked
> bay back of Port au Prince, blue vitreol
> streaked with paler streams, shabby as loose
> hair, badly dyed—like chemical waste
> mixed in, eating out the shores . .
>
> He pointed it down and struck the rough
> waters of the bay, hard; but lifted it again and
> coming down gradually, hit again hard but
> remained down to taxi to the pier where
> they were waiting—
>
>   (Thence Carlos had fled in the 70's
> leaving the portraits of my grandparents,
> the furniture, the silver, even the meal
> hot upon the table before the Revolutionists
> coming in at the far end of the street.)[136]

The first stanza describes the Haitian seascape in terms of the artificial color spectrum of chemical pollution. Noxious sulfuric compounds ("blue vitreol") color the waters, not natural beauty or the play of light that Stevens celebrates in "The Idea of Order at Key West." Like such contaminations, the diction ("shabby as loose hair," "mixed in") also suggests the Haitian "headwaters" of racial discourses, which, as we'll see, become central to Williams's translations in this period. The next stanza lands "hard" on this seascape, and rough descent triggers genealogical commemoration in stanza three. This rhythm of rough descent aligns with the entire "catastrophic" historical rhythm proposed by the waterfall at the center of *Paterson*. The parenthetical in stanza three refers to Doctor Carlos Hoheb, Williams's maternal uncle and namesake, who escaped a popular revolution in Santo Domingo in 1879, ultimately leading to the family's relocation to New York.[137] Williams analogizes Uncle Carlos's abrupt political flight to his own rough landing aboard the "flying boat." The waters pattern a long history of non-assimilations and of "mingling" without mixing: streaky contaminants, rough landings, and overthrown social orders. Observations of his family's counter-revolutionary place in its convulsive past and fractious present guide Williams's hemispherism at every turn.

Taking their cue from Williams, the following pages offer an aerial view of the issues at stake in Williams's wartime poems of the Caribbean, which bounce like a seaplane across several "mingling" but not well-mixed discourses: first, his cultural diplomacy work; second, his penchant for genealogical self-commemoration; third, his constructions of Afro-Caribbean discourse; and fourth, his halting attempts to vindicate a counterrevolutionary liberalism. In these mingling but unmixed discourses, Williams affirms a cultural hemispherism riven with insuperable contradictions.

Williams's understanding of cultural diplomacy came into focus during his attendance at the First Inter-American Writers Conference, an event that has never benefited from a historical reconstruction. The conference kicked off, symbolically, on Pan American Day (April 14), and promised auspicious contacts for isolated Puerto Rican literary aspirants, while promoting the inter-American wartime ethos of "fuller understanding and mutual appreciation among the writers and intellectuals of the American Republics" who were to "unite for the defense of their cultures and traditions."[138] Archibald MacLeish and Muna Lee, in consort with the Cuban senator, philosopher, and biographer Jorge Mañach, organized the conference. Mañach delivered an encomium to José Martí and attempted to leverage tepid international attention as a rallying point for imprisoned nationalist Albizu Campos.[139] Several belle-lettristic US government attendees, opposed to Puerto Rican independence, countered his efforts.[140] MacLeish, serving these interests, used his floor time to deliver "The American Writers and the New World," an argument against what he called the "colonial theory" of literature that veiled a neocolonial theory in its place. MacLeish sought to disprove the belief that the literature of a transplanted culture was inferior to that of its origin country, a point he made in a rhetoric of possession, arguing that the New World "in process of creation" made obligations on its writers, whose imaginative job was to "occupy" the world in the spirit of conquistadors such as Juan Ponce de León.[141] Putnam critiqued the Writers' Conference in the *Daily Worker* and *New Masses* by arguing that MacLeish's neocolonial inter-Americanism, handmaiden to the "Rockefeller committee," turned off most of the respected writers invited to attend, such as Carl Sandburg, Alfonso Reyes, and Ciro Alegría.[142] He also felt it made no real place for the Puerto Rican writers to whom it supposedly catered. One young Puerto Rican writer, Carlos Carrera Benítez, scandalized the audience at the lone "manuscript session" by speaking impassionedly about US colonial language policies that neglected Castilian and vernacular Spanish, thereby producing "a nation of stammerers."[143]

Carrera Benítez's passionate diagnosis of a Puerto Rican cultural stammer enters into an ongoing dialogue in Puerto Rican poetry of the years immediately before and after the conference, one that hinges on a question of poetic commitment: how could a language be adequate to the passions or *ardors* of a literature struggling to come into being? For example, the stammer evokes Luis Palés Matos's use of the trope in his 1937 "Preludio en Boricua," one of the most famous Puerto Rican poems of the day, which devastatingly likens the voices of Puerto Rican literary aspirants to bleating goats stewing in a cauldron of unrest:

> ¿Y Puerto Rico? Mi isla ardiente,
> Para ti todo ha terminado.
> En el yermo de un continente,
> Puerto Rico, lúgubremente,
> bala como cabro estofado.[144]

When Williams, impressed by Palés Matos at the conference, translated the poem for Lloyd Mallan and H. R. Hays's 1942 "Pan-American" number of *American Prefaces*, he rendered this stanza "And Puerto Rico? My burning island/for thee all has indeed ended./Among the shambles of a continent/Puerto Rico, lugubriously /you bleat like a roast goat."[145] In his translation, the sonorous echo of "roast goat" outweighs the fact that a roast *crackles*, whereas stew *bleats*. In

The Wedge, Williams would soon find in *ardor* a metaphor for modernist war-time innovation. By contrast, for others the ardor of Puerto Rico aroused questions of decolonial justice. In "Campo," Julia de Burgos likewise described Puerto Rico as an island aflame, *scorched* by injustice, where a people is unquenchably *burning* (in the ardor of a protracted gerundial present) between tradition and political futurity:

> ¡La tradición está ardiendo en el campo!
> ¡La esperanza está ardiendo en el campo!
> ¡El hombre está ardiendo en el campo![146]

> (Tradition is burning in the countryside!
> Hope is burning in the countryside!
> Man is burning in the countryside!)

Burgos did not see, in the ardor of Puerto Rico, the sound and syntax of animal incomprehensibility, as did Williams via Palés Matos, nor "a nation of stammerers," as did Carrera Benítez. Rather, she saw a popular, furious linguistic image of revolutionary justice.

In the midst of the conference's political jostling, Williams delivered a refreshingly literary lecture entitled "An Informal Discussion of Poetic Form." Treating his aesthetic doctrine of Objectivism as a partial, unsatisfactory improvement on Imagism, he described a program for poetic form that would be commensurate with the plurality of American languages. He also mused on the "function" Latin America might "exercise toward the United States and Canada" with respect to poetic innovation, speculating that it would lead Anglo-American poets to the "forms" of Spanish and Portuguese literature, and "shake us free for a reconsideration of the poetic line." An immersion in the "shorter, four stressed line rather than the pentameter" as well as a taking of "hints from the romancero" would allow Anglo-American poets to "finally discover something more acceptable to our temperament, manner of thought and speech." Pound famously wrote, "To break the pentameter, that was the first heave."[147] To situate Williams's "shaking free" in the history of modernism is to see him describe Spanish-language poetry as a second "heave."

Although he intended to recite poems that exemplified the "new poetic forms," Williams instead chose to read aloud a group of seven poems, published between 1923 and 1936, organized thematically rather than formally around his familial connections to the island. Describing these familial connections, Williams once wrote that his mother, Raquel Hélène Hoheb, "was born neither in Spain nor South America but in Porto Rico."¹⁴⁸ The daughter of a Dutch-Jewish father and a Basque mother, she grew up in Mayagüez, Puerto Rico, before studying painting in Paris. His father, William George Williams, was a Spanish-speaking Englishman who had lived in the Spanish Caribbean "*desde que tenía cinco años*" (from the age of five), as his son later wrote. After the family moved to New Jersey in 1881, William George traveled extensively in Latin America advertising for Murray & Lanman's popular Florida Water cologne. In 1883, Williams was born into a family newly displaced from Spanish America, but whose language, livelihood, and identity all very much depended upon it. He grew up bilingual at home, the slinger of a "choice Rutherford Spanish" with "a peculiar Hackensack accent," as he described his linguistic capacities as a young man.¹⁴⁹ If later he became a quintessentially "American" poet, as late as 1917 Pound called him a "blooming foreigner" with "enough Spanish blood to muddy up your mind, and prevent the current American ideation from going through it like a blighted colander."¹⁵⁰ In 1916, Williams published his first translations of modernista poems in Alfred Kreymborg's little magazine *Others* in collaboration with his father. Some, like R. Arévalo Martínez's "The Sensation of a Smell," could have passed for Florida Water advertising copy in their focus on olfactory effluvia.¹⁵¹ Williams maintained a miscellaneous practice of translation throughout his career, though almost always in collaboration—first with his father, and later with his mother and with Rutgers University professor José Vázquez Amaral.

The poems Williams chose to read in Puerto Rico thus constitute a partial corpus of Caribbean "origin poems." Many imagine his mother's decorous, Spanish colonial Antilles steeped in late-nineteenth-century genteel arts, including "All the Fancy Things" ("That's all they thought of/in Puerto Rico in the old Spanish/days when she was a girl"); "Brilliant Sad Sun" ("And Patti, on her first concert tour/sang at your house in Mayagüez"); and "The Flower" ("Another petal reaches/into the past, to Porto Rico/when my mother was a child bathing in a small/river and splashing water up on/the yucca leaves"). As centerpieces to his recital, he placed the complementary poems "Adam" and "Eve" (from *Adam & Eve in the City*, 1936), which Williams described as "tributes to my father and mother," and which imagine the Caribbean as a Columbian Eden, while associating his own family's migrations from the West Indies to New Jersey with the fall from a prelapsarian tropic. In all, Williams freighted his participation in wartime inter-American cultural exchange with overdetermined familial commemorations. Samuel Putnam surmised as much when he wrote of Williams: "fine poet and prose writer that he is, and one who has never had his just meed of appreciation, he at the same time has never been noted for the clarity of his social

78 THE POETRY OF THE AMERICAS

and political thinking. He seems to have been lured into the present dubious adventure out of sentimental reasons: his mother was a Porto Rican."[152]

Here, it bears repeating that the *politics* of Williams's bicultural self-fashioning during his trip to Puerto Rico—executed under the terms of wartime inter-American cultural policy—has elicited little attention since Putnam noticed it.[153] Champions of his biculturalism hardly note that his origin story tracks shifts in the exertion of US soft power over several generations, dating back to his familial ties to prominent pro-annexationists in New York's Puerto Rican colonia. In 1941, Williams waxed nostalgic for the Puerto Rico his mother had left behind, but his political attitude to the island more closely mirrored that of the physician Julio Henna, Williams's first employer at the French Hospital in lower Manhattan in 1906, and president of the Spanish American Club, where he often entertained Williams. Williams later mythologized Henna as one of the anticolonial "revolutionists who the Spanish had made it hot for" in the early 1880s, when Henna had founded Puerto Rico's branch of the Cuban Revolutionary Party.[154] But by the time of the Spanish American War, the revolutionist was a self-appointed Puerto Rican "commissioner" who first lobbied for US intervention, and then negotiated personally with William McKinley on behalf of US annexation. Williams's wartime cultural ambassadorship replays Henna's interest in assimilating Puerto Rico into what Henna called, following Thomas Jefferson, the "empire of liberty."[155] Williams's nostalgic self-portrait screens out how his cultural diplomacy fits into longer patterns of US hegemony.

Thus, a few years later, counterrevolutionary sentiment lingers in an aside in Williams's *Autobiography* disclosing ambivalence about Hispaniola's future: "It is hard to think of old things surrounded by the affections of a noonday sun in the tropics. Trujillo the tyrant, hard to know what to think in view of the benefits he has occasioned—and even here, back in the hills, there is talk of warfare across a trivial border."[156] In this remark, note how the dash tellingly halts the sentence from enumerating any "benefits" Rafael Trujillo may have brought about. Recalling his work as a Good Neighbor emissary, Williams validates the policy's worst moment of permissiveness toward Trujillo, who Eric Roorda calls "the dictator next door."[157] Williams's inconclusiveness compares unfavorably to the outrage on the Puerto Rican literary left.[158] Burgos, for example, channels Neruda's anti-authoritarian vituperations in her "Himno de sangre a Trujillo:" "General Rafael, Trujillo General,/que tu nombre sea un eco eterno de cadáveres,/rodando entre ti mismo, sin piedad, persiguiéndote" (General Rafael, Trujillo General/ may your name be an eternal echo of cadavers/wandering within you, without pity, pursuing you).[159]

Williams's ambivalence over Hispaniola brings us back, here, to his seaplane poem's aquatic metaphors for Haitian métissage (racial mixture), for Williams's cultural ambassadorship fueled his broader interest in Afro-Caribbean transcultural motifs. Palés Matos gave Williams a copy of *Tuntún de pasa y grifería: Poesía afroantillana* (Tomtom of Kinky Hair and Black Things: Afro-Caribbean Poetry, 1937), and Williams translated "Preludio en Boricua" on his return to New Jersey. His striking "not-to-be-called translation" of Palés Matos's Dada-inspired, negrista poetry, which Williams deferentially admitted lacked the music of the original, offers equivalences between Antillean and Afro-American sociolects:

> Tuntún de pasa y grifería
> y otros parejeros tuntunes.
> Bochinche de ñañiguería
> donde sus cálidos betunes
> funde la congada bravía.[160]

> (Mixup of kinkhead and high yaller
> And other big time mixups.
> Messaround of voodoo chatter
> Where their warm black bodies
> Loosen the savage conga).[161]

Palés Matos's poem affiliates with a modernist current with which Michael North also associates Williams, namely a perturbing use of "linguistic imitation" as a form of "racial masquerade."[162] While mainland US writers have been found guilty of cultural appropriation for such linguistic gestures, parallel tendencies in Puerto Rican poetry since the late 1920s led to local debates as to whether *negrista* poetry reproduced or subverted racial discourses.[163] The racial epistemology characteristic of the Puerto Rican Generation of 1930 eludes mainland discourses of racial imitation.[164] Williams's translation adds a secondary masquerade by exporting this complexity across linguistic boundaries. The proliferation of mashed diction—*mixup, kinkhead,* and *messaround*—scars the poem's surface with the semantic struggle of that exportation. Thus a new racial form enters Williams's work, coding his racial poetics through translation and cultural export, a poetics that will inform Williams's work in *The Wedge* and *Paterson* as well.

In sum, the portrait of Williams's hemispherism can no longer simply be premised on the recovery of his bicultural identity, for US cultural diplomacy propels him to influence the drift of Puerto Rican nationalism, his racial politics float indecisively between minstrelsy and *negrismo*, and the harbors of Port au Prince prompt his confession that he harbors undemocratic political aspirations for the Caribbean. The violent reorganization of Caribbean states that Williams records in island-hopping air travels, racial imitations, and ancestral inquiries all subsequently flood into *The Wedge*, Williams's volume of war poems, which doubles as a draft for *Paterson* Book I (1946). Readers know the Passaic Falls in *Paterson*, lyrically evoked and interspersed with historical chronicles, as an icon of the localist "sources" for postwar US poetic language. By oscillating in the coming pages between *The Wedge* (1944) and *Paterson* (1946), I'll show how the latter poem's localist vision of Americana emerges from the revisionary effacements of the profuse Caribbean concerns that marked his wartime drafts.

Beleaguered by wartime paper shortages, Harry Duncan's Cummington Press published *The Wedge* in a small, bright orange volume limited to an edition of 380.[165] Several poems in it, written just before and just after the Inter-American Writers' Conference, thematize Williams's Caribbean genealogy. "Catastrophic Birth" describes the 1902 eruption of the Martinican volcano Mount Pelée that Williams claimed "wiped out the last of my mother's family."[166] "Paterson: The Falls" offers Gulf Stream origins for Williams's burgeoning long poem. And "Rumba! Rumba!" offers a negrista imitation poem setting the table for Williams's interest in Palés Matos. Antillean identity supplies thematic, formal, and translational sources for his inter-American poetics, linked at every turn to *The Wedge*'s overarching concern with total war.

Like many of Williams's Caribbean sources and symbols, the title of *The Wedge* hides a pun behind an erasure: the working title was "The (lang) WEDGE: A New Summary." Williams introduced the volume by soliciting his readers to regard it as war poetry: "The war is the first and only thing in the world today. The arts generally are not, nor is this writing a diversion from that for relief, a turning away. It *is* the war or part of it, merely a different sector of the field."[167] Notwithstanding his clear antipathy to the primacy of the war in the world, Williams welcomes its aesthetic implications, inviting the war theme to radically preempt and reconfigure unrelated poetic subjects. If the main theme of *The Wedge* is war, the central link between war and form is the violence or *ardor* of poetic revelation. Reframing *ardor* as a keyword of Puerto Rican poetics, to Williams, the perceiving mind of the poet who "ardors" that his perceptions "may constitute a revelation in the speech that he uses" marries poetic composition to war.[168] The volume's proem, "A Sort of a Song," articulates Williams's most durable dictum "(No ideas/but in things) Invent!" Williams's exempla for "No ideas/but in things" are violent lines like "Saxifrage is my flower that splits/

the rocks."[169] In such lines, he links ardor to the violence of nature, furnishing a matrix for the kinesthetic action of language.

The next poem in *The Wedge*, "Catastrophic Birth," similarly suggests a volcanic eruption as the natural symbol for ardor understood as the quality of poetic form:

> Fury and counter fury! The volcano!
> Stand firm, unbending. The chemistry
> shifts. The retort does not fracture.
> The change reveals—change.
> The revelation is compact—
> compact of regathered fury.[170]

North persuasively argues that Williams's "crabbed" syntax and passion for violent verbs had long been mechanisms through which his poems expressed creative innovation.[171] North shows how *In the American Grain*'s portraits of the extermination of pre-Columbian peoples and cities by Ponce de León and Hernán Cortés figure modernism's violent novelty. Williams now found the war context adaptable to his old impetus. The eruption of Mount Pelée, a primordial symbol of New World natural violence, metaphorizes genealogical annihilation, a metaphor he marshals as a theory of wartime art. Puerto Rico, too, was the "isla ardiente," as Palés called it. "Burning the Christmas Greens" trades on the same theme of burning rebirth ("ourselves refreshed among/the shining fauna of that fire") through an absolving post-holiday conflagration: "Violence leaped and appeared. /Recreant! roared to life/as the flames rose through and/our eyes recoiled from it."[172]

In 1942, the economist Joseph Schumpeter suggested a theory of capitalism as a process of "Creative Destruction" in its incessant search for new foreign markets and technologies and its attempts to destroy old economic structures and to create new ones.[173] It is tempting to suggest that Williams's modernist language of "recreation" offers a striking verbal mimesis of Schumpeter's conception. Yet, as *The Wedge* reiterates Williams's fixation on violent verbal action, it primarily associates these conflagrations with the composition of *Paterson*. Williams wrote to James Laughlin in 1943: "I am burned up to do it but don't quite know how. I write and destroy, write and destroy."[174] In this period of intensive revision, *The Wedge* supplies descriptive language Williams reapplies to *Paterson*'s Passaic Falls. The plummeting volcanic action of Mount Pelée now becomes "the catastrophe of the Falls itself."[175] Williams understood the etymology of *catastrophe* as a downward turn. Fluvial and volcanic action are natural "catastrophes," and like the volcanic catastrophe of Mount Pelée that "wiped out" Williams's maternal ancestry, the entire first book of *Paterson* emphasizes the torrential deluge of the falls, among whose victims are Williams's previous references to his West Indian origin story:

> they leap to the conclusion and
> fall, fall in air! as if
> floating, relieved of their weight,
> split apart, ribbons; dazed, drunk
> with the catastrophe of the descent
> floating unsupported
> to hit the rocks: to a thunder,
> as if lightning had struck
>
> All lightness lost, weight regained in
> the repulse, a fury of
> escape driving them to rebound
> upon those coming after—[176]

The entire lexical world of "Catastrophic Birth" repeats here in *Paterson*: the *re*-verbs (*regained, repulse, rebound*), the "fury," and the purification through catastrophic language in the lines "Around the falling waters the Furies hurl!/ Violence gathers, spins in their heads summoning them."[177] As the poem progresses, its "events" repeat the diluvial feeling of the catastrophe, from the landing of Williams's aircraft in Haiti to the plummet of Sarah Cumming and the leap of Sam Patch. "Falling" unites the narrative action of *Paterson* I.

When Williams performed *Paterson*, he chose to read the lyrical passages aloud and leapt over the prose, distinguishing between poetic invention and historical source material.[178] In his fine critical edition of *Paterson*, Christopher MacGowan follows the poet's impulse by annotating this prose more extensively than the verse. But this decision has at least one unintended consequence. It suggests to readers that locodescriptive poems of the falls are natural and lyrical as opposed to historical and intertextual. On this reading, Williams diverges from Poundian historicism's transformation of historical data into lyric material, for Williams's poem includes history but does not countenance it in voiced lyric language. However, by recycling lyric language from his previous poems on the destruction of Martinique while discarding their geographic references, *Paterson*'s descriptions of the Passaic reveal local history through translocal occlusions and a rhythm of historical obliteration itself.

In *The Wedge*, the short lyric "Rumba! Rumba!" follows on the inter-American genealogies of "The Catastrophic Birth" and "Paterson: The Falls," while inviting a different set of attentions and explanations. Not simply another symbol of Williams's poetics of genealogical annihilation and rebirth, the Cuban dance craze suggests a sound poetics of "downfall" rather than an imagistic instance of natural "catastrophe":

> No, not the downfall
> of the Western World
> but the wish for its
>   downfall
> in an idiot mind—
> Dance, Baby, dance!
>
> thence springs the conflict,
> that it may crash
>   hereafter;
> not submit and end in
> a burst of laughter—
> Cha cha, chacha, cha!
>
> to hide the defect—
> the difficultly held
> burden, to perfect!
> melted in a wish to die.
> Dance, Baby, dance
>   the Cuban Rumba![179]

This poem's standpoint is ambiguous, for the poem is not obviously *about* Caribbean life in quite the same way as the poems of Palés Matos. For example, the "idiot mind" that choreographs the symbolic downfall of the West might be a Cuban or an American, and white or black. In the first case, Williams might be depicting the kind of anti-imperialist rumbero who speaks in the poems of Nicolás Guillén. He might be the kind of figure we find chided, for instance, in "Tú no sabe inglé (Don't Know No English)." In this case, Williams offers a negrista exercise like Guillén's "Pequeña oda a un negro boxeador cubano" (Little Ode to a Black Cuban Boxer):

> Y ahora que Europa se desnuda
> para tostar su carne al sol

y busca en Harlem y en La Habana
jazz y son
lucirse negro mientras aplaude el bulevar,
y frente a la envidia de los blancos
hablar en negro de verdad.

(Now that the white world
toasts its body in our sun
and looks for *rumbas* in Havana,
shine in your blackness, kid,
while the crowd applauds.
Envied by the whites,
speak for the blacks indeed!)[180]

I quote from the translation of Langston Hughes and Ben Carruthers, who clearly take significant liberties, aggregating European tourists as the "white world," and consolidating "Harlem y Havana," "jazz y son"—isomorphic pairs of Afrocentric metropolises and musical forms—as "rumbas in Havana." Most importantly, they transform the idea of speaking *in* a "true" black sociolect ("hablar en negro de verdad") into representational speech: "speak *for* the blacks indeed!" (emphasis added). Perhaps, Williams's "Rumba! Rumba!" likewise essentializes a Cuban dancer "envied by the whites" while the crowd applauds. But Williams's rumbero could just as soon be a white participant in a commodified US version of the rumba dance craze. In this case, Williams's embrace of Afro-Cuban tropes rejects their commensurability with Anglo-American cultural norms. In the first case, his poem sympathizes with Guillén's. In the second, Guillén dismisses it as naive tourism.

Resolving this indeterminacy requires an inquiry into what *rumba* was to US audiences circa 1940, when Williams first published his poem in *The New Republic* amid notices on the Nazi offensive in Europe and occasional commentaries about Good Neighbor diplomacy. For at least a decade, *rumba* had already been an overextended cover term for diverse forms of commodified Cuban music and dance, just as Hughes inserts *rumbas* as a cover term for the marginally more distinct "jazz y son." Rumba experienced a 1934 US popularity boom, and a 1935 Carole Lombard film capitalized on the craze in a sequel to her hit *Bolero*. As Timothy Brennan notes, North American musicians borrowed Caribbean rhythms as early as the mid-nineteenth century, but these borrowings became culture industry hallmarks beginning in the early 1930s, intensifying rather than eroding the distinction between high and low culture. In *La música en Cuba* (1946), Alejo Carpentier argues that Cuban music was prominent in the internationalization of both popular and highbrow music, leading Brennan to observe that "like all the cultural worlds that found their origin in slavery, the Afro-Latin sound typically hovers like an indistinct echo, a sort of 'background music' simultaneously highbrow and lowbrow, rarefied and pop."[181] By 1940, that sound fueled the huge popularity of Xavier Cugat's band, a major culture industry vehicle for Good Neighbor cultural diplomacy.

Williams's poem acknowledges the rumba craze in morbidly Spenglerian terms. The qualifications of the first stanza ("No, not the downfall of the Western World/but the wish for its/downfall") critique a death drive in Western civilization, whose awkward adoption of the dance craze portend the "catastrophe" of the war. Rumba choreographs Spenglerian "downfall" as a dynamic self-immolation, "melted in a wish to die." Here is the old trope of civilization reverting into barbarism: decline from within, not from without. The rumbero's "idiot mind" does not then refer to a Cuban, but to a US dancer observed in a discomfiting cross-cultural choreography or "misplaced idea."[182] "Rumba! Rumba!" tacitly accepts antagonisms between Afro-Latin and Anglo-Saxon cultures, and implies that their mutuality—a US rumba craze as a form of wartime inter-Americanism—reveals a deadly psychology. Even prior to *The Wedge*, Williams observes scenes of nonacculturation between Afro-Latin and Anglo-Saxon music, linking it to his father in the poem "Adam." "On a hot island/inhabited by negroes—mostly," his father preserves an unassimilated musical cultural life by building himself "a boat and a separate room/close to the water/for a piano on which he practiced."[183] Incompatible Anglo and Latin cultural norms led Williams to associate the Caribbean with personal "catastrophe" in his father's era:

> Underneath the whisperings
> of tropic nights
> there is a darker whispering
> that death invents especially
> for northern men
> whom the tropics
> have come to hold.[184]

The Wedge also fatalistically links war and dance outside of the Caribbean locus: "What is war,/the destroyer/but an appurtenance // to the dance? ... When terror blooms—/leap and twist/whirl and prance—."[185]

"Rumba! Rumba!" relies on this overblown semantic nexus between desire and war. It maps the poles of sensual musical experience and civilization crisis onto North/South cultural divides. This nexus is interrupted by the poem's onomato-poeic, imperative title and refrain: "Rumba! Rumba!," "Dance, Baby, dance!," and "Cha cha, chacha, cha!" Interjections like these have led Fredric Jameson to remark, "We need, incidentally, not merely a study of Williams' punctuation [. . .], but more importantly some disquisition on the philosophy of the exclama-tion point in Williams."[186] Jameson claims that such exclamation points threaten to "tear through the fabric of syntax," marking the "non-metaphorical attention" of Williams's poems to the present. In these exclamations, Cuban music does not, as Brennan writes, "hover indistinctly." Rumba tears through the poem's lyrical program like radio static or war news. The interruptions of rumba foment a cri-tique of culture industry entertainments as the basis of wartime inter-American cultural diplomacy. In fact this cultural export process was often recognized as a political cover device in films and novels of the period.[187]

Williams's syncopated "cha cha, chacha, cha!" refrain also places his poem in relation to the Caribbean poetic device known as the jitanjáfora. Jitanjáforas are onomatopoeic nonce words, often of African provenance, inaugurated by Mariano Brull's poem "Leyenda" in 1927 ("Filiflama alabe cundre"). Theorized by Alfonso Reyes's essay "Las Jitanjáforas" (1942) and serving as prevalent fea-tures of the poetry of Nicolás Guillén and Luis Palés Matos, jitanjáforas link Caribbean poetics to the Euro-American modernist poetics clustered around Eugène Jolas's journal *transition* and his program for "the revolution of the word."[188] Carruthers and Hughes's translations of Guillén in *Cuba Libre* (1948) shy away from jitanjáfora-heavy poems, but in its heyday the device bears com-parison to the contemporaneous development of *scat* in the United States.[189] However, in "Rumba! Rumba!" no such wider social meaning for sound obtains. Here, jitanjáforas are neither ritual linguistic inventions nor marks of ludic tex-tual play. Instead, they are histrionic thuds, evocative of the aerial bombings Williams remarks across the rest of *The Wedge*. No longer an Afro-Cuban poetic trope, the repetitive *cha-cha-chá* refrain in Williams's poem indexes the colo-nization of jitanjáfora by the culture industry.[190] Williams' nonce words often signal the failure of lyric tradition to account for mass-cultural soundscapes, or the short-circuiting of Anglo-American lyric standards by modern noise. "Rumba! Rumba!" signals an unintelligible circuit between Afro-Caribbean and Northeast culture. Afro-Cuban poetry feeds the cultural commodification happening all along the US Eastern Seaboard, but Williams elicits Anglo/Latin poetic exchange only to dismiss it. "Rumba! Rumba!" erects a sound barrier between good neighbors. It suggests, as Williams had in "Adam," that the islands would never cease their ardors: "never, never, never would/peace come as the sun comes/in the hot islands."[191]

In *The Wedge*, war, cultural expropriation and commodification mingle together as creative diplomacy. Williams implicates poetry in these processes, yet his recreant modernist language observes the "catastrophic" rhythm of exchanges without envisioning coherent alternatives. Now and again, Williams's occluded Caribbean sources in the local history of *Paterson* come to the poem's surface as signs of this linguistic failure: "The language is missing them/they die also/incommunicado."[192] Here, the denizens of *Paterson* are transformed into Caribbean prisoners held "incommunicado"—as if in Cuban solitary confinement in the waning days of Spanish rule. A postwar failure of modernist language mirrors a failure to know the ardors of the "minority island."

Lysander Kemp and the Gunboat Good Neighbor

In their own ways, Julia de Burgos, Pablo Neruda, and William Carlos Williams show how Good Neighbor diplomacy foundered when confronting facts of military mobilization in the hemisphere. But conscription and volunteer military service were also major sites of inter-American encounter. To speak of Good Neighbors was often to speak of GIs. Over 500,000 US Latinos served active duty in World War II, not counting related domestic war work or the bracero worker exchange that began in 1942.[193] CIAA and the OWI concertedly propagandized about the sacrifices of US Latinos on behalf of the war. Several years before he became a key outsider voice of postwar poetry, Charles Olson worked at the OWI, where he collaborated with left front artist Ben Shahn on *Spanish Speaking Americans in the War* (1943) (Figure 1.10). Olson's athletic prose describes "1 out of every 2 Spanish speaking males" north of the Rio Grande—as well as countless women engaged in domestic work—who "gave their full complement" to US efforts.

GIs were tacit figures of inter-Americanism in poems of the era. Octavio Paz, traveling during his Guggenheim year in Berkeley, transformed the US/Mexico borderlands into the surreal dreamscape of leave-taking US soldiers in "Conscriptos USA" (1944).[194] Reciprocally, the looming cosmology of war was the subject of Muriel Rukeyser's Mayan-themed lyric "A Game of Ball" (1944).[195] Whereas poets such as Rukeyser and Olson found themselves in domestic positions propagandizing about the military's amenability to Good Neighbor

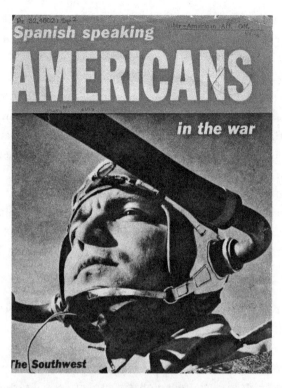

Fig 1.10   Charles Olson and Ben Shahn, *Spanish Speaking Americans in the War* (Office of War Information, 1943). Courtesy of Stanford University Libraries.

diplomacy, young GIs were in positions to offer stringent poetic critiques of the US military presence in Latin America. This was especially true of the young poet Lysander Kemp.

Lysander Schaffer Kemp, Jr. (1920–1992) is remembered mainly as what Paul Blackburn called "a one-man factory of translations of incredible beauty." His achievements include Juan Rulfo's *Pedro Páramo* (1959), Octavio Paz's *Labyrinth of Solitude* (1961) and Mario Vargas Llosa's *Time of the Hero* (1966).[196] He later edited University of Texas Press's Pan-American series. Besides Gregory Rabassa and Harriet de Onis, he is the most prolific and important—if least heralded— US broker of Boom-era Latin American literature. But Kemp's early career is so forgotten that even his papers at the Harry Ransom Center fail to report a brief biographical statement. As was true for many, World War II–era exigencies drew Kemp to inter-American letters. The aspiring poet enlisted in the Army in October 1942, and by early 1943 he was stationed in the Caribbean Defense Command (CDC), serving at several outposts of strategic US military interest, from Guayaquil and the Pacific coast of Ecuador to the Panama Canal Zone and Puerto Rico. During his tour, Kemp wrote nearly all of the forty-one poems in his first volume, *The Northern Stranger* (1946). Random House published it in a wave of titles by returning servicemen soon after Kemp submitted it in fulfillment of a Master of Arts degree at Boston University.[197]

The Northern Stranger is a lyric travel diary that begins with the rhetorical idealism of Good Neighbor diplomacy, but which subsequently reroutes this idealism through the messy encounters between Latin Americans and the 130,000 US uniformed personnel that served the CDC during the war—including 68,000 in the Canal Zone alone at its peak in 1943.[198] Kemp ranges widely across meters and forms, from cross-national emulations of décimas and guarachas to pentametric landscape poetry and bathetic protest verse. This variation does not validate Williams's belief that the short Spanish line might ground a new phase of modernist innovation. Rather, Kemp sought a poetic idiom to make vivid the ironies of wartime inter-Americanism, especially the irony that a US military presence far vaster than the small forces of Marines occupying Nicaragua in 1912 or Haiti in 1915 now mingled with the Good Neighbor rhetoric of nonintervention. Kemp's poems candidly argue, like few writers of his time, that Good Neighbor diplomacy did not supersede the gunboat era, as diplomatic historians schematically assert. Instead, it provided a rhetorical alibi for the largest and most sustained influx of US armed personnel into Latin America in all of history.[199]

Kemp's proem "Good Neighbor" contrasts the lyric persona of the "Northern Stranger" against that of the "Good Neighbor," suggesting that the closest a GI on the ground in Guayaquil might come to a successful investment in good neighborliness was self-aware strangerhood. Trawling the affective regions of alienation, pity toward Latin American underclasses, and impudence toward Good Neighbor rhetoric, Kemp asks:

> Who will unbend and how will he unbend
> to neighborly ways the body that slides in shadow
> lightly like a column of mist or a ghost,
> but fronts the Northern Stranger stiff as a post?[200]

The stanza's syntactic contortions and enjambments enact the noncompliant physicality of the Latin American "body" they describe, splaying and evanescing across the stanza rather than regimenting within the strophe. The poem characterizes the object of Good Neighbor diplomacy ("the body") as a figure of double reticence: first, an uncontainable haunting ("a column of mist or a ghost"), but also its opposite—a fixed, unflinching post. This wooden fence post does not belong to the wall Robert Frost ironized in his 1914 poem "Mending Wall" as the figure of the good neighbor, but it certainly recalls Frost's attempt to ironically deflate the "good fences make good neighbors" cliché that the neighbors in Frost's poems bring into being.

Kemp's book received split reviews. William Rose Benét stooped to regard it as a good first effort by a "sensitive" and "photographic" poet, and Vivienne Koch lauded "visual composition" with better feeling for paradox and exactitude than those of other returning servicemen.[201] Ruth Stephan, the editor of *Tiger's Eye*, a journal of New World surrealism, compared Kemp's protestant rectitude unfavorably to Jorge Carrera Andrade's *A Secret Country*. Howard Moss, measuring *The Northern Stranger* against contemporaries such as Lowell's *Lord Weary's Castle*, Williams's *Paterson* I, and H. D.'s *Trilogy*, regarded the imagery as vague and fuzzy, characterizing the spectacle of his "naive shock" before Central American poverty as "simple humanitarianism," unobjectionable except that "technically he leaves much to be desired."[202] True, Kemp humiliatingly allegorizes the Latin American body politic as an unapproachable "slouch" to be propped by the "northern stranger":

> Who from our easier cities will come to his crumbling
>   tragic city and stand him straight and strong
>   from love and goodness of heart, for nothing, a song?[203]

The phrase "for nothing, a song" locates the spirit of "humanitarian poetry" in the ambiguity of a popular idiom. Kemp calls the poem a "song" according to the popular meaning "gratis." He conflates discourses of aesthetic autonomy and spiritual charity. However, Kemp's attempts to be a poetic helpmeet to liberal developmentalism thereafter stumble on neo-imperial topoi. His description of a "crumbling/tragic city" (the phrase itself "crumbles" across the line break) suggests a longer tradition of writers and artists depicting decadent, ruined Spanish colonial edifices to signal the reciprocal health of an ascendant, US-centered, hemispheric empire.

Kemp elsewhere emphasizes the dichotomy between crumbling colonial infrastructure and the vernacular architectures of underdeveloped communities. In Latin America, "Nothing/is middling, as in New England. Buildings are stone/flowery and huge, or else of split bamboo."[204] Instead of the baroque religious monuments theorized by poets such as José Lezama Lima as a discourse of "counterconquest," Kemp highlights ramshackle, vernacular architecture at the center of several poems of moral outrage regarding the San Juan slum of El Fanguito. "Scenery for a Nice Lady" and "The Faulty Hag" are especially concerned with this scene of impoverishment. In the shadow of the postcard panoramas of San Juan, Kemp describes destitution:

> But there in San Juan is the frightful swarming section
> of stilted rickety shacks constructed of rubbish
> above polluted water and stinking flats.
> Its name is not The Mud, it is *El Fanguito*—
> The Little Mud. . . . When I first heard it, I winced
> at the tragic laugh in the diminutive of affection.[205]

In *The Crime of El Fanguito* (1948), the open letter of protest that Communist Party chairman William Z. Foster wrote to Harry Truman in 1948 after visiting the spreading slum, he translated *El Fanguito* as "The Mudhole," but Kemp the blooming translator lingers on the phrasal strangeness of "the diminutive of affection."[206] He situates *El Fanguito* in a poem called "Scenery for a Nice Lady," beside other poems entitled "Postcard For Ruth" and "Landscape." His imagined readership consists of middle-class humanitarian ladies (like those in Frances Grant's salons), not labor activists or politicians. The poem signals a growing genre of poetic poverty tourism hooked into the plans and projects of liberal developmentalism (see Chapter 5). Kemp does better in the Puerto Rico sugar poem "Tumbando Caña," notable for its denunciations of the circuits between cane field labor practices and table delicacies, hinging on the half rhyme that moves the reader from rational knowledge that "sugar is profitable and sweet" to a conflicting "taste of human sweat."[207]

In all, *The Northern Stranger* offers a doubtful, deflating scenography of Good Neighbor diplomacy viewed from a warship or troop transport. "A Headful of Scenes," a poem written aboard a gunboat steaming from Puerto Rico to St. Thomas, gets at this deflationary gesture: "my eyes were entranced, but it was only looking."[208] Ultimately, the GI persona closes the volume with "Fragments of an Impossible Poem," where the accumulation of the poet's failed cross-national identifications and the emptiness of touristic locodescription inform a statement of "impossible" planetary identity:

> I think I can only want and try to know my country, Mexico, any land
>   on earth;
> let nothing, no Northern blindness, no Western bias,
> keep me from knowing more of anybody.
> *Yo soy mejicano*—I am Turkish Peruvian Russian
> Chinese Liberian, my skin is black white brown.

> The planet Earth is my home. I like it here,
> I have many neighbors. I look to know them better.[209]

"Fragments of an Impossible Poem" stitches together the emphases of several years of attempts at a poetry fit for the Good Neighbor era: a multilingual, multinational, racial pluralism that evades the poetic speaker's ideological inheritances.

In all, the inter-American cultural diplomacy initiatives of World War II had a remarkably varied effect on poems and poetic careers. Through Fitts's anthology, Carrera Andrade's poems, or Williams's bicultural self-commemoration, hemispheric democracy absorbed avant-garde impulses into certified images of literary reciprocity. It could also be turned on its head—by Hughes and Frank's paeans to racial democracy, or by Neruda's and Burgos's moral identifications with hemispheric minority communities. Likewise, we can see in its agencies the seed of careers that were later preoccupied with the common situation of the Americas, including Kemp's, Bishop's, Olson's and Paz's. Good Neighbor diplomacy may have seemed a flash-in-the-pan, propagandistic expedient of wartime antifascism, incapable of generating the deeper, more lasting inter-American culture that critics such as O'Gorman called for. But it sponsored the "fragments of an impossible poem" whose effects could be seen long after the 1945 divestments in most of the Good Neighbor–era cultural programming. Those effects—manifesting obliquely but importantly among a large cohort of postwar poets—are the subjects of the next chapters of this book.

2. A Xenoglossary for the Americas

Benjamin spoke of the author inserting the silver rib of the foreign word into the body of language. What seems inorganic here is in actuality only histori-cal evidence, evidence of the failure of that unification.

—Theodor Adorno, "*Wörter aus der Fremde*
(Words from Abroad)" (1959)[1]

The previous chapter described the complex roles of poets in the expansive project of wartime inter-American cultural diplomacy. By contrast, this chap-ter constellates three notable lyric poets from distinct cultural situations across the Americas—Wallace Stevens in Hartford, Connecticut; José Lezama Lima in Havana, Cuba; and Jorge Luis Borges in Buenos Aires, Argentina—who main-tained an elliptical disposition toward cultural diplomacy as it unfolded in the midcentury. Variously hailed by its appeals and institutions, they largely repudi-ated cultural diplomacy. Yet each fashioned a theoretically complex poetic sys-tem enlacing the cultural diplomacy project in the life of the poem. Drawing attention to affinities between these poets suggests a mode of reading that locates the negotiation of geopolitical desires in semiautonomous poetic elements rather than institutional or political affiliation. I argue that these poetic elements, which may be as fragile as the small cluster of foreign words and lexemes I will call a "xenoglossary," point in themselves toward an early Cold War history of inter-American relations viewed from the standpoint of its language politics. The questions arising here are these: do the "foreign words" scarring the surfaces of midcentury poems of the Americas furnish evidence for histories of linguistic and cultural conjuncture? Or, as Theodor Adorno speculates, do foreign words index the failures of such conjunctures?

The following pages begin by contextualizing ideas about the internationalization of language in the bloc politics of the early Cold War. Subsequently, I demonstrate how such contexts spur the imaginative poetic formulae of Stevens, Lezama, and Borges as their poems participate in processes of interlingual dissolution and agglutination. Despite their distinct corpuses, their scattered allegiances, and a remarkable penchant for disavowing one another, they share a convergent emphasis on the foreign word as a poetic institution made consequential by midcentury language ideologies. Stevens, Lezama, and Borges are not poets conventionally associated with the neo-macaronic, vanguard styles of multilingual modernism that scholars often peg to the poetics of Ezra Pound, Mina Loy, and Vicente Huidobro (and their international cast of inheritors), nor do they flaunt a broader cultural politics of multilingualism investigated by scholars such as Joshua Miller, Kirsten Silva Gruesz, Doris Sommer, and Marc Shell.[2] Some critics have eagerly absorbed Stevens into the flexible aesthetic framework of periphrastic counterquest theorized by Lezama and Severo Sarduy as the "neo-baroque"; others see in Stevens and Borges a shared project of sensual linguistic alterity. By contrast, I argue that all three poets cultivated a distinctly "post-symbolist" poetics of cognitive "fluency" achieved through linguistic exogamy. A prominent dimension of this discourse applies unique pressures to foreign words as a symbolic order of linguistic knowledge.

Foreign Words and Bloc Politics

To a previously unimaginable degree, the development of supranational political blocs following World War II penetrated the mobile boundary that Mexican diplomat-poet Alfonso Reyes called "la frontera lingüística" (the linguistic border), making the Hispanization of American English and the Anglicization of Latin American Spanish increasingly conceivable realities.[3] The multilingual poet and *transition* editor Eugène Jolas optimistically predicted that all hemispheric languages would be welded into "a Super-American expression," and he mused: "The Super-Occidental, or the Atlantic Language—is this not Walt

Whitman's vision of a great democracy?"[4] In some respects, the internationalization of language appeared possible as never before.

Yet the prospect of supranational expression was mediated by the language ideologies—the shifting normative standards—of the linguistic communities into which foreign words wandered, intruded, or petitioned for membership.[5] Indeed, the advent of the Cold War power blocs marks a sea change in the idea of a language community precisely in so far as certain national languages—preeminently American English—were rescaled on supranational terms. Accordingly, across a spreading Anglophone world, foreign words no longer marked a resistance to the nationalism of World War I, or the exuberant cosmopolitanism of the interwar age of global tourism, or even the diasporic and hybrid multilingualism of melting pots and border zones. Whereas Delmore Schwartz hypothesized, in 1938, that the Wallace Stevens of the 1910s and 1920s wrote in the cosmopolitan language of an era in which one "knew French with pride, discussed sophistication, feared to be provincial, and aspired to membership among the elite," by the end of World War II the "middle generation" of US writers, to which Schwartz belonged, often railed against foreign words.[6] Concurrently, Allen Tate diagnosed a "new provincialism," whereby restrictive, provincial conceptions of language and culture at home governed the disposition toward huge geographical regions abroad.[7]

Many English writers, too, fell back upon a culture of nativistic retrenchment associated with the flagging empire, and they excoriated foreign words with new fervor.[8] Arthur Koestler wrote of English writers who suffered from "the French flu," quarantining French as an international language of literature and diplomacy.[9] In 1946, George Orwell remarked that "except for the useful abbreviations *i.e., e.g.,* and *etc.*, there is no real need for any of the hundreds of foreign phrases now current in English," and he took aim at promoters of international auxiliaries such as Lancelot Hogben.[10] Although the movement to create international auxiliary languages for an emerging "democratic world order" continued with works such as Hogben's *Interglossa* (1943) and Frederick Bodmer's attempts at "Language Planning for a New Order" in *The Loom of Language* (1944), World War II largely gaveled a judgment against auxiliary language enterprises such as Esperanto and Linguo Internaciona, promoted by linguists such as Edward Sapir and Otto Jespersen as late as the 1930s.[11]

After the war, we see instead the supranational projection of English as a global language in I. A. Richards's diffusion of C. K. Ogden's Basic English and the anticommunist left's fear of the totalitarian language announced by Orwell's Newspeak. While English sought to rinse off its foreignisms, it also sought to bathe the world in English. "American English," wrote William Empson in 1953, "is somehow taking over the whole world."[12] Anglophony reigned in poetry too. Writing in *The Purity of Diction in English Verse* (1952), Donald Davie contended: "I derive from this poetry a pleasure which I can only describe by saying that the diction is pure. I feel, when I read some other poetry, a peculiar discomfort which I can define only by saying that the diction is impure."[13] John Ciardi's anti-McCarthy poem "In the Witch-Hunting Season" (1956) rebranded Pound's institutionalization as part of a Cold War inquisition against multilingualism: "Ask Ezra at St. Elizabeth's mismanaging/a dozen languages in a rage of tricks/to pile all Hells into one dictionary."[14] For Ciardi, *The Cantos'* foreign lexicon was a heresy to power-bloc politics.

While the promotion of American English as a global idiom hinged on its identity as a mechanism of universal democracy and international business, commitments also grew to national languages, creoles, and vernaculars as sites of resistance to Americanization. On this complex geolinguistic map, I highlight a set of vectors for foreign words along the North/South situation of the Americas. Flourishing and often antidemocratic nationalisms policed linguistic boundaries, such as Argentine Peronism and Cuban insularism (and insularism's stylistic correlative, known as conversationalism). Yet these boundaries were permeated by borderlands, immigration routes, and cosmopolitans, as well as by a succession of bloc political arrangements: the Good Neighbor policy and its impetus toward hemispheric solidarity, the United Nations and UNESCO, the Organization of American States, and the economic development project. In such a world, under what conditions could a Pan-American language be conceived or dreamed by poets and artists? To what ends?

By the early 1940s, Argentine writers and artists theorized Pan-American language as a coarse allegory of bloc politics.[15] Artist Xul Solar had imagined an artificial romance language called neocriollo (Neo-Creole) as a game in the tertulias (literary salons) of the early 1920s, creating an extensive series of "visions" from which he published small fragments in avant-garde magazines. By the late 1930s, however, he had scaled up the political pretenses of his linguistic inventions, coming to describe a metalanguage called panlengua (Pan-Language) with the modest auxiliary aim of uniting the world's linguistic megaregions. Xul's friend and erstwhile collaborator Jorge Luis Borges politicized Neo-Creole, deploying Solar's imaginary language in his utopian metafiction "Tlön, Uqbar, Orbis Tertius."[16] There, the imaginary country Tlön's "conjectural *Ursprache*" is based on Solar's inventions. Borges describes "Tlön" and its successor "Orbis Tertius" as geopolitical allegories of language after the conspiratorial advent of an enormous political bloc. Permeating the real world over the pace of centuries, the new country presages an age when "English and French and mere Spanish will disappear from the globe. The world will be Tlön."[17] Borges and Solar's friendship soured in 1946 over Solar's tacit support for Peronism, but by 1951 Solar joined Borges in affirming the political ambitions of his two imaginary languages, coming to believe that Neo-Creole was a potential metalanguage for the hemisphere, the "futur lenguo del Contenente."[18] Wrote Solar: "We are living in the epoch of the great blocs: Pan America, Pan Europe, Pan Asia," and in such a situation, " 'Creole' or 'neocreole' could be the auxiliary idiom of Pan-America. 'Pan-lengua' would then be the complementary language between the three blocs."[19] A decade later, Solar again forecast a Pan-American superlanguage with signature utopianism: "one can anticipate for our Pan America—and the rest of the planet—that Spanish, Portuguese, and English, with their great majority of common voices between them, could come closer to one another, to the point of melting in a single popular language."[20] Across the postwar period, Borges affirmed Solar's auxiliary inventions, and his essays also playfully champion an English tradition of universal language philosophy from John Wilkins to Hogben that he links to Solar.[21]

Sylvia Molloy has elegantly described how, in the booming rioplatense cultural mood of the 1920s, Borges and Solar each began "to reformulate notions of the *patria*, of foreignness and national belonging" through the cultivation of new linguistic idioms and " *faux-naif* geographies," forging what Beatriz Sarlo has called a "national universalism" and what Molloy describes as "cosmopolitan *criollismo*."[22] This chapter proposes that these prominent interwar experiments in negotiating between local and foreign languages and their traditions shaped an auxiliary poetics. Through this poetics, Borges went on to cultivate an oblique hemispherism during the insularist retrenchments of the early Cold War that became a key part of his explosive global prestige in the cultural diplomacy networks of the 1960s. Indeed, "Borges is another of the new 'esperantists,' " remarked George Steiner by 1971.[23]

A handful of Borges's poems join dozens of others that, in the 1940s and 1950s, refract the debates over the language ideology of the Americas that I sketch above. These poems advance the foreign word as a poetic institution with a distinct language politics, specifying the nature and function of foreign usages from the purposes to which they are put in the quotidian record of multilingualism. The premise of poetic speech alters the valence of foreign words, removing them from the sphere of the ordinary and diverging from the straightforward ambition of communicative referentiality. Sometimes, poems flaunt what Roman Jakobson called literature's "*differentia specifica*," which is to say that poems mark them-selves as foreign language performances per se.[24] In other cases, poems promote their fidelity to natural, popular language, circumscribing an internal quotient as exogamous. In either case, poems operate as a linguistic performance whose foreignisms can be upheld or abandoned by a speech community according to its changing historical whims or necessities. Poems alternately shelter or dissolve foreign words, and in the midcentury Americas, communities of poets, critics, and readers were diversely receptive to poems that enact such processes.

Lyric poets like Stevens, Borges, and Lezama persisted in writing a form of symbolist poetry long after its ostensible expiration. This post-Mallarméan poetry utilizes foreign words as a symbolic intercultural optic, responsive to a deficit of more obvious frameworks of transnational cultural participation. Retrospectively, such poetic languages might be regarded as attenuated ver-sions of Solar's panlengua. That is, while Solar's formulation has an obvious purchase on works such as Oliverio Girondo's elastic, neologism-laden *En la masmédula* (In the Moremarrow, 1954), it can be extended beyond its express influence: domestically to the poems of Borges; abroad to those of Lezama; and, at a further extreme, to the poems of Wallace Stevens. To do so is to recast Stevens's Latinization of American English as an effort to entangle US poetry with a hemispheric linguistic fabric rather than a baroque habit of exoticizing the sumptuousness of Latin American life. It is to read the Spanish of Lezama's "Pensamientos en la Habana" (Thoughts in Havana, 1949), rigged with mock English-language citations, as establishing a relationship to a cosmopolitan modernism newly centered in the United States, even as it avowedly resists US neo-imperialism. And it is to begin to account for Borges's "Englishness" not simply as a genealogical accident or a lamentation for the so-called "land that England lost," but as a tightly crafted philosophy of language that highlights poetry's capacity to mark out interlinguistic vitality in the flux of time. For such poets, foreign words may often amplify or confirm geopolitical divisions, but they cumulatively construct a xenoglossary: a shared auxiliary lexicon open to poets across the Americas.[25]

Stevens's "Lingua Franca et Jocundissima"

A daunting bipolarity in the critical literature on Wallace Stevens can lead his readers into conflicting accounts of what Stevens knew of foreign places and for-eign poets—indeed, of his entire disposition toward worldliness on the one hand, nativism on the other. Alan Filreis meticulously historicizes a dependency on a "postcard imagination" and a powerful desire to "experience and write about 'longed-for lands'" percolating through much of Stevens's late work.[26] Yet Helen Vendler prefers to read Stevens as a lifelong nativist with an occasional flirtation with French and no contact with other literatures whatsoever:

> For reasons not entirely clear, Stevens never set foot in Europe, yet he sub-scribed to French and English periodicals, and bought, when he could afford it, beautifully printed editions of French poetry and (sight unseen) French paintings. In spite of these tastes for the European and the exotic (tea from Ceylon, etc.), Stevens was a tenaciously nativist poet, who never ceased to think about the situation of the American poet from his first book (as in the Tennessean "Anecdote of the Jar") to his last (as in "The River of Rivers in Connecticut").[27]

It is one thing to state that Stevens was a poet "who never ceased to think about the situation of the American poet," a statement that could as easily be made about most every poet of Stevens's cohort. But it is quite another to describe Stevens as a lifelong nativist on the order of James Whitcomb Riley or Robert Frost, a poet whose imagination is coextensive with the naturalistic verisimil-itude of American landscape. In fact, Stevens consistently filtered his thought about "American reality" through his writing about a larger entity that his poems so often describe as a "world." His poems are dramatically populated with the multilingual fragments he culled to describe this worldly figure, and his delight in this heterogeneous sphere brings many of his major poems to a climax or a close. In the collection of aphorisms Stevens entitled *Adagia*, he went so far as to remark: "French and English constitute a single language." In describing an undifferentiated, "exotic" exterior, Vendler flattens the global feedbacks and interlingual admixtures that structure Stevens's writing.

For example, it will not do to think of Stevens's well-documented and increas-ing contact with poets and writers of Latin America across the 1940s and 1950s—most prominently with Cuban writer José Rodríguez Feo, but also with Jorge Carrera Andrade, Lezama, and Borges—as a "taste for the exotic." Stevens per-tains to a network of inter-American writers who find their way into his poetry through citation, allusive style, and nomenclature. Such citations have invited critics to make astute comparative gestures that trumpet relation and connec-tion, as Christopher Winks does in his study of the comparative baroque aes-thetics of Stevens and Lezama, and Eric Keenaghan in his study of their mutual ethic of "queer vulnerability."[28] Here, by contrast, I focus on a mutual diffidence between Stevens and his Latin American contemporaries, aiming to move the appraisal of his inter-American poetics beyond a record of intertexts, correspondents, and affinities. Stevens's linguistic ideology, what he calls "lingua franca et jocundissima," captures a moment in the linguistic identity of the Americas at large, a conceptual commonality he shares with Lezama and Borges in a field of resemblances, not influences or filiations.

In the 1940s, a new relation between Stevens and Latin American writers emerges, and both his correspondence and his poetry register a hemispheric drift that scholars either idealize or ignore. Whereas in *Parts of a World* (1942) the fictional "Mrs. Alfred Uruguay" bestrode a donkey down the premodern pathways of "the ultimate elegance: the imagined land," by *Transport to Summer* (1947) such fantastications embroider a core of Latin American literary figures with global prestige.[29] "Description Without Place," for one, makes a cagey reference to Pablo Neruda: "Things are as they seemed to Calvin and to Anne/Of England, to Pablo Neruda in Ceylon,/To Nietzsche in Basel, to Lenin by a lake."[30] Even so, Stevens most likely did not read Neruda before delivering this valedictory poem at the 1945 Harvard commencement ceremony, learning of Neruda circuitously from Leonard van Geyzel, his correspondent in Ceylon, where Neruda was stationed in the late 1920s.

Simultaneously, Stevens data-mined his lengthening correspondence with a young, enterprising Cuban editor of the Havana-based journal *Orígenes* in order to write "A Word with José Rodríguez-Feo." The poem enshrines an inter-American address in its title, no matter how coded the poetic conversation that follows it (Rodríguez Feo himself wrote to ask Stevens for clarification).[31] By the time Stevens's collected *Letters* were published in 1966, readers would have been hard-pressed to deny the liveliness and intimacy of his exchange with Rodríguez Feo from 1944 until Stevens's death in 1955. Their full correspondence, published in 1986, offers continuing authority for some critics to regard Stevens as a poet thickly—if privately—enmeshed in the circuitry of inter-American cultural relations.[32]

However, Stevens attenuated his participation in such networks with much more skepticism than recent scholars allow, excluding himself from the pantheon of World War II–era inter-American cultural workers that I track in Chapter 1, even as that network begs his participation. Stevens and Rodríguez Feo were not in touch until the end of 1944, and prior to Stevens's brief, admiring exchange with Carrera Andrade in 1943, his attitude toward Latin American writers was extremely chilly. In 1938, he warned the editor and publisher Ronald Lane Latimer not to move the Alcestis Press to Mexico: "I am very much afraid that you might as well take your press to the bottom of the sea as to take it to Mexico City, but that Mexico City is a wonderful place to visit goes without saying."³³ He sought to intensify the absurdity of an inter-American publishing venture by postulating the impossibility of the reciprocal move: "What chance would a Mexican have who brought his press to New York City with the idea of publishing works of Mexican poets?"³⁴ Later that year his antipathy to Mexico grew ever harsher. Ignoring the literary renaissance underway in one of the decade's key cosmopolitan meeting grounds, he quipped: "In Mexico life is altogether without a thesis; it is a lot of scenery and economics based on charity."³⁵

By September 1942, his aversion extended to a Latin American literary gestalt. When Stevens received an inquiry from the influential Argentine journal *Sur*, whose lost details likely amount to a request from Borges and Adolfo Bioy Casares to publish their translation of "Sunday Morning" in the porteño periodical, Stevens leveled a blanket judgment against "South American" writers, charging them with Francophile posturing:³⁶

> Everybody has a kind of understanding of the English, French, Germans, etc., but I cannot say that I have the slightest understanding of anything in South America. In a general way, I have a feeling that the people down there are not yet themselves. For instance, there is nothing South American about the poetry of Mr. [Jules] Supervielle. He is a Parisian and, in being Parisian, is typical of the sophisticated writers and thinkers of South America, except possibly when they write and think of politics. The result is that one skips them and goes to the Parisians themselves.³⁷

Supervielle exemplified Stevens's point in a conveniently tautological way. He was a Uruguayan who naturalized as a French citizen of his own volition, much like Ramón Fernández, the Mexican-born French intellectual whom Stevens apostrophizes in "The Idea of Order at Key West" (1936), and whom Stevens would have read not in *Sur* or *Cuadernos Americanos* or *Orígenes* (although later he subscribed to all three) but in the pages of the *Nouvelle Revue Française*.³⁸ Despite the interchanges that Stevens's famous poem stages between Northern severity and Southern sensuality, its climactic queries to "pale Ramon [*sic*]" about the play of light and sound along the Floridian littoral were tinged with a poetic conversation pointed obliquely at French interlocutors, not inter-American ones.³⁹

Stevens's skepticism toward North/South cultural exchange as of late 1942 proves especially notable when considered in relation to the many poets drawn into the network of inter-American cultural activity primed by state institutions in the early 1940s. Even Vice President Henry Wallace brought inter-American rhetoric to the very center of statements of foreign policy, making frequent public speeches as early as 1939 to the effect that a transcendent hemispheric culture was near:

> The events of Europe and Asia have waked us up. We are challenged to build here on this hemisphere a new culture which is neither Latin American nor North American but genuinely inter-American. Undoubtedly it is possible to build up an inter-American consciousness and an inter-American culture which will transcend both its Anglo-Saxon and its Iberian origins. As long as we were looking across the Atlantic Ocean, this was not possible, but now that we are looking north and south, everything is possible.[40]

Stevens mistrusted this inter-American culture, especially in the realm of literature, and instead went "to the Parisians themselves." If "inter-American culture" exists, Stevens triangulates it with the cosmopolis Pascale Casanova calls the capital of "the World Republic of Letters." Borges too—despite attempts to foster inter-American literary understanding through his translations—later confessed to a similar "mental Gallicism," in the phrase of Rubén Darío.[41] In 1942, Stevens projected his Gallic mindset onto Latin America, but in the following pages I track the evolution of this mindset across the next few years.

We can read the narrow Latin American apertures of "Notes Toward a Supreme Fiction" in light of this reticence, given that it was composed contemporaneously with Stevens's harsh judgments of Latin American writers. And these apertures cast light on the volume *Transport to Summer* (1947) that "Notes" brings to a close. Composed in the summer of 1942 and first published in October by the Cummington Press, "Notes" precedes active endorsement of cultural inter-Americanism by Stevens, and instead exhibits his desultory exotification of Latin America, which led Yvor Winters to notice that Stevens's "protagonists" often ended up "finally and irretrievably on a small but beautiful planet, floating like a tropical island in boundless space."[42] Yet the climactic apostrophe of "Notes," after much throat-clearing, addresses itself to a newly Hispanized world: "at last, I call you by name, my green, my fluent mundo." In so doing, the poem revalues "worldliness" in the historically determinate semantics of inter-American cultural policy. While, at the time he wrote "Notes," Stevens had yet to embrace Latin American poetry as an autonomous cultural resource, his struggle to write a major modernist poem can nonetheless be read as a discursive negotiation with the construction of the Americas as a world. Scholars commonly understand Stevens's "mundo" in philosophical terms.[43] Here, I argue that we need to attend to the semantics of the "world" as a language politics—an inter-cultural vision that plays out not when we regard Stevens's poems as plain-style philosophy ornamented by foreign flourishes, but as lexical maps encoding forms of global cognition in poetic diction.

The "fluent mundo" figure describes the main poetic activity of "Notes Toward a Supreme Fiction" itself. The poem's famously doctrinal sense of its own abstraction, pleasurability, and dynamism often consigns "Notes" to be read according to the rubrics that Stevens headlined. Yet the thirty-one neatly ordered cantos comprise a poem that strives toward the verbal formula of the "fluent mundo" and reflects on its phenomenal reality in the life of the poem. The following remarks on the "fluent mundo" divide into two parts. First, I describe Stevens's language ideology as the production of an unfettered verbal "fluency." This language ideology—tending toward a plastic, denationalized language of foreign words—brings Stevens to confront the problem of the poetry of the Americas. Second, I examine "Notes" in a historical conversation about the semantics of "worldliness" (or perhaps "mundialismo" is better) from the poem's appeal to perceive "the idea/Of this invention, this invented world" to its moments of Adamic vision, when Adam and Eve find themselves "In heaven as in a glass; a second earth;//And in the earth itself they found a green," to the final name Stevens gives to that green, "fluent mundo."[44]

Stevens aspired early to "fluency" as a linguistic ideal, opposing it to his propensity for modernist difficulty. Writing to Harriet Monroe in 1922 about the poems he collected in *Harmonium* the following year, he remarked that he wished "to keep on dabbling and to be as obscure as possible until I have perfected an authentic and fluent speech for myself."[45] However private the poet's sense of linguistic "fluency" remained, he held it in tense opposition to the quality of obscurity. Soon, Stevens also linked fluency to the "ambrosial latitude" of the tropics.[46] Following the publication of *Harmonium* in September 1923, Stevens embarked on a two-week cruise with his wife Elsie from New York to Havana and then on to Tehuantepec and California via the Panama Canal, the farthest south he ever traveled. "In that November off Tehuantepec," the sea's "paradisal green" and "too-fluent green" insistently met his gaze as he wrote the poem "Sea Surface Full of Clouds."[47]

Many critics note that some variant on "fluency" is an operative motif in Stevens's poetic system, if not its main procedure, though its significance is often buried by the self-importance of Stevens's epigrammatic philosophizing. Frank Kermode intuited "fluency" as the key to Stevens's late-career profusion of writing, treating the conjecture of a "fluent mundo" as a hypothetical world that Stevens continually approached in lucid, "fluid" style.[48] J. Hillis Miller similarly describes Stevens's "universal fluctuation" or constant "oscillation."[49] Such a motion, I would argue, finds its shape in Stevens's rarefied diction, especially in mispluralized nouns for movement and the play of light on water, words that tug on the limits of American English: *ensolacings, brilliances, versicolorings, infuriations, ravishments, enflashings*. Once the reader accepts that such usages have a special, metasymbolic status in Stevens's poems as naturalistic descriptions of linguistic motion, it becomes clear that Stevens similarly activates seemingly neutral usages, such as *resemblances, balances*, or *excitements*.

Fredric Jameson builds on Hillis Miller in offering a provocative account of Stevens's "flow." Unlike the "flow" developed by the surrealists, Jameson sites Stevens's fluidity in a structuralist associative system like that which Claude Lévi-Strauss calls "pensée sauvage." Exotic reference and binary opposition are two hallmarks of this structuralist metalanguage, as are what Jameson calls "signifying fields" or "vocabulary fields," a set of "neutral counters for the exercise of poetic speech."[50] Casting Stevens's verse as expositions of structuralist linguistics, Jameson concludes that the exercise of "flow," surmounting of oppositions, and incorporation of "the foreign" bring the poems to "know global closure." Stevens fluently incorporates many distinct codes of linguistic material into a poetic system that endlessly produces sonorous output, and Jameson's inventory of these codes is compelling though partial. It could be expanded to include Stevens's propensities for philosophical terminology, binary oppositions, place names, fabular personae, foreign diction (especially simple Spanish, complex French, rarefied Anglo-Saxon, and binomial Latin), luxury products, single alphabetic letters (especially c, x, and z),[51] mispluralized nouns, ideophones, and syllabic nonsense. Strangest is Stevens's pervasive verbal habit of transforming forced superlatives and comparatives into poetic speech. In *Transport to Summer, plentifullest, loudlier*, and *closelier* are but three of the thirty-odd words he thus shoehorns into his metrical fluidity.

These linguistic features recombine across his work, no less so in "Notes Toward a Supreme Fiction." Take Cantos IV and V of *It Must Change*. These "planter poems" depict a typically tropical Caribbean scene. Amid a list of binaries, Stevens offers an image of easy commerce between North and South, writing that "North and South are an intrinsic couple" walking "away as one in the greenest body." Keenaghan argues—optimistically—that these lines imagine an "erotic" union of the Americas.[52] If so, how does one understand Caribbean indices that do not stage erotic coupling so much as division or remove?

And là-bas, là-bas, the cool bananas grew,

Hung heavily on the great banana tree,

Which pierces clouds and bends on half the world.[53]

Erotic paronomasia here, too, is low-hanging fruit, for the reader who picks it. Yet surely the banana tree's crescent-like halving action offers as much an image of division as it does of unity. Who is Stevens's planter if not the United Fruit Company? What joins the "intrinsic couple" besides its Great White Fleet of reefer ships? It hardly takes Stevens to eroticize the banana trade. Sexualized bananas are stock wartime tropes, as in Carmen Miranda's "The Lady in the Tutti Frutti Hat" from Busby Berkeley's technicolor musical *The Gang's All Here* (1943), where women parade large papier-mâché bananas through a kaleidoscopic performance (Figure 2.1). The singing, anthropomorphic "Chiquita Banana" (1944) also enlists her sexy linguistic masquerade in the service of hemispheric solidarity: "I'm Chiquita Banana and I've come to say/I come from little island down equator way/I sail on big banana boat from Caribe/to see if I can help Good Neighbor policy."

Fig 2.1 Screen capture from Carmen Miranda, "The Lady in the Tutti Frutti Hat," in *The Gang's All Here*, dir. Busby Berkeley (Twentieth Century-Fox, 1943).

Stevens anticipates the United Fruit Company's inter-American pidgin with his own, pointing "là-bas" at Latin America through another Francophile screen. The title of "Notes Toward a Supreme Fiction" elevates deixis—language that points towards spatiotemporal phenomena—as an essential poetic act. Here, Stevens codes geographical deixis in terms of decadent Parisian airs, given that *Là-bas* was also the title of a novel by Joris-Karl Huysmans. Such distancing effects smooth over his coarse descriptions of Latin American writers as "the people down there." In the nuanced fluency of "Notes," no prominent arrow marks the way, as it does on the cover of *Sur* (Figure 2.2), where Borges hoped to publish Stevens. Some years later, Rodríguez Feo described Borges to Stevens as "one of the most brilliant and queerest writers down Argentina way," an idiom popularized by another Miranda musical *Down Argentine Way* (1940) and the Chiquita Banana song's "down equator way." Rodríguez Feo transformed Borges, who was then in a state of professional, political, and romantic despair, into a handsome literary Lothario whose stories could be equated to the eroticized mass cultural crazes CIAA sold

Fig 2.2 *Sur* No. 113–114 (March–April, 1944), special number dedicated to US literature.

to the United States as the stock imaginary Latin America. "Là-bas" swaps an artificial register for the vernacular idioms pointing "down" to Latin America.

Of course, "Là-bas, là-bas" serves purposes in the poem beyond ornamental Gallicism. It also activates consonance and assonance in a sound scheme that doubles on the repetitions of "banana," naturalizing the Caribbean's exportable commodity-world in the poem's abyss of Jabberwocky, or "gorgeous nonsense," to use a phrase from Stevens's essay "The Noble Rider and the Sound of Words."[54] Stevens's poems take frequent refuge in this ideophonic realm, drawing signifying relationships between Romance languages and the natural phenomena of the Americas, as in the chirpy cacophony of "Cock-robin's at Caracas./Make o, make o, make o,/Oto—out—bre," or the windy, alliteratively Antillean scheme "Parlparled the West-Indian weather."[55] A chain of critics from Yvor Winters to Fredric Jameson assign "Notes" the distinction of being at once a poem and a theory of poetry.[56] Yet, in a canto that curiously fails to draw more attention from such critics, Stevens suggests that the work of the poem is precisely the transformation of nonsemantic or preverbal content into a fiction of total, fluid comprehensibility. "The poem goes from the poet's gibberish to/The gibberish of the vulgate and back again," he declares, finding in such movement a way of "compounding the imagination's Latin with/The lingua franca et jocundissima."[57] His poems enact a lingua franca—an auxiliary language—that is common precisely in so far as it is ludic or "jocundissima." The fact that Stevens names "language" here is itself important. The persona behind the fluent incorporation of foreign words into common speech is the "beau linguist," who habitually hears sound as pure speech, and vice versa:

> As if the waves at last were never broken,
> As if the language suddenly, with ease,
> Said things it had laboriously spoken.[58]

Here, fluency is a trick of the end rhyme *broken/spoken*, which repairs a "broken" world by transforming nature into language. Elsewhere, ideophonic nature sounds, such as the sparrow's "Bethous" or the bee's "green juvenal," produce fluency out of noise. Yet Stevens most clearly associates fluency as a linguistic ideal with the foreign speech of Romance languages. To be fluent is not simply to command a foreign language but to weave and dissolve languages into a singular global language. Stevens must be understood as richly multilingual, a poet bent on "the beau language without a drop of blood," the "palabra of a common man," the "fluent mundo," a poet whose xenoglosses are microcosms of the global auxiliary language he calls "lingua franca et jocundissima." His "supreme fiction" continually hooks up exogamous utterances to the production of "a single text" defined by the aesthetics of fluency.

If *fluency* describes a collaborative hemisphere in the realm of verbal aesthetics, *mundo* calls attention to a conflict in naming the world. Responding to this problem in "The Noble Rider," Stevens writes: "we recognize, even if we cannot realize, the feelings of the robust poet clearly and fluently noting the images in his mind and by means of his robustness, clearness and fluency communicating much more than the images themselves. Yet we do not quite yield. We cannot. We do not feel free."[59] Stevens's inability to "yield" to the aesthetics of fluency suggests that the further his poems work dynamically toward the achievement of fluid sonority, the more they abstract from a referential grounding. In "fluent mundo," Stevens rewrites the problem of inter-Americanism as a fundamental quality of poetry itself: a friction between sonorous pleasure and meaningful reference.

The ways in which sonority begets referential indeterminacy were hardly lost on Stevens. For all his poem's claims to dramatize the ease or fluency of speech, the early reception of "Notes" is marked by the bewildered questions of his literary correspondents. Stevens admitted to Hi Simons that "[t]here are several things in the *Notes* that would stand a little annotating," and he viewed Simons as an authorized outlet for his eccentric annotations to reach wider audiences. For example, one poem in "Notes" offers a xenophobic sound image of Arabic language in the lines "At night an Arabian in my room,/With his damned hoobla-hoobla-hoobla-how," but Stevens confided to Simons that "the fact that the Arabian is the moon is something that the reader could not possibly know."[60] Even should a given reader become aware of this meaning—or others around it, such as the seeming accident that the word *room* in this line is a palindrome for *moor*—does it make the sound-image of Arabic any more intelligible as a synesthetic proxy for moonlight? Stevens's jabber in this instance approximates what Borges calls, drawing on the lexical world of Moorish Spain, an *algarabía*, a word for gibberish formed from the sound-image of Arabic. Here, foreign speech invades the image of the sublunary natural world. Elsewhere, Stevens suggests to Simons that even ostensibly pedestrian usages connote foreign meanings. In "[t]he glitter-goes on the surface of tanks," he specifies, "the word tanks would be obscure to anyone not familiar with the use of that word in Ceylon," where it indicates a water reservoir.[61] This obscurity holds doubly true for a public newly exposed to images of the Pacific theatre of the war. A few weeks later Stevens returned home from a funeral in the company of a woman whose husband was "in the Tank Corps, and has been in Hawaii for the greater part of a year so that he hasn't yet seen his daughter."[62] The idiom of troop transport even haunts the volume title *Transport to Summer*, to which we could compare Kemp's poem titled "Transport to Ecuador."

Stevens's referents, though grounded in the world, abstract from their hold on realism toward a metalinguistic order, and it does not get a reader very far to become a dutiful initiate into his self-professed records of observation. Syntactical and grammatical sparseness often produces this semantic difficulty. Stevens does not create long, subordinated, hypotactic clauses. Rather, his syntactical simplicity amplifies his semantic difficulty, packaging the burden of interpretation in the unit of diction. The interpretive challenge posed by Stevens's "Notes" is to understand not merely how the poem produces a symbolic order out of referential material, but how it is interlaced with a secondary conversation about that very process. The poem produces abstraction out of reference, but it must also describe how it does so. The most complexly distorted "referent" in "Notes"—the world as such—is the key site of this negotiation.

No poem in "Notes" perorates at such length on the semantics of the "world" as its climactic, penultimate poem, Canto X of *It Must Give Pleasure*:

> Fat girl, terrestrial, my summer, my night,
> How is it I find you in difference, see you there
> In a moving contour, a change not quite completed?
>
> You are familiar yet an aberration.
> Civil, madam, I am, but underneath
> A tree, this unprovoked sensation requires
> That I should name you flatly, waste no words,
> Check your evasions, hold you to yourself.
> Even so when I think of you as strong or tired,
>
> Bent over work, anxious, content, alone,
> You remain the more than natural figure. You
> Become the soft-footed phantom, the irrational
>
> Distortion, however fragrant, however dear.
> That's it: the more than rational distortion,
> The fiction that results from feeling. Yes, that.
>
> They will get it straight one day at the Sorbonne.
> We shall return at twilight from the lecture
> Pleased that the irrational is rational,
>
> Until flicked by feeling, in a gildered street,
> I call you by name, my green, my fluent mundo.
> You will have stopped revolving except in crystal.[63]

The "fat girl," imagined bending over her work, is a contingent and polysemous figure, plausibly evoking a Sorbonne librarian or an impressionistic peasant digging in the fields of a Van Gogh painting. By contrast, Stevens tellingly glossed the "fat girl" as an allegory of the terrestrial globe in a letter sent to Henry Church immediately after the publication of the poem. "The fat girl," wrote Stevens, "is the earth: what the politicians now-a-days are calling the globe, which somehow, as it revolves in their minds, does, I suppose, resemble some great object in a particularly blue area."[64] If Stevens apostrophizes "the earth" in his own symbolic language, he also recognizes that the earth's discourse can be politically co-opted for the projection of supranational power.

Stevens refracts this politics by talking around the earth's name, refusing to settle for *globe, world,* or other variants. Instead, he offers "fat girl," "terrestrial," "my summer, my night," "madam," "more than natural figure," "rational distortion," "fiction," and finally, "at last," the "fluent mundo." For a poem that professes to "waste no words," it perambulates to great excess. Even Stevens's admonition to laconic directness comes as a verbose profusion: "That I should name you flatly, waste no words, check your evasions, hold you to yourself." The speaker's evasive prolixity belies his point. The poem's lyric "I" hardly constitutes itself as a speaking subject so much as a wandering sound image or an echo of the "world." The key phrase in this respect is "madam, I am," which calls out to be pronounced as two rhyming, iambic feet (or trochaic, depending on whether the speaker Anglicizes the pronunciation of "madam"). "I am" suggests "iamb": a homophonic description of the poem's metrical foot rather than a subjective expression of being. The poetic self figures sonic repetition, echoing and talking its way around the feminized world it apostrophizes. Stevens uses the word *world* forty-six times in *Transport to Summer,* but when he professes to name it "flatly," he instead offers sheer sphericity, for the poem's pleasure comes in changing the world's name until it has been three-dimensionalized.[65] In a previous poem, Stevens proposes that his poetics creates a mimesis of convexity through reiteration:

> One of the vast repetitions final in
> Themselves and, therefore, good, the going round
>
> And round and round, the merely going round,
> Until merely going round is a final good.[66]

"Notes" therefore offers a fine-tuned rhetorical meditation on the linguistic processes and pratfalls of "globalizing" speech. This relies on a misogynistic topos of feminized verbal rotundity at least as old as the kitchen wench in Shakespeare's *Comedy of Errors* ("she is spherical, like a globe; I could find out/countries in her"). But a point to stress is that the "fluent mundo" is not a locus amoenus such as Winters declares to be the telos of many Stevens poems. It is not another palm at the end of Stevens's mind. Rather, a spherical globe slows on its axis: an incipient allegory of globalization at the moment in which such a discourse harmonizes with the inter-American cultural project. The "fluent mundo" therefore reneges on a previous dictum from his poem "Academic Discourse in Havana": "The world is not/The bauble of the sleepless nor a word/That should import a universal pith/To Cuba."[67] Here, Stevens abandons himself to precisely the "universal pith" of globalization.

I introduce the term "globalization" because Stevens's worldmaking is not merely analogous to political debates about globalization. In speaking of what "the politicians now-a-days are calling the globe," Stevens has in mind the purveyors of the precise discourse that would come to be named "American globalization." Juan Trippe, the founder of Pan American World Airways, iconically presided over Latin America in "his legendary globe-gazing pose" in period photographs (Figure 2.3).[68] His friendship with Henry Luce led him to endorse the American Century by way of unilateral dominance of the world's skyways. Henry Wallace named his multilateral alternative to the American Century "The Century of the Common Man," focusing on the extension of Roosevelt's "four freedoms" to the developing world. We hear its echo in a Stevens line such as "palabra of a common man who did not exist" in the poem "Holiday in Reality." Wallace and political rivals like Wendell Willkie were equally fixated on aviation, and Wallace spoke of a "network of globe-girdling airways," an international, deterritorialized airspace opposed to the visions of Trippe, Luce, and Willkie.[69] When Henry Luce's wife Claire Booth Luce was elected to Congress in Stevens's home state of Connecticut in November 1942, she captured attention by declaring Wallace's multilateral view of geopolitics "globaloney."[70] Her neologism indicates that the semantics of the world was a feverish object of public discussion. For all of its lyrical autonomy, Stevens's "Notes" comes close to congressional disputes on the semantics of globalization.

Oddly, Stevens's postwar critics roundly rejected the "fluent mundo" formulation on precisely the grounds that it misnamed the world, especially as Orwellian language politics made global English, rather than Stevens's sophisticated metalanguage, the auxiliary language of choice for postwar globalization. In this spirit Dudley Fitts, the prolific translator and editor of the *Anthology of Contemporary Latin American Poetry* (1942), first singled out Stevens's use of foreign words as

Fig 2.3 Juan T. Trippe, President of Pan American World Airways, in his "'legendary' globe-gazing pose," in Josephson, *Empire of the Air* (1943). Wikimedia Commons.

an artifice of "affectation" that lent the poems "a certain preciosity [. . .]. Thus a fine apostrophe to the world ('Fat girl') precariously names the globe 'my fluent mundo.'"[71] For a translator who had spent two years rendering Spanish-language poems into literalistic translations in the service of inter-Americanism, the "precarious" multilingual pollution of *world* struck him as an overly concessionary synthesis. Or, perhaps, any ornament seemed misplaced amid wartime austerity measures.

After the war, comparable critiques emerged. Reviewing *Transport to Summer*, Robert Lowell anatomized the "reality" underlying Stevens's poems as a collection of "places visited on a vacation," "Tennysonian sound effects," and "exotic vocabulary."[72] He may have had in mind a passage from "The Pure Good of Theory":

> Then came Brazil to nourish the emaciated
> Romantic with dreams of her avoirdupois, green glade
> Of serpents like z rivers simmering,

Green glade and holiday hotel and world
Of the future, in which the memory had gone
From everything, flying the flag of the nude,

The flag of the nude above the holiday hotel.[73]

If Brazil is synecdoche of the postwar "world/Of the future" (a phrase Stevens wrests from its semi-ironic usage in Stefan Zweig's 1941 *Brazil: Land of the Future*), its "nude" flag has been stripped of its national markers only by the luxury of being a Pan American World Airways port of call, not by, say, the achievement of social equality. "Avoirdupois," the kind of word that led Lowell to decry Stevens's "exotic" vocabulary, entered English from Old French to define the standard English system of weights. Is Brazil a "weight" for the "emaciated/Romantic?" Is it, too, a kind of "fat girl?" Or is "avoirdupois" a sound image rather than a semantically meaningful word, onomatopoeically describing the natural phenomenon of a river snaking through the glade? Is it an auditory icon for some Amazon River of the mind, just as the letter *z* is a visual icon for it? For that matter, is *z* a Latinized homophone for the definite article *the*? "Avoirdupois" hides semantic connotations of instrumentality in a rarefied and flexible cloak of sonority.

In 1953, William Empson broadcast the same critique as Fitts and Lowell to different effect: "There is one unfortunate feature of [Stevens's] style which ought to be noticed, what he calls 'beau-linguist' perhaps, as in the line 'I call you by name, my green, my fluent mundo.' "[74] Empson accepted Whitman's use of ornamental foreign words in that they offered an "all-inclusively democratic" use of the "mother tongue," but by the early 1950s, Stevens was "out of date because American English is somehow taking over the whole world." Randall Jarrell hammered another nail in the coffin of Stevens's auxiliary style the same year. To him, Stevens's poetics connoted the professoriate's faux worldliness:

All his *tunk-a-tunks*, his *hoo-goo-boos*—those mannered, manufactured, individual, uninteresting little sound-inventions—how typical they are of the lecture-style of the English philosopher, who makes grunts or odd noises, uses homely illustrations, and quotes day in and day out from *Alice*, in order to give what he says some appearance of that raw reality it so plainly and essentially lacks. These "tootings at the wedding of the soul" are fun for the tooter, but get as dreary for the reader as do all the foreign words—a few of these are brilliant, a few more pleasant, and the rest a disaster: "one cannot help deploring his too extensive acquaintance with the foreign languages," as Henry James said, of Walt Whitman, to Edith Wharton.[75]

To Empson, Stevens was an undemocratic Whitman, his "fluent mundo" an unwelcome revision of Whitman's "O vast rondure swimming in space." To Jarrell, he was a mannered professor-poet hobbling on the cosmopolitan crutches of Victorian gentility. By regarding Stevens's foreign diction as Whitmanian, both suggest the influence of F. O. Matthiessen's critique of Whitman's foreign words. To Matthiessen, Whitman's "belief in the need to speak not merely for Americans but for the workers of all lands seems to have given the impetus for his odd habit of introducing random words from other languages, to the point of talking about 'the ouvrier class'!"[76] Matthiessen thought Whitman's usage gave way to "an intoxication with the mere sound" that ran counter to his general tendency toward Emersonian Cratylism—Emerson's belief, in *Nature*, that words were natural signs of things. Foreign words, by contrast, only evoked the word's abstraction.

Stevens's late poems accept the critique of his diction by dramatizing movements away from foreign speech. His late poems are like the young French protagonist of a poem he named obscurely for a Rodin sculpture, "Celle Qui Fût Héaulmiette" (She Who Was Héaulmiette): effortlessly exorbitant once upon a time, but now prone to "another American vulgarity.//Into that native shield she slid."[77] No poem crouches so carefully behind the "native shield" as Stevens's final poem, "Of Mere Being." Offering another phrasal map of the hemisphere in the image of the "palm at the end of the mind," Stevens nonetheless avoids all traces of linguistic exogamy. The bird in the palm "sings a foreign song," and "its feathers shine," as if to exaggerate the shrinking away from verbal play. The "luminous flittering" of all things gives over to droll description. The alliteration of the poem's final, Phoenix-like image ("the bird's fire-fangled feathers dangle down") belatedly resurrects the ludic sounds midcentury readers rejected. An unremarked irony closes Stevens's career: he pushed back against the inter-American cultural project until after the war, only to belatedly offer it, in the sonorous global language of his "lingua franca et jocundissima," an interlinguistic style discarded by Anglophone poets. "Fluency" as a language ideology had stronger affinities with poets, such as Lezama and Borges, on the far shores of English.

Post-Symbolists

Stevens's fluency bears stronger resemblance to the lyric modes of a number of midcentury Latin American poets than it does to his US critics and epigones.

A major company of poets, including Jorge Luis Borges (Argentina), José Lezama Lima (Cuba), and Alfonso Reyes (Mexico), course the stylistic terrain that Lezama calls "el flujo calmoso/de la tierra que no está navegada" (the calm flow/of the unnavigated land). This poetic territory toggles between abstraction and reference, between mellifluous Gallicism and gravelly nativism, between Hispanized English and Anglicized Spanish. In this territory, poems propose syntheses between vernacular and vehicular languages, offering a novel hemispheric lexical geography.

Of course, I am not the first to propose reading Stevens together with Lezama. Julio Ortega claimed that Lezama was like one of Stevens's "Mayan sonneteers" in "The Comedian as the Letter C."[78] Christopher Winks offers the most recent and compelling account of their relation, taking up neo-baroque theories by Severo Sarduy, Lezama, and Édouard Glissant to imagine Stevens's poetry in relation to a latent North American yearning for the baroque, seen as a style informed by "proliferating contact of diversified natures," paradisiacal nostalgia, Caribbean hedonism, and the elliptical "philosophical implications of tropical landscape."[79] In Winks's account, Stevens renounces baroque language aesthetics soon after *Ideas of Order* (1936), just as it emerges among his postwar Latin American interlocutors. The neo-baroque has much explanatory value, but as with critics who note that the baroque is a retrojection onto the aesthetics of counterreformation and counterconquest, we risk anachronism in calling Stevens's poetic system neobaroque. By the late 1950s, when the Cuban discourse of the neo-baroque solidified, the Stevens-Lezama relationship was over. In its day, it was mediated by a shared symbolist inheritance. Both poets unapologetically amplified adherence to linguistic abstraction in the face of politicized critiques of poésie pure. This inter-American resemblance emerged from Mallarméan and Valéryan models belatedly circulating in literary enclaves throughout the Americas, as much or more than it did from the baroque.

I have referred to such poets as "post-symbolists," a term requiring further clarification. It may also be unclear why the symbolist inheritance experiences an aesthetic resurgence in the 1940s. Scholars often narrate the history of modern poetry with a premium on its rhythms of novelty and innovation, but its rearguard actions furnish epochal styles. Diverse critics such as Hugh Kenner, Paul De Man, and Robert Alter variously use the term "post-symbolist" across the 1960s and 1970s to denote the French poets of the 1890s, as well as resurgent tendencies in poetry that have subsequently been silenced under period rubrics like "modernism." By the 1940s, symbolism had been killed off or grafted into new poetic movements many times, in many national contexts, for over half a century.[80] So too had symbolism's Latin American cousin modernismo. Nonetheless, a spate of pronouncements on symbolism's fate in the Americas arose, and the death of Paul Valéry in 1945 heralds the last post-symbolist currents in poetry.

In 1946, Hi Simons noted Mallarméan debts in Stevens's early poems, and Horace Gregory observed that "one source of freshness and delight in Stevens has been derived from what seems to be a careful and highly selective reading of Corbière."[81] Charles Feidelson saw Stevens's poetry as an articulation of the fundamentally "problematic" stance of the symbolist tradition as it reached aesthetic exhaustion and took itself up, self-critically, as a subject.[82] Despite the Cold War era's propensity for modes of symbolic reading, these views did not take root to a notable degree. By the 1980s, Marjorie Perloff was at pains to remind readers why the "Supreme Fiction" marks Stevens as a "belated *Symboliste*," against critics like Harold Bloom, Vendler, and Joseph N. Riddell, who read his "romantic intoning" as Whitmanian.[83]

The post-symbolist poetic thought that emerged in the 1940s revived a Mallarméan poetics of alien words and "inanité sonore," and a Valéryan poetics of cognitive fluidity and prolixity. Reyes inaugurates a period truism about Valéry in the Americas—one that also describes Stevens's fluency—when he opens "Paul Valéry Contempla a América" (1938) by describing the French poet in "fluid" contemplation:

> Aun la volubilidad y fluidez de su habla revelan en él esta capacidad inmediata de pensamiento: cuando habla (mientras fulguran los ojillos garzos desde donde Atenea, sin duda alguna, nos acecha), se desliza sobre las palabras—acuaplano o trineo acuático—arrastrado por su velocidad mental.[84]

> (Even the volubility and fluidity of his speech reveals his immediate capacity for thought: when he speaks (while his cerulean little eyes blaze from where Athena, without a doubt, lies in wait for us), he flows over the words—an aquaplane or water sled—towed along by his mental velocity.)

The comic image depicts Valéry "aquaplaning" over his own vocabulary. Reyes likens Valéryan thinking not to surfing or waterskiing, but to the calisthenics of a soon-obsolete water sport. Reyes casts Valéry as a symbolist master transported into a trendy tropical vacation activity. Symbolism equates to "fluency" in the "holiday hotel world." Revitalization through transport to the Americas is the theme of Reyes's short essay on Valéry. He described a respeciation of European culture ("a natural selection that permits the transfer of the most viable and transportable species from European to American soil") and a new process of engrafting ("the consoling hope that, in the face of a bellicose destruction of Europe—taken as it is, today, with brutality—Europe, somehow, can go on living in America"). These biological metaphors for literary respeciation echo older debates about the autonomy of literary culture in the Americas and prefigure Richard Morse's description of inter-American cultural history as a struggle between a " 'horticultural' im- or transplantation" which seeks to be dispelled by "a baroque or Baudelairean vision of 'correspondences' that allow transtemporal, transcausal juxtapositions and mediations to reveal ancient, continuously self-renewing identities."[85] Facing the wartime devastation of Europe, Reyes esteems the prospect of implantation hybridizing European traditions with American democracy.

Valéry's death in 1945 was not symbolism's end point so much as a flashpoint. In New England, Washington, Havana, Mexico City, and Buenos Aires, literary establishments transfigured and digested the symbolist legacy with renewed vigor. When *Sur* dedicated its October 1945 issue to a commemoration of Valéry, Borges contributed the essay "Valéry como símbolo" (Valéry as Symbol).[86] Borges mirrors Reyes's images of liquid mental capacity, contrasting the persona of Valéry, the European poet of infinite technique and sublime intellectualism, and that of Whitman, caricatured by spontaneous felicity and corporeality. For Borges, the legacies of Valéry and Whitman reside in the symbol of a "possible man." Valéry left behind "the symbol of a man who is infinitely sensitive to every fact and for whom every fact is a stimulus that can sustain an infinite series of thoughts."[87] Such renewals of Valéryan poetry throw into relief T. S. Eliot's pronouncement on the death of the symbolist tradition during a 1948 lecture in Washington, DC. "The *art poétique* of which we find the germ in Poe, and which bore fruit in the work of Valéry, has gone as far as it can go," writes Eliot, "I do not believe that this aesthetic can be of any help to later poets."[88] Here, Eliot describes a generational closure more than a formal one. His remark responds to an elegiac sense that the symbolist "phase"—described as a process of increasingly self-reflexive technique driving toward pure poetry—has "come to an end with the 1945 death of Valéry." Eliot prognosticates that postwar poetry cannot be "spontaneous and irreflective" (*à la* Whitman), but should work toward the symbolization of the symbolist tradition itself: "We should have to have an aesthetic which somehow comprehended and transcended that of Poe and Valéry." Borges, Stevens, and especially Lezama exemplify Eliot's invitation to write an unspontaneous, reflective poetics in the midcentury Americas. For Lezama, foreign words are unique pressure points in post-symbolism's self-reflective system.

Lezama's Citations

Lezama's first published poem, *Muerte de Narciso* (1937) rewrites Valéry's "Narcisse parle," and Lezama goes on to elaborate his Valéryan debts in the essays "Valéry y el acto poético" (1938) and "Sobre Paul Valéry" (1945), but it is not until the volume of poems *La fijeza* (Fixity, 1949) that he transfigures the symbolist legacy into his own mature poetic system. The keystone poem in *La fijeza*, "Pensamientos en la Habana," exemplifies the poetry of "an infinite series of thoughts" Borges calls for. It is also a poetic theory of inter-Americanism premised on foreign-language citations, offering a homology to Stevens's "Notes" and specifying how poets differently mediate national speech through the use of foreign words.

Lezama was born in 1910 in Havana, where, like the famously domestic Stevens, he lived without traveling abroad, aside from brief trips to Mexico in 1949 and Jamaica in 1950. First a poet, later a cultural theorist and novelist, he rose to prominence as the author of five volumes of poetry between 1937 and 1960 (and one published posthumously in 1977) and as the director of the journal *Orígenes* between 1944 and 1956, a responsibility he shared with José Rodríguez Feo. *Orígenes* doubled as a platform for the *origenista* group of mostly Catholic Cuban writers and as a conduit for the translation and dissemination of international modernism in Cuba. Simultaneously charged with forging Cuban literary nationalism and deprovincializing it, *Orígenes* published a dazzling inter-American array of writers and intellectuals. Anglo-American contributors included Marianne Moore, Elizabeth Bishop, Katherine Anne Porter, F. O. Matthiessen, Harry Levin, Allen Tate, Wallace Stevens, William Carlos Williams, W. H. Auden, and T. S. Eliot; Latin American and Antillean contributors included Aimé Césaire, Gabriela Mistral, Octavio Paz, Alí Chumacero, Efrain Huerta, and Alfonso Reyes. This New World ecumene also included Europeans exiled in the Americas such as, Vicente Aleixandre, Luis Cernuda, Jorge Guillén, Juan Ramón Jimenez, Saint-John Perse, and Pedro Salinas, and extended to the French poetry of Aragon, Char, Éluard, Michaux, and Valéry. This slim, peripheral quarterly convened major exponents of international modernism to breach a bulwark of Cuban insularity.

Cuban insularity might itself be compared to several varieties of midcentury national retrenchment. When US poets were not excoriating the exogamies of Wallace Stevens, they often sheltered in the nativistic Americana emblematized by Williams's *Paterson*, while British modernists adopted forms of insularism Jed Esty describes in *The Shrinking Island* (2004). By contrast, Cuba's island condition offered a port of entry for a post-national Spanish-American literature to flow into the currents of international modernism, one that included the very same British and US figures contemporaneously undergoing nativist turns. Octavio Paz recognized the delicate balance *Orígenes* struck when he wrote Lezama after first reading an issue: "I find it very intelligent, very sensitive, very universal and at the same time very much ours, very much of Hispanic America.[89] By 1956, a rift between Lezama and Rodríguez Feo led to the latter's splinter journal *Ciclón*, and both journals ended their runs by 1959. Lezama's reputation, however, grew around his role as a theorist of the Latin American aesthetic of the neo-baroque, the vision he foregrounded in the lectures collected as *La Expresión Americana* (1957) and his Boom novel *Paradiso* (1966).

As a poet, Lezama shares Stevens's systemic features such as meditative prolixity; a heavy burden placed on metaphor and image; and a fluent appropriation and arrangement of what I call Stevens's "global feedbacks." Gustavo Pérez Firmat calls them Lezama's "cultural blocks," which construct a proliferative, systemic process of "creative assimilation."[90] The notion of a poetic system was something else the two poets shared. Lezama formulated it in the prose poems concluding *La fijeza*, just as Stevens was described as interlacing *Transport to Summer* with a theory of poetry. Both systems bridge prewar international modernism and postwar literary theory.[91] The aphoristic promotion of a cult of difficulty is one pillar of these twin systems. Stevens's dictum "the poem must resist the intelligence/almost successfully" mirrors Lezama's gnostic motto: "sólo lo difícil es estimulante" (only the difficult is stimulating).[92] Lezama's poetry rejects a growing Cuban preference for anti-ornamental directness (conversacionalismo), just as Stevens challenges a demotic poetic realism ascendant in Jarrell. If Stevens retains sophistication in the era of "Basic English," Lezama responds to Cuban conversacionalismo with a like defense of difficulty in his debate with Jorge Mañach, who rebuked *Orígenes* for obscurantism.[93]

Ironically, the cult of difficulty impeded exchange between Lezama and Stevens, even after Lezama sought to forge a relationship. Beginning around 1945, Lezama occasionally promoted his own reputation in the United States, sending *Enemigo rumor* and *Aventuras sigilosas* to Dudley Fitts, who undertook translations on José Rodríguez Feo's advice and included them in his anthology's second edition.[94] He similarly sent *La fijeza* to Wallace Stevens in 1949, perhaps hoping to slipstream behind Stevens's friendship with Rodríguez Feo. The response was polite but tepid:

> Although I do not read Spanish, I wish I did because there may well be something in common between your point of view and mine. This is suggested particularly by the Variations On A Tree. The truth is that one gets a good deal from the mere reading of poetry without being able to gather fully the meaning of what one reads and, in that sense, although I am not able to evaluate your book (*La fijeza*), it gives me pleasure, for which I must thank you.[95]

"Variaciones del árbol" is a sequence of four unrhymed sonnets that abstractly circle about the tree as an emblem of cognition.[96] While its seriality is Stevensian, in the opaque linguistic textures of *La fijeza* it stands out for its clarity. Stevens's scene of encounter with Spanish-language poetry takes pleasure in "mere reading" prior to full semantic competency, but gravitates toward Lezama's most semantically restrictive stanzas. As if neither remembered this exchange, four years later Lezama sent his essay collection *Analecta del reloj* (1953) to Stevens, and Stevens replied with amnesiac repetition: "I do not read Spanish well enough to be able to get much out of it [. . .] But all your pages tantalize me."[97] If Lezama offers sonorous pleasure straining his reader's semantic intelligence, this is true for native and second-language readers alike, and Spanish-language critics routinely lament the lack of annotated editions. All readers of Stevens and Lezama are Tantalus.

The association of poems with islands offers a final point of affinity. Cintio Vitier defines Lezama's images of islands as an "insular teleology."[98] Vitier highlights his ability to sunder the poem from historical location without consigning it to an ahistorical present, suggesting that Lezama limns extreme sensations of distance, "situating the poem in the reminiscence of the mythical image of the island."[99] Lezama adopts a standpoint of "reminiscence" under the Greek figure of Mnemosyne, mother of the muses. In Vitier's view, Lezama's insular teleology treats poetry as "an absolute cognitive medium" (an unmistakably Valéryan phrase) whose excessive slowness and refinement defines an "eclogic substance of the island." Titles like "Un obscuro prado me convida" (An Obscure Meadow Lures Me) and "Noche insular: jardines invisibles" (Insular Night: Invisible Gardens) analogize poems to this species of locus amoenus, much as Winters saw the Stevens protagonist "floating like a tropical island in boundless space."

Vitier claimed that Lezama's "insular teleology" operates as a national figure for Cuban poetry, inscribing origenismo in the island's diachronic national literary history. Others take Lezamian insularity as a figure for a "Caribbean discourse," a node in the Pan-Antillean intellectual tradition running from Puerto Rican essayist Antonio S. Pedreira's *Insularismo* (1934) to Antonio Benítez Rojo's *The Repeating Island*.[100] But the idea of intensely cognitive, archipelagic poetry is not innately Cuban or Pan-Antillean, so much as it is a stock feature of a deracinated post-symbolist poetics. Julio Cortázar suggests to Lezama in a 1957 letter from Paris that "insularity" is a condition marking writers across the Americas:

> En estas islas a veces terribles en que vivimos metidos los sudamericanos (pues la Argentina, o México, son tan insulares como su Cuba) a veces es necesario venirse a vivir a Europa para descubrir por fin las voces hermanas. Desde aquí, poco a poco, América va siendo como una constelación, con luces que brillan y van formando el dibujo de la verdadera patria, mucho más grande y hermosa que la que vocifera el pasaporte.[101]

> In these often terrible islands, where we South Americans are stuck living (Argentina, or Mexico, are really just as insular as Cuba), sometimes you have to go to live in Europe in order to finally discover your sister voices. From here, little by little, America becomes like a constellation, with lights that shine and begin to form the outline of a true homeland, much larger and more beautiful than the one shouted out by a passport.

Lezama did not become a rootless cosmopolitan like Cortázar, but his insularist poems are best regarded from this standpoint, constellating the potentialities of the Americas in rhythms of baroque profusion and Baudelairean correspondence. As I discuss in Chapter 4, Cortázar also takes up post-symbolist motifs in his key work *Historias de cronopios y de famas* (1962).

"Pensamientos en la Habana" does not foreground Lezamian insularity, though it variously encodes it. First published in *Orígenes* 3 (1944) and then in *La fijeza*, its publication history lags two years behind Stevens's "Notes," the poem it most deeply resembles. Written in twelve long stanzas, many of the sentences are less baroquely hypotactic than the Gongorine precedents with which they are associated, while others strain comprehensibility. It opens with a speaker *in medias res cogitans*, answering an unasked question:

> Porque habito un susurro como un velamen,
> una tierra donde el hielo es una reminiscencia,
> el fuego no puede izar un pájaro
> y quemarlo en una conversación de estilo calmo.

(Because I dwell in a whisper like a set of sails,
a land where ice is a reminiscence,
fire cannot hoist a bird
and burn it in a conversation calm in style.)[102]

If a question prompts this flight of metasymbolic discourse, it is "why do you speak in so difficult a fashion?" The poem answers in a defensive posture linking poetic style with a negative definition of Cuban climatology, connoted by "una tierra donde el hielo es una reminiscencia" (a land where ice is a reminiscence). Cuba is a Petrarchan oxymoron: neither "hot" nor "cold" style provokes the speaker's ambitious desires for a phoenix-like regeneration of poetic language.

The unobtainable "estile calmo" (calm style) owes something to the stylistic disjuncture that marked Eliot's *Four Quartets*, a poem Lezama partially translated and knew intimately. He reflects metapoetically on his style, much as Eliot writes "That was a way of putting it—not very satisfactory:/A periphrastic study in a worn-out poetical fashion,/Leaving one still with the intolerable wrestle/With words and meanings."[103] Lezama installs "style" as the poem's subject, and subsequently as its agent. Negatives and double negatives accrue so rapidly around the poem's self-concept of style that the first stanza dramatizes an Adornian modern art, negating itself in the making:

Aunque ese estilo no me dicte un sollozo
y un brinco tenue me deje vivir malhumorado,
no he de reconocer la inútil marcha
de una máscara flotando donde yo no pueda,
donde yo no pueda transportar el picapedrero o el picaporte
a los museos donde se empapelan los asesinatos
mientras los visitadores señalan la ardilla
que con el rabo se ajusta las medias.
Si un estilo anterior sacude el árbol,
decide el sollozo de dos cabellos y exclama:
my soul is not in an ashtray.[104]

(Though that style doesn't dictate to me a sob
and a tenuous hop lets me live in bad humor,
I will not recognize the useless movement
of a mask floating where I cannot,
where I cannot transport the stonecutter or the door latch
to the museums where murders are papered

while the judges point out the squirrel
that straightens its stockings with its tail.
If a previous style shakes the tree,
it decides the sob of two hairs and exclaims:
my soul is not in an ashtray.)[105]

In 1946, Horace Gregory suggested that Wallace Stevens often led his critics "in small and closely herded droves into the bogs of metaphysical discussion."[106] Lezama's arabesques likewise lead his readers down a *via negativa* into ashtrays of metaphysical discussion, and coming to the single line of mock English poetry at the end of this stanza, he seems to do so as a Stevens parody.

In some respects, the first stanza is a false start, for the developing relation of the solitary poetic "I" to "style" swells into a plural set of poetic agents. An insular "nosotros" and an external "ellos" structure the poet's relation to style:

Como sueñan humillarnos,
repitiendo día y noche con el ritmo de la tortuga
que oculta el tiempo en su espaldar:
ustedes no dicidieron que el ser habitase en el hombre;
vuestro Dios es la luna
contemplando como una balaustrada
al ser entrando en el hombre.
Como quieren humillarnos le decimos.
the chief of the tribe descended the staircase.[107]

(Since they dream of humiliating us,
repeating day and night with the rhythm of the tortoise
that conceals time on its back:
you didn't decide that being should dwell in man;
your God is the moon
watching like a banister
the entrance of being into man.
Since they want to humiliate us we say to them:
el jefe de la tribu descendió la escalinata.)

By this point the poem flaunts its most conspicuous surface feature: a string of italicized phrases, most in foreign languages, which end all but the penultimate stanza of the poem. These phrases function like "hypograms," though not in the sense defined by Paul de Man, who regards hypograms as ciphers distributed beneath the textual surface. Rather, Lezama's hypograms are subtexts inscribed "below" the stanza.[108] They bear resemblance to the epigrammatic citations *Orígenes* poets habitually include above their poems, but here they define the poem's stanzaic structure, flattening distinctions between text and paratext. The first three are mock quotations from nonexistent English poems (*"my soul is not in an ashtray"* and *"the chief of the tribe descended the staircase"*) or artless sound schemes (*"we don't choose our shoes in a show-window"*). They may derive from the French line Stevens inserted at the end of the fourth stanza in each of the numbered poems comprising his sequence "Sea Surface Full of Clouds" (indeed, one such line apostrophizes the ocean as the poet's soul: "C'etait mon enfant, mon bijou, mon ame"). Lezama begs the reader's feelings of hermeneutic inadequacy, though his foreignisms hint at determinate US topics such as Greenwich Village bohemianism, Indian assimilation, and consumer choice. The fourth and fifth stanzas end in an italicized Spanish line that closes on the phrase *"no descifra"* (do not decipher), directing the reader not to take the hypograms seriously as interpretable citations from verifiable source material. The sixth stanza ends in a line of French, the seventh and eighth in Spanish, and the ninth, tenth, and twelfth stanzas repeat the initial English phrases in Spanish translations. The last translates the first: *"my soul is not in an ashtray"* becomes *"Mi alma no está en un cenicero."*

As they accumulate, the hypograms therefore methodically Hispanize the poem. Lezama invents apocryphal French and English poetic worlds, and then domesticates them. Reasonably enough, Ben Heller understands this maneuver as a "subversive" or resistant use of translation.[109] Yet it might as easily dramatize the assimilation of cosmopolitan poetic norms, establishing two poles for the poem's use of foreign speech. The first pole resists the language ideology of global English to forge a Cuban national identity, while the second relates the poem to what Juan Ramón Jiménez contemporaneously described as "universal modernism." To Jiménez, universal modernism paradoxically structures national renewal: "Universal modernism, in the varied countries of Europe, is a return to the national tradition. It is so in France, in Germany, in Italy, in the United States. In Hispano-America the same thing happens."[110] Lezama's citations assimilate universal modernism and redeploy it on behalf of insular specificity.

In the same way, the third stanza clarifies the nosotros/ellos duality as an invasive culture characterized by the capitalistic logics of "vitrinas" (show windows), imposed upon a "we" who seeks an authentic style:

> Ellos tienen unas vitrinas y usan unos zapatos.
> En esas vitrinas alternan el maniquí con el quebrantahuesos disecado,

y todo lo que ha pasado por la frente del hastío del búfalo solitario.

Si no miramos la vitrina, charlan

de nuestra insuficiente desnudez que no vale una estatuilla de Nápoles.[111]

(They have some show windows and wear some shoes.

In those show windows they alternate the mannequin with the stuffed
> ossifrage,

and everything that has passed through the forehead of the lonesome
> buffalo's boredom.

If we don't look at the show window, they chat

about our insufficient nakedness that isn't worth a figurine from Naples.)

On local culture's behalf, the poet recasts the show window as a space of oneiric
figuration rather than consumer spectatorship. In it, a "mannequin" alternates
with an "ossifrage," part of a string of toys and taxidermy animals that litter the
poem. The ossifrage, or bearded vulture, takes its name from its diet of bone
marrow, scavenged from the broken bones of carrion that it drops from a great
height. Ossifragic poetics nourishes itself on fragmentation, in a display of Eliotic
modernist coherence. Lezama associates the witness of this spectacle of modernist fragmentation with the perpetual boredom of a "lonesome buffalo," as if
window-shopping prolonged the dynamics of US westward expansion, as viewed
from the standpoint of an animal decimated by it. Perhaps this lonely buffalo
also thus figures the modern reader. For the minority "we" in this stanza, not to
shop in this window is to invite the derision of a hegemon, who accuses "us" of an
"insufficient nakedness." This speaker refuses to be anthropologized or treated as
"native." The final calque *We don't choose our shoes in show windows* critiques
economic hegemony even as it concedes to cultural hegemony.

Lezama did not see his hypograms quite this way. He ascribed them to a "contrapuntal" poetics, a practice with a lively career in Cuban culture.[112] Lezama
explicitly identifies his poetic surfaces with such processes: "Expressions that in my
poetic world are points of reference form [. . .] a contrapuntal projection to reach
their unity in this new conception of world and image, of enigma and mirror."[113]
He also glosses his hypograms as part of a poetics of ritual incantation, suggesting
that *"the chief of the tribe descended the staircase"* references Mallarméan poetics:

> Already in my introduction to the first issue of *Orígenes* [in 1944] I tried
> to stress that. I wanted the poetry appearing in that magazine to be the
> poetry of a return to magic spells, to rituals, to the living ceremony of
> primitive man. It's very curious that a poet like Mallarmé, who enjoyed

the benefits of a great tradition, should have come in his mature years to long for the magical art of a tribal chieftain.[114]

For Lezama, behind the English citation resides Mallarmé's old enjoinder to "donner un sens plus pur aux mots de la tribu" (to give a purer sense to the words of the tribe). In the post-symbolist context for foreign words, that enjoinder makes peculiar sense in English. Lezama's own account of his poetics as contrapuntal juxtapositions or ritual incantation do not do justice to their work as an intercultural poetics of resistance and accommodation in the symbolic order of diction. Thus "Pensamientos en la Habana" fixes and unfixes meanings in the "flujo" (flow) of poetic style, and metaphors of weaving and braiding are legion in the poem, as are countermetaphors of impeded "transport" and fragmented style. Lezama associates memory with processes of stitching and unraveling, welding and fracture. Like Penelope, the poem writes and unwrites words in the mnemonic rhythm of reading. The Lezamian Penelope-poet weaves and unweaves fields of signification—a chain of taxidermy and toy animals, a string of italicized foreign words. He offers a vision of the poet in provincial contemplations of an oxymoronic world picture. He "hoists" and lowers, burnishes and tarnishes, melts and freezes his phoenix-like images in a tessellating mindscape.

A final Valéryan poetic institution that brings Lezama's poem into the post-symbolist orbit is "secondary Cratylism." If "primary Cratylism" draws natural signifying links between the sounds of words and the things they describe, as does Plato in the *Cratylus* or as does Walt Whitman (following the theory of language set forth in Emerson's *Nature*), secondary Cratylism proposes poetry as the self-conscious creation of this illusory sound relationship.[115] "Secondary Cratylism" in the tradition of Mallarmé and Valéry understands language as "fallen" from an original state of total phonosymbolic relatedness, and instead marshals language in poetic space in order to generate illusions of relatedness. Lezama makes sonic associations a meaningful logic within his poem less frequently than Stevens, but he does so purposively at several moments, in which sound associations level parts of speech or grammatical categories. As though finding small glitches in the poem's "flow," the reader experiences the sonic identity of an occupation and a household object: "[. . .] donde yo no pueda transportar el picapedrero o el picaporte" (where I cannot transport the stonecutter or the door latch). Later, a preposition and an animal converge: "pero el perro" (but the dog). And then again, an indefinite participle ("una") mirrors a body part ("uña"): "pero yo continúo trabajando la madera, /como una uña despierta" (but I go on working the wood,/like a[n indefatigable] fingernail). These phrases appear with enough regularity to sustain the possibility that the poem shuttles the reader around by sound logic rather than grammatical logic. It might be tertiary Cratylism: so cautious and self-aware as to be unconvinced the Cratylic illusion can be maintained even for the length of the poem.

In one of his last great poems, "El pabellón del vacío" (The Pavilion of Nothingness), published posthumously in *Fragmentos a su imán* (Fragments Drawn by Charm), Lezama returns to the figure of the "uña" (fingernail) as the figure of post-symbolist poetics, but he shifts its emphasis from Cratylism to the creation of the foreign word in the poem. There, the poet's fingernails repeatedly and impetuously scratch from the everyday surfaces around him. What they make is something the poet calls a "tokonoma," a Japanese word for hollow or alcove that is traditionally used to display a scroll text.[116] Here, we might justly invoke the etymology of *stanza* as *room*. For the very room surrounding the poet—the walls, the surfaces of the desk—all become spaces in which to insert and to display the hollow of the "tokonoma." If Stevens shrank away in his final poems from "lingua franca et jocundissima," Lezama, by contrast, affirms the foreign word as the institution of poesis itself.

Borges and the Dawn of English

Sylvia Molloy has linked Jorge Luis Borges's writing to precisely the condition Gustavo Pérez-Firmat describes as Lezama's "transcultural" dimension, and which I earlier aligned with Steven's "global feedbacks." Molloy makes Borges exemplary of a post-colonial view of Latin American culture as a "disruptive transculturation" that "avoids permanent positioning, chronological determination, and, above all, fixed representations.'"[117] For her, this relational culture became paradoxically susceptible, as it entered the world literary marketplace of the 1960s via figures such as Lezama and Borges, to a reading that saw only rooted localism or deracinated universality, rather than the persistent staging of a translational friction between these very terms. Borges himself stages these transcultural dynamics in a staggering variety of philosophical and narrative registers across his career as a writer, varieties that exceed the scope of my concern. In the final section of this chapter, I will propose that the view of language ideology developed in my discussions of Stevens and Lezama inflects Borges's poetry, where he describes ceaseless transcultural relations between the English, Spanish, and French languages. This language ideology plays out as another poetics of foreign words—a poetics premised on a diction that restores the alien freshness to common words, or which invents uncommon words from whole cloth, and which therefore reshapes the static word-symbols of the dictionary into a living casebook of lexical freshness—another xenoglossary.[118] For Borges, poetry is a project of lexical animation that relies on processes of linguistic transculturation.

In Molloy's account, Borges's linguistic project takes on a Latin Americanist politics, but Borges himself characterized it within a different political orbit, to which he became drawn late in his career: that of the state-sponsored liberal world culture of the Cold War. As his global prestige consolidated following the 1961 award of the Prix International, Borges often narrated his literary autobiography as a story about the priority of the English language in its development. He especially enjoyed flattering US audiences with this tale during his high-profile lecture tours and cultural diplomacy junkets of the late 1960s and early 1970s.[119] Probably the most significant version of this story is the lengthy "Autobiographical Notes" that Borges published in *The New Yorker* in 1970 with the help of his companionate translator Norman Thomas di Giovanni. Borges reports that "both English and Spanish were commonly used" in his childhood home, and that "If I were asked to name the chief event in my life, I should say my father's library."[120] There, he began reading English and American literature, as well as world literature in English translation, including *Don Quixote*. Borges so thoroughly stressed the priority of these English-language works in the attunement of his literary ear that he recalls finally reading *Don Quixote* in its original, only to discover that it struck him as a lousy translation.

Borges's Anglophilia was filial. He took after his father Jorge Guillermo Borges, son of a Staffordshire Englishwoman named Frances Haslam, as well as his Argentine mother, who, once she learned English, did most of her reading in it. He claimed to inherit from his father his belief in "the power of poetry," namely "the fact that words are not only a means of communication but also magic symbols and music."[121] As he put it: "Poetry came to me through English— Shelley, Keats, FitzGerald, and Swinburne, those great favorites of my father, who could quote them voluminously, and often did."[122] From there, Borges's claim to Englishness stretched across his literary career, beginning with his first literary venture at age six, setting down "in quite bad English a kind of handbook on Greek mythology" and translating Oscar Wilde's "The Happy Prince" at age nine. These pursuits led him to distrust the orthodoxies of his early education, predicated on an Argentine nationalism that ignored "knowledge of the many lands and many centuries that went into its making."[123] It led him to sustain his private reading in English during his classical primary education in Geneva, where his first attempts at poetry were written in imitation of Wordsworth's sonnets and French symbolism. While he was in Spain in 1919–1920, his first published poem imitated Whitman, who for a time he regarded "not only as a great poet but as the *only* poet."[124] As he later said, "I was quite old when it occurred to me that poetry could be written in a language other than English."[125] In retrospect, he faulted the Spanish Ultraists who formed his first literary cohort for their lack of grounding in French and English literature. Borges translated widely from English and American literature in the late 1930s and early 1940s, which positioned him as a key sluice gate in the Good Neighbor–era projects of hemispheric literary intercommunication. This culminated in his work as a journeyman lecturer on English literature in the early years of the Perón administration and his later decade as a professor of English and American literature at the University of Buenos Aires. Borges even maintained an interlingual phonetic understanding of his own name, remarking that pronunciation of *Jorge* included a "'g' sounding like a strong Scottish 'h.'"[126]

I stress Borges's biographical and professional allegiances to English in order to point out that he regarded Spanish as an "unavoidable destiny" rather than an endowment. In effect, Borges's language philosophy prizes Spanish not as a natural language or native ground, but as a surface or a medium through which to stage relations to other languages. Borges's 1970 narration of his Englishness to his US audiences also suggests that his thought on language migrated from the "national universalism" of interwar Argentina to the pan-linguistic project of hemispherism. In that very moment, US discussions of Borges noted his resemblances to Stevens.[127] Alfred Kazin pointedly homologized parodic impulses in their inter-linguistic styles:

> But a point about Borges is his constant transmutation and extension— often as parody—of his father's library. He is in fact "English" only in the sense that some American writer in Texas or Wyoming, some Wallace Stevens in Hartford who absorbed and mimicked French poetry without going to France—can be called "French."[128]

As Stevens transfigures Romance languages, Borges transfigures English. Yet this resemblance hardly stems from genetic influence. After translating "Sunday Morning," Borges neglected to mention Stevens in his 1967 *Introduction to American Literature*, and in late-career interviews he averred no knowledge of Stevens at all, even when reminded of his translations: "since I don't know him, why should I slander him?" Their career narratives, furthermore, seem to progress in reverse directions. Stevens begins as a cosmopolitan and matures into the philosophical regionalist of "An Ordinary Evening in New Haven." Borges, by contrast, matured toward universalism, but he began by writing a "cultivated nativism," as Jorge Carrera Andrade characterized his first three books (*Fervor de Buenos Aires* [1923], *Luna de enfrente* [1925], and *Cuaderno San Martín* [1929]), or what Borges himself called a "sham riot of local color."[129] In truth, these early books crafted an artificial form of criollo localism, marking lunfardo and gaucho dialect registers as their own exogamous lexicons. But use of "extranational" foreign words marks the point of convergence in their careers, waxing in Borges as it wanes in Stevens.

The intensification of English sources, words and themes dawn in Borges's poems slowly across his career, from the two published English love poems "To I. J." (1934) to his myriad translations of North American poets in the 1940s, and finally to his poems about his struggles to learn Anglo-Saxon in the 1950s. Ronald Christ describes Borges's "curious intimacy" with English as a "personal" and "subjective" aspect of childhood, but the eclectic array of poems Borges wrote in his late phase commemorating North American writers, places, and occasions are highly self-conscious negotiations of his new relationship to North American readerships, academic communities, and the cultural diplomacy apparatus of the CCF (see Chapter 5).[130] Borges frequently links these confrontations with English to the poetic genre of dawn songs known as *alba* or *aubade*.

The lyric corpus of the polygeneric and prolific Borges first took shape in *Fervor de Buenos Aires* (1923), and across the 1920s he adumbrated his regionalist ultraism. Two newly revised and slightly expanded collected poetry editions followed in 1943 and 1954, and a substantial new body of poetry developed in the 1950s, beginning with the miscellaneous *El Hacedor* (1960) and continuing through eight successive volumes. Poetry preoccupies the main current of Borges's late work, from highly formal Shakespearean sonnets to popular forms such as milongas. All told, Borges wrote more than four hundred extant poems in fourteen books. In the hiatus between *Cuaderno San Martín* (1929) and *El Hacedor* (1960), so the story goes, Borges developed his *Ficciones* and excelled in other forms: metaphysical detective stories; aporetic philosophical essays; even collaborations on film scripts. These mid-career successes can override a continuous image of Borges as poet, sundering a youthful regionalist from a senescent bard.[131] Yet Borges maintained that the poems of *Fervor de Buenos Aires* contained the nuclei of most of his later preoccupations in any genre, and he persistently revised, reorganized, and added to his poetic corpus, lending a Petrarchan flare for lyric organization to his poetry until it becomes a kind of cancionero or songbook. These revisions and reorganizations extrude the poems from a ground in historical specificity. "Chronology will lose itself in a sphere [orbe] of symbols," he writes in his dedication of *El Hacedor.* Accordingly, there is still no critical edition of his complete poetry.

These ahistorical compilations enabled insertions and revisions that record augmented relations to the English language. For example, Borges retitled the early poem "Último resplandor," from *Fervor de Buenos Aires*, preferring to call it *"Afterglow"* in all Spanish editions after Norman Thomas di Giovanni supplied him with this word during their collaboration on *Selected Poems 1923–1967* (1972).[132] Borges had already long expressed his interest in English compound words like "afterglow," alongside English's capacity for neologism and other forms of concise complexity. In his 1946 review of Joyce's *Ulysses*, Borges expresses concern that "neo-Latin idioms, and in particular Spanish," were comprised of "unmanageable polysyllables," and his Harvard lecture on "Poetry and Thought" singled out the Joycean flare for the invention of words (as in "glittergates of elfinbone") as a definition of poetry's capacities.[133] He persistently weighed English words against their Spanish counterparts, and his theory of translation came to be built on this comparative disposition toward diction.

Borges gives a theoretical shape to his lyric corpus in the introduction to his English-language *Selected Poems*, written while he was visiting Brigham Young University in Salt Lake City in 1971, by which time his presence had saturated the US university system. Poetry, Borges writes, appeals to the imagination, while prose appeals to reason. Prose contemplates externals, and once it is "dreamed and shaped" it is "sent out into the world," while verse records personal tastes, hobbies, and habits. "In the long run," he writes, "perhaps, I shall stand or fall by my poems." A characteristically Borgesian distinction inheres in this "I." He does not suggest his literary reputation will "stand or fall" by his poems. Rather, his poetic legacy is the record of himself "as a possible man," as he once wrote of Valéry and Whitman. The phrase "I shall stand or fall by my poems," written in English to an English-speaking public, increases the intensity of personal memory in his poetry, while walling it off from the "public" face of his prose fictions. Borges recalls Goethe's quotation that "all poetry is occasional poetry," yet, with playful relish, he forgets the occasion for Goethe's comment. He insists that poems begin in the contingency of lived experience, but he undermines this insistence by neglecting to memorialize these occasions in the life of the poem. Poems unreliably contain the languages, feelings, and occasions the poet designates them to record. Yet poetry, as an art devoted to the excavation of latencies in the lexical world, is an art of foreignizing words—of restoring to them their etymological freshness.

"Englishness" designates one unreliable collection of this sort. Experiences of forgetting often follow the advent of English in Borges's poems, as does the mood of the dawn. "Englishness" doubles as a biographical priority and a carefully constructed artifice. English virtualizes language in a symbolic order that creates dynamic relationships between nativity and alterity. As early as 1931, Borges expressed the desire to enliven Spanish through Anglicization. *Las kenningar*, a study of kennings, links Xul Solar's metalinguistic inventions to an Anglicization of Spanish:

> Así también, hasta que las exhortaciones gramaticales de nuestro Xul-Solar no encuentren obediencia, versos como el de Rudyard Kipling: "In the desert where the dung-fed camp-smoke curled" or this other from Yeats: "That dolphin-torn, that gong-tormented sea" serán inimitables e impensables en español.[134]

> So also, as long as our Xul Solar's grammatical exhortations are not obeyed, lines like this from Rudyard Kipling: "In the desert where dung-fed camp-smoke curled" or this other from Yeats: "That dolphin-torn, that gong-tormented sea" will be inimitable and unthinkable in Spanish.

Borges's bilingualism and Anglophilia begins to seep into his poetry contemporaneously, soon after the publication of *Las kenningar*. "Prose poems for I. J." are two of the six new poems to appear in Borges's first collected volume, *Poemas, 1922–1943*. They were later retitled "Two English Poems" and rededicated in *Poemas, 1922–1953*.[135] In these love poems, Borges uses English as a language of escape from the precise Spanish of his metaphysical detective narratives, indulging in dreamy, semi-private emotional excess. Like Neruda's *Veinte poemas de amor y una canción desesperada* (1924), "Two English Poems" move forward in vast metaphors that transfer poetic desire from environments to love objects and back: night becomes sea, surges forth in the memory of the love object, and subsides. The poem is an aubade of unrequited rather than consummated desire:

> The useless dawn finds me in a deserted street-corner; I have outlived the night.
> Nights are proud waves: darkblue topheavy waves laden with all hues of deep spoil, laden with things unlikely and desirable.
> Nights have a habit of mysterious gifts and refusals, of things half given away, half withheld, of joys with a dark hemisphere. Nights act that way, I tell you.

> The surge, that night, left me the customary shreds and odd ends: some
>   hated friends to chat with, music for dreams, and the smoking of bitter
>   ashes. The things my hungry heart has no use for.
> The big wave brought you.
> Words, any words, your laughter; and you so lazily and incessantly
>   beautiful.
> We talked and you have forgotten the words.
> The shattering dawn finds me in a deserted street of my city.[136]

Here, perfunctory poetic flourishes, like the "darkblue topheavy" wave of night, aspire to the roughened Anglophone cacophony that interests Borges in *Las kenningar* and in the poetry of Cummings. However, most of the poem struggles through ineffectually placed declamations ("I tell you") and dangling prepositions ("The things my hungry heart has no use for"). This imprecision matches the speaker's mood of dreamy excess. The dawn, sign of the alba, is "useless," invested with the same arbitrariness as words themselves ("Words, any words"). If words are arbitrary, they are correspondingly forgettable. They fail to shoulder the burden of human interaction as a mnemonic occasion: "We talked and you have forgotten the words." The forgetting of English remained a deep preoccupation in Borges's fiction as well, something which criollo culture must be warned against. In his late story "El evangelio según Marcos" (The Gospel According to Mark), a bourgeois medical student from Buenos Aires named Espinosa comes to know a family of gauchesque country people on the pampa named "los Gutres," a corruption over several generations of a Scottish surname (the Guthries). In their capacity for the obsolescence of their English patrimony lies their facility for the shocking scene of crucifixion that they mete out on the story's protagonist.[137]

As in "Two English Poems," Borges elsewhere stages the aubade as the scene of language's failure to bear the weight of memory, and he rehearses this topos with continual associations to English as the object of loss. Even where English words appear in his poetry seemingly at random, he collocates them with the mood of dawn. In a wartime sonnet on the theme of the London Blitz, "Para la noche del 24 de diciembre de 1940, en Inglaterra," he writes of the bombs falling through the night: "Que los bélicos 'crackers' retumben hasta el alba" (That the bellicose 'crackers' boom until dawn).[138] A 1951 essay treats the first English poet, Layamon, as dispossessed from his own literary inheritance.[139] Here he associates the dawn of English itself with the loss of a linguistic predecessor.

Borges sought to rectify this dispossession in his study of Anglo-Saxon in the 1950s, re-envisioning the emergence of the English language. Edwin Williamson recounts these circumstances for the composition of the poem "Al iniciar el estudio de la gramática anglosajona" (On Beginning the Study of Anglo-Saxon Grammar): "From about 1958, four or five students, mostly girls, would come to the National Library on Saturday mornings to accompany Borges in the deciphering of Old English texts [. . .]. His first encounter with the language produced a strange exhilaration—he sallied forth into the street with his students declaiming a passage they had succeeded in deciphering that morning."[140] The corresponding poem Borges wrote to commemorate this self-described "intimate" experience of language learning probably takes its title from John Keats's "On First Looking into Chapman's Homer," which links it to Borges's autobiographical sense of the emergence of poetry in his own life. Borges's poem takes shape as a metalinguistic dawn song for the emergence of the ancestral English language that so interested him.[141] The speaker plunges through a temporal abyss of fifty generations to an atavistic Anglo-Saxon society, prior to the birth of vernacular English:

> Al cabo de cincuenta generaciones
> (Tales abismos nos depara a todos el tiempo)
> Vuelvo en la margen ulterior de un gran río
> Que no alcanzaron los dragones del viking,
> A las ásperas y laborisas palabras
> Que, con una boca hecha polvo,
> Usé en los días de Nortumbria y de Mercia,
> Antes de ser Haslam o Borges.[142]

> (After some fifty generations
> (Time opens such abysses before us all)
> I return to the far shore of a vast river
> Never reached by the Viking's dragoons,
> To the harsh and work-wrought words
> Which, with a tongue now dust,
> I used in the days of Northumbria and Mercia
> Before becoming Haslam or Borges.)[143]

In this domain of poetic anteriority, the poet reencounters and retrieves ancestral words in their vivid, imagistic, ritual freshness. Words reconnect to their primordial metaphoric functions and ritual utilities. For Borges, every dictionary yet invented is merely a metasymbolic placeholder for the figural degradations words have undergone as they pass from language to language. That is, words are "symbols of other symbols":

Símbolos de otros símbolos, variaciones
Del futuro inglés o alemán me parecen estas palabras
Que alguna vez fueron imágenes
Y que un hombre usó para celebrar el mar o una espada;
Mañana volverán a vivir,
Mañana *fyr* no será *fire* sino esa suerte
De dios domesticado y cambiante
Que a nadie le está dado mirar sin un antiguo asombro.

(Symbols of other symbols, they appear as variants
On their English or German future, these words
That once were images
And a man used them to celebrate the sea or a sword.
Tomorrow they will come alive again,
Tomorrow *fyr* will not become *fire* but rather that kind
Of tamed and changeable god
Whom no one can look upon without ancient astonishment.)

The poet casts the English word *fire* as the echo of its predecessor, granting *fyr* imaginative priority. Borges thus subscribes to the orthodoxy of poetic apologists such as Vico and Herder who view poetic language as preceding prosaic language. The poem works against the falling from concretion into abstraction. Robert Harrison calls this process "lexification," or the process through which human beings are thrown into the history and historicity of the most basic words.[144]

Ultimately, the dawning of English words in Borges's poems dramatizes how all words are estranged foreigners with respect to their own etymons. Thus, words become magically redolent inter-linguistic amulets. For Borges, they convoke an ahistorical poetic temporality in which the poet can return over and over to the scene of language at its dawn:

Alabado sea el infinito
Laberinto de los efectos y de las causas
Que antes de mostrarme el espejo
En que no veré a nadie o veré a otro
Me concede esta pura contemplación
De un lenguaje del alba.

(Praise be to the infinite
Labyrinth of causes and effects

Which, before displaying the mirror for me
In which I will see no one or will see some other self,
Has granted me this pure contemplation
Of a language at its dawn.)

Again, here, is "pure contemplation" in the unmistakably Valéryan, post-symbolist mode. Again, too, Borges links it to the meditation on the exogamous character of words.

We can imagine Borges's poetic meditations on foreign words, with their English priorities displaced from the geographical scene of the Americas, having been written without the promises and disappointments of an inter-American era of cultural diplomacy. But the pressure system of this front, shuttling like Stevensian weather across the linguistic frontiers of the hemisphere, made foreign words unique points of discussion and meditation in midcentury poems: pollutions and addenda in the space of the waning, late-symbolist ethos of "pure poetry." It is striking that Borges consolidated his account of the role of the English language in his work during his cultural-diplomatic tours of the United States in the late 1960s and early 1970s, and in works such as his Charles Eliot Norton lectures and his "Autobiographical Notes" in the *New Yorker*. In these instances he pulled the reading of his work out of the transcultural project of "cosmopolitan criollismo," and pushed it into the domain of the hemispheric cultural diplomacy project. In Hartford, Havana, and Buenos Aires, even poems that dramatized their "insular" sense of enclosure from inter-American affiliation, or their hermetic rejection of demotic speech, or their contemplations of language's emergence in the deep past suddenly pinned their hopes to the foreign word as an institution of poetic knowledge.

3. The Ruins of Inter-Americanism

They'll cry, these fat & supported characters: "Oh, they are all over the place, these, ruins!" Which is quite, quite the big & astounding fact
—Charles Olson, *Mayan Letters* (1954)

I argued in Chapter 1 that World War II entailed an efflorescence of literature around wartime "hemispheric solidarity," giving bite to a previously toothless Good Neighbor policy. Yet, as Chapter 2 began to suggest in its portrait of the language politics of poets who turned away from cultural diplomacy, much of the Good Neighbor era's rhetoric and associated cultural programs fell into neglect just after the war. This neglect struck many on the literary left as a stark abdication of promising convictions. For example, in 1953, when Pablo Neruda sent a copy of *Canto general* to Waldo Frank and invited Frank to Chile in the spirit of their earlier inter-Americanism, Frank declined while bemoaning the Cold War's "subtle technics of exile" and "shrinking of American consciousness."[1] Lewis Hanke, who was one of the very architects of wartime inter-Americanism in his role at the Library of Congress, would later describe a "drought" in which Latin American nations experienced academic and cultural marginalization within the hemispheric system.[2] Likewise, Cuban poet-critic Roberto Fernández Retamar looked back on the interval 1945–1959 as a moment of reduced literary "intercommunication."[3] Seeking to explain this drought, Deborah Cohn has mapped the obstructive effects on US–Latin American literary relations of the McCarran-Walter Act of 1952, which denied visas to foreign nationals suspected of communist ties, to which we can add the domestic roles of the Smith Act and the Hatch Act in suppressing inter-American communists.[4] Although aspects of political and economic inter-Americanism were formalized by the Chapultepec Conference (1945), the United Nations Charter (1945), the Rio Treaty (1947), the Bogota Charter of the OAS (1948), Harry S. Truman's Fair Deal, and the boom in consumer-export Americanization, these institutions and initiatives all tended to reject Good Neighbor diplomacy's rhetorical and cultural dimensions. In all, it was clear that hemispheric modernization no longer had cause to enlist literary modernism in its projects as it had only a few years before. Meanwhile, the Congress for Cultural Freedom and allied information services and international education programs installed a depoliticized canon of high modernists as an official export literature of US diplomacy.[5] A literary historian might well look at the midcentury and see only a void in cultural hemispherism, one in which national entrenchment, economic globalization, reduplicating forms of cultural insularity, politicized visa policies, and a formalist literary quietism all reinforced one another.

In this chapter, however, I will argue that several prominent postwar poets sought to allegorize the "interregnum" in hemispheric democracy itself. They did so by staging a bardic retreat into the recesses of the hemisphere's indigenous civic architectures, which became paradoxical figures of alternate futurities in their poems. From mutually inflected states of ruin—the collapse of political and cultural inter-Americanism in the early Cold War, and the attempt to renew literary aesthetics in the wake of modernism—there emerged a notable poetic genre in postwar hemispheric literary history: the meditation on ruins. Rejecting the appropriation of the pre-Columbian ruin as a reliquary of romantic nationalism, poets recast it as a site for performances of cultural inter-Americanism and as a space to critique an intensifying rhetoric of modernization that relegated expressions of humanism and transnational solidarity to Cold War receivership.

Ruins were indeed "all over the place" in postwar poems and manifestos. Readers may call to mind some of the most canonical poems in twentieth-century Latin American letters, such as Neruda's *Alturas de Macchu Picchu* (The Heights of Macchu Picchu, 1946), Octavio Paz's *Piedras sueltas* (Loose Stones, 1955) and *Piedra del sol* (Sunstone, 1957), Alberto Hidalgo's *Patria completa* (1960), Martín Adán's *La mano desasida: Canto a Machu Picchu* (The Unclenched Hand: Song to Machu Picchu, 1964), and Ernesto Cardenal's *Homenaje a los indios americanos* (Homage to the American Indians, 1969). Yet a coeval US poetry invites comparison, including Charles Olson's "postmodern" manifesto-poem "The

Kingfishers" (1949), his poetic essay "Human Universe" (1951), and his epistolary book *Mayan Letters* (1954). Allen Ginsberg's "Siesta in Xbalba and Return
to the States" (1956), his most significant poem before "Howl" (1956), is a ruin
meditation that crucially informs his conception of a "destroyed" generation
in "Howl." Subsequently, ruin poems ripple through Philip Lamantia's *Ekstasis*
(1959) and his "Destroyed Works" typescript, Lawrence Ferlinghetti's *Starting
from San Francisco* (1961), and the emerging ethnopoetics of Jerome Rothenberg.
On the whole, in a surprisingly multidirectional network of relations and affinities, Spanish-language and English-language instances of the emerging ruin-
poem genre influence and reorient one another by turns. The bulk of this chapter
maps out these relations through extended discussions of the midcentury poets
who visited ruins and wrote meditations upon them. But first, we need to define
the broader historicity of what I will call *a midcentury culture of pre-Columbian
ruins*, as these ruins came to be perceived as sites and icons of cultural diplomacy
through the crisscrossing discourses of archaeology, art history, economic modernization, and poetry.

Privileged Observatories: A Midcentury Culture of Pre-Columbian Ruins

Especially in lands known to indigenous peoples as Anahuac (Mesoamerica) and
Tahuantinsuyu (highland Peru), a newly fortified, postwar hemispheric transportation network opened formerly remote areas to heightened archaeological
attentions, fueling what a director of Harvard's Peabody Museum called "the
post-World War II boom in 'primitive' art."[6] "Open Sesame to the Maya," the
title of a 1947 *Bulletin of the Pan American Union* article on the excavation of
Bonampak, captured this booming mood.[7] Archaeologists and art markets
drove the boom, but poets encouraged and critiqued it in key ways. For them,
indigenous iconographic, chirographic, and artifactual heritages redressed the
attenuation of inter-American political discourses. Poets working in modernist
traditions detoured atavistically from wartime roles in state projects into archaeological zones, where they meditated on pre-Columbian antiquity. For Neruda,
Paz, Olson, Ginsberg, and Cardenal, the prenational architectonics of ruined
cities organized postnational idealizations. Accessing remote ruins on new
highways in the 1960s, Cardenal ruminated in his *Homenaje* on the difference
between pre-Columbian carreteras supporting processional rites and those now
in service to commercial automobility.[8] Even so, from Machu Picchu, Chichén

Itzá, Palenque, Uxmal, and Mesa Verde, poets grounded poetry's public voice on visionary filiations to indigenous reality, and attested to an inter-American map that could be understood as a striking alternative to accelerating modernization and nuclear endangerment. I bring together discrete Maya, Inca, and Anasazi cultural worlds in the list above and in the pages below in the spirit of poets such as Cardenal and critics such as Brotherston who articulate the trans-indigenous affinities of a hemispheric "fourth world."[9]

To be sure, pre-Columbian aesthetics intermittently characterized the writing and art of the preceding decades. At the height of modernismo, Rubén Darío staked divisions in the Americas on the existence of ruins: "Si hay poesía en nuestra América ella está en las cosas viejas, en Palenke y Utatlán, en el indio legendario, y en el inca sensual y fino, y en el gran Moctezuma de la silla de oro. Lo demás es tuyo, demócrata Walt Whitman" (If there is poetry in our America it is in the old things, in Palenque and Utatlán, in the legendary *indio*, and in the fine and sensual Inca, and in the great Moctezuma on his golden throne. The rest is yours, democratic Walt Whitman).[10] Yet the opposition between the hemispheric democracy emblematized by Whitman and the poetry of pre-Columbian antiquity gave way in the age of muralism and the aestheticized anthropology that James Clifford calls "ethnographic surrealism."[11] Rivera's panoramic inter-Americanism proposed, in Jeffrey Belnap's analysis, "to sublate U.S. technology and reorganize the American lifeworld according to the socio-aesthetic principles of a revived and resilient Native American civilization."[12] Alongside Rivera's muralism, ethnographic surrealism reworked indigenous architecture as a universal heritage implicated in rather than opposed to political modernity, just as inter-American cultural diplomacy initiatives took up these discourses.

As an art collector, Nelson Rockefeller was among the grand patrons of these aesthetic attentions. Expressly in the context of the Rockefeller-led wartime hemispheric democracy campaigns, several artists and writers placed pre-Columbian heritage at the center of projections for inter-American political futures. When painter Barnett Newman organized a 1944 exhibition of pre-Columbian statuary, his catalogue essay suggested that wartime "friendship between the Americas," if made permanent, needed a "moral" foundation:

> It is a hopeful sign for our cultural rapprochement to watch the grow-
> ing aesthetic appreciation of pre-Columbian art. For here we have ready-
> made, so to speak, a large body of art which should unite all the Americas
> since it is the common heritage of both hemispheres. [. . .] Here in this art
> is the moral base for that intercultural community that is the foundation
> of permanent friendship.[13]

Newman's Duchampian, "ready-made" theory of pre-Columbian aesthetics as the ground of postwar inter-Americanism was less morally foundational than he supposed. Duchamp's readymades decommissioned mass-produced consumer products from their primary forms of utility and revalued them in the marketplace of the collector and museum, but the new prizing of pre-Columbian artifacts extracted a cultural commons from underfoot of native communities, and fragmented pre-Columbian history to satiate private collectors.

An eclectic company including struggling artists and Hollywood directors stoked these dynamics. In June of 1950, when abstract expressionist painter Emerson Woelffer traveled from the Yucatán to Pensacola, Florida, on a steamer carrying a cargo of mahogany, he brought rolls of painted canvases from an artistically productive half-year stay in Lerma, Campeche, but he also smuggled "boxes and boxes of Mayan artifacts."[14] Filmmaker John Huston, whose multifarious relations to Mexico dated back to 1925, began collecting pre-Columbian art when he filmed *Treasure of the Sierra Madre* (1948) in Tampico and Jungapeo, Michoacán. His interests enlarged with his studio budgets. By *The Unforgiven* (1959), filmed in Durango, Huston moonlighted by running a smuggling operation that brought three large Veracruz sculptures to Texas.[15] Now, the Western film set had itself become the scene of inter-American cultural expropriation.[16]

US poetry follows a similar trajectory, careening from wartime inter-Americanism to postwar fortune-hunting. Following the Buenos Aires PEN International Conference in 1936, Harriet Monroe, sadly, died en route to Machu Picchu, prefiguring a connection between ruins and cultural diplomacy. Morton Zabel's obituary stated "no one could think it wrong that she died [. . .] climbing the steep slopes of the Andes toward the shattered halls and temples of the Incas."[17] William Carlos Williams, speaking in Puerto Rico in 1941, anticipated Newman's call for a pre-Columbian reliquary as the inter-Americanism of last resort:

> And if everything else that I have said is wrong-headed, destructive to that precious soul of things which the true poet should cherish! If I have been mechanical and crass in my concepts, relying for my argument on mere techniques and materials—Well, in that case, from the old and alien soul of America itself, may the reliques of its ancient, its pre-Columbian cultures still kindle something in me that will be elevated, profound and common to us all, Americas. There is that path still open to us.[18]

Here autochthony becomes a transnational figure, marking a break with the era of New World modernisms that sought to build national literatures on the forced genealogical connection to an imagined indigenous past. Williams, Hart Crane, Vachel Lindsay, and Mary Austin all put versions of this project on offer in the

United States, as had Oswald de Andrade in Brazil and Miguel Ángel Asturias in Guatemala.[19] Despite Williams's commitments to modernist form, viewed as a new technical attention to strategies of typography, lineation, prosodic variability, and demotic diction, he suggests that the horizon for a New World cultural commons resides somewhere other than in "techniques." Fretting that modernist innovation could be too crassly "mechanical," he offers a neoromantic alternative, "kindled" by pre-Columbiana.

Stephen M. Park sensitively traces Williams's thinking about Mesoamerican architectures to his 1920s work, but for his late poems, forms of ruination define the "catastrophic" rhythm of language itself.[20] Williams did write a Mesa Verde poem in the 1940s entitled "The Testament of Perpetual Change," just as Robert Frost wrote the short lyric "Cliff Dwellers," each poet visiting Southwestern ruin sites during academic reading tours. Yet the inter-American ruinology Williams names was more common in other poets. Transnational pilgrimage to "the old and alien soul" of the hemisphere characterized major inter-American postwar poems. Neruda's ascent to Machu Picchu—"entonces en la escala de la tierra he subido" (and then the ladder of the earth I climbed)—was one version of this pilgrimage.[21] So was Olson's New World archaism: "shall you uncover honey/where maggots are?//I hunt among stones."[22] Even Ginsberg's retrospect on his postwar cohort's failure in the opening line of "Howl" grew from the "Byronic meditation on ruins" he called "Siesta in Xbalba," written in Yucatán and Chiapas in 1954. Spurning "New York rotting/under the tides of Heaven," he scrawled "skully meditations" on the "sacred ruin of the world" in his notebooks at Palenque:

> on a time-rude pyramid rebuilt
> in the bleak flat night of Yucatán
> where I come with my own mad mind to study
> alien hieroglyphs of Eternity.[23]

From this ruin, Ginsberg began to observe wider circuitries of his "destroyed" generation.

These neoromantic poems, in flight from techno-modernity toward indigenous textual traditions and civic architecture, act out adventuresome fantasies for poets unable to earn a living from their craft. When Olson and his wife Connie slipstreamed behind the Woelffers, whom they knew from Black Mountain College, into a rental home in Lerma in 1951, looting enthralled Olson. In letters judiciously excluded from Robert Creeley's edition of *Mayan Letters*, Olson writes, "And figure another thing, on profit: the natives have Mayan pieces, to offer (as well yrself, may, dig) ((if you skip the law)) If one smuggles out, no telling, how much MAKE! Museums, here, like very much—& don't ask, questions."[24] Only in later works by Adán and Ferlinghetti do these attitudes yield to reciprocity. Meditations on ruins could recapitulate colonial violence in their way of configuring poetic indigeneity, but they also obliquely sowed a fallow era of inter-American consciousness.

Whoever names an aesthetic category of "ruins" invokes a long European tradition of poetic and theoretical meditations. Rose Macaulay remarked in 1953, at the height of postwar *Ruinenlust*, "down the ages men have meditated before ruins, rhapsodized before them, [and] mourned pleasurably over their ruination." Macaulay qualified this universalizing claim with a specific one: "the main strand is, one imagines, the romantic and conscious swimming down the hurrying river of time, whose mysterious reaches [. . .] glimmer suddenly into view with these wracks."[25] Thomas McFarland argued that forms of "diasparaction" (incompleteness, fragmentation, and ruin) saturate the entire cultural imaginary of the romantic era.[26] These romantic intensifications mask a longer tradition, from the imperial memento mori and the "talking ruins" of the enlightenment to the ruin as the imagined foundation of romantic nationalism, or what Ángel Rama terms "originalism."[27] Gothic ruins, modernist fragments, postmodern tourism, and the post-industrial urbanism known as "ruin kitsch" all manifest afterlives of these discourses.[28] Andreas Huyssen succinctly argues that "The cult of ruins has accompanied Western modernity in waves since the eighteenth century," and he concludes that "nostalgia for ruins" is modernity's most tenacious, auratic desire.[29] Octavio Paz further links modern nostalgia to a transtemporal ruinology:

> Las catedrales son las ruinas de la eternidad cristiana, las estupas lo son de la vacuidad budista, los templos griegos de la *polis* y la geometría pero las grandes ciudades norteamericanas y sus arrabales son las ruinas vivas del futuro. En esos inmensos basureros industriales han parado la filosofía y la moral del progreso. Con el mundo moderno se acaba el titanismo del futuro, frente al cual los titanismos del pasado—incas, romanos, chinos, egipcios—parecen infantiles castillos de arena.[30]

> (Cathedrals are the ruins of Christian eternity, stupas are those of Buddhist emptiness, Greek temples those of the *polis* and geometry, but the great North American cities and their suburbs are the living ruins of the future. In these immense industrial wastes philosophy and moral progress have halted. In the modern world the titanism of the future has been completed; confronting it, past titanisms—Inca, Roman, Chinese, Egyptian—seem like infantile sand castles.)

This remark comes as an aside in Paz's account of American modernist poets such as Pound, Crane, and Williams. He describes the whole project of American modernism as a rhapsody of linguistic ruination that, in responding to the ruin of industrial modernity, diminishes the ruins of the past.

The postwar poems that I discuss here can be placed in these transtemporal traditions of meditation on ruins, yet they also interrupt and reorient them. In the late 1940s, Machu Picchu and Chichén Itzá no longer grounded foundational nationalisms or imperial romances, nor were they yet mass tourist destinations or UNESCO-designated world heritage sites. New World ruins remained partially excavated and deciphered, offering Western modernity a projection not of its own anteriority, but an alterity from which it deviated. Postwar ruin poems do not trope or thematize ruins, but rather "site" poetic enunciation in their architectonic network of prenational spaces, which organize hemispheric imagination.[31] Among the Maya, Olson evades the "blueberry America" he associates with Williams's *Paterson* and the old "yurrup" he links to Pound's *Cantos*.[32] Reciprocally, Neruda approaches Machu Picchu to harbor the transnational feeling of being "Chilean, Peruvian, American." Ginsberg, in the "Xbalba" (limbo) of Mayan Mexico, which he codes geographically as an orphic underbelly to US techno-capitalism, awakens nostalgia for the "ancient continent I have not seen."[33]

Many facets of this prenational nostalgia interlock in postwar ruin poems. First, such poems critique a modernization project, which had been an articulate network for hemispheric ideals, but whose new gospel was Truman's Fair Deal.[34] Poetic critiques of modernization proffer alternative humanisms. Paz, decrying technology in 1956, calls the Mayan temple a "privileged observatory from which man could contemplate the world and the transworld as a totality."[35] Olson taps a midcentury desire to reground definitions of the person against dehumanizing techno-capitalism and a "spectatorism" that diminishes "participation" as a cultural good.[36] Rallying a discourse Mark Greif has named "the age of the crisis of man," Olson asks: "Can one restate man in any way to repossess him of his dynamic?"[37] Neruda makes the same restatement:

> Qué era el hombre? En qué parte de su conversación abierta
> entre los almacenes y los silbidos, en cuál de sus movimientos metálicos
> vivía lo indestructible, lo imperecedero, la vida?
>
> (What was man? Where in his open talk
> amid shops and whistling, in which of his metallic motions
> lived the indestructible, the imperishable—life?)

On this view, "being" is "threshed" and "siloed" in the "inacabable/granero de los hechos perdidos, de los acontecimientos/miserables" (the bottomless/granary of wasted deeds, of shabby/incidents). For the Olson of "Human Universe," likewise, "all individual energy and ingenuity is bought off" and "passivity conquers all." Confronted by Mayan ruins, Olson remarks: "for I come on, here, what seems to me the real, live clue to the results of what I keep gabbing about, *another* human-ism."[38] Amid modernization's threat to traditional folkways, ruined cities propose counteractive dispositions for humanist crises.

A second facet of the ruin poem takes shape here as an identification with hemispheric indigenism. That is, Olson's alternative humanism echoes, and borrows from, Latin American poetry's allegiances to indigenism, a movement especially strong in Peru and Mexico that sought greater social visibility and political autonomy for indigenous peoples.[39] Midcentury ruin poems champion indigenous communities and link pre-Columbian ruins complexly—but affirmatively—to the cultural politics of a trans-indigenous "Fourth World," even as they loosely appropriate indigenist discourses for other purposes. Latin American poets could be as guilty of ethnopoetic appropriations as Anglo-Americans, while Anglo-American poets could cultivate an indigenism not easily dismissed by critics who see only nostalgia-mongering and neo-imperial adventuring. A decade ago, Manuel Martinez argued that Allen Ginsberg and William S. Burroughs were merely psychotropic treasure hunters replaying imperialist adventures.[40] More recently, Mexican poet, essayist, and cultural critic Heriberto Yépez indicted Olson's errant travels to Mexico as the root of a generalized embodiment of several generations of US imperialism.[41] To the contrary, I argue that US ruin poems belong to an inter-American circuit seeking alternative humanisms, anticipating sociolinguistic and native practices involved in decolonizing indigenous textual traditions of the Americas.

Third, postwar ruin poems replace an East/West gaze on the wartime ruination of Europe with meditations on New World cultural autonomy. Paz's "Himno entre ruinas" (Hymn among the Ruins) juxtaposes diverse eras of European ruination, including the overrun postwar Naples where the poem was written, to images of Mexican youth smoking marijuana "en lo alto de la pirámide" at Teotihuacan:

> *Mis pensamientos se bifurcan, serpean, se enredan,*
> *recomienzan,*
> *y al fin se inmovilizan, ríos que no desembocan,*
> *delta de sangre bajo un sol sin crepúsculo.*

(*My thoughts are split, meander, grow entangled,*
start again,
and finally lose headway, endless rivers,
delta of blood beneath an unwinking sun.)[42]

These are nesting scales of metaphoric ruination ("ruins alive in a world of death in life!," as translated by Williams). In them, the germinal movement of poetic thought is rooted in the specificity of New World experience, much as in Williams's own poetic credo "No ideas/but in things," exemplified by the exclamation "saxifrage is my flower that splits/the rocks." Paz's "Himno entre ruinas" is followed in some editions by "En Uxmal," a cubist haiku sited in a naturalistic Yucatecan ruin. In *Piedras sueltas* (Loose Stones, 1955), where the latter poem first appeared, Paz metaphorizes the chapbook itself as a rubble heap. Muriel Rukeyser, translating these poems, likens them to the "riprap" of Gary Snyder's western trails, but for Paz, the word *piedra* carries with it the long cultural memory of Aztec civilization. Such historical resonances are not similarly layered in Snyder's rocky berms in virgin wilderness.[43]

Finally, poets surveyed ruins to site an embodied public voice for postwar poetry through access to visionary experience. The ruin's visionary locus frames the voiced poetry that Ginsberg calls "spontaneous bop prosody," the embodied, breathy poems that Olson defines as "projective verse," and Neruda's attempts to ground his populist politics through the compulsive, prosopoeic act of speaking by and for the voices of the dead. Ruin poems were premised on the clamorous presence of the male poet transfiguring his physical proximity to ruins into auratic vision, and into an authority beyond nationalism.

The following pages arrange in succession four interludes in a postwar hemispheric literary history of ruin poetry: Neruda's 1943 visit to Machu Picchu and his pursuant composition of *Alturas de Macchu Picchu* in 1945; Olson's 1949 composition of "The Kingfishers," the prelude to his sojourns in the Yucatán peninsula in 1951 and the *Mayan Letters* (1954); Ginsberg's poetic development from the composition of the long poem "Siesta in Xbalba" in 1954 to that of "Howl" (1956); and Adán's writing of his hectoring and obscure epic *La mano desasida* in Lima, and his pursuant exchanges with Ginsberg and Ferlinghetti. I intersperse these episodes with briefer accounts of others less well known: US communist poets from George Oppen to Walter Lowenfels who worked at moments in Neruda's shadow; the anthropologist-poet Robert H. Barlow in Mexico City in the years before his 1951 suicide; Lamantia's Tenochtitlan poems; and finally, Cardenal's composition of the *Homenaje*, a capstone of the ruin-poetry tradition. As postwar national literatures abandoned inter-Americanism, ruins housed residues of hemispheric belonging, and the accrual of a tradition of ruin poetry became a resonant echo chamber of inter-American literary relations.

Dead Mouths: Neruda at Machu Picchu

In 1972, Peruvian scholar Hugo Montes compiled a book on the image of Machu Picchu in Latin American poetry, discussing Neruda and Adán alongside Alberto Hidalgo, Mario Florián Díaz, and Gonzalo Humberto Mata. Intriguingly, Montes claimed that ruin poems held a discursive and imaginative priority over ruin architecture. Tourists may now throng the Inca Trail, he remarks, but Chileans primarily associate the phrase "Machu Picchu" with Neruda's poem, not the actual "Incan fortress" of the Peruvian sierra. Montes celebrated "a curious case in which the poetic word has come to substitute for geographical reality and historical meaning."[44] To him, Hiram Bingham's 1911 archeological expedition to Machu Picchu, described in his *Lost City of the Incas* (1930), merely presaged Neruda's "poetic discovery."[45] Montes's remark points to the parochial perspective of some of the poem's Chilean readership, to whom "Machu Picchu" is firstly a metonymy for the poetry of Pablo Neruda, and only secondly a nominative representation of a physical place located in highland Peru. One of the jobs of *Alturas de Macchu Picchu*, beginning with Neruda's insertion of an extra *c* in "Macchu" to lend the phrase orthographic symmetry, was to make it real in the associational logics of its readers.

Written in 1945, partially published in Spanish and French in 1946, and only fully published in 1948, *Alturas* was quickly hailed as the major poem of twentieth-century Latin America, and heralded by one reviewer as the "punto culminante del indigenismo" (peak of indigenism). The poem elevates the idiom of the native Americas, shaping a transnational, public imagination about the spiritual value of ruins.[46] As if to compensate for this impoverished public imaginary, the first oversized limited edition published in 1948 by Ediciones Librería Neira in Santiago supplemented "the poetic word" with surreal illustrations by Chilean communist artist José Venturelli. Another *demi-luxe* edition of 1954, in an exaggeratedly large font, incorporated a copious photographic dossier by the Andean photographer Martín Chambi (Figure 3.1). The clandestine Chilean edition and the deluxe Mexican subscriber edition of Neruda's epic *Canto general* (1950) likewise accorded it a prominent place, and two English versions were translated by 1950, one by H. R. Hays for the surrealist magazine *Tiger's Eye* (1948) and the other in the communist pamphlet *Let the Railsplitter Awake* (Masses and Mainstream, 1950).[47] These editions suggest that *Alturas* fueled a public imagination for ruin spaces wherever it traveled, transmuting hemispheric

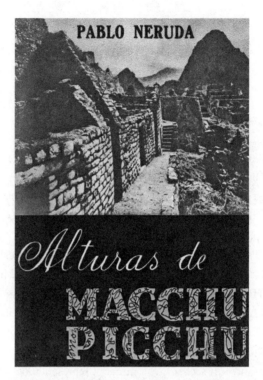

Fig 3.1 Pablo Neruda, *Alturas de Macchu Picchu* (Santiago: Nascimento, 1954). Photograph by Martín Chambi. Used by permission of the Archivo Fotografico Martín Chambi.

antiquity into inter-American novelty for surrealists, elites, and leftist solidarity movements alike.

Alturas offers a myth of spiritual regeneration by reorienting epistemological problems of being toward an antiquated externality rather than a Cartesian ego. The poem's resolutions to entrust itself to "piedra persistente" (persistent stone) opposes "propio pensamiento" (the thought of the self), as critic Santiago del Campo pointed out in an early review.[48] In so doing, *Alturas* proposes a meditative counterweight to extractive imaginaries linked to Machu Picchu. The years immediately after its publication saw the Spanish-language edition of Bingham's *Ciudad Perdida* (1950) and the Charlton Heston adventure picture, *The Secret of the Incas* (1954). Heston's proto–Indiana Jones turns archeology into a cover for profiteering. Apprised of a priceless relic, his Austrian love interest asks him, "Is there really such a sunburst?" Heston flies a stolen plane to Machu Picchu to seek it out, callously replying, "Well, if there isn't, archaeologists have dug up half of Peru just to look at some old ruins and mummies." For Neruda, by contrast, ruins incite a hemispheric "principle of faith."

Scholars often rehearse the origin story of *Alturas de Macchu Picchu* by beginning with the autobiographical portrait Neruda supplies in his memoirs, *Confieso que he vivido* (I Confess that I have Lived) (1974).[49] In this telling, the October 1943 trip to Machu Picchu came during his multi-city airplane tour from Mexico home to Chile:

> I stopped in Peru and made a trip to the ruins of Macchu Picchu. There was no highway then and we rode up on horseback. At the top I saw the ancient stone structures hedged in by the tall peaks of the verdant Andes. Torrents hurtled down from the citadel eaten away and weathered by the passage of the centuries. White fog drifted up in masses from the Wilkamayu River. I felt infinitely small in the center of that navel of rocks, the navel of a deserted world, proud, towering high, to which I somehow belonged. I felt that my own hands had labored there at some remote point in time, digging furrows, polishing the rocks. I felt Chilean, Peruvian, American. On those difficult heights, among those glorious scattered ruins, I had found the principles of faith I needed to continue my poetry. My poem *Alturas de Macchu Picchu* was born there.[50]

Some slight falsifications in this account must be noted. Neruda suggests "my poem ... was born there," but he conceived it at least three years prior. Marxist indigenista philosopher José Uriel García wrote to Neruda in February 1940 to convince him to stop in Cuzco on his way to Mexico. Although Neruda could not make the trip, Uriel García implies that he and Neruda discussed *Canto General*, and that Neruda already slotted Incan sites into his plans for the poem:

> No olvido de su ofrecimiento de su visita al Cuzco, en cuanto emprenda Ud. la marcha a su nuevo destino diplomático. Si no voy a México, al congreso indigenista que se efectuará el 14 de abril, para aquella fecha yo estaré en el Cusco y esperaré allí su visita para acompañarlo en la urgente necesidad suya y nuestra también de que conozca las raíces y las columnas sustendoras de *nuestra* América.[51]

> (I do not forget your offer to visit Cuzco as you begin your march to your new diplomatic destination. If I don't go to the Indigenist congress taking place in Mexico on April 14th, I'll await your visit to Cuzco in order to accompany you on your urgent need—and ours as well—to know *our* America's sustaining roots and columns.)

Uriel García further declares: "Qué fecundas sugerencias recibiría Ud. para su canto a América, que todos los que tenemos fe en su talento creador esperamos" (what fertile suggestions you'll receive for your song to America, which all of us who have faith in your creative talent are awaiting). Thus, Neruda's ascent to Machu Picchu in 1943 was not the scene of hemispheric epiphany transforming his 1938 "Canto general de Chile" into the hemispheric amplitude of his epic chronicle *Canto General*. Uriel García had already bestowed globalizing encomia on Neruda by 1940, regarding him as "a great personality and great citizen of America and the world, sublime poet of the masses and lands of the Americas."[52] Literary historians conveniently herald his Machu Picchu visit as an epiphany, but it built on several years of alignment between Marxist indigenism and Pan-Americanism.[53]

Neruda's posture of romantic solitude among "glorious scattered ruins" also deserves clarification. Neruda's stop in Peru included visits to Lima and Cuzco for a series of readings and lectures with leftist Peruvian writers, and his horseback tour through the Urubamba valley (the "Hiram Bingham Highway" was not completed until 1948) stopped at other Incan sites such as Sacsayhuamán. His companions included his second wife, Delia de Carril, and Uriel García, who led Neruda to associate the ruins with an indigenist vision of unalienated labor instanced by contemporary Quechua peoples. In one photograph from their site visit, the three travelers rest on a stone wall. Neruda, perhaps winded, sits at a remove from Delia, who poses in a fashionable coat and white sunglasses (Figure 3.2).

Fig 3.2 José Uriel García, Delia del Carril, and Pablo Neruda (from l. to r.) at Machu Picchu, October 1943. Photographer unknown. Used by permission of Archivo Fundación Pablo Neruda.

The most iconic photograph depicts Neruda alone, gazing past the camera, cloaked in Andean poncho and beret (Figure 3.3). It ambiguously expresses indigenist identification, while suggesting that Neruda traveled as the performative protagonist of his own Andean costume drama. Santí points out that a few years earlier, Juan Ramón Jiménez had accused Neruda of an "artificial indigenism."[54] Other post-symbolists similarly rebuffed indigenism in poetry of the period. Stevens inveighed against "the appalling interest in the Indians: [...] One sees pictures of the Mayas, and this, that and the other. These things never take one below the surface and I have yet to feel about any Maya that he was made of clay."[55] Yet Neruda felt the cosmopolitan universalism of post-symbolists entailed a dangerous "denationalization."[56] As if fending off charges of indigenist artifice or an inability to "take one below the surface," *Alturas* stages "deep" union through acts of digging and reknotting with humic elements. *Alturas*'s first canto insists on this rhythm of sinking and plunging: *hundiendo; más abajo; hundí; en lo más genital; descendí.* Del Campo astutely describes this as the poem's drama of "reabsorption," although

Fig 3.3 Pablo Neruda at Machu Picchu, October 1943. Photographer unknown. Used by permission of Archivo Fundación Pablo Neruda.

his judgment proves false that this "curious phenomenon" lacks "comparison with any other hemispheric poet."[57]

Romantic solitude and ethnological identity coexist uneasily in *Alturas* and in "La lámpara en la tierra," the poem preceding it in *Canto General*. No one saw this more clearly than anthropologist-poet Nathaniel Tarn, who corresponded extensively with Neruda while translating the poem in 1966, but whose essay "Pablo Neruda and Indigenous Culture" later critiqued it on the grounds that it makes strategic, appropriative use of indigenous materials.[58] Tarn suggests that although Neruda came from Hispanic bloodlines, and despite Chile's acculturated Indian and Mestizo populations (estimated to be 10 percent and 65 percent of the national Chilean population respectively in 1941), "the root of enablement he requires is Indian."[59] "La lámpara" brings Chile into *Canto General* as a solitary, divided place in a hemispheric system of indigenous consciousness. In "Los Hombres," the sixth and final canto of "La lámpara," Neruda assigns the generalizing status of "men" to the indigenous peoples of the hemisphere, giving a willy-nilly portrait of hemispheric indigeneity. Successive stanzas name the Caribs, Tarahumara, Aztecs, and Maya, interspersed with stanzas on the ruins of Chichén Itza, Machu Picchu, and Cuzco, and finally Arauco (or Araucanía), the Mapuche lands of central Chile. Crucially, Neruda does not portray Machu Picchu, Cuzco, and Arauco as populous arenas of indigenous life but as elegiac spaces of ruination. "No hay nadie" (no one is there), he repeats in his litany for Arauco, a metonym for "el gran Sur solitario" (the great solitary South). Neruda pocks his representation of the Fourth World with lacunae.

Therefore, despite his commitments to indigenism, Neruda's posture of romantic solitude at least partially predicates indigenous identification on irrecoverable loss. Tarn points out that this sense of loss serves strategic (and politically efficacious) ends. Neruda subsumes most instances of indigeneity into generic social categories that underlie the stance of Pan-American Marxism: if indigenous peoples are grouped as "el hombre" in "La lámpara," in *Alturas* the indigene becomes *el pobre, el pueblo, el antiguo ser, el servidor, el dormido*, and most importantly *hermano*. Tarn concludes that Neruda's real triggers are in the natural world and in the oppositional logics by which he names figures of conquest, authority, and imperial adventure. By contrast, "When man, Indian man, appears, we almost have anti-climax. We have to await the *conquistadores* [in Book III] who *do* arouse his ire and his inspiration."[60] In all, argues Tarn, "Neruda is a good ethnopoet, i.e., one who, [. . .] sees and uses the symbolic value of the Indian root of Americanicity while continuing perforce to dwell in his own non-Indianness."[61]

The politicized social occasions behind Neruda's romantic indigeneity—his position as an ethnopoet—deserve adumbration because in the intervening two years between his tour of Machu Picchu and the composition of his poem, Neruda increasingly performed his poetry in front of vast crowds, and *Alturas de Macchu Picchu* is a poem pitched dialectically between imagined poles of romantic solitude and the representational politics of poesía comprometida, as instanced by his large audiences. For example, over five thousand people reportedly thronged his farewell banquet upon his fall 1943 departure from Mexico.[62] Robert Pring-Mill describes the rhythm of his homecoming: "His return to Chile in October 1943 was a triumphal journey, on which he found himself acclaimed in capital after capital by huge crowds for whom his poetry seemed to voice the sufferings and aspirations of all the Latin American peoples."[63] And the crowds only grew. In March 1945 Neruda was elected senator, representing mining districts in the northern provinces of Tarapacá and Antofagasta. In July he joined the Communist Party, and he spent the summer in Brazil and Argentina. In São Paulo on July 15, at an event in the Pacaembú stadium honoring the dissident Carlos Prestes, he read in front of an audience of 130,000 people, with Jorge Amado translating beside him. "After each line of my slow reading," he recalled, "there was an explosion of applause from the Brazilians. That applause had a deep resonance in my poetry. A poet who reads his poems to 130,000 people is not the same man."[64] An event photograph suggests one of the largest audiences for modern poetry ever amassed (Figure 3.4). The "electric atmosphere" of these public readings powered Neruda's collective poetic voice, committed to populist intelligibility.[65]

Six weeks after the Pacaembú reading, which Neruda memorialized in a poem in *Canto General*, he began to compose *Alturas de Macchu Picchu*, and the poem's twelve cantos recapitulate the movement from the imagined scene of romantic solitude to one of representational commitment. The first five of the poem's twelve cantos work through a series of lyric topoi defined by alienation and spiritual decay. At the outset, the poetic self goes "Del aire al aire, como una red vacía" (From air to air, like an empty net), caught in a meaningless rhythm of arrival and departure as though coming from nowhere and going nowhere. No simple traveler, this meta-Neruda describes a transit through his own poetic career in one and the same moment as he describes transit through a city of spiritual death—"solo,/rodé muriendo de mi propia muerte" (I paced alone/dying of my own death).[66] Neruda's persona here reworks the peripatetic hermeticist of

Fig 3.4 Pablo Neruda's view as he reads in front of approximately 130,000 people at Pacaembú Stadium, São Paulo, Brazil, July 14, 1945. Photographer unknown. Used by permission of Archivo Fundación Pablo Neruda.

the first *Residencia en la tierra*, a persona found throughout his work until the rumblings of social commitment enter it via the popular front in the mid-1930s, when the conversion to a poetry of dissent and social solidarity occurs decisively in "Reunión bajo las nuevas banderas" (Meeting under new flags). Given Neruda's large corpus of vituperative political poetry, from *España en el corazón* to "Nuevo canto a Stalingrado" (1942) and from "Que despierte el leñador" (1948) to *Canción de gesta* (1961) and "Incitación a Nixoncidio" (1973), *Alturas* notably returns to the meditative opacity of his earlier writing at the very moment in which Neruda declaratively sheds his meditative allegiances. The poem opens a secondary, alternative ideation of inter-American faith—a conversion that does not explicitly summon the modes of protest or defiance so prevalent in *Canto General*'s enumerations of "La arena traicionada" (The sand betrayed) by conquistadors, caudillos, and corporate plunderers. *Alturas* offers a meditative antechamber to the defiance of "Que despierte el leñador," as if the ruin preludes and prepares a ground for anti-US invective. The same dynamic informs Ginsberg's maturation from "Siesta in Xbalba" to "Howl."

Canto I of *Alturas* serves as a proem to the twelve-poem sequence by a prolepsis of the action that the speaker replicates upon his ascent to Machu Picchu in Canto VI: the act of sinking his hand into the humic core of the earth ("hundí la mano turbulenta y dulce/en lo más genital de lo terrestre" (I sunk my sweet, turbulent hand/into the genital quick of the earth).[67] After this overtly sexualized action, the poetic subject transforms in the following stanza from an empty net to a seminal drop ("descendí como gota"), sinking blindly into the "gastada primavera humana" (exhausted human springtime). While the poem drives toward an ascendant voyage of spiritual discovery, it first performs a subterranean descent or *katabasis*—a reabsorption by a maternal world and a return to a world of dead souls. The gesture's erotism returns at the moment of ascent, as the speaker entreats the hemispheric desire he calls "amor americano" (American love), to rise and vivify the Incan ruin.[68]

Only in Canto VI does the speaker shift from flâneur to mountaineer: "Entonces en la escala de la tierra he subido" (Then the ladder of the earth I climbed). There, too, his sequence detours through flights of New World surrealism, often impeding or frustrating legibility. A few spare, sublime epithets in Canto VI—"Alto arrecife de la aurora humana" (high reef of the human dawn)— snowball into Canto IX, a poem consisting entirely of forty-three lines of paired epithets for Machu Picchu.[69] Here are the first five lines, which Neruda performed at a lugubrious pace:

> Águila sideral, viña de bruma.
> Bastión perdido, cimitarra ciega.
> Cinturón estrellado, pan solemne.
> Escala torrencial, párpado inmenso.
> Túnica triangular, polen de piedra.
>
> (Interstellar eagle, vine-in-a-mist.
> Forsaken bastion, blind scimitar.
> Orion belt, ceremonial bread.
> Torrential stairway, immeasurable eyelid.
> Triangular tunic, pollen of stone.)[70]

Such lines are bound by a loose hendecasyllable and strict isomorphism, but they are also deeply riven by relentless caesuras that divide them like mortarless space between stones (William Carlos Williams similarly remarked that *In the American Grain* featured prose blocks massed like "Inca masonry"). Santiago del Campo observed that lines like these create "a plastic modeling of the theme in the symmetry of the verses."[71] Neruda voices an interpretive "obscurity" through his accumulating metaphors. Machu Picchu alternates as a fortress and sacred worship space, a site from which to experience a synthetic cosmology, and a dialectical relation between the natural world and human enterprise.

Such obscurity surrounded Machu Picchu due to the absence of a written Quechua language in pre-conquest Peru. As the scholar George Kubler wrote in 1960:

> The purpose of the settlement is not clear. Its strategic and demographic conditions are unknown; its economic relationship to other communities is unclear; and the town has been variously regarded as a fortress, as a temple, as a nunnery-town and as a resort. [. . .] we know less about the history of the Andean peoples than we do about predynastic Egypt four millennia earlier.[72]

Canto IX's heap of metaphors therefore reveal the speculative attitude of the scholarly establishment. Kubler makes one further speculation that bears comparison to Neruda. He offers a Marxist interpretation of Machu Picchu in Incan society: "Only the architectural forms escape from the grim sameness of Inca manufactures. The escape took the form of extreme rhythmic and plastic variety within narrow technological limits directed towards a poetic vision of the natural setting."[73] The final two cantos of *Alturas* explicitly define Neruda's investment in Macchu Picchu as a genetic social myth in touch with Kubler's insights. There, Neruda, who often recited the poem in front of miners and trade unions, retrojects a vision of laborers building the city. By a prosopoeic device that confers a voice on the site, Neruda comes to speak for this group: "Yo vengo a hablar por vuestra boca muerta" (I come to speak for your dead mouth). Neruda repeats the same gesture elsewhere, part of a career-long preoccupation with humanitarian voicings of the torment of the poor, the speechless, and the victims of political violence. This tendency mitigates the criticism of Tarn, who argues that "Indians have to have been oppressed, enslaved, and killed *in order that* he can speak."[74] The force of Neruda's gesture can be alternatively understood to assume the burden of reawakening horrors he does not endeavor lightly to poeticize. It is not the speechlessness of the indigenous subject so much as the ruin's lack of iterability that occasions the poet's capacity for representational speech. *Alturas* offers a visionary reconstruction of poetry's public voice in autochthonous American reality, a voice quavering between a panoramic faith in the hemisphere and a representational poetry of universal political commitment.

While the ruin allegorized Neruda's Marxist conception of hemispheric history, the poem's publication history and fragmentary circulation record also bears out the ruined promise of hemispheric communism, continuing the narrative of his lost relations with US leftist poets that I began in Chapter 1. The first Mexico edition of *Canto general*, published soon after Neruda's exile to Mexico in 1950 (with murals by Diego Rivera and David Alfaro Siqueiros adorning the boards), was supported by a large subscription list acknowledging over three hundred individuals and institutions from fourteen American nations and eight European ones. Reading the extensive list of US subscribers, one is struck by how comparatively few notable names appear, aside from a few committed editors of US communist publications and Latin Americans living in the United States. Frank apologized to Neruda in a letter for failing to subscribe, so we know that many must have received the invitation. One might wonder, for example, at the absence of writers contemporaneously popularizing Neruda in *Masses and Mainstream* and *Tiger's Eye*, or else other communist writers in touch with Neruda's network, like George Oppen and Walter Lowenfels. In fact, both these poets have shadow relations to *Canto general* defined by their ruinous experience of the Cold War.

Oppen was thrown into his own exile to Mexico in 1950. Together with his wife Mary and daughter Linda, he arrived in July, within a few weeks of Neruda, having fled from Redondo Beach, California, under the threat of prosecution under the anticommunist Smith Act. Nothing suggests that Oppen and Neruda met, and Oppen's decade in Mexico is famous primarily for its reticence.[75] Their failure to meet is surprising, because they shared friends in Siqueiros and in the illustrator José Venturelli, both also in Mexico City at the time, and both collaborators on Neruda's books. The Oppens were neighbors with Venturelli's brother-in-law Rafael in Redondo Beach, and met Venturelli through Rafael immediately upon relocating.[76] When Venturelli exhibited his etchings, silkscreens, woodcuts, and watercolors in October, Oppen helped to mount the show.[77] In gratitude, Venturelli gave Oppen a picture of a puma from a collection of thirty illustrations made in 1946 for a deluxe Losada edition of *Alturas* that never came to fruition.[78] The rest of those illustrations remain a set, but one lost fragment of *Alturas* landed in Oppen's Mexico City home, touching a poet whose sense of ruin was so strong he had temporarily abandoned writing altogether.[79]

Consider one further example of communist disparaction in the poetry of the Cold War Americas. In poems such as "Que despierte el leñador," Neruda critiqued naive US government support of oligarchical Latin American dictators willing to toe the Cold War line of anticommunist allegiance, but US poets found they were constrained from publishing or expressing support for Neruda's positions. Avant-garde poet and communist Walter Lowenfels was, like Waldo Frank, unable to attend Neruda's July 12, 1954, fiftieth-birthday celebration in Chile, owing to what he wryly described as "a previous commitment in the United States District Court of Eastern Pennsylvania, together with eight co-defendants, for 'subversive thoughts.'" While in the courtroom standing trial for conspiracy under the Smith Act, he composed "Voyage to Chile," an imitative reply to "Que despierte el leñador," to "send to Chile in [his] place." One exemplary excerpt reads:

> Wait, wait, Pablo Neruda, tell the people of the Orinoco
> I am with you
> tell the workers of Brazil my prison is the heartbeat of your song
> Tell the gauchos of the Pampas
> I am the freedom of your dreams. Whisper to the Negroes
> of the Deltas
> the ghettos of Chicago will not last a thousand years.[80]

Lowenfels's poem, in its stuttering attempts to express hemispheric solidarity, in its final call for the ruin of Chicago poverty (one of Octavio Paz's images of North American industrial ruin), and in the poem's very repression by a Cold War legal regime, suggests how far the hemispheric democracy campaigns of World War II had fallen into ruin, and how deeply Neruda's poems sought an idiom of imaginative rectification.

Repossessed Dynamics: Olson and Barlow among Stones

Guy Davenport once observed that after World War II, Neruda's *Alturas* proved "that there was life and a new relevance in a genre which had been a standard feature of the Victorian sensibility," and he named this genre the "meditation on ruins," a "poetic form worked to death between the late eighteenth and mid-nineteenth centuries."[81] According to Davenport, Neruda directly influenced another hallmark postwar ruin poem, Charles Olson's "The Kingfishers" (1949), although ensuing squabbles over influence have inhibited more extensive studies of the ruin poem's generic significance to postwar hemispheric literary history.[82] One exception is Brotherston, who places both poets in a broad tradition of the "great song" of the Americas, the epic poem of moral identification with hemispheric geography.[83] More precisely, the genre Davenport describes as Olson's "meditation on ruins" names the same discourse Jill Kunheim calls Neruda's "postmodern *indigenismo*."[84] For Kunheim, "postmodern" signifies the aesthetic regime that Frederic Jameson links to emerging cultural logics of late capitalism, but Olson's poetic archaeology of the Maya led him to gloss the term himself in 1951: "any POSTMODERN is born with the ancient confidence that he does belong."

The collapse of hemispheric solidarity furnishes the structure of feeling that links the postmodern indigenism of the Chilean Neruda as he ascended the Peruvian Sierra en route from his consular position in Mexico to Santiago and the ruin meditations of the American Olson, whose disaffections five years after his release from wartime state employ led him to descend to the limestone lowlands of the Yucatán. Transnational literary history itself stands to learn from Neruda's and Olson's strategies of poetic retrieval, "unearthing" a shared project of regrounding the creative potential of poetic voice in pre-conquest space. Just as Neruda imagined a postnational Latin American poetic culture in the even broader panorama of the hemisphere, US poets saw ruins as cultural challenges to the confining authority of state formations. In 1951, Olson wrote from Campeche: "I keep thinking it comes to this: culture displacing the state."[85]

Resituating Olson in this field of hemispheric resemblances requires a denaturing of a career narrative strictly linked to national accounts of postwar US poetry. A 6'8" scholar-poet born in Gloucester, Massachusetts, in 1910, Olson towered over the postwar scene as the tutelary spirit and elder statesman of Donald Allen's anthology *The New American Poetry* (1960). By the time he began writing poetry in the late 1940s, already into his middle age, he had accrued an eclectic biography linked to national literary projects: he was among the first American Studies graduate students at Harvard under the tutelage of F. O. Matthiessen; he held a Guggenheim fellowship for his contributions to Melville scholarship, culminating in the publication of *Call Me Ishmael* (1947); he served in low-level posts at the ACLU, the OWI, and the Roosevelt administration; and from 1951 to 1956, he was the terminal rector of Black Mountain College. When Allen enshrined him in *The New American Poetry* based in part on his influential articulation of an action poetics in the 1950 manifesto "Projective Verse," he had spent two decades swinging from the center to the fringes of national literary culture.

Certifications of this national narrative sideline the hemispheric drift of Olson's cultural geography and its complex dialogues with the human sciences. Putting this drift at the center of his work leads us to what Olson called his "field-trip," in January of 1951, to Lerma, Campeche, on the Yucatán peninsula, where he worked for more than six months as a boastful, self-taught epigrapher of Mayan glyphs. Some critics belittle this "murky" archaeological research, but in the Yucatán Olson actualized the "on-site investigation" he deemed necessary to furthering his immersions in historical geography. [86] James Clifford's description of ethnographic surrealism helpfully describes the epistemological shift that Olson also sought: "a crucial modern orientation toward cultural order" viewed as "a situation in which ethnography is again something unfamiliar and surrealism not yet a bounded province of modern art and literature."[87] Midcentury Mayan Mexico was an unfamiliar cultural margin conducive to Olson's still-unbounded poetic program.

Olson's main achievement in this respect is *Mayan Letters*, an experimental epistolary volume edited and published by Robert Creeley for Divers Press in January 1954 (Figure 3.5). *Mayan Letters* inherits the traditions of modernist mixed-genre and prosimetrical books like Williams's *Spring and All* (1923) and

Fig 3.5 Charles Olson, *Mayan Letters* (Mallorca: Divers Press, 1954). © The Estate of Charles Olson. Used with permission.

In the American Grain (1925), romances of Mexican antiquity such as those of
D. H. Lawrence and Katherine Anne Porter (who Olson read assiduously), and
intercultural theories of poetic writing like Pound's edition of Ernest Fenollosa's
The Chinese Written Character as a Medium for Poetry (1918). It mingles short
Maya-themed lyrics with aphoristic prose meditations on other writers, ethnographic observations, archaeological enigmas, and a theory of glyphic writing
as an alternative to logocentric discourse. The title holds these issues together in
a pun, indicating the epistolary genre while analogizing experimental writing
to Mayan glyphs. If Ed Dorn once read Olson "from Gloucester out,"[88] *Mayan
Letters* makes it possible to read from Campeche *in*, adjoining the letters to
poems like "The Kingfishers" and "To Gerhardt, There, Among Europe's Things
of Which He Has Written Us in His 'Brief an Creeley und Olson,'" to a grant
proposal for further study entitled "The Art of the Language of Mayan Glyphs,"
and to the essay "Human Universe" (1951). By 1952, this matrix of texts led Olson
to declare an epithet for his vocation, not strictly as a "poet or writer," but as an
"archaeologist of morning": an excavator of New World origins.[89]

Olson's pre-Columbian interests partly derived from Black Mountain anthropologist Paul Radin and the Berkeley cultural geographer Carl Sauer, who made
him aware of the anthropologist-poet Robert Barlow.[90] Barlow had modeled the
kind of work Olson intended to conduct in Mexico, and so it was particularly
painful that Olson found himself abruptly eulogizing him in a letter to Creeley
soon after arriving in Mérida in January of 1951:

> the news hit me the 1st night Merida:
>
> that Barlow, my boy Barlow, the finest
> Americanist of them all (I'm sure I must have sounded off to you abt
> him—put out mag called Tlallocan [sic] all by himself, & mostly in
> Nahuatl—wrote fair verse—was the best (the sort of thing, Parkman
> almost, given the necessary difference of 100 yrs)
>
> a month ago, he told his boys (Indians, he lived at 34 alone
> Atzacopozatcalco) to go away for the night, wrote them a letter (in Mayan
> I am told) and took a full bottle of the pills which sleep
>
> dead/Barlow dead/ the goddamndest loss to the necessary
> knowledge of precisely these parts & peoples, precisely such things & fixes
> you and I know are of value

Barlow, a professor of anthropology at Mexico City College, committed suicide
on New Year's Day by overdosing on Seconal, supposedly fearing that a student
was preparing to out his homosexuality. According to Hart, a note in Mayan

was found pinned to his door that read "Do not disturb me, I want to sleep a long time."

The suicide abbreviated a polymath and precocious career, beginning when Barlow wrote to H. P. Lovecraft about his love of weird fiction at the age of thirteen. Lovecraft became a friend and, upon his death, appointed the nineteen-year-old Barlow his literary executor. Barlow apprenticed briefly to the painter Thomas Hart Benton, then fell in with the Activist group of poets spearheaded by the provocateur Lawrence Hart in San Francisco during World War II. *Poems for a Competition* (1942), Barlow's first poems written in the surrealistic free verse of the Activists, won a Bay Area literary prize. At Berkeley, Barlow also discovered a talent for anthropology and studied Nahuatl. He moved permanently to Mexico in 1943, where he published only one more small chapbook of poems entitled *View from a Hill* (1947), but worked closely with Nahuatl and Mayan communities to compile several hundred anthropological pamphlets, including glossaries of Mayan glyphic writing and guides to Nahuatl; collected Nahuatl songs and stories; and, from 1943 until his death, *Tlalocan*, a journal of "source material—chiefly manuscripts—having a definite bearing on the aboriginal cultures of Mexico."[91] Hart suggests that Barlow ultimately "carried on a surprising career as a sort of minor culture hero among the Nahuatl Indians of that region."[92] Olson's regard for Barlow as an "Americanist" points to the way in which both scholar-poets understood the nascent American Studies as a hemispheric project.

Hart claims that Barlow's indigenous attentions account for his poetic originality: "the whole impedimenta of the archeology of the Mexican Indians is brought into his work in such a way as to give it a romantic flavor which was almost as strong in esthetic quality as the poetry itself." But the relation of Barlow's verse to indigeneity is not casually romantic. In high modernist form, Barlow limns disjunctures between technomodern and mythic understandings of the Americas. The poem entitled "Of the Names of the Zapotec Kings" ironically resigns itself to the standpoint of techno-modernity: "Ah, Zapotecs and Dominicans, how could they have endured life/Before the automat?"[93] The prose poem "The Gods in the Patio" treats Mexico City's Museo Nacional de Arqueología, Historia y Etnografía as a site that heightens this disjuncture. There the "impedimenta of the archeology of the Mexican Indians" are displayed like Eliot's etherized patient: "Fifty bones of a murdered world are on view today at eleven. Guests will please smuggle cameras and check their tips." In the elegy "For Leon Trotzky and Huitzilopochtli," he blends the hero of the Fourth International and the Fourth World's Aztec God of War:

Was death square then, or did it have blue fronds?

Were the preliminary feathers and flutes preferable to a hatchet?

Where the idol lies sealed in a pod of mud, where the delivery trucks go
  over it,

*Aquí, a las 17 horas se rindió homenaje póstumo a León Trotzky. El velorio
en el mismo lugar esta noche.*

Barlow assigns a Joycean mythical parallelism to Trotsky's assassination and Aztec
ritual sacrifice, but portrays modern transportation occluding memory of sacrificial ritual, "sealed in a pod of mud, where the delivery trucks go over it." Italicized
newspaper copy further deflates the poet's prospect of ritual captivation. Barlow
uses these modernist resources to heighten the reader's perception of economic
development's obliteration of indigenous knowledge. Elsewhere, Barlow's poetry
exhibits nostalgia for romantic revitalization of pre-Columbian perspectives. The
imagistic "Nostalgia," which Barlow marked "*(to be translated into Nahuatl)*," and
his late, unpublished poems written in Spanish at Chichén Itzá play out the desire
that Brotherston calls translating "into the language of America."[94] His poems stage
transculturation in reverse, pointing into and toward American language traditions.

Olson's interest in Barlow was not in his "fair verse" so much as *Tlalocan* and his
glossaries of Mayan glyphs, for the epigraphic enigma of the Maya fueled Olson's
work. In 1951 only the calendrical frame of the glyphic system had been deciphered,
one-third of the extant record of writing. Yuri Knorozov's groundbreaking article
on Mayan phonetics, which led to decipherment over the next twenty years, was
published in Russia in 1952, after Olson returned to the United States.[95] Olson dili-
gently assumed the office of amateur epigrapher and archeologist. His studies of
Mayan writing belong to a predisciplinary moment in which the human sciences
and literary aesthetics cross-fertilized. In late March 1951, for example, Olson wrote
Creeley from Lerma to boast that his poetic interpretation of Mayan culture was
more significant than the whole of archeological inquiry following the 1839 "rediscovery" of Mayan ruins by John Lloyd Stevens and Frederick Catherwood:[96]

These Maya are worth remembering because they were hot for the world
they lived in & hot to get it down by way of a language which is loaded to
the gills of the FIRST GLYPH with that kind of imagination which the ker-
ekters have a way of calling creative yet I have yet to find *one* man among all
who have worked this street in the last century who is, himself, confident of
his taste, is even possessed of that kind of taste, or drive towards a hot world
which is called creative power.[97]

These overheated, hard-bop prose rhythms are intrinsic facets of his Mayan interpretive strategy. He believes that advancement in Mayan epigraphy requires "taste," a word he associates with "creative power," "imagination," and "hot" language.[98] Taste signals poetic judgment and romantic vigor, not the "cold" language of scientific analysis. To Olson, poetic knowledge has more vital purchase on the interpretation of Mayan antiquity than nascent methods in anthropology, cultural geography, and archaeology, because the human sciences fail to note the plastic character of Mayan writing and its central role in the synthetic organization of civic life.

Olson had previously linked romantic, visionary "taste" to Mayan inquiry at the conclusion of his key poem "The Kingfishers":

> I am no Greek, hath not th'advantage.
> And of course, no Roman:
> he can take no risk that matters,
> the risk of beauty least of all.
>
> But I have my kin, if for no other reason than
> (as he said, next of kin) I commit myself, and,
> given my freedom, I'd be a cad
> if I didn't. Which is most true.
>
> It works out this way, despite the disadvantage.
> I offer, in explanation, a quote:
> si j'ai du goût, ce n'est guères
> que pour la terre et les pierres
>
> Despite the discrepancy (an ocean courage age)
> this is also true: if I have any taste
> it is only because I have interested myself
> in what was slain in the sun
>
> I pose you your question:
>
> shall you uncover honey / where maggots are?
>
> I hunt among stones[99]

These stanzas grandiosely reject European cultural traditions. In the phrase "I am no Greek, hath not th'advantage," the rejection borrows stylistically from Ezra Pound, even as Olson quarrels with him in the same mood as William Carlos Williams, who wrote in *Spring and All*, "If I could say what is in my mind in

Sanscrit or even Latin I would do so. But I cannot."[100] Further, Olson's New World alternative repurposes a quote from Rimbaud's poem "Fêtes de la faim" (Feasts of Hunger), namely "Si j'ai du goût, ce n'est guère/que pour la terre et les pierres" (if I have any taste, it is only for earth and stones), as a credo of postwar Mayan studies. Olson's partial translation attends to a poetic economy of ritual sacrifice: "if I have any taste/it is only because I have interested myself/in what was slain in the sun." Rimbaud's "taste for the earth" translates into Olson's search to refound knowledge in direct observation of hemispheric geography, following cultural geographer Carl Sauer. Apostrophizing the Pound of *The Pisan Cantos*, who wrote elegiacally of Mussolini "that maggots shd/eat the dead bullock," Olson pointedly blends popular front antifascism and Cold War ruin discourse to revise Pound: "I pose you your question: shall you uncover honey/where maggots are?/I hunt among stones." Fortified with Rimbaudian vision and Poundian belief in the facticity of language, the poet abandons them for the New World.

"The Kingfishers" stages these swerves to the cultural priorities of the Americas as a rapid series of cultivated allusions and distracted juxtapositions obstructing the poem's legibility as a hypotactic statement. In fact, it thematizes a history of endlessly shifting human attentions in terms of overgrown Mayan cities. "When the attentions shift," Olson writes, "the jungle/leaps in."[101] Discussing Olson's tenure at Black Mountain, Martin Duberman locates his distractibility in an obstreperous classroom method, a "grandiloquent [. . .] parading of cross-cultural references" that exaggerates a "hot language" of excitement toward cultural materials for his students and readers.[102] Where it frustrates, it pushes these acolytes past the poetic page to investigate the source materials the poem organizes. "A Bibliography on America for Ed Dorn" lays out Olson's pedagogical premises of saturation and excavation: "to dig one thing or place or man until you yourself know more abt that than is possible to any other man." The hipster idiom "to dig" gains methodological resonance in the context of Olson's archaeological poetics.

Olson's paratactic "hot language" emphasizes an excitable kinesthesia linked to the poetics of ruins and glyphs. One of his letters to Creeley from Lerma begins with the hurried neologism "christamiexcited," as if making an orthographic identification between his poetics of excitement and the cultural body of "Mexico," here identified by a near homophone.[103] Olson's own orthographic eccentricity physicalizes poetry's drama of investigation. He imagines orthographic proximity to Mayan writing as a scandal to middle-class US reading values: "Our fellow cits are, I take it, quite easily thrown off by any noun which contains Z's and X's."[104] The US citizenry's bourgeois reading norms recapitulate the violent colonial alphabetization of indigenous language. Aiming to reverse that transcultural flow, he reinscribes the textures of his poetry with taunts to standardization, or "the internationalizing of language" he associates with a "worship of IARichards."[105] From "christamiexcited," he continued on to the observation that "my nerves are so bunched toward these ruins." The possibility of an alternative humanistic disposition relies on physical proximity and site-specific investigation.

Signs of how modernization jeopardized indigenous communities and archeological sites scarred the Yucatecan landscape. On a stroll with his wife Connie, Olson chances on a "hill where the sea's winds reach, where the overlook is so fine, these Maya had once built what appears to have been a little city," but he qualifies: "I say appears, for now, after six years of the Sanchez Construction Co. crushing the stones of that city, we were able to see only one piece of one column of what (the Indian workers told us) was once, six years ago, many many such columns in place."[106] Similarly, Mayan men find their livelihood in grinding a dispossessed cultural heritage into bags of white cement. He faults the archaeologists of the "Peabody-Carnegie gang," who laughed him off when he proposed "a total reconnaissance of all sites" on the peninsula, for Olson believed that only the total geographical distribution of archeological remains could underlie a morphology of Mayan cultural life, or "these ignored, or smiled at, spots where, 1500 years ago, for, o, say, 500 years, a people went about human business."[107] Olson hardly fetishized pre-contact cultures, interesting himself in the "perdurables" of the "living Maya speech" and Mayan appropriations of global commerce, so that "coca-cola tops are the boys' tiddley-winks . . . [and] old tires are the base foot-wear of this whole peninsula (the modern Maya sandal is, rope plus Goodyear)."[108] Here, Olson vexatiously acknowledges the Maya's "coevality" with himself, in the term of anthropologist Johannes Fabian.[109] Cold War modernization—then known in Europe as "Coca-Colonization"—rendered that coevality unmistakable.[110]

Olson's alternative is a "reading" of Mayan sites. In "The Art of the Language of Mayan Glyphs," his grant proposal to the Viking Fund, he claims: "For the sites are more to me than ruins to be visited or excavated or reconstructed: they are quite literally 'libraries' and 'museums.'"[111] Disparaging the romantic ruinology of landscape tourism and scientific archaeology, he offers to recover the entextualized experience of Mayan architecture. The phonetic content of Mayan glyphs was not yet widely recognized, and Olson perspicaciously argued that glyphs encode phonetic content available in living Maya speech. Immersed in epigraphic scholarship, he promises a program for advancing decipherment by considering glyphs from the perspective of the plastic arts. Glyphs chiseled into

stone slabs or brush-painted into screen-fold books cannot be divorced from
the artistic processes of sculpture and painting. Olson's claim about "the double
nature of this unusual writing," which "is at once object in space (the glyph) and
motion on stone in time (the glyph blocks)," offers to assimilate Mayan writing
into a synthetic account of the plastic arts, consonant with other assimilationist
aesthetic theories from Horace to Fenollosa, who Olson read vigorously.[112]

The "plastic" examination of glyphs makes "text" its guiding object: "let this
language itself—not even any other hieroglyphic system—declare what, for itself,
are its own laws." To study Mayan writing is to study the architectural and cultural organization of the Mayan city, whose lintels, stelae, and stairways are the
physical archives of written language. The Mayan city organizes around its textuality. By these standards, Olson's insistence on the "resistance" and "solidity" of
the stones as live records of a people going about "human business" argues more
radically for the textual autonomy of the Maya than does Neruda's indigenist
appropriation of "piedra persistente." Olson's Mayan laborer is no "dead mouth,"
but a creative, protomodern avatar of New World culture. Olson appreciates
glyphs as "a graphic discipline of the highest order" that demonstrates Mayan
"exactness about all the solid things which nature offered them." For Creeley, he
translates this claim as a romantic theory of creativity in the language of hard-
bop prose: "these Maya are worth remembering because they were hot for the
world they lived in & hot to get it down."[113]

Here, Olson lays track for an aggressive, pre-Derridean polemic against logo-
centrism in the essay "Human Universe," which opens: "We have lived long in a
generalizing time, at least since 450 B.C." During that time, for Olson, "Logos,
or discourse [. . .] has [. . .] so worked its abstractions into our concept and use
of language that language's other function, speech, seems so in need of restoration that several of us go back to hieroglyphs or to ideograms to right the balance."[114] The forms of generalization and abstraction he finds damaging in the
Western narrative end in a midcentury quagmire of machine-age rapacity, where
"fun" and "spectatorism" crowd out work and participation "as the conditions
of culture." The glyph resolves the question: "Can one restate man in any way to
repossess him of his dynamic?" This restoration endows cultural livelihood with
engaged citizenship and artistic labor. Mayan chirographic exemplarity promises
to revitalize dissipated linguistic energies. Here it also bulwarks a tirade against
scholarly disciplines consigning the Maya to history:

> [The Maya] will be the subject of historians' studies or of tourists' curios-
> ity, and be let go at that, no matter how much they may disclose values

> he and his kind, you would think, could make use of. [. . .]. All that is
> done is what a Toynbee does, diminish the energy once here expended into
> the sieve phonetic words have become to be offered like one of nature's
> pastes that we call jewels to be hung as a decoration of knowledge upon
> some Christian and therefore eternal and holy neck. It is unbearable
> what knowledge of the past has been allowed to become, what function of
> human memory has been dribbled out.[115]

Olson hopes to forestall the domestication of Mayan culture into the global
order through the radical foreignization of writing. Glyphic writing promises
the poetic value of restoring material substance to words that are empty filters.
In glyphs, Olson sought new foundation for an illusory and dormant art of participatory citizenship.

Oddly, Olson directed much of his writing on the Maya to interlocutors in
Europe. Creeley was in Mallorca, while another of Olson's correspondents was
in Freiburg, namely Rainer Maria Gerhardt, a young poet-editor creating a lively
German reception for Poundian modernism. Gerhardt's little magazine, aptly
named *Fragmente*, fomented debates on European diasparaction in Olson and
Gerhardt's correspondence. "To Gerhardt, There, Among Europe's Things of
Which He Has Written Us in His 'Brief an Creeley und Olson'" is Olson's most sustained poem written in Mexico. While relishing dialogue with a foreign admirer,
he juxtaposes notions of cultural genesis in the tradition Antonello Gerbi called
"the dispute of the New World."[116] To this end, Olson indicts Gerhardt for dissi-
pating language in the manner of Toynbee, and too lightly inheriting Poundian
modernism's Eurocentric cultural historiography. Gerhardt's own poems facilely
transcribe hallmark modernist citations like Pound's "the Chinese written character" and Eliot's "my end is my beginning," and Olson and Creeley agreed they
were too full of "Pound tags." [117] Thus, Olson admonished the extraction of poetic
materials

> [. . .] from a time on the other side of yourself
> from which you have so lightly borrowed men, naming them as though,
> like your litany of Europe's places, you could take up
> their power: magic, my light-fingered faust,
> is not so easily sympathetic. Nor are the ladies
> worn so decoratively.[118]

Recalling the "Christian and therefore holy neck" bejeweled with the sieve of
phoneticism in "Human Universe," Gerhardt's wan discursiveness uses "words

as signs worn/like a toupee on the head of a Poe cast/in plaster."[119] By witheringly comparing Gerhardt's poetry to a hairpiece atop Poe—the first US poet to enter the French canon—he suggests that European modernism makes false improvements on the American Renaissance.

Olson, who once called Homer "that late European poet," often plays with poetic priority, and the image of the Poe bust suggests an entire disposition toward cultural priority that privileges archaeological imagination:

> Admitting that among the ruins
>> with a like schmerz in every vessel of his throat,
>> he repeated, "Among the ruins, among them
>> the finest memory in the Orient"
> one will go about picking up old pieces
>> bric-a-brac, he snorted, who did not know whereof he spoke,
>> he had so allowed himself to be removed, to back-trail
> or put it immediately out of the mind, as some can,
> stuff the construction hole quickly with a skyscraper[120]

The jarring, undermining parataxis between "one will go about picking up old pieces" and the following "bric-a-brac, he snorted" suggests an opposition between those who linger in ruin spaces contemplating the fractures of cultural memory, and those who see digging as the foundation for the phallic, vertical modernization of the skyscraper. Olson valorizes a poet-archaeologist-bricoleur, while opposing a phallic, rapacious developer. If modernism plugs the stratigraphy of historical consciousness, postmodernism digs in the ruins to reprioritize lost humanist perspectives. Seeing modernization's fallout throughout Mexico, Olson's poem imagines a mock-heroic alternative.

By July of 1951, funds depleted and grant proposals denied, Olson returned to his post as a writing instructor at Black Mountain College, where he hoped his faculty position would boost his application. By the time he was finally awarded the long-sought Wenner-Gren Foundation grant in late 1952, he had assumed Black Mountain's rectorship, the institutional affiliation that, ironically, was the key to his award, and a string of personal and economic troubles made a return to Mexico untenable. A symbolic gavel was pounded against his projected return to Mexico when a Treasury Department representative pursued Olson's failure to submit a tax return on the grant money in early 1954.[121] Creeley published *Mayan Letters* in Mallorca that same month, just as an unhappy, unsuccessful young poet named Allen Ginsberg arrived in the Yucatán on his way to San Francisco.

Mechano Hells and Mayan Isms: Ginsberg, Lamantia, Cardenal

Neruda's myth of representational speech and the "ancient confidence" of Olson's projectivism both draw breath from pre-Columbian ruins, but a third, still more influential articulation of the performance standards for midcentury poetry emerged partly from like circumstances: the "spontaneous bop prosody" Allen Ginsberg made famous with "Howl." In this section, I'll argue that Ginsberg generates the core proposition of "Howl" in the two-part sequence "Siesta in Xbalba and Return to the States" in early 1954, a poem Ginsberg described to John Hollander as a "Byronic meditation on ruins."[122] Such a demonstration will require some toggling between "Siesta in Xbalba" and "Howl," revealing how key ideologemes of midcentury ruin poetry inflect the latter poem. I'll then show how ruin poems by Philip Lamantia and Ernesto Cardenal also emerged from the same set of concerns, in a complex network of relations with Ginsberg, Neruda, and others.

Like Neruda's ascent to Machu Picchu, the popular literary history around the composition of "Howl" has an overfamiliar quality. "Howl," it is agreed, exploded into public consciousness during Ginsberg's performance at the October 7, 1955, Six Gallery reading in San Francisco. Its social origins reside in the disaffections of postwar middle-class youth, the pathologization of homosexuality as deviance, and Cold War anticommunism, felt throughout *Howl and Other Poems* as sentimentality for the Old Left.[123] Yet *Howl*'s retrospective description of these damages frontloads a cosmological yearning that also puts it in dialogue with the discourse of ruin poems: "I saw the best minds of my generation destroyed by madness, starving hysterical naked,/dragging themselves through the negro streets at dawn looking for an angry fix,/angelheaded hipsters burning for the ancient heavenly connection to the starry dynamo in the machinery of night."[124] Ginsberg called the poem's anaphoric repetition of the word "who" its "fixed base," enabling a breathless catalogue of subcultures. This formal architecture builds on psalmody, overloaded with imagist generational portraits that compound the feeling of a moment lived promiscuously and disastrously.

Critics build accounts of the poem's protest against the repressive world of the Eisenhower-era United States on little more than intuitive glosses of the poem's title.[125] But interpretations of "howling" have had remarkable variance. The Whitmanian "yawp" is a common touchstone, but for William Carlos Williams, who introduced the first edition, Ginsberg's "howl of defeat" registered the

abjection of a queer, melancholic Jew.[126] Kenneth Rexroth and Olson each beati-
fied Ginsberg as a minor prophet, Rexroth associating the howl with the tradition of "Hosea or the other, angry Minor Prophets of the Bible,"[127] while Olson
described a fiery chiasmus ("Flame was his tongue and his tongue was flame")
that linked to the political outsiderism of the Adullamites:

> Howl, howl, howl, howl! O, you are men of stone:
> Had I your tongues and yes, I'd use them so
> That heaven's vault should crack.[128]

Only the poem's detractors shaped its express meaning as a defiant howl against
Cold War social repression. For Richard Eberhart, Ginsberg made a miscalculated
attempt to raise his voice on the loud factory floor of modernity: "a howl against
everything in our mechanistic civilization which kills the spirit, assuming that
the louder you shout the more likely you are to be heard."[129] M. L. Rosenthal in
The Nation laments the poem's "sustained shrieks of frantic defiance," noting
"the danger that he will screech himself mute any moment now."[130] Hollander,
despite his hatred of the poem, at least noticed the title's ambiguities and allusions. Remarking "on the utter lack of decorum of any kind in his dreadful little
volume," he summoned Ginsberg's self-conscious use of Whitman's line: "What
living and buried speech is always vibrating here, what howls restrain'd by decorum?"[131] Hollander believed "that the title of his long poem "Howl," is meant to
be a noun, but I can't help taking it as an imperative," disparaging Ginsberg as
something like the protagonist of Camus's *L'étranger*, who, in Stuart Gilbert's
1946 translation, would be greeted with "howls of execration."[132] Defenders like
Mark Schorer valued the poem's mood of "diatribe or indictment," while detractors disparaged a frantic shriek of misplaced rebellion.[133]

For all of this commentary, no one seems to make philological inquiries as to
how the word emerged in Ginsberg's body of writing. For example, early readers of
"Howl" did not know the semantic matrix of associations Ginsberg loaded onto the
word in his journals and notebooks. It begins to accrue stable meaning in December
1953, at the outset of Ginsberg's six-month sojourn to Cuba and Mexico.[134] There,
howling connotes exotic outpourings of ritualized foreign speech. In the louche
prerevolutionary Cuba of "Havana: 1953," Ginsberg observes a cafe rumba scene:

> white men and women
>   with standing drums,
>   mariachis, voices, guitars—
>   drumming on tables,

knives on bottles,
    banging on the floor
        and on each other,
with wooden clacks,
        whistling, howling[135]

This poem is among the first in which Ginsberg employs Williams's laddered lines, so perhaps it is fitting that he also follows Williams in making "rumba" his topic. Ginsberg affiliates "howling" with Caribbean sonic motifs, not unlike Williams's diagnosis of a wartime death drive in the presemantic textures of jitanjáforas.

A week later, during a fitful night of reveries in a hammock atop the castle at Chichén Itzá on New Year's Day, 1954, Ginsberg penned a journal entry entitled "Chichén Itzá Soliloquy," in which he changes out the rumberos for a visionary scene of a pre-Columbian polity:

> Everywhere in this dead city the clap of hands reechoes from half dozen temples laid out at acoustical angles made for jazz and poetry and religion: the projection of a voice of stone, the echo of eternity—so that some man in plumes and frenzied calm stood up on monuments that echoed to each other in front of a silent mob and suddenly started to yell his head off in a dancebeat scream—toward what end other than howls of joy that answered him I dont know[136]

Now "howls" are the Mayan polity's enraptured answers to a priest-poet in a city engineered for "jazz and poetry." By 1955, scenes of poetic call-and-response were familiar to the attendees of San Francisco and New York poetry readings, but collocations of midcentury "jazz poetry" with fantasized pre-Columbian scenes also circulated in early-1950s popular culture. Les Baxter's exotica star Yma Sumac, the five-octave Peruvian singer of the 1951 album *Voice of the Xtabay* (flaunting Olson's scandalous letter *x*), howled and warbled at Machu Picchu in *The Secret of the Incas* (1954). Ginsberg stands in contrast to Neruda's "La lámpara en la tierra," which links an Aztecan priestly "howl" to ritual sacrifice: "En un trueno como un aullido/caía la sangre por/las escalinatas sagradas" (In a thunder clap like a howl/the blood fell/down the sacred steps). By contrast, Ginsberg's sense of priestly *howling* sanctified a kind of civics in the rhythms of a primordial bebop.

By itself, the link between pre-Columbian ruin sites and Ginsberg's use of the term "howl" is enough to renew attention to his six months in Yucatán,

Campeche, and Chiapas in early 1954, the trip to which I'll now turn. But such attention pays dividends beyond the reinflection of a single word, helping to make sense of several aspects of the architecture of "Howl."

Inspirations for Ginsberg's trip to Mexico were eclectic. Early in 1953, he corresponded extensively with Burroughs, whose hallucinogenic misadventures hunting for yagé in Colombia, Ecuador, and Peru later led them to compile an epistolary narrative, "In Search of Yage," published as *The Yage Letters* (1963).[137] Burroughs (who once studied briefly with Barlow in Mexico) spurred Ginsberg south, as did the conclusion of his brief employment at a New York literary agency. Possibly, too, that agency tacitly awakened his desire for transnational tramping through their representation of B. Traven, the reclusive German writer of Mexican adventure narratives such as *The Treasure of the Sierra Madre* and indigenous labor fictions of Chiapas such as *The Rebellion of the Hanged*.

Ginsberg flew from Havana to Mérida with three hundred dollars to his name, as well as the address of an archaeologist given to him by the Museum of Natural History in New York, who granted him a pass to "stay on archeologist's camps, free, everywhere there's a ruin I go."[138] Thus Ginsberg enjoyed free access to ruin sites, the golden ticket to shoestring travel, on an itinerary he painstakingly distinguished from that of the "touristas [*sic*]" whose company he enjoyed at the kitschy Mayaland Hotel at the foot of the Chichén Itzá castle. Had he arrived two weeks earlier, he might have met the young anthropologist Nathaniel Tarn, who stopped at Chichén Itzá en route home from fieldwork in Guatemala.[139] Instead, Ginsberg spent his time alone at Chichén Itzá and Uxmal, mounting his hammock in the elevated cradles of ruins: "in high room in Uxmal alone." He recorded dreams and hard-boiled conceits for noir films in his notebook, took copious photographs, and wrote letters and journalistic travelogues to Jack Kerouac, Neal Cassady, and Lucien Carr. He soon pieced together a poetic sequence from the journals: "Havana: 1953," "My Green Valentine," and "Siesta in Xbalba and Return to the States."

Ginsberg's detours correspond to an intensified era for Mayan archaeology, led by the "Peabody-Carnegie gang" that Olson denounced, but also by Alberto Ruz Lhuillier's stewardship of INAH (Mexico's National Institute of Archaeological History), which led to the 1952 discovery of Pakal's tomb at Palenque.[140] The scaffolding of Ruz's team can be observed in Ginsberg's photographs from Palenque, where he lent an unknown photographer his camera to snap a photo of him staring out in solitude at unexcavated mounds (Figure 3.6). Impressed by the acoustics of Mayan cities, Ginsberg walked about such sites clapping his hands and listening for echoes, describing the best-known archaeological features of the

Fig 3.6 Photograph of Allen Ginsberg at Palenque, Chiapas, Mexico. Spring 1954. Courtesy of the Allen Ginsberg Papers at Stanford University, used by permission of The Wylie Agency LLC.

"ruined skin of stones" in clipped notes, and wandering up the intense pitch of the pyramids "always a little afraid of these steep stairs." Tourism did not seem to him a repellent strategy for Mexican statecraft: "Reconstructing the whole of this city Uxmal, they'd have a tourist attraction so vast & magical it would put their economy on a working basis." Despite Ginsberg's valorization of spontaneity, his poem "Siesta in Xbalba," carefully rebuilt from his notebooks, was also a model of painstaking reconstruction, much like Ruz's archaeology.

In Palenque, Ginsberg met Karena Shields, an archaeologist who he believed had played Jane in the Tarzan films of the 1930s (in fact she appears only to have voiced Jane for radio programs). In his "monthlong guesthood" on Shields' cocoa finca, Ginsberg delved into deeper study of Mayan societies ancient and contemporary. He also engaged in private moments of sylvan eroticism, leaning "against a tree inside the forest expiring of selfbegotten love," and finding a heart-shaped leaf around which he composed the Rodgers-and-Hart-style blues poem "My Green Valentine."[141] This same leaf emblematizes sexual frustration in "Siesta in Xbalba," where Ginsberg asks "but to whom shall I send this/anachronistic valentine?"[142] In letters to Carr and Cassady, Ginsberg carried on an extensive, unpublished scientific adventure travelogue, acting out Travenesque, resource-extractive fantasies that recall interwar mobile transnational labor networks.

After working Shields's finca, he schemes to Lucien Carr about starting his own farm on the model of Truman's "Point 4" (or "fair deal") development programs.[143] In correspondence with Burroughs, the "Point 4 man" is a common postwar sight. Ginsberg later imagines himself as a dealer in antiquities, as in this scene from "Siesta in Xbalba":

> And had I mules and money I could find
>> the Cave of Amber
> and the Cave of Gold
>> rumored of the cliffs of Tumbala[144]

Here, Ginsberg evokes the luckless, Tampico-stranded Humphrey Bogart in Huston's *Treasure of the Sierra Madre,* or the kind of interwar transnational laborer Crane experienced as a mesmeric Ancient Mariner in the poem "Cutty Sark." While Ginsberg felt deep nostalgia for the lost cultures of the Old Left, he wrote as though webs of radical transnational laborers were unbroken networks in which he could participate through Mexican tramping. Later, tracing these networks back to the Bay Area in the "tincan banana dock" of "Sunflower Sutra," they appear as their own kinds of archaeological fragments, obsolete amid "rusty" piles of industrial ruin.[145]

Ginsberg weaves these labor narratives together with scientific-adventure reportage and, increasingly, a romantic adventurism he associates with Shelley's revolutionary legacy. One report recounts his expedition in the company of a group of Tzeltal Maya to discover a cache of relics in a limestone cave near Aguas de Salto, which area archaeologists had yet to survey.[146] In "Siesta in Xbalba," Ginsberg transfigures his observational report into the poem's mood of mock prophecy:

> I alone know the great crystal door
>> to the House of Night,
> a legend of centuries
>> —I and a few Indians.[147]

Here the mock prophecy is a bit cringeworthy, but it tests out a strategy that would underlie the bardic indictment of "Howl."

Defending "Siesta in Xbalba" to John Hollander in 1958, Ginsberg described his compositional practice as the purification of language he field-tests in his notebooks: "Xbalba is fragments of mostly prose, written in a Mexican school copybook, over half a year—then rereading, picking out the purest thoughts, stringing them together, arranging them in lines suitably balanced, mostly measured by the phrase, that is, one phrase a line [. . .]."[148] But Ginsberg located the poem's value elsewhere:

> the fact that Xbalba is "carefully made" is its most minor virtue—it's technically no improvement on Williams, except its application of free verse to Wordsworthian meditation long poem—Tintern Abbey type, or Byronic meditation on ruins. But the real technical advance is in the long line poems, they proceed inevitably and naturally from the earlier poems, it's just a sort of COMPOUND imagism—compounded cubist images, and compounded rhythmic long lines.[149]

In other words, the value of "Siesta in Xbalba" is its blend of neoromantic ruinology with a "COMPOUND imagism" that presages "Howl." Xbalba, a misspelling of Xibalba that Ginsberg elected not to fix in later editions, is a word for the Mayan underworld that furnishes the poem's controlling metaphor. He codes it geographically as an orphic underground to the shrill reality of the United States, which he increasingly associates with the impediment to his literary progress. "Oh I am damned to hell/what alarmclock is ringing" closes the New York dawn poem "My Alba," a title that rhymes with "Xbalba" not by accident. Contrasting New York's antipoetic, waking nightmare, Xbalba proceeds through "crude night imaginings" in which glyphic "entablatures of illegible scripture" prompt ecstatic verbal reveries elaborated through imagistic compounds. In "reconstructing" Williams's imagism from the standpoint of ruins, Ginsberg counted a stanza on a palm tree his biggest success: "Palms with lethargic feelers/rattling in presage of rain,/shifting their fronds/in the direction of the balmy wind,/monstrous animals sprayed up out of the ground/settling and unsettling."[150] Strikingly, Ginsberg recapitulates the same indecision Williams expressed in his Puerto Rico lecture toward a hemispherism of technical innovation and one of romantic origins.

These experiments with a longer line also mark the first time Ginsberg approaches his "chain of strong breath'd poems" that "Howl" later solidifies:

> and only the crude skull figurement's
>   gaunt insensible glare is left
> with broken plumes of sensation,
> headdresses of indecipherable intellect
>   scattered in the madness of oblivion
> to holes and notes of elemental stone,
> blind face of animal transcendency

> over the sacred ruin of the world
> dissolving into the sunless wall of a blackened room

These breathless lines overspill the imagism Ginsberg modeled on Williams, as if what Williams called the "old and alien soul" common to the Americas outran the clipped, technical phrasing of the imagist program. In the early 1980s, as the design of Ginsberg's *Collected Poems* came together out of the miniature installments that shaped his publication history in the City Lights Pocket Poets series, Ginsberg metaphorized his corpus as a global landscape, a "panorama of valleys and plateaus with peaks of inspiration every few years." "Siesta in Xbalba" preceded "Howl" in the range of "inspired" or strong-breathed peaks.[151]

Perhaps most importantly, "Siesta in Xbalba" also offers the first glimmer of the retrospective vision that frames Part I of "Howl." The seemingly innocuous "Howl" opening "I saw" arise nowhere in Ginsberg's early poetry except in "Xbalba," where it describes a color snapshot, a technological pictogram that parallels Mayan glyphs:

> Dreaming back I saw
> an eternal kodachrome
> souvenir of a gathering
> of souls at a party,
> crowded in an oval flash[152]

Mock prophecy works better here in the juxtaposition of eternity with the cheap "kodachrome/souvenir," and the metonymic spiritualization of partygoers as "souls." The poem goes on to name them "posturing in one frame," crowding into "Xbalba" as though into a "Howl" miniature:

> Anson reading Horace
> with a rolling head,
> white-handed Hohnsbean
> camping gravely
> with an absent glance,
> bald Kingsland drinking
> out of a huge glass,
> Dusty in a party dress,
> Durgin in white shoes
> gesturing from a chair,
> Keck in a corner waiting
> for subterranean music,

> Helen Parker lifting
>   her hands in surprise[153]

This is the first time Ginsberg versifies a collective portrait of the Beat "generation," bunching them into an alliterative retrospect. He does so by contrasting New York's "noise of a great party [. . .] the culture of my generation" to his Chiapas overlook:

> And I in a concrete room
>   above the abandoned
> labyrinth of Palenque
>   measuring my fate,
> wandering solitary in the wild
>   —blinking singleminded at a bleak idea—[154]

The temporal distance of Ginsberg's nostalgia for the postwar decade in "Howl" relies on this geographical distance—a view from Palenque's symbolic prospect. The first line of "Howl" encodes the snapshot imagined from the Palenque hammock, a correlate to Olson's "hunt among stones" and Neruda's "ladder of the earth." We cannot understand Ginsberg's elaborate nostalgia for his destroyed generation—a generation in ruins—without a thicker sense of Ginsberg's auratic nostalgia for Mayan Mexico.

Mexico has a scarce thematic presence in "Howl" itself, which passingly mentions those "who got busted in their pubic beards returning through Laredo with a belt of marijuana," those "who disappeared into the volcanoes of Mexico leaving behind nothing but the shadow of dungarees and the lava and ash of poetry scattered in fireplace Chicago," and those "who retired to Mexico to cultivate a habit."[155] The last alludes to Burroughs; the first two allude to the poet John Hoffman, a friend of Philip Lamantia who disappeared in Mexico and was presumed dead in 1952, leaving behind a small sheaf of metaphysical poems in Lamantia's care. Fittingly, Lamantia's recital of Hoffman's Yucatan seaside poems directly preceded Ginsberg's own famed performance at the Six Gallery in October 1955. Lamantia himself was the source of a single line in "Howl": "Who bared their brains to heaven under the El and saw Mohammedan angels staggering on tenement roofs illuminated."[156] The very destroyed lives scoring "Howl" here join, in a ruinous circuit, the first ecstatic experiences of hearing "Howl."[157] Critics regard Ginsberg's early work as uneven, but "Siesta in Xbalba" and "Havana: 1953" are his first major poems. Ginsberg himself maintained a high regard for "Siesta in Xbalba." Immediately following the publication of *Howl and*

Other Poems, Ginsberg printed it in its own mimeograph edition aboard a merchant ship off the coast of Alaska, republished it in full in *The Evergreen Review* in 1957, and included it in *Reality Sandwiches* (1963). Mayan Mexico awakened Ginsberg's nourishing identification with hemispheric space, a "nostalgia/for the classic stations/of the earth." If there was a "god/dying in America," ruins suggested "an inner/anterior image/of divinity/beckoning me out/to pilgrimage."[158]

Lamantia's first transits through Mexico beginning in 1954 echo Ginsberg's, and by 1963 Ginsberg reflected that "Philip Lamantia and I share old friendship and similarity of sources—our insight into an American *voice,* its *mechano hells* (his words)."[159] Lamantia's interest in Mexico was fueled in part by readings of Antonin Artaud's *Voyage to the Land of the Tarahumara* (1936) and by his early 1950s residence in the late Jaime d'Angulo's Berkeley home, where he had access to d'Angulo's anthropological library and where he began experimenting with peyote. Recalling this scene in an uncollected poem from the late 1950s, he wrote: "It was peyote! Peyote!/Jaime's pad, anthropological apocalypses/farout stone readings on glyphs/theAirswelling!"[160] In 1955 he visited the Cora and Nayeri Indians as an amateur ethnographer, filling his notebooks with lexicons and taking snapshots.[161] The poems recording these ethnographic interests were largely discarded, but then reassembled at the end of the 1950s as part of a typescript entitled "Destroyed Works," placing them in an allusive dialogue with Ginsberg's "destroyed" generation. At the same time, Lamantia subordinated his ethnography into several ruin poems that identify with the pre-Columbian contexts for Ginsberg's "Howl." In the second canto of "Howl," a ritual excoriation of "Moloch," Ginsberg offers a biblical figure for the overwhelming spiritual sacrifice demanded by North American industrial capitalism. "Moloch" gains a flexible status in Lamantia's own ruin poems, sometimes posited as an alternative to indigenous rituals and sometimes aligned with Aztecan sacrificial forms. "Poem for Indians" ends with the ritual incantation "I will teach you the path away from Moloch/hi a yi! hi ya ha! cotzil-i-man!"[162]

In the long Tenochtitlan poem "Ceylonese Tea Candor (Pyramid Scene)," Lamantia renders the links between Moloch and the ruin site explicit in a pyramidal visual poetics derived from a marijuana-fueled vision:

<blockquote>
north of
Mexico City
once called Ten
och tit lan built one
thousand AD by the Toltecs
</blockquote>

after destruction of Teotihuacan
city of the gods . and conquered by
witch/driven Aztecs, bloody blackmagic
nazi/moloch worshipping sun devils of old
mexico who took the remains of Toltec High
Religion and turned it into degenerate center of Hell's
cult of bloody hearts torn open for the pleasure of all the
demons of the seven circles of the seven thousand webs of the
seven million fallen angels of God's solar paradise
And I say to you all take care on this continent that the
Hordes shall not descend who have been prepared by
Fiends who for 6 centuries officiate their rites of
rapine child sacrifices and blackmagic murders from
these heights of stone
BEWARE AND LISTEN TO MY MESS-
AGE OH POORE MANKINDE ON
THIS CONTINENT OF THE PEO-
PLE OF THE HOLY PERSON LIS-
TEN AND PREPARE AND
CHANGE!!! CHANGE!!![163]

Lamantia first experimented with visual poetry in pyramidal and cross forms in *Ekstasis* (1959), combining a metaphysical devotional poetry with debts to George Herbert and an anthropological feeling derived from his trips to Mexico. Here, in his vision of Teotihuacan, the accretion of the double pyramid structure encodes multiple strata of pre-Columbian history, one that paradoxically degenerates into Aztec ritual sacrifice as the poem builds or assembles as a pyramid. The poem presents an impacted or stepped view of history, linking Aztec sacrifice to the biblical metaphor of capitalism that Ginsberg names Moloch, as well as to Nazi genocide. The ruin poem reveals twentieth-century forms of violent sacrifice as recapitulations of Aztec rites, and these revelations prelude a hemispheric ethic of care ("take care on this continent") that the poet prophesies in an apocalyptic mood.

Nicaraguan poet Ernesto Cardenal came to know Lamantia in Mexico in 1959 after leaving his studies at Thomas Merton's Trappist monastery, the Abbey of Gethsemani, near Bardstown, Kentucky. Cardenal translated "Ceylonese Tea Candor" among many other poems as he and José Coronel Urtecho prepared *Antología de la poesía norteamericana* (1963), an influential anthology notable for beginning with translations of Native American poems before surveying seventy-five modern American poets from Poe, Whitman, and Dickinson to Lamantia, Levertov, and Ashbery. Cardenal's poetic New World historicism of this period is the single most innovative and important response to the prevalent models of Pound and Williams, and he names his reinvention of their external-izing poetics "exteriorismo" in 1961. In *Homenaje a los indios americanos* (1969), a book-length celebration of the transnational indigenous Americas, Cardenal offers a capstone and a critique of midcentury ruin poems.

While *Homenaje* is unimaginable without the ruin poems of Neruda, Paz, Ginsberg, and Lamantia to build from, and without the poetic historicism of Pound and Williams, Cardenal's circumspect epistemological relation to ruins critiques the bardic, visionary inhabitations of the ruin poets who preceded him. In the Tikal poem "Las Ciudades Perdidas" (Lost Cities), howls do not emit from priests, but rather from jaguars and mountain lions inhabiting the abandoned Tikal, along with Pan American Airways planes overhead. Cardenal questions the reconstructive urge to write ruination into a new poetry: "¿Pero cómo escri-bir otra vez el jeroglífico [. . .]/Reconstruir otra vez nuestras acrópolis tropicales [. . .]?" (But how to write hieroglyphs again [. . .]/How to rebuild again our tropi-cal acropolises?).[164] Tikal's ruins, described in the densely repetitive sound tex-ture of "acrópolis tropicales," are intelligible not through decipherment but as a scene of didactic contrast to secular modernity. Cardenal privileges the Mayan penchant for building highways that answer needs for religious procession rather than commodity transport, and the Mayan cosmovision's disregard for linear temporality makes it conducive in Cardenal's reading to reawakening Tikal's value within modernity.

In the Poundian page layouts of the long poem "Mayapán," Cardenal comes to the strategies for poetic rewriting and reconstruction of the pre-Columbian ruin. He celebrates ruined cities as prototypes of Fourth World consciousness, which is itself a new avant-garde:

> Un artista oscuro en su estudio
> encorvado ensayando otras líneas
> otro estilo, *avant-garde*
> poetas con nuevos ismos
> ismos mayas
> creando
> otra etapa de civilización para el pueblo maya
>
> (An obscure artist in his studio
> hunched testing other lines

> another style, *avant garde*
> poets with new isms
> > Mayan isms
> creating
> > another stage of civilization for the Maya people)[165]

These experimental "ismos mayas" translate ceremonial and aesthetic functions into homophonic rebuttals to North American commercialism and industry. Surveys of Mayan stelae parody the language of real estate speculation. If
stelae are "artificial volcanos" to the Maya, Cardenal refigures them with the
epithet "rascacielos/sagrados" (sacred/skyscrapers), part of a "Building Boom"/
"Estela Boom" remaking "el skyline de Tikal" as one remakes the New Jersey
skyline. These anachronisms heighten the contradictions of modernity in sound
play. Cardenal contrasts "Commercial Centers" with "centros ceremoniales,
Ceremonial Centers," and neon advertisements with the "poemas en las piedras"
(poems in the stones) of Mayan architecture. Cardenal's ruinology sets itself
apart from the developing tradition of ruin meditations by offering a didactic
spiritualism encoded in sonic parallels and phonemic entanglements: a sound
poetry of ruins to complement Lamantia's visual poetry.

Hidden Doors: Ferlinghetti and Adán at Machu Picchu

Lamantia and Cardenal are not alone in testifying to a new inter-American ethos
organized by the reception of ruin poems in the late 1950s. In 1958, the Bay Area
Chilean scholar Fernando Alegría invited Ginsberg and Lawrence Ferlinghetti
to attend a leftist writers' congress in Concepción de Chile. Because of Alegría's
efforts, "Howl" was first translated in Chile in 1957. While in Chile, Ferlinghetti
began a lengthy imitation of Neruda's *Alturas* that he entitled "The Hidden
Door," which he completed en route home from the conference in February of
1960, when he stopped at Machu Picchu. "The Hidden Door" is structured as a
litany like "Howl," as are many of Ferlinghetti's poems. But it also moves along
on Nerudian expressions of labor solidarity for the "lost door of Lota coal mines"
and surrealist observations such as "Hidden door sea-angel cast-up Albatross/
spouting seasperm of love in thirty languages/and the love-ship of life," which
is surely a friendly parody of Neruda's wince-worthy epithets for Machu Picchu
such as "Madre de piedra, espuma de los cóndores."[166] When Ferlinghetti's

speaker summits the "Hidden door of the Andes at ten thousand feet/in a ragged mist of ruins and red horizons," a droll imagist stanza terminates the litany by depicting an Yma Sumac–inflected scene of exotica music in the ruined city, deflating the prophetic mood:

> It is dusk
> by the time we get to
> Machu Picchu
> Some Indians go by dancing
> playing their flutes
> and beating drums[167]

Published in *Starting from San Francisco* (1961) with a 7″ record of Ferlinghetti reading, the iconic image of Machu Picchu adorned the cover.

It is tempting to view "The Hidden Door" as a weak entry into the ruin poem genre, Beat posturing of the kind that led Ginsberg to call American Beats "rebels" in distinction from Latin American "revolutionaries," and which led Alegría to reflect that in Chile Ginsberg was regarded "as a melancholy, black-bearded Boy Scout in exile."[168] But Chileans received "The Hidden Door" as serious cultural diplomacy. Back in San Francisco, Alegría and Ferlinghetti discussed the Concepción conference on KPFA, and Ferlinghetti argued that his recital of "The Hidden Door," which was greeted by enormous applause, assuaged the anti-American sentiment that Cuban literary critic José Antonio Portuondo stirred up on behalf of a resolution in support of the Cuban government. Alegría specified:

> I was presiding at that meeting and I saw this old man getting up. The audience was taking part in the debate also and he said exactly what Ferlinghetti is saying now, and he added that he was not sympathetic to the United States but that after he heard the poem "Hidden Door" that Ferlinghetti wrote in Chile, and Ginsberg talking about American literature, he had changed his viewpoint. And he added that these two poets were the best ambassadors that the United States could send down to Chile.[169]

The State Department had tried to counteract the influence of the Beat writers by sending a commercial theater director and Cold Warrior named Stanley Richards along with them, and the Chileans had invited Archibald MacLeish, who could not attend. But the Beats, who were covered vigorously by the press throughout the week (Figures 3.9 and 3.10), were received much the same way that

Fig 3.7   Allen Ginsberg, Nicanor Parra, and Ernesto Sábato in Concepción de Chile. "Se inició encuentro de Escritores Americanos," *El Sur* (Jan. 19, 1960). Photographer unknown. Lawrence Ferlinghetti Papers, UCB.

Louis Armstrong and other Cold War cultural diplomats were received elsewhere in these years—as "true" emissaries of cultural freedom outside the endorsement of the state.[170]

On his return trip, Ferlinghetti recited his poems in Lima, but was received with less fanfare. A newspaper article called him a representative of the "beater" generation, confusing this for "bitter" (amargo).[171] But while Ferlinghetti's poem may have derived from Ginsberg and Neruda, it still flowed in to currents of the Latin American ruin poem as conceived by Peruvian poet Martín Adán (1908–1985). During an indeterminate interval between 1950 and 1961, while suffering from alcoholism and mental illness, Adán composed a poem in a jumble of notebooks and loose-leaf pages titled *La mano desasida: Canto a Machu Picchu* (The Unclenched Hand: Song to Machu Picchu). One of the longest, most obsessive, and most obstreperous poems in twentieth-century Latin American letters, it sustains a hectoring apostrophe to the Incan ruin and ruminates philosophically on the possibility of interchanging the Andean citadel's stony reality with the

ALGO SOBRE LOS MINEROS DE LOTA
En amable plática Fernando Alegría con el norteamericano Lawrence Ferlinghetti. Al resumir el Encuentro, Ferlinghetti dijo:
"Espero que el aspecto y los rostros de los mineros de Lota se
verán transformados por el Encuentro, aunque en ello no pongo
muchas esperanzas.

Fig 3.8 Lawrence Ferlinghetti and Fernando Alegría in Concepción de Chile.
Photographer unknown. "Algo sobre los mineros de Lota," *Cronica* (Jan. 23, 1960).
Lawrence Ferlinghetti Papers, UCB.

poet's own ontological being, his forms of perception, and the linguistic habits
he inherits from Western humanism. "¿Qué eres tú, Machu Picchu,/Almohada
de entresueño?. . ./¿Yo Mismo,/Si me acuerdo y no me acuerdo?" (What are you,
Machu Picchu,/Drowsy pillow?. . ./I Myself?/If I remember and do not remember?).[172] *La mano desasida* awaits a much fuller study than I can offer here, but
this brief quotation is enough to establish some of the poem's hallmark features,
such as an insistent and repetitive address to Machu Picchu and its series of long
passages of interrogatives that shift paratactically between exterior qualities of
stone and interior investigations of subjective being.

Some of these ruminations are staged as deflationary swipes at traditions of
Latin American vanguard poetry. For example, Adán takes aim at the Neruda
who wrote of Machu Picchu "sube a nacer conmigo" (rise to be born with me),
hectoring the stone instead to join the poet in the mutuality of their catastrophe:

Cáete, si eres, Machu Picchu,
Cáete conmigo. Te lo digo: no sigas

Presidiendo las cosas
Y los cielos, con tus piedras caedizas.[173]

(Fall down, if you are, Machu Picchu,
Fall down with me. I say to you:
Preside no longer, neither over things
Nor heavens, with your tottering stones.)

Other swipes come at the expense of the tourist with his Kodak, but also the "cholo" Indian, as if the poet must clear all social angles of vision away from his absorptive, penetrating lyricization of the ruin.

The poem's manifold difficulties are exacerbated by its odd publication history, for it was scribbled—often as Adán drank alone in bars—without the author designating clear ordering principles. Consequently, among the few scholars who have paid the poem serious attention, Greene suggests that its ungainliness points toward a "rude, seemingly aimless thrashing" that "seems to risk everything, even its own interest and outcome," while Anchante grants it an intentional design enacting aesthetic ideals of limitlessness, circularity, and impregnability.[174] Three successively larger texts of the poem circulate. The first consists of 150 lines printed alongside selections from Neruda's *Alturas* and Alberto Hidalgo's *Patria Completa* (1960) in *Nuevas Piedras para Machu Picchu* (1961), a pamphlet published by Adán's friend and editor Juan Mejía Baca to commemorate the fiftieth anniversary of Hiram Bingham's "rediscovery" of Machu Picchu.[175] Despite its brevity, Adán's poem won a national prize. Then, in 1964, Mejía Baca published an augmented, 638-line poem in a multimedia book that included a seven-inch record on which Adán declaimed passages of the poem. Adán chose neither the text nor its ordering as it appeared in this edition. Rather, Mejía Baca asked three critics, whose names he never subsequently disclosed, to pick their favorite fragments of the poem. Apparently, no one at the time, nor at any time since the 1964 edition was published, noticed that the multimedia book object Mejía Baca created was an uncanny homage to Ferlinghetti's *Starting from San Francisco* (where Ferlinghetti first published "Hidden Door"), right down to the red, sans serif typeface adorning the cover and the inclusion of a seven-inch recording of the poet reading (Figures 3.9 and 3.10).

When Ginsberg sought out Adán in Lima in early 1960, no fragments of *La mano desasida* had been published, and Adán's reputation relied on his avant-garde novella *La casa de cartón* (The Cardboard House, 1928), some early experimental lyric poems and reviews that appeared in journals such as *Amauta* in the late 1920s, a doctoral study on baroque aesthetics in Peru, and three volumes of

Fig 3.9 *Starting from San Francisco* by Lawrence Ferlinghetti, © 1961 by Lawrence Ferlinghetti. Reprinted by permission of New Directions Publishing Corp.

poems marked by his abandonment of avant-garde practices in favor of the careful subversions of fixed forms such as décimas and sonnets: *La rosa de espinela* (1939), *Sonetos a la rosa* (1942), and *Travesía de extramares (sonetos a Chopin)* (1950). Ginsberg's poem to Adán, "To An Old Poet in Peru," dated May 19, 1960, suggests that his acquaintanceship with Adán's work was limited to the mid-career sonnets:

> Your clean sonnets?
> I want to read your dirtiest
>   secret scribblings,
>   your Hope,
> in His most Obscene Magnificence. My God!

Ginsberg, therefore, like the rest of the reading public, did not yet understand the scope of Adán's *La mano desasida* if he knew it at all. Only a third edition, prepared by Ricardo Silva-Santisteban and published in *Obra poética* (1980),

Fig 3.10 Martín Adán, *La mano desasida: canto a Machu Picchu* (Lima, 1964).
Photograph by Baldomero Pestana. Used by permission of the Estate of Baldomero
Pestana.

clarified that scope. There, it ballooned tenfold to over 5,000 lines, or nearly two
hundred pages. The text of this poem, now monumental, roughly follows the
chronology in which Mejía Baca received the manuscripts from Adán prior to
1961, divided into thirteen cantos, ten of which are titled. This monumental poem
should not be confused for a critical edition, which is yet to be distilled from the
unbound manuscripts Mejía Baca left to the Pontificia Universidad Católica del
Peru in 1986. A critique of Neruda, an homage to Ferlinghetti, what Greene calls
an "obversal" to Ginsberg, and a monument to the ruin of Adán's own psychology and standing in Peruvian letters, *La mano desasida*'s very history of neglect
absorbs and redirects the energies of the genre.

In 1963, a year after Lamantia's *Destroyed Works*, Ginsberg's *Reality
Sandwiches* appeared from City Lights with the full run of his Mexico and Peru
poems. In 1966, Tarn published his translation of *Alturas de Macchu Picchu*,
and, as an editor at Jonathan Cape, brought into alliance Olson's and Neruda's

anthropological poetics and the French post-structuralists by republishing *Mayan Letters* in 1968 alongside *The Scope of Anthropology* by Claude Levi-Strauss and *Elements of Semiology* by Roland Barthes. Cardenal's *Homenaje*, composed across the 1960s, appeared in 1969 and in English in 1973. Thus the ruin poem may in hindsight appear to be a 1960s vogue. In truth, however, the pre-Columbian ruinology of *Alturas*, "The Kingfishers," "Howl," "Ceylonese Tea Candor," "Mayapán," "The Hidden Door," and *La mano desasida* came together piecemeal in the early Cold War as an answer to the declining geopolitics of inter-Americanism itself. From the "privileged observatories" each of these poets sought out in the indigenous architectures of the Americas, they arrived at the decaying wartime dream of hemispheric democracy. Their bardic efforts to reconstruct the promises of hemispherism and to align it with the new textures of postwar poetry laid the groundwork for the profusion of 1960s relations I describe in the next chapter under the rubric "The New Inter-American Poetry."

4. The New Inter-American Poetry

Ferlinghetti's and Ginsberg's visits to Chile and Peru prelude a sizeable outburst of 1960s inter-American poetic dialogues, institutions, small-press magazines, and translations. In 1962, Margaret Randall and Sergio Mondragón founded the bilingual literary magazine *El Corno Emplumado* (The Plumed Horn) in Mexico City, promising to "tune the world in" on a new hemispheric "network" at a moment—following the Bay of Pigs invasion—when "relations between the Americas have never been worse."[1] In a letter to *El Corno*, Ernesto Cardenal defined their emergent relation to political inter-Americanism: "I told you: you are creating the true Pan American Union. The Pan American Union is of the poets [...] If the poets do not actualize Pan-Americanism nobody else will."[2] Even the new PAU Cultural Director Rafael Squirru endorsed this account, asking Paul Blackburn for help in making "this Pan American Union the only union that I believe in, which is that of the poets."[3] And Blackburn likewise viewed poetry as a cultural front in the Kennedy administration's Alliance for Progress, writing: "Is it an impossible dream to think of a bilingual America stretching from Tierra del Fuego to the Arctic Ocean, comprised of eighty-three states instead of fifty? Not by conquest but by union."[4] These youthful countercultural poets sought imaginative protocols to integrate hemispheric literary cultures across and through shifting political winds, contrary aesthetic genealogies, and the global Cold War's checkered institutions of cultural diplomacy.

This chapter tells the story of the leftist poetic hemispherism called for by Blackburn, Cardenal, Randall, and many others at the outset of the 1960s: San Francisco Beats and Cuban barbudos; New York experimentalists and their Argentine and Mexico City associates; Midwestern surrealists and Peruvian guerrilleros. To make visible this multidirectional history, the chapter considers an unusually hefty volume of poems in an uncommonly large spatiotemporal frame. I justify these magnitudes in several respects. The time span of a "long hemispheric 1960s" follows Claudia Gilman's description of "catorce años prodigiosos" (fourteen prodigious years) of revolutionary fervor from the January 1, 1959, Cuban revolution to the US-backed September 11, 1973, coup d'état against Salvador Allende's socialist government in Chile.[5] Leftist poetic inter-Americanism partly follows this geopolitical tempo, decentering the US-centric 1965 civil rights moment and the 1968 anti–Vietnam War protests as the main vertices of the decade's self-conception, permeating the aesthetic imagination with revolutionary identifications between guerrillero, Beat, and African-American poetry early in the decade, and exhibiting bracing anger at state policies by decade's end. The enlarged spatial configuration acknowledges how a Good Neighbor imagination of a neighborly and navigable hemisphere gave way to what Charles Bernstein calls "innumerable overlaying, contradictory or polydictory, traditions and proclivities and histories and regions and peoples and circumstances," even as claims to spatial mobility continued to inform poets through the Alliance for Progress and the relaxed visa policies of the Brezhnev-era Cold War thaw.[6] Enlarging the map also acknowledges that Havana's outsized place in the countercultural hemispheric imagination wove together with inter-American enclaves such as Lima, Mexico City, and New York. Above all, 1960s leftist hemispherism brings together a huge number of poets, minor and canonical, metropolitan and marginal, apolitical and armed. These poets contributed to local coteries, national anthologies, and site-specific literary practices, but many also participated in international gatherings and translocal circuits.[7] This was clear to Kenneth Rexroth, who wrote in a 1961 cover story on the New Americans: "For the first time in a generation, American poetry is once more a recognizable part of world poetry."[8] To echo Karl Marx's description of world literature, from the many national poetries there arose a "new inter-American poetry."

In order to expediently sketch the contours of this spatiotemporal enlargement, I'll begin the chapter by resituating the poets of Donald Allen's watershed anthology *The New American Poetry 1945–1960* (1960)—a standard feature of national histories of postwar US poetry—in a hemispheric panorama. Reprovincializing

The New American Poetry in the discourse network I am calling "the new inter-American poetry" revivifies the transnational dimensions of the era's poems and poetic group formations. By its own account, *The New American Poetry* united out of disparate small-press publications a "third generation" of US modernists. When Grove published it in May 1960, it implied a rebuke to the academic formalism of *New Poets of England and America* (1957), and inflamed decades of US poetry scholarship conceding partisan intra-national factions, as if refracting Cold War logics of conflict in the realm of verbal art. Robert Lowell's 1960 National Book Award speech construed these divisions between "the cooked and the raw," whereas later poet-critics speak of margins and mainstreams, expressivism and constructivism, quietism and experiment.[9] Reviewing this "overfamiliar" story, Oren Izenberg deftly shows how scholars are now at pains to "dissolve" the two traditions into a fuller national picture. Yet the category of the national canon—to which poems can be pluralistically admitted or from which they can be discriminated against—often remains the residual premise for Izenberg's and others' analyses.[10] The limits of this national picture come into view when we consider the ways in which the anthology's contributors exited and re-entered the US poetry scene in the very moment that Allen was assembling it for publication.

At least one-third of the contributors to *The New American Poetry* participated in it from hemispheric removes, or attested to an array of transnational enmeshments. Mexico was a key site and source of poetic material. Denise Levertov spent 1956–1958 in Guadalajara and Oaxaca, began an intensive correspondence with Octavio Paz, and planned her volume of poems *With Eyes at the Back of Our Heads* (1960) around Mexican cultural structures.[11] Philip Lamantia convened a Mexico City reading circle through 1961, including Homero Aridjis, Sergio Mondragón, Randall, Cardenal, and others.[12] Jack Kerouac's first book of poetry, *Mexico City Blues*, was written in Mexico in 1955 and published in 1959. With the motto "if you know what I/p a l a b r a," Kerouac's sequence of 241 "choruses" offers a lettristic and often asemantic rumble through a North American inter-language, as if each poem were "The Airplane in the Pan/American night –."[13] Gregory Corso's slightly dated *vida* in *The New American Poetry* ends with his writing of "most of *Gasoline*" from Mexico in 1958.[14] With haiku-like condensation, Corso's "Mexican Impressions" remark the temporal incongruities of Americanization:

> Through a moving window
> I see a glimpse of burros
>   a Pepsi Cola stand,
> an old Indian sitting
>   smiling toothless by a hut.[15]

Meanwhile, Corso's "Puma at the Chapultepec Zoo" rewrites Rilke's "Der Panther" for the Americas, joining the animalization discourses of other Beat poetries such as those of Michael McClure, who also passed through Mexico in 1962, attending the incantatory mushroom ceremonies of Maria Sabina in Oaxaca, writing pieces of the "beast language" of *Ghost Tantras* (1964), and reciting them in a corrida.

Robert Creeley spent most of 1959–1961 in Guatemala, teaching English to the children of wealthy Anglo-Americans on a coffee finca near Lake Atitlán.[16] He wrote much of *For Love* (1962) there, although this volume of reticent miniatures mostly avoids cross-cultural poetic influence, despite interest from his correspondents (such as Blackburn, Ed Dorn, Elsa Dorfman, Ginsberg, Levertov, and Olson) in Guatemala's contemporary poets and the civil conflicts that battered its rural poor after the US intervention of 1954.[17] Oddly, given the phenomenological particularism Creeley describes in a 1961 statement of his poetics as "the most scrupulous localism—because only the particular instance proves free," the only poem in *For Love* that registers its Guatemalan occasion is "The Pool."[18] The speaker, embarrassed to lounge poolside among naked white bodies in his "own white flesh" produces refractory, multiplying feelings of segregation: "The sense of myself/separate, grew/a white mirror/in the quiet water."[19] Creeley's neo-colonial observations amplify and perpetuate his whiteness. To Dorn, he comments: "we stagger on with the white man's burden—and the Indians look more distant, out of it (good for them) daily."[20] "The Pool" thus takes Guatemala as "the dilemma of some literal context," stirring the poet toward self-obliteration in anonymous song, "at last free of [the poet's] own time and place."[21]

Creeley's self-magnifying white guilt distinguishes him from Ferlinghetti's upbeat politicization of a trip to Cuba in 1960. Both Ferlinghetti and Ginsberg made lasting contacts with Latin American poets, including Ernesto Cardenal, Nicanor Parra, Martín Adán, and Pablo Armando Fernández. LeRoi Jones likewise visited Cuba in July 1960 on a tour cosponsored by the Fair Play for Cuba Committee (FPCC) and Casa de las Américas, meeting major Cuban poets. In New York, Joel Oppenheimer and Ron Loewinsohn joined Jones in contributing to pro-Cuba poetry pamphlets. Paul Blackburn also worked with the FPCC and translated Octavio Paz, Julio Cortázar, and the protest poems of Nicolás Guillén against the segregationist policies of Governor Faubus in Arkansas, which Blackburn was dismayed to find he could not place in a "USIS-backed publication."[22] By 1960, attendees at Les Deux Magots poetry readings heard Blackburn debut translations of Cortázar's unpublished, jazz-inspired prose poems *Historias de cronopios y de famas* (1962).[23]

Mexico's vagaries as a New American muse also attracted many young poets not included in Allen's anthology. Clayton Eshleman hitchhiked from Indiana to Mexico City and Acapulco in 1959 and to Jalisco the next summer.[24] In 1961, Randall left for a decade-long residence in Mexico City. Such poets registered Latin American poetry as a transformative novelty, or what Weinberger calls a "discovery."[25] Working in the shade of Allen's anthology, they conflated this novelty with the very idea of a new American poetry. In Robert Bly's journal *The Sixties*, Louis Simpson parodied an Anglo poet's death and rebirth as a Nerudian surrealist. Modeling this resurrectionary transculturation, the poem is titled "Death, Death, Death, Death" in the table of contents, but retitled "Keeping Abreast, or Homage to Pablo Neruda Perhaps" at the back of the magazine. The speaker meets a fellow poet, "Thomas," a "nice Jewish boy" from Amherst, who mopes about in cliché Beat postures, strums a guitar, wears a cloak, and smokes dope.[26] But Ginsberg's poems do not precipitate his Beat transformation so much as Neruda's, which Thomas carries charm-like "in his hip pocket." Shifting the terms of the anthology wars to a capacious hemispherism, Simpson's doubting speaker confronts Thomas's resolute belief in a New World poetics: " 'Thomas,' I said, 'is this the new poetry?'/'It is the new world, he replied.' " The send-up likely alludes to Jack Hirschman's *Hip Pocket Poems* 1, a 1960 pamphlet featuring Eshleman's Neruda translations.[27]

The trope of a pocketful of foreign poetry itself leads us to the story of how inter-Americanism was valued by the New Americans and their widening cohort circa 1960. Ferlinghetti's City Lights Pocket Poets Series was practically born under the sign of Spanish-language poetry. Second in the series was Kenneth Rexroth's *Thirty Spanish Poems of Love and Exile* (1955), a slender volume including Neruda, Guillén, Mariano Brull, Antonio Machado, Rafael Alberti, and Arturo Serrano Plaja. The first volume City Lights devoted to a single Latin American poet was a slim sheaf of Parra's *Anti-Poems* (1960), translated by Jorge Elliot. Parra's wry, mock-moralizing observations in poems such as "Vices of the Modern World" point up the doctrinal unrest between Marxism and the Catholic Church on matters of sexuality and foreign policy, and Ferlinghetti's 1961 poem "Overpopulation" exploits the same matrix of concerns. Ferlinghetti and Parra must be read in tandem, circa 1960, as poets with strong Catholic cultural backgrounds whose poems ironically redefine Christian "vice" against discourses of political demography, economic underdevelopment, and foreign policy.

In my view, these extranational coordinates pull *The New American Poetry*'s pages from its binding, placing them back in dialogue with other anthological projects: the portfolios of new Latin American national poetries that routinely populate the pages of *El Corno*, José Coronel Urtecho and Ernesto Cardenal's *Antología de la poesía norteamericana*, Rafael Squirru's support of PAU anthologies such as *Young Poetry of the Americas* (1965), Octavio Paz's *Poesía en movimiento* (1966), and Heberto Padilla's *Cuban Poetry, 1959–1966* (1967). If many New American poets enmeshed themselves in inter-American exchanges just as the anthology hit the shelves, these were exchanges that multiplied, bringing poets such as Mondragón, Cardenal, Cecilia Vicuña, and Mario Benedetti into dialogue with the United States. Rescaling *The New American Poetry* within the new poetry of the Americas, "overfamiliar" questions about its stake in the divisions in US poetry can be refocused on the question of its availability to internationalist discourses.

These anthologies and poetic communities sought to enact what I have called an "integrationist literary history," one that privileges the proximities between diversified kinds of poems around a shared term of collective integrity. Integration, as an aim of civil rights movements, inspired anthological and editorial debates about transnational literary community formation across the decade. For example, Eshleman privately critiqued Randall's inclusiveness, claiming that rendering visible a hemispheric literary culture came at the expense of aesthetic discrimination: "One can't be a segregationalist & an integrationalist at the same time. For you to say 'there is room for all' is intellectual sloppiness."[28] However, others found the integrationist aesthetics of journals such as *El Corno* massively appealing. In a twinned parody of Eliotic impersonality and patriotic fervor, Creeley gestured toward the configuration in a poetics statement in *The New American Poetry*: "The issue is the poem, a single event—to which, as to the Battle of Gettysburg, or the Pan American Highway, many men may well contribute."[29] In Cuba, Padilla wrote: "But after all, didn't Valery propose the compilation of a history of poetry with no name attached to any poem, so that it could be read as the work of one poet?"[30] Taking my cue from these accounts of the hemispheric poem as a "single event," this chapter argues for a scalar shift from Allen's nation-based integration to that of the hemisphere.

Hemispheric integration is an implicit conceptual standpoint as often as it is an active premise, but many key poetic projects of the 1960s wrote from this standpoint. The pages that follow outline six gatherings of writers attempting to integrate the new inter-American poetry (among many more possible configurations). With a flexible sense of scale, we can locate these gatherings in overlapping sociological institutions of hemispheric counterculturalism: political tourism, experimental correspondence, militant cells, poetic coteries, cultural-diplomatic conferences, and especially a lively culture of translation and an explosion of hemispheric little magazines. I begin by surveying the imaginative and political solidarities of Beats and Cuban barbudos; next, I take up the epistolary and translational exchanges of Blackburn and Cortázar; third, I recover the founding and dissemination of the little magazine *El Corno Emplumado*; fourth, I consider the case of the slain Peruvian militant poet Javier Heraud, and translator Clayton Eshleman's pursuant relations with Heraud's Lima cohort; fifth, I reconsider a broad and competitive interest in translating Pablo Neruda. Of course, these elements of a networked, countercultural hemispherism had their limits. I briefly take up these limits in a sixth and final section that compares Frank O'Hara's poetry of Manhattan to a kindred poetry of pedestrian New York authored by O'Hara's Latin American and Caribbean coevals.

Beats and Barbudos

In 1965, the young poet Santiago Mathieu celebrated the Cuban revolution's sixth anniversary with the words "*todas las poesías del mundo están llenas de cuba*" (all the poetries of the world are full of cuba).[31] While Castro's revolution permeated poetic and cultural imaginations of the 1960s across national and gender lines in and beyond Latin America, one of the first and most habitual ways of articulating a transnational solidarity with Havana was a masculine "beard" motif that analogized Beat and barbudo style. Introducing the "Generación Derrotada" (Beat Generation) to the readers of the Cuban weekly literary supplement *Lunes de Revolución*, Cuban poet Oscar Hurtado wrote: "Los barbudos del Norte están hermanados en rebeldía a los barbudos de Cuba" (the bearded ones of the North are brothers in rebellion with Cuba's bearded revolutionaries).[32] New Left activist Tom Hayden looked back on the era through the same lens: "the bearded ones in the Sierra Maestra touched our bearded ones in the Haight-Ashbury."[33] Robert Lowell famously distinguished between two competing poetries, "a cooked and a raw," but in a draft of his speech, he defined these poetries this way: "The cooked, marvelously expert and remote, seems constructed as a sort of mechanical or catnip mouse for graduate seminars; the raw, jerry-built and forensically deadly, seems often like an unscored libretto by some bearded but vegetarian Castro."[34] Lowell's division between silent academic poetry and coffee house declamatory poetry, a poetry of "pedantry" and a poetry of "scandal," also marked out those who were in active sympathy with the barbudos of the Sierra Maestra and those who were not. One kind of poetry expertly dramatized national exceptionalism; another messily reached for new transnational solidarities and identifications.

Historian Van Gosse defines this latter tendency as "Yankee *fidelismo*," both within the organizational New Left represented by the Fair Play for Cuba Committee (FPCC) and within what Gosse called "the extrapolitical world" of hipsterism.[35] Gosse argues that "*fidelismo* was a destabilizing and eventually radicalizing force in the United States, as well as in Cuba," and he focuses on the sociology of a middle-class US youth reorienting their sense of Cuba as a glamorous vacation destination into an adventuresome New Left site of solidarity. Recent scholars such as Rafael Rojas and Todd Tietchen expand Gosse's insights in important book-length studies. Rojas considers the full collection of "New York intellectual" responses to Castroism; Tietchen defines a genre of travel writing he calls the "Cubalogue," amplifying Beat and Afro-American vectors to suggest that Havana "momentarily emerged as an inter-American haven, or oppositional public sphere."[36] However, expressions of Yankee fidelismo in Beat-affiliated poetry and its reception among Cuban writers go beyond the purview of New York intellectuals and are not always manifested in travelogues. In a history of inter-American poetics, we can speak of a flexible subgenre of Beat-barbudo poetry, written by or apostrophically addressed to Cuban revolutionaries, celebrating their struggles, appropriating their symbolic styles, and seeking poetic idioms of commitment dormant since the 1930s. This poetry often lit on the figure of the beard itself, the figure of a tenuous intercultural tangle that endured as long as Castro's cultural policy remained open, especially from 1959–1962. Three examples will have to stand in for a larger complex of relations: LeRoi Jones, Lawrence Ferlinghetti, and the single issue of the League of Militant Poets magazine *Pa'Lante: Poetry, Polity Prose of a New World* (1962).

In 1958, Jones and his wife Hettie Cohen, living in Manhattan, acquired an offset press with which they began to publish the little magazine *Yugen* (1958–1962) and the chapbooks of Totem Press. The revolution of January 1, 1959 filled Jones with a cinematic sense of Castro's heroism, which he likened to Errol Flynn's *Robin Hood*: "The Cuban thing seemed a case of classic Hollywood proportions."[37] Flynn, incidentally, often used the "little island" as a "refueling stop" en route to his private ranch in Jamaica, and was commissioned by the Hearst Press to write a series of articles on "the rebel leader Fidel Castro," resulting in a semi-documentary B movie, *Cuban Rebel Girls* (1959), his last film. Jones's first enthusiastic contribution to the culture of Beat-barbudo solidarity was comparatively modest: an eight-page "blue plate" pamphlet entitled *Jan 1st 1959: Fidel*

Castro (Figure 4.1). Named "blue plate" for the cheap daily specials in American diners and priced accordingly at five cents, it included six contributors: Jones, Joel Oppenheimer, Max Finstein, Gilbert Sorrentino, Ron Loewinsohn, and Jack Kerouac. Oppenheimer's lead poem "For the Barbers" ironizes the Beat/barber relation:

> tenderly as a
> barber trimming
> it off i
> sing my songs, like
> a barber stropping
> a razor, i rage.

This stanza tentatively identifies with the barber, finding similes for poetic craft in middle-class professional life. Enjambed lowercase lines pattern gerunds and *o-* and *i-* sounds, likening the barber's trimming and stropping to the poet's vocalizations. Aural symmetry magnifies metaphor, as in the explosive line "a razor, i rage." But Oppenheimer then turns on the barber, recasting him as a figure of "calculation" and "cunning," ending the poem with a plaintive celebration of beardedness. Crucially, the beard is not a form of revolutionary identification but one of noncommittal deprofessionalization: "oh the/professionals what we/should fear." Similarly, Finstein's poem "Animal Vegetable Mineral" ends by punctuating ruminative stanzas of New York life in January with an exclamatory celebration of revolutionary Cuba's possessive romantic potency, not its eradication of inequality: "los barbudos!/the pretty girls/will belong/to you."

Jones's poem "For You" also juxtaposes romantic possibility with the situation of a cold New Year in New York, but it leads him toward an ambiguous vindication of revolutionary commitment: "& come the revolution/it will be the same,/ Miles Davis &/bourbon. Sunday mornings;/after we have won." Jones recalled sharp pushback in his liberal individualist Beat enclave against this stanza's committed political stance. In fact the pamphlet's remaining poems disidentify with the revolution. Sorrentino imagines the fate of "Major Hoople"—a proprietor in the long-running comic strip "Our Boarding House"—suddenly dispossessed by the revolution: "when will they possess/your useless yard and send/you out to work, to/work!/lovely Major Hoople." Kerouac warns Cubans against coming to Florida on account of dangers emblematized by coral snakes, alligators, and fire ants, which lurk beneath the state's leisurely sheen. When Ferlinghetti later traveled to Cuba, Kerouac reportedly told him "I got my own revolution out here—the American Revolution." While preserving these disengaged voices in his coterie publication, Jones unexpectedly found that Cuba's revolution awakened for him the cause of US civil rights. As he later put it, "perhaps the intensification of the civil rights movement, the daily atrocities which fat sheriffs in Dumbbell, Georgia, could run on blacks, began to piss me off much more deeply than I thought."[38]

Jan 1st 1959: Fidel Castro interested Oscar Hurtado, the most dedicated purveyor of Beat literature in Cuba in the early days of the revolution. Hurtado translated and annotated all but one poem in the weekly literary supplement *Lunes de Revolución*. His introduction describes the "young North Americans" of the Beat Generation writing a consoling literature of experience that stops short of revolt, while acknowledging that condemnations of nuclear-age politics lead to natural sympathies with fidelismo. The point is true enough, although Hurtado's annotations of the six poems reach for nonexistent symbolic readings in orthodox service to Cuba. Of Oppenheimer's "For the Barbers," he writes: "notamos el simbolismo del barbero . . . que no comprende la riqueza natural de la selva pilosa del 'barbudo'" (we note the symbolism of the barber . . . who does not comprehend

Fig 4.1 LeRoi Jones et al., *Jan 1st 1959: Fidel Castro* (New York: Totem Press, 1959).

the natural richness of the hairy jungle of the 'barbudo' ").[39] Hurtado recasts these poems as warnings about the proximity of the Cuban Revolution to the centers of US imperial power. These readings bear out Jones's own hopes for the pamphlet, which marked the first ambivalent inklings of his radicalization.

Therefore, when Jones received an invitation from FPCC and Casa de las Américas to travel to Havana in July 1960 along with a group of African-American intellectuals, he leapt at the opportunity. Langston Hughes and James Baldwin declined the invitation, but Jones reconnected on the trip with Harold Cruse, Sarah Wright, and photographer Leroy McLucas, and he met Richard Gibson of the FPCC and the militant civil rights activist Robert F. Williams, who proved to be a powerful model for him. *Lunes de Revolución* published a major dossier entitled "Los negros En U.S.A." in advance of their arrival, including Jones's otherwise uncollected "Nick Charles habla desde la muerte."[40] The special issue is notable in many ways, perhaps not least as the first publication to identify Jones as an African-American writer first and a Beat writer second. Cuba's literary public sphere conscripted his writing outside the Beat coterie in the broader panorama of African-American anti-imperialism. In "Cuba Libre," his prize-winning essay chronicling his trip, Jones contrasts uniformed barbudos to the cultural rebels of the United States, "merely people like myself who grow beards and will not participate in politics."[41] This awakening owed much to critiques of literary disengagement Jones heard from Gibson, Williams, Pablo Armando Fernández, and Nicolás Guillén, who asked Jones if his old friend Langston Hughes had abdicated his revolutionary sympathies. Jones particularly credits his awakening to a fourteen-hour train ride to celebrate the July 26th movement at a campesino rally in eastern Cuba, where he briefly met Castro. On that ride, he endured grueling political challenges from Mexican poet Jaime Shelley and from the Mexican graduate student Rubi Betancourt.[42]

The poems of *Preface to a Twenty Volume Suicide Note* (1961) barely record Jones's pursuant racial awakening and political conversion, with the exception of "Betancourt," a three-part lyric dated July 30, 1960, dedicated to "Rubi," which commemorates seaside dialogues in Havana. Jones concedes the inadequacy of verbal art to his emerging politics, metaphorizing poems as harbor bulwarks: "To/ contain even that/madness (within/some thrown wall/of words.)"[43] The poem climaxes in an avowal of political conversion, declaring "That/there are fools/ who hang close/to their original/thought." In a note to *Lunes* celebrating his visit, Jones decried this same figure of the "idiota" (fool), noting that Cuban youth found a margin of creativity "en un mundo cuya belleza está constantemente amenazada por idiotas profesionales (y amateurs)" (in a world whose beauty is constantly threatened by professional (and amateur) fools).[44] His poetry now "turns" toward social participation:

> Think
> about it! As even
> this, now, a turning
> away. (I mean I think
> I know now
> what a poem
> is) A
> turning away . . .
> from what
> it was
> had moved
> us . . . [45]

In "How You Sound??" (1959), written for the notes on poetics in *The New American Poetry*, Jones announced, "MY POETRY is whatever I think I am." Grounding a subjective ontology in poetic speech, Jones suggests a process of projectivist discovery modeled on Olson: "'Who knows what a poem ought to sound like? Until it's thar.' Says Charles Olson . . . & I follow closely with that."[46] In "Betancourt," he crucially revises this process-oriented view of poetry. In the triad "I mean I think/I know," the very ground of knowing slips shakily into an iambic colloquial idiom of indecision, one that morphs between signification, cognition, and knowledge. Verse's etymological sense of "turning away" dramatizes shifts of perceptual self-discovery through the restless "turns" of enjambment. This turning, however, does not avert from the social, as it does most often in thought on the social form of lyric. Rather, it turns away from prior self-conceptions. For Jones, apostrophic aversion achieves conversion rather than isolation. This turn entails a disavowal of Beat disengagement and the affirmation of revolutionary social participation, spurred on by his epiphanic seaside Havana conversations with Betancourt.

Lawrence Ferlinghetti also visited Cuba in December 1960, and promoted its cause in the following months before the Bay of Pigs Invasion. On his first night in Havana, he was eating his own blue plate special at a local restaurant when he was surprised to "see big guy with beard wearing fatigues and smoking cigar come out of restaurant kitchen: it's Fidel."[47] They spoke warmly, Ferlinghetti describing himself as a "*poeta norteamericano*" in his self-described "taxi-cab Spanish." His visit was devoted to literary reconnaissance, hoping to right a lack of interest in younger Latin American writers among the New York publishers. Prior to the trip, his New Directions publisher James Laughlin, for example, wrote to him: "I'm afraid I can't tell you very much of anything about Cuba, except that Octavio Paz, when he was here not long ago, spoke highly of two 'pro-Castro-Catholic poets' named Vitier and Lezama Lima [. . .] Otherwise, I'm afraid I just know about Cuba what I read in the papers, and probably a lot of that is strongly distorted."[48] While Laughlin sought out the fairer account of C. Wright Mills's journalistic experiment *Listen, Yankee: The Revolution in Cuba* (1960), he also mirrored the mass media anticommunist view, accusing Castro's "fancy antics" of threatening the Cuban poor he claimed to serve.[49] Ferlinghetti reproached Laughlin's anti-Fidel sentiment, conscripting him to furnish Havana's Casa de la Amistad intercultural center with names of US poets and intellectuals to combat the disinformation campaigns of the US press.[50] Laughlin complied, and worked assiduously to sell Ferlinghetti's "Poet's Notes from Cuba," although its eventual placement in *Liberation* was less prominent than he'd hoped.

Ferlinghetti took meetings at the *Lunes de Revolución* offices and at Casa de las Américas, exploring Cuban poetry's slow adoption of revolutionary themes and its interest in US writing. Among new Cuban poets, Ferlinghetti most admired Pablo Armando Fernández, whose *Armas (Poemas en voz alta)*—choral poems for rally recitations—he saw in typescript. Their performance initiatives and typographic versatility impressed him more than José Alvarez Baragaño's *Poesía: revolución del ser* (1960), which he understood as "growing out of *los años del terror* leading up to the Revolution." Fernández told him that the Beat rebellion's apoliticism muted his enthusiasm for the "weird dissent" of the Beats.[51] Such comments impacted Jones's and Ferlinghetti's search for new models of politicized solidarity. Indeed, Ferlinghetti had already sought an answer to this critique in his broadside poem "Tentative Description of a Dinner Given to Promote the Impeachment of President Eisenhower," where he reconciled Beat nonchalance with a poetics of "engagement" that harkened to the 1930s literatures of revolutionary socialism. As Ferlinghetti wrote in the liner notes to a recording of the poem (later collected as a statement of his poetics in *The New American Poetry*): "And this is where all the tall droopy corn about the Beat Generation and its being 'existentialist' is as phoney as a four-dollar piece of lettuce. Because Jean-Paul Sartre cares and has always hollered that the writer especially should be committed. *Engagement* is one of his favorite dirty words."[52]

Ferlinghetti's stopover coincided with a visit by Pablo Neruda, who was writing the protest poems of *Canción de gesta* (Song of Protest, 1960) in honor of the revolution. These include occasional poems summoning a unitary hemispheric voice to celebrate the barbudo victory: "voy a pedir un minuto sonoro,/por una

vez toda la voz de América,/sólo un minuto de profundo canto/pido en honor de la
Sierra Maestra" (I will ask for a sonorous minute,/for once with the whole voice of
América,/but one minute of deepest song/do I ask in honor of the Sierra Maestra.")[53]
Delighted to meet Ferlinghetti after following the Beat splash in Concepción the
previous year, Neruda strategized with him during their brief meeting about how
to support the revolution in the United States. A few days later, the editors of
Lunes conducted a group interview with Neruda, and Hurtado questioned him
on his regard for Beat literature. Neruda replied that he had heard quite a bit
about Ginsberg the previous year, but had read little. He compared Beat rebellion
to Wildean aestheticism as a revolution of lifestyle that broke "el molde de . . . la
manera trumaniana de ver la vida" (the mold of . . . the Trumanian way of looking at life), just as Wilde broke Victorian social norms.[54] He found that the few
Beat poems he had read were of high quality, and tended toward scandalous titles
like "Cinco maneras de matar al Presidente Eisenhower" (Five Ways of Killing
President Eisenhower). Here Neruda's error, which conflates Stevens's "Thirteen
Ways of Looking at a Blackbird" with Ferlinghetti's "Tentative Description of a
Dinner Given to Promote the Impeachment of President Eisenhower," notably
replaces lawful processes of political redress with incitements to political violence. I suspect this conflation remained in Neruda's mind when he wrote his
final, scathing poem "Incitación a Nixoncidio" (Incitation to Nixoncide, 1973).

Ferlinghetti certainly did not advocate Eisenhower's assassination, but rather
feared a US strike against Castro. Returning to San Francisco in January, he
wrote "One Thousand Fearful Words for Fidel Castro" (1961) (Figure 4.2), read it
at a San Francisco political rally on January 13, and published it as a City Lights
broadside with a note informing readers there were less than one thousand words
in order to leave "room for a happier ending, in case the relentless hostility of
government and press in the U.S. should somehow not triumph in the end."
Ferlinghetti's poem opens in homage to W. H. Auden's "September 1, 1939," the
most important poetic expression of the world-historical anxieties marking the
onset of World War II. Auden's poem begins "I sit in one of the dives/On Fifty-
second Street/Uncertain and afraid/As the clever hopes expire/Of a low dishon-
est decade."[55] Ferlinghetti's poem, ringing in the close of the "Eisenhower era,"
draws its force from the same well of apprehension as Auden, but its deflationary
and dark humor punctures Auden's bardic seriousness with absurd details:

> I am sitting in Mike's Place trying to figure out
>   what's going to happen without Fidel Castro
>   Among the salami sandwiches and spittoons
>   I see no solution[56]

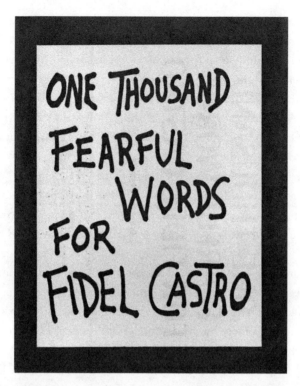

Fig 4.2 Lawrence Ferlinghetti, "One Thousand Fearful Words for Fidel Castro" (San Francisco: City Lights, 1961).

Auden's poem, furthermore, voices the collective and depersonalized agony of a global humanistic "we," which organizes around the voiceless and "unmentionable odour of death." By contrast, Ferlinghetti personalizes the figure of revolutionary collectivity in the dashing figure of Fidel, addressing the poem to him with increasing apostrophic force.

To cut the mood of portent and to play into the glamorous tropes attending Fidel, Ferlinghetti positively valorizes the interchange of Beat and barbudo style, gently chiding Fidel for appropriating his style from the Beats rather than the other way around:

> They're going to fix you, Fidel
>   with your big Cuban cigar
>   which you stole from us
>   and your army surplus hat
>   which you probably also stole
>   and your Beat beard

Meanwhile, Ferlinghetti's premonition of an imminent counterrevolutionary strike against Castro underscores the poem's strategies of verbal and historical repetition. Twin refrains pepper the poem, one premonitory ("They're going to fix you, Fidel"), and the other an ironic rehabilitation of the Declaration of Independence ("When in the course of human events"). These verbal repetitions work in counterpoint to a historic echo of the media imperialism of 1898: "And Hearst is dead but his great Cuban wire still stands." Distributed experimentally as a broadside, as a rally recitation, and as part of the popular multimedia book *Starting from San Francisco*, the poem itself carves out an alternative mediascape to Hearst's "Cuban wire."

A culminating expression of Beat-barbudo solidarity is the single issue of the magazine *Pa'Lante* (or "Onward"), edited in spring 1962 by Howard Schulman with the Cuban-American author José Yglesias (who briefly studied at Black Mountain College in 1945–1946) and the Chicana activist Elizabeth Sutherland Martínez (Figure 4.3). It included contributions from Jones and Leroy McLucas, both veterans of the same July 1960 FPCC trip to Cuba; New American poets Michael McClure, John Wieners, Allen Ginsberg, Joel Oppenheimer, and Paul Blackburn; the older American socialist poet Thomas McGrath; *Lunes*-affiliated Cuban writers Escardo, Pablo Armando Fernández, Elvio Romero, Nicolas Guillén, and Guillermo Cabrera Infante; and the Cuban literary critic and UNEAC functionary José Antonio Portuondo. As Rojas insightfully notes, McLucas's cover photograph of a coffee-sipping barbudo, gun holstered low on his hip, encapsulates the hybrid, symbolic imaginary of Beat-barbudo solidarity. A manifesto by the League of Militant Poets announced twin aims of publishing "guerilla writing from Latin America" in order to "demolish the walls put up in fear between men's minds" alongside that of "young Americans" to affirm "the bloom of art in our country as indication of radical economic and social change to come."[57] Importantly, the issue was published just after *Lunes*'s closure, following the First Congress of Cuban Artists and Writers in August 1961 (see Chapter 5). Thus the inclusion of Portuondo's address to the congress "A New Art for Cuba" did not outline "the liberal attitude toward art-forms which prevailed at the Congress" as emphatically as *Pa'Lante*'s editors claimed.[58] More accurately, it signaled an attempt to forge an integrationist response to the revolution that encompassed antagonistic old-line communists and younger socialists in Cuba and New York.

Other contributions heightened the issue's contradictions. Michael McClure's center-justified poem "Fidelio" outlined hip stylistic Beat-barbudo symmetries by likening Fidel to the protagonist of Beethoven's opera but also to an avatar of

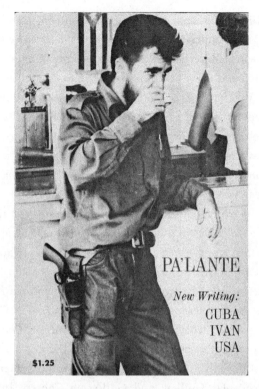

Fig 4.3 *Pa'Lante: Poetry, Polity, Prose of a New World*, eds. Howard Schulman et al. (New York: League of Militant Poets, 1962). Photograph by Leroy McLucas.

the apocalyptic feast, as well as one of the lion-addressees of his contemporaneous *Ghost Tantras*:

> Charming bearded singer! Make the beast's tune
> that precedes the triumphal ending of mankind's symphony.
> We hold our breath & listen to the roar.
> Your tongue is ruby meat and vibrates a new melody
> of new virtue to the starving and poor.
> Eyes are mild within your lion's face.[59]

Even if McClure's apocalyptic animalization of Fidel's revolutionary speech was part of a sympathetic portrait of a "charming" and "mild" leader, this poem was perhaps the most patently extraneous extension of McClure's new concepts of vocalization and his theories of the ecology of revolution, developed contemporaneously in *The Meat Science Essays* (1963) and *Ghost Tantras* (1964). Still other Beat contributors seemed indifferent to the cause (as was the case with John

Wieners), or put upon to be included. Ginsberg's "Prose Contribution to the Cuban Revolution" argued that politics did not matter so much as the revolutions of "being" and "consciousness": "I'm NOT down on the Cubans or anti their revolution, it's just that it's important to make clear *in advance, in front*, what I feel about life. Big statements saying Viva Fidel are/would be/meaningless and just 2-dimensional politics."[60]

Ginsberg, of course, sported the prime Beat beard, and often signed his letters with ecstatic mock-political notations about it, writing to Robert Creeley "Peter & I have big huge frizzy beards, his is RED."[61] For him, the beard transcends intercultural identifications. In "To an Old Poet in Peru," addressed to Martín Adán in May 1960, Ginsberg turns landscapes of revolutionary facial hair into surreal prophecies of death. Ginsberg contrasts Adán's "old face needing a shave" to an image of his own youth that oxymoronically likens the vitality of his new beard to archaic, pre-Incan cultures: "And my young beard sprouted/magnificent as the dead hair/in the sands of Chancay."[62] "To an Old Poet in Peru" contrasts two prophecies of death—one for the aging Peruvian poet and the other for the young US bard. Their common fate will be to die under the sign of revolution, "Both surrounded by screaming/communists with flowers/in their ass."[63] For Ginsberg, inter-American poetries were countersigns to Cuban revolution, not expressions of it. Ginsberg finally visited Cuba in 1965 to judge a literary prize for Casa de las Américas alongside Nicanor Parra. There, he flaunted his revolutionary sexual politics in the face of state orthodoxy and developed a relationship with the queer "El Puente" poets before his outspokenness led to his banishment from the island.[64]

Few poems capture the symbolic interchange between Beat expression and barbudo revolution that Ginsberg critiqued as completely as Edward Field's "Ode to Fidel Castro," from his Lamont Prize–winning volume *Stand Up, Friend, With Me* (1963). Field queers Fidel as the "Rebellisimo and darling of the Spanish-American lower classes," noting that Fidel, in his "work clothes of the buck private and the beard of the saints" was at times cinematic, at times "like a poet writing an ode." Field identifies his own surname anagrammatically with "Fidel," and compares their mutual desire for the "spotlight" and for "the crowds to chant my name."[65] His symbolic politics compensate for a sense of political inadequacy. The end of his ode derails into an elegy with affinities to Ferlinghetti's "Fearful Words":

> By the time you see this, Fidel, you might not even exist anymore
> My government is merciless and even now
> The machine to destroy you is moving into action

The chances are you won't last long
Well so long pal it was nice knowing you
I can't go around with a broken heart all my life
after I got over the fall of the Spanish Republic
I guess I can get over anything
My job is just to survive.[66]

In making casual reference to the 1939 exile of the Spanish loyalists (when the poet was fifteen), Field's romantic youth declares its anachronistic foreclosure of commitment, a generation born under the banner of political disillusionment. His ode preempts itself, transforming Castro's revolution into a revolution of symbolic politics: "So you're not perfect, poets don't look for perfect/It's your spirit we love and the glamour of your style." Field offers a disarmed simulacrum of militant revolution: a symbolic political resolution.

One of the few really militant poems of fidelismo by a US writer did not make it into *Pa'Lante*, though its author was associated with the editors. In "Juan Pedro Carbo Servia Running Thru the Palace Gate," Marc Schleifer offers a hagiographical poem that turns the barbudo's revolution into a scene of heavenly gatecrashing:

Juan Pedro Carbo Servia
running thru the Palace Gate
yours is a futurist beauty
that found itself
alley-trussed by a hundred bullets.
Not time yet to sing praises
of your pothead poetry
(& was it junk-high)
that you'd have a 3 cent coffee
in the streets
with all Havana's fuzz
out gunning.
Yr a cool one, Carbo
sitting in hotel lobbies
jumping out of elevators, stairways, windows
silent or shooting.
Fangio bowing before your grace
Blanco Rico before your fire.

No statues now, Carbo
100 years
safe in a communist world
when the state has withered
there will be gardens of love
for you
roses, dreamy lakes
perfumes of a new race.[67]

Schleifer's poem draws a poetic equation between something like Frank O'Hara's "personism" and the compañerismo of revolutionary life. It converses casually with the protagonists of the revolution, and coolly connects to Cuban martyrology in the style of Fernández's *Libro de los héroes* (1964). The only poem written by a US citizen in Randall and Mondragón's Cuban dossier in *El Corno Emplumado 7*, it glamorizes the symbolic politics of Yankee fidelismo, but also prefigures a late-decade boom in US translations of militant verse. Schleifer's utopian optimism diverges from Jones's vision of the poet's death in the machinery of American imperialism and contrasts the teleology of death in Javier Heraud's guerrillero poetry with a casual prediction of revolutionary accomplishment, while its homosocial jouissance ignores Cuba's emerging repressive policy toward homosexuals.

Cortázar, Blackburn, and All the Village Cronopios

Paul Blackburn's contribution to *Pa'Lante* was but one facet of his extensive promotion of inter-American poetry. As poetry editor at *The Nation* in 1962, he formulated his conception in an essay entitled "The International Word." Summoning "an impossible dream ... of a bilingual America stretching from Tierra del Fuego to the Arctic Ocean," he tied this dream to Kennedy-era institutions at odds with the oppositional public sphere of *Pa'Lante*:

> What the Alliance for Progress, the Organization of American States and the new, still small Latin American Free Trade Association are beginning to accomplish today, may they not prove the basis for a gradualized Plan for Union tomorrow? The ducts of free exchange are already open in literature. [...] What is happening when Allen Ginsberg and Lawrence Ferlinghetti are invited to address a writers' conference in Santiago, Chile? Or when

Octavio Paz, the great Mexican poet and a functionary in the Mexican Embassy in Paris, reads at the YMHA Poetry Center in New York? [. . .] *Evergreen Review* and the *Texas Quarterly* have both published Mexican numbers, and *New World Writing* (No 14) a Latin American number. [. . .]. Even individual efforts count for something, if they manage to achieve a continuity of publication. I am thinking of Robert Bly's insistence on the seminal value of translation in *The Sixties* (formerly *The Fifties*), even though the quality of the translations is uneven; and the new bilingual *The Plumed Horn* (*la primera revista bitnik*, someone called it) out of a bilingual marriage in Mexico City [. . .]. The sole literary magazine in Guatemala is, I believe, backed by USIA funds. So it is taking place on all levels.[68]

Blackburn typified the new sensibility he described. A veteran of the Fulbright program in France and Spain in the early 1950s, he began participating in a project he gently chided as the "sack of world literature . . . by the American publishing business." His earliest spoils include the troubadour translations of *Proensa*, first suggested by Ezra Pound, published by Creeley's Divers Press in 1953 and subsequently expanded in manuscript until his premature death in 1971. His troubadour poetics permeate many of his best poems in the projectivist and New York school observational modes, such as "Pre-Lenten Gestures" and "Sirventes," as well as the title of the little magazine *Trobar*, with which he was associated.

By the late 1950s, Blackburn's knowledge of Romance languages led him to a miscellaneous practice of translating Latin American poetry and fiction. Over the next decade, he translated poems and stories by Julio Cortázar, Manuel Duran, Nicolás Guillén, Javier Heraud, Leandro Katz, Federico García Lorca, Pedro Mir, Vinicius de Moraes, Heberto Padilla, Octavio Paz, Jaime Sabines, and others.[69] Paz came to regard him as his favorite US translator of the hour. For Cortázar, he acted as agent and translator. Teaming with Sara Golden Blackburn, an editor at Pantheon who was married to Paul from 1963 to 1967, he brokered English-language book deals for Cortázar's *Los premios* (The Winners, 1960) and *Rayuela* (Hopscotch, 1963) and translated *Final del juego* (End of the Game and Other Stories, 1956), *Historias de cronopios y de famas* (Cronopios and Famas, 1962), and Cortázar's lesser-known poems.

Though Blackburn's poetry has long attracted simmering if subterranean interest, and while his use of the new portable tape recorder to document the Lower East Side poetry scene is rightly celebrated, the foregoing achievements as a translator and as a cultural broker of inter-American literature have largely escaped critical notice.[70] However, Cold War institutions of cultural diplomacy took note in their day, and Blackburn served as their strategic collaborator. Reading Blackburn's translations in the Mexican number of *Evergreen Review*, Ramón Xirau of the Centro Mexicano de Escritores approached him with other projects, and when Squirru took the helm of Cultural Affairs at PAU in 1963 he made Blackburn an important associate. Although Blackburn for a long time found the National Translation Center at UT Austin hostile to his promotion of Cortázar, they warmed to him after the Cold Warrior Keith Botsford took over from Jim Dimoff in 1966 (on Botsford, see Chapter 5).[71]

Blackburn paired with Cortázar in especially sympathetic ways, and Cortázar became his most active Latin American collaborator and correspondent. Cortázar's own journeyman academic years and work in Paris as a freelance translator for agencies such as the UNESCO and Interpol paralleled Blackburn's work as a freelance editor and translator for PAU and the New York publishing houses. Cortázar first wrote to Blackburn in spring 1958 hoping to find a translator for his unpublished *Historias de cronopios y de famas*, remarking "Si se decide a traducir algo mío al inglés, me dará una grandísima alegría, y mis cronopios hablarán un nuevo idioma" (if you decide to translate something of mine into English, it will bring me great joy, and my cronopios will speak a new language).[72] A bilingual epistolary friendship quickly blossomed, doubling as a formalized professional relationship of agent and author. Signing an agent contract, Cortázar wrote:

> No te imaginas la alegría que me da, porque sé que es algo que te interesa personalmente antes que profesionalmente. De poeta a poeta, y de amigo a amigo, eso occurre muy pocas veces en el literary market. De manera que acepto con mucho gusto tu propuesta, y desde ya te puedes considerar como mi AGENTE. Hallo, Mr. Agent! How do you do, Mr. Agent? It sounds kind of strange, no? What is an Agent? What is an Author? If an Author sees an Agent/coming through the rye. . .[73]

> (You can't imagine the joy you bring me, because I know it is something that interests you personally before it interests you professionally. Poet to poet, and friend to friend, this occurs too infrequently in the literary market. So I accept your proposal with great pleasure, and from now on you can consider yourself my AGENT. Hallo, Mr. Agent! How do you do, Mr. Agent? It sounds kind of strange, no? What is an Agent? What is an Author? If an Author sees an Agent/coming through the rye. . .)

Cortázar's musings on the sociological functions of agent and author reveal a canny sense of his correspondence as the staging ground for entry into the world literary marketplace. When he eventually settled on a satisfactory definition of *agent*, it was this: "you're the absolute pilot of my soul in the States."[74] Blackburn and Cortázar defined their relationship as an overcoming of professional obligation through the flux of intimate bilingual experimentalism, beginning with Blackburn's first Spanish-language note to Cortázar, who replied: "As you wrote me in a magnificent Spanish, I am going to answer in a no less remarkable English. I suppose that a half dozen of good dictionaries and a great deal of patience will help you to decipher this letter. ¡Salud, amigo! (This little Spanish is just to get my second wind, as they say.)"[75]

Underlying Cortázar's adroit bilingualism and reflexive disposition toward the literary marketplace, he expresses an affinity for the post-symbolist strategies of lyric difficulty and the magic charm of foreign words discussed in Chapter 2. He had translated Henri Brémond's important treatise on the topic, *La poésie pure* (1925); he knew Borges; and he corresponded with Lezama, from whose difficult poetry he gleaned what he called the "imminence of comprehension." Praising aesthetic difficulty to Blackburn, Cortázar also arrives at an extended reflection on Wallace Stevens:

> Speaking of difficult poets, I have been reading for a long time Wallace Stevens' poems. Sometimes I like them a lot, sometimes I find them rather overworked, if that is the word for a poetry like his. (This typewriter gets funny ideas sometimes.) Cuando digo *overworked* quiero decir demasiado fabricado, demasiado artificial . . . Pero en cambio casi siempre me gusta la música de Stevens.[76]
>
> (. . .When I say *overworked* I mean too fabricated, too artificial. . . But on the other hand I almost always like the music of Stevens.)

Cortázar's cautions about Stevens's excessive artifice did not prevent him from signing over his poetry manuscript "Circunstancias Generales" for Blackburn's translations with an epigraph from Steven's "Connoisseurs of Chaos" (Figure 4.4). The poets' names, their exaggerated initials ornamented with Daoist spirals, traverse through and visually mirror Stevens' mock syllogism: "A. A violent order is disorder; and/B. A great disorder is an order. These/Two things are one. (Pages of illustrations.)."

The mediation of post-symbolism offers a way of understanding Cortázar's language game in *Historias de cronopios y de famas*. While Cortázar regarded *Historias* as a collection of short fiction, his glosses suggest how he enlaced it

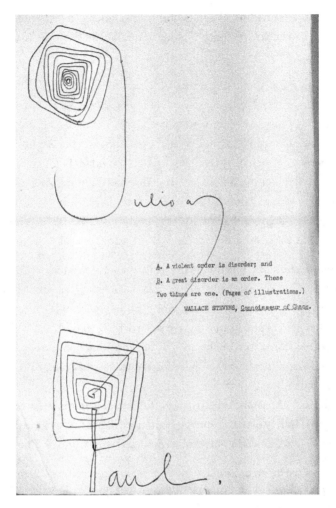

A. A violent order is disorder; and
B. A great disorder is an order. These
Two things are one. (Pages of illustrations.)
      WALLACE STEVENS, Connoisseur of Chaos.

Fig 4.4 Manuscript inscription by Julio Cortázar for Paul Blackburn.
Paul Blackburn Papers, UCSD.

with qualities of poetic difficulty and lyric charm. When Blackburn sent him a
philological speculation about the invented word *cronopio*, Cortázar replied with
an early explanation of the word's origin story, namely a premonition he experienced while listening to Louis Armstrong at the Théatre Champs Elysées in
1952: "Why Paul, you shouldn't ask that kind of thing! How can I know? . . . They
just arrived, body and soul. The only difference with their final form is that at the
beginning they were rather like a kind of balloons to me. Green and humid."[77]
In effect, *cronopio* was a post-symbolist foreign word. When Blackburn confronted a confusing conceit by which the strange microbial *cronopios* "bailaba

tregua y bailaba catala," he literalized his translation as "dance truce and dance catalan," but Cortázar responded that literalism failed to capture his attempts at lyric charm:

> Para mí eso es simplemente una frase with a certain magic of rhyme, a sort of "runic rhyme" in Poe's sense. Claro que ahora que he leído tu división entre los negociantes [españoles], catalanes y madrileños, me pregunto si no tendrás razón tú. Who is right, the Agent or the Author? No use to scan the contract. No explanatory clause provided. But, Paul, if Cortázar's Famas dance catalan, is that fundamentally wrong? The Author SAYS, no. Famas may dance catalan and dance truce. I think your philological enquiry is delightful and quite true in the poetic sense of Truth, which is the ONLY sense of Truth. (I am speaking like Shelley, I'm afraid.)[78]

In addition to the sonic inventions of words such as *cronopios, tregua,* and *catala,* others, such as the rhymed greeting "buenas salenas," are coinages Cortázar invents for purely rhythmic reasons: "un puro *nonsense,* que en español, tiene valor mágico solamente" (pure nonsense, which in Spanish has value only as magic).[79] These words mirror the abysses of "gorgeous nonsense" celebrated by Stevens, and the difficulties they pose for the translator require post-symbolist strategies of metalinguistic gimcrack.

Consider a brief passage from Cortázar's third story in the collection, "Alegría del cronopio" (Gaiety of the Cronopio) containing these nonsense exchanges, followed here by the translation Blackburn finalized with Cortázar's input:

> Encuentro de un cronopio y un fama en la liquidación de la tienda
>   *La Mondiale.*
> —Buenas salenas cronopio cronopio.
> —Buenas tardes, fama. Tregua catala espera.
> —¿Cronopio cronopio?
> —Cronopio cronopio.
> —¿Hilo?
> —Dos, pero uno azul.
> El fama considera al cronopio. Nunca hablará hasta no saber que sus palabras son las que convienen, temeroso de que las esperanzas siempre alertas no se deslicen en el aire, esos microbios relucientes, y por una palabra equivocada invadan el corazón bondadoso del cronopio.[80]
>
> (An encounter between a cronopio and a fama at a liquidation sale in a shop called La Mondiale.

—Gray day, cronopio cronopio.

—Grade A, fama. Respite catalan hopeful.

—Cronopio cronopio?

—Cronopio cronopio.

—Thread?

—Two, but one blue one.

The fama considers the cronopio. He will not utter a sound until he's certain the words are precisely correct. Fearful that the always alert esperanzas, those sparkling microbes, will simply slip into the air, and through one mistaken word invade the cronopio's good-natured heart.)[81]

This portrait of quotidian Parisian commerce has some affinity with New York School observational poetry in the mode of Frank O'Hara or Blackburn's own "Pre-Lenten Gestures." Primarily, however, the "liquidation sale" at *La Mondiale* suggests Cortázar's way of deflating Stevens's linguistic allegories of globalization even as he adopts their stance. The encounter verges on total linguistic abstraction, and Blackburn's inventive translation matches the sonic abstraction of "buenas salenas" with the front rhymes "gray day" and "grade A." Out of the microbial encounter of the cronopio and fama, an attempt to translate metalinguistic gaming in the literary marketplace of "La Mondiale" ensues. Only the mot juste avoids the invading "mistaken word." Here, Cortázar and Blackburn collaborate to rewrite post-symbolist artifice as an allegory for translation in the world literary marketplace.

These inventive usages inflect Cortázar's practice of assigning honorary "cronopio" status to artists and writers he admires, addressing his letters to "Cronopio Paul." After Blackburn introduced him to the East Village literary scene grouped around the little magazine *Trobar*, including Jerome Rothenberg and Robert Kelly, Cortázar began signing off letters with salutations such as "Abrazos para KELLY, JERRY AND ALL THE VILLAGE CRONOPIOS."[82] The Village cronopios responded in kind. By 1962, Blackburn occasionally wrote his own cronopio-style accounts of Lower East Side life, such as "The Cronopios in America–1," published in LeRoi Jones and Diane DiPrima's newsletter *Floating Bear*:

After having picked up his letters at General Delivery, a cronopio went across to a bar in Christopher Street to peruse them quietly. The first was a letter from the cronopio's father containing money; the second was a long, woeful communication asking for money, from an acquaintance, a heroin addict, stranded in St. Louis; the third was an holiday extra-special subscription offer from TIME magazine; and the last was a letter from a cronopio friend of his in Argentina with a funny drawing on the back.[83]

Blackburn's "cronopio" describes the circuit of translation and epistolary exchange through which the Lower East Side poetry scene imagines exorbitant relations to world literature.

Blackburn and Cortázar's transatlantic dialogue also includes a fascinating tape exchange. Beginning on New Year's 1960, Blackburn composed anthology tapes for Cortázar. The first contained readings of his translations of *Historias de cronopios y de famas*, jazz musical interludes with Blackburn's commentary, ambient urban noise, and twenty-six of his recent poems, mostly those collected in *Brooklyn-Manhattan Transit* (1960). At this point, the small Divers Press pamphlet *The Dissolving Fabric* remained Blackburn's only book-length publication, and so the tapes offered an experimental publication format focused on immediacy, liveness, and the role of Blackburn's dispersive typographic layouts in producing performance scores. Another experimental New Year's tape for 1963 includes a dossier of Blackburn's poems and translations alongside conversations with other poets such as Jerome Rothenberg, An Anselm Hollo poem describing the translator as the Faustus of the 1960s, Zukofsky's *"A" 1–12*, and English translations of Guillén, Borges, Neruda, Celan, and others. In Paris, Cortázar took breaks from the writing of *Rayuela* by listening to Blackburn's tapes, and by sitting with friends such as Octavio Paz to listen to others. Paz came away from New York with a tape of his YMHA reading: "Octavio me hizo escuchar la banda donde tú lees (maravillosamente!!) *The Salamander*. It was a very moving experience for me, dear Paul, and your voice walked around in my house and did all kinds of tricks with the spoons in the kitchen." Cortázar linked the tapes to an emerging phonographic literary public sphere, though not quite the "midcult" one described by Jacob Smith.[84] Compiling Caedmon spoken-word albums and memories of Joyce reading from *Finnegans Wake*, he sought out transgenerational, international modernism in recorded speech. Scenes of "the group" listening to records in *Rayuela* carry with them something of this tape exchange. Blackburn, too, found in Cortázar's taped readings and jazz solos a "beautiful moyen de correspondence, baby."[85] That "beautiful" way of corresponding stands in for a large experimental epistolary culture that stoked the inter-American poetry of these years.

The True Pan-American Union: Margaret Randall and *El Corno Emplumado*

Blackburn and Cortázar show how countercultural correspondence laid the groundwork for major debuts in the booming world literary marketplace. But these writers' experimental letters, translations, and tape exchanges textured 1960s literary hemispherism as much as the popular Cortázar paperbacks that resulted. In other words, coffee shop and private apartment readings, along with the small-press "mimeograph revolution" that built on cheap commercial printing and recording technologies, stimulated a wide network of counterculturalists to embrace hemispherism. The new inter-American poetry is located in these small institutions of countercultural self-fashioning as much as in the Boom stoked by the large publishing houses.

One site of such exchange was Beat surrealist Philip Lamantia's Zona Rosa apartment in Mexico City, where bilingual readings often occurred between 1958 and 1961. Participants included Ernesto Cardenal, Homero Aridjis, Efraín Huerta, Juan Bañuelos, Leonora Carrington, Margaret Randall, and Sergio Mondragón, alongside less well-known poets such as Harvey Wolin, Sandra Rutman (Kraus), and Mary Lou Austria. Randall's reminiscences furnish one of the few records of this ephemeral scene, but in Lamantia's archive a folder marked "Poems by Others" contains some of the poems read, circulated, and translated.[86] In a poem by Aridjis that Lamantia translated, the speaker begins with what may be a description of this very scene: "Cirabel/llego siempre a tu aposento/con una confusión de bocas" (Cirabel/I always come to your rooms/with a confusion of mouths). Indeed, the "confusion of mouths" bears resemblance to the "Babbel" sound poetry Lamantia wrote with Wolin and Rutman, which, though inspired by Dadaism and Antonin Artaud, responded more particularly to the confusion of tongues he found in his coterie.[87] Another of Lamantia's untitled draft poems in the archive moves from the tiny apartment outward to a capacious hemispherism: "America it's because you are intelligent from the fingers up/all the way from Tierra del Fuego/to the Canadian border."[88] Here Lamantia blends the apostrophe of Ginsberg's "America" with the proprioceptive insight of Charles Olson to summon the new inter-American poetry.

Formalizing the intercultural pleasures of Lamantia's reading circle, Mondragón and Randall founded the most vital small-press journal of the new inter-American poetry, namely *El Corno Emplumado*, a bilingual quarterly that published thirty-one numbers from 1962 to 1969 (Figure 4.5). The biggest of the

(a)

el corno emplumado   the plumed horn   el corno e mplumado   the plumed h orn   el corno emplumado the plumed horn   el corn o emplumado   the plume d horn   el corno emplum ado   the plumed horn   el

bartra - creeley - eshleman - mondragón - solís - k aplan - blackburn - bañuelos - randall - ginsberg - co rrington - mejía sánchez - blossom - castellanos - k elly - cárdenas peña - wolin - bruenner - vallejo - g avronsky - bremser - frank - rainer - di suvero - c lark - macgrégor - coffeen - goeritz - tobias - conner

(b)

Fig 4.5 *El Corno Emplumado* 2 and *El Corno Emplumado* 22 (with cover art by Felipe Ehrenberg). Courtesy of Margaret Randall.

littles, it featured hundreds of poets and managed to find distributors across the Americas. Eshleman called it *"the* big table that *Big Table* never became."[89] The wide discourse radius was a result of each issue's letters at the back of the magazine, and of its multidirectional translations, most by Randall and Mondragón. It synthesized and redisseminated tendencies of local journals from around the hemisphere, while inspiring like-minded inter-American projects, such as Thelma Nava's *Pájaro Cascabel* (Mexico City), Miguel Grinberg's *Eco contemporáneo* (Buenos Aires), Richard Greenwell's *Haravec* (Peru), and Thomas Merton's *Monk's Pond* (Abbey of Gethsemani, Kentucky). It only shuttered after losing government support when it protested the 1968 Tlatelolco massacre. By then, Randall and Mondragón's marriage had drifted apart along with their aesthetico-political outlooks, Mondragón toward Zen spirituality and Randall toward a commitment to the Cuban state.

Randall, the daughter of Jewish New Yorkers, grew up in Albuquerque, New Mexico, where, in the mid-1950s, she befriended Robert Creeley and Elaine de Kooning. She subsequently spent three years on the Lower East Side of New York (1958–1961), frequented the Cedar Tavern, worked for Nancy MacDonald's Spanish Refugee Aid, and sympathized with the FPCC, whose offices were next door. During Castro's April 1959 visit to New York City, Randall cooked Castro an extravagant paella and lugged it uptown by subway, only to have the delivery thwarted by his security detail.[90] When Randall found that the gender politics of the Lower East Side scene stopped short of the "all poets welcome" motto that looms over Daniel Kane's account of the period, she left for Mexico by bus, in the company of her young son Gregory, whose father was the poet Joel Oppenheimer. MacDonald supplied a few contacts, such as the anthropologist Laurette Séjourné.[91]

"Relations between the Americas have never been worse," wrote Mondragón, Randall, and Harvey Wolin in a headnote to the inaugural issue in early 1962.[92] "*El Corno Emplumado* will be a showcase (*outside politics*) for the fact that WE ARE ALL BROTHERS." The journal's name wedded the jazz horn to the quetzal feather, symbolically yoking a US culture of improvisation to an indigenizing Mexican cultural nationalism. The improbable conceit was lost on many correspondents, who habitually misidentify it as "The Fluted Horn," "The Fluted Serpent," "La Scorza Emplumada," "El Cuerno Emplumado," or "El Cornado." Most settled into knowing it as *El Corno*, and some of the magazine's house illustrators, such as Jaime Carrero, often added to a growing imaginary of jazz-poet-quetzal creatures wedded to portraits of many poets affiliated with the magazine (Figure 4.6). Such images allegorize easements of inter-American poetic

Fig 4.6 Jaime Carrero, "Meg" (Margaret Randall), and "Sergio Mondragón,"
El Corno Emplumado 17 (January 1966): 44–45. Courtesy of Margaret Randall.

communication and the overcoming of stark rifts in the months after the counterrevolutionary Bay of Pigs invasion in Cuba. The self-funded poetry journal
proposed a semi-autonomous counterpublic, emphasizing a common humanity
"above" and "outside" politics. Even now, Randall continues to emphasize "our
freedom from institutional sponsorship," although as we will see, the magazine's
financing was a bit more complicated, challenging inherited accounts of the
"mimeo revolution."[93]

Randall and Mondragón had a loose editorial agenda at the start, articulating an "unpolitical" enthusiasm for inter-American cultural relations, nourished
by their Beat enclave. Seeking funds for the inaugural issue, Randall described
the emerging journal to the poet James Merrill, one of many unlikely financiers
(another was Mexican poet José Gorostiza in his role working for a government
ministry):

> I am a young American poet, having spent the last three years in New York,
> recently arrived in Mexico — more or less for good. I came to find more
> writing time, more time for my small son, more time to live [. . .]. I found
> all this, but much more: a landscape of silently screaming young Mexican

poets, some of them excellent, writing in the solitary isolation of a world without a "scene," without publications to speak of, without communication of any kind. This is a world which hangs between centuries — vitally involved in the new American poetry and involved too in the mystic roots of its own country. There are some American poets here too, and recently there have been readings: marathon sessions of bi-lingual music, from which germinated the idea for a bi-lingual magazine.[94]

El Corno therefore first rendered visible an eclectic Mexico City countercultural community driven by lofty, hemispheric idealism. This idealism streamed into the first issues, which refigured ad hoc community as literary network and featured cross-cultural dialogues and juxtapositions of aesthetically divergent, neo-avant-garde coteries.

In its first four years, *El Corno* published substantial portfolios of the Brazilian Noigandres group's concrete poetry (Haroldo de Campos served as the magazine's "representative" in Sao Paolo); concrete and visual poems by Mexican artists from Mathias Goeritz to Felipe Ehrenberg; proto-conceptual work by young poets like David Antin, Vito Acconci, and Jackson Mac Low; US and Mexican surrealists; guerilla poetry from Guatemala, Cuba, and El Salvador; dossiers of experimental poetry from Canada, Nicaragua, Argentina, Uruguay, and Peru; the Colombian nadaista (nothingist) group; selections of so-called "tribal" poetries, which appeared well before the ethnopoetic anthologies of the late 1960s; US poets affiliated with the Beat, Black Mountain, and Deep Image groups, such as Creeley, Dorn, Blackburn, Ginsberg, Ferlinghetti, Snyder, and Rothenberg; translations of high modernists from Vallejo and Neruda to Pound and Williams; and single-author issues spotlighting offbeat choices such as Raquel Jodorowsky, Robert Kelly, and George Bowering.

El Corno also built transgenerational bridges to an older cast of leftist and avant-garde poets from the Popular Front days, including the poet Walter Lowenfels in New York, Catalan exile Agustí Bartra, and Yiddish-Mexican poet Jacobo Glantz. Glantz's delicatessen, facetiously known as the Jacobo Glantz Gallery, featured art appearing in early issues of *El Corno*, such as assemblages by Bruce Connor, loosely inspired by the mummies of Guanajuato, bearing wry titles like "Portrait of Allen Ginsberg" and "The Bride."[95] However, the visual repertory of the magazine in its early days skewed more toward the surreal drawings of Leonora Carrington, Carlos Coffeen Serpas, and especially José Luis Cuevas. In its later years, *El Corno* became a key outlet for still younger writers, perhaps most importantly the Chilean poet and artist Cecilia Vicuña, then the barely twenty-year-old author of the "No manifiesto de la Tribu No" (No Manifesto of Tribu No) and a sheaf of erotic lyric poems whose publication was planned and scuttled in both Chile and the United States, where she visited Sergio Mondragón in 1968.[96]

The magazine's inclusiveness gave it an integrationist allure. Diane Wakoski wrote, "everyone in New York is very impressed [. . .] We, they, people, LIKE the fact that you have an open mind, not favouring any school or type of writing."[97] However, these inclusions turned off other readers. Bly disdained "the Beat emphasis" and unhelpfully suggested: "You are serving up steaks from a long dead horse. The poetry of people like Lamantia is almost too bad to believe. But I like the Spanish work."[98] Octavio Paz publicly supported the magazine and reprinted his 1968 protest of the Tlatelolco massacre in its pages, even after expressing private reservations when it had previously bungled translations of some of his poems. In 1967 he argued that the kinds of Latin American poets found in its pages, with the exception of Brazilian Noigandres, amounted to Beat "acolytes" instead of an authentic avant-garde: "Imitating Olson or Ginsberg in Lima, Caracas, Buenos Aires, Santiago, Mexico City, or Tegucigalpa is tantamount to ignoring—or, what is worse, forgetting—the fact that this poetic revolution has already taken place in the Spanish language."[99] Paz also privately rebuked Bly by the end of the 1960s, disparaging an antiwar reading by "that Minnesota milkman or hog butcher" which he saw while teaching at the University of Pittsburgh.[100] Bly and Paz joined a debate: did El Corno's integrationist stance abdicate aesthetic acumen? Robert Kelly gave a sober analysis in "Enstasy: Poem for El Corno Emplumado at the Tenth Issue." "It is likely that you print many bad poems," he admitted, but ecumenicalism and integration were still key:

At some point all the work, good work & bad work & work that fails to be either, has to be melded, thrown together in the teeth of the world (and its literary values) in the name of the new age. *England's Helicon*. Tottel's *Miscellanie, transition*, are not interesting as history but *in* history, at the moment of their joining together that which is. Of value.)[101]

Kelly's comparisons, from Tottel's *Miscellanie* to Eugène Jolas's avant-garde *transition*, offer a useful genealogy for the spirit of El Corno's attempts at hemispheric integration.

Randall and Mondragón indeed threw the journal "in the teeth of the world." Writing to US foundations for support in 1964, Randall reported impressive numbers: "we print 3,000 copies of *El Corno Emplumado* and we distribute these between some 600 subscribers and 250 bookstores in 23 countries."[102] Beyond these official circulation numbers, young artists often confessed to pilfering the magazine as an illicit form of cultural currency. Marco Antonio Flores called it the most commonly stolen magazine from the Casa de las Américas library. Perhaps the most interesting thief was Rolando Peña, a Venezuelan art student in New York who frequented the Warhol Factory (where other *El Corno* correspondents included Al Hansen). Peña's New Year's postcard to Randall and Mondragón in 1965 merits quotation:

> Aunque no los conozco personalmente estoy seguro que en el Nirvana caótico neural que habitamos nuestras proyecciones defecativas higiénicas se encuentran y eso es lo importante. Soy asiduo lector del Corno aunque siempre ha sido prestado o robado. [...] Reciban mi mensaje desde este cementerio hermoso de urinarios."[103]

> (Even though I don't know you personally, I am sure that in the chaotic neural nirvana where we abide, our defecatory, hygienic projections meet, and that's what's important. I am an assiduous reader of Corno even though I always borrow or steal it. [...] Accept my message from this beautiful urinal cemetery)

The "urinal cemetery" refers to Peña's Duchampian self-portrait in a urinal factory, beneath a billboard advertising a volcanic pat of butter drenching a spaghetti mountain (Figure 4.7). *El Corno* joined a global countercultural network seeking alternatives to an age of commercial abundance that could border on the grotesque.

By the time they were wrapping up the first volume, Cardenal wrote Randall and Mondragón from his mission in Colombia to suggest that *El Corno* was righting the deficit of political inter-Americanism noted in the journal's first editorial:

> Te diré: ustedes están creando la verdadera Unión Panamericana. La Unión Panamericana es la de los poetas, no la de esos que se sientan en los banquetes y "devoran a mi pueblo como si fuera pan," como dice el Salmo. Los poetas son los que se entiende, a pesar de las barreras del idioma, porque ellos son los que tienen los órganos de comunicación, son la voz de la tribu. Si los poetas no realizan el Panamericanismo nadie más lo hará. Y lo están haciendo. Y por primera vez en la historia se comenzarán a entender el pueblo norteamericano y el hispanoamericano, en un verdadero entendimiento de pueblos, porque se entienden sus poetas. En Washington no se han dado cuenta todavía de que las grandes naciones

Fig 4.7 Rolando Peña, New Year's postcard, 1965. El Corno Emplumado Collection, HRC. © 1965 Rolando Peña. Used by permission of Rolando Peña.

(los EE.UU. incluso) han sido hechas por los poetas. Un cambio de métrica produce grandes consecuencias sociales como dice Pound.[104]

(I told you: you are creating the true Pan American Union. The Pan American Union is of the poets, not those who sit at banquets "devouring my people like bread," as the Psalm says. The poets are the ones who know this, despite language barriers, because they sustain the organs of communication. They are the voice of the tribe. If the poets do not bring Pan-Americanism into being nobody else will. And they are. And, for the first time in history, North Americans and Spanish Americans will begin to understand one another, a true understanding of peoples, because their poets understand one another. In Washington they still do not realize that the great nations (including the US) were made by poets. A change of metrics has great social consequences, as Pound says.)

Here, Cardenal invokes numerous poetic warrants that reconfigure the poetry of the Americas for the Alliance for Progress years. He intimates a Whitmanian, bardic enthusiasm; he suggests a Mallarméan "purification" of the voice of an enlarging hemispheric "tribe"; he professes a Nerudian desire to speak for the hungry, the voiceless, and the poor; and from some chimerical combination of

Ezra Pound and Che Guevara he borrows the notion that metrical transformation implies social transformation—that stitched in the textures of the "new poetry" lay the social landscape of the New Man in the revolutionary history of the New World. For Cardenal, the alternative poetry press articulated and disseminated the new inter-Americanism as a tiny institution of hemispheric democracy, the 'true' alternative to the Pan American Union (PAU), which since 1948 had remained the physical seat of the Organization of American States (OAS) in Washington, DC, and which, as Fox documents in *Making Art Panamerican*, threw most cultural support into the visual arts section, neglecting poetry in the Cold War.[105]

El Corno published many letters like Cardenal's, sometimes without permission. Levertov objected: "you tend to print an awful lot of letters praising the magazine. What I call hysteria is an attitude of fervent poetic brotherhood which, while I am in sympathy with the desires that give rise to it, seems to me more than a little inflated."[106] Levertov's charge of "fervent poetic brotherhood" could have singled out Miguel Grinberg of Argentina, who "raved" so much upon reading Cardenal's declaration that he founded a "League of International Poets" (also called Nueva Solidaridad), and spoke immodestly of accomplishing in twelve months what the official "servicio cultural diplomático" had not accomplished in twelve years.[107] True enough: the first issue of Grinberg's "revista inter-americana" *Eco contemporáneo* went to press just months after *El Corno*. In spring 1964, over three hundred young poets from fifteen American nations embarked on a pilgrimage to a "First Encounter of American Poets" in Mexico City, organized by Grinberg, Randall, and Mondragón (Figure 4.8).[108]

Initially, even the PAU itself supported Grinberg's League. Squirru joked to Blackburn: "by then I hope our Organization will have something concrete to offer. Among the ideas I have launched is one of military forces at the service of culture which would translate itself in the Air Force providing transportation for poets, writers, intellectuals and students, for cultural purposes. . . If this job proves anything less than the possibility to bring us poets all together, I want no part in it."[109] Accordingly, Squirru hoped to turn the PAU magazine *Américas* into "a formidable weapon with which to promote the new writers, poets [and] painters." At Grinberg's invitation, Cortázar addressed a manifesto full of mock outrage "A los cronopios de la acción poética inter-Americana" (To the Cronopios of the Inter-American Poetic Happening). He portrayed a furtive and anarchic network with the promise to flower into a hemispheric counterculture:

> En vista de todo lo cual, mi indignada aportación a este nefasto primer
> encuentro de la Acción Poética Interamericana es la siguiente: Cronopios
> de la tierra americana, muestren sin vacilar la hilacha. Abran las puertas

Fig 4.8 Alex Rode at the International Gathering of Poets, Fuente de Don Quijote, Parque de Chapultepec, Mexico City. From left: unidentified, A. Fredric Franklyn, Alex Rode, Barbara Jacobs, Homero Aridjis, rest unidentified. Courtesy of Margaret Randall.

como las abren los elefantes distraídos, ahoguen en ríos de carcajadas toda tentativa de discurso académico, de estatuto con artículos de I a XXX, de organización petrificadora. Háganse odiar minuciosamente por los cerrajeros, echen toneladas de azúcar en las salinas del llanto y estropeen todas las azucareras de la complacencia con el puñadito subrepticio de la sal parricida.[110]

(In view of all this, my indignant contribution to this nefarious first meeting of the Inter-American Poetic Happening is the following: Cronopios of American lands, do not hesitate to show your true colors. Open the doors like distracted elephants, drown in cackling rivers every attempt at academic discourse, all statutes with articles I to XXX, all lapidifying organizations. Be meticulously scorned by locksmiths, throw tons of sugar in the salt of tears and break all the sugar bowls of complacency with furtive handfuls of parricidal salt.)

Randall and Mondragón described *El Corno* as a textual supplement to such happenings, a shadow institution of the inter-American system. As they wrote: "If Ernesto Cardenal in Colombia is right in saying 'the poets are the true Pan-American Union' and Miguel Grinberg in Argentina is promoting this vision into reality [. . .], the mirrors most publicly reflecting this common vision are the NEW MAGAZINES."[111]

Here we need to pause for a reflection on standard histories of the so-called mimeograph revolution. In his preface to the 1998 exhibition *A Secret Location on the Lower East Side: Adventures in Writing, 1960–1980*, the *El Corno* contributor Jerome Rothenberg argued that US literature often migrates from periphery to center. For Rothenberg, the mimeo revolution extended a US tendency toward self-publication at the margins prior to consecration by the mainstream, which he links to Whitman's "self-published" *Leaves of Grass*, and to the historical avant-garde's "network" of "noncommercial, often poet-run" publications, such as the Objectivist Press and *transition*. The "new poetry" of the 1960s was also "at a necessary distance from the commercial hub of American publishing (the concentration of media power in mid-Manhattan)." For him, "the Lower East Side & environs," fed by cheap rents, photostat, ditto, mimeograph duplication, and cheap postage, describes a real concentration of energies, as well as a metonym for global DIY enclaves from Jonathan Williams's Jargon Society in North Carolina to Cid Corman's *Origin* in Kyoto, Japan. Rothenberg stresses noncommercial and anti-institutional oppositions to state-sponsorship. To him, "dependence on support from institutional & governmental sources" begins with the National Endowment for the Arts of the 1980s, imposing a "gloss of professionalism on the alternative publications" in their twilight.[112]

Yet when we return to some archives of the mimeo revolution, Rothenberg's anti-institutional portrait seems only partially true. Our first clue is in the existence of such archives at all. The fifty boxes comprising *El Corno*'s archives at the Harry Ransom Center and the Fales Library are products of yearly sales that partly financed the journal. Felix Pollak at the University of Wisconsin's Little Magazine Archive helped where he could, too. Randall realized the value of her trove of letters through Ted and Eli Wilentz of the Eighth Street Bookshop and Corinth Press in Manhattan. Many of these letters were marked "not for publication": Lawrence Ferlinghetti chastises Randall for violating City Lights copyrights with translations of Ginsberg poems; Octavio Paz discreetly critiques Mondragón's translation work and prefers to remain out of the journal; Ernesto Cardenal, recently ordained as a priest, confesses to an incurable anticlericalism. The editors did not publish these letters, but partly sustained the journal through their sale.

Cardenal's claim that *El Corno* was "the true Pan American Union" offers the other clue. As I have suggested, PAU became another unlikely patron for the magazine. Squirru approached the magazine on the advice of Blackburn, who told Randall he'd asked "that swinging bureau-cat" to "get his platoons of monies into the line, en la lucha!"[113] He offered a 500-copy PAU subscription, enough to finance a quarter of the journal's yearly production. *El Corno's* apoliticism briefly melded with the Alliance for Progress's liberal anticommunist cultural programming, but stress fractures soon appeared, as *El Corno* dashed off barbs at PAU-style cultural diplomacy, and Squirru wrote to denounce a reprinting of Castro's "Speech to the Intellectuals."[114] But the journal's ecumenical agenda meant that Squirru himself contributed poems, even as he immediately pulled the subscription. Randall only fully broke with Squirru after her first visit to Cuba in 1967, by which time it was clear that *El Corno* aligned more closely to Havana's *Casa de las Américas* magazine than to *Mundo Nuevo* or *Cuadernos*, the latter two being journals exposed in 1967 for accepting CIA backing. Randall wrote to the PAU journal *Américas* denouncing the "cultural politics of the Alliance for Progress and the O.A.S.," which, she argued, put young intellectuals in a CCF-like dilemma. *El Corno* thus transformed from an "apolitical" expression of countercultural brotherhood to a key site of neo-avant-garde cross-fertilization, and then into a shadow institution of hemispheric cultural diplomacy, toggling across the decade between Mexican state bureaucracy and Alliance for Progress cultural programming, and finally embracing Cuban revolutionary nationalism.

This embrace of Cuba characterizes Randall's chapbook *So Many Rooms Has a House But One Roof* (1968), written after her visit to Havana in 1967 for the "Encuentro con Rubén Darío" centennial (Figure 4.9). With a cover illustration by Felipe Ehrenberg, the twelve-poem sequence expresses the poet's meditative sympathy for the revolutionary project, described in alliteratively Ginsberg-inspired terms as "men against moloch" and as an effort to "create/a new language" adequate to revolutionary society, a single "roof" over the proliferating misconceptions about the island circulating in US mass media. Many of the sequence's stanzas describe crumbling or repurposed homes occupied by poets, figures of a "new language" of fleeting revolutionary domesticity. The closing poems are sited at the garish seaside "Xanadu" mansion in Veradero abandoned by the wealthy industrialist Irénée du Pont, president of the DuPont Company.

The "Encuentro con Rubén Darío" took place at Xanadu, repurposing a palatial expression of US economic influence for an international gathering of poets to revive Darío's hemispheric spirit:

> dupont built this fortress
> of a house
> a wide gull floats beside the cupola

Fig 4.9 Margaret Randall, *So Many Rooms Has a House but One Roof* (New Rivers Press, 1968). Cover by Felipe Ehrenberg. Courtesy of Margaret Randall.

dupont prepared the golf course
where egrets and wild hens nest
and poets walk. we sit, it is
different now
dupont was mason, paid the help, drank
daiqueries
but the gull turned, the change came

brute
and sure
dupont fled this peninsula and died
and poets sit, keep company
with this gull
stayed with revolution on his wing.

At this meeting, Randall first met the Uruguayan poet Mario Benedetti and heard a young Nancy Morejón read from *Richard trajo su flauta*. Under this "one roof," a near rhyme with "one truth," she figures the Cuban revolution as a habitus for the imperial ironies and restorative imaginaries of an inter-American poetics. Soon, Randall's embrace of the Cuban revolution came to encompass a feminism that powerfully revised the forms of intercultural revolutionary identification preceding hers in the early 1960s.[115]

Transnational Martyrology: Heraud, *Quena*, Eshleman

Part of Randall's turn toward Cuba involved her work to promote so-called "guerril-lero poetry." Cuba offered one kind of inter-American "oppositional public sphere" when it came to Beats, and another when it came to stoking guerilla revolution and training revolutionaries in the Americas. Over the course of the 1960s and 1970s, several militant Latin American poets passed through Cuba en route to guerilla activity, and many of their lives later came to an end at the hands of repressive state forces, local police, or leftist factionalism. The finest among these poets were Otto Rene Castillo (Guatemala, 1934–1967), Roque Dalton (El Salvador, 1935–1975), Javier Heraud (Peru, 1942–1963), Lionel Rugama (Nicaragua, 1949–1970), Rita Valdivia (Bolivia, 1946–1969), and Che Guevara himself (Argentina, 1928–1967). Various historical scales furnish contexts for their poetry and its reception, from models of troubadour and crusade lyric as old as vernacular poetry in the West to romantic career narratives premised on the revolutionary patriotism of José Martí, and espe-cially the popular front martyrdom of Federico García Lorca.[116] In particular, the 1963 death of Javier Heraud keenly reinflected the Lorca paradigm of martyrological reception, now premising it on a hemispheric community of poets united against Cold War anticommunism. Heraud's posthumous canonization established an ele-giac strain of New Left hemispherism premised on the body of the mourned poet.

A promising poet from Lima, Heraud published two chapbooks in 1960 and 1961, trained as a guerilla in Cuba, and died in the abortive actions of his revo-lutionary cell as it entered southern Peru in 1963. The few surviving pictures of him show a young university student in an ill-fitting suit, the dutiful, petit bour-geois son of a prominent Lima family. These images fed Heraud's mythologiza-tion as a "trascendente símbolo de la joven poesía peruana" (transcendent symbol of Peruvian youth poetry), for his friends and family in Lima had not grasped the extent of his rapid radicalization when news of his death reached them.[117] His first book, *El Rio* (1960), is a tiny sixteen-page chapbook, printed in a hand-stitched edition by Javier Sologuren's small press Cuadernos del Hontanar. The work of a confident eighteen-year-old student, its brown wraps and peach paper house five slender poems. The nine-part "El Rio" is the centerpiece. A deceptively simple, excessively enjambed poem, "El Rio" transforms an epigraph of Antonio Machado ("la vida baja como un ancho río" (life runs like a wide river) into the refrain "yo soy el río [que. . .]." The poem offers a serial, extended conceit of the poet's growth, personified by the course of a river toward the sea. In a lethargic, continuous announcement of the poet's fluid presence, it winds from a "source" toward a turbid scene of dissolution in a greater oceanic flux: "Llegará la hora/en que tendré que desembocar en los/océanos,/que mezclar mis/aguas limpias con sus/aguas turbias" (The hour will come/when I must flow into the/oceans,/must mix my/clean waters with its/murky waters).[118] Narrating the poet's maturation, it climaxes in social self-abnegation. Like a tributary, the individuating process of aesthetic education trickles toward the oceanic flux of social collectivity. Unlike major modernist river poems such as Langston Hughes's "The Negro Speaks of Rivers," Giuseppe Ungaretti's "I fiumi," Fernando Pessoa's "O Tejo é mais belo que o rio que corre pela minha aldeia," or Vicente Huidobro's "Exprés," Heraud's poem does not make the planetary river system an allegory of racialized, diasporic self-commemoration. For Heraud, rivers model bourgeois individualism's dissolution in collectivity.

In light of Heraud's untimely death—gunned down in the middle of a river—the fluvial motif haunts his work from beginning to end. His second chapbook, *El viaje* (1961), variously extends *El Río*'s figurative waterways. The book is slightly longer, the paper stock is cheaper, and the cover's splash of green print vaguely evokes a rifle. Twin epigraphs from T. S. Eliot and the Peruvian surrealist Emilio Adolfo Westphalen renew the sense that Heraud struggles to break free from modernist models. With no table of contents, it nimbly invites readers to limpidly wade into this riverine body of work anywhere along its course. Heraud conjures a troubadour tradition of song composed on the march under the idle sun. Compare, for instance, Guillaume IX's "Farai un vers de dreyt nien," here in Blackburn's translation: "I shall make a vers about/nothing,/downright nothing, not/about myself or youth or love/or anyone. I wrote it horseback dead asleep/ while riding in the sun."[119] However, in Heraud's poems, idleness is counterpastoral, provoking contemplations of death. Heraud often taunts death, and styles morbidity as the poem's telos. In the exemplary "Poema," the word *río* shifts homophonically from "river" to "I laugh":

Yo no me
río de
la
muerte.
Sucede

> simple-
> mente,
> que no
> tengo miedo
> de morir
> entre
> pájaros
> y arboles.

(No, I don't/laugh at/death./It's/just/that/I'm not/afraid/to die/among/birds/and trees.)[120] These light-footed lines, rarely more than a foot or two in length, are enjambed with a minimalist persistence that evokes Creeley. However, Heraud calibrates this fleetness to the foot-by-foot "pace" of the labored revolutionary march amid fecund nature.

   Much guerrillero poetry evokes rural marches. "Vámonos patria a caminar," Otto Rene Castillo titled his signature poem.[121] Che Guevara's 1956 "Canto a Fidel" also incites the march: "Vámonos, ardiente profeta de la aurora,/por recónditos senderes inalámbricos/a liberar el verde caimán que tanto amas" (Let's go, burning prophet of the dawn, along recondite, wireless paths, to liberate the green alligator you so love). Like Heraud's "Poema," "Canto a Fidel" links marching to mortality, establishing acceptance of death in the service of history's Hegelian slaughter bench: "Y si en nuestro camino se interpone el hierro,/pedimos un sudario de cubanas lágrimas/para que se cubran los guerrilleros huesos/en el tránsito a la historia americana" (And if iron stands in our way/we ask for a sheet of Cuban tears/to cover our guerrilla bones/on the journey to American history).[122] Heraud fuses the "walking" measure, the perceptual unit of the *paso*, to the death march:

> Y sin embargo,
> caminando un poco,
> volteando hacia la izquierda,
> se llega a las montañas
> y a los ríos.
> No es que yo quiera
> alejarme de la vida,
> sino que tengo
> que acercarme hacia la muerte.
>
> (So, walk on a while
> turn to the left

and you reach the mountains
and the rivers.
Look it isn't that I want
to leave life back there—
but I must follow a path
that death is known to stalk.)[123]

Leaving bourgeois Lima society behind, the poet figures walking as a compulsory revolutionary energy. "Las Moscas," a description of a fly feeding on the putrefying soldier, ends with Heraud's clearest vision of his own death: "Solo espero no alimentarla/y no verla en mis entrañas,/el día que si acaso/me matan en el campo/y dejan mi cuerpo bajo el sol" (Because I have this recurrent hope/not to feed you/I don't want to see you/in my entrails/the day they cut me open/in the countryside/and leave my body under the sun).[124] Here Dorn and Brotherston's translation lends the poem drama by transforming the description of the fly into a second-person address. Heraud himself, in resorting to the image of the fly, draws on Neruda's "gusano" (worm) and other figures of bourgeois and fascist rapaciousness common to 1930s traditions of committed poetry.

In summer of 1961, a few weeks after the publication of *El viaje*, Heraud attended the communist anticolonial World Youth Forum in Moscow, followed by three months in Paris and Madrid. Shortly after his return to Lima in October, he collaborated with César Calvo on his last poem, *Ensayo a dos voces* (Essay for Two Voices), published posthumously in 1967. Antonio Cisneros describes it as an experiment in two poets meeting as one, in contrast to the automatism of the surrealists, and it returns again to the river theme as the terms of dialogic self-abnegation. Before 1961 was out, Heraud won a scholarship alongside fellow poet Rodolfo Hinostroza to travel to Havana to study cinema. Unbeknownst to his family, and possibly unbeknownst to Heraud himself, "cinema" was code for "foquismo" training, a Guevaran practice defined by the deployment of vanguard paramilitary cells to infiltrate and radicalize local networks of peasants.[125] Heraud returned from Cuba in a foco that crossed Brazil, armed in Bolivia, and entered the Puerto Maldonado area in the Amazonian basin of southern Peru. Peruvian foquistas of the Army of National Liberation (ELN) applied Guevaran principles too impetuously, overestimating local peasant and unions support for a cadre of bourgeois Limeño students trained in Cuba. Ultimately, a squad of armed forces and local landowners ("plantation policemen" in Clayton Eshleman's phrase) anticipated the infiltration and chased down the ELN cell for several days. On May 15, 1963, they detained some of the cell and killed Heraud as he snuck past Puerto Maldonado along the Rio Madre Dios in an oarless dugout canoe. A hail of gunfire from the riverbank executed him, an explosive dumdum bullet ripping open his stomach. He was naked, and his comrade allegedly waved a white cloth.[126]

News of Heraud's death chilled Lima, sparking debates over the validity of revolutionary action. Pedro Beltrán, the corporate liberal former premier and editor of Lima's *La Prensa*, criticized Cuba's insidious role as a communist staging ground: "Peru, and every American country including the US, will remain subject to grave danger as long as Cuba is permitted to operate as a center of ideological, military, and economic subversion for Communism." Javier's father Jorge Heraud, a prominent lawyer, rebuked the hard-line anticommunist depiction of Javier's death. In an angry open letter to Beltrán, he charged the Peruvian army with taking criminally repressive measures against a nude, unarmed boy:

> Nosotros sabíamos que nuestro hijo Javier estaba hondamente preocupado porque aspiraba a tener una vida útil y creadora. Lo prueba sus libros de poemas, pero nunca supimos que él pensara, al irse a Cuba, en otra cosa que estudiar cinematografía. Por eso las noticias de Puerto Maldonado nos fulminaron, y yo fui al lugar de los hechos porque me resistía a creerlos. Allí tuve la trágica certidumbre de la muerte de Javier. Pero mi pena, con ser insondable, se ha agrandado más aún al saber que mi hijo [. . .] pudo ser detenido sin necesidad de disparos.[127]

> We knew that our son Javier was deeply concerned with aspirations to lead a useful, creative life. This is proven by his books of poems. But we never knew he was considering, upon going to Cuba, anything other than the study of cinematography. So the news from Puerto Maldonado came as a bolt from the blue, and I went to the scene, because I refused to believe it. There I gained the tragic certainty of Javier's death. But my unfathomable sorrow was further deepened by the knowledge that my son [. . .] could have been arrested without the necessity of a shot being fired.

Jorge's paternal grief touched off an outpouring of panegyric from Lima's literary community, including Mario Vargas Llosa and Heraud's poet friends and professors, such as Washington Delgado. Transnational messages of solidarity and homage rushed in from Nicolás Guillén and Fayad Jamís in Cuba. Neruda sent a message from Isla Negra condemning the "fuerzas oscuras" of "nuestra América oscura" (dark forces of our dark Americas) that peppered bullets into a child.

At first, the story received little notice in the United States aside from a brief article in *Time*. Buttressed by Beltrán's remarks, "Biography of a Lost Poet" portrayed Heraud as a talented but misguided youth whose ideological folly could be blamed on his Marxist mentors who shilled for Castro's program to "export" communism.[128] Yet by 1969, Heraud had undergone a transnational martyrology, sainted through translations by Randall in *El Corno*, Maureen Ahern de Maurer in *Haravec*, Blackburn in *TriQuarterly*, and Dorn and Brotherston in *Palabra de guerrillero*. His poetry's sacrifice to history touched off debates about poetry's relation to revolutionary politics on the one hand, and toward state-funded literary culture on the other. His recuperation is due in part to the nine months that aspiring poet-translator Clayton Eshleman spent in Peruvian literary circles in 1965–1966, where he was employed by the USIA-sponsored Instituto Cultural Peruano Norteamericano (ICPNA) to produce the bilingual magazine *Quena* (Flute), and where he hoped to woo César Vallejo's notoriously obstreperous French widow Georgette de Vallejo into sharing the *Poemas humanos* worksheets for his projected translations.[129]

Eshleman had discovered jazz and poetry as an undergraduate at Indiana University, where he transformed the literary magazine *Folio* into a space for the New American writing of Ginsberg, Zukofsky, Hirschman, Bly, and Mary Ellen Solt, all glad to find a rare Midwest publication venue. He also encountered poems by Neruda and Vallejo in Dudley Fitts's *Anthology of Contemporary Latin American Poetry*, and armed with the vague awareness that Beat poets often went to Mexico, traveled south in the summers of 1959 and 1960, experiencing a rapid expansion of his creative faculties as poet and translator. As he later recounted to Randall, he found a "breakthrough" after "the dullness and disgust in Bloomington": "to see all that cactus, land, past, the walking blood, was as they say too much: I must have written 200 poems in a couple of months, including gobs of the *Res* [*Residence on Earth*] (starting from scratch in *both* languages)."[130] When he contracted hepatitis and returned early to Indiana, he asked a Guadalajara bookseller to refund his down payment on a leather-bound edition of Neruda's *Obras completas* for his bus fare.

A second summer included coffee-shop readings with Beat acolytes in Mexico City, a chance encounter with James Baldwin in Acapulco, and an evening with Lysander Kemp in Jalisco. In these travels, translation went hand in hand with novice attempts at poetry in *Mexico & North* (1962), self-published in a hand-stitched edition and distributed by Trobar Books. The title promised a cardinal reorientation of US poetry in the geography of greater Mexico. Eshleman's rootless, summering poet stalks around Lake Chapala in Jalisco, peppering picturesque observations about his amazement at the fecundity of semi-rural Mexico with soaring metaphors and citations from Vallejo and Neruda poems.

In 1962, Eshleman began a two-year stint teaching English in Japan, befriending Gary Snyder, Cid Corman, and Ginsberg while there. Modeling himself on stone lithographer Will Peterson, who designed *Mexico & North*'s cover, he "apprenticed" to poetry through his translations of Vallejo and Neruda, with whom he corresponded cordially. He mythologized his "encounter" with Vallejo as a violent clash of wills in "The Book of Yorunomado," a long poem named for the coffee shop where he usually worked on his translations. Drawing on Japanese discourses of ritualized violence, it describes Vallejo as the "dead cholo//eating into my cord."[131] Back in the United States in 1964, Eshleman found readjustment difficult. Blackburn connected him with Squirru at the PAU, who contracted Eshleman to translate an anthology of Latin American poets chosen by Squirru. Viewing it as a distraction from his work on Vallejo, he never completed it, but his resume that year listed his occupation as "Translator of contemporary Latin-American Poetry for the Pan American Union." In 1965, PAU released an anthology similar to the one planned by Eshleman.

By then, Eshleman had set out for Lima. With a flair for romantic self-fashioning, he flew his pregnant wife Barbara from Indiana to Cuzco, while he hitchhiked along the Pan-American Highway from Indiana to Panama City before flying the rest of the way. He first dropped in on Mondragón and Randall in Mexico City, with whom he had begun a voluble correspondence in 1962. They furnished him with introductions to Raquel Jodorowsky in Mexico City; Marco Antonio Flores, who was hiding out from the police in Guatemala; and Ernesto Cardenal and José Coronel Urtecho in Nicaragua. Eshleman argued with Cardenal at lunch over his perception of gender bias regarding his plans for the male-only Solentiname community, where Cardenal would move the following year. Eshleman regarded Cardenal as stiff and old-fashioned, whereas Urtecho, who he later commissioned to translate Olson's "Projective Verse," struck him as cosmopolitan.[132]

In Lima, his editorship of *Folio* helped him secure a job to create a bilingual magazine under the auspices of the Instituto Cultural Peruano Norteamericano (ICPNA), directed by a man named Conrad Spohnholtz.[133] He evidently modeled his magazine on his experience with *El Corno*, though he hoped to exercise greater discernment regarding the relations of New American and experimental Latin American writing. Through this position, he developed friendships with Calvo, Julio Ortega, and Cecilia Bustamante. But his ICPNA affiliation backfired. Soluguren and Carlos Germán Belli at first agreed to work as advisors, but suspected Eshleman's ties to the Instituto. At a lunch in the countryside, Soluguren ostentatiously accused Eshleman of being a CIA spy, perhaps to secure his own political standing among Peruvian leftists. Despondent, Eshleman walked back to Lima.[134]

Eshleman was neither spy nor anticommunist. He was a young and reasonably opportunistic free expression advocate. ICPNA received funding from a few official USIA positions and worked in consort with the State Department to promote free-market business interests through politically neutral cultural programs. Spohnholtz required Eshleman to keep *Quena* "apolitical," though after a few drinks he confessed that this requirement supported US anticommunist policy. Indeed, to be "apolitical" was regarded as a stance of moral abdication on the revolutionary left. Otto René Castillo's poem "Intelectuales apolíticos," which imagines a future where these "sterile" existentialists are interrogated by the poor, was among the classic indictments of apoliticism.[135] Eshleman came to understand this apoliticism through Juan José Arévalo's *Antikomunismo en América Latina* (Antikommunism in Latin America), describing it as a "kind of non-Spanish, non-English jargon that in itself shows the lack of ground for relation."[136] In one poem in *Walks* (1967), he recalls his vexing shudder upon encountering the anticommunist apparatchik Spohnholtz reaching to co-opt the stance of hemispheric idealism that Eshleman had come to admire through his *El Corno* associates:

> Over candles at the Director's house
> while I pull & pare my stroganoff, sold
> what the traffic'll bear, Sponholz [sic]
> leaned into taper, the dark elegance
>   of dining—
> smiling 'We're all here. . . I'm
> reminded. . . to fight against. . .'
>   one's uneasy shudder
> hearing a man mouth policy
>   who's hired one
> for one's own purposes:
> that the united States of the Spiritual Kingdom of America
> begin Tierra del Fuego end Canada light.
>   The flame weaving in the light
>   'the blue light cleaving
> to the white and consuming fat and flesh of
> burnt-offering beneath it . . .'[137]

Through the image of flickering candlelight and the innuendos of anticommunism presented here as elliptical quotations, Eshleman reads the neglectful consequences of anticommunist attitudes. He associates the "burnt-offering" consumed too eagerly by Spohnholtz with the Peruvian poor who did not benefit from the US in the region. Years later, he expressed the cutting view that poetry's "peristaltic body" cannot "simply 'flow'" amid suffering: "I break my teeth on Apollo as long as my taxes issue forth as a blowtorch into the face of a Guatemalan peasant."[138]

Quena, he hoped, would be a cure for anticommunist doublespeak through its bicultural attention to linguistic innovation. The 250 typescript pages he assembled included Eshleman's and Blackburn's translations into English of Vallejo, Germán Belli, Cisneros, Delgado, Heraud, and others. Complementarily, he commissioned José Coronel Urtecho and the Argentine poet Halma Cristina Perry to translate into Spanish key works by Corman, Olson, Zukofsky, Robert Duncan, Rothenberg, and Ted Enslin. Nonetheless, Eshleman found Peruvians indifferent to Quena until he floated the idea of publishing a Heraud cluster. Calvo suggested Washington Delgado's essay "The Death of Javier Heraud," a sensitive inquiry into the artist's role in Peruvian society. Delgado, a self-described "petit bourgeois professor," does not advocate revolutionary violence, but defends the poet's rights of conscience to engage with it. Rebutting the view that Heraud's actions were misguided, he argues that guerrillas do not perpetrate violence, but only seek to ameliorate the violence and immiseration already pervading the world.[139] Eshleman and Spohnholtz sparred over the inclusion of Delgado's essay until a US embassy representative scuttled the entire issue, disallowing material "that *deals with any activity not in support of American foreign policy.*"[140] After Quena imploded, some of it ended up in five issues of *Haravec: A Literary Magazine from Peru* (1966–1968), edited by Maureen Ahern and Richard Greenwell without ICPNA support, as well as a Cuzco pamphlet entitled *Poetas norteamericanos* (1966).[141]

From the start, Eshleman regarded Quena as a distraction from his real purpose in Peru: the translation of Vallejo's *Human Poems*, eventually published by Grove Press in 1968 and revised for nearly forty years in the run up to *The Complete Poetry of César Vallejo* (2007). Three months into his trip, a newspaper announced it (Figure 4.10), though Eshleman was nowhere near finished. The scope of this story exceeds my concern here, and involves a labyrinth of complicated interactions with Vallejo's difficult widow Georgette, her ad hoc group of literary advisors (such as César Moro, Emilio Adolpho Westphalen, and Washington Delgado), a period of wrangling between Maureen Ahearn and Georgette, and a postpublication backlash.[142] The following section of the chapter takes up Eshleman's role as a translator of Neruda, which ties into this story as well. First, I'd like to emphasize how Eshleman's eight months in Peru came into focus in a sequence of poems.

VALLEJO EN INGLES

ESCRIBE: CESAR LEVANO

Clayton Eshelman, joven poeta norte-americano, ha venido al Perú para vivir un año en el país de Vallejo. Lleva ocho de sus 28 años admirando y trabajando en traducciones del trascendente personaje de Stgo. de Chuco.

Fig 4.10   César Levano, "Vallejo en Inglés," *Caretas: Ilustración peruano* (Nov. 22, 1965): 62. Clayton Eshleman Papers, UCSD.

Eshleman's *Walks* (1967) was self-published in an oversized edition as the tenth pamphlet under the "Caterpillar" imprint "in the year of the Burnt Child." An antiwar silkscreen "glyph" of a "small napalmed Vietnamese child" branded each of the Caterpillar books until such time as the war ended, a sign that Eshleman now connected his brush with Cold War cultural policy to broader circuits of US interventionism. *Walks* are "kinetic poems" written in the "suitcase Lima was at that time," as he wrote in an inscription of the book to a fellow poet. Woven together with other short lyrics and two works addressed to Eshleman's Peruvian friends, the ten numbered poems entitled "Walks" offer telegraphic notations of the squalor of Lima's barriadas (shantytowns). Eshleman describes impoverished hillsides as Dantean hells:

> the hill. The hill is
> the skeleton of a hill. A woman's breast
> suckling as we climb looking for a
> way to climb, to penetrate shacks
> ringwormed straw nailed into dry dirt
> bolgia upon bolgia up

This slum tourism seeks visionary truth unavailable to the poet from institutions of poverty mitigation like the Alliance for Progress and the Peace Corps. In his social concern, Eshleman inscribes himself in a poetics reaching back to Neruda and Vallejo.

Walks also pays a passing homage to Charles Olson and the culture of pre-Columbian ruins in so far as it maintains an interest in Incan ceramics and especially the collections of Andean erotica contemporaneously popularized by the Larco Herrera Museum. Eshleman recounts an episode in which Alfred Kinsey visits the museum and redefines sexually explicit works not as pornographic but as erotic. Pages of Eshleman's poem describe the museum's collections of surreal erotic objects: "—owl with penis growing out/its nose—"; "Two Pumas Frontally Fucking."[143] As the poet indulges in "the/foolishness of walking around/facing cases writing notes" he imagines what Olson calls a "human universe," but he connects this poetics of rehumanization to a 1960s vogue for revisionary ideas of human sexuality.[144] He yearns after sacramental piety in lines written for his newborn Matthew, and funnels his demons into lyrics of surreal erotism and marital crisis.

The book's most effective element occurs when Eshleman addresses Peruvian writers and his interactions with cultural policy, especially the long prose section in the book's center, "Letter to César Calvo Concerning the Inauguration of a Monument to César Vallejo," and the closing poem "For Carlos Germán Belli among the Lima Dead." The letter to Calvo sounds off about every one of Eshleman's grievances with the Peruvian literary community: his struggles with the legacies of Vallejo and Heraud, and his quarrels with Georgette, Delgado, Westphalen, Quena, and the ICPNA. "I am sorry, I just can't write you about love or anything so nice and clean as Tom Merton writes his S.A. chums," he confides, distinguishing his inter-American jeremiad from other visions of cultural fellowship circulating around the Trappist monk Thomas Merton, who Cardenal had popularized in Latin America after his period of study with Merton at his Gethsemani monastery. The title of the poem to Belli evokes Olson's "To Gerhardt, There among Europe's Things," part of a transnational epistolary poetics through which the US poet articulates difference through relation, inscribing thwarted scenes of intercultural fellowship. At the conclusion, he announces a détente with Belli:

> You struggle, you wind archaic
> Spanish tighter, the clock never explodes, the days
> flash down Ica, Puno, Lima's Kechuan street names thru
>
> the city you'll never leave, you grab
> for a girl's hand, you collapse
> in the gutter, yet
>
> you're the best I
> met there, you are kind, there is a sweetness
> in you screams like the tiger-lily

a hundred yards from the sea blue
blue against the desert you're
always leaving

& suspect me of being a spy.[145]

Like the taut sonnets of Belli's *¡Oh hada cibernética!* (1961)—apostrophes to a muse of electronic modernity full of arcane diction—Eshleman's poem winds up tighter in these stanzas than at any point in his early career. Energized by antagonisms, the poems of *Walks* tendentiously describe a well of intercultural bad feeling and a national culture squandering and martyring its literary talents. In doing so, Eshleman records a restless aspiration toward hemispheric cultural citizenship, which hopes to strip away all baggage of idealization and residues of parochialism.

Neruda, Deep Image, and the Politics of Translation

The US popularization of Vallejo trailed behind Neruda's widespread Anglophone reception after 1959. In 1960 William Carlos Williams, now that he was "all but blind," wrote a "Tribute to Neruda the Poet Collector of Seashells," inscribing Neruda all too typically in his vision of a hemispheric reality addressed commemoratively to his mother, and portraying Neruda as the naive, localist poet of Isla Negra collecting "seashells on his/native beaches," which, "like the/sea itself, gave/his lines the variable pitch/which modern verse requires."[146] As the aging Williams shoehorned Neruda into his "variable pitch" theory of the modernist line, Robert Lowell in the United States quipped to Bishop in Brazil as late as 1962 that "No one here except for the young enthusiast knows even Neruda."[147] Yet the rolls of Neruda's US enthusiast-translators grew very large, coming to include Rothenberg, Eshleman, Bly, Wright, Stephen Berg, Ben Belitt, and W. S. Merwin, not to mention UK translators such as Nathaniel Tarn and Alasdair Reid. These competitors made Neruda a whetstone that sharpened allegiances and enmities. While renewing translation as a form of hemispheric cultural diplomacy, they also bent it into something new: a prestige game in the sociology of the literary marketplace. Here, I build on Neruda's correspondence archive to reveal the competition over Neruda's poems across the 1960s. "Translation" exceeded dynamics of fidelity and license, defining Neruda's belated US canonization as a symbolic Cold War thaw.

Some US poets regarded Neruda as an alternative to Williams's modernism, not an example of it. "American poetry resembles a group of huge spiral arms whirling about in space," Bly remarked in his 1963 essay "A Wrong Turning in American Poetry," scolding US poets for extending Anglo-modernist legacies. Bly lamented US poetry's turn to facts (Pound), precision (Moore), pseudo-positivism (Eliot's "objective correlative"), and "projective verse" (Olson). Such poets "whirled about so far out that anyone who follows them will freeze to death."[148] Even Williams, who Bly championed by comparison, was in his objectivism "as much caught up in destructive expansion as the others."[149] To Bly, such conceptions of the poem verged too closely on the impersonal, anti-lyric, industrial ideal of the "automated and flawless machine," an anti-humanistic language ideology as well as a neocolonial language politics of expansion. For instance, Pound's epic idea of the *Cantos* as a poem "including history" was better understood as a process that "annexes other people's ideas, facts, other languages." The loose cohort of Deep Image poets associated with Bly (including Eshleman, Wakoski, Jerome Rothenberg, Robert Kelly, James Wright, and Galway Kinnell) did not all share his overarching critique, but most advocated with him for an inward-turning poetry with a wide array of coordinates drawing on Hispanophone poets like Neruda, Vallejo, Lorca, and Alberti. The Deep Image, a phrase Rothenberg coined from Lorca's "cante jondo" (deep song), was in part a belated US wing of a revolutionary New World surrealism. While Marjorie Perloff identifies divisions in US poetry criticism of this era between followers of Pound's externalized, factic poetics and followers of Stevens's internalized, imaginative poetics, Deep Image poets instead saw choices between Pound and Neruda. Neruda valorized "inwardness" as itself revolutionary, rather than resistant to "reality" as it was in Stevens's terms.[150] Influences now took inter-American shapes. Wrote Bly, "A man cannot turn his face at the same moment toward the inward world and the outer world: he cannot face both south and north at the same moment."[151] Ironically, in these same years, Latin American poets, including Cardenal, Parra, and Rodolfo Hinostroza, all broke with Neruda's model in order to cultivate an anti-lyric inspired by the same fact-oriented Anglo-American modernism that Bly rejected.

Neruda returned to the United States in 1966 for the first time since 1943, owing to Archibald MacLeish's intercession with the Johnson administration at the moment it relaxed its visa dispensations. His visit was heralded as the literary event of the year, as well as evidence of the Cold War's end. In New York, he polemically appeared at the New York PEN Club meeting, where he rebuffed

Ignazio Silone's hot contestations with agility, and he gave a thronged reading at the 92nd Street YMHA, introduced by MacLeish, the aging guru of US cultural diplomacy.[152] There, "a battery" of five English translators appeared on stage beside him: Eshleman, Wright, Bly, Belitt, and the old wartime inter-Americanist H. R. Hays.[153] These men barely masked their animosities for the occasion, and their appearance papered over the grievances of their competitive associations. As Belitt promised Neruda, it "should be very gala: a veritable congress of your translators, each claiming the other knows nothing whatever of the mysteries of translating Neruda *truly*, and all ready to cut throats and march under banners in behalf of their own versions."[154] As Eshleman remembers it, "I was the only one Neruda embraced. After I read my translations he walked over and put his arm around me, and he didn't do that to the others."[155]

Belitt was referring to a story that begins with the network of readers forged out of Fernando Alegría's invitations to Ginsberg and Ferlinghetti to attend the 1960 Concepción de Chile conference. Ginsberg read Neruda in late 1959, reporting to Creeley:

> he's better than I thought, especially a long howl-like poem 'Let the Railsplitter Awake' [. . .]. I've seen a lot by him lately & he's very powerful. I think the younger chileans put him down now as being too full of romantic-political bullshit, and are more apt at concision & fact images etc, rather than his public-address system.[156]

Ginsberg admired Neruda's transformation of Cold War realpolitik into his poetry's hemispheric idealism, the move from "exaggerated surrealistic odes of Molotov & Howard Fast & politics" toward an interruption in the Cold War's rhetorical echo chamber, which Ginsberg saw in the closing lines of "Que despierte el leñador": "let us think of the whole world/and pound the table with love [. . .] I didn't come here to prove anything/I just came here to sing/to you/and for you to sing with me." Ginsberg's reception of Neruda highlights a depoliticized cultural freedom, transcending sectarianism in poetic autonomy.

But the translation surge was often mired in politics. In the mid-1950s, Laughlin insisted to Angel Flores that a New Directions reissue of *Residence on Earth* would have to leave out Neruda's political poems.[157] In 1959 Alegría sought to shepherd Carlos Lozano's edition of Neruda's *Odas elementales* through publication at the University of California Press (it appeared through the PAU's Las Américas Publishing Corporation in 1961). Neruda gave permission to Alegría, while admonishing him for failing to provide for Neruda's compensation given a slack Chilean economy.[158] Rothenberg's cordial letter may have thus dismayed Neruda soon after, for it included translations Rothenberg published in *Floating World* alongside the announcement that more were to be published in the upcoming issue of *The Fifties*.[159] Rothenberg, along with Bly and Wright, unwittingly began to build cultural capital on Neruda translations while Neruda painstakingly reminded other translators to secure his rights. Eshleman requested permissions the same September for his translation of poems from the first two *Residencias*, announcing his desire to transform "estos humildes trabajos en un pequeño volumen que creo necesario hoy en los Estados Unidos." He praised Neruda's "naturaleza" over an emotionless, archaic, intellectual US language, which "drowned the natural qualities of the soul."[160] Nerudian surrealism was an antidote to US academicism.

Anti-academic interest in Neruda among Deep Image poets can explain the security of Neruda's relationship with Ben Belitt, whose best-selling editions of Lorca and Neruda were reviled for their license, errata, and overblown, arcane diction.[161] Belitt's relationship with Grove Press lent *Selected Poems of Pablo Neruda* (1961) a patina of seriousness and a financial promise that younger translators could not match. It also ignited a squabble between Eshleman and Grove editor Richard Seaver, the former accusing Seaver of torpedoing his efforts to publish translations with Indiana University Press, while Seaver called Eshleman "unorthodox" in pursuing publication without rights held by Grove.[162] Eshleman wrote Neruda from Japan announcing his alternative intention to release his translations in a small-press edition to be published by George Hitchcock that autumn.

When Neruda's agent approached W. S. Merwin in August 1962, Merwin (who eventually translated *Twenty Love Poems and a Song of Despair*) admitted to Neruda: "I am aware, [. . .] as I believe you are, that most of the translations of your writing which have appeared in English have been shamefully inadequate."[163] Eshleman concurred in *The Nation*, attacking Belitt's role in Neruda's "strange and sad history of translation in English," and suggesting drolly of many passages that "I don't think this is quite what Neruda was getting at."[164] One of Belitt's egregious errors, the unaccountable translation, in the poem "Walking Around," of "origen y ceniza" (beginning and ash) as "clinkers and causes," became the title of Eshleman's negative review. To Neruda, Eshleman ramped up his anger: "I have nothing but disgust for that translation and said so in a review."[165] He qualified: "I'm not complaining but getting out [. . .] what I should have said to you a year ago: that poetry and the translation of poetry in America has become another matter of prestige and sham."[166]

The differences between Bellit and Eshleman are on display in "Caballero solo," one of Neruda's early poems of frank sexuality, written in India in 1927 and collected in his first *Residencia en la tierra* (1933). Belitt translated it "Gentleman Alone," while Eshleman rendered it "Lone Gentleman," included it in his Amber House pamphlet, and read it with minor variations to open the YMHA evening in 1966. Here is the first stanza in Neruda's Spanish, followed by Belitt's and Eshleman's translations:

> Los jóvenes homosexuales y las muchachas amorosas,
> y las largas viudas que sufren el delirante insomnio,
> y las jóvenes señoras preñadas hace treinta horas,
> y los roncos gatos que cruzan mi jardín en tinieblas,
> como un collar de palpitantes ostras sexuales
> rodean mi residencia solitaria,
> como enemigos establecidos contra mi alma,
> como conspiradores en traje de dormitorio
> que cambiaran largos besos espesos por consigna.[167]

> The young homosexuals and languishing girls,
> the tall widows frantic with sleeplessness,
> the matrons still tender in years, now thirty hours pregnant,
> the gravel-voiced tomcats that cross in the night of my garden
> like a necklace of sexual oysters, atremble,
> encircle my lonely environs—
> antagonists stalking my soul,
> schemers in nightgowns,
> exchanging long kisses, packed in like a countersign.[168]

> The young homosexuals and the hot girls,
> the gaunt widows suffering from delirious insomnia,
> and the young wives pregnant thirty hours,
> and the hoarse cats crisscrossing my garden in darkness
> like a necklace of throbbing sexual oysters
> they surround my lonely house
> like enemies set up against my soul
> like conspirators in pajamas
> exchanging countersign of thick French kisses.[169]

Belitt's archaicizing syntax, prepositional phrases, and odd word choices ("matrons still tender in years," "gravel-voiced tomcats," "night of my garden") stand in stark contrast to Eshleman's sensitivity to Neruda's natural speech rhythms and colloquialisms ("the young wives," "hoarse cats," "my garden in darkness"). Belitt imputes oxymorons ("frantic with sleeplessness") where literalism serves better ("delirious insomnia"), and in all Eshleman preserves the spirit of Neruda's youthful candor with his own New American idioms, even if he perhaps overly domesticates Neruda as a New American forebear. My comparative reading here owes something to a method Eshleman himself developed in his "Test of Translation," a conceit he adapted from Zukofsky's A Test of Poetry, which became a staple column in his magazine Caterpillar.

In 1965, more divisions ensued, as Nathaniel Tarn and Alasdair Reid began to translate Neruda following his summer visit to London and to the PEN conference in Bled (where Keith Botsford arranged for many of Neruda's doings, revealing how Neruda was exhibited and contained by a wide array of ideological projects). Soon, Tarn wrote to Neruda as he translated Alturas de Macchu Picchu: "English-language poetry is very quiet at the moment, as you know; this bears down on us a great deal and it is not easy to pass into the full flood of your soaring language."[170] Tarn was partisan toward his own efforts over those of Belitt, and Neruda's own disquiet with Belitt appears to have emerged for the first time by 1966, to such an extent that Belitt recredentialed himself by sending Neruda a large and unseemly packet of testimonials on behalf of his translations.[171]

When Neruda arrived in New York in summer 1966, he thus dropped into a maelstrom of partisan debates. Belitt sidelined Tarn's British Neruda in New York, while the exceptionalist MacLeish "claimed" him as "American." MacLeish's Neruda belonged to the academy and the diplomatic circuit, even as a countercultural Neruda winked at the New American generation, reading in private to younger poets at the Academy of American Poets director Elizabeth Kray's apartment on the Upper West Side and holding court at long Italian dinners with Eshleman, Antin, and Rothenberg. There was Neruda the neutralized pawn of cultural diplomacy, leashed by the Cold Warrior literary journalist Selden Rodman and reading at the Inter-American Development Bank in Washington, DC, and Neruda the bearer of repressed Old Left memory, ruminating on the legacies of the IWW and singing Paul Robeson to young US poets, as José Yglesias noted in a long report on the visit for The Nation.[172] In short, Neruda fed a US anticommunist agenda even as he defended revolutionary Latin American values. In a Life photograph by Inge Morath, he posed in "comic glasses," derisively depicted as a Communist with a "Snake-eyes' view of the U.S.," who Johnson's administration had granted a perhaps unwise visa in its efforts to ramp up a "rhetorical rejuvenation" of its foreign policy (Figure 4.11).[173]

Fig 4.11 Pablo Neruda, "Snake-eyes' view of the U.S." *Life* (June 24, 1966).
© Inge Morath/Magnum Photos.

It is a wonder it took the United States so long to permit Neruda's visit. Blackburn noted in 1960 that the unwillingness of various "USIS" funded magazines to publish his translations of the "Kommunist" poet Nicolás Guillén probably means "not any Neruda either etc," but wondered "whatinhell, wdn't it be SMART even to publish such a piece? [. . .] The brilliant politics of our state dept. eludes me completely."[174] MacLeish's introduction of Neruda at the YMHA marked a new attitude, arguing that the "American commitment" envisioned a unitary hemisphere, whatever motivated a poet's politics. "Neruda's presence here necessarily reminds us of Neruda's absence over a long count of years when functionaries in Washington seem seriously to have believed that it was the duty of government to protect the American people against a poet who the most American of all North American poets would have loved."[175] MacLeish called Neruda a denizen of a "magnificent double continent" and "a great American poet in the precise and particular sense of the word American . . . which includes not only the United States but Chile and not only Chile but the United States." Finally, he too referred to the decisive lines of "Que despierte el leñador" to vindicate Cold War liberalism's version of cultural freedom: "Let us think of the world's wholeness, pounding the table with love."

But MacLeish's grandiloquent hemispheric idealism, renewed now a quarter century after he first spearheaded it, negatively framed the public idea of Neruda's poetry for Latin American critics. Neruda's visit to the United States galvanized divisive Latin American responses. On a stop in Mexico en route back to Chile, Elena Poniatowska staged a feminist hit-piece interview with Neruda's third wife, Mathilde de Urrutia.[176] Cuban writers took the occasion to describe Neruda as a pawn of US cultural imperialism.[177] Neruda argued back sharply that he had won numerous points on behalf of revolutionary conceptions of poetry at the PEN conference.[178] A few years later, as Allende's ambassador to France, he returned to New York's PEN club to give a blistering account of the Chilean debt crisis that did make his cultural diplomacy in 1966 seem accomodationist. By 1974, a year after Neruda's death, Michael Wood wrote of Neruda's translators "they really are many [. . .] and they are not, on the whole, very good." Wood bemoaned the mislaying of Neruda "in a limbo between languages, in that translators' territory where people speak of 'irreplaceable rapture' and an 'innumerable mouth,' say things like 'He was dazzling, that bony one,' and 'My sad tenderness, what comes over you all at once?' "[179] Only this "mislaying" of Neruda clarifies the impact of John Felstiner's *Translating Neruda* (1980), which sought to wrestle from the competition a marriage of scholarly accuracy to translational praxis. Yet Neruda's afterlife in English facing-page editions never fully overcame this era of soupy translationese, and still belongs in large to aesthetico-political debates about 1960s US poetry and Cold War policy.

One final example may serve to clarify how these politicized and competitive negotiations around Neruda's US image distorted his poetic project. At the YMHA reading in 1966, Bellit remarked with an abundance of self-deprecation that at least two words of his reading of Neruda's famous poem "Walking Around" were correct: specifically, the title, which Neruda originally gave in English. "Walking Around" owes debts to the French flânerie of Charles Baudelaire and Guillaume Apollinaire: "Sucede que me canso de ser hombre./Sucede que entro en las sastrerías y en los cines/marchito, impenetrable, como un cisne de fieltro/ navegando en un agua de origen y ceniza" (It so happens I'm tired of being a man./It so happens I go into the tailor's shops and cinemas/withered, impenetrable, like a felt swan/navigating waters of origin and ash).[180] In truth, neither Belitt nor any other of this stanza's dozen or so translators (including my own effort in the previous quotation) has been resourceful enough to replicate the sonic device through which Neruda shows how commerce with idle doings of metropolitan life produces and transfigures the poet's alienation. In the epistrophic play of the near homophones *cines* (cinemas), *cisne* (swan), and *ceniza* (ash), Neruda makes dreary entertainment (*cines*) transform the modernista swan-poet (*cisne*) into a damned voyager in a sea of ash (*ceniza*). A profound meditation on urban poetry after the advent of the culture industry, this stanza is also not such a bad description of Neruda's voyage among US translators.

Manhattan Poems Beyond the New York School

This chapter has focused on countercultural attempts to integrate hemispheric literary culture in the political context of the Cuban revolution, the print-cultural context of the "mimeo revolution," and the market for translation. To be sure, that integrationist imagination in service to the idealism of hemispheric community had its limits, and I've noted some: Beat indifference to political commitment, aesthetic critiques of *El Corno*, Eshleman's antagonism toward Peruvian poets, and competitions among translators. A further limit can be adduced in a genre of poetry often associated with the energizing of literary community, namely the "coterie poetics" of a prominent kind of Manhattan "walking around" poem in the traditions of Neruda's poem above. I conclude this chapter with a comparative exercise in reading Manhattan "walking around" poems by O'Hara and Blackburn alongside similar poems by Mario Benedetti, Alcides Iznaga, Eugenio Florit, and Derek Walcott.

In early 1960s New York, the most distinguished practitioner of poetry as urban choreography was Frank O'Hara, whose poems are organized around the chatty observations of a metropolitan flâneur suffering from none of Neruda's anomie. O'Hara's untroubled poetic speaker relates more promiscuously to Manhattan's shop windows and streetscapes than any previous flâneur, as in the humorous blurb on the back cover to *Lunch Poems* depicting him writing poems as he shops: "often this poet, strolling through the noisy splintered glare of a Manhattan noon, has paused at a sample Olivetti to type up thirty or forty lines of ruminations." Further, in his "personist" use of what Lytle Shaw calls a "coterie poetics" (wresting from "coterie" a term of art rather than a pejorative usage for a restrictive audience), O'Hara energizes poetry's social currency through acts of naming.[181] These twinned poetic features—a rehabilitation of the "walking around" poem and a strategy of coterie naming—underscore O'Hara's reputation for metropolitan sociality.

But O'Hara's sociality had limits, and its coordinates—with the notable exception of his close relationship with the damaged young Puerto Rican poet Frank
Lima—were largely Europhilic. Previously, I wrote of the "pocket" trope's ties to
hemispheric literary culture. A different instance of the trope occurs in O'Hara's
memorable walking around poem "A Step Away from Them" (1956), fittingly
collected in the Pocket Poets Series in *Lunch Poems* (1964). "My heart is in my/
pocket, it is Poems by Pierre Reverdy," concludes the poem.[182] In his classic case
of midtown lunch-break flânerie, he reserves Europhilic closeness for Reverdy in
marked contrast to the Latin American immigrants and imports that he keeps
at a distance across the rest of the poem. When O'Hara notes "there are several Puerto/Ricans on the avenue today, which/makes it beautiful and warm," it
seems like an eroticizing gaze on migrant figures derived from Hart Crane, but
when he next observes the "posters for BULLFIGHT" and hurriedly downs a "glass
of papaya juice" before returning to work, Borinqueño New York forms part of
a kitschy, Hispanized urbanity that lubricates his poem's propulsive, observational logic without igniting or inspiring it.[183] O'Hara keeps a "step away" from
unnamed Latin American coevals who wrote their own classics of New York
flânerie.[184]

In a 1963 sequence "The Selection of Heaven," Blackburn likewise conflates
Latin American immigrants, writers, and commodities. He writes: "ROYAL
EBONY/is the name of a carbon paper. Is/also the title of a poem by Nicolás
Guillén."[185] In fact it was precisely the carbon paper on which he typed his Guillén
translations, now flattening that material process into the stuff of his poems.
Elsewhere, Blackburn observes a Latina woman bicycling by, and keys his typog-
raphy to a mimesis of her motion through the street:

> MESTIZA: brown, olive and black.
> Scudding clouds the sun rides against.
> The wind wins / brown, olive, and black
> wind of bicycle-March against her jacket
> shape of her top
> revealed
>
>   /
>
>   the legs push .[186]

Here too, Spanish-Caribbean New York renders colorful the mechanisms of composition: the visual prosody of the Latina cyclist embodies the poem's kinetic pace
of disclosure. Poems by O'Hara and Blackburn premised on coteries, flânerie,

and projectivist typewriter composition often yoke together Latino immigrants and Latin American commerce in the mechanics of poetic observation. Other Anglophone poets treat similar subjects as a threat to a Europhile aestheticism. As Gregory Corso stared into a puma's eyes at the Chapultepec Zoo, the animal's caged, ballerina-like grace reminded him of "Ulanova/locked in some small furnished room/in New York, on East 17th Street/in the Puerto Rican section."[187]

The lone Latino poet to align himself with the New York School by the early 1960s was Frank Lima, whose first book *Inventory* was published by the Tibor de Nagy Gallery, owing to the patronage of the painter Sherman Drexler, Kenneth Koch, and Frank O'Hara, with whom Lima became especially close. Lima's fledgling poems take up New American methods with strong affiliations to Beat junkie culture and New York School urbanity, but their impetus is not to beautify barrio street life in the mode of O'Hara so much as it is to puncture and deflate it through an aesthetic of disgust, as in this stanza from the poem "Inventory—To 100th Street":

I see window-people
        hanging out of gooey-stick slips
                sweating
                strange
        below-the-button drawers
                crouched junkies in hallways
                with monkey backs
                eating cellophane bananas
                        on a g-string
                                waiting
                        for that last bust
        Spics with cock-comb
                hair fronts
                ear-gulping mambo music
                eye-lapping pepperican flower
                        crotches[188]

Here O'Hara's tropical warmth mutates into an inescapably sticky and torpid heat, his tropical fruit mutates into a grotesque vision of addiction, and the poet finds the image of the man on the street taking in Caribbean music and sexualizing the Latina passersby not as a pleasing sensory matrix but as an "ear-gulping" and "eye-lapping" form of gluttonous overload. The poem's sonic agglomerations of compound words and alliterative phrases reinforce its aesthetic of ravenous consumption.[189]

We can compare O'Hara's observational logics to Manhattan poems by Latin American visitors to the island in the same years. Uruguayan poet Mario Benedetti's "Cumpleaños en Manhattan" (1959) likewise dialogues intensely with "A Step Away from Them."[190] Benedetti's speaker strolls New York on his birthday despairing at the ten cents it costs for "otro jugo de fruto/con gusto a Guatemala" (another fruit juice/the taste of Guatemala). The successive stanzas emplace Latino/a immigrants of diverse origins on the avenues, but not as props in O'Hara's tropical set pieces. Rather, Benedetti's poet jolts the Puerto Ricans out of "su belicoso miedo colectivo" (collective warlike fear) in so far as they "reconocen mi renguera" (recognize my limp) and "se aflojan un momento" (relax for a moment). These Puerto Ricans find in the metropolis only a fleeting and apprehensive community.

Similarly, Cuban poet Alcides Iznaga's "Estamos solos en Manhattan" (We're Alone in Manhattan) records the poet's 1959 attempts, during a visit to Manhattan, to find what he calls "dos fuerzas como tus ríos/estrechando mi corazón" (two forces, like your two rivers/clutching my heart): namely Langston Hughes and Eugenio Florit, the Cuban-American poet, translator, and Columbia University professor.[191] He metaphorizes these poets as contrasting currents circling the island, building on Hughes's own imagination of Manhattan as an island in the greater Caribbean and on his riverine conceits in "The Negro Speaks of Rivers." However, Iznaga's rivers do not produce a Hughes-like statement of planetary identity so much as an obstructed relation: he walks around 127th Street in Harlem asking for Hughes's home, only to find that the denizens of the street do not know the existence of a famous world poet in their midst. A police officer knows the way, but Iznaga finds Hughes is not at home, nor is Eugenio Florit on another occasion:

> Yo salí en busca de dos poetas como dos ríos,
> Y me quedé en Manhattan solo.
> Yo que quería conocer a Frost y a Richard Wright,
> a Cumming y a Sandburg,
> quería conocerlos acompañado de Langston o de Eugenio.
>
> Y estoy solo
> y la calle 42 no es nada
> ni Madison ni Broadway Avenues,
> sólo la niebla lejana que en sus

extremos la envuelve,

es algo.[192]

(I went out in search of two poets like two rivers.

And I ended up alone in Manhattan.

I who wanted to meet Frost and Richard Wright,

Cumming [sic] and Sandburg,

Wanted to meet them in the company of Langston and Eugenio.

And I am alone

and 42nd Street is nothing,

neither Madison nor Broadway Avenues,

only the distant fog, enveloping

all in its extremities

is something.)

For Iznaga, flânerie alienates: it fails to forge a poetics of coterie he reasonably expects from his sensitive readings of New York's literary world and from his comparative understanding of Cuba's own coterie-like social cohesion. These deficits appear to Iznaga as metaphors for racial ills, in the common integrationist motif of the hour:

yo estaba pensando en los rótulos

del Sur: "WHITE ONLY"

que separaban como los dos ríos

a Manhattan

(I was thinking of the signs

of the South: "WHITE ONLY"

which separated like the two rivers

of Manhattan.)

Florit wrote a more famous, slightly patronizing epistolary poem in reply to Iznaga, entitled "Los poetas solos en Manhattan" (Poets Alone in Manhattan, 1959).[193] It amplifies and clarifies Iznaga's comparison of Havana's clannish sense of social cohesion to Manhattan street life's loneliness, exposing the deep interpersonal and intercultural shortfalls (such as a cordial but toothless amity between Florit and Hughes) that would have made O'Hara's "Personism" such an attractive manifesto.

Derek Walcott also visited New York in 1958–1959 at the fringes of the New York School. His poem "A Village Life" (a purposefully ambiguous reference to the faux

254 THE POETRY OF THE AMERICAS

small town–ness of Greenwich Village) is an elegy dedicated to the memory of theater actor John Robertson, who Walcott met when Robertson attended Trinidad's
1958 Arts Festival Week as a lighting designer. Robertson helped bring Walcott on
a Rockefeller theater fellowship to New York, where he met poets and artists such
as O'Hara, Robert Frank, and Alfred Leslie at the Cedar Tavern. Leslie included
Walcott's work in his "One Shot" magazine *The Hasty Papers*, and Walcott also
made an abortive contact with Donald Allen, who liked "A Far Cry from Africa"
enough to publish it in *Evergreen Review* and briefly championed him at Grove,
but broke with him over a minor insult.[194] On balance, Walcott was as alienated
by New York as Benedetti or Iznaga. In "A Village Life," Walcott composes poems
in a loft in winter: "Behind my back/a rime of crud glazed my cracked coffee-
cup,/a snowfall of torn poems piling up/heaped by a rhyming spade."[195] The image
joins a symbolic system of seasonal migrations announced in the first poem of *The
Castaway* (1965), but migratory freedom gives way to a pariah status. Homesick,
Walcott compares himself implicitly to the cat-like fog threading through the first
stanzas of Eliot's "The Love Song of J. Alfred Prufrock": "I floated,/a cat's shadow."
Flirting with and then fleeing from Beat and New York School models, by 1966
Walcott complained about Beat imitators in Trinidad: "Too much of the verse of
these younger poets shows no such struggle. Most of it settles for the 'hip' effect,
the 'with-it' coolness of diluted American poetry. Lines, arbitrarily sliced, irreso-
lute 'haiku', wispy impressions meant to impress us by their fragility like someone
blowing smoke rings, are what we are given."[196] As I show in the next chapter,
Walcott reciprocates O'Hara's decisive "step away" in his flight from New York
school interlocutors toward Robert Lowell's tragic psycho-political model. That
drift was influenced by his sense of limits to New York School coterie poetics
in particular, and to the wider orbit of the integrationist, "new inter-American
poetry" that I have sketched across the length of this chapter.

5. Questions of Anticommunism

Hemispheric Lyric in the 1960s

In a 1962 photograph adorning the frontispiece to *Words in Air: The Complete Correspondence Between Elizabeth Bishop and Robert Lowell*, the two poets walk barefoot in the breaking surf on a Rio de Janeiro beach, Guanabara Bay stretching out behind them, but little else.[1] A candid vacation shot, it evokes the warmhearted light of gregarious intellectual intimacy overcoming private torment and sociopolitical engagement. It also intimates what Derek Walcott once called Lowell's verbal style, defined by "the casual symmetry of a jacket draped on a chair, genius in shirtsleeves."[2] The cover of Bruce King's biography, *Derek Walcott: A Caribbean Life*, displays a related image of a lone Walcott pensively strolling a Trinidadian beach, gazing into the distance, as if emphasizing a lyric persona he sought to define in these years as an alienated virtuoso steering Anglo-Caribbean poetry's entrance into the world literary marketplaces of London and New York (Figure 5.1).

As portals into the intellectual biographies of Lowell, Bishop, and Walcott, these photographs emplace their subjects at large in the Americas while abstracting or alienating them from geopolitical life. And yet the photographs are linked precisely by Cold War institutions of inter-American statecraft: both were taken near the time of Lowell's visit to Trinidad, Brazil, and Argentina on behalf of the Congress for Cultural Freedom. Putting aside newfound skepticism about state-funded culture, he traveled with Elizabeth Hardwick and their daughter Harriet.

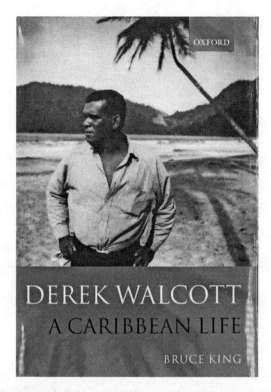

Fig 5.1 Derek Walcott in Trinidad, ca. 1962. Photographer unknown. In Bruce King, *Derek Walcott: A Caribbean Life* (Oxford University Press, 2000). Used with permission.

Their first stopover, at Robert Giroux's suggestion, was to meet Walcott and his wife Margaret, with whom they were so taken that they extended their visit by a week. Later, after an extended summer lecture circuit alongside Bishop in Brazil, Lowell continued to Argentina with Keith Botsford, the CCF's South American liaison. This last visit became infamous, due to an incident first narrated in Ian Hamilton's biography of Lowell and popularized by Frances Stonor Saunders's account of the CCF's quixotic efforts to "weaponize" culture as a front in the Cold War. As Saunders tells it:

> It was in Buenos Aires that the trouble started. Lowell threw away the pills prescribed for his manic depression, took a string of double martinis at a reception in the presidential palace, and announced that he was "Caesar of Argentina" and Botsford his "lieutenant." After giving his Hitler speech, in which he extolled the Führer and the superman ideology, Lowell stripped naked and mounted an equestrian statue in one of the city's main squares.[3]

Saunders viciously scripts this manic episode as a symptom of the semi-covert, anticommunist cultural program in Latin America. Here, her unforgiving stance towards Lowell's psychological anguish perhaps stems from her mirthful suggestion that, in this case, one of the CCF's intellectual weapons had turned into a rogue—or a dud—missile.

If the seaside photographs soften the relation between poetry and anticommunist cultural policy in the Cold War Americas by rendering it as a postcard, the verbal image of a nude Lowell astride a porteño liberator statue hyperbolizes the same relation. But it's a critical relation nonetheless. The question of anticommunism powers major collections of so-called middle generation lyric poetry, such as Bishop's *Questions of Travel* (1965) and Lowell's *For the Union Dead* (1964). By invoking "the question of anticommunism," I mean to ask how this pervasive yet undertheorized counter-ideology shaped poetic agendas at formal and thematic levels. The first half of this chapter charts how, for Bishop and Lowell, anticommunism redefined poetry as a cultural-diplomatic activity; how, for Bishop, it could be presented as anti-poverty humanitarianism in her poetry's most ludic figural logics and auditory schemes; and how, for Lowell, its psycho-political dynamics landed in the realm of his confessional verse, ratifying the views of liberals such as Arthur Schlesinger who held that only alienated, anxious man could be the subject of a genuine art.[4] Furthermore, as Benjamin Kohlman and Matthew Taunton argue, when anticommunism solidified during the Cold War into a term of opposition to "Communist ideology" in particular and "ideology in general," it often went by other names, such as "creative autonomy" and "freedom of expression," and enacted resistance to anti-colonialism.[5] The second half of the chapter considers how anticommunist diplomatic attitudes toward form and expression instigated major Caribbean works such as Heberto Padilla's *Fuera del juego* (Out of the Game, 1968) and Derek Walcott's *The Gulf* (1970). These volumes belong to an extended family of 1960s lyric, forged in the teeth of anticommunist literary institutions across the hemisphere.[6]

In these works, anticommunism does not constitute a political unconscious so much as an active component of poetry's political imaginary. Transfiguring middle-generation formalism, Walcott created the flexible phenomenological, racial, and geographic figure of "the gulf." In this figure, he lyricized his increasingly vexed relation to movements of independence and racial uplift from the standpoint of the world poetry congresses and hemispheric reading junkets he attended with support from the CCF and the Farfield and Rockefeller Foundations. Likewise influenced by the lyric model of Lowell, Padilla's critiques of Soviet Russia and revolutionary Cuba aggravated a crisis of cultural

permissiveness in the state bureaucracy known as "the Padilla Affair" after the
poet was imprisoned and forced to recite a coerced confession as a condition
of his release. The Padilla affair showed, dialectically, how strategies of liberal
poetic subjectivity, when practiced by Second World poets, defined an aporia in
Cuba's revolutionary imagination.

Lyric sequences by Bishop, Lowell, Walcott, and Padilla all display new
strategies of hemispheric cultural diplomacy by enacting crises of confessional
lyric formalism as an aesthetic ideology in service to anticommunist policy.
These displays had unpredictable and contradictory consequences. While the
liberal bourgeois subjectivity of some hegemonic US poems proved the poet's
heedlessness to a reasonable historical materialist discipline, poems produced
within the historical materialist discipline of Second World and Third World
states proved reasonably deserving of a right to express a bourgeois lyric self.
Put differently, the anticommunism of Bishop and Lowell is often an ideological or ethical abstraction; for Walcott or Padilla, writing amidst and sometimes
on behalf of the decolonization project, anticommunism is a concrete practice
of position-taking within a volatile political domain. The poems and episodes
I emphasize in the following pages thus stretch, like a tangled length of chain,
in several directions over the diverse local and international cultural politics of
Brazil, Argentina, Trinidad, Guyana, the United States, and Cuba. Some poems
and episodes are chain links bound by structures of poetic influence, institutional relation, or intellectual affiliation, while others rub against one another
abrasively and unintentionally in the tangle of aesthetic and ideological vectors
that marked hemispheric poetry relations in the decade.

Bishop's First Anticommunist Shudder

The title of this chapter alludes to Bishop's *Questions of Travel* (1965), a volume
of poems consisting of two parts grouped "Brazil" and "Elsewhere." Alluding to
Questions of Travel in this fashion, I mean to call attention to Bishop's central
place in an inter-American anticommunist poetics. Indeed, I will argue that the
eleven-poem "Brazil" sequence, written between 1951 and 1964, develops an anticommunist poetics that is in many respects paradigmatic of the relation between
lyric formalism and Cold War cultural policy. This poetics is especially exemplified by the poems "Manuelzinho," "Squatter's Children," and "The Burglar
of Babylon," but it operates across the length of Bishop's sequence. While hers
is the liberal, humanitarian anticommunism of the Alliance for Progress, in

some of the Brazil poems, the particular flavor of anticommunism dominates the ideological mix. Bishop's celebrated aesthetic formalism—especially poetic features including rhyme, homophony, and simile—does not lift her poems into an autonomous realm of literariness. Rather, it harbors her political dispensations and helps her to elaborate her developmentalist anticommunist stance. My argument about her poetic anticommunism is supported by several facts about her turn as a would-be cultural diplomat for the CCF, a turn that has gone almost entirely unremarked in the voluminous bodies of scholarship on Bishop and on the Cultural Cold War. Nevertheless, the most important consequences of her anticommunist efforts are not visible in her advocacy of particular writers or in her brokerage role as a cultural diplomat, but in the highly particular forms of her verbal art.

To emphasize Bishop's 1950s and early 1960s anticommunism is, of course, to challenge an increasingly accepted sense of her progressive political identifications, if not to potentially rankle many of her liberal celebrants. Since the mid-1990s, several scholars elegiacally recuperated Bishop's *North & South* (1946) as the work of a socially conscious young poet whose political commitments might be described as those of a fellow traveler (a CPUSA sympathizer in the cultural front).[7] In part, these scholars deepened and extended Adrienne Rich's generous reading of Bishop as a feminist outsider; mostly, they sought to upend a broader Cold War consensus, beginning with Randall Jarrell in 1946, that Bishop's poems traced an apolitical genealogy to Marianne Moore's precisionist formalism.[8] Yet, while it is true (as I argued in Chapter 1) that Bishop was mixed up with more writers tied to the Third and Fourth Internationals during World War II than we commonly remember, it is also true that when McCarthyism and Schlesinger's "vital center" each rendered "fellow traveler" inert as a US political category in the early 1950s, Bishop did not renew her progressive identifications. The "World War II to Cold War view" from her Library of Congress office overlooking the Capitol during her tenure as Poet Laureate Consultant in 1949–1950 has not been understood as an abdication of these leftist credentials, but Bishop needed no Koestlerian apostasy to grow more determined as a liberal anticommunist.[9] At the very least, Bishop's political development ratifies an observation by her acquaintance Nicolas Nabokov (Secretary General of the CCF): "the philo-Communism of the mid-thirties was a passing fad."[10] Diverging starkly from Bishop's US critics, the popular Brazilian musician, poet, and intellectual Caetano Veloso has observed another purpose in Bishop's scattered writing on Brazilian politics in the early 1960s—including her approval of the 1964 anticommunist "golpe de estado" that sent leftist students and intellectuals to jail. Veloso suggests that by this point in her Brazilian sojourn Bishop sought nothing less than a vindication of "right wing good intentions."[11]

Furthermore, my title "Questions of Anticommunism" ought to interrupt an overreliance on the keyword *travel* in understanding Bishop's Brazil. Few critics have failed to note how several of the "Brazil" poems flaunt their complicity in a formula we might write as "tourism reenacts colonialism."[12] The schematic and tropological engines of Bishop's poems, such as the numerical near-anagrams of "Arrival at Santos," dated 1952, and the subsequent ekphrasis of a tapestry of colonial violence in "Brazil, January 1, 1502," often reinforce this formula. "Questions of Travel," which Robert von Hallberg appointed the single best poem of postwar American tourism, enlists insistent, self-interrogative enjambment to complete this triptych of poems invested in unmaking the conventions of colonial ufanismo (boosterism) and the imperial romanticism of landscape description.[13] Yet Bishop's self-critical, neo-colonial tourist persona gives way across the Brazil sequence to several rooted standpoints. "Squatter's Children" observes the social system of the favela with a measure of authority earned by her proximity, and in "Manuelzinho" Bishop ventriloquizes her aristocratic lover Lota Macedo de Soares venting exasperated condescension at "the world's worst gardener since Cain." "The Riverman" works through fabular forms in the mode of a lettered ethnographer, and "The Burglar of Babylon" takes up the ballad, the pre-distressed genre of bardic nationalism. Bishop avowedly remained "a New Englander herring-choker bluenoser" through her fourteen years in Brazil, but the progress of the multiple forms and personae she employs across her lyric sequence implies a narrative of Brazilian self-authentication, from the uncomfortable tourist of "Arrival at Santos" to the folk balladeer of "The Burglar of Babylon."[14] We ought to therefore forestall the questions of travel and outsiderhood that drive most accounts of Bishop's social being for the questions of power, poverty, and politics that she makes the driving questions of her polyvocal sequence.[15] This is not to say that the principal vehicle of Bishop's politics is the submission of diverse Brazilian voices to a unitary speaker. To the contrary, her poems disperse anticommunism's drift in ludic sound schemes such as homophony and rhyme. Anticommunism circulates as what Michel Foucault called a "dispositif" (apparatus), a discourse that secures relations between social behaviors, institutional affiliations, and poetic devices.[16]

One anecdote indexes the relation between anticommunism's social life and its poetic form with particular force. In 1961, Bishop wrote to Lowell that she felt her first "really cold shudder of fear and horror of Communism" at a garden party hosted by landscape architect Roberto Burle Marx in honor of Carlos Lacerda,

the governor of the state of Rio and a close friend to Lota and Bishop. The anecdote Bishop recounts to Lowell is especially notable for the linguistic party game
at its center:

> Unfortunately someone had had the idea of bringing along a Chinese Trade
> Commission that had just arrived from a stay in Cuba—8 or 10 small-sized,
> slovenly-looking, youthful, long-haired Chinese who wouldn't touch
> alcohol and *pinned people down*, in French or bad English. (Mão-Mão—
> pronounced like Mow—means "bad-bad" in Portuguese and is a common
> expression. After they all refused Scotch and wine, again, looking grim-
> mer & grimmer, Roberto said "Mao-Mao-Tse-Tsung.") I tried talking to
> one whose English was very limited and when he told me "Castro-strong-
> strong" shaking his fist, and "Batista bad-bad" (as if I wouldn't have heard
> of *him*, probably) for the first time, I think, a really cold shudder of fear
> and horror of Communism went down my spine.[17]

It should come as no surprise that Bishop's anti-Communist "shudder" occurs at
a benefit for Lacerda. John Dos Passos, who published a book about a 1962 tour of
Brazil, heroized Lacerda as "Brazil's most accomplished anti-Communist," and
Bishop privately called Lacerda "the only real hope" for liberalism as Brazil swept
left after 1959. She linked his anticommunism to expressive freedom, calling him
a "Dynamic Crusader" who "long combatted left-wing elements and all forms of
dictatorship."[18] In the anecdote above, the triggers for Bishop's anticommunist
frisson include youthful marks of underdevelopment (long hair and uncleanli-
ness), a dubious yellow-peril discourse, and the famously boozy Bishop's account
of teetotaling as a form of social cheerlessness she associates with the adjective
"grimmer." Most of all, her shudder turns on the homophonic jests volleyed by
Burle Marx and the Chinese man. Her description of the language game thus
merits a closer look.

First, we should note that Bishop strangely litters her report to Lowell with
errata. The nasal *mão* means *hand*, whereas *mau* means *bad*. Moreover, the redu-
plicated *mau mau* is not an especially "common expression" in Portuguese at
all. There was of course a considerable Kenyan Mau Mau Uprising in approximately 1952–1960, carried on by a large secret society of aggressive, armed anti-
colonialists. After the murder of the British Ruck family, the Mau Mau were
sensationalized as boogeymen within late colonial discourses. Linguists debate
the etymon of the name Mau Mau—perhaps an anagram of uncertain derivation,
or perhaps a meaningless ideophone, as susceptible as *dada* had been in 1916 to

semantic predications of several kinds. Ceremonial oaths and secretive language games often figure into origin stories for it, and in some respects it appears to emerge as a preferred term for the Kikuyu insurrectionaries among British anti-communists precisely because it harbored a ritual linguistic atavism.[19] By the time Rock Hudson, Dana Wynter, and Sydney Poitier starred in the film *Something of Value* (1957, reissued as *Africa Ablaze*, 1962) and Jamaican novelist Victor Stafford Reid allegorized the Ruck story in *The Leopard* (1958), the Mau Mau Uprising had global currency, the ideophonic quality of the name linked to the circumscription of anticolonial revolt within the domain of presemantic irrationality. "Kikuyu, quick as flies,/Batten upon the bloodstreams of the veldt," wrote Walcott in his early poem "A Far Cry from Africa."[20] His title implies what he once called his squandered compassion for the "scream of pain" by those involved "on both sides of that revolt," as well as the distant violence that his poem alliterates.[21] Burle Marx's joke amplifies the etymological problem of *mau mau*, confusing an anagram of Kenyan insurrection with Sino-Portuguese homophony. Is Burle Marx expressing tautonymic negativity in Portuguese, or an ideophonic idyll of guerilla insurrection in Kikuyu? Just how multilingual is "Mão-Mão?" And why does Bishop misinterpret the letter—if not the spirit—of the joke?

Stranger still is this: the "limited English" that Bishop attributes to the Chinese delegate contains quite a bit of poetic ingenuity. "Castro-strong-strong" (with its involuntary, echolalic reduplication of *stro-stro-stro*) and the likewise alliterative "Batista bad-bad" seem like artful ripostes to Burle Marx's "Mao-Mao-Tse-Tsung" (which misspells *Tung* as *Tsung* in order to reduplicate the sound of *Tse*). The Chinese delegate's mirrored sound figures each glean a nonaccentual syllable (*stro* and *bat*) from the names of two Cuban political leaders that hide structures of political feeling as homophones in their spoken cadences. Therefore, the inventor of the phrases "Castro-strong-strong" and "Batista-bad-bad" must have a fairly vigorous sense of the visual iconicity of the words *Castro* and *Batista*, for the syllables emphasized in the language game are not emphasized in speech. The man Bishop describes as a slovenly, long-haired Chinese speaker with "limited English" and no Portuguese seems unlikely to have invented the phrases at all. Carefully composed verbal art masquerades in her account as halting scraps of dogmatism.

Bishop's homophonic play deserves such close scrutiny because her "Brazil" poems often advance forms of analogic thinking invited by homophones, as well as closely related auditory schemes such as rhyme. Rhymes and homophones habitually amass in her poems—like the dockside sacks of *green* coffee *beans seen being* exchanged for Miss *Breen* in "Arrival at Santos," or like the ramshackle houses on the favela hillsides of "The Burglar of Babylon," or the huts of "Squatter's Children." The long ballad "The Burglar of Babylon" includes a makeshift *ars poetica* for Bishop's emphasis on homophony. There, the "fearful stain" of the "poor who come to Rio" "cling and spread like lichen."[22] In the curious phrase "like lichen," a rhopalic sound analogy short-circuits a larger, conservative analogy, in which favela squatters (described ironically as a "stain") are likened to undesirable, fragile fungal growth. In an obvious sense, the rhopalic phrase "like lichen" expresses a marvelous accident: how coincidental it is that *like* sounds like *lichen*. It also emphasizes a banality: to say *like* "likens" things to one another. But the observation is weightier if we view the homophone the other way around, seeking to understand the way that "lichen" is "like" "likening." Bishop's poems wear the fungus of similitude as a habit of mind with great pride. The poem comes to abhor the visual architecture of the favela, "piling" up on the hillside behind the Copacabana, but the poem is paradoxically content to massify analogies as the poem's primary activity. The cover of the June 16, 1961, issue of *Life*, with a special feature on "Latin America," declared "SHOCKING POVERTY SPAWNS REDS." And, as Jay Prosser points out, Bishop's understanding of the favela later came to owe a debt to Gordon Parks' *Life* photo-essay on the children of the da Silva family, "A Beaten Family in Rio Slum" (Figure 5.2).[23] By the time readers came to the poem in *Questions of Travel*, it would have seemed an extension of the implications of Michael Harrington's 1962 exposé of domestic poverty, *The Other America*, a poetic buttress to Parks's photographs, and the generalized anticommunist discourses of the Alliance for Progress's developmentalism.

Hodge-podge accumulation is also the emphasis of the earlier poem "Squatter's Children" (1956), in which Bishop describes the squat where Lota allowed her gardener Manuelzinho and his children to live on her Samambaia property. Here, too, "up" sounds "pile up," again like hillside tenements, and now also like ominous weather:

> On the unbreathing sides of hills
> they play, a specklike girl and boy,
> alone, but near a specklike house.
> The sun's suspended eye
> blinks casually, and then they wade
> gigantic waves of light and shade.
> A dancing yellow spot, a pup,
> attends them. Clouds are piling up;
>
> a storm piles up behind the house.[24]

Fig 5.2 "Freedom's Fearful Foe: Poverty," *Life Magazine* (June 16, 1961). Photographs by Gordon Parks. Courtesy of and © Gordon Parks Foundation.

It is as if Bishop has preempted "Castro-strong-strong" with "Bishop-up-up." An implicit intolerance analogizes the gathering storm to the squatter's children as a metonym for an emergent social class. However, Bishop's analogy between poor children and a communist storm equivocates much more than do Parks' photographs. For example, the phrase "Their laughter spreads/effulgence in the thunderheads" suggests an auditory analogy in which laughter is like thunder. The resonance of rhyme as what Susan Stewart calls a "rich cognitive moment on the brink of realized structure" creates strong illusions of this conservative coupling.[25] But *effulgence* is a term of visual rather than auditory illumination, and *thunderheads* are cumulus repositories of thunder that precede it. They make possible a sonic eruption; they are not the eruption itself. If laughter "spreads" (like lichen) through the thunderhead, it is the light sensory event that threatens a dark and heavy sensory event. The concluding stanza of the poem likewise raises the expectation of an intolerant analogy that goes unfulfilled. "Children, the threshold of the storm/has slid beneath your muddy shoes" likens immiserated children to the looming storm, but only until the syntactically belated possessive pronoun "your" reorients the analogy as an apostrophic address to the children.

The squatter's children abide in this world of amassing auditory repetitions, sound schemes that often describe their own status as schemes. When the clang of a dropped "mattock with a broken haft/the two of them can scarcely lift" triggers the poem's focus on the children's laughter, *haft* and *lift* are conjoined by a half rhyme. *Haft* is not only a handle, but also the preterit *halved*, or a homophonic representation of its particular status as rhyme. This phonaesthemic device builds across the poem:

> weak flashes of inquiry
> direct as is the puppy's bark.
> But to their little, soluble,
> unwarrantable ark,
> apparently the rain's reply
> consists of echolalia[26]

The rhyme words *bark* and *ark* cross in a semantic and sonic chiasmus: *ark* is not only a boat, but also the echo of an arf; *bark* is not only an arf, but also a synonym for a boat. These porously bivalent words are leaky vessels in which the children weather yet another self-conscious figure for sound: the "echolalia" of the rain's reply. "Squatter's Children" insists on abiding in the childish, puerile malformations of sound. This puerility flirts willy-nilly with the analogy of subjects of social concern to blackening skies, or the official metaphors of Cold War anticommunist poverty discourses: to find a child in a cold rain is to observe a risk of political radicalization. The sounds in Bishop's poems, as a space of thematic development, are a presemantic music of Cold War developmentalism.

Several other poems in the Brazil sequence chime with the scene of observation in "Squatter's Children," but certainly none more than the contemporaneous "Manuelzinho," which Brett Millier euphemistically calls a "portrait of the endearingly unreliable gardener" that Lota employed at her Samambaia home.[27] In fact, Bishop witheringly portrays the Brazilian underclasses. The poem ventriloquizes an unfashionably illiberal Brazilian aristocrat so subtly that Bishop gave paratextual stage directions: *"Brazil. A friend of the writer is speaking."* This wasn't clear to many readers, and so she often added in correspondence "It's supposed to be Lota talking."[28] The dramatic monologue renders class relations as a verbally playful litany of patronizing grievances, but it struggles to demarcate the social status of its own speaker:

> Half squatter, half tenant (no rent)—
> a sort of inheritance; white,
> in your thirties now, and supposed
> to supply me with vegetables,
> but you don't; or you won't; or you can't
> get the idea through your brain—
> the world's worst gardener since Cain.[29]

The halting rhythm of internal, off-beat and half-rhymes such as *tenant* with *no rent* reinforce the poem's imbrication of class analysis with sonic play; even the structure of complaint is rendered as interchangeable rhyming anapests ("but you don't; or you won't" or you can't"). The poem ends with a brief apology, but this is buried under the extended relish it takes in disclosing the gardener's failings. Translating a Brazilian aristocrat's condescension into exquisitely patterned formalist verse, the poem parades the misfit domestic comedy of Brazilian class stratification before its readers. The poet does not stand in judgment of this comedy per se, but her own bonds of affection and allegiance are nearly indistinguishable from the patroness whose voice she inhabits.

In these instances, Bishop's paradoxically rich acoustical imagination of poverty prepares her for a tendency to identify poetry as a mode of Cold War cultural diplomacy. In the letter to Lowell where Bishop describes her first shudders of fear at communism, she also affirms a dawning desire to become a cultural policy strategist for the CCF, a desire "Not immediately connected with [the Chinese trade commission] but perhaps partly":

> We have done, are doing, such stupid things here, absolutely incredible folly, some of it, and as far as "cultural exchanges" go we couldn't present ourselves in a worse light, usually, and I think I could really be of some use, if they'd want me.[30]

She hopes to show the Brazilian government "what kind of cultural importations the Brazilians would *really* like" as a way "to be a 'poet engagée,'" and reports

Lota's reply that she only "wanted to be engagée to Kennedy's insolent chariot." Thus, for Bishop, the CCF and the Alliance for Progress each reframed the legacy of World War II–era resistance poetry. Political commitment became anticommunist cultural policy, requiring a disfiguration of Jean-Paul Sartre's key term "engagement." Bishop claims the mantle of engagement even as her poems exemplify Sartre's admonition that "the poet is forbidden to engage himself" on the grounds that it is the "poet's business to contemplate words in a disinterested fashion."[31]

The political genealogy for Bishop's concept of poetic engagement here issues directly from the Good Neighbor diplomacy of World War II, which remained an important framework for her ideas about cultural policy in the early 1960s, more than a decade after the policy's demise. How immediate? In February 1962, aghast at the Brazilian foreign ministry's vocal support of "the insane Castro" at the recent Punta del Este Conference (where Brazil's Goulart administration sought to normalize political relations with the communist bloc and oppose sanctions against Cuba), Morton Zabel wrote to Bishop to ask: "What happened to all those *boas vizinhanças* [good neighbors] I helped churn up back in the 1940s?? Have they *all* gone down the chute?"[32] Zabel, a former editor of *Poetry* and a sometime University of Chicago professor, inaugurated the Chair of North American Literature at the National University of Brazil in 1943 during a wave of exchanges sponsored by the Office for the Coordinator of Inter-American Affairs. By 1962, when her fondness for Zabel led her to propose "Why don't *you* be the cultural attaché for a year or two," Bishop revived these networks to craft the role of ad hoc cultural diplomat.[33] She falls into a curious category: a poet not employed by the CCF who actively sought its support. She once speculated naively to Lowell about who funded it, but by 1962 Botsford had cannily schooled her on how to talk about the CIA alignment:

> My connexions, which I'm sure you overestimate, with official bodies in the US, is something one may talk about (speculation), but should not put on paper. I mean, supposing one were involved: privacy & discretion, no? Finally, the Congress *can* be mentioned by name, & is not supported *only* by the Ford Foundation, far from it.[34]

This back and forth implies Bishop's increasingly willful participation in cultural diplomacy in all of its semi-covert caginess. In 1962, for example, Bishop hosted CCF director Nicholas Nabokov when he attended the Rio de Janeiro Music Festival in August and September, the biggest event sponsored by the CCF in Brazil that year.

Bishop also wrote to Botsford to seek feedback on her *Brazil* book for the Life World Library (1962), one of her principal contributions to cultural diplomacy. Later she disowned this "awful little book," stressing to Zabel "please never make any attempt to see it," but her depiction of the Rio favelas captions Parks's photograph by highlighting the proximity of the "vertical slums" to "Rio's luxury apartment houses" as "reminders of the rural squalor behind Brazil's industrial progress."[35] Underscoring her fear of an unruly electorate susceptible to leftist political demagoguery, she juxtaposes the favela photo with one of a riotous pro-Castro rally organized by the Peasant League in Recife, which attracted "a small but militant turnout of laborers, who were harangued by anti-U.S. speakers."[36] Most historians regard Communist agitation as a minor phenomenon in the poverty-stricken Brazilian Northeast, but Bishop's analysis chimed well with Kennedy's couching of aid in the area in the rhetoric of red menace, reinforcing oligarchical sway over political modernization in the process.[37] Her formulaic analysis posits that "revolutionary fervor" feeds on rural "misery," a lynchpin ideologeme of the Alliance for Progress. The anticommunist captions of her glossy Time-Life World Library spreads are subtexts for the complex sound play elaborated in her poems of poverty tourism. She registered one note of contrition, when, in the wake of her Time-Life debacle, she reversed her poor opinion of Allen Ginsberg to take solace in one "brilliant" strophe from "America," Ginsberg's unapologetic avowal of Old Left nostalgia: "Are you going to let your emotional life be run by Time Magazine?"[38]

In these years, exiled Guatemalan president Juan José Arévalo's *Antikomunismo en América Latina* stingingly indicted how press coverage of Latin America was coopted by the mechanisms of "anti-Kommunism" (for him, the *k* signaled a cartoonish mass media version of a more substantive counter-ideology). Writing in parables conducive to his philosophy of "spiritual socialism," Arévalo lampooned the Time-Life flavor of US Cold War influence in the region, along with its violent undercurrent of covert interventions.[39] In its pages, Carlos Lacerda exemplified the trajectory from free speech advocacy to anticommunist politics. Bishop's Brazil poems can be imagined as subjects of an unwritten chapter in Arévalo's striking polemic.

Lowell's Imperial Phantasmagoria

Bishop's other big contribution to cultural diplomacy was her role in enabling Lowell's CCF-sponsored visit to Trinidad, Brazil, and Argentina in 1962. Robert Frost and Stephen Spender made similar visits to Brazil in the 1950s, muted affairs compared to Waldo Frank's 1943 tour or the institution-building visits of Samuel Putnam and Morton Zabel. Lowell himself had previously joined the Congress's efforts in Western Europe, teaching in the Salzburg Seminar in American Civilization in 1952.[40] In December of 1958, Lowell and Bishop first discussed leveraging the cultural attaché at the US Embassy in Rio to arrange a trip for Lowell to visit Bishop and to lecture around Brazil and the Southern Cone, but the idea was tabled until three years later. In the interim, Lowell appeared at Kennedy's 1961 inauguration alongside fifty other writers and the aging Robert Frost. Arthur Schlesinger paraphrased the poem Frost had been too blinded by winter glare to read, when he wrote that the inauguration prefigured "a new Augustan age of poetry and power."[41] Lowell returned to the White House for a dinner honoring André Malraux on May 11, 1962, where his disillusionment sharpened. As he wrote to Edmund Wilson (and paraphrased to Bishop), "It was all good fun but next morning you read that the President [. . .] might have invaded Cuba again—not that he will, but I feel we intellectuals play a very pompous and frivolous role—we should be windows, not window-dressing."[42] By 1965, when asked to return to the Lyndon Johnson White House for a Festival of the Arts, he publically declined the invitation in protest over US foreign policy. The following pages show how a feverish Latin American sequence in *For the Union Dead* renders visible Lowell's transformation.

Bishop clearly associated Lowell's writing with her emerging endorsement of anticommunist cultural policy. When Lowell asked her to blurb *Life Studies* in 1959, she described his poems as exportable inoculations for leftist foreign nationals like the "grimmer and grimmer" Chinese trade commission she would encounter two years later:

> Whenever I read a poem by Robert Lowell I have a chilling sensation of here-and-now, of exact contemporaneity: more aware of those "ironies of American history," grimmer about them, and yet hopeful. If more people read poetry, if it were more exportable and translatable, surely his poems would go far towards changing, or at least unsettling, minds made up against us.[43]

Bishop's description closely mirrors the one she offered to Lowell of the garden party: another "chilling sensation," this time not her shudder at communism itself but her frisson when encountering a poetry fit to staunch communism's anti-imperialist discourses, which she recast as anti-Americanism. Aesthetic frissons and anticommunist cultural policy were never far from one another in her mind. And so poems were the best way to refute her sense that agencies such as USIA promoted only cultural images of American democracy that undermined the project of preventing Brazilian realignment.[44] Poetic form—and sound play in particular—was Bishop's privileged site of a transnational, democratic, anti-communist cultural diplomacy.

Bishop's foray with Lowell into cultural diplomacy work can also be understood as her attempt to cope with a dawning awareness, as a US citizen abroad, that agencies such as USIA exported deleteriously cartoonish visions of American literature, unreciprocated by a Brazilian literary scene she found wanting. Bishop felt that inter-American poetic exchange was embryonic. Of Brazil's poets, she reserved her praise to Lowell almost exclusively for João Cabral de Melo Neto. And although she merely tolerated him in her correspondence, she was the first English-language translator of Carlos Drummond de Andrade, who had written three key volumes of committed communist verse, from *Sentimento do mundo* (Feeling of the World, 1940) to *A rosa do povo* (Rose of the People, 1945), but who renounced his membership after the party newspaper he wrote for in 1945 censored one of his editorials. She likewise tolerated Manuel Bandeira and Vinicius de Moraes. All four of these writers assumed privileged places in her *Anthology of Twentieth-Century Brazilian Poetry* (1972). However, Bishop reviled the Noigandres school of Concrete Poetry (which in 1962 she called "something god-awful called *Neo-Concretionism*—pure 1920's Parisian"), nearly matching her scorn for Charles Olson, who, after he'd rented her home in Key West in the early 1940s, she came to regard as "one of the three or four people in this world I really hate."[45] Concomitantly, she opined that the Brazilian mixture of anti-Americanism and provincialism led to no more knowledge in Brazil about English-language poetry than a handful of canonized modernists: "Frost and Millay and E. Dickinson—Pound, Cummings—And Eliot, *well*"). Crane and Stevens were known "vaguely," Dylan Thomas "yes—but they don't really understand him," and "the ignorance of any American poets under fifty is pretty general."[46] To Bishop, government agencies dulled the promise of interchange, and only Lowell could rectify that dullness.

Correspondence between Bishop, Botsford, Hardwick, and Lowell in early 1962 reveals a tellingly frustrated effort to create a context for Lowell's visit by translating his poems alongside a teaching anthology of Anglo-American verse for Brazilian readers. Botsford first solicited Bandeira, who he trumpeted as "the foremost translator in this country," to translate a book-length selection of Lowell's works.[47] When Bandeira dropped out, Botsford conscripted Mauro Faustino, who found Lowell's poems too difficult, at which point Botsford himself attempted several translations with Afranio Coutinho, president of the Congress's Brazilian section. When they were likewise stymied, Botsford sprayed blame in every direction: "they just don't know enough English to handle you," he wrote. "It took us five hours to do forty lines, *literally*—what's an ice-house for a Portuguese, and more so, a Brazilian?"[48] In the end, Maria Augusta Costa Ribeira did most of the uncredited translation work (after the trip, Hardwick graciously pressed Botsford to compensate her). The resulting twenty-nine-page pamphlet, entitled *Quatro poemas*, featured an introduction by Bishop entitled "Algumas notas sobre Robert Lowell," an unattributed essay by Botsford, and four poems, with prose translations, sampled from Lowell's first three collections. It was the pilot publication in the CCF's *Série cadernos brasileiros*, followed that summer by Walmir Ayala's anthology *Novíssima poesia brasileira*.

Lowell simultaneously entertained his own idea to have an anthology's worth of Anglo-American poems translated from "Frost through say Snodgrass; Hardy through Larkin and [Ted] Hughes." He intended to print them for "S. American distribution," discussing the matter with John Hunt of the Farfield Foundation, though it never came to fruition. He also anxiously imagined how to handle his performances, asking Botsford: "How well will the audience understand English? I have sinking feeling about not connecting, of my voice being unintelligible, of assuming knowledge of what they want to know, of telling what they know as well as I, or else can't follow."[49] Botsford repeatedly brushed Lowell's reasonably sensitive concerns aside by demeaning the Brazilian reading public. "Latins," he pronounced, "and especially Latin-Americans, are far more at home in abstractions than we are ... They are used to talking about poetry as though they were all hugger-muggering each other up on Parnassus."[50] Boundlessly condescending, Botsford continued: "they have very little experience of very complex verse—their language not being up to the complex ambiguities ... of English; thus you seem strange to them, rich and admirable, but difficult." When Lowell and Hardwick departed in June, they were undeterred by the thwarted attempt to manufacture a context and reception for Lowell's verse. Their correspondence repeatedly references "the whole meaning of our trip," without explicating that meaning as anticommunist intercultural understanding.[51]

After Trinidad, to which I will turn in the next section of this chapter, Lowell first stopped in Recife, where the press hailed him as the United States' "major Catholic poet." Anthropologist and politician Gilberto Freyre, who joined Lacerda and Bishop at the anticommunist center, attended Lowell's reading at the Joaquim Nabuco Institute for Social Research on June 26 and wrote a long "salute" to Lowell in the *Diário de Pernambuco*.

It followed on the heels of "Misconceptions of Brazil," published in *Foreign Affairs* that spring, in which Freyre situated Brazil's leftward drift not as part of "supranational" Latin American trends, but rather as part of a local history of monarchical republicanism. He excoriated the populist ex-president Jânio Quadros's neutral foreign policy, which had normalized relations with the "*caudillo*" Castro. He endorsed Quadros's far more pro-US successor João Goulart and his openness to the Alliance for Progress, but only so long as it could make a quick impact. "For instance," Freyre wrote, "the Brazilian Northeast, the country's number one problem region, has recently been visited by so many official and semiofficial groups from the United States, without any significant positive results, that the matter is becoming the subject of humorous comments."[52] Far from laughable by contrast, Lowell's "complex, curly, twisted, dense, restless, contradictory" poetry promised to ease geopolitical sectarianism:

> Mas há nos seus poemas profundidades [. . .] características tanto do modo de ser, de pensar e de sentir da sua gente—a anglo-americana particularmente a da Nova Inglaterra—como da sua geração e do seu tempo: o tempo que com maior ou menor intensidade vivemos todos nós americanos de tôdas as Américas, homens de todas as fés e de todas as negações de fé, ocidentais e orientais, brancos e gentes de cor, homens e mulheres, povos de varias raças, gentes de varias culturas, nações de varios passados, grupos todos êsses, cada vez mais aproximados uns dos outros pela crescente desmoralização das distâncias físicas pela técnica moderna de comunicações; cada vez mais perto uno dos outros, pela crescente redução das distâncias políticas e sociais entre os povos arcaicamente denominados capitalistas e os povos inadequadamente chamados socialistas, tanto é o que de uns transborda nos outros, tornando ridículos os muros simplemente políticos levantados entre êles pelos puristas de uma ou de outra seita: a seita comunista e a seita capitalista.[53]

> (But there are profundities in your poems . . . as typical of the modes of being, thinking and feeling of your people (Anglo-Americans of New England, particularly) as they are of your generation or your age: the age that, with more or less intensity, all of us Americans live in throughout the Americas, people of all faiths and of all denials of faith, Eastern and Western, white and colored people, men and women, people of various races, people of various cultures, nations of varied pasts, all these groups increasingly approximate each other by the growing demoralization of physical distances by modern communication technologies; made ever

closer by the increasing reduction of political and social distances between people archaically called capitalists and people improperly called socialist, so much so that some overflow into the other, rendering absurd the merely political walls erected between them by purists of one or another sect: the communist sect and the capitalist sect.)

In Lowell's lyric complexity, Freyre found a metonymy for the hemisphere's matrix of sociopolitical contradictions. It offered solace for technology's homogenizing pressure and for clashing Cold War universals washing over heterogeneous New World cultures.

Lowell discontinued his letters to Bishop while in Brazil, so the details of his summer in Rio are scant: a leisurely stay in a modern high-rise overlooking the Copacabana, and a small slate of recitals and press conferences. Drinking heavily by mid-August, he strained his friendship with Bishop, and his subsequent trip to Buenos Aires on September 4 was disastrous, leading to the manic imperial episode fueling accounts of his failed weaponization by historians of the cultural Cold War.[54] Yet these accounts neglect evidence of Lowell's trip among Argentine sources. For example, according to Adolfo Bioy Casares, he scandalized the anticommunist Jorge Luis Borges in a reception at Borges's home by womanizing, insulting Borges's decor, and expressing sympathy for Castro. Wrote Bioy Casares in the diary of his meetings with Borges: "Me cuenta que un poeta norteamericano Robert Lowell, pagado por los Estados Unidos, está aquí, habla en favor de Fidel Castro y es un imbécil" (He tells me that the North American poet Robert Lowell is here, paid for by the United States; he speaks out in favor of Fidel Castro and he's an imbecile).[55] An Irish physician later sequestered Lowell during a lunch with Argentine writers, including the novelist Luisa Mercedes Levinson, to whom Lowell attached himself. Hospitalized and sedated with Thorazine, he continued to harangue Botsford by obsessing over the theme of an imperial American Rome until Botsford arranged his return to New York.[56] On letterhead from Compañía Argentina Shell de Petróleo's "Servicio Médico," Lowell pretended to be stricken with flu and malaria as he asked Harvard to cover his fall classes.[57] Hospitalized in New York in October, he missed the Cuban Missile Crisis.[58] By then, Botsford had apologized to Bishop, lamenting Lowell's role in scuttling most of his organizing work for the CCF in Argentina: "I got back to Buenos Aires to find the PEN fled: Madariaga having told Spender Brasil's Congress was full of communists." However, by 1964 Botsford had re-enticed Borges himself into some of the CCF's activities (Figure 5.3). Lowell likewise apologized to Botsford that winter for "the rough house and phantasmagoria at the end of Argentina."[59]

Fig 5.3 Joachim G. Jung, Photograph of Keith Botsford and Jorge Luis Borges, Berlin International Conference of Poets, 1964. Box 542, Folder 13, IACF.

Lowell's trip has therefore been regarded as disastrous for the Congress, but in fact he was effective in Trinidad and Recife, a nonentity in Rio de Janeiro, and only ruinous to the CCF's work in Buenos Aires because of his scandalous pro-Castro outbursts. These sudden shifts underscore Lowell's understanding of the "phantasmagorical" rhythm of his trip. He transfigured his cultural-diplomatic efforts into a patently phantasmagorical triptych of poems toward the close of *For the Union Dead*: "July in Washington," "Buenos Aires," and "Dropping South: Brazil." They offer a collection of political fantasies experienced as though in a fevered dream state. These dreamscapes bend the psycho-political mechanisms of the confessional lyric toward a retrospective expiation of his imperial guilt with an ambivalent revolutionary disposition. Ian Hamilton suggests the poem "For the Union Dead" is Lowell's "first step towards extending the possibilities of his self-centeredness: towards treating his own torments as metaphors of public, even global, ills." In fact, *For the Union Dead* as a volume repeatedly recasts confessionalism in terms of foreign policy engagements with Latin America, monumentalizing the poetic self in a US-centered hemispheric imperium produced out of Lowell's ambivalent agency as a cultural diplomat.

Although "July in Washington" leads this sequence, it was probably written in July 1964, well after the other two poems it anticipates. In ten unrhymed couplets, it figures US imperialism: "The stiff spokes of this wheel/touch the sore

spots of the earth."⁶⁰ By envisioning Washington in terms of its radial geom-
etry, Lowell recalls Pierre Charles L'Enfant's 1791 spoke-and-hub master plan
for the city. However, he depicts this plan as an inflexible wheel on a rude cart
reaching out to "touch the sore spots" around the globe. The verb "touch" jars
by interrupting the alliterative symmetry of "the stiff spokes" and "the sore
spots." The word's neutral valence suggests that the spokes are irritants, not
root causes. The rough-hewn US capital rides over a world figured as an inde-
terminately wounded body. The hemispheric imperium is uncontrollably violent, but not intentionally so. The next stanza updates a central image of Latin
American modernismo—the swan—as one of weekend boating in this imperial
capital: "On the Potomac, swan-white/power launches keep breasting the sul-
phurous wave."⁶¹ Claiming the weekend warrior boats as Parnassian symbols,
Lowell suggests that even the Capitol's leisure activities reflect its naive consolidation of world power.

Lowell's capital is also in a metadiplomatic dialogue with Latin America:

> On the circles, green statues ride like South American
> liberators above the breeding vegetation—
>
> prongs and spearheads of some equatorial
> backland that will inherit the globe.⁶²

Here, the poem envisions the Age of Liberty, resituating Lowell's fixations with
DC in a monumental, Bolivarian image of the revolutionary Americas. Chilean
poet Nicanor Parra glibly dismisses gestures such as these, describing "USA" in
an epigrammatic postcard poem as the nation "Donde la libertad/es una estatua"
(Where liberty/is a statue).⁶³ But in Lowell's complex and monumental hemispherism, the statuary's "prongs and spearheads" reorient his centrifugal image of
spokes on a wheel as centripetal forces that menace back at the capitol. The noun
"backland" refers to Euclides da Cunha's Os Sertões (Rebellion in the Backland,
1902), which, at Bishop's suggestion, Lowell devoured in Samuel Putnam's 1944
translation, neither aware that Putnam chose this project as one conducive to
his communist inter-Americanism.⁶⁴ The "stiff spokes" image of urbanism quietly dialogues with the urban plan of Brazil's just-completed inland capital city,
Brasilia, which Lowell had seen in Bishop's Life book. Yet, in Lowell's poem, neither early-1960s Brazil nor the early-1960s United States evoke a fecund, revolutionary future of "breeding vegetation" (an image that sonically recalls Lowell's
description of Beat poets as writing the poems of some "bearded but vegetarian
Castro"). Instead, they emblematize a revolutionary past in the patina of oxi-
dized statuary, allegories of a political form the United States was now quelling

abroad. These ruinous and regenerative statues are hemispheric analogues to the Civil War monument on the Boston Common in "For the Union Dead," which "sticks like a fishbone/in the city's throat."[65] While "For the Union Dead" imagines Boston's symbolic resolution of Civil War divisions, "July in Washington" equivocates on Lowell's stance toward hemispheric unity.

In "Buenos Aires," Lowell's speaker looks out from his room in a famous neo-classical hotel onto one of the "backlands" evoked in the previous poem:

> In my room at the Hotel Continentál
> a thousand miles from nowhere,
> I heard
> the bulky, beefy breathing of the herds.
>
> Cattle furnished my new clothes:
> my coat of limp, chestnut-colored suede,
> my sharp shoes
> that hurt my toes.[66]

Lowell adds a gratuitous accent to "Continentál," authenticating Spanish-language pronunciation by ignoring its orthography. The cloistered speaker imagines his lyrical solitude, inhabiting the Petrarchan topos of remove from the vulgar *popol tutto*, who Lowell egregiously likens to Argentine cattle in a profusely alliterative scheme ("bulky, beefy breathing of the herds"). In this, Lowell renders Argentina's social body inarticulate, voiced only by a stuttering alliteration, much like Bishop's sound schemes for her "Squatter's Children" or Walcott's "Kikuyu, quick as flies." But Lowell portrays the speaker dressed in the same leathers to which he analogizes Argentine society, thus charting how the social body he denigrates yields the luxury export commodities he wears. No "genius in shirtsleeves" here, Lowell's leather goods alternately slacken and constrict the poem's metrical progress.

The poem proceeds through other paradoxes and tragic visions designed to expiate the speaker's psycho-political guilt. For one, the poet's capacities as a cultural diplomat fail to interrupt a military dictatorship. As in "July in Washington's" Parnassian Potomac, the Argentine capital surges into view as a typological imitation of the late nineteenth century: "A false fin de siecle [sic] decorum/snored over Buenos Aires." Such "decorum," or the obligatory style of state-sponsored cultural work, is "false" because behind it lurk the "coups d'état/of the leaden internecine generals." Indeed, the provisional government controlled by José María Guido between March 1962 and October 1963 declared General Juan Carlos Onganía commander in chief of the Argentine military in

September 1962. To Lowell, General Onganía's splash across the daily newspapers ironizes a tradition of "Republican martyrs" that the poet observes as statuary in a visit to the famous Recoleta cemetery. There, the poem's phantasmagorical quality comes through as busts of "soldier bureaucrats" contrast the liberators of "July in Washington" and the "leaden" Onganía:

> Along the sunlit cypress walks
> of the Republican martyrs' graveyard,
> hundreds of one-room Roman temples
> hugged their neo-classical catafalques.
>
> Literal commemorative busts
> preserved the frogged coats
> and fussy, furrowed foreheads
> of those soldier bureaucrats.[67]

Alliterative phrasal clusters of *s-*, *r-*, *c-* and *h-* sounds in the first stanza and *f-* and *b-* sounds in the second stanza align elite Argentine classes with the senseless "bulky, beefy breathing" of the masses. Lowell belittles this nobility when compared to the "nobles certidumbres del polvo" (noble witnesses of the dust) ironized by Borges's 1923 cemetery poem "La Recoleta" for having presaged the "deseable/dignidad de haber muerto (the appealing/dignity of having died)."[68] The architectural term *catafalque* alliterates *neo-classical* and rhymes with *walks*, but the term's propriety in the sound scheme is belied by semantic imprecision. A *catafalque* is a temporary funeral structure that imitates the monumental tomb while a notable personage lies in state, but the preponderance of Recoleta tombs negates the occasion for a catafalque. Neither impermanent nor notable, only the "fussy, furrowed foreheads" of the "soldier bureaucrats" reside in them, cheapening the Age of Liberty's unfulfilled ideals.

The poem's penultimate stanza extends the Recoleta scene while winking at the manic episode Lowell suffered in Argentina:

> By their brazen doors
> a hundred marble goddesses
> wept like willows. I found rest
> by cupping a soft palm to each hard breast.[69]

This is not the same as the nude poet riding a liberator statue. Lowell reassigns the "Caesar of Argentina" role to Onganía's junta, if not the Republicans enshrined in their personal "Roman temples," opting instead for a failed gesture of consolation. The soft palms of soft power take cold comfort in republican monuments.

No effective "window" onto statecraft, Lowell's speaker stands in the wings molesting the muses of history, copping a feel from the goddesses guarding the buried martyrs. The molestation of the statue's breast is a site of "rest," an odd desideratum for the speaker, who previously asserts no need for repose. In the poem's citywide "snore," the poet's leisurely slog through the newspaper in the comfort of the hotel room is the closest thing to work. In this sense, "rest" implies Arnoldian solace, or else a tormented expression of bad faith, as if Lowell were vindicating the resignation expressed by Guadeloupe-born French poet Saint-John Perse in his 1960 Nobel Prize lecture: "it is enough for the poet to be the guilty conscience of his time."[70] Here, Lowell's poem comes closest to an auto-biographical description of what he called "rough house and phantasmagoria," ending on a cheap pun about his leather-clad, psychologically disturbed state: "I was the worse for wear,/and my breath whitened the winter air."[71] The speaker's dreamscape rehearses his psycho-political damage. An alternate version of the poem published in the *New York Review of Books* in 1963 heightens the sexually multifarious scene. The speaker walks the streets fighting off "seduction from the dark/python bodies of new world demigods," imagines Perón as a bull who continues to inflame a city of "nymphets," and observes that the city's "obelisk/ rose like a phallus/without flesh or hair" as a lighthouse beacon, navigating him to the safe port of the hotel. [72] In another republican monument, the poet finds a symbol of his own phallic arousal, which paradoxically safeguards him from feminine sexual predations.

Lowell's third Latin American poem also privileges fevered dream as the stage for confessional guilt. "Dropping South: Brazil," depicts a nocturnal reverie of return to the Copacabana beach he called home across the summer of 1962, but one that is comically written in the Stevensian mode Lowell earlier disparaged. He stands over a spinning globe ogling what Stevens calls a "holiday hotel world":

> Walking and walking in a mothy robe,
> one finger pushing through the pocket-hole,
> I crossed the reading room and met my soul,
> hunched, spinning downward on the colored globe.[73]

This tightly rhymed, pentametric quatrain loosens over the rest of the poem, and in come semaphoric signals that Stevens's "fluent mundo" has expired. Stevens's "flag of the nude" yields to Lowell's beach where "red flags forbade our swimming"; Steven's inland of "z rivers simmering" yields to Lowell's interior where, in an allusion to Claude Lévi-Strauss, "people starved, and struck, and died— unhappy Americas, ah *tristes tropiques*!" Lowell had previously characterized two competitive strands of American poetry, "a cooked and a raw"; now the "cooked" Lowell makes a poetic votive to the "raw," Afro-Brazilian rites of macumba, in a wild, mid-dream self-quotation: "'I am falling./*Santa Maria*, pray for me, I want to stop,/but I have lost my foothold on the map.'" In a letter to Botsford, Lowell highlights this phantasmagorical distance:

> Brazil is far away, and yet it has somehow accompanied us: yellow, blue and red boat streamers hang from our balcony, our big silver slave's bangle is handed to visitors [. . .], and whenever we give a dinner [. . .] [w]e try to describe Goulard, Aledjadinho (?), Burly Marx, Rebellion in the Backlands. I've written a poem about walking in my sleep, leaning on a large standing globe, and then falling through the air southward till I land on the Copacabana.[74]

Lowell's *mauvaise foi* expiation of the United States' cultural diplomatic project suggests that no matter where he slid, having lost his foothold on the map, the American flag in some sense flew—in the creature comforts, the grand hotels, the CIA leashes, the old friends.

Lowell put this problem darkly in his stage adaptation of *Benito Cereno*, cowritten with William Meredith in 1961 and first performed in 1964.[75] Delano exhorts: "There goes the most beautiful woman in South America."[76] When his greenhorn bosun corrects him, saying that only the "smothering, overcast equator" and the "flat dull sea" are in view, Delano specifies: "I wasn't talking about women,/I was calling your attention to the American flag." In "this absentee empire," the Captain claims, "We are home. America is wherever her flag flies." In elevating personal anguish to global ill, Lowell's confessionalism harnesses a "wounded" lyric subjectivity to expiate the "sins" of cultural diplomacy, and to remake a neo-imperial project of free-market democracy as a fevered dream of self-torment.

Walcott in the Gulf

Although Lowell's model of liberal self-compromise and confessional phantasmagoria mainly failed to breach the intellectual and poetic formations of continental Latin America, it influenced at least two of the most important lyric poets in the 1960s Caribbean: Derek Walcott (St. Lucia, 1930–) and Heberto Padilla (Cuba, 1932–2000). Patricia Ismond rightly claims that the 1960s and 1970s were Walcott's period of greatest regional commitment to indigenizing the Caribbean artist, yet that commitment, forcefully articulated in his prolific journalism, clearly conversed with the Cold War cultural policy apparatus that simultaneously conscripted him.[77] Other scholars, noting Walcott's hemispherism, place him in the genealogy of numinous Adamic poets to whom he expresses allegiance in "The Muse of History" (1974), including Borges, Neruda, and Césaire.[78] Yet these affinities, too, emerge from the situation of the cultural Cold War: Walcott's first reading of Neruda and Borges was due to a friendship with Cold Warrior Selden Rodman, and a key encounter with Césaire occurred at a 1964 CCF conference. Lowell's underremarked model—his openness to imitation, his relaxed lineation strategies, and what Walcott calls the "brutal honesty" of his attention to the fictional power of ordinary detail—offers an alternate point of departure for Walcott's poetic project in this period.[79] Walcott once "confessed" that Lowell's "influence was irresistible" precisely because his openness to appropriation enabled Walcott's revaluation of postcolonial mimicry.[80] Most importantly, Lowell modeled for Walcott a stance toward participation in the CCF and primed his entrance into the New York literary marketplace. Walcott borrows from Lowell, Bishop, and Hardwick the model of a self-compromising, verbally dense confrontation with a tragic view of hemispheric history, amid what Cary Fraser calls the era's discourse of "ambivalent anti-colonialism," or independence claims subordinated to "Cold War imperatives."[81] Through these years, anticommunism is one of Walcott's red threads. In 1957, he denounced the "Communist" verse of Afro-Guyanese poet Martin Carter.[82] By 1967, he describes himself as a "pretty dull bourgeois," and claims "the tragic view of history . . . is the view the greatest poets hold, except the Communists."[83] These views diffusely inform *The Gulf* (1970), a lyric chronicle of Walcott's passage through the 1960s.[84]

Walcott met Lowell in Port of Spain at the outset of Lowell's 1962 CCF lecture tour, less than two weeks after the collapse of the Federation of the West Indies and just two months before the formal achievement of independence for Trinidad and Tobago. In a postcard to Bishop, Lowell describes Trinidad's racial complexity as "a world rather like Louisiana turned on its head with an inset from *Passage to India*."[85] Botsford warned Lowell and Hardwick that in Trinidad "the Congress can do little in the way of organizing. You do your own, as representatives of the Fortress, and we'll be grateful. . . . Any talking you do about what the Congress is & what it stands for, will be appreciated." He further sought to assure Lowell, with his characteristically graceless and patronizing racism, that the tour couldn't fail: "In small islands, it's like the praise-drums up African rivers: the word will be passed along."[86] In the end, Lowell secured speaking appearances at the University of the West Indies and at the public library, but the highlight was Walcott, who acclaimed Lowell in the *Guardian* as "Poet from the Land of the Bean and the Cod," while finding in "For the Union Dead" a "fervently moral critic of nuclear politics and . . . industrial vulgarity."[87] "We've had a really incredible time," wrote Hardwick to Botsford. "Walcott was just about waiting on the steps of the hotel when we arrived—and thank heaven. We've had a tremendously intimate picture of the island."[88] Walcott was flustered at their meeting at the Queen's Park Hotel, calling Hardwick "Edna St. Vincent Millay."[89] He later recalled seaside evenings discussing *Imitations* with Lowell: "I don't think any of the biographies have caught the sort of gentle, amused, benign beauty of him when he was calm."[90]

Over the next year the couples corresponded and Robert Giroux solicited Lowell's glowing report on Walcott's *In A Green Night* in advance of publication. In fall 1963, Walcott returned to New York on a Rockefeller grant for meetings with Giroux. "The Derek Walcotts are here in New York for a few weeks," wrote Hardwick to Botsford. "We had a cocktail party for them and everyone loves them here as much as we do. How noticeably different they are from American Negroes—they dislike England instead of the US."[91] At this debut, clearly a peculiar dialogue about hemispheric race relations had inflected the cocktail party banter. For, soon after they returned to Port of Spain, the Walcotts reflected back on the party in a startling letter to "Cal and Lizabeth," in which they fabricate a *Paris Review* interview conducted by Malcolm X with the Lowell's "cook Teresa," who speaks in pidgin, and Hardwick, who speaks in a drawl that may be a linguistic racial masquerade:

> Dear Cal and Lizabeth,
>
> We came across this:
>
> PARIS REVIEW NO. 52227
>
> (An interview: The Lowells live in a high-vaulted monastery near Lincoln Center, from which one can hear, if one leans out, Elia Kazan quarrelling with Leonard Bernstein. When we came in, Mrs Lowell, a secret drinker, was hiding a half-empty bottle of Bourbon under her record player, on which there was a Billie Holiday record. We asked the distinguished critic if she knew the late singer.
>
> "Did ahknowthelateBILLIEHOLIDAY?' she muttered.
>
> In as much as all Miss Hardwick had to say was for the most part either incomprehensible if not genteely profane, especially on the subject of race (the human race, one must emphasize), we tried to learn about the Lowells' writing methods from their Spanish cook Teresa.[92]

This mock editorial note displays "genteel" ironies of an elite liberal angle of vision on civil rights: a Billie Holiday record doubles as a cover for alcoholism; a coy sentimentalism shifts "the subject of race" from the register of national grievance to that of United Nations–brand universalism; and a middlebrow conversation about literary craft is recast as domestic service work. The "genteely profane" status of Hardwick's drawl scandalizes the entire situation.

In the subsequent interview, X's literary queries bleed into Teresa's nonsensical responses, such as "Exactamente. A las cinquos [sic] de la tarde." A cocktail party farce about race in the Americas ensues:

> MALC. X: But is that not also the cocktail hour?
>
> TERESA: 'Scusi?
>
> MALC. X: Let me put it this way. You state, more or less unequivocally, that around every cinquos de la tarde, Senorita Hardwick composa sara syntactica de Boston y el tunderclappo y Senor Roberto de Lowello y Winslow de la Bostonidad, y composo sas poemas also? Would that be right?
>
> TERESA: Tristo Tropique.
>
> MALCOLM: Comprende! Then it would be correct to imply that one Saturday evening a las cinquous de la tarde, (to coin a bolivar), un large cocktail party was given en this residence, for a Senor y Senora Diricho MuroBracho, y Margaretha Muro Bracho, with William Meredith, Frederick Seidel, Susan Sontag, Robert Silvers, Jack Benny, Jack Thompson, Howard Mosquito y Henry Rago?
>
> TERESA: Henry Rago, non! Excusi.
>
> (AT THIS POINT MRS LOWELL INTERPOSED AND SEEMED READY TO BE INTERVIEWED. SHE HAD THIS STATEMENT TO MAKE:)
>
> MISS HARDWICK: Sho ah know the Walcotts, honey. Whah, they's some of mah best friends. The wife cant read and the husband cant write, but that don't matter, does it?
>
> MALCOLM X: Did you notice if they was colored, ma'am?
>
> MISS HARDWICK: Sho ah noticed they was colored, Malcolm. But so's Carson Mac Cullers, ah'm sho, so's Tenesse Williams, so's Alex Pushkin. But to me, they's simple people, that's all. We like them for what they are.
>
> MALCOLM X: And what are they?
>
> MISS HARDWICK: Why, just plain colored people, that's all.[93]

Some of the same homophonic humor in Bishop's account of Roberto Burle Marx's "garden party" peppers this interview's obscure in-jokes. A pigeon Romance language floats between Spanish and Italian, as if the Walcotts cannot decide whether to mock a monolingual cook or to send up their own interlinguistic deficits. "Tristo Tropique" misspells Claude Lévi-Strauss's book title *Triste Tropiques,* alluding to Lowell's use of this epithet for the "unhappy Americas" in "Dropping South: Brazil." The guest list includes attendees (Silvers, Sontag, Meredith, Seidel) alongside celebrities not in attendance (Benny) and hokey nicknames, such as Margaretha Muro Bracho, a loose translation of Margaret *Wall*cott's name, and a mangling of muy borracho (very drunk). When Malcolm X broaches race, Hardwick assimilates the question by comparing the Walcotts to the southern regionalist writers McCullers and Williams. The interview format conventions are undermined by supplanting questions of writing with the cocktail party's linguistic tumult. How Lowell and Hardwick write—questions of poetic form and practical craft—give way to the hemispheric noise of racial masquerade and clashing pidgins. That noise, the Walcotts suggest in a note following the interview, "can be obtained at Cliff Sealy's Bookshop on Marli Street as anti-American propaganda."[94] The mock-interview traces a circuit through which a concentrated social expression of New York's elite literary-institutional life could be transmuted into an illegible clatter of Cold War cultural propaganda, the kind that might trickle in to the counter-institution of John Clifford Sealy's Trinidad Bookshop.

In the following years, some of Walcott's best poems stage the same drama. "Laventille" (1965) takes its name from an impoverished community on a steep hillside in Port of Spain (named, in turn, for the stiff breeze the hill form generates). It is a close cousin to Bishop's "Squatter's Children," a poem Walcott likely read in *Questions of Travel,* which he named one of 1965's five best books in a year-end questionnaire.[95] "Laventille" begins:

> It huddled there
> steel tinkling its blue painted metal air,
> tempered in violence, like Rio's favelas,
>
> with snaking, perilous streets whose edges fell as
> its episcopal turkey-buzzards fall
> from its miraculous hilltop.[96]

While Bishop's favela "piles up," Laventille "huddles," a social form of snug destitution. Here, the neighborhood's famous reputation as the originator of steel pan music ("steel tinkling its blue painted metal air") does not wrest it from squalor, in contrast to the relationship between music and poverty on offer, say, in Brathwaite's syncopated vernacular "riddims" in *Rights of Passage* (1967) or in the Brazilian film *Orfeu Negro* (1959), which Walcott praised, in one of his many articles about state-funded culture, for balancing "Soviet-dominated art and the medieval and capitalist idea of the artist as a pauper in search of a patron."[97] Instead, Walcott's "tinkling" sound scheme echoes the "peddlers' tin trinkets," a thin acoustical imagination that fails as a basis for local culture. In his 1964 article "Spreading Our Culture Abroad," Walcott lampoons a local philistinism that elevates calypso and carnival over the "whorish modesty" of state-funded high culture.[98] The poem's modest acoustics, reinforced by tercets and cross-stanza enjambments that exaggerate a rhythm of descent, echo Walcott's diagnosis of Trinidad's cultural deficits.

The poem's descending tinkles are likened to its presemantic noise, as in the hill's microclimatological propensity to produce precipitation:

> From a harsh
> shower, its gutters growled and gargled wash
> past the Youth Centre, past the water catchment,
> rigid children's carousel of cement.[99]

Here the poem directly announces its affiliation to Bishop's anticommunist poverty acoustics. Runoff from the poorly engineered hill streams around the paltry social provisions of the Youth Centre in a "guttural" phonology of growls and gargles, a linguistic register susceptible to phonosymbolic play, since "guttural" and "gutter" have no etymological connection, only the glottological connection linked by the production of the hard *g* in the throat.[100] Bishop's poetics of likeness also arises here, as when Walcott writes: "where the inheritors of the middle passage stewed/five to a room, still clamped below their hatch,/breeding like felonies,//whose lives revolve round prison, graveyard, church."[101] Metaphorizing tenement shacks as the holds of a slaver, Walcott sketches a circle between a felonious imagination of unbreakable poverty and racial slavery. The roundabouts of carousels, the massification of bodies, and the insensible sound of drainage all render these cycles as poetic structure.

While amassing more and more of this whirl of babble, Walcott highlights how poems allegorize class structures in poetic sound:

> Below bent breadfruit trees
> in the flat, coloured city, class

>
> escalated into structures still,
> merchant, middleman, magistrate, knight. To go downhill
> from here was to ascend.[102]

Laventille respatializes the rhetoric of economic uplift as a paradoxical form of descent. The enjambed phrase "class//escalated into structures" acknowledges how a particular hill materializes class as "structure," while the verb "escalated" evokes anxious Cold War logics of the "SHOCKING POVERTY SPAWNS REDS" variety, even as the mechanisms of poetic art relax that reading through the delayed, descending placement of the cross-stanza enjambment. For Walcott, vertical axes of economic mobility give way to a circular poetic logic of "ritual, desperate words,/born like these children from habitual wombs,//from lives fixed in the unalterable groove/of grinding poverty."[103] The poem's lexical and acoustical imagination mirrors repetitive cycles of Third World poverty. Poetic form articulates through the malformed slum. The poem's closing line, "and in its swaddling cerements we're still bound," offers a slight phonemic variation on the revolving cement carousel from earlier in the poem. The child's playground, "the unalterable groove/of grinding poverty," and the death shroud at the close of the poem all imagine confining circularities. "Laventille" finds its place in Walcott's lyric corpus among a pattern of repeated exiles and returns to the islands, which he calls an "open passage" contradistinguished from the amnesiac circularities and overcoded repetitions of the middle passage.

At the time of the 1963 cocktail party, Lowell secured money for Walcott from the Farfield Foundation, one of the CIA's philanthropic fronts for cultural funding.[104] King's biography minimizes these facts on the grounds that "most of the writers and editors were innocent about the ultimate source of American aid."[105] Walcott *was* probably innocent of the covert sources, but he was also overtly cozy with the anticommunist cultural apparatus, publishing poems in *Encounter* in 1963, and accepting subsequent Farfield Foundation support to read at the CCF's September 1964 International Congress of Poets in Berlin and at New York's Solomon R. Guggenheim Museum on October 15, 1964.[106] Walcott saw in the well-heeled anticommunist lecture circuit a potential pipeline for Trinidadian state culture. He began dreaming up a congress of "international blend" in Trinidad with pluralistic and anticommunist coordinates. Enthusing that "I am not one for passing up a conference or congress with Pan prefixed to it," he imagined "a salt-and-pepper combination of white liberals, mulatto middle-of-the-roaders, Irish freeloaders, Hindu masseurs, all raging at injustice, colonialism, and after Independence what do you

Fig 5.4 Joachim G. Jung, Photograph of Roger Caillois, Derek Walcott, and an unidentified woman, Berlin International Conference of Poets, 1964. Box 542, Folder 13, IACF.

drink?, like one thousand guests of honour at a cocktail party with Pan beating in the background."[107] Lowell's cocktail party scales up here to a ludic world poetry congress. "I'm not knocking the idea. I just want to be asked," he concluded.[108]

Asked he was. Attending the Berlin International Conference of Poets in September 1964, he was star-struck by Auden, Borges, and Césaire, even as he grew cognizant of the conference's goal of preventing postcolonial writers from cultivating Soviet sympathies (Figure 5.4). The uniform "business suits" in which modern poets expressed their "careful anonymity" appeared to him to comprise a liberal economic forum—a "Chamber of Commerce Convention."[109] Yet there was real value in "points of human exchange where each poet recognized in the other the distance and solitariness of his calling."[110] By 1966, he produced savvier self-reflections about participation in Cold War cultural diplomacy:

> Congresses have become popular of late. The Cold War divided its intel-
> lectuals into separate camps, not with any precise definition, but it con-
> structed arenas of opinion in which writers could challenge foreign
> policy, in which they could dramatize ideological shifts. Sponsors like
> the Congress of Cultural Freedom, sometimes obliquely, sometimes

forthrightly, state their political position by arranging international seminars on the artist and politics.[111]

Despite its avowed aims of intellectual weaponization, Walcott again affirmed the Congress's value: "underneath it all there is a real invisible community, a private commonwealth."[112] The Cold War cosmopolitan congress as an interface between solitary poetic calling and literary community increasingly inflected Walcott's lyric fiction in *The Gulf*.

The Gulf, a poetic chronicle of the 1960s, lyricizes revolutionary and racial uprising and the hemispheric geopolitics of Guyana, Trinidad, Bolivia, Cuba, and the United States. One of the capstones of the hemispheric lyric impulse, it is both a symptom and an agent of inter-American cultural-diplomatic activity, pushing the problematic to new limits through its strategies of alienated remove and its eclectic range of self-compromising attentions. It participates in the crisis of anticommunist liberal subjectivity we see in Bishop and Lowell's contemporaneous sequences, while synthesizing the autochthonous New World vision of Neruda and the Cratylist impulses of Stevens, Lezama, and Borges. For example, "A Map of the Continent" describes "the one age of the world" as if it veers "Between the Rupununi and Borges,/Between the fallen pen-tip and the spearhead"—that is, between indigenous Guyanese irredentists (Rupununi) and conservative Cratylists (Borges) who share only a faith in New World vision.[113]

At the center of the volume, Walcott titled a three-canto poem "The Gulf," layering a symbolic system around this figure. First, *gulf* signals the disparity between phenomenal and noumenal reality, which Walcott elaborates around the biblical locution "Between me and thee is a great gulf fixed," quoted as an epigraph in Walcott's poem "Crusoe's Journal."[114] This gulf divides the alienated poet from society, and he attempts to breach it through ritual immersion in New World experience. Second, *gulf* signals economic, racial, and geographical chasms between the US north and south in the age of civil rights. Third, *gulf* metaphorizes the Gulf of Mexico geography as that which divides islands of the Anglophone Caribbean that had recently failed to confederate, and further separates the United States from this archipelagic Caribbean. Fourth, *gulf* is a metonym for an oil industry (as in the massive Gulf Oil Company) that Walcott links to filling station signage from Port of Spain and Guyana to Tampico and New Orleans. Inferentially, oil therefore links him to the foundation moneys that fund his "open passage" around the gulf system, furnishing him with friendly grant officers and recipients who find their ways into his poems as dedications. Finally, *gulf* divides Walcott's attitude toward his own poetic development, as the speaker of *The Castaway* (1965) gives way to a looser, more confident versifier. *The Gulf* narrates a metropolitan self-authentication, from the self-denigrating "rhyming spade" of "A Village Life" who experiences sexual frustration, spurned publishing efforts ("a snowfall of torn poems piling up"), and racist attacks ("Blues"), to the business-class traveler who accepts foundation speaking engagements.[115] In all, *The Gulf* signals Walcott's arrival as a hemispheric poet for whom the lyric sequence's spatiotemporal fiction emplaces him in the interlocking frameworks of liberal anticommunism, commonwealth, postcolonial, revolutionary, and civil rights discourses, and Caribbean, New York, Texas, and London literary marketplaces.

The Castaway staged its alienation through the hilltop prospect of Laventille, the snowy New York loft window of "A Village Life," or the beach of "Crusoe's Journal." By contrast, in "The Gulf," air travel offers a privileged standpoint for the poet's staging of his alienation. Walcott dedicates "The Gulf" to Barbara and Jack Harrison, who pioneered a translation grant program in the Rockefeller Foundation Humanities Division which kick-started University of Texas Press's Pan American book series. In 1962 he accepted a position as head of the University of Texas Institute of Latin American Studies, where the foundation grant dollars followed him.[116] Walcott most likely read at UT Austin at Harrison's invitation in October 1968, and "The Gulf" imagines his return to Trinidad, stirring together inter-American literature, race, politics, and economics through a slow circling, distancing action. "The airport coffee tastes less of America," it begins, as if commodity exchange weakens the phenomenal reality of New World experience, which the poet's "exhausted soul" seeks to "reclaim" from its detachment.[117] As part of his curative imagination, the speaker carries a talismanic "book of fables by Borges, its prose/a stalking, moonlit tiger," probably *Dreamtigers* (1964), the University of Texas Press's translation of *El hacedor* (1960), featuring a stalking tiger woodcut cover image by the Uruguayan artist Antonio Frasconi. In the image-matrix of Walcott's poem, Frasconi's tiger has oracular knowledge of the Kennedy assassination: "What was willed/on innocent, sun-streaked Dallas, the beast's claw curled round that hairspring rifle is revealed/on every page as lunacy or feral law."[118] Borges's visiting professorship at UT Austin in 1961 gives Walcott a model to impute to the *Dreamtigers* miscellany a tragic political prophecy.

Here is the second canto of "The Gulf," in which the poet departs from Dallas's Love Field for Trinidad:

> The cold glass darkens. Elizabeth wrote once
> that we make glass the image of our pain;
> I watch clouds boil past the cold, sweating pane

above the Gulf. All styles yearn to be plain
as life. The face of the loved object under glass
is plainer still. Yet, somehow, at this height,

above this cauldron boiling with its wars,
our old earth, breaking to familiar light,
that cloud-bound mummy with self healing scars

peeled of her cerements again looks new;
some cratered valley heals itself with sage,
through that grey, fading massacre a blue

light-hearted creek flutes of some siege
to the amnesia of drumming water.
Their cause is crystalline: the divine union

of these detached, divided States, whose slaughter
darkens each summer now, as one by one,
the smoke of bursting ghettos clouds the glass

down every coast where filling-station signs
proclaim the Gulf, an air, heavy with gas,
sickens the state, from Newark to New Orleans.[119]

This canto's aerial perspective integrates Walcott's role as a cultural diplomat between Caribbean independence movements and US literary elites with his commentaries on US civil rights and the unrest of radical black nationalists undergoing forms of state suppression ("smoke of bursting ghettos"). On high, the poet hopes to bridge these "detached, divided States," states that must be read as both jurisdictional and experiential. One index of this integrationist disposition is Walcott's reuse of the word "cerements." Whereas cerements stifle Laventille, here, unswaddled, they reveal a glorified nature.

To understand Walcott's integrationist gambit we need to follow the allusion contained in the first line: "Elizabeth wrote once/that we make glass the image of our pain." I believe that Walcott has in mind Elizabeth Hardwick's 1963 essay "Grub Street: New York," in which she writes, "Glass is the perfect material of our life." Hardwick's glass signifies a display window that converts suffering into identification. She writes of how "each unutterable day of suffering and humiliation" that James Baldwin exposed to his *New Yorker* readership in his 1962 essay "Letter from a Region in My Mind" fashioned a liberal literary public sphere of therapeutic tolerance. As she specifies: "Everyone talked about [Baldwin's essay] and seemed to feel in some way the better for it. The guerrilla warfare by which the weak become strong, or at least destructive—even the threat of that could be taken, apparently, accepted, turned into glass. Only Russia and Communism arouse—there, writer, watch out."[120] Glass therefore manages collective agony; it diagnoses how 1960s theaters of social revolution are smoothed into liberal strategies of therapeutic identification, though these capacious identifications always stop shy of the communist state.

Hardwick offers one last example of her "glass" conceit in a portrait of an anonymous, excessively romantic Brazilian cultural diplomat "come forth from some mute backland," just the sort of writer her CCF participation often led her to meet:

> The poor, the hungry, fly in by air, brought on official visits, missions of culture. A South American in a brushed, blue serge suit, wearing polished black shoes and large cufflinks of semiprecious stones. [. . .]. He had arrived, by hideously hard work, at an overwhelming pedantry, a bachelorish violence of self-control. The pedantry of scarcity. This pale glacier had been produced in the tropics, a poor man in a poor country, trying to lift himself into the professions, to cut through the jungle of deprivation, save a few pennies of ambition from the national bankruptcy.[121]

Hardwick blends poverty mitigation as anticommunism, cultural diplomacy as anticommunism, and intercultural literary criticism as anticommunism. Her condescending portrait of this Third World cultural emissary hinges on the price of his emergence from an assumed scene of poverty, not unlike the Walcott that Lowell introduced during a poetry reading at the Guggenheim as "lucky" to be born in Trinidad if the island does not "bury" him (apparently ignoring Walcott's St. Lucian place of birth).[122] While Hardwick suggests the cost of the diplomat's success is "overwhelming pedantry," Walcott suggests another self-presentational pathway, defined by his absorption of Hardwick's therapeutic liberal public sphere and its redeployment on behalf of a commonwealth literary public.

Walcott's poem literalizes Hardwick's "glass" as the jet window, even as he gives it new metaphorical extensions. The window "pane" is the sound image of "pain"; only the word *plane* itself is conspicuous by its absence in the rhyme scheme. Walcott's mature liberal optic comprehends social suffering only at a cool distance. Although the poet yearns to link the therapeutic optics of glass with a foundational "plain style," the social agonies of civil rights continually cloud that style in the "smoke of bursting ghettos." The poet's many identifications with the liberal hemispheric order ("the South felt like home") yield to acknowledgment of "my status as a secondary soul./The Gulf, your gulf, is daily widening." He fears a final breach, envisioned as a vengeful black nationalism:

> each blood-red rose warns of that coming night
> when there's no rock cleft to go hidin' in
> and all the rocks catch fire, when that black might,
> their stalking, moonless panthers turn from Him
> whose voice they can no more believe, when the black X's
> mark their passover with slain seraphim.

These lines transform Borges's moonlit "Dreamtigers" into the moonless Black Panthers, and Malcolm X's assassination into the lamb's blood on the doors of the Jewish Passover, wherein a vengeful god promises to deliver the violence that Anglo-America has wrought. The scene portrays an ethnonational revolt that is simultaneously sparked and repressed, inevitable but self-damaging, like the waves of militant black power that almost toppled the Trinidadian government in 1969–1970. Here the poem's "gulf" conceit reappears as a leaden cauldron, as still as the "waved lead" sea that opens Melville's *Benito Cereno* with its premonitory climate of failed revolt: "The Gulf shines, dull as lead."

Walcott's mature and tragic view of history, which he thus models on Hardwick, Bishop, and Lowell, records other scenes of failed revolt in several poems of violent revolutionary repression, including "Junta" and two elegies to Che Guevara. The fascinating but unsuccessful poem "Junta" turns on an extended homophonic transformation between the words "Caesar," "siegheil," and "Julius Seizure," creating a dense thicket of sound play that likens a dictatorial regime to an extended epileptic fit.[123] "Che" is a short ekphrasis of Bolivian journalist Freddy Alborta's photograph of Che's body lying Christ-like on a stone bier, surrounded by the Bolivian soldiers and the CIA agents who killed him on October 9, 1967. It presents a stock portrait of what Margaret Randall calls the "emotional iconography" of Che's martyrdom.[124] By contrast, Walcott dates the other Che poem, "Elegy," eight months later on June 6, 1968, a date notable (though no critics seem to note it) as the day of Robert F. Kennedy's assassination. Immediately following "The Gulf," "Elegy" magnifies the theme of political assassination in the architecture of the book. Of a "black singer" who wails through several stanzas of the poem, Walcott writes "and yearly lilacs in her dooryards bloom," alluding to Whitman's Lincoln elegy, as if Guevara, Robert F. Kennedy, and John F. Kennedy in the previous poem each inhabited dimensions of the integrationist, Republican ethos of Bolívar and Lincoln, "howling" the traumatic repetition of their murders. "Elegy" also opens with an integrationist image that the poem rapidly undermines: "Our hammock swung between Americas,/ we miss you, Liberty. Che's/bullet-riddled body falls." The hammock suggests a meta-geography of the Caribbean archipelago linking North and South America, each foiled in its bid to keep the promises of Republicanism:

> and those who cried the Republic must first die
> to be reborn are dead,
> the freeborn citizen's ballot in the head.
> Still, everybody wants to go to bed
> with Miss America. And, if there's no bread,
> let them eat cherry pie.[125]

Here, the failure of electoral politics and a sexualized mass culture, linked by thudding end rhymes, suggest a movement away from a hemispheric idealism that the sequence elsewhere struggles to cultivate. The dignified and tragic distance with which Walcott coolly observes revolutionary failures begins to signal his stance of anticommunist self-compromise.

The hammock in "Elegy," like the figure of the gulf itself, suggests the ways in which Walcott regarded Trinidadian poetry as occurring at the "crossroads of sensibility." As he explains, "in the last few years a number of American and a few English poets have become interested in the complexities and the metaphoric arrogance of foreign poetry, the poetry of the Romance languages," particularly Vallejo, Neruda, and Paz. "We are located at the crossroads of these exchanges," he writes, ". . . closer to Brazil than we are to England, not only in geography but also in sensibility."[126] Many poems in *The Gulf* approximate "the complexities and the metaphoric arrogance" of poetry in Spanish. In "The Corn Goddess," a serpentine drive around the island comes to a physical crossroads where grilled corn is sold: ". . . Jeer, but their souls/catch an elation fiercer than your desolate/envy; from their fanned, twisting coals/their shrieks crackle and fly. The sparks/are sorrowing upward though they die."[127] These lines embody Walcott's Lezamian sense that the process of naming the world anew amounts to a spark, fire, or ritual conflagration—a bonfire of sounds, memories, images, and objects. He imagines a paradox: all must be burned to keep the light of luminous contemplation alive. *The Gulf* clarifies this thought about Caribbean language's ritual self-becoming in the Ovidian registers of four etiological folk poems: "Moon," "Serpent," "Cat," and "Hawk." In "Moon," the poem self-generates through assonantal repetitions of the apostrophic vowel "O," likened to the full moon's shape in the sky:

Resisting poetry I am becoming a poem.
O lolling Orphic head silently howling,
my own head rises from its surf of cloud.

Slowly my body grows a single sound,
slowly I become
a bell,
an oval, disembodied vowel,
I grow, an owl,
an aureole, white fire.[128]

An *ars poetica* for building image-forms out of sound schemes, this poem stops just short of intimating the political application of such processes in "Laventille." The "Serpent," likewise, conducts "its self-seducing sibilance," and "Cat" insists on "-ill" sounds, linking the poet's desire for future-oriented action ("I'll") to "still"-ness, "ill"-ness, and orthography itself ("Spell it"). Even the poem's invocation of "Carlos Williams" and his famous cat poem hinges on the sound of the name *Will*iam. "Hawk," dedicated to Barbadian diplomat Oliver Jackman, loosens the sound scheme and renders it macaronic, foregrounding the "crossroads of sensibility" through the Trinidadian form of folk caroling, imported from Venezuela, known as the "parang." The parang's onomatopoeic "treng-ka-treng," from the four-stringed guitar called the cuatro, emerges from "rum-guzzlers, country fiddlers" who are weirdly linked to Yucatecan mythology.

Walcott's tragic view of history, his casual anticommunism, his ritual poems of linguistic self-becoming, and his zealous advocacy for state-sponsored culture are all blended in *The Gulf*'s other most important poem, the six-part sequence "Guyana." Guyanese decolonization in 1953–1964 and independence, achieved in May 1966, were of ongoing fascination to Walcott. His earliest anticommunist literary statements, such as the conviction that "nearly all of Communist poetry" is guilty of the "tendency to simplify individual experience into exhortation," were articulated in critiques of the Afro-Guyanese anticolonial poet Martin Carter.[129] When Carter's *Poems of Resistance* (1954) was reissued in 1964, Walcott again called them "sadly ironical" in the context of the "racial chaos of today's headlines."[130] The chaos Walcott had in mind was several years of racially motivated violence between East Indians and Africans of British Guiana covertly stoked by the CIA in order to thwart Dr. Cheddi Jagan's electoral victory, since the zealously anticommunist Kennedy administration suspected the head of the People's Progressive Party (PPP) as a "sleeper"

Soviet sympathizer. Carter's anticolonial and anticapitalist sentiments therefore hardly merited Walcott's rearguard critique, and were predictive rather than naive about the extent of neocolonial manipulation of the Guyanese democratic process. Yet Walcott found in Carter a "simplifying prophetic fury" and a "sense of duty that makes Marxist verse so dull, so deliberately pedestrian and dated." In place of these committed values, Walcott suggests that Carter's notes of racial plurality were the only insights of his verse: "African-Amer-Indian, this is Guyana's one voice." Yet, concomitant with his dismissive attitude toward Marxism, Walcott ended up supporting the ascendancy of the anti-pluralist People's National Congress (PNC) led by the Afro-Guyanese strongman Forbes Burnham.

Early on, Walcott offered muted support for Burnham, who became the nation's first president over Jagan. According to Stephen G. Rabe, the US State Department and the CIA now largely regret Burnham's two decades of autocratic misrule (1964–1985), yet the CIA itself, working with the Kennedy and Johnson administrations, engineered Burnham's rise over Jagan, ironically through its support of labor unions, and atrociously inflamed racial tensions between Indo-Guyanese and Afro-Guyanese in the years 1962–1964. As Rabe has it, "In the name of anticommunism, the Kennedy administration took extraordinary measures to deny the people of British Guiana the right to national self-determination."[131] Even as Kennedy and his allies advocated racial justice in the United States, "they were fostering policies that fueled racial hatred between blacks and Indians in British Guiana," a paradox enabled only by anticommunist paranoia.[132] By 1967, the CIA interventions were public record.

Walcott visited Guyana to judge a theater festival in November 1965, and returned to direct a play at the Georgetown playhouse in March 1969. He also took a keen interest in Guyanese independence in 1966, writing two extensive essays for the Trinidad Guardian in the week following May 26, Independence Day. There, he celebrates Burnham's sponsorship of a Caribbean Writers and Artists Conference inviting a cast of pan-Caribbean intellectuals and endowing "artists with a dignity and responsibility that has rarely been granted by any government, old or new." Effectively, he saw in a rostrum that featured Césaire, Hearne, Guillén, and Hughes the Afro-Caribbean replay he had long sought of Kennedy's inaugural or the CCF congress in Berlin. He simultaneously critiqued leftist commentators such as C. L. R. James, writing: "Guyana for a long time will be the favourite subject of political apologists, of Marxists with logorrhea, and advocates of further violence directing operations behind their academic barricades." These charges suggest that Walcott uncritically accepted Burnham's

PNC leadership, and badly misassigned responsibility to the PPP for the racial violence in the run up to the PNC victory. Then again, Walcott's grievance with Marxism was stylistic, not substantive. He worried most about "what John Wain has called 'creeping exegesis,' or the 'love vines' of critics will cripple us all."[33] In "A Georgetown Journal," the concluding section of "Guyana," Walcott returns to this critique:

> And the prose of polemics grows, spreading lianas of syntax
> for the rootless surveyor,
> the thunderous falls have been measured,
> the thickening girth of the continent has been buttoned

Prefiguring the argument of his famous essay "The Muse of History" (1974), Walcott suggests that a proper poetic stance toward Guyana obliterates history. Other poems in the sequence such as "The surveyor. . .," "The Falls," and "A Map of the Continent" favor a cartographer's innocent visions alongside the catastrophic sublimity of a waterfall. By contrast, he links Marxist historicism to weedy lianas. Gordon Rohlehr was perhaps the only critic of the hour to argue that Walcott's frenzy to secure state arts patronage blinded him to the historical processes unfolding in Guyana. In sum, Walcott's Adamic vision could be an obtuse form of ahistorical Cold War liberalism.

Padilla in Difficult Times

On March 20, 1971, the poet Heberto Padilla was arrested and sequestered in the Villa Marista political prison outside of Havana, Cuba, where state security agents presented him with a dossier of his counterrevolutionary statements, including several taped conversations with the Chilean novelist Jorge Edwards, then serving as Salvador Allende's diplomatic appointee to Cuba. Padilla was subsequently interrogated, administered psychotropic drugs, left in isolation, and beaten to the point of requiring hospitalization. His wife Belkis Cuza Malé was also briefly arrested and interrogated, and Edwards was declared a "persona non grata." On April 9, an impressive group of European and Latin American leftist intellectuals published an open letter to Fidel Castro in Le Monde requesting Padilla's release, arguing that by repressing writers who exercised a right to critique from within the revolution, Cuba would undermine its leadership of the Latin American and global left. They received no response. Padilla was eventually released on April 25, but only after he wrote a coerced confession of his guilt on the typewriter his captors had ransacked from his home.

This document, often called his "autocrítica" (self-criticism), began as a one-page statement of "deviation" from ideological principles, but his captors rejected it until he filled thirty typescript pages with self-accusations, retractions, and indictments. Two days after his release, he recited it at a session of the Union of Writers and Artists of Cuba (UNEAC), and it was released in partial form by the Cuba's state news agency. The autocrítica renounced Padilla's penchant for provocative "critiques" of the revolutionary government, which began to imperil him around 1967, but which I will trace in the following pages back to his liberal anticommunist intellectual formation in late 1950s New York. What some called the right to critique, he now confessed, had been his self-important inclination to level a series of "injurias y difamaciones" (insults and slanders) against the Revolution. His most significant defamatory expression, he further admitted, was his prize-winning book of poetry *Fuera del juego* (Out of the Game, 1968), which he now recast as puerile exercises in "el resentimiento, la amargura, el pesimismo" (resentment, bitterness, and pessimism), all synonyms for a counterrevolutionary "desencanto" (disenchantment).[134] Padilla confessed that after *Fuera del juego*, he had become a popular magnet for liberal anticommunist foreign intellectuals who used his disaffected poetry in order to analyze Cuba's situation sonorously but not rationally.

Padilla suggested that one photograph in particular captured this symbolic place in a hemispheric anticommunist order (Figure 5.5). As readers we should be wary of potential irregularities in the transcription of his remarks as well as exaggerations in the loose English translation released by Prensa Latina:

> Por ejemplo, yo recuerdo el libro de Lee Lockwood el periodista norteamericano, donde aparece mi foto con un tabaco y un periódico granma, una foto muy hábil, muy inteligentemente hecha, que aparece con un pie de grabado que dice: Heberto Padilla, poeta y enfant terrible.

> For example, I remember the American, Lee Lockwood's book, where my photo appears. I have a cigar and a copy of the newspaper *Granma*—it's a clever photo and I don't want this photo to demean in any sense Lee Lockwood himself, but under this photo is a caption which perfectly sums up the pose that I adopted in this photo. It says: Heberto Padilla, poet and enfant terrible. I fell in love with this image.[135]

Fig 5.5 Lee Lockwood, "Herberto [*sic*] Padilla, poet and political *enfant terrible*," in *Castro's Cuba, Cuba's Fidel* (New York: Vintage, 1969). © The Lee Lockwood Estate. Used with permission.

The photograph, taken in 1966 as Lockwood prepared *Castro's Cuba, Cuba's Fidel*, was not published until the 1969 edition—a year after *Fuera del juego* won UNEAC's Julián del Casal Prize over bureaucratic objections. Lockwood was sympathetic to the Cuban state, even downplaying internal intellectual dissidence. In his memoir, Padilla once idly suggested that "where the paths of poetry and politics cross there is little room for reconciliation," but the photograph posits the poet's freedom to mirthfully digest political reality.[136] Comically chewing his cigar, the poet leisurely consumes an unknown news item. The demagogic speechifying of Castro on the reverse page of *Granma* is displayed for US viewers, out of the poet's sight. It bears comparison to Lowell reading of "leaden internecine generals" in "Buenos Aires," only Padilla's stance is upbeat, suffering none of the same confessional weariness. A coercive state presence corrodes every sentence of Padilla's self-criticism, and yet that coercion cannot corrode Padilla's true-enough reading of the photograph as a negotiation between a critical, anticommunist expressive self confined by Cuban cultural policy, and the fact that his critical standpoint permits ideological misappropriations by international intellectual communities.

When Prensa Latina released the partial transcripts of Padilla's autocrítica, denunciations of Cuba's cultural policy reached fever pitch. The repercussions of "el caso Padilla" thereafter came to allegorize the promises and disappointments of the Revolution as a discursive project of participatory empowerment. Lillian Guerra argues that such empowerment required Cuban culture to decolonize at all levels of popular and public life in order to break with a neocolonial past of indenture to US economic and cultural hegemony. Thus Padilla's self-criticism targets even a sympathetic US journalist. But, as Guerra specifies, Cuban cultural policy split between the promise of shaping new social perceptions and the need to police the boundaries of the sayable.[137] For Euro-American anticommunist intellectuals, the Padilla affair was clear international proof (more than dawning awareness about maltreatment of homosexuals) that Cuba's inhospitable stance toward expressive freedom veered into neo-Stalinist territory. For pro-Cuban intellectuals of the Latin American left such as Ernesto Cardenal, Gabriel García Márquez, and Julio Cortázar, it precipitated balancing acts between humanitarian critiques of the government's repressive streak and ongoing support for the revolution.

Lost in the well-rehearsed details of the Padilla affair is the extent to which Padilla's decisions as a lyric poet were closely linked to traditions of anticommunist lyric in the hemisphere, confronting state orthodoxies in terms inassimilable to a national analysis of revolutionary discourses.[138] Padilla's poems self-consciously perform his critical freedom by borrowing liberal anticommunist scripts, yet most accounts of the Padilla affair lose sight of his poetry altogether (as well as difficult-to-access archives of his journalistic and editorial work). Clare Cavanagh points out how dynamics of lyric expressivity that Marxist scholars rebuke as romantic ideology or bourgeois subjectivity are often important mechanisms of dissent in Second World contexts such as Russia and Poland that limit the possibilities of expressive speech.[139] This dynamic partially captures Padilla's place within Cuba's antagonistic literary public sphere, where he was committed to a project Guillermo Cabrera Infante called the unmasking of the "encarnación del alma es(c)lava en el trópico" (incarnation of the Slav(e) soul in the tropics).[140] Reading Padilla's poetry requires a careful reconstruction of the subjective and formal dynamics of his poetic choices, often inherited from cosmopolitan, anticommunist models. Only braced against the full resonance of these tensions do his journalism for *Lunes de Revolución*, his first book *El justo tiempo humano* (The Time of Human Justice, 1962), and finally *Fuera del juego* make sense as preludes to the scandalous state repression that overdetermines his place in literary history.

Rarely has the mere reading of a Robert Lowell poem been a risky political act, but there is a quiet transgression in the scene of recitation that opens Padilla's intellectual autobiography, *La mala memoria* (*Self-Portrait of the Other*, 1989). When news of the Cuban Revolution reached the twenty-six-year-old on New Year's Eve, 1958, he was in his New York apartment reading Lowell's "Man and Wife": "Oh my *Petite*,/clearest of all God's creatures, still all air and nerve."[141] Later in the long stanza referred to by Padilla, Lowell's speaker recalls his failure, on a Greenwich Village evening in the late 1940s, to seduce Elizabeth Hardwick, a botch mirroring Padilla's own extramarital flirtations in New York. Lowell's evening ends instead with the speaker recalling how he "outdrank the Rahvs," aligning Padilla's quotation with scores of midcentury men who wrote uncomfortably about fidelity and seduction. But behind the romance is his allegiance to the sociopolitical milieu of the *Partisan Review*—that is, to the anti-Stalinist coordinates of New York intellectuals as they "devolved" from critical socialism into liberal anticommunism.[142] To these affinities, Padilla's memoir heaps other anecdotes of his attraction to liberal anticommunist poets and intellectuals, far from the revolutionary hue and cry of Cuba in which his work is customarily and necessarily read. "Mis amigos afirman que [mi cultura] es inglesa" (My friends say my culture is English), he wrote in *Fuera del Juego*, by which time he was defending himself from charges of Anglophilia, held to be synonymous with counterrevolution.

Padilla spent long stretches of time in New York and Miami between 1949 and 1959. In New York at seventeen years old, he found a mentor in Eugenio Florit, who modeled cosmopolitan openness toward British, American, and French modernisms, an openness that Padilla solidified in Juan Ramón Jiménez's courses on international modernism at the University of Miami in 1955.[143] In Washington in 1958, Padilla watched firsthand as Ezra Pound was released from St. Elizabeth's (owing to a concerted campaign by Archibald MacLeish, Robert Frost, Saint-John Perse, and Dag Hammarskjöld).[144] "I wanted to speak to him," Padilla recalled of the scene at Pound's release, "but I couldn't bring myself to approach this man who had been vanquished by his own contradictions and afflictions."[145] Padilla's inscription of his witness to the closing moment of the Pound affair retroactively presages his own scandal, the defining moment of postrevolutionary cultural repression in Cuba. If Padilla's poetic family tree was shattered by the revolution, it was possible that he could recuperate a genealogy of poets running afoul of the state.

When the Revolution succeeded, Padilla was teaching business Spanish at a Rockefeller Center Berlitz School to US employees of companies such as Anaconda Copper. He was also translating Perse, and he recalls how his efforts to discuss his versions of *Anabase* and the early Caribbean poems of *Eloges* were frustrated by Perse's interest in using Padilla as a Cuba informant. This advisory role also structured his meetings with Archibald MacLeish, to whom he later dedicated "Una época para hablar" (A Time for Speaking), a lament for poetry's retreat from participation in public fora of argument. His memoir offers pride of place to these moralizing public poets tied to the liberal state. More than other Cubans in the United States such as Pablo Armando Fernández, Padilla owed his intellectual debts to Cold War modernism. His memoir figures his troubled twelve years of revolutionary participation up to his 1971 arrest as a disruption in a liberal hemispheric order.

These tensions mark *El justo tiempo humano* (The Time of Human Justice, 1962), written between 1959 and 1962, of which he later claimed, "Entre Estados Unidos y Cuba surgieron esos poemas, y se mueven en esos mundos" (These poems emerged between the United States and Cuba, and they move in these worlds). *El justo tiempo humano* must also be read alongside Padilla's contributions to *Lunes de Revolución*, the literary supplement to the government paper *Revolución*, edited by Guillermo Cabrera Infante and Pablo Armando Fernández from March 1959 to November 1961. The first three of Padilla's sixteen contributions to *Lunes* triangulate the self-contradictory hemispherism on offer in his early verse: first, the key poem from *El justo tiempo humano*, entitled "Infancia de William Blake" (Childhood of William Blake); second, the interview he conducted with the inter-American intellectual Waldo Frank during the tour of Cuba arranged for Frank by Alcides Iznaga; and third, his attack on *Orígenes*.

"Infancia de William Blake" displays a cosmopolitanism married to a broad history of the socialist hemispherism visible in his interview with Frank, which preserves the artist's intellectual autonomy from revolutionary commitment. Padilla asked Frank for advice about the attitude Cuban writers should adopt toward the new Cuban reality, and Frank responded:

> Escritores deben trabajar por sus países. Si hay que darles conferencias a los campesinos, dénselas, pero que no se pierda la independencia, que el compromiso no vele la función crítica que le corresponde al escritor. Su deber es reflejar artísticamente la realidad [. . .] Un arte de propaganda es un arte de traidores ¡Cuidado con eso. . .![146]

(Writers should work for their countries. If there are courses to give to the peasants, give them, but do not lose your independence; the compromise should not veil the critical function of the writer. His responsibility is to artistically reflect reality [. . .] An art of propaganda is an art of treason. Beware it. . .!)

Even among guarded supporters of the revolution such as Frank, its permissiveness toward self-critique emerged as a key question of a cultural policy in process of formation. Two months later, Padilla first inhabited Frank's "critical function" with overcompensatory zeal. In "La poesía en su lugar" (Poetry in Its Place), he lashed out at the *Orígenes* poets, scorning the 1944 emergence of Lezama and his epigones. To his mind, the extravagant metaphysical argument of *Enemigo rumor* and the works it influenced set the clock back on Cuban poetry at the very moment Stevens, Perse, Eliot, and Rene Char were announcing the triumph of international modernism. Padilla's critique barely holds, given *Orígenes*'s own affinities with Padilla's vaunted conception of international modernism. It also revives Jorge Mañach's 1948 debate with Lezama. But Padilla was in no mood to acknowledge these complexities, stressing instead that "'Orígenes' es el instante de nuestro mal gusto más acentuado, es la comprobación de nuestra ignorancia pasada, es la evidencia de nuestro colonialismo literario y nuestro servilismo a viejas formas esclavizantes de la literatura" (*Orígenes* is the moment of our most accentuated bad taste, it is the verification of our past ignorance, it is the evidence of our literary colonialism and our servility toward old enslaving forms of literature).[147] Correspondingly, for Padilla, *Orígenes* gave form to Cuba's place in the early Cold War's hemispheric "drought." Between the failed revolution of 1933 and the victory of 1959, it opened "un vacío pesando sobre la obra de creación, anulándola" (a void weighing on the work of creation, annihilating it). Lezama's name, Padilla declared, "se quedará en nuestras antologías ilustrando las torpezas de una etapa de transición que acabamos de cancelar en 1959" (will remain in our anthologies illustrating the torpidity of a transitional phase that we have just ended in 1959).[148]

In truth, the conversational economy of the *Lunes* poets did not represent a decisive break. Virgilio Piñera's lively participation in *Lunes* as well as the contributions of Lezama and José Rodriguez Feo marked continuities. Accordingly, Piñera found it easy to rebut Padilla, suggesting that "Padilla. . . en estos días está de turno para encarnar el papel de lobo feroz de nuestras letras" (Padilla . . . these days is on duty to play the part of the ferocious wolf of our literature).[149] The exchange gives birth to the figure of Padilla's increasingly self-mythologizing contrarianism, here as a posture of generational revolt blending international modernist aspirations with strategic endorsements of a pro-Revolutionary, conversational directness. In Padilla's later poem "A J. L. L.," dedicated to Lezama, he rejects this posture in order to recast himself as a naive youth in revolt: "un muchacho enfurecido frente a sus manos atareadas/en poner trampas" (a boy infuriated by his own hands at work/setting traps).[150]

While rejecting Lezama, Padilla turned to Lowell, Blake, Dylan Thomas, and Randall Jarrell. He called Lowell's *Life Studies* "a revelation to me," and distinguished his confessional stance toward personal experience from Ginsberg's "strident and self-pitying formula."[151] These sensibilities diverged from Padilla's *Lunes* cohort, who took an interest in Ginsberg's circle over Lowell's. In *Lunes*, Ambrosio Fornet and Oscar Hurtado translated and featured Beats as various as Ginsberg, Ferlinghetti, LeRoi Jones, A. B. Spellman, Michael McClure, and John Wieners. Yet Padilla found in liberal formalist poets such as Lowell and Jarrell a way out of the dual bottlenecks he saw in Lezama's Gongorism and Ginsberg's Lorquismo (*Howl*, according to Padilla and to a common Hispanophone critique, owed its surrealism to the facile influence of Lorca's *Poeta en Nueva York*). "Infancia de William Blake" focused on the social insistences of Blake's sooty London, not on the prophetic pose that Ginsberg adopted from Blake.

In this regard, consider Padilla's 1961 poem "Playa Girón" (Bay of Pigs), a poem on a topic that attracted dozens of revolutionary versifiers to extol the martyrological virtue of Cuban troops in the Bay of Pigs invasion. It belongs to Padilla's brief moment of revolutionary orthodoxy, written a few months after his New Year's contribution to *Lunes*, "Un día de reafirmación revolucionaria" (A Day of Revolutionary Reaffirmation), and amid Padilla's several forgotten patriotic contributions to journalism in the immediate wake of the invasion.[152] The poem's refrain "Muerte,/no te conozco" (Death,/I do not know you), heightens the sacrifice of the Cuban soldier by underlining Padilla's civilian status, a poetic subject position consolidated by Euro-American poets of World War II seeking alternatives to Great War trench poetry.[153] Incompatible epigraphs drive home the point: Roberto Fernández Retamar's "Nosotros, los sobrevivientes,/¿A quiénes debemos la sobrevida?" (We, the survivors/to whom do we owe our survival?) is paired with Randall Jarrell's emphatic *"THESE DIED THAT WE MIGHT LIVE/ —that I may live!—."*[154] Padilla's elegy nullifies the ideological poles of the Playa Girón conflict by borrowing elegiac material from the literature of the aggressor. Dueling currents of revolutionary commitment and liberal centrism script his poetic stance.

El justo tiempo humano earned Padilla glowing reviews in *Verde Olivo*, the official organ of the Revolutionary Armed Forces, where communist poet Manuel Navarro Luna championed its drama of conversion to the cause of revolutionary justice. In *Casa de las Américas*, Salvadoran militant poet Roque Dalton also enthused, issuing only one demurral: "¿está situado en el mejor camino usando la severa expresión, resultado de sus preferencias europeas?" (is he on the best path, employing the severe expression of his European preferences?)[155] Even Piñera was cautiously optimistic, but warned that the volume's transformation from reflections on childhood to the decisive phase of revolution still adhered to an "estética personalista" (egoistic aesthetic). Padilla's personal experience came at the expense of collective aims: "No negamos que el 'yoísmo' nos haya regalado obras maestras, pero es el caso que en los tiempos que corren no estamos para 'yoizar' " (We don't deny that 'yoísmo' [I-ism] has given us masterpieces, but it is the case that in the age currently passing by we are not about to 'yoizar'). Anglophile influences were responsible for this yoísmo, specifically British "Angry Young Men" such as Philip Larkin: "Padilla es un 'angri man' cubano, pero sin 'rencor al pasado' " (Padilla is a Cuban 'angri man,' but without 'rancor for the past.')[156] Piñera concluded by expressing his disquiet at the idea that more Cuban poetry might be written in Padilla's style.

The state did what it could to police the individuating sources of Piñera's disquiet. Despite the committed turn of *El justo tiempo humano*, Padilla's romance of revolutionary participation had already been deflated when *Lunes* came under fire in May of 1961 from the government bureaucracy's increasing reticence toward cultural freedom (by November, the magazine was shuttered). The controversy flared over *P.M.*, an unsanctioned documentary about Cuban nightlife filmed by Guillermo's brother Saba Cabrera Infante. It set off a wave of extreme cultural policing by old guard Communists, and a spate of fears among defenders of cultural liberties. *P.M.* was a proxy for a larger attack on *Lunes*, which according to Carlos Franqui, the editor of *Revolución*, suffered from its polemical thesis that "the barriers that separated elite culture from mass culture" could be broken down through glossy spreads on figures such as Marx, Borges, Sartre, Neruda, Faulkner, Lezama, and Martí. Indeed, *Lunes* married the typographical sensibilities of Cubo-Futurism and the anti-imperialist tendencies of the revolution to the mass-market communications strategies of *Life* or the *New York Times Sunday Book Review*. Now, *Lunes*'s largely anticommunist editorship saw that their socialist leanings could not prevent an "old-line" communist "crackdown" that rejected their model of Cuban acculturation to the norms of international modernism.[157]

At meetings at the National Library in late June 1961, some hoped to dispel the fears enflamed by the *P.M.* debate, but only found them fanned. Castro presided, flanked by an emergent cultural bureaucracy.[158] Padilla attended the meeting with the Russian poet and filmmaker Yevgeni Yevtushenko, and recalled sparring with Carlos Rafael Rodríguez, editor in chief of the Communist daily *Hoy*, over his suggestions that *Hoy* would suppress publication of T. S. Eliot and Ezra Pound given their respective reactionary and fascist politics. "I objected," recalls Padilla, "noting that such prejudicial zeal against T. S. Eliot was excessive."[159] Padilla pointed out Rodríguez's hypocrisy by reminding him of his earlier plan to write a comparative study of Eliot and Neruda, but this small rhetorical victory was outweighed by *Lunes*'s closure, and Padilla again found his adherence to the expressive freedoms of Euro-American writers at odds with Cuban state policy, especially as old guard Communist Party members revived the censure of right-wing modernism as a proxy discourse for US Cold War influence.

The fracture led Padilla to five years of work abroad as one among many quasi-exiled nonconformist Cuban writers. He worked first as a journalist in London for the state news agency Prensa Latina, but rumors of collaboration with the Associated Press scuttled his attempt to open a London office of Prensa Latina. His subsequent appointment in Moscow benefited from his friendship with Yevtushenko, but also cemented his disillusionment with the cultural tactics of the Russian state. When Padilla returned to Cuba briefly in 1964, Che Guevara appointed him to CUBARTIMPEX, "a subdivision of the Ministry of Foreign Commerce concerned with the exporting and importing of all items related to art and culture."[160] He worked as a kind of book importer in Prague until 1966, when he returned to Cuba coincident with the intensifying "Stalinization" of the Cuban state bureaucracy. This included shuttering of alternative outlets of intellectual dissent, centralizing the progress of socialism around Castro's personality, and retreating from the prospect of hemispheric revolution, in part by initiating the lateral solidarity of the Tricontinental, viewed by some as a new international face of nationalist retrenchment.[161]

Padilla struggled with the new terms of cultural participation, although at the very moment that the deepest fissures in Padilla's own relationship to the state begin to emerge, he offered an orthodox revaluation of Cuban revolutionary literature that judges all works according to their participation in history. In 1967 he contributed the preface and author vitae to a 788-page anthology entitled *Cuban Poetry, 1959–1966*, published bilingually in English and Spanish by the Havana Book Institute. The anthology never rates a mention in Padilla scholarship, but it is worth noting how it promises a selection guided exclusively "by the Revolution's impact on our poets," or, put differently, "a criterion of historic evaluation rather than an aesthetic one." Padilla's proposal to take the Revolution as a criterion of literary historical selection appears to be a strategy more than a conviction, but he plays out the consequences, insisting on the historical criterion "over and above ... the different ways and means of poetic expression." Revolution thrusts "diverse poets in a relationship of unusual alliance; a shared atmosphere of tensions and emergent problems which finds its reflection in a range of poetry, running from those of most careful structure and the strictest vocabulary to those interspersed with fragments of dialogue, loose and disarrayed."[162] That same year, the journal *El Caimán Barbudo* invited Padilla to write an admiration of Lisandro Otero's novel *Pasión de Urbino*, but he chose to pan it as the work of a mediocre state functionary, pointing out the hypocrisy of publishing it when the government suppressed superior works such as Guillermo Cabrera Infante's *Tres tristes tigres*. He could no longer sustain the tempered commitment of his anthology. As Padilla later recalled, it "was just what State Security had been waiting for to finish me off."[163]

The events surrounding his poetry collection *Fuera del juego* made his marginalization permanent. Convinced he would be barred from entering it into the Julián del Casal Prize competition at UNEAC that summer, Padilla snuck the manuscript into the pile through Belkis and an intermediary at UNEAC. Acting independently from UNEAC leadership, the five judges—Cuban poets José Lezama Lima, Manuel Díaz Martínez, and José Z. Tallet, along with the Peruvian poet César Calvo and the British critic J. M. Cohen—unanimously declared Padilla's victory, withholding honorary mentions. Their citation highlights the book's aesthetic merits, fending off counterrevolutionary charges by calling Padilla "un poeta en plena posesión de sus recursos expresivos" (a poet in full possession of his expressive resources) with a dramatic and agonic vision of man's role in history that constitutes a form of revolutionary art: "en *Fuera del juego* se sitúa del lado de la Revolución, se compromete con la Revolución y adopta la actitud que es esencial al poeta y al revolucionario; la del inconforme, la del que aspira [. . .] más allá de la realidad vigente" (in *Fuera del juego* he locates himself on the side of the Revolution, he is committed to the Revolution, and he adopts the attitude essential to both the poet and the revolutionary: the attitude of the nonconformist, who aspires [. . .] beyond prevailing reality."[164] UNEAC's directors disagreed, but avowing to maintain respect for freedom of expression up to the very limit in which it becomes the freedom of counterrevolutionary expression, they chose not to censor publication. Instead, they issued a lengthy counter-citation lambasting the poet's counterrevolutionary stance. In this way, *Fuera del juego* fractured a détente between intellectuals and the Cuban state.[165]

Fuera del juego's attempts to personalize historical experience in a complex, gnomic poetry of critical dissent provoked murky and polarized reactions. One poem, "En tiempos difíciles" (In Difficult Times), first appeared unobjectionably in *Casa de las Américas* in a 1967 dossier of twenty revolutionary poems dedicated to Rubén Darío, but by the time it landed as the proem to *Fuera del juego* it was a lively point of contention.[166] The poem is a conventional blazon or heraldic enumeration of body parts—hands, eyes, lips, legs, breast, heart, shoulders, and tongue. However, the poem swaps out the love poet of the blazon for the revolutionary state, swaps the beloved out for the revolutionary subject, and observes the relationship between them in a grammar of impersonal remove:

> Le pidieron sus labios
> resecos y cuarteados para afirmar,
> para erigir, con cada afirmación, un sueño
> (el-alto-sueño)

> (They asked him for his lips,
> his dry, cracked lips, to affirm
> and with each affirmation to build a dream
> (the 'high dream'))

Early modern blazons often use the device for the epideictic celebration of a beloved. However, the blazon is also a violent form in its synecdochic enumeration of its subject, scattering female beauty misogynistically into constitutive "parts." Padilla relocates this violence in state monopolies on physical labor and expressive freedom: lips parched from hard work must be put to mouthing orthodoxy; legs must be employed in digging trenches. And the revolutionary subject's "donación resultaría inútil/sin entregar la lengua,/porque en tiempos difíciles/nada es tan útil para atajar el odio o la mentira" (gifts would be useless unless he surrendered his tongue,/since in difficult times/there is nothing more useful for warding off hatred and lies).[167] UNEAC rejected the blazonic conceit of "dismemberment," arguing instead that the individual's submission was best understood as a form of sacrifice:

> Cuando Padilla expresa que se le arrancan sus órganos vitales y se le demanda que eche a andar, es la Revolución, exigente en los deberes colectivos quien desmembra al individuo y le pide que funcione socialmente. [. . .] El despegue económico que nos extraerá del subdesarrollo exige sacrificios personales [. . .]. Esta defensa del aislamiento equivale a

una resistencia a entregarse en los objetivos comunes, además de ser una defensa de superadas concepciones de la ideología liberal burguesa.[168]

(When Padilla expresses that 'they' strip out his vital organs and demand that he go to work, he refers to the Revolution's need for collective debts that dismember the individual by asking him to function socially. [. . .The] economic uplift that will extricate us from underdevelopment demands personal sacrifices [. . .]. His defense of isolation equates to a resistance to communal objectives, and it furthermore amounts to a defense of outdated conceptions of liberal bourgeois ideology.)

This response accurately acknowledges the poem's critique of the revolutionary state as a "dismembering" institution, though it fails to recognize the traditional resources on which the poem draws. It suggests that Padilla misrepresents the rhetoric of individual sacrifice as the rhetoric of mutilation. In his memoir, Padilla recalls the scene immediately following the writing of his self-criticism with the remark that the guards knew "En tiempos difíciles" by heart, and engaged in the "macabre ritual" of reciting lines of the poem by heart as they beat upon those individual parts of his body.[169] The state absorbs and redeploys the blazon's critique of state power against the poet himself.

The poem's oppositional force comes in part from its way of standing at a critical distance from the game of revolutionary participation. To be "fuera del juego" (out of the game) is a strategy of poetic observation committed to the individual autonomy of the artist to inhabit various personae and to speak to a range of social subjects. Some poems, such as "Oración para el fin de siglo" (Prayer for the Turn of the Century) speak from the standpoint of an ambiguous "we"—a class of intellectuals as decadent as those of the fin-de-siècle in their penchant for intraparty conflict, even as they posture as revolutionary instruments of decadentism's end, excoriating "el culo remendado del liberalismo" (the mended rump of liberalism). "Oración para el fin del siglo" bears the signs of Lowell's influence, looking backward on the same snoring fin de siècle as "Buenos Aires." If Lowell's Recoleta was the scene of bad-faith visions of the Americas as an "absentee empire," Padilla's modernist bourgeois subject highlights the bad faith of revolutionary cultural participation. Other poems further model the speaker's revolutionary bad faith. One offers an epitaph of the poet as a failed Anglo-modernist:

Definitivamente él no fue un poeta del porvenir.
Habló mucho de los tiempos difíciles
y analizó las ruinas,
pero no fue capaz de apuntalarlas.[170]

(Most certainly he was no poet of the future.
He said a great deal about the difficult times
and anatomized the ruins,
but could not shore them up.)[171]

Padilla rejects the voice of progressive collectivity, observing himself allusively in the rearguard position of a failed Eliot. In a wasteland of Cuban cultural production, he foresees the failure of his own perorations about difficult times, which is to say the failures of his own poems.

In "Los poetas cubanos ya no sueñan" (Cuban Poets No Longer Dream), the poet stands outside the collectivity of Cuban poets in an indeterminate form of judgment, lamentably among the dreamless poets even as he accuses them. These poets' service to history places phantasmagoria beyond their reach, for even in the solitude of night, history appears to them in a nightmarish, traumatic repetition, as if through the burning napalm of Vietnam war photographs. The poet's expressive subjectivity withers into mute witness:

> unas manos los cojen por los hombros
> los voltean,
>> los ponen frente a frente a otras caras
> (hundidas en pantanos, ardiendo en el napalm)
> y el mundo encima de sus bocas fluye
> y está obligado el ojo a ver, a ver, a ver
>
> (hands grab them by the shoulders,
> spin them around,
>> place them before other faces
> (drowning in swamps, burning in napalm)
> and the world flows over their mouths,
> and their eyes are obliged to see, to see, to see)

The poem could plausibly be understood as a simple indictment of historical violence or an Adornian condemnation of poetry's ability to comprehend unspeakable atrocity. However, the final line of the poem contains a critique of that very view. In the repetition of "a ver, a ver, a ver" Padilla's visual stutter makes a compressed allusion to Pablo Neruda's "Explico algunas cosas" (I Explain A Few Things), a Spanish Civil War–era harangue on new forms of violence perpetrated against civilians. Neruda's final lines also trebly repeat the injunction to "Venid a ver la sangre por las calles" (Come and see the blood in the streets), a decisive conversion in Neruda's career toward an "impure poetry"

that abandons hermetic surrealism for messy entanglements with social struggle and historical witness. Padilla was fond of Neruda's poetry, participating
in a *Lunes de Revolución* roundtable interview with Neruda in 1960.[172] By 1966,
however, Cuban writers censured Neruda for participating in the International
PEN Conference in New York (just as they would disinvite Nicanor Parra from
jurying a poetry prize in 1970 after Parra visited with Pat Nixon at the White
House). Unlike his compatriots, Padilla's poetic censure does not accuse Neruda
of insufficient anti-imperialist solidarity with Cuba. Instead, it indicts Cuban
poetry's traumatic repetition of Nerudian witness, denying poetry's access to
historical phantasmagoria. This critique of his literary cohort combines with
others portraying Padilla as the victim of that cohort's own judgments, such as
the aforementioned poem "Mis amigos no deberían exigirme. . ." (My friends
should not ask me. . .).

Fuera del juego balances metacommentary on Cuban literary politics with
poems of second-person instruction, usually directed toward bourgeois women.
"El discurso del método" (Discourse on Method) and "Para aconsejar a una
dama" (Advice for a Lady) offer hypothetical scenarios for women in various
states of fear or flight from revolution. "El discurso del método" borrows the
title of Descartes's treatise on the process of arriving at a subjective ontology and
turns this "method" into an ironic script for a member of a liberal bourgeoisie to
flee a revolutionary locale that looks a lot like Cuba, but which the poem strategically fails to name or place. The poem highlights the same structure of feeling as
Elizabeth Bishop's "Manuelzinho" in its scathing portrait of a class war burbling
beneath domestic fealty: "Ten desconfianza de la mejor criada./No le entregues
las llaves al chofer, no le confíes/la perra al jardinero" (Do not trust your favorite
maid./Do not give your keys to the chauffeur, do not entrust/your dog to the
gardener).[173] The domestic staff's betrayal, as they are swept up in revolutionary
chauvinism, is to take over the roles of police and passport control and to therefore wield state power over their former employers. "El discurso del método"
also echoes Bishop's "Manuelzinho" in its ambivalence toward subjects of social
concern. The speaker lampoons the bourgeois exile even as he expresses a clear
measure of classist allegiance with her. An omnidirectional scorn for the realities
of social stratification ensues. "Para aconsejar a una dama" reads as the inverse
of "El discurso del método," working through the script of bourgeois acculturation to new revolutionary norms: "Y si empezara por aceptar algunos hechos/
como ha aceptado—es un ejemplo—a ese negro becado/que mea desafiante en su
jardín?" (Suppose you begin by accepting certain facts/as you have accepted, for
example, that black scholarship boy/who pees defiantly in your garden?).[174] The

poem's disdainful premise of "downward" acculturation leads to an angry final charade of cross-class sex and stagy, ironic sloganeering.

UNEAC's critique of Padilla found this one of two troubling strategies that "traditionally served as instruments of counterrevolution." First, they noted how the poems situated "su discurso en otra latitud" (his discourse in another latitude) through devices such as dedications (to the imprisoned Greek poet Yannis Ritsos in the title poem, and elsewhere to the American poet-statesman Archibald MacLeish). Thanks to this "clumsy expedient," they wrote, "cualquier descripción que siga no es aplicable a Cuba" (any description that follows is not applicable to Cuba), and the comparison can only be supplied in the dirty conscience of the poem's interpreter: "Exonerada de sospechas, Padilla puede lanzarse a atacar la revolución cubana amparado en una referencia geográfica" (Exonerated of suspicion, Padilla can launch an attack on the Cuban Revolution protected by geographical reference."[175] UNEAC further accused Padilla's critical attitude of draining the revolutionary's characteristically active "commitment" and installing an antihistoricism expressed through "la exaltación del individualismo frente a las demandas colectivas del pueblo en desarrollo histórico" (the exaltation of the individual before the collective demands of the people in the progress of history). Padilla's sidelong critiques of Stalinizing cultural orbits that often appear to be Cuba, coupled with UNEAC's disavowal of the very book they have honored, make *Fuera del juego* a whirlpool of murky accusations chasing one another into nothing. One of the many shortcomings of UNEAC's analysis is its inability to grapple with a complex lyric sequence which disperses the unitary speaker into several dialectical stances—who sings by turns with and against his fellow poets, with and against elites and peasants, with and against international communism. This speaker turns dogmas, catechisms, and statements of ideology into stagy instructions in the manner of Parra, but also indulges in Eliot's prematurely weary and infernal view of social collectivity. If Elizabeth Bishop's "Brazil" sequence drifts toward the authentication of a polyvocal Brazilian speaker, Padilla's *Fuera del juego* de-authenticates revolutionary discourse's ability to contain the variegated postures of poetic internationalism.

At least UNEAC's critiques were openly exegetical, but in November 1968, a series of five articles in *Verde Olivo* written pseudonymously by Leopoldo Ávila attacked Padilla on an ad hominem basis.[176] The first described Cabrera Infante as a Cain-like counterrevolutionary, and argued that only CIA backing of *Mundo Nuevo* accounted for the popularity of *Tres tristes tigres*. Padilla, after defending Cabrera's novel, was guilty by association of CIA sympathies.[177] The next article, titled "Las provocaciones de Padilla," viciously argued that Padilla's first volume, with its wan revolutionary spirit and nine-year gestation period, only saw the light of day through the largesse of expanded state publishing programs. It accused Padilla of subsequently wasting government money on a luxurious travel schedule, and suggested that the six years between *El justo tiempo humano* and *Fuera del juego* signaled the poet's lack of industriousness:

> Parecía que [. . .] el andar, despreocupado y boquiabierto por capitales europeas gastando alegremente dólares que se le entregaban para otra finalidad, no le dejaba tiempo para las musas. Y esto lo decimos con tristeza: no desconocemos la relación directa que hay entre los dólares que gastaba Padilla y el sudo de nuestros macheteros.[178]

> (It seems [. . .] the leisurely, gape-jawed going about European capitals, happily spending dollars that were given to him for other ends, did not leave him time for the muses. We say this with sadness: we do not fail to recognize the direct relation between the money Padilla spent and the sweat of our cane cutters).

The article further lambasted Padilla's pompous belief in self-torment (one with debts to the damaged confessionalism of Lowell), while pointing out that the revolution had not censored or arrested him, unlike the persecuted poets Boris Pasternak and Yannis Ritsos with whom he identifies. To the contrary, the revolution allowed "frankly counterrevolutionary" poems such as "En tiempos difíciles" and "Discurso del Método" to appear in state-sponsored magazines. Rancorously, Ávila even accuses Padilla of putting this falsely persecuted persona on offer in order to pander to outlets of liberal anticommunism with international cachet. In this, Ávila likens Padilla's poems to a form of intellectual Tuzex, the Czech hard-currency stores where in the communist period one could purchase foreign luxury goods.

After Ávila's attack, Padilla was denied work for a year, finally appealing directly to Castro for a post at the University of Havana. In response to Ávila, Padilla began to group the poems he continued to write under the heading of "Provocaciones." Eventually, a small volume was published under that title, although they were collected by J. M. Cohen as "Later Poems" in his translation *Sent Off the Field*. In 1971, two months before his arrest, Padilla read his "Provocations" for Nicolás Guillén's UNEAC reading series. A large and varied diplomatic presence attended the packed reading, including Chinese and Chilean diplomats. One of the "Provocations," a poem entitled "Travelers," written in March 1970 and first published in Paul Blackburn's translation, seemingly responds to Ávila's charges. Padilla does not cozy to the parade of intellectuals who visit the island. Rather, he scorns their claims to expertise in the island's language, cultural politics, and structure of agrarian reform, indicting the entire subgenre of travel writing that Tietchen calls the "Cubalogue":

> They have taken the plane illegally, i.e., no passport,
> but are the most comfortable travelers of the future.
> They feel delightfully subversive
> and at peace with their consciences.
> Their Nikons, Leicas, Rolliflexes (a
> matter of individual taste) gleam
> perfectly competent to handle
> the tropical light, to handle the
> underdevelopment.[179]

Padilla's "traveler" figure flexibly includes the journalists and intellectuals he knew and befriended, such as Lockwood, Robert Scheer, and Robert Silvers. But even as he casts aspersions on them, he offers a harsher rebuke of Cuba, which will not issue the exit visa needed to secure a similar mobility. Padilla is but the "damned" subject of the travelers' photographs, posing roguishly in a manner that recalls Lockwood's shot:

> There are a lot of photos of that ilk throughout the world
> of me: I
> look like a mountebank. One eye
> stares resentfully at the camera,
> the other looks anywhere else.
> Wives, sons, friends of the energetic traveler look
> and suppress their disgust: I'm trapped in
> the photo, a caged lion
> roaring against words of importance:
> (Eternity, History).
> But I cannot transmogrify
> file clerks from universities, nor clarify
> anything. I'm damned.[180]

This is the kind of poetic "Tuzex" indicted by Ávila. Indeed, it was one of two poems Paul Blackburn translated for *The New York Review of Books* in the weeks following Padilla's imprisonment, designed, alongside José Yglesias's article "The

Case of Heberto Padilla," to draw attention to his situation. But it also dissents from the liberal outlet of the *New York Review* as much as it does from communist outlets of Cuban state culture. The poem antagonizes the very figures drawing attention to Padilla's case, as if siding with Castroite critiques of the bourgeois intellectual left. Padilla would recast this self-portrait into the "torpid masquerade" of his "self-criticism," but as a poem it lashes out at communist orthodoxies and anticommunist habits alike, opening a Pasternakian space of the doomed poet's expressive autonomy.[181] Padilla's poem highlights how the image of a boldly international anticommunist poet is contingent on the mechanisms that delimit his expressive freedom within the Cuban state. Rejecting the revolutionary role of "poet of the future" while denied access to an attractive liberal hemispheric order, he antagonizes both perspectives, arriving at an aporetic self-condemnation.

The New York Review of Books drew attention to Padilla's case in the spring and summer of 1971, the onset of Cuba's so-called "quinquenio gris" (five gray years). *Le Monde*'s open letter to Castro of April 9, protesting Padilla's imprisonment, was signed by a cast of European and Latin American intellectuals including Simone de Beauvoir, Italo Calvino, Julio Cortázar, Hans Magnus Enzensberger, Carlos Fuentes, Gabriel García Márquez, Octavio Paz, and Jean-Paul Sartre. However, some abstained from signing a follow-up letter protesting Padilla's bizarre self-criticism. One particularly notable abstention was Octavio Paz. Despite his agreement with the letter's principled support of free expression and its condemnation of the Revolution's stifling of critique, he claimed that he did not suffer from "the deception that motivated it": the ongoing partisan enthusiasm for the Revolution shared by its many distinguished signatories.[182] He instead wrote a "small individual reflection" focused on the irony that even if Padilla's confession was uncoerced, the accounts of his "defamations" of the Revolution in café chatter with friends and intimates hardly seemed threatening in comparison to the elaborate international intrigues that Stalin's trials forced upon its confessors. Cuba impoverished the horror of Stalinist tactics even as it perpetuated them.

Those with greater revolutionary enthusiasm than Paz sought to redefine the aims of "critique" within it. Julio Cortázar's essay-poem "Policrítica en la hora de los chacales" (Polycritique in the Hour of the Jackals) proposed a "policritical" response to the emerging cultural repression.[183] To Cortázar, the yoking of politics and critique inserted a "cri" (cry) syllable in the midst of politics, a howl of good-faith commitment that might pierce the disenchanted spin of liberal corporate media as it tore every story to bits like a pack of jack-als. Padilla's own poems are difficult to place in Cortázar's account—part vic-tim to the jackals and part jackals themselves. Works like Cortázar's speak to the deep crisis of commitment (and *crisis* is another word audible in the *cri* of "policrítica") that Latin American intellectuals faced in the aftermath of the Padilla Affair. "I've wanted to erase your case from my mind" is what Gabriel García Márquez reportedly told Padilla in 1980, as he began to help Padilla's family, Robert Silvers, Ted Kennedy, and others advocate for the poet's permis-sion to leave Cuba.[184] Márquez's amnesiac desire stemmed from the friendships that foundered over debates about the case's meaning in the trajectory of the Cuban project. The remark suggests what Lillian Guerra calls Mario Benedetti's famous "prescription for overlooking—and writing over—the 'errors'" of the revolution in process of formation: "Corrected or not, admitted or not, the truth is that the possible mistakes and deficiencies of the Cuban Revolution count very little when compared with its achievements."[185] Padilla's liberal commit-ments make these errors unmistakable, but one of the costs of his critique is the inter-American cultural project itself.

Stations in the Gulf

The foregoing readings show that no monolithic "anticommunist poetics" emerged in the Cold War Americas. Rather, the counter-ideological drift of anticommunism shaped formal agendas and strategies of enunciation at sev-eral levels of literary expressivity, exceeding the national domains of Cold War orthodoxy and covert influence where literary scholars presumed them to reside. Anticommunism operated at large in poems of Brazil, Guyana, Argentina, Cuba, Trinidad, and other fronts of the global Cold War. Such poetry orbited around the value of "expressivity" itself, and around ephemeral poetic sound features. If expressive values and poetic devices can organize an understanding of these issues, so can sites of enunciation. In this respect, consider in conclusion the fol-lowing selective comparison of several poems sited in cars and at filling stations.

Here is a well-known imagistic moment in Bishop's poem "Filling Station," which is organized around a sound figure that will be familiar from the interpre-tation of "Squatter's Children" earlier in this chapter:

> . . . Somebody
> arranges the rows of cans

so that they softly say:
ESSO—SO—SO—SO
to high-strung automobiles.
Somebody loves us all.[186]

The orderly filling station display case "lubricates" the anxious everyday commerce of cars with the gentle whispers of a corporate lullaby. The soothing sonic arrangement is made possible by a "somebody," rendered impersonal perhaps because Bishop's anti-workerist tendencies are allergic to the coarse lexicons of labor forms such as "attendant" or "worker," or perhaps because corporate personhood itself supplies her sound figure. That is, Standard Oil's brand name ESSO is from the start a phoneticized pronunciation of its initials. Bishop elevates this branding mechanism into the poetry of chance echoes—part of what I earlier called the presemantic music of US developmentalism. We might compare Lowell's grotesque imagination of automobility in "For the Union Dead":

The Aquarium is gone. Everywhere,
giant finned cars nose forward like fish;
a savage servility
slides by on grease.[187]

Here a civic commons defined by the scientific wonder of an aquarium transforms into a grotesque, ichthyoid account of machine-age slavishness. Bishop's anxiety-soothing phonemes yield to Lowell's jaunty lines of horrified premonition.

Walcott was moved by Lowell's lines, and it is not hard to see them ramify through the poems opening *The Gulf*, such as "The Corn Goddess," where "Silence asphalts the highway, our tires hiss/like serpents."[188] Likewise in "Ebb," he laments "the afterbirth/of industry," or his sense that the natality of independent Trinidad's new "pioneer factory" industries, supported by preferential tax treatments, was likewise grotesque, or "scurf-streaked."[189] To Walcott, this was particularly so because no parallel "pioneer" funding primed the pump of Trinidadian cultural life. As he rewrites Lowell's confrontation with banality: "From this car/there's terror enough in the habitual," lines that echo with the newspaper articles to which he gave titles such as "Down By the Old Gas Pump," which laments the lack of state-private cultural investments. "One tires of making the frustration of a new generation of young actors, writers, artists, and entertainers clear to big business and Government," he wrote.[190] On the rare occasion that big business stepped up, as in British Petroleum's $5,000 Trinidadian novel competition in 1964, Walcott celebrated them: "What BP have

shown is that large firms owe a debt to the country that they can repay by fostering its self-expression."[191]

Contrast Padilla's "Paisajes" (Landscapes), one of his most imagistic poems:

> Se pueden ver a lo largo de toda Cuba.
> Verdes o rojos o amarillos, descascarándose con el agua
> y el sol, verdaderos paisajes de estos tiempos de guerra.
> El viento arranca los letreros de Coca-Cola.
> Los relojes cortesía de Canada Dry están parados en la hora vieja.
> Chisporrotean, rotos, bajo la lluvia, los anuncios de neón.
> Uno de Standard Oil Company queda algo así como
> S   O   Compa y
> y encima hay unas letras toscas
> con que alguien ha escrito PATRIA O MUERTE.[192]
> (You can see them from one end of Cuba to the other.

> Green, red, or yellow, defying the water
> and the sun, the true landscapes of these times of war.
> The wind tears down the Coca-Cola posters.
> The clocks courtesy of Canada Dry have stopped
> at the old time.
> The broken neon advertising signs splutter in the rain.
> One of the Standard Oil Company is reduced to something like
> S   O   Compa y
> and above it is
> a rough inscription MY COUNTRY OR DEATH)[193]

Revolutionary sloganeering overwrites the abandoned signposts of US commerce
in Cuba following the blockade. Like Bishop's "ESSO-SO-SO-SO," Padilla's
Standard Oil is a scrap of lipogrammatic found poetry emerging from the commercial vernacular world of postmodern signage. The implications, however,
are different. Does "Compa" reveal—in the obstructed unfolding of the word
"Company"—a lost lane into the revolutionary solidarity of the term *compadre*?
That reading chimes with the prorevolutionary graffiti, but then again no anti-
revolutionary graffiti is allowed. Does Padilla present the rough sloganeering
as an impoverishment of the corporate found poem, or an improvement on it?
State-sponsored mottos overwrite corporate patronage at a moment when Padilla
is observing the collapse of the Cuban cultural policy project.

To be sure, one thing that links these poems is a networked hemispheric infrastructure space of refineries and filling stations created in consort with the hemispheric modernization project. What is striking here is to see how poets diversely ironize their forms of faith that expressive life must ultimately be "primed at the pump" of the capitalist state's infrastructure space. Each poet allows for the fact that petroleum fuels public culture even as it debases it and, to some degree, places it in cross-cultural entanglements. As a corollary to their low-grade anticommunist convictions, each of these poets forges a self-compromised dependency on stations in the gulf for their free exercise of poetic art.

6. *RENGA* AND HETERONYMY

Cosmopolitan Poetics after 1967

As we have seen, poets of the 1960s attended a sequence of high-profile, often well-funded world literary symposia, poetry festivals, and diplomatic junkets abetting the association of a new cosmopolitan community that was conscious of writing beyond the nation to a degree rarely equaled in modern poetry. If the elite intellectual programs of state-sponsored cultural diplomacy across the 1950s and 1960s emphasized cosmopolitanism's Kantian terms of art (universalism, exilic detachment, cultural autonomy, rights of association, and peace), some poets writing concurrently offered an alternative cosmopolitanism grounded in formal dimensions of poetics. By 1969, the year Octavio Paz assembled a "quadrilingual quartet" in Paris to collaboratively author *Renga: A Chain of Poems* (1971), Paz had emerged as this community's most vocal idealist. In 1961 he claimed: "nationalism is not only a moral aberration; it is also an aesthetic fallacy."[1] Now he went further: "in German, Polish, Roumanian, or Portuguese, the poets of our time write the same poem." Announcing a succession of zeitgeists that exceeded languages or nations, Paz declared "There is not (there has never been) a French poetry, an Italian, Spanish, or English: there was a poetry of the Renaissance, a Baroque poetry, a Romantic poetry. There is a contemporary poetry written in all the languages of the West."[2] In convening a network of contemporaries, Paz suggested a wholesale challenge, modernist in its enthusiasms, to the romantic belief that the poet's speech expresses national particularity. This concluding chapter elaborates on the cosmopolitan provocations enacted by Paz and the poets of his network. To do so is to reroute our understanding of Cold War cosmopolitanism through several nesting scales of a self-reflexive poetics at once: language, form, translation, performance, authorship, and community. In keeping these multiple dimensions in focus, I aim to bring this book to a close by remapping some of the hemispheric traffic of the cultural Cold War, as reported in previous chapters, onto a cosmopolitan history of poetic form.

Go Home, Octavio Paz!

To call poetic practices "cosmopolitan provocations" is to stress that even in their most benign form they often aggravated national recalcitrance or Cold War fissures in the conditions of international congresses. For example, writing in the *Guardian* in July 1967, on the eve of London's Poetry International '67, poet-critic Donald Davie fired an editorial warning shot across the bow of the poets soon slated to gather at Royal Albert Hall. The headline ran "Go home, Octavio Paz!" and continued with a would-be valedictory:

> Go home, Octavio Paz! And go home also, Neruda, Yves Bonnefoy, Hans Magnus Enzensburger [sic], Ungaretti, Bella Akhmadulina, Anthony Hecht. Go home, every good poet who has been lured to London this week for Poetry International '67.
>
> If it is too late for them to stay home, as Voznesensky and Yevtushenko have done, let them take a leaf out of Charles Olson's book, and hop a plane at once. They have been brought here under false pretenses.[3]

In part, Davie's barbs were directed at Malcolm Muggeridge, a notorious cultural conservative who served as the festival's master of ceremonies. But the commentary went further in its suggestion that Paz's vision of a singular, cosmopolitan poetics was constructed upon "false pretenses." To Davie, the principal architect of inauthenticity was the poet Ted Hughes, who, despite having ambitiously transformed a local Poetry Book Society soirée into an international gala, now stood accused of a toothless, detached universalism. "However rootedly national in detail it may be," Hughes wrote, poetry "is beginning to represent, as an ambassador, something far greater than itself." Summoning the rhetorical boilerplate of Cold War cultural diplomacy, Hughes grandiloquently described poetry as "a universal language of understanding, coherent behind the many languages, in which we can all hope to meet."[4] This viewpoint had distinguished apologists, as when T. S. Eliot remarked in 1942: "We can be deeply stirred by hearing the recitation of a poem in a language of which we understand no word."[5] Nonetheless, a commonsensical faction of the Anglophone literary public, weaned on the New Criticism, treated Hughes as something of a sideshow hawker for expressing it. A certain Alfred Läutner's informal account of the festival sniped at the "apparent conviction that some useful purpose was to be gained from listening to a poet reading his work even when one couldn't understand the language."[6] And despite Davie's healthy dread of parochialism, he too inveighed against the "delusion" that the barriers to international understanding were overcome by the effects of authorial presence: "Clearly, it cannot be true that if you have no Spanish, Pablo Neruda's presence and his voice will magically enlighten your darkness."[7]

Only a few commentators lucidly denounced this insular backlash. To Nathaniel Tarn, naysayers like Davie were insulated too willfully in a "new wave of little-Englandism." Tarn was a veteran of the mid-1960s CCF conferences and a polyglot poet, anthropologist, and editor who contributed to the festival organization and concurrently piloted two far-reaching new series of international poetry and theory for Jonathan Cape (Cape Editions and the Cape Goliard Press). He lamented a tendency to circumscribe cosmopolitan perspectives within the liberal domestic polity: "the British have a genius for leaving foreigners to typecast specialists: the rest of us need never give a damn."[8] Poetry International '67 confronted such local standards with a worldly vision of poetry as mass-mediated, institutional, transgenerational, aesthetically catholic, and geopolitically ameliorative.

This popular cosmopolitanism drew on global countercultural exuberance. The nightly readings at the Royal Albert Hall echoed in the aftermath of the seminal rock concerts that strained the venue's acoustics in the mid-sixties. The readings seemed implicitly designed to harness and tame the spirit of the June 11, 1965, "International Poetry Incarnation," also at the Albert Hall, a happening preserved as cinema vérité by Peter Whitehead's film *Wholly Communion* (1965). There, a reported 6,000 people ("what must have been the largest audience ever assembled to hear poetry in this country," according to one news agency) took in readings by Allen Ginsberg, Gregory Corso, Lawrence Ferlinghetti, Anselm Hollo, and the Austrian sound poet Ernst Jandl. Ferlinghetti's performance figured cosmopolitanism as the "Holy Proposal" of a transgressive sexuality penetrating the nation-state's "obscene boundaries" through facile agglutinations of rhymed suffixes:

> And blessed be the fruit of transcopulation
> and blessed be the fruit of transpopulation
> and blessed be the fucking world with no more nations![9]

Ferlinghetti's "fucking world" is not only an epithet; it is also a sexual politics that brings to a culmination his farcical proposal for replacing state-sponsored cultural and exchange programs (such as the Peace Corps) with a "mass exchange fuck." Rerouting the object of obscenity from the discourse of sexuality to the exercise of national power, Ferlinghetti's poem suggests that only national "boundaries" are obscene. This appetitive cosmopolitan proposition arrived in London that summer hand in hand with Allen Ginsberg, in London after his performances of unrepressed homosexual rhetoric in the public arena precipitated his banishment from Cuba, where he'd been invited to jury a Casa de las Américas poetry prize alongside Nicanor Parra, and Czechoslovakia, where he was crowned "the King of May."

By sexualizing their cosmopolitan itinerancy, Ginsberg and Ferlinghetti revealed Cold War fractures in the circuitry of transnational assembly. According to Tom Raworth's account of the International Poetry Incarnation, avowed communist poets from whom Ferlinghetti had borrowed poetic strategies just a few years earlier, including Pablo Neruda, Andrei Voznesensky, and Pablo Armando Fernández, were all supposed to participate, but backed out (although Voznesensky observed from the audience). "The rumours seem to be that Neruda had been told Allen might take off his clothes, thus didn't want to be associated w/it, and that the others were in a way warned not to read, maybe because of Allen's expulsion from Cuba and Czechoslovakia."[10] In Ferlinghetti's performance, he responded to their absence by ad-libbing "I am waiting for Voznesensky to turn on with us and speak love tonight," and "I am waiting for Neruda to answer/and I am waiting for the rebirth of wonder." Ginsberg scrawled an invitation for Neruda at his London hotel, which Neruda did not answer: "I hope this time we will at last have a chance to look in each other's eyes—If you have a free hour please do phone me and perhaps we can drink some chicha or whiskey or pure water?"[11] Two summers later at Poetry International '67, such fractures were surmounted by quiet institutional sponsorship, while little more than the psychedelic calligraphy of the festival's program notes (Figure 6.1) evoked the freewheeling, erotic concept of the "Spontaneous planet-chant carnival" or "immaculate supranational Poesy insemination" two summers earlier.[12]

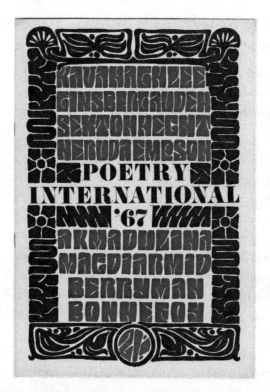

Fig 6.1 Poetry International '67. Poetry Book Society, London. Used with permission.

The older, prominent poets attending Poetry International '67 were in a position to note far greater intervals of frustrated cosmopolitan desire. Neruda, Paz, W. H. Auden, and Stephen Spender all bookended careers that early on led them to the Second International Congress of Anti-Fascist Writers in Madrid in 1937. Paz reconnected with Spender for the first time since 1937 when Spender commissioned Paz's contributions for a special Latin American number of *Encounter* in 1965.[13] At events such as Poetry International, what had thirty years earlier been an expression of cultural front "commitment" now came under the rubric of improvisatory "cultural freedom." Irish poet Patrick Kavanagh's "Extempore at Poetry International '67," written on Bastille Day, captured this new mood in light verse: "But since the arrival of the Beatles and the Stones/Anything goes/ And I am glad/That freedom is mad [. . .]."[14] This jingly-jangly poem, impacted with easy rhymes, wryly contends that liberal cultural cosmopolitanism, as a guarantor of "freedom," has gone "mad." As with Davie's "false pretenses," Kavanagh critiques cultural freedom's delusive pathology.

Historian Christopher Lasch suggested one reason for this delusiveness at the close of the summer, when his article "The Cultural Cold War" contributed to the discrediting of the Congress for Cultural Freedom.[15] Lasch argued that the values of prominent literary intellectuals had become indistinguishable from anticommunist statecraft, and he detailed CIA support, via dummy foundations, for a massive web of cosmopolitan cultural committees and journals—*Encounter* preeminent among them—whose editors stood accused of failing to divest from or to denounce their secret funding sources. Lasch postulated that by the early 1950s, a definition of culture as a form of democratizing universalism produced the "defection of the literary intellectuals" from the project of meaningfully critiquing political institutions: "Men who have never been able to conceive of ideas as anything but instruments of national power" came to be "the sponsors of 'cultural freedom.'"[16] These were the rationales now employed by *Encounter* contributors such as Hughes, Muggeridge, Spender, and to some extent Paz in their benedictions of Poetry International '67.

If such cultural freedoms, which tugged ideals of literary and intellectual autonomy into the domain of state-sponsored cosmopolitanism, were already contested when they were formulated in the late 1930s by propagandist-diplomats such as MacLeish, now they came to manifest a crisis in the formula of state-sponsored "world culture," a crisis that some recent cosmopolitan theory skirts. One touchstone of cosmopolitan theory suggests that "cosmopolitanism and statism are natural opposites."[17] Moreover, some attribute the durability of cosmopolitan theory itself to post-1989 reconfigurations. To Bruce Robbins, until 1989 cosmopolitanism consisted of the "detached" enlightenment variety, "underpopulated if not socially empty," only to be "filled up" by global subjects enacting multiform, particularized attachments in the years after 1989.[18] This periodization circumvents forms of committed cosmopolitanism peculiar to the Cold War itself, which, as Lasch suggested, consisted in a regime of not-so-covert alliances between states and cosmopolites. On the heels of a brief Cold War thaw, 1967 marked a first wave of intensive retrospection about Cold War cultural diplomacy as a significant mode of cosmopolitan sociality by a group of literary actors that remained partially and sometimes inadvertently in its grips.

Revelatory though Lasch's argument was ("in all, quite a fertile field for historical research," wrote Malcolm Cowley in 1967), its scholarly impact took hold slowly in particularized domains of cultural and institutional history.[19] By now, landmark studies (including those of Kozloff, Guilbaut, Franco, Saunders, von Eschen, and most recently Cohn and Fox) have developed the historiography of midcentury regimes of cultural diplomacy and cosmopolitan exchange, describing paradoxical alliances between the ideologies and institutions of Cold War cultural diplomacy and major modes of aesthetic production like Hollywood cinema, abstract expressionism, jazz, and the Latin American Boom novel. Such accounts expose literary and artistic expressions of "cultural freedom" as complex soft-power mechanisms of cultural imperialism—often despite their professed aesthetic politics—undergirding the United States' Cold War promotion of universal democracy.

But little poetry scholarship sufficiently digests the historiographical framework of the cultural Cold War. Fredric Jameson begins and ends his discussion of Cold War poetry in *A Singular Modernity* with the suggestion that the US academy installs Wallace Stevens ("abstract enough to enable transfers and translations, export strategies") over Ezra Pound and T. S. Eliot, which seems neither entirely true to the story of Stevens's emergence as a poet of transnational significance in the 1940s nor a significantly capacious way of understanding the currents of poetic modernism reconvening in the Cold War world of arts and letters.[20] The sequence of congresses with which I begin this chapter opens one aperture on the multivectored transnational traffic of Cold War poetry. To render it more fully visible has led me across this book to recover the spectacle of anticommunist maneuverings behind beloved volumes of poetry such as Lowell's *For the Union Dead*, Bishop's *Questions of Travel*, and Walcott's *The Gulf*; to explore the chimerical and contradictory international careers of poets such as Neruda and Heberto Padilla; and to highlight the wide array of abortive associations between the "New American" poets, their Latin American contemporaries, and institutions of cultural diplomacy like the PAU. While I have endeavored to keep the formal agency and interpretive complexity of these writers' poems in full view as I recount their intersections with cultural diplomacy, the stories herein can compel the historicist edge of criticism to overshadow the formalist explanations to which it ought to be linked. How, then, to sustain a meaningful connection between the work of poets in the cultural Cold War and the practice of comparative poetics as a scholarly project committed to recuperating a cosmopolitan history of poetic form?[21]

In other words, one challenge poetry scholars face in the study of the heteroclite poetries produced during what Odd Arne Westad calls the "global Cold War"[22] is to locate rubrics that bridge the methodological gap separating Cold War cultural and institutional history from a close attention to the formal work of poetic cosmopolitanism in the modernist traditions. When we look across a canon of "world poetry" that coalesced in the late 1960s and early 1970s, what class of poems self-consciously, openly enacted cosmopolitan protocols? What corpus of forms manipulated the corrupted and corruptible terminologies, such as "translatability," that grounded cosmopolitan desires? How did use of these forms variously challenge, confirm, or disperse the geopolitical configurations within which they were composed? Did there emerge in poetry what Rebecca Walkowitz has, in her work on novelistic style, called a "critical cosmopolitanism," one that not only describes detached, universalizing cosmopolitan desiderata, but negotiates the paradoxes of cosmopolitanism with multiple attachments and embodied affects at various levels of literary form?[23]

This chapter concludes the book by proposing at least two such poems: first, the collaboratively authored *Renga* (1971) and second, Kenneth Koch's sequence "Some South American Poets," a heteronymous collection of hoax "translations" from *The Pleasures of Peace* (1969). *Renga* and "Some South American Poets" proffer antithetical formal responses to the tenor of cultural diplomacy at the heart of the global Cold War. Each lays claim to complex genealogies distributed across the comparative history of modernism, proposing renga and heteronymy as practical resolutions to crises in the terms of cosmopolitan reunion. These resolutions also appear to be two of the gathering gestures of a midcentury moment in the poetry of the Americas that reached a point of exhaustion.

La Renga de Occidente

Octavio Paz never heeded Davie's imperative to go home. Instead, his attendance at Poetry International cemented his friendly collaboration with British poet Charles Tomlinson, who first discovered Paz's poems through *Encounter*.[24] Along with Jacques Roubaud and Edoardo Sanguineti, they comprised the "quadrilingual quartet" that met in a Parisian hotel basement in April 1969 to compose *Renga: A Chain of Poems*.[25] The Mexican, British, French, and Italian poets were all ecumenical experimentalists in their respective national situations. Their communal reinvention of the medieval courtly Japanese chain poem was among the most concentrated postwar attempts to link cosmopolitanism to modernist experiment. A reviewer for *Books Abroad* deemed the result of this experiment "the most unique and least accessible poem of the twentieth century."[26]

Two momentous years separated Poetry International '67 from the composition of *Renga*. In 1967, Paz was in his twenty-second year of employment in the Mexican Foreign Service, having served as ambassador to India since 1962. In October 1968, he loudly resigned from the diplomatic corps in dissent over the student massacres at Tlatelolco, ten days before the Mexico City Olympic Games.[27] Having previously declined to compose a poem on the theme of the Olympiad for a largely unsuccessful "World Meeting of Poets" that formed part of the cultural programming in the run-up to the games, he now typed out a short, seething, widely circulated poem that metonymically evoked the horrors of the massacre only in a parenthetical image of its solubility: "(City/Employees wash away blood/ In the Plaza de los Sacrificios)." This pointed toward his developing mythical inter- pretation of the massacre as an Aztecan rite of ritual sacrifice: "Los viejos dioses andan sueltos otra vez y nuestro Presidente se ha convertido en el Gran Sacerdote de Huitzilopochtli" (The ancient gods are once more let loose and our President has been transformed into the High Priest of Huitzilopochtli).[28] Paz later wrote a book-length essay for the Hackett Memorial Lectures at UT Austin, critiquing the Mexican state's repression of the student protesters ("the only true international group") in its blind publicity for the Olympiad's false internationalism.[29]

Following his resignation, Paz left Delhi on a slow boat to France, where *Renga* was soon conceived and composed. He then went on to periods of residency as a visiting scholar at European and US universities, where he admitted to Tomlinson that he would be captive to the "horrible oro norteamericano" (horrible North American gold) of its "marmóreas Universidades" (marbled Universities).[30] These residencies included Pittsburgh and the University of Texas at Austin in 1969, Cambridge in 1970, Oklahoma in 1971, and Harvard on and off between 1971 and 1975, by which time he returned to Mexico to found and edit the newspaper sup- plement *Plural*. At Austin, Paz was welcomed owing largely to the critical acu- men of CCF affiliate Roger Shattuck and Paz's own translator Lysander Kemp, as well as to the National Translation Center, directed by Botsford since 1965. In Austin, Paz helped to organize a low-key reprise of Poetry International '67 that included the participation of Robert Duncan, Louis Zukofsky, Robert Creeley (standing in for the ailing Charles Olson), Jorge Luis Borges, Czesław Miłosz, and Alberto de Lacerda (Figure 6.2).

Although these were the several institutional contexts in which Paz conceived, convened, edited, translated, and finally published *Renga*, he did not publicize his debts to US academia. Rather, his resignation from diplomatic service trans- formed him, in the words of Claude Roy, into a paragon of cosmopolitan detach- ment: "a roving poet, a wandering scholar exiled from everything except poetry." While *Blanco* (1966), *Ladera este* (Eastern Slope, 1969) and *Le singe grammair- ien* (The Monkey Grammarian, 1972) all register Paz's diplomatic residencies in Japan and India, primarily through his explorations of non-Western religious and poetic materials, we can see in his poem "Mexico: The XIX Olympiad" how Paz now crafted an explicit divorce of cosmopolitan discourse from state-sponsored

Fig 6.2   Flyer for International Festival of Poetry, The University of Texas at Austin, November 17–22, 1969. Kemp/Paz Collection, Container 3.6. Used by permission of Harry Ransom Center, The University of Texas at Austin.

diplomacy of all kinds, translating it instead into semi-autonomous poetic forms and performative social rituals.

This formal and performative cosmopolitanism led him to assemble the "international foursome" who composed *Renga* in Paris in April 1969. He first conceived the idea that February, probably as he read "memorable examples" of renga in Donald Keene's *Anthology of Japanese Literature*, published by Grove Press (who also published Paz). He intended to gather a quintet, but could not secure Paul Celan's participation.[31] As Paz first proposed to Tomlinson: "La Renga de Occidente (hay que buscar otro nombre, quizá) debe componerse por varios poetas de distintas nacionalidades pero que, aunque en *lenguas diferentes, hablen un mismo lenguaje*" (the Renga of the Occident (we might need to look for another name) should be composed by various poets of distinct nationalities, but who, even if in *different tongues, speak the same language*).[32] Paz guided the quartet through five days of collaborative writing as the subway rattled by a Left Bank retreat at the Hôtel Duc de Saint-Simon. The poets perceived the act of sitting together as a tonic to the modern pathology of writing in private. As Paz wrote in the book's introduction: "I write in front of the others, the others in front of me. Something like undressing in a cafe, or defecating, crying before strangers."[33]

Together, they composed a sequence of twenty-seven interlocking sonnets. Swapping the sonnet in for the Japanese tanka as the base form for the chain, the four poets worked one poem at a time, composing half an octave or half of a sestet before passing the poem to the next writer. Each poet led one seven-sonnet cycles, and concluded it alone. Thus Paz begins the first sonnet and writes the entire seventh one, Roubaud initiates the eighth and the fourteenth is exclusively his, and so on. Sanguineti declines the final poem to end on a communal note.

The poets claimed to have broken a record by writing the first "Renga de Occidente," although in some ways the poem was belated. At least a century of Euro-American borrowings from Eastern poetics was in their frame of reference. Paz well knew how the French prose poem emerged from "the spirit of Japanery."[34] He learned from the French colonial consul poets Paul Claudel, Victor Segalen, and Saint-John Perse, studied the misprisions of haiku and tanka by Anglo-American imagism from Arthur Whaley and Jun Fujita to Ezra Pound, and recovered Mexican haiku from the *japonaiserie* of José Juan Tablada, Xavier Villarutía, Jaime Torres Bodet, and José Gorostiza. He studied the legacies of the ideogram in Ernest Fenollosa, Pound, Tablada, Guillaume Apollinaire, and the Brazilian concrete poets, and approved the Westernization of Zen in John Cage, writing *"John Cage es japonés."*[35] He followed with interest the 1960s cult of Japan that led Corman, Eshleman, Ginsberg, Kerouac, and Snyder, following in the footsteps of Kenneth Rexroth, to experiment with Eastern spirituality and poetic form. Paz was a scholar and an adept of Mexican haiku, an essayist on Japanese literature, and one of the first Western translators (before Corman) of renga master Matsuo Basho's *Oku no hosomichi* (Back Roads to Far Towns). From this vantage point, *Renga* exemplifies the *arrière-garde*, consolidating a long tradition of East-West poetic exchanges, translations, and misprisions.[36] Eliot Weinberger—who is at once Paz's great vindicator and *Renga's* most biting critic—has considered the poem in this light, which Weinberger regards as Western modernism's alternative to its own premium on innovation: "the discovery of all that poetry is not (but could be) and the recovery of all that poetry (it is imagined) was."[37]

However, to stress the genealogical coherence of this tradition imposes an order that the poets of *Renga* frequently ignore. Rather than lay claim to it (as Paz does elsewhere), they postulate a profusion of rationales about the poem's cosmopolitanism that clamor for rehearsal, even threatening to negate one another and to moot the writing of the poem. Claude Roy oxymoronically claims that *Renga* is possible because Paz has "the natural cosmopolitanism of a mind naturally rooted in his native Mexico."[38] Although Paz generally rejects this viewpoint, Roy's odd phrase suggests Kwame Anthony Appiah's conception of a "rooted cosmopolitanism" that refutes the opposition between cosmopolitanism and nationalism.[39] For the pithy Tomlinson, the European ego was not so easily suppressed without "several centuries of Buddhist self-abnegation behind one."[40] Provocatively downplaying Paz's *Mexicanidad*, Tomlinson wonders how "four Europeans (Octavio Paz is both Mexican and European)" will manage to dissolve their egos in the flux of Eastern epistemology. By the poem's finale, he announces the achievement of his theophany: "I have become four voices that encircle/a common object, defining a self/lost in a spiral of selves, a naming."[41] This mythologized encounter between Europe and Asia allows Tomlinson to metaphorize the poem's many post-Babelic images of linguistic reunification, its "tree of tongues" and "twining of voices," as a "discovery" of America out of the dialectics of East and West. Toward the end of the poem he synthesizes it in language that recalls John Donne's "To His Mistress Going to Bed": "language of silence; sufficiency of touch,/o my America, my new-found-land explored,/unspeaking plenitude of the flesh made word."[42] Tomlinson effectively figures Paz as European in order to figure the body of the *Renga* project as a New World of undissociated sensibility.

Paz himself was doctrinaire about *Renga*'s cosmopolitanism. In his introduction, "collective poetry" emerges as the natural telos of poetry in the West: "One has no need to state that [collective poetry] is one of the modern obsessions." However, Paz carefully shields "collective" poetry from more acute political overtones by distinguishing it sharply from "collectivist poetry," a distinction designed to bulwark *Renga* from being interpreted as a benediction of Second World politics.[43] The distinction also marks a waning of the utopian optimism that Paz's private correspondence expresses in the weeks immediately following May '68 through the horror of Tlatelolco. In lieu of politics, Paz explains the transvaluation of collectivity first in terms of *translation* and second in terms of a revision of the concept of the *author*, which emerges here as the true kernel of his cosmopolitan thinking.

Paz credited the Anglophone modernists Pound and Eliot with marrying poetic creation to the process of translation. By the late 1960s, surrounded by his own competitive associations of translators of the kind I discussed in Chapter 4, Paz grandiosely proclaimed "our century is the century of translations," and "history itself seems to us an imperfect translation." These credos oddly jar with *Renga*'s actual strength: the ways it restricts and even eschews translation. The multilingual poem was "retranslated" by Paz, Roubaud, and Tomlinson for facing-page editions by George Braziller in New York, Gallimard in Paris, and J. Mortiz in Mexico City (the Italian Feltrinelli edition was never completed), but the poem actively resists this process. For example, the "trait that radically distinguishes it from the Japanese model," wrote Paz, was multilingual

composition. Stanzaic juxtapositions are conceived as linguistic juxtapositions.[44]
Moreover, by the third poem of the sequence, a mode of intralingual citation
develops within the stanza, what Weinberger calls "leakage." While Weinberger
believes that authorial presence re-emerges in the convention of italicized foreign
speech, this is not always the case. To the contrary, languages themselves become
the agents of intralinguistic dialogue in the manner of marginal scholia:

> [*Nota (¿en nahuátl?): Occidente dice:* "Eros and Ceres,
> hand in hand etc." but *practica (sin decirlo) los* 120 journées. . .
> *Sade: lo que no decimos; Rousseau: lo que no hacemos.*]

Here, a scholastic bit of Nahuatl apocrypha (or perhaps a language that cannot
be positively identified at all) offers an ironic commentary on the West's false
consciousness. No sketchy allegory for the "Third World," Nahuatl connotes
the indigenous Fourth World that Brotherston describes in terms of transin-
digenous textual practices across the hemisphere.[45] The Fourth World's written
accusation suggests that *Occidente* is a regime of speech rather than of writing,
inverting conventional distinctions between "oral" and "literate" societies while
calling the West to account for masking allusively Sadistic practices in the language of erotism and fertility (Eros and Ceres). The presumptive textuality of
the absent Nahuatl commentary indicates a Fourth World that emerges in the
poem as if revived, philologically, from the dead, rather than in the manner of
vocal collaboration with indigenous coevals that Rothenberg's nascent ethnopoetics promoted in *Technicians of the Sacred* (1968). This is the kind of stanza
that clearly evokes Ezra Pound, but not Pound's translations, as Paz claims, so
much as the hypercondensed, multilingual mythologies of history that Pound
wove into the fabric of the *Cantos*. The difference between the *Cantos* and this
stanza is that Poundian multilingualism proposes to resolve world poetic history through the cultural heroism of a single poetic ego, while *Renga* experimentally repopulates the multilingual poem with a cast of authentic speakers
and informants.[46] "Not as a tapestry," wrote Paz, "but as body in a perpetual
state of change."

In Paz's cosmopolitan self-accounting, *Renga* also relies on a new concept
of authorship. If surrealism "put into brackets the notion of the author," Paz
imagines *Renga* as a cross-cultural double of the surrealist game known as the
exquisite corpse. Bracketing authorship is not merely a compositional procedure
in *Renga*, but an entextualized mode of presentation. Parentheticals proliferate
throughout the poem. Sanguineti, in particular, almost always leaves his stanzas
bracketed, and thematizes the bracket as a metapoetics in *Renga* II.5:

(mi distendo sopra il tuo corpo, come queste parole
sopra il secondo verso di un sonetto rovesciato:
ti stringo con le deboli dita di queste mie parentesi)

je te serre sans force avec de l'ozone avec de la paille
je répète ta musique au début de chaque laisse
jour à jour (les nuits sont cette canso capfinida)

abres y cierras (paréntesis) los ojos como este texto
da, niega, da (labios, dientes, lengua) sus sentidos:

in this branchwork labyrinth of glance and feature,
these lines that are life-lines,
these veins vines.

(I stretched myself out over your body, like these words
along the second line of a mirror sonnet:
I grasp you with the weak fingers of these brackets of mine)

I grasp you without force with ozone with straw
I repeat your music at the start of each laisse
day by day (the nights are this *canso capfinida*)

you open and close (brackets) your eyes, and this text
gives, denies, gives (lips, teeth, tongue) its meanings

in this branchwork labyrinth of glance and feature
these lines that are life-lines,
these veins vines. (tr. Charles Tomlinson)

In Sanguineti's opening apostrophe, the parenthesis distends over the "body" of the poem and encloses or "grasps" it with weak fingers. The parenthesis reveals the expressive author comprehending his own textuality. Roubaud, in the following stanza, enlarges this grasping action, equating it to the diurnal cycle, "jour à jour," repetitions bound loosely together like the free medieval French stanza the laisse. A cosmological rhythm takes hold, in which nights offer parenthetical respites that link the days like "cansos capfinidas" (the medieval "head-finishing" device that rhymes a stanza's end word to the beginning word of the successive stanza). As Paz puts it in the third stanza, parentheses bracket authors while establishing a rhythm of aperture and closure, rooted at once in medieval French verse forms, in Roubaud's diurnal cycles, and in the erotic body's "ojos," "labios," and so on.

Perloff passingly critiques Paz's eroticized, corporeal images of textuality (as visible above or in phrasings like "the female body naked as a syllable").[47] Paz corporealized text as an erotic body in *Blanco* (1966), and here this tendency reemerges as what Tomlinson dubs, in a liturgical reversal, "the flesh made word." These erotics encode the balder seductions of poems such as Ferlinghetti's "Holy Proposal" in cultivated textual traditions. They too easily rewrite erotic experience as intercultural understanding, reflecting a poetic crisis of masculinity as much as they approximate cosmopolitan resolution.[48]

The Oulipian poet Jacques Roubaud's interpretation of *Renga* offers the crucial alternative. Roubaud argues that the practice of renga relies on effectively surmounting the textual gulf between poets: "a poet writing renga must strain to bridge the gap which exists between the preceding verse written by someone else and one's own."[49] Such linking procedures in classical renga are called *tsukeai*. Although the authors of *Renga* never name the concept, Roubaud clearly evokes tsukeai as the courtly protocol through which a poet artfully breaks into a circumscribed space of poetic dialogue. Here, contemporary scholars of the art of renga regard "La Renga de Occidente" sympathetically. Esperanza Ramirez-Christensen suggests that if renga is an art of formalized sociality, its main institution is tsukeai, which she elaborates as a structure of linkage that amplifies "tension," in which tension is understood as a mode of mutual constitutiveness, of the "coming into appearance of phenomena, or meaning, through correlation."[50] *Renga* offers nothing less than an alternative to the Western lyric's medieval emergence. In the notable account of Giorgio Agamben, Western lyric, as defined by the possibility of enjambment, must confront the paradoxical status of its exhortations and endings (in which the possibility of enjambment is obliterated and the poem is hurled into silence or passes into prose).[51] *Renga*, by contrast, reconstitutes the ground of poetic making around the gaps between poetic speakers and the silences between poems.

We can reevaluate *Renga* II.5 according to these protocols of linkage between the poem's speakers. Roubaud enters the poem through a loosely interpreted "canso capfinida," translating Sanguineti's final line "ti stringo con le deboli dita" with his first line "Je te serre sans force," while enlarging the field of phenomena that the poet "grasps" from the blank space of the page to poetic history and the rhythms of diurnal time. Paz subsequently interprets linkage as a return to Sanguineti's initial theme of the parenthesis. Only Tomlinson breaks with tsukeai in favor of totalization. Pretending to offer a complete description of the *Renga* project, his stanza relies on the ludic homophony of the phrases "lines that are lifelines" and "veins vines." He diverts the poem's energy from cross-stanzaic dialogue between languages to monolingual sonic correspondence between individual words.

The uneven application of self-arbitrating dialogue was bound up in political dimensions that *Renga* sought to evade. The formalization of poetic sociality here facilitates the coalition of Western languages, but not the languages of East and West. *Renga* does not include a Japanese renga practitioner in its coterie. In this regard, Paz was explicit:

> In the present moment of its history the West is meeting with the East at various points—meeting without touching, moved by the logic of its own destiny. One of these points is poetry. Not some idea of poetry, but its practice.[52]

To appropriate poetic practices was to meet ethically "without touching," whereas West and East were also "touching," not least in violent conflicts in Southeast Asia that prompted—the very month that the poets descended to their writer's den—the beginning of the Paris Peace Talks on Vietnam. Paz wished to insulate the poem from politics, but Claude Roy's tongue-in-cheek description of the poem as a "'united nations' of four poets" indicates the poem's structural longing for rule-based, courtly protocols of international arbitration.

Perhaps the strangest claim Paz made of *Renga* was his regard for it as a poem "which effaces itself as it is written, a path which is wiped out and has no desire to lead anywhere." Contemporary theorists of renga draw on this formulation: "like a pen that erases even as it writes, it takes away as much as it adds with every verse."[53] Eager to write poetry that removed itself from the ideological polarizations of his day, Paz's poetics of erasure strike me as a muffled critique of teleology. Jean Franco argues that Latin American writers at the peak of the global Cold War confronted the "conflicting universals" of Soviet collectivism and American democracy.[54] Paz swapped these Cold War aims with a wager, formalized in the art of renga, that humanity tended toward self-regulating, self-erasing cosmopolitan dialogue. Call this view *manifest cosmopolitanism*, a view moving toward his conviction that modern poetry was singular rather than multiple. *Renga* hastens to dissolve poetic egos and national poetries in one wishful sweep. Bracketing authorship, Paz and company figure the poet as a metonym for natural language in the stream of dialogic contact with the other languages of the world. Paz simplified these elaborate formal protocols in his introduction to the 1971 Charles Eliot Norton lectures that he delivered at Harvard University: "despite language and cultural differences, the Western world has only one modern poetry."[55]

Heteronyms and Literary History

From the hotel where Paz and company composed *Renga*, it was just a kilometer down Boulevard Saint-Germain to the offices of the *Paris Review* at 17 rue de Tournon.[56] In the summer 1969 issue, readers stumbled over a curious sheaf of testimonials about an obscure Latin American poet named Jorge Guinhieme, reputed to be a leading writer of the Argentine vanguard.[57] New York School poet Kenneth Koch's "translations" from Guinhieme's *The Streets of Buenos Aires* follow, touted as Guinhieme's "continuing life work." If readers were bound to quickly spot this as a poorly disguised hoax, it was all part of the fun. The poems stirred up no particular scandal, and Koch disclosed his authorship by quickly publishing an enlarged version in *The Pleasures of Peace* (1969). Koch situates the Guinhieme corpus in a fabricated "anthology" entitled "Some South American Poets," recasting Guinhieme as a bridge between modernismo and vanguardismo and creating a host of poets writing in Guinhieme's large shadow: a second generation in which nearly everyone is named Luis, and an enfant terrible third generation led by Juan Garcia [*sic*], the twenty-two-year old author of a precocious work titled *The Mistresses of Garcia*, a work that hyperbolizes the twin love objects (*marisol* and *marisombra*) of Neruda's lyric sequence *Veinte poemas de amor y una canción desesperada* (1924). Koch's heteronyms reduce hazy contours of Latin American poetic history to the imitable stylistic tics of so many of the kinds of poets I have surveyed across this book: a late Parnassian, a tellurian popular front surrealist, a nativist, a diplomat, and a young Marxist guerrillero.

Here is "Cabana Ailanthus," one of Guinhieme's shorter poems:

> At the Cabana Ailanthus when night breezes are stilled
> One old commonwealth teacher remains fastened to his desk.
> Through the night come the sounds of the frog
> As if someone, or as if an entire people, had learned a Romance language.

The Ambonese (Indonesian) phrase *ai lanto* means "tree of heaven," but also denotes a tree considered invasive in North America (Eliot, in "The Dry Salvages," writes of "the rank ailanthus of the April dooryard"). In Koch's poem, it also connotes a translator-persona overly indebted to Eliotic locutions, and perhaps emplaces the poem in Southeast Asia. Guinhieme's *Streets of Buenos Aires* bears more than its share of resemblance to Borges's 1923 *Fervor de Buenos Aires* (here as if the wistfully Anglophile Borges had written a poem in the persona of a British colonial administrator). But it might also be taken as evocative of "Pablo Neruda in Ceylon" (in Stevens's phrase), or Paz in India. The scene of convulsive language instruction (an "entire people" learning a Romance language) evokes the colonial birth of Francophone Indochina or the Hispanophone Philippines, but the poem also lampoons a US scene of translation as an endorsed activity of Cold War cultural diplomacy. The poem's baggy translationese conjures the ranine croaking of US translators like Belitt and Bly who have loudly discovered Spanish-American poetry and begun to assert its revolutionary depth against the "cold" precision of Anglophone modernism.[58] When Koch writes "But a foundation of anachronistic feathers/Darkens the blood of the priest gown before speechlessly he utter the ungracious words [*sic*]," his hoax targets a US translator's obtuse literalism, improperly subordinated syntax, mannered imputations, and mechanical errors.

Koch also furnishes a mock poetics for "Some South American Poets" in Guinhieme's manifesto "The Hasos in Argentine Poetry." "*Hasosismo*," or "the art of the fallen limb," is "the art of concealing in one line what has been revealed in the previous line." As Guinhieme stresses, this fact has eluded all previous "explicators of the *hasosismo*." They have "made often the error of seeing this function as the reverse of what it actually is: the revelation in one line of what was concealed in the preceding—or, the concealing in one line of what is to be revealed in the next." The *hasos* thus lays a tiger trap for critics. At the peril of falling into it, I note that the little critical attention occasioned by "Some South American Poets" places the *hasos* at the center of Koch's project. Jonathan Mayhew, for example, rightly regards *hasos* as a parody of the *duende* (Federico García Lorca's "deep song") in light of a rampant mid-century vogue for kitschy, American Lorquismo.[59] Yet the appeal of the *hasos* depends little on how it alludes to particular source texts, Lorca or otherwise, and depends much on how it ably torpedoes poetic attitudes beyond its allusive field. Consider how neatly the *hasos* takes aim at the credos of *Renga*. If Roubaud stresses a diurnal rhythm of poetic disclosure in *Renga*, writing "day by day (the nights are this *canso capfinida*)," Koch targets this overwrought sense of distinction in an emphatically capitalized remark: "HASOSISMO IS THE MYSTERY OF NIGHT COVERED BY THE DAY; IT IS NOT THE DAY, WHICH IS REVEALED AFTER BEING HIDDEN IN THE NIGHT." And whereas Paz calls *Renga* a poem "which effaces itself as it is written, a path which is wiped out and has no desire to lead anywhere," the *hasos* adopts an "art of concealment" in order to expose it as a syntax of obfuscation.

"Some South American Poets" conjures these several connections at once: it sympathetically parodies Borges, Lorca, and Neruda; witheringly disparages US Cold War translation culture; and seriously critiques the "manifest cosmopolitanism" of Paz. The long, narrative title poem in *The Pleasures of Peace* likewise evokes a cast of fictionalized exilic poets coming together in cosmopolitan salons. It reads as a parodic recapitulation of the fissures in the Cold War idea of the cosmopolitan poem. Here Koch emphasizes how peace—from Kantian cosmopolitanism's distant aim of "perpetual peace" to Picasso's "Dove of Peace," which came to symbolize the international communist response to American ideologies of liberal freedom—functions as a resigned Cold War poetic mandate:

> So now I must devote my days to The Pleasures of Peace—
> To my contemporaries I'll leave the Horrors of War,
> They can do them better than I—each poet shares only a portion
> Of the vast Territory of Rhyme. Here in Peace shall I stake out
> My temporal and permanent claim.

In the ensuing catalogue of ill-defined "empeacements," a nameless Russian poet reads a mock Soviet apostasy ("Complaint About the Peanut Farm") in the service of a cosmopolitan peace, and a certain Italian "Giorgio Finogle" defenestrates himself, after the fashion of Yves Klein's "Leap Into the Void," also "for peace." As an aesthetico-political goal, "peace" leads international poets to quixotic, contradictory, and absurd acts of poetic self-invention and self-immolation.

But just as *Renga* reaches back into the entire history of modernist appropriations of East Asian poetic forms, "Some South American Poets" evokes another cosmopolitan modernist genealogy at a deeply formal rather than an allusive level. I have in mind the entire poetic program of heteronymy, which comes into focus in this post-1967 moment as another decisive invention of cosmopolitan modernism, albeit one mapped in scholarly accounts with less precision than the adoptions of East Asian poetics. Fernando Pessoa, coiner of the concept of heteronymy as it relates to the poetic persona, defined his project as the creation of "an inexistent coterie," and he furnishes a fictional collection of influences and interrelationships whose paradoxical effect is to make the author himself "the lesser presence."[60] Pessoa reroutes attention from his authorial presence to the fictive and dramatic aspect of poetic speech, while undermining the cadastral fiction that such speech is primarily intended for a national community. Pessoa's ultra-Lusophone heteronyms evoke Walt Whitman, Filippo Tommaso Marinetti, Antonio Machado, Alfred, Lord Tennyson, and, perhaps most importantly, Valéry Larbaud.

The way in which Kenneth Koch later refigures heteronymy as a major legacy of cosmopolitan modernism is illegible without retracing the history of this device prior to and beyond Pessoa. Paz, who is one of Pessoa's best critics, speculates that Larbaud's *Livre de M. Barnabooth* (1908) inaugurates the device, opening poetry "a los vientos políglotas de la modernidad" (to the polyglot winds of modernity).[61] When Larbaud published Barnabooth's poems, prefaced by a critic of his own invention, he offered the foundational personality of a conservative cosmopolitan modernism. A. O. Barnabooth was a stateless subject of the Americas, born in Arequipa during the 1879 War of the Pacific and reared in New York, where he earns an enormous fortune in some unspecified form of hemispheric commerce, only to wander the railways and seas of a late-imperial globe dreaming up a modernist poetic idiom to map his ecumene. Against Barnabooth and Pessoa's Alberto Caeiro, the "Spectra" hoax of Witter Bynner and Arthur Davison Ficke (1916–1917) suggests another origin for the polygenetic heteronym, and all appear as faces of the intensifying modernist pressure on the poetic persona as such in Ezra Pound's *Personae* (1909) or Edgar Lee Masters' *Spoon River Anthology* (1914). Heteronymy consciously edges up against anonymity, pseudonymy, and the persona poem, multiplying this inventory of effects.

This drive to de-author the poem does not inevitably tend toward cosmopolitanism. If Larbaud and Pessoa invent a cosmopolitan heteronymy, Masters creates a populist national collection of voices with global afterlives in Pablo Neruda's "La tierra se llama Juan," a sequence of worker- and prisoner-authored poems published heteronymously in Chilean newspapers in 1948 before they found their place in the epic *Canto general* (1950).[62] With "La tierra se llama Juan," dissident and surreptitious heteronyms register proletarian social totality, subjecting the device to an ideological polarity that was only latent in Pessoa's "inexistent coterie." The Salvadoran poet Roque Dalton's posthumous *Poemas clandestinos* carries this tendency to its limit. Returning home in the late 1960s after periods of political agitation in both Czechoslovakia and Vietnam and foquismo guerilla training in Cuba, by 1974 (the year before his death) Dalton began publishing as five radically heteronymic students, preserving his own anonymity while amplifying a chorus of revolutionary voices.[63] Dalton's collection of revolutionary voices includes coded conversations with expatriates from the United States. The only woman among them, "Vilma Flores," responds to Dalton's debates with Margaret Randall about Kate Millett and revolutionary feminism.[64]

In one sense, Koch's "Some South American Poets" could not be farther from Dalton's *Poemas clandestinos*, despite their shared satirical and parodic leanings. Koch's collection intervenes in Latin American literary history, which it manipulates as a discrete corpus of postures, a bravura simulacrum of the waning era of cultural diplomacy. In this regard it belongs to a conservative cosmopolitan tradition of heteronymy founded with Larbaud and Pessoa. But in another sense, Koch's project comprehends the multiple refractions of heteronymic writing,

re-entangling the cosmopolitan conservatism and Marxian collectivism of previous heteronymic collections with one another under the integrationist rubric
of a fake "area" anthology.

Renga and "Some South American Poets" each respond to a 1967 crisis in cosmopolitan performance by reaching back and formalizing complex and crisscrossing genealogies in a singular, global literary history of modern poetry. They
refract and reactivate that transnational literary history to offer new, contingent
Cold War cosmopolitanisms that refute one another when they do not attempt to
"erase" themselves. Even as they quarrel with one another, both *Renga* and "Some
South American Poets" also seem to quarrel with the moment in literary history
so powerfully—if reductively—defined by Roland Barthes's essay "The Death of
the Author." While *Renga* sometimes enacts Barthes's suggestion that writing is
the "negative where all identity is lost," recasting the "text" as "a tissue of quotations drawn from the innumerable centres of culture," *Renga* and "Some South
American Poets" hardly exemplify the author's death so much as they bracket
or multiply authorship in transnational space.[65] In *Renga*, gone is the unitary
author of a solipsistic, semiprivate lyric. Here, four authors approach the poem
as a cosmopolitan meeting ground, projecting unitary lyric codes into a ritualized structure of multilingual dialogism. In "Some South American Poets," the
long-gone Ossianic compilers of bardic nationalism are revived in the guise of
a prank compiler of out-of-focus, authorless globalism. *Renga* and heteronymy
loosen up the ground that roots poetry in the stability of natural language formations, treating the units of poetic form as ceaselessly negotiated by translational
practices. If *Renga* offers a well-regulated, collaborative fantasy of cultural syn-
chronization, "Some South American Poets" hastily appropriates a geolinguistic
area called "South America" in which the US poet freely creates, intervenes, and
manipulates.

These two images of poiesis are situated alongside one another uneasily, but
certainly more than scholars have ventured to admit. Precisely in this form of
uneasy resemblance, they also resemble the many other forms of poetic imagination that this book has endeavored to record: first, the poets that flew diverse
flags while sharing the banner of hemispheric solidarity during the antifascist
struggles of World War II; second, the poets that were subsequently scattered
by the early Cold War's various theaters of insularity, where they researched the
symbolic power of the word or the allegorical force of the indigenous past as
oblique ways of sustaining the creative diplomatic energies of the Good Neighbor
era; and third, the poets that gathered together again in a 1960s moment of complex and contradictory efforts at hemispheric integration. In Paz's collaborations

and in Koch's heteronyms, we see in particular an effort to rework the intensive era of poetic cultural diplomacy into a performative cosmopolitanism playing out in an especially self-conscious use of form. In this, poets such as Paz and Koch close an era in the history of the poetry of the Americas, bringing it to a point of exhaustion by reaching back toward the origins of poetic modernism, only to outline a set of poetic postures and forms that shake the reader's faith in the diplomatic value of poetry, precisely as they enlace such cross-cultural possibilities in the elements of poetic artifice.

Notes

Introduction

1. See especially "The Washington Pan-American Congress" in José Martí, *Inside the Monster: Writings on the United States and American Imperialism*, tr. Elinor Randall, ed. Philip S. Foner (New York: Monthly Review Press, 1975): 339–367.
2. José Martí, *Versos Sencillos/Simple Verses*, tr. Manuel A. Tellechea (Houston: Arte Publico Press, 1997): 15.
3. José Martí, "Nuestra América," *La Revista Ilustrada* (January 10, 1891): 1–6.
4. For this view, see Theodor Adorno, "On Lyric Poetry and Society," in *Notes to Literature*, Vol. 1, ed. Rolf Tiedemann (New York: Columbia University Press, 1991): 37–54, and Jonathan Culler, *Theory of the Lyric* (Cambridge: Harvard University Press, 2015): 296.
5. These factors include machinations over sovereignty in Cuba, Puerto Rico, and the Panama Canal Zone; US gunboat diplomacy and military interventions in Mexico, Haiti, and Nicaragua; and the economic policy of Pan-Americanism.
6. On such characteristics, see, for example, Haun Saussy, "Exquisite Cadavers Stitched from Fresh Nightmares," in *Comparative Literature in an Age of Globalization* (Baltimore: Johns Hopkins University Press, 2006): 21.
7. Pablo Neruda, *Canto General* (Madrid: Catedra, 1990): 134; Wallace Stevens, *Collected Poetry and Prose* (New York: Library of America, 1997): 351.
8. Muna Lee and Ruth McMurry, *The Cultural Approach: Another Way in International Relations* (Raleigh: University of North Carolina Press, 1947).
9. See Ángel Rama, *The Lettered City*, tr. John Charles Chasteen (Durham: Duke University Press, 1996), and Ericka Beckman, *Capital Fictions: The Literature of Latin America's Export Age* (Minnesota: Minnesota University Press, 2012): xix. Franco describes the postwar breakdown of this sociopolitical role for intellectuals. See Jean Franco, *The Decline and Fall of the Lettered City: Latin America in the Cold War* (Cambridge: Harvard University Press, 2002): 187.
10. See Anna Brickhouse, *Transamerican Literary Relations and the Nineteenth-Century Public Sphere* (Cambridge: Cambridge University Press, 2004); David Luis

Brown, *Waves of Decolonization: Discourses of Race and Hemispheric Citizenship in Cuba, Mexico, and the United States* (Durham: Duke University Press, 2008); John Patrick Leary, *A Cultural History of Underdevelopment: Latin America in the U.S. Imagination* (Charlottesville: University of Virginia Press, 2016); Stephen M. Park, *The Pan American Imagination* (Charlottesville: University of Virginia Press, 2014); Julio Ramos, "Hemispheric Domains: 1898 and the Origins of Latin Americanism," *Journal of Latin American Cultural Studies* 10.3 (2001): 237–251.

11. On the drought, see Delpar's discussion of Lewis Hanke. Fox argues against the consensus view about the drought (or "interregnum" in her terminology). Cohn studies the legal institutions that produced it. Helen Delpar, *Looking South: The Evolution of Latin Americanist Scholarship in the United States, 1850–1975* (Tuscaloosa: University of Alabama Press, 2008): 129 and 184; Claire Fox, *Making Art Panamerican: Cultural Policy and the Cold War* (Minneapolis: University of Minnesota Press, 2013): 13; Deborah Cohn, *The Latin American Literary Boom and U.S. Nationalism during the Cold War* (Nashville: Vanderbilt University Press, 2012): 37–65.

12. See Mariano Siskind, *Cosmopolitan Desires: Global Modernity and World Literature in Latin America* (Evanston: Northwestern University Press, 2014): 3.

13. Samuel Guy Inman, *Inter-American Conferences, 1826–1954: History and Problems* (Seattle: University Press of Washington, 1965).

14. *The First Inter-American Writers' Conference of the University of Puerto Rico, April 14–23, 1941* (Rio Piedras: The University of Puerto Rico, 1941).

15. Jorge Teillier, "Conversación 'Beat' con Allen Ginsberg," *Ultramar* 3 (1960): 3. See also Fernando Alegría and Lawrence Ferlinghetti Interviewed by Dale Miner (Berkeley: KPFA, n.d.). Fernando Alegría Papers, M0651, Box 86, Tape 7, SUL.

16. Ernesto Cardenal to Sergio Mondragón, *El Corno Emplumado* 5 (1964): 146.

17. William Carlos Williams, "By the Road to the Contagious Hospital," in *Spring and All* (Dijon: Contact, 1923): 12.

18. José María Torres Caicedo, "Las dos Américas," *El Correo de Ultramar* (February 15, 1857). See also Arturo Ardao, *Génesis de la idea y el nombre de América Latina* (Caracas: Centro de Estudios Latinoamericanos Rómulo Gallegos, 1980): 175–185.

19. For example, in 1925 Inman shifted the "problem" of hemispheric unity from geography to ethnocultural difference by remarking: "There are two Americas—not North and South, but Anglo-Saxon and Latin." Samuel Guy Inman, *Problems in Pan Americanism* (New York: G. H. Doran, 1925): 2.

20. Richard M. Morse, *New World Soundings: Culture and Ideology in the Americas* (Baltimore: Johns Hopkins University Press, 1989): 1.

21. In this respect, I model the recuperation of "inter-American poetics" as a transnational extension of post-1989 historicist recovery of politicized leftist, diasporic, and minority literary formations. See, for example, Michael Denning, *The Cultural Front: The Laboring of American Culture in the Twentieth Century* (New York: Verso, 1997); Winston James, *Holding Aloft the Banner of Ethiopia: Caribbean Radicalism in Early Twentieth Century America* (New York: Verso, 1999); William J. Maxwell, *New Negro, Old Left: African-American Writing and Communism Between the Wars* (New York: Columbia University Press, 1999); Cary Nelson, *Repression and Recovery: Modern American Poetry and the Politics of Cultural Memory, 1910–1945*

(Madison: University of Wisconsin Press, 1992); Ramón Saldívar, *The Borderlands of Culture: Américo Parédes and the Transnational Imaginary* (Raleigh: Duke University Press, 2006); and Alan Wald, *Exiles from a Future Time: The Forging of the Mid-Twentieth-Century Literary Left* (Chapel Hill: University of North Carolina Press, 2002).

22. Barthes: "a little formalism turns one away from History, but a lot brings one back to it." Roland Barthes, *Mythologies* (New York: Farrar, Straus and Giroux, 1972): 111–112. See also Caroline Levine, *Forms: Whole, Rhythm, Hierarchy, Network* (Princeton: Princeton University Press, 2015).

23. Édouard Glissant, *The Poetics of Relation* (Ann Arbor: University of Michigan Press, 1997): 23.

24. On the distinction between institutions and formations, see Raymond Williams, *Marxism and Literature* (Oxford: Oxford University Press, 1977): 117.

25. Bernstein similarly describes "a simultaneity of inconsolable co-existences," and Greene writes of "obversals." See Rachel Price, *The Object of the Atlantic: Concrete Aesthetics in Cuba, Brazil, and Spain, 1868–1968* (Evanston: Northwestern University Press, 2014): 76–108; Bernstein, "Poetics of the Americas," *Modernism/modernity* 3.3 (1996): 1–23; and Greene, "Inter-American Obversals: Allen Ginsberg and Haroldo de Campos circa 1960," in *The Lyric Theory Reader: A Critical Anthology*, eds. Virginia Jackson and Yopie Prins (Baltimore: Johns Hopkins University Press, 2014): 618–631.

26. Salomón de la Selva, "The Dreamers Heart Knows Its Own Bitterness," in *Tropical Town and Other Poems* (New York: John Lane, 1918): 38.

27. Salomón de la Selva (ed.), *Pan American Poetry: A Magazine of Song in English and Spanish* 1 (1918): 1.

28. Octavio Paz, *Children of the Mire: Modern Poetry from Romanticism to the Avant-Garde* (Cambridge: Harvard University Press, 1974): vi.

29. José Martí, "Poesía," in Juan Antonio Pérez Bonalde, *El poema del Niágara* (New York, 1883).

30. See Fernando Alegría, *Walt Whitman en Hispanoamerica* (Mexico: Studium, 1954); Gay Wilson Allen and Ed Folsom (eds.), *Walt Whitman and the World* (Iowa City: University of Iowa Press, 1997), esp. 96–106; Enrico Mario Santí, *Ciphers of History: Latin American Readings for a Cultural Age* (New York: Palgrave, 2005): 66–83.

31. Pedro Mir, *Countersong to Walt Whitman & Other Poems*, tr. Jonathan Cohen and Donald D. Walsh (Washington, DC: Azul Editions, 1993): 46–99.

32. Octavio Paz, *Obras Completas*, Vol. 15 (Mexico City: Fondo de Cultura Económica, 1993): 527.

33. Gordon Brotherston, *Latin American Poetry: Origins and Presence* (Cambridge: Cambridge University Press, 1975): 27.

34. Kirsten Silva Gruesz, *Ambassadors of Culture: The Transamerican Origins of Latino Writing* (Princeton: Princeton University Press, 2002).

35. See Martin W. Lewis and Kären Wigen, *The Myth of Continents: A Critique of Metageography* (Berkeley: University of California Press, 1997).

36. Watt Stewart and Harold Peterson, *Builders of Latin America* (New York: Harper & Brothers, 1942): 258.

37. Archibald MacLeish, *The American Story: Ten Broadcasts* (New York: Duell, Sloan and Pearce, 1944): v.

38. Paul Robeson, *Here I Stand* (London: Dennis Dobson, 1958): 111.

39. See, for example, *Tiger's Eye* (1947–1948): 124 and *The Pan American* 3 (1943): 94.

40. Gruesz, *Ambassadors of Culture*, 9.

41. Edmundo O'Gorman, "Do the Americas Have a Common History?" tr. Angel Flores, *Points of View* 3 (1941). Less equivocal studies followed, such as Vera Kutzinski, *Against the American Grain: Myth and History in William Carlos Williams, Jay Wright, and Nicolás Guillén* (Baltimore: JHU Press, 1987); Morse, *New World Soundings*; Julio Ramos, *Desencuentros de la modernidad en América Latina* (Mexico City: Fondo de Cultura Económica, 1989); José Davíd Saldívar, *The Dialectics of Our America: Genealogy, Cultural Critique, and Literary History* (Durham: Duke University Press, 1991); Mary Louise Pratt, *Imperial Eyes: Travel Writing and Transculturation* (New York: Routledge, 1992); and Lois Parkinson Zamora, *The Usable Past: The Imagination of History in Recent Fiction of the Americas* (Cambridge: Cambridge University Press, 1997).

42. T. S. Eliot, "The Social Function of Poetry," in *On Poetry and Poets* (London: Faber and Faber, 1957): 8.

43. See, for example, José David-Saldívar, *Trans-Americanity: Subaltern Modernities, Global Coloniality, and the Cultures of Greater Mexico* (Durham: Duke University Press, 2011): xv–xvi.

44. On translation, see Vera Kutzinski, *The Worlds of Langston Hughes: Modernism and Translation in the Americas* (Ithaca: Cornell University Press, 2012); Ignacio Infante, *After Translation: The Transfer and Circulation of Modern Poetics Across the Atlantic* (New York: Fordham University Press, 2013); and Gayle Rogers, *Incomparable Empires: Modernism and the Translation of Spanish and American Literatures* (New York: Columbia University Press, 2016). On "new world poetics," see Roland Greene, "New World Studies and the Limits of National Literatures," *Stanford Humanities Review* 6.1 (1998); Charles Pollard, *New World Modernisms: T. S. Eliot, Derek Walcott, and Kamau Brathwaite* (Charlottesville: University of Virginia Press, 2004), and George Handley, *New World Poetics: Nature and the Adamic Imagination of Whitman, Neruda and Walcott* (Athens: University of Georgia Press, 2007). On "hemispheric poets," see Justin Read, *Modern Poetics and Hemispheric American Cultural Studies* (New York: Palgrave, 2009). On "transnational poetics," representative accounts include Jahan Ramazani, *A Transnational Poetics* (Chicago: University of Chicago Press, 2009), and Matthew Hart, *Nations of Nothing But Poetry: Modernism, Transnationalism, and Synthetic Vernacular Writing* (New York: Oxford University Press, 2010).

45. Charles Bernstein, "Our Americas: New Worlds Still in Progress," in *Attack of the Difficult Poems* (Chicago: University of Chicago Press, 2011): 65. See also Bernstein, "Poetics of the Americas," *Modernism/modernity* 3.3 (1996): 1–23.

46. As Santí explains, Paz's "América" encompassed the hemisphere, "taking at face value the Foundation's stated criteria for 'strengthening interamerican cultural relations.'" Santí's otherwise astute study makes the aside that Paz "mercifully" never completed

his investigation, wrongly reducing it to "the Whitman question in Spanish America." See Santí, *Ciphers of History*, 67.

47. Octavio Paz, "Visita al Poeta Robert Frost," *Sur* 14 (1945): 33–39; Octavio Paz, *Crónica trunca de días excepcionales*, ed. Antonio Saborit (Mexico: UNAM, 2007).

48. Paz, *Children of the Mire*, 116.

49. Paz, *Children of the Mire*, 121.

50. Mark Wollaeger with Matt Eatough (eds.), *The Oxford Handbook of Global Modernisms* (London: Oxford University Press, 2012): 12.

51. George Steiner, *Extraterritorial: Papers on Literature and the Language Revolution* (New York: Atheneum, 1971): 3.

52. See Edward Kamau Brathwaite, *History of the Voice: Development of Nation Language in Anglophone Caribbean Poetry* (London: New Beacon Books, 1984); Haroldo de Campos, *Novas: Selected Writings* (Evanston: Northwestern University Press, 2007); Glissant, *Poetics of Relation*; Jerome Rothenberg, *Eye of Witness: A Jerome Rothenberg Reader* (Boston: Black Widow Press, 2013); Jerome Rothenberg and Diane Rothenberg, *Symposium of the Whole: A Range of Discourse Toward an Ethnopoetics* (1983); and Nathaniel Tarn, *The Embattled Lyric: Essays and Conversations in Poetics and Anthropology* (Stanford: Stanford University Press, 2007).

53. Bernstein, *Attack of the Difficult Poems*, 72.

54. See also Paz's meditation on the constellation as motif and method. Paz, *Children of the Mire*, 67 and 150.

55. Earl Miner, *Comparative Poetics: An Intercultural Essay on Theories of Literature* (Princeton: Princeton University Press, 1990): 5.

56. However, these attentions need not be pegged to categorical debates on the naturalized status of lyric as a false synonym for many kinds of poems, a process that Jackson calls "lyricization." See Jackson and Prins, *The Lyric Theory Reader*, 3, and Virginia Jackson, *Dickinson's Misery: A Theory of Lyric Reading* (Princeton: Princeton University Press, 2005): 8.

57. For a related conception of how poems create linguistic images of alternate historical experience, see William Rowe, *Poets of Contemporary Latin America: History and the Inner Life* (Oxford: Oxford University Press, 2000): 12–18.

58. Roland Greene, "Poem," in *The Princeton Encyclopedia of Poetry and Poetics: Fourth Edition*, eds. Roland Greene, Stephen Cushman, Clare Cavanagh, Jahan Ramazani, Paul F Rouzer, Harris Feinsod, David Marno, and Alexandra Slessarev (Princeton: Princeton University Press, 2012): 1047.

59. On some of these approaches, see Jeremy Braddock, *Collecting as Modernist Practice* (Baltimore: Johns Hopkins University Press, 2011); M. L. Rosenthal and Sally M. Gall, *The Modern Poetic Sequence: The Genius of Modern Poetry* (New York: Oxford University Press, 1986); Lytle Shaw, *Frank O'Hara: The Poetics of Coterie* (Iowa City: University of Iowa Press: 2006); and Stephen Voyce, *Poetic Community: Avant-Garde Activism and Cold War Culture* (Toronto: University of Toronto Press, 2013).

60. On domestic sociologies of assimilation, see John Alba Cutler, *Ends of Assimilation: The Formation of Chicano Literature* (New York: Oxford University Press,

2014). On the postcolonial geopolitics of integration, see Gary Wilder, *Freedom Time: Negritude, Decolonization, and the Future of the World* (Durham: Duke University Press, 2015).

61. Wilder, *Freedom Time*, 2.

62. Pablo Neruda, *Canto General*, 445.

63. Perry Anderson, "Internationalism: A Breviary," *New Left Review* 14 (2002): 15

64. Ernesto Cardenal and Jose Coronel Urtecho, *Lincoln de los poetas* (Managua: El Hilo Azul, 1951).

65. Charles Olson, *The Collected Poems of Charles Olson*, ed. George F. Butterick (Berkeley: University of California Press, 1987): 335–336.

66. For a key critique of national canon formation through anthologization, see Jed Rasula, *The American Poetry Wax Museum: Reality Effects, 1940–1990* (Urbana, IL: NCTE, 1996).

67. On the "state-private network," see Cohn, *The Latin American Literary Boom*, 30; Helen Laville and Hugh Wilford, eds., *The US Government, Citizen Groups, and the Cold War: The State-Private Network* (London: Routledge, 2006).

68. Christopher Lasch, "The Cultural Cold War," *The Nation* (Sept. 11, 1967); Serge Guilbaut, *How New York Stole the Idea of Modern Art: Abstract Expressionism, Freedom, and the Cold War* (Chicago: University of Chicago Press, 1983); Max Kozloff, *Cultivated Impasses: Essays on the Waning of the Avant-Garde, 1964–1975* (New York: Marsilio, 2000); Frances Stonor Saunders, *The Cultural Cold War: The CIA and the World of Arts and Letters* (New York: New Press, 2000); Jean Franco, *The Decline and Fall of the Lettered City: Latin America in the Cold War* (Cambridge: Harvard University Press, 2002); Penny von Eschen, *Satchmo Blows up the World: Jazz Ambassadors Play the Cold War* (Cambridge: Harvard University Press, 2004); Hugh Wilford, *The Mighty Wurlitzer: How the CIA Played America* (Cambridge: Harvard University Press, 2009); Patrick Iber, *Neither Peace nor Freedom: The Cultural Cold War in Latin America* (Cambridge: Harvard University Press, 2015).

69. Louis Menand, "The Unpopular Front," *New Yorker* (October 17, 2005); Andrew Rubin, *Archives of Authority: Empire, Culture, and the Cold War* (Princeton: Princeton University Press, 2012).

70. Fox, *Making Art Panamerican*, 12.

71. Cohn, *The Latin American Literary Boom*, 32.

72. Greg Barnhisel, *Cold War Modernists: Art, Literature, and American Cultural Diplomacy* (New York: Columbia University Press, 2015): 18.

73. Darlen Sadlier, *Americans All: Good Neighbor Cultural Diplomacy in World War II* (Austin: University of Texas Press, 2012): 21.

74. On semi-autonomy, see Fredric Jameson, *A Singular Modernity: Essay on the Ontology of the Present* (New York: Verso, 2002): 160.

75. Luis-Brown, *Waves of Decolonization*, 7; Park, *The Pan-American Imagination*, 12.

76. Jorge Fornet, *El 71: Anatomía de una crisis* (Havana: Letras Cubanas, 2013).

77. Jorge Edwards, *Persona Non Grata: A Memoir of Disenchantment with the Cuban Revolution*, tr. Andrew Hurley (New York: Paragon House, 1993): xi.

78. See, for example, Alfred Arteaga, *Chicano Poetics: Heterotexts and Hybridities* (Cambridge: Cambridge University Press, 1997); James Smethurst, *The Black Arts Movement: Literary Nationalism in the 1960s* (Chapel Hill: University of North Carolina Press, 2006); Urayoán Noel, *In Visible Movement: Nuyorican Poetry from the Sixties to Slam* (Iowa City: Iowa University Press, 2014).

Chapter 1

1. The phrase "inter-American solidarity" was popularized by the "Declaration of Principles of Inter-American Solidarity and Cooperation" adopted by the 1936 Inter-American Conference for the Maintenance of Peace at Buenos Aires. See Mary St. Patrick McConville, *A Primer of Pan Americanism* (Washington, DC: Pan American Union, 1937).

2. Edmundo O'Gorman, "Hegel y el moderno panamericanismo," *Universidad de la Habana* 22 (1939), tr. *Do the Americas Have a Common History?* (Washington, DC: Pan American Union, 1941).

3. Hubert C. Herring, *Good Neighbors: Argentina, Brazil, Chile and Seventeen Other Countries* (New Haven: Yale University Press, 1941): vi. Herring directed the New Haven–based Committee on Cultural Relations with Latin America.

4. See Matthew Josephson, *Empire of the Air: Juan Trippe and the Struggle for World Airways* (New York: Harcourt, Brace and Company, 1943); Roger Stephens, *Down That Pan American Highway* (New York: s.n., 1948); and Alan L. Heil, Jr., *Voice of America: A History* (New York: Columbia University Press, 2003).

5. Easterling describes infrastructure as architectural "organization space" that conforms to notions of network interactivity rather than to fixed lexicons of sited buildings. Recently she has extended her thesis to transnational infrastructures. See Keller Easterling, *Organization Space: Landscapes, Highways and Houses in America* (Cambridge: MIT Press, 2001); Easterling, *Extrastatecraft: The Power of Infrastructure Space* (New York: Verso, 2014).

6. Mildred Adams, "Poetry of Latin America," *The Nation* (Jan. 30, 1943): 168.

7. Archibald MacLeish, "The Art of the Good Neighbor," *The Nation* (Feb. 10, 1940): 170–172.

8. On Good Neighbor cultural diplomacy, see Catherine Benamou, *It's All True: Orson Welles's Pan-American Odyssey* (Berkeley: University of California Press, 2007); Amy Spellacy, "Neighbors North and South: Literary Culture, Political Rhetoric and Inter-American Relations in the Era of the Good Neighbor Policy, 1928–1948" (PhD dissertation, University of Iowa, 2006); and Sadlier, *Americans All*.

9. Dudley Fitts to Xavier Abril (Mar. 1, 1943). Dudley Fitts Papers, Box 1, Folder 1. YALE.

10. Skeptics like Moffatt plainly understood "our official agency of good neighbor-liness" and its "plane-loads of professional and amateur good neighbors" as a form of cultural imperialism: "These new literary Columbuses rediscovered South America [. . .]. And of the languages, the *mores,* the civilization, the background of the continent which they are 'interpreting,' they have just as much

knowledge as did the original Conquistadores." See Lucius Gaston Moffatt, "Two Books on Latin America," *Virginia Quarterly Review* 19 (1943): 446.

11. Santí, *Ciphers of History*, 67.

12. Ramón J. Sender, "A Rhapsodic Age?," tr. Dudley Fitts, *Partisan Review* 12.1 (1945): 109.

13. See the "Pan-American number" of *American Prefaces* (Winter 1942), guest-edited by Lloyd Mallan; H. R. Hays, *12 Spanish American Poets* (New York: MacMillan, 1943); Lloyd Mallan, Mary & C. V. Wicker, and Joseph Leonard Grucci (tr.), *3 Spanish American Poets: Pellicer, Neruda, Andrade* (Albuquerque: Swallow & Critchlow, 1942); the Latin American sections of *Fantasy* magazine in 1942 and 1943; and Sidonia Carmen Rosenbaum, *Modern Women Poets of Spanish America* (New York: Hispanic Institute, 1945). On competition among translators, see Dudley Fitts to Jorge Carrera Andrade (April 28, 1942). Jorge Carrera Andrade Collection, Box 6. SBUL.

14. Américo Castro, "On the Relations between the Americas," *Points of View* 1 (1940): 1

15. Alegría, *Walt Whitman en Hispanoamerica*, 10.

16. David Green, *The Containment of Latin America: A History of the Myths and Realities of the Good Neighbor Policy* (Chicago: Quadrangle, 1971): 85.

17. See Office of Inter-American Affairs, *History of the Office of the Coordinator of Inter-American Affairs: Historical Reports on War Administration* (Washington, DC: GPO, 1947).

18. Cary Reich, *The Life of Nelson A. Rockefeller: Worlds to Conquer, 1908–1958* (New York: Doubleday, 1996): 233.

19. As Bishop wrote, "the Coordinator's office seeks, as it has from the beginning, to find outlets for desired publications through established publishing houses. Only they have the necessary means of distribution." John Peale Bishop to Jorge Carrera Andrade (March 12, 1943). Jorge Carrera Andrade Collection, Box 2. SBUL.

20. See Simon Schaffer, Lissa Roberts, Kapil Raj, and James Delbourgo, *The Brokered World: Go-Betweens and Global Intelligence, 1770–1820* (Sagamore Beach, MA: Science History Publications, 2009).

21. Braddock, *Collecting as Modernist Practice*, 29–70.

22. Dudley Fitts to CV Wicker (Oct. 5, 1941). Dudley Fitts Papers, Box 3, Folder 78, YALE.

23. Dudley Fitts, *The Poetic Nuance* (New York: Harcourt Brace, 1959): 7.

24. James Laughlin to Dudley Fitts. Dudley Fitts Papers, Box 1, Folder 35, YALE.

25. Muna Lee, *A Pan-American Life*, ed. Jonathan Cohen (Madison: University of Wisconsin Press, 2004): 42.

26. On Muñoz Marín, see Thomas Aitken, *Poet in the Fortress: The Story of Luis Muñoz Marín* (New York: New American Library, 1964). For Lee's views on cultural diplomacy, see Lee and McMurry, *The Cultural Approach*.

27. Dudley Fitts to Angel Flores (1951). Angel Flores Collection, HRC.

28. Fitts, *Anthology*, 609.

29. Fitts to Carrera Andrade (Dec. 29, 1942). Jorge Carrera Andrade Collection, Box 6, SBUL.

30. Lloyd Mallan, "The Poets of Latin-America," *New York Times Book Review* (Feb. 7, 1943). Adams added: "The number of people who have tried to be helpful about it, if each bought a copy, should insure its financial success. But something went wrong." See Adams, "Poetry of Latin America," 168.

31. Lloyd Mallan to Harry Duncan (April 21, 1944). Cummington Press Records and Harry Duncan Papers, Box 2, Folder 9, EU.

32. Muna Lee to Dudley Fitts (Dec. 4, 1942). Dudley Fitts Papers, Box 1, Folder 36, YALE.

33. Jorge Luis Borges to Waldo Frank (Nov. 2, 1946). Waldo Frank Papers, PENN. On Borges's rights, see also Dudley Fitts to John Peale Bishop (Oct. 3, 1941). John Peale Bishop Papers, Box 21, Folder 5, PUL.

34. Jorge Luis Borges, "Los Libros," review of *An Anthology of Contemporary Latin American Poetry, Sur* 102 (1943): 65.

35. Fitts to Carrera Andrade (March 16, 1942). Jorge Carrera Andrade Collection, Box 6, SBUL.

36. Bishop to Fitts (July 31, 1941). Dudley Fitts Papers, Box 1, Folder 7, YALE.

37. *Sur* 113–114 (March–April 1944) included a "panorama" of US literature edited by former *Poetry* editor Morton Dauwen Zabel and translations of Crane, Cummings, Moore, Penn Warren, Porter, Schwartz, Shapiro, Stevens, Thurber, Welty, and Whitman.

38. George Dillon to Jorge Carrera Andrade (Sept. 9, 1941). Jorge Carrera Andrade Collection, Box 5, SBUL.

39. Fitts to Carrera Andrade (Jan. 24, 1942). Jorge Carrera Andrade Collection, Box 6, SBUL.

40. Quoted in Jorge Carrera Andrade, *Century of the Death of the Rose*, tr. Steven Ford Brown (Montgomery: New South Books, 2002): 19.

41. William Carlos Williams to Muna Lee (July 6, 1942). Jorge Carrera Andrade Collection, Box 17, SBUL.

42. Wallace Stevens to Carrera Andrade (May 19, 1943). Jorge Carrera Andrade Collection, Box 16, SBUL.

43. Hays to Carrera Andrade (n.d.). Jorge Carrera Andrade Collection, Box 8, SBUL.

44. Carrera Andrade to Hays (n.d.). H. R. Hays Correspondence with Latin American Writers, Box 1, Folder 1, PUL.

45. "Rediscovery" is a popular trope of the period. See, for example, Ángel Guido, *Redescubrimiento de América en el arte* (Rosario: Universidad del Litoral, 1941).

46. Jorge Carrera Andrade, "The New American and His Point of View toward Poetry," tr. H. R. Hayes, *Poetry* 62.2 (1943): 88–104.

47. Jorge Carrera Andrade, *To The Bay Bridge/Canto al Puente de Oakland*, tr. Eleanor Turnbull (Stanford: Hoover Library on War, Revolution and Peace, 1941). Another translation by Carlos Reyes followed Turnbull's translation in 1976. Muna Lee also translated the poem in 1941, and Carrera Andrade's letters to Turnbull imply that he may have substituted Lee's version at the last moment.

48. David E. Nye, *American Technological Sublime* (Cambridge: MIT University Press, 1994).

49. Nelson A. Rockefeller to Jorge Carrera Andrade (Oct. 24, 1941). Jorge Carrera Andrade Collection, Box 14, SBUL.

50. On Niagara as inter-American "icon," see Gruesz, *Ambassadors of Culture*, 35–48.

51. On Rivera's mural, see Silvia Spitta and Lois Parkinson Zamora, "Introduction: The Americas, Otherwise," *Comparative Literature*. 61.3 (2009): 189–208.

52. For a canonical account of these dynamics, see Stephen Kern, *The Culture of Time and Space, 1880–1918* (Cambridge: Harvard University Press, 1983).

53. Hart Crane, *Complete Poems and Selected Letters*, ed. Langdon Hammer (New York: Library of America, 2006): 39.

54. Hart Crane and Harriet Monroe, "A Discussion with Hart Crane," *Poetry* 29.1 (1926): 36.

55. Brian Reed, *Hart Crane: After His Lights* (Tuscaloosa: University of Alabama Press, 2006): 128.

56. In 1942, Carrera Andrade read a translation of *The Bridge* by Diomedes de Pereyra, Bolivian novelist and Bishop's co-director of the publications division at CIAA, but no scholarship notes connections between Carrera Andrade's poem and Crane or Rivera. Jorge Carrera Andrade to Muna Lee (1942). Jorge Carrera Andrade Collection, Box 9, SBUL.

57. See Harris Feinsod, "Vehicular Networks and the Modernist Seaways: Crane, Lorca, Novo, Hughes," *American Literary History* 27.4 (2015): 698.

58. Herbert Bolton, "The Epic of Greater America," *American Historical Review* 38.3 (1933): 448–474.

59. Jorge Carrera Andrade, *El volcán y el colibrí: autobiografía* (Puebla: Editorial J. M. Cajica, Jr., 1970): 154–155.

60. Carrera Andrade refers to the architectural meaning of *zócalo* as "plinth" or "pillar" (as opposed to "plaza"), evoking the enormous support in the middle of the bridge's West Span.

61. Muriel Rukeyser, *The Life of Poetry* (New York: Current Books, 1949): 209.

62. H. R. Hays, "Jorge Carrera Andrade, Magician of Metaphors," *Books Abroad* 17.2 (1943): 101–105.

63. Borges, "Los Libros," 62.

64. Borges, "Los Libros," 63.

65. Paz, *Crónica trunca*, 85.

66. A final typescript of the book was completed in March 1943. It was held up when CIAA transferred publications to the State Department, and a rejection from James Laughlin contributed to the delays. Carrera Andrade later inquired if Laughlin was a fascist, to which Fitts responded, "No, J. Laughlin is no Fascist. He's really a buen hombre." See Bishop to Carrera Andrade (March 2, 1943) and Fitts to Carrera Andrade (March 30, 1942), Jorge Carrera Andrade Collection, Boxes 1 and 6, SBUL. See also Carrera Andrade, *El volcán*, 142.

67. Jorge Carerra Andrade, "Boletín de viaje," in *A Secret Country*, tr. Muna Lee (New York: MacMillan, 1946): 54–55.

68. John Peale Bishop, "The Poetry of Jorge Carrera Andrade," in Carerra Andrade, *A Secret Country*, v.

69. Sadlier, *Americans All*, 48.
70. Babette Deutsch, "Lyrics from Ecuador and New England," *New York Times* (Feb. 16, 1947).
71. Kutzinski, *Worlds of Langston Hughes*, 3.
72. Alain Locke, "The Negro in the Three Americas," *Journal of Negro Education* 13.1 (1944): 10.
73. Langston Hughes, "Greetings, Good Neighbors" (Pan-American Women's Club Dinner, n.d., 1943). Langston Hughes Papers, Box 485, Folder 12320, YALE.
74. Most likely, the visa was denied on the grounds of the 1939 Smith Act. Nicolás Guillén to Langston Hughes (May 15, 1941). Langston Hughes Papers, Box 70, Folder 1366, YALE.
75. Langston Hughes, *The Collected Poems of Langston Hughes*, ed. Arnold Rampersad (New York: Alfred A. Knopf, 1995): 273 and 648.
76. For example, Hughes compared himself to Claude McKay for West Indian audiences during a 1943 reading for OWI, and read "Harlem Sweeties," "The Negro Speaks of Rivers," and "Captain Mulzac," his occasional poem for Hugh Mulzac, the first black captain to command a vessel in the merchant marines. "Radio Broadcast" (n.d.). Langston Hughes Papers, Box 485, Folder 12325, YALE. For other details, see Arnold Rampersad, *The Life of Langston Hughes: 1941–1967, I Dream a World* (New York: Oxford University Press, 2002): 39–45.
77. Early US designs for international shortwave broadcasting were pioneered in Latin America, although much wartime broadcasting was transatlantic. On shortwave, see Heil, *Voice of America*, 33; On CIAA's Radio Division, see, for example, MacLeish, *The American Story* ix–xii, and Sadlier, *Americans All*, 84–118. See also Thomas McEnaney, *Acoustic Properties: Radio, Narrative, and the New Neighborhood of the Americas* (Evanston: Northwestern University Press, 2017).
78. See, for example, the pamplets *El Salvador, Land of Eternal Spring* (Washington, DC: CIAA, 1944), and *Venezuela, Land of Oil* (Washington, DC: CIAA, 1944).
79. Federico García Lorca, *Collected Poems*, ed. Christopher Maurer (New York: Farrar Strauss & Giraux, 2002): 652.
80. Barry Carr, "'Across Seas and Borders': Charting the Webs of Radical Internationalism in the Red Circum-Caribbean, 1910–1940," in *Exile and the Politics of Exclusion in the Americas*, eds. Luis Roniger, James Naylor Green, and Pablo Yankelevich (Brighton: Sussex Academic Press, 2012): 217.
81. On Hughes as translator, see Brent Hayes Edwards, "Langston Hughes and the Futures of Diaspora," *American Literary History* 19.3 (2007): 689–711, and Ryan Kernan, "Lost and Found in Black Translation: Langston Hughes's Translations of French- and Spanish-Language Poetry, His Hispanic and Francophone Translators, and the Fashioning of Radical Black Subjectivities" (PhD dissertation, UCLA, 2007).
82. Vaughn Rasberry, *Race and the Totalitarian Century: Geopolitics in the Black Literary Imagination* (Cambridge: Harvard University Press, 2016): 10.
83. Ramazani, *A Transnational Poetics*, 61.
84. Kutzinski, *Worlds of Langston Hughes*, 4.
85. William J. Maxwell, "Global Poetics and State-Sponsored Transnationalism: A Reply to Jahan Ramazani," *American Literary History* 18.2 (2006): 360.

86. Waldo Frank, *South American Journey* (New York: Duell, Sloan and Pearce, 1943): xvii.

87. Frank hounded the agency for months after the trip to collect a balance of $850. Waldo Frank to Nelson Rockefeller (January 1943). Waldo Frank Papers, PENN.

88. Natalie Robins, *Alien Ink: The FBI's War on Freedom of Expression* (New York: William Morrow, 1992): 84

89. Waldo Frank, "Our Island Hemisphere," *Foreign Affairs* 21.3 (1943): 522.

90. In reality, the political landscape of democracy in the Americas was shifting rapidly. As Grandin points out, in 1944 only five Latin American nations could claim nominally to be democracies, whereas by 1946 only five nations could not. See Greg Grandin, *The Last Colonial Massacre: Latin America in the Cold War* (Chicago: University of Chicago Press, 2011): 5; Frank, "Our Island Hemisphere," 517.

91. Lewis Mumford, "Lewis Mumford Pays Tribute to Waldo Frank," *New York Times* (May 23, 1943): 88.

92. Frank, *South American Journey*, 92.

93. Frank, *South American Journey*, 77.

94. Frank, *South American Journey*, 386.

95. Frank Ninkovich, *The Diplomacy of Ideas* (New York: Cambridge University Press, 1981): 61–86.

96. Vicente Barbieri, "Salutación a Waldo Frank," *Argentina Libre* (May 7, 1942): 6.

97. Ezequiel Martínez Estrada, "A Waldo Frank," *Argentina Libre* (May 7, 1942): 7.

98. Frank, *South American Journey*, 72–73.

99. Borges to Frank (Nov. 1, 1946). Waldo Frank Papers, PENN.

100. See Ezequiel Martínez Estrada, *Panorama de los Estados Unidos*, ed. Joaquín Roy (Buenos Aires: Torres Agüero, 1985).

101. In Montevideo, Frank met Juana de Ibarbourou in the "little bourgeois home" she never left, "overstuffed with bad bric-a-brac." He suggested that "in the United States a poetess of the stature of Juana would have ten thousand readers: the scattered minority who are not satisfied with the twice-hundred-times-told refrains of Edna St. Vincent Millay." In Chile, where the United Front leveraged his visit against a government that had yet to break with the Axis, Frank escaped public view hiding out "in Vicente Huidobro's cottage by the sea." See Frank, *South American Journey*, 160 and 235.

102. Vinicius de Moraes to Waldo Frank (December 1942). Waldo Frank Papers, PENN.

103. de Moraes to Frank (December 1942). Waldo Frank Papers, PENN.

104. Frank, "Our Island Hemisphere," 519.

105. Frank, *South American Journey*, 362.

106. The fullest previous account is David Schidlowsky, *Neruda y su tiempo: Las furias y las penas*, Vol. 1, *1904–1949* (Santiago de Chile: RIL, 2008): 545–549.

107. Neruda's impressively varied leftist US contacts exceed his biographers' reports. See Marian Bachrach to Pablo Neruda (Nov. 16, 1945), FPN.

108. Pablo Neruda to Marjorie Carr Stevens and Elizabeth Bishop (December 1942). Elizabeth Bishop Papers, F. 16.14, VUL.

109. Pablo Neruda, *Memoirs*, tr. Hardie St. Martin (New York: Farrar, Straus & Giroux, 1974): 165.

110. Brett Millier, *Elizabeth Bishop: Life and the Memory of It* (Berkeley: University of California Press, 1995): 165–169.
111. Elizabeth Bishop, "El Primitivo Gregorio Valdés," *Orígenes* 6 (1945). See also Joelle Biele, *Elizabeth Bishop: Objects & Apparitions* (New York: Tibor de Nagy Gallery, 2012).
112. Elizabeth Bishop, "To Marianne Moore [For M. M.] [Invitation to Marianne Moore]," MS, Elizabeth Bishop Papers, F. 56.8, VUL.
113. Elizabeth Bishop, *One Art: Letters*, ed. Robert Giroux (New York: Farrar, Straus & Giroux, 1994): 108. While Neruda was not formally a part of the surrealist movement, critics such as Juan Larrea tightly link the poet's development to the traditions of New World surrealism. See Juan Larrea, *El surrealismo entre viejo y nuevo mundo* (Mexico City: Cuadernos Americanos, 1944), and Juan Larrea, *Del surrealismo al Machu Picchu* (Mexico City: J. Mortiz, 1967).
114. Armando Zegri, "Noche de las Américas," *La Hora*, Santiago (March 15, 1943).
115. Marc Eliot, *Walt Disney: Hollywood's Dark Prince* (New York: Birch Lane Press, 1993): 170.
116. Philip Murray and Vicente Lombardo Toledano, *Labor's Good Neighbor Policy* (New York: Council for Pan American Democracy, ca. 1943): 9.
117. Samuel Putnam, "Pablo Neruda," *New Masses* (March 16, 1943): 23
118. Samuel Putnam to Juan Antonio Corretjer (n.d.). Samuel Putnam Papers, Box 13, SIUC.
119. Pueblos Hispanos, "Pablo Neruda—Hombre de Pueblos Hispanos," *Pueblos Hispanos* (Feb. 20, 1943); Pablo Neruda, "Canto de amor a Stalingrado," *Pueblos Hispanos* (Feb. 27, 1943): 7.
120. For an expanded study of Burgos's Good Neighbor–era poetry and her FBI file, see Harris Feinsod, "Between Dissidence and Good Neighbor Diplomacy: Reading Julia de Burgos with the FBI," *Centro: Journal of the Center for Puerto Rican Studies* 26.2 (2014): 98–127.
121. Maxwell defines the bureau's practice of ghostreading as "a duplicitous interpretive enterprise [. . .] grasped through its effects if not always caught in the act." He argues that the FBI ought to be regarded as "perhaps the most dedicated and influential forgotten critic" of African-American writing. My term "ghost-translators" extends Maxwell's account. See William J. Maxwell, *F. B. Eyes: How J. Edgar Hoover's Ghostreaders Framed African American Literature* (Princeton University Press, 2015): 5, 127.
122. Julia de Burgos, "Campo," *Pueblos Hispanos* (July 3, 1943): 10.
123. United States Federal Bureau of Investigation. Julia de Burgos file deposited by Jack Agüeros in the Jack Agüeros Papers, Assorted documents dated July 6, 1944, to March 1, 1955. Internal case file no. 100–60530. CUL.
124. "Scrapbook." Frances R. Grant Papers, Box 22, RUL.
125. Edwin Honig to Angel Flores (d. 1943). Angel Flores Papers, HRC.
126. Earl Browder, *Victory—and after* (New York: International Publishers, 1942); Earl Browder, *Victoria y post-guerra*, tr. Juan Antonio Corretjer (Havana: Editorial Paginas, 1943). Compare the weight Browder gives Puerto Rico to Republican politician Wendell Willkie's bestselling travelogue *One World* (New York: Simon

and Schuster, 1943), whose global voyage does not mention Puerto Rico, despite the fact that it was the first extra-continental stop of his plane, "The Gulliver."

127. Browder, *Victory*, 218–219.

128. Pablo Neruda, "Watergate, Watergate Everywhere," tr. Nathaniel Tarn, *New York Times* (July 20, 1973).

129. Pablo Neruda to Dudley Fitts (Feb. 8, 1942). Dudley Fitts Papers, Box 2. YALE; Pablo Neruda, *7 de noviembre: Oda a un día de victorias* (Mexico City: España Popular, n.d. [1941])

130. Julia de Burgos, "Campo," *Pueblos Hispanos* 3 (July 10, 1943).

131. United States, Federal Bureau of Investigations. Julia de Burgos file deposited by Jack Agüeros in the Jack Agüeros Papers. Assorted documents dated July 6, 1944, to March 1, 1955. Internal case file no. 100-60530. CUL.

132. The first works to call attention to Martí's achievement in the United States include Jorge Mañach, *Martí: Apostle of Freedom*, tr. Coley Taylor (New York: Devin-Adair, 1950), and José Martí, *The America of José Martí*, tr. Juan de Onís (New York: Noonday, 1953).

133. The spelling "Jeronymo's House" follows the first published edition of the poem. Later editions change it to "Jeronimo's House." Elizabeth Bishop, "Three Key West Poems," *Partisan Review* (Sept. 1941): 383.

134. Marzán's laboriously documented book deepened and prolonged Williams's genealogical self-portrait and cemented it as a major paradigm for understanding Williams as a "bicultural" poet, along with Cohen's recent edition of Williams's translations from Spanish. By contrast, Morse and Read resist identity-driven narratives of Williams's relation to Latin America in order to triangulate Williams's uses of form and history with Brazilian and Chilean vanguards. Lowney adds a nuanced discussion of Williams in the US/Mexico borderlands. Alongside this view of a "hemispheric" Williams, Denning describes his participation in cultural front leftism premised on his regular presence in its periodicals. See William Carlos Williams, *By Word of Mouth: Poems from the Spanish, 1916–1959*, ed. Jonathan Cohen (New York: New Directions, 2011); Julio Marzán, *The Spanish American Roots of William Carlos Williams* (Austin: University of Texas Press, 1994); Richard M. Morse, "Triangulating Two Cubists: William Carlos Williams and Oswaldo de Andrade," *Latin American Literary Review* 14.27 (1986): 175–183; John Lowney, "Reading the Borders of 'The Desert Music'" in *The William Carlos Williams Review* 24.2 (2004): 61–77;. Denning, *The Cultural Front*, 212–213.

135. Williams's *Autobiography* describes his aerial view as a nostalgic trigger for remembrances of his West Indian origins, the New World history of *In the American Grain* (1925), and Hart Crane's "abortive visit to such Carib seas," a muffled reference to Crane's 1932 suicide off the coast of Florida from the SS *Orizaba*. William Carlos Williams, *The Autobiography of William Carlos Williams* (New York: Random House, 1951): 313–315.

136. William Carlos Williams, *Paterson*, ed. Christopher MacGowan (New York: New Directions, 1992): 25–26.

137. Paul Mariani, *William Carlos Williams: A New World Naked* (New York: W. W. Norton, 1990): 449.

138. *First Inter-American Writers' Conference*, 3.
139. *New York Times* (April 22, 1941).
140. Organizers included Robert Morss Lovett, Government Secretary of the Virgin Islands, and "Honorary President" Guy J. Swope, former Democratic Congressman, acting governor of Puerto Rico, and the Department of the Interior's incoming Director of the Division of Territories and Island Possessions. See *First Inter-American Writers' Conference*, 1.
141. *First Inter-American Writers' Conference*, 55.
142. Samuel Putnam, "Carl Sandburg, Other Writers Guess Mr. MacLeish's Real Aims," *Daily Worker* (April 15, 1941): 7.
143. Samuel Putnam, "The Spanking of A. MacLeish," *The New Masses* (May 20, 1941): 21–24.
144. Luis Palés Matos, *Tuntún de pasa y grifería: Poemas afroantillanos* (San Juan: Biblioteca de autores puertorriqueños, 1937): 27.
145. William Carlos Williams, *The Collected Poems of William Carlos Williams Volume II, 1939–1962* (New York: New Directions, 1991): 46.
146. Julia de Burgos, "Campo," *Pueblos Hispanos* (July 3, 1944).
147. Ezra Pound, "Canto LXXXI," in *The Cantos* (New York: New Directions, 1970): 538.
148. William Carlos Williams to Bob Brown (May 11, 1930). Philip Kaplan and Bob Brown Papers, SIUC.
149. Williams, *By Word of Mouth*, 129.
150. William Carlos Williams, *Kora in Hell: Improvisations* (Boston: The Four Seas Press, 1920): 14.
151. R. Arevalo Martinez, "The Sensation of a Smell," tr. William Carlos Williams and William George Williams, *Others* 3.2 (1916): 42.
152. Putnam, "Sandburg," 7.
153. Marzán amplifies the brief, factual discussion in Mariani's *New World Naked*.
154. Williams, *Autobiography*, 71.
155. José Julio Henna and Manuel Zeno Gandía, *The Case of Puerto Rico* (Washington, DC: Press of W. F. Roberts, 1899): 21.
156. Williams, *Autobiography*, 315.
157. Eric Roorda, *The Dictator Next Door: The Good Neighbor Policy and the Trujillo Regime in the Dominican Republic, 1930–1945* (Durham: Duke University Press, 1998).
158. Baraka recalls East Village life a decade later: "you could look out of Tim's window at a big billboard with a picture of Trujillo on it, then dictator of the Dominican Republic. US support for Trujillo was great in those days [. . .]. Some days we'd sit there drinking wine . . . staring out at Trujillo." Amiri Baraka, *The Autobiography of LeRoi Jones* (New York: Freundlich, 1984), 131.
159. Julia de Burgos, *Song of the Simple Truth*, ed. Jack Agüeros (Willimantic, CT: Curbstone Press, 1997): 392–393.
160. Palés Matos, *Tuntún de pasa y grifería*, 25.
161. Williams, *Collected Poems Vol. II*, 45.
162. Michael North, *The Dialect of Modernism: Race, Language, and Twentieth-Century Literature* (London: Oxford University Press, 1992).

163. Julio Marzán, *The Numinous Site: The Poetry of Luis Palés Matos* (Madison, NJ: Fairleigh Dickinson University Press, 1995).
164. César Ayala and Rafael Bernabe, *Puerto Rico in the American Century: A History Since 1898* (Chapel Hill: University of North Carolina Press, 2007).
165. William Carlos Williams, *The Wedge* (Cummington, MA: Cummington Press, 1944).
166. Williams, *Collected Poems Vol. II*, 455.
167. Williams, *Collected Poems Vol. II*, 53.
168. Williams, *Collected Poems Vol. II*, 53.
169. Williams, *Collected Poems Vol. II*, 55.
170. Williams, *Collected Poems Vol. II*, 55.
171. North, *The Dialect of Modernism*, 151–152.
172. Williams, *Collected Poems Vol. II*, 64.
173. Joseph A. Schumpeter, *Capitalism, Socialism and Democracy* (New York: Harper & Brothers, 1942): 83.
174. Williams, *Paterson*, xi.
175. Williams, *Paterson*, xiii.
176. Williams, *Paterson*, 8.
177. Williams, *Paterson*, 10.
178. "William Carlos William Reading at NBC Studios, Washington DC, for the Library of Congress Recording Laboratory" (October 18, 1947).
179. Williams, *Collected Poems Vol. II*, 75.
180. Nicolás Guillén, *Cuba Libre*, tr. Langston Hughes and Ben Carruthers (Los Angeles: Anderson & Ritchie, 1948): 113.
181. Alejo Carpentier, *Music in Cuba*, ed. Timothy Brennan, tr. Alan West-Durán (Minneapolis: University of Minnesota Press, 2001): 8.
182. Roberto Schwartz, *Misplaced Ideas: Essays on Brazilian Culture*, ed. John Gledson (London: Verso, 1992).
183. William Carlos Williams, *Collected Poems Volume I, 1909–1939* (New York: New Directions, 1991): 407.
184. Ibid, 409.
185. Williams, *Collected Poems Vol. II*, 43.
186. Fredric Jameson, *The Modernist Papers* (London: Verso, 2007): 20.
187. In John Huston's film *We Were Strangers* (1949), a Cuban-American man returns to Cuba in 1933 to sow revolution, disguised as a musical talent scout. In Carpentier's novel *Los Pasos Perdidos* (The Lost Steps 1953), the protagonist laments his participation in jingle writing ("poor music used for detestable purposes"). See Alejo Carpentier, *The Lost Steps*, tr. Harriet de Onis (New York: Knopf, 1956): 15.
188. Alfonso Reyes, "La jitanjáfora," in *La experiencia literaria* (Buenos Aires: Losada, 1942); see also Eugène Jolas, "From Jabberwocky to 'Lettrisme' (1948)," in *Eugene Jolas: Critical Writings, 1924–1951*, ed. Rainer Rumold (Evanston: Northwestern University Press, 2009): 184.
189. See Brent Hayes Edwards, "Louis Armstrong and the Syntax of Scat," *Critical Inquiry*. 28.3 (2002): 618–649.
190. "Cha cha, chacha, cha!" borrows from an onomatopoeia common to Cuban danzón, but the now-ubiquitous "*cha-cha-chá*" dance, attributed to Enrique Jorrín's "La Engañadora," was popularized ten years after Williams's poem.
191. Williams, *Collected Poems Vol. I*, 409.

192. The Spanish-American War of 1898 gave the term *incommunicado* idiomatic cur-
     rency, as the US yellow press critiqued the Spanish practice of holding prisoners
     incommunicado. Williams, *Paterson*, 11.
193. Ruiz argues that wartime conscription signals a threshold for regarding Latino
     history as United States history. Vicki L. Ruiz, "Nuestra América: Latino History
     as United States History," *Journal of American History* 93.3 (2006): 666. On bra-
     ceros, see Alicia Schmidt Camacho, *Transnational Imaginaries: Latino Cultural
     Politics in the Mexico-US Borderlands* (New York: NYU Press, 2008): 62–111.
194. Octavio Paz, *Libertad bajo palabra, 1935–1957*, ed. Enrico Mario Santí
     (Madrid: Cátedra, 1988): 376.
195. Muriel Rukeyser, *The Collected Poems of Muriel Rukeyser*, eds. Janet E. Kaufman
     and Anne Herzog (Pittsburgh: University of Pittsburgh Press, 2005): 235.
196. Other significant translations include Miguel León-Portilla, *The Broken Spears*
     (Boston: Beacon Press, 1962); Ricardo Pozas Arciniega, *Juan the Chamula: An
     Ethnological Recreation of the Life of a Mexican Indian* (Berkeley: University of
     California Press, 1962); Rubén Darío, *Selected Poems* (Austin: Texas University
     Press, 1965); Carlos Fuentes, *Aura* (New York: Farrar, Straus and Giroux, 1965);
     Mario Vargas Llosa, *The Time of the Hero* (New York: Grove, 1966); Xavier
     Domingo, *The Dreams of Reason* (New York: G. Braziller, 1966); Paz, *The Other
     Mexico: Critique of the Pyramid* (New York: Grove, 1972); Paz, *The Siren and the
     Seashell: And Other Essays on Poets and Poetry* (Austin: University of Texas Press,
     1976), as well as several major poems by Paz in various collections.
197. Two poems ("Reveille Here and Now" and "On a Wall in Puerto Rico") were
     published in *Poetry* (August 1945), and three others ("Fashions of la Libertad,"
     "Landscapes by Lorca and Disney" and "Little Portrait" were published in *Kenyon
     Review* (Autumn 1945). "Landscape, Puerto Rico," appeared in *Poetry* (April 1946).
198. Donald A. Yerxa, *Admirals and Empire: The United States Navy and the Caribbean,
     1898–1945* (Columbia: University of South Carolina Press, 1991).
199. Studies of the US military in the Americas tend to map distinct local interven-
     tions. See, for example, Mary Renda, *Taking Haiti: Military Occupation and the
     Culture of U.S. Imperialism, 1915–1940* (Chapel Hill: University of North Carolina
     Press, 2001), and Harvey R. Neptune, *Caliban and the Yankees: Trinidad and
     the United States Occupation* (Chapel Hill: University of North Carolina Press,
     2007). Several essays in *Close Encounters of Empire: Writing the Cultural History
     of U.S.—Latin American Relations*, eds. Gilbert M. Joseph, Catherine C. LeGrand,
     and Ricardo D. Salvatore (Durham: Duke University Press, 1998) discuss GIs and
     marines in Central America and the Caribbean, but to my knowledge few or no
     scholars have investigated the writings of WWII-era GIs in Latin America.
200. Lysander Kemp, *The Northern Stranger* (New York: Random House, 1946): 9.
201. William Rose Benet, "Three American Poets," *Saturday Review* (Aug. 31, 1946): 21.
     Vivienne Koch, "Poetry Chronicle," *Sewanee Review* 54.4 (1946): 714.
202. Howard Moss, "Ten Poets," *Kenyon Review* 9.2 (1947): 297.
203. Kemp, *Northern Stranger*, 9.
204. Kemp, *Northern Stranger*, 44.
205. Kemp, *Northern Stranger*, 16.
206. William Z. Foster, *The Crime of El Fanguito: An Open Letter to President Truman
     on Puerto Rico* (New York: New Century, 1948): 3.

207. Lysander Kemp, "Tumbando Caña," *Poetry* 71.1 (1947): 28.

208. Kemp, *Northern Stranger*, 47.

209. Kemp, *Northern Stranger*, 76–77.

Chapter 2

1. Theodor W. Adorno, *Notes to Literature*, tr. Rolf Tiedemann (New York: Columbia University Press, 1991): 174–185.

2. On multilingualism in ethnic modernism, see Joshua Miller, *Accented America: The Cultural Politics of Multilingual Modernism* (New York: Oxford University Press, 2011). On multilingualism in vanguard modernism, see Yunte Huang, *Transpacific Displacement: Ethnography, Translation and Inter-Textual Travel in Twentieth-Century American Literature* (Berkeley: University of California Press, 2002), and Marjorie Perloff, "'Logocinéma of the Frontiersman': Eugene Jolas's Multilingual Poetics and its Legacies," in *Differentials: Poetry, Poetics, Pedagogy* (Tuscaloosa: University of Alabama Press, 2004). Brian Lennon critiques publishing industry use of translation over multilingualism in *In Babel's Shadow: Multilingual Literatures, Monolingual States* (Minneapolis: University of Minnesota Press, 2010). These works avow a poetics of "compression" with debts to Pound's concept of condensation (reducible to the trans-lingual dictum "dichten = condensare"). Touchstones for hemispheric multilingualism include memoirs like Richard Rodriguez's *Hunger of Memory* (New York: Bantam, 1982) and Ilan Stavans's *On Borrowed Words: A Memoir of Language* (New York: Penguin, 2002), and critical accounts such as Gustavo Pérez Firmat's *Tongue Ties: Logo-Eroticism in Anglo-Hispanic Literature* (New York: Palgrave Macmillan, 2003) and Doris Sommer's *Bilingual Aesthetics: A New Sentimental Education* (Durham: Duke University Press, 2004). For a plurilinguistic approach to US literature, see Marc Shell (ed.), *American Babel: Literatures of the United States from Abnaki to Zuni* (Cambridge: Harvard University Press, 2002).

3. Alfonso Reyes, *Última Tule* (Mexico City: Imprenta Universitaria, 1942): 225.

4. Eugène Jolas, "Super-Occident and the Atlantic Language (June 1941)," in *Critical Writings*, 441.

5. Gruesz outlines a shifting history of "language ideologies attaching to Spanish from the colonial period through World War II." She defines language ideology as any interested conception of language in service to a social group, or to an ideal such as the belief that language constitutes nationhood or exemplifies beauty. See Kirsten Silva Gruesz, "Alien Speech, Incorporated: On the Cultural History of Spanish in the US," *American Literary History* 25.1 (2013): 20.

6. Delmore Schwartz, review of *The Man with the Blue Guitar, and Other Poems*, by Wallace Stevens, *Partisan Review* 4.3 (1938): 49–52.

7. Tate: "Our Utopian politics is provincial. It is all very well to meet at Dumbarton Oaks or on the Black Sea to arrange the world, but unless the protagonists of these dramas of journalism have secret powers the presence of which we have hitherto had no reason to suspect, the results for the world must almost necessarily be power politics." Allen Tate, "The New Provincialism," *Virginia Quarterly Review* 21.2 (1945): 262–272; Tate, "El Nuevo Provincialismo," *Orígenes* 8 (1945): 32–40.

8. See Jed Esty, *The Shrinking Island: Modernism and National Culture in England* (Princeton: Princeton University Press, 2004).

9. Arthur Koestler, "The French Flu," in *The Yogi and the Commissar* (London: Jonathan Cape, 1945): 21–27.

10. George Orwell, "Politics and the English Language," *Horizon* 13.76 (1946): 252–265.

11. Herbert Shenton, *International Communication: A Symposium on the Language Problem* (London: K. Paul, Trench, Trubner, 1931); Lancelot Hogben, *Interglossa: A Draft of an Auxiliary for a Democratic World Order, Being an Attempt to Apply Semantic Principles to Language Design* (London: Penguin, 1943); and Frederick Bodmer, *The Loom of Language: An Approach to the Mastery of Many Languages*, ed. Lancelot Hogben (New York: Norton, 1944): 487–521.

12. William Empson, "An American Poet," *Listener* (March 26, 1953).

13. See Donald Davie, *The Purity of Diction in English Verse* (London: Chatto & Windus, 1952): 1–2. "Pure poetry" is a legacy of symbolism in multiple national traditions. See, for example, *An Anthology of Pure Poetry*, ed. George Moore (London: Nonesuch, 1924) and Henri Brémond, *La Poésie pure* (Abbeville: F. Paillart, 1925). See also the polemical response to Spanish pure poetry, such as Pablo Neruda, "Sobre una poesía sin pureza," *Caballo Verde para la Poesía* (October 1, 1935).

14. John Ciardi, *As If: Poems, New and Selected* (New Brunswick: Rutgers University Press, 1955).

15. Hoyos similarly describes Borges's "Aleph" as a metaphor for globalization. Héctor Hoyos, *Beyond Bolaño: The Global Latin American Novel* (New York: Columbia University Press, 2015): 2–5.

16. For Solar's relation to Borges, see John King, "Xul Solar: Buenos Aires, Modernity and Utopia," in *Xul Solar: The Architectures*, ed. Christopher Green and Dawn Ades (London: Courtauld Institute Galleries, 1994); Mario Gradowczyk, *Alejandro Xul Solar* (Buenos Aires: Ediciones ALBA, 1996); and especially *Xul Solar and Jorge Luis Borges: The Art of Friendship*, ed. Gabriela Rangel (New York: Americas Society, 2013).

17. Jorge Luis Borges, *Labyrinths*, tr. James Irby (New York: New Directions, 1961).

18. Lindstrom catalogues features of Solar's language, especially rare neologisms and compound words, prefixes, suffixes, infixes, and Greek and Latin scientific substrates. Patricia Artundo (ed.). *Alejandro Xul Solar: Entrevistas, articulos y textos ineditos* (Buenos Aires: Corregidor, 2005): 170; Naomi Lindstrom, "Xul Solar: Star-Spangler of Languages," *Review* 25–26 (1980): 117–121.

19. Artundo, *Solar*, 77.

20. Artundo, *Solar*, 198.

21. Jorge Luis Borges, "The Analytical Language of John Wilkins," in *Other Inquisitions, 1937–1952*, tr. Ruth L. C. Simms (Austin: University of Texas Press, 1993). Borges links Solar to Wilkins in Jorge Luis Borges, "Autobiographical Notes," *The New Yorker*, with Norman Thomas di Giovanni (Sept. 19, 1970): 77.

22. Sylvia Molloy, "'I Long for Patria': Jorge Luis Borges and Xul Solar," in *The Art of Friendship*, 38.

23. Steiner, *Extraterritorial*, 5.

24. Roman Jakobson, "Closing Statements: Linguistics and Poetics," in Thomas A. Sebeok, *Style in Language* (Cambridge: MIT Press, 1960): 350.

25. My word *xenoglossary* emphasizes diction and individual lexical choices, as distinct from recent scholarly stress on *xenoglossia*, or the performance of foreign language by a speaker who has not learned the language she writes or speaks. See Jennifer Scappettone, "Xenoglossia," in Greene et al., *Princeton Encyclopedia of Poetry and Poetics*, 1543–1544.

26. Alan Filreis, *Wallace Stevens and the Actual World* (Princeton: Princeton University Press, 1991): xv and 187–242.

27. Helen Vendler, "Ice and Fire and Solitude," *New York Review of Books* (Dec. 4, 1997).

28. See Christopher Winks, "Seeking a Cuba of the Self: Baroque Dialogues between José Lezama Lima and Wallace Stevens," in *Baroque New Worlds: Representation, Transculturation, Counterconquest*, eds. Lois Parkinson Zamora and Monika Kaup (Raleigh: Duke University Press, 2010): 597–621, and Eric Keenaghan, *Queering Cold War Poetry: Ethics of Vulnerability in Cuba and the United States* (Columbus: Ohio State University Press, 2009): 31–57.

29. Wallace Stevens, *Collected Poetry and Prose*, eds. Frank Kermode and Joan Richardson (New York: Library of America, 1997): 226.

30. Stevens, *Collected Poetry and Prose*, 298–299.

31. Filreis shows how several poems in *Transport to Summer* build from Stevens's correspondence with Rodríguez Feo. "Paisant Chronicle" defines "major men" for him, while "Attempt to Discover Life" builds on Rodríguez Feo's epistolary portrait of his mother and their house at San Miguel de los Baños. "The Novel," from *The Auroras of Autumn* (1950), borrows at greater length, transcribing Rodríguez Feo's letters directly into the poem. "Someone Puts a Pineapple Together," from *A Necessary Angel* (1951), is an ekphrasis of a painting by the *Orígenes*-affiliated artist Mariano Rodriguez that Stevens owned. See Filreis, *Actual World*, 187–242.

32. Beverly Coyle and Alan Filreis, *Secretaries of the Moon: The Letters of Wallace Stevens and José Rodríguez Feo* (Durham: Duke University Press, 1986).

33. Wallace Stevens, *Letters of Wallace Stevens*, ed. Holly Stevens (Berkeley: University of California Press, 1966): 329.

34. Stevens, *Letters*, 329.

35. Stevens, *Letters*, 331.

36. See Wallace Stevens, "Domingo a la mañana," tr. Jorge Luis Borges and Adolfo Bioy Casares, in *Sur* 113–114 (March–April 1944), a number dedicated to US literature.

37. Stevens, *Letters*, 418.

38. Ramón Fernández also broke through to English-language readerships with *Messages* (New York: Liveright, 1927).

39. Stevens, *Collected Poetry and Prose*, 106.

40. Henry Wallace, "Pan America," in *Democracy Reborn*, ed. Russell Lord (New York: Reynal & Hitchcock, 1944): 159.

41. Pascale Casanova, *The World Republic of Letters* (Cambridge: Harvard University Press, 2004): 96–97.

42. Yvor Winters, *The Anatomy of Nonsense* (Norfolk, CT: New Directions, 1943): 90.

43. See Joseph Leonard, *The Fluent Mundo: Wallace Stevens and the Structure of Reality* (Athens: University of Georgia Press, 1988).

44. Stevens, *Collected Poetry and Prose*, 329–331.

45. Stevens, *Letters*, 231.

46. Stevens, *Collected Poetry and Prose*, 83.

47. Stevens, *Collected Poetry and Prose*, 82–85.

48. Frank Kermode, *Wallace Stevens* (Edinburgh: Oliver and Boyd, 1960).

49. J. Hillis Miller, *Poets of Reality: Six Twentieth-Century Writers* (Harvard University Press, 1965): 226.

50. Jameson, *The Modernist Papers*, 209.

51. Philip Furia and Martin Roth, "Stevens' Fusky Alphabet," *PMLA* 93. 1 (1978): 66–77.

52. Keenaghan, *Queering Cold War Poetry*, 36.

53. Stevens, *Collected Poetry and Prose*, 340.

54. Stevens, *Collected Poetry and Prose*, 644.

55. "West-Indian weather" is the philosophical trope through which Stevens articulates time in his late work: "Time will stand still for a few weeks as the weather itself stands still in August before it removes to Charleston, where it will stand still a little longer before it removes to some place in South America like Cartagena, which is, I suppose, its permanent abode." Stevens, *Collected Poetry and Prose*, 239–241 and Stevens, *Letters*, 642.

56. Winters claims that Stevens might "justifiably be treated [. . .] in a series of essays on literary theorists." Matthiesson calls Stevens more "esthetician" than poet. Perloff links *Transport to Summer* to the emergence of a new US tendency toward theoretically austere poetry. Jameson also regards Stevens as a poet-theorist. See Winters, *The Anatomy of Nonsense*, 88; F. O. Matthiessen, "Wallace Stevens at 67," *New York Times* (April 20, 1947); Marjorie Perloff, "Pound/Stevens: Whose Era? Revisited," *Wallace Stevens Journal* 26.2 (2002): 135–142; Jameson, *A Singular Modernity*, 168.

57. Stevens, *Collected Poetry and Prose*, 342–343.

58. Stevens, *Collected Poetry and Prose*, 335.

59. Stevens, *Collected Poetry and Prose*, 644–645.

60. Stevens, *Collected Poetry and Prose*, 331; Stevens, *Letters*, 434.

61. Stevens, *Letters*, 434.

62. Stevens, *Letters*, 440.

63. Stevens, *Collected Poetry and Prose*, 351.

64. Stevens, *Letters*, 426.

65. John Serio and Greg Foster (eds.), Online Concordance to Wallace Stevens's Poetry, available at http://www.wallacestevens.com/concordance/WSdb.cgi (accessed Feb. 27, 2017).

66. Stevens, *Collected Poetry and Prose*, 350.

67. Stevens, *Collected Poetry and Prose*, 116.

68. Trippe, whose Hispanic first name was a prophetic parental lark, built, from a single mail contract between Key West and Havana in 1927, the planetary system of routes known as Pan American World Airways. From early on, the history of Pan American World Airways was linked to the international avant-garde. Matthew

Josephson's key study of Trippe, *Empire of the Air*, is dedicated to Philippe Soupault (a signatory of the first surrealist manifesto). An avant-garde writer turned muck-raking historian, Josephson was Guillaume Apollinaire's first English translator, and friend of Hart Crane and Allen Tate. His wife Hannah was a friend of Neruda, who visited the Josephsons in New York in 1943. See Hannah Josephson to Pablo Neruda (December 1942). FPN.

69. Henry Wallace, *The Century of the Common Man* (New York: Reynal & Hitchcock, 1943): 59.

70. On "globaloney," see Josephson, *Empire of the Air*, 12. On broader debates over aviation, see Wendell Willkie, *One World* (New York: Simon and Schuster, 1943), and Jennifer Van Vleck, *Empire of the Air: Aviation and the American Ascendancy* (Cambridge: Harvard University Press, 2013).

71. Dudley Fitts, *Saturday Review* 26.35 (August 28, 1943): 9.

72. Robert Lowell, "Imagination and Reality," *The Nation* 164 (April 5, 1947).

73. Stevens, *Collected Poetry and Prose*, 289.

74. Empson, "An American Poet."

75. Randall Jarrell, *Poetry and the Age* (New York: Vintage, 1953): 129.

76. F. O. Matthiessen, *American Renaissance: Art and Expression in the Age of Emerson and Whitman* (New York: Oxford University Press, 1941): 529.

77. Stevens, *Collected Poetry and Prose*, 376.

78. Julio Ortega, "The Poetry of José Lezama Lima," tr. Claudia J. Elliott, typescript deposited by Clayton Eshleman in the Clayton Eshleman Papers, Box 126, UCSD.

79. Winks, "Seeking a Cuba of the Self," 599.

80. Kenner describes these structures in F. S. Flint's "Contemporary French Poetry" (1912), including Yeatsian syntax, Pound's metonymic fragments, and Eliot's diction. See Hugh Kenner, *The Pound Era* (Berkeley: University of California Press, 1971): 178–181, and Kenner, "Some Post-Symbolist Structures," in Garrick Davis, *Praising it New: The Best of the New Criticism* (Athens: Ohio University Press, 2008): 169–182.

81. Hi Simons, "Wallace Stevens and Mallarmé," *Modern Philology*, 43.4 (1946): 235; Horace Gregory and Marya Zaturenska, *A History of American Poetry: 1900–1940* (New York: Harcourt Brace, 1942): 330.

82. Charles Feidelson, *Symbolism and American Literature* (Chicago: University of Chicago Press, 1953): 73.

83. Marjorie Perloff, "The Supreme Fiction and the Impasse of Modernist Lyric," in Albert Gelpi, *Wallace Stevens: The Poetics of Modernism* (Cambridge: Cambridge University Press, 1985): 50.

84. Reyes, *Última Tule*, 167–168.

85. Morse, *New World Soundings*, 3.

86. Jorge Luis Borges, "Valéry como símbolo," *Sur* 120 (1945): 30–32.

87. Williamson characterizes Borges's post-symbolism in his discussion of the rival *tertulias* of Cansinos-Asséns and Ramón Gómez de la Serna in the Spain of the late teens. Borges fomented post-symbolism through his allegiance to Cansinos-Asséns's group, "who never managed to shake off the symbolist-derived aesthetics of Hispanic *modernismo*." See Edwin Williamson, *Borges: A Life* (New York: Viking, 2004): 77.

88. T. S. Eliot, *From Poe to Valery* (New York: Harcourt Brace, 1948).

89. José Lezama Lima, *Órbita de Lezama Lima*, ed. Armando Álvarez Bravo, (Havana: UNEAC, 1966): 50.

90. Pérez Firmat, "The Strut of the Centipede: José Lezama Lima and New World Exceptionalism," in *Do the Americas Have a Common Literature?*, 318.

91. When Armando Álvarez Bravo interviewed Lezama in 1964, he remarked: "[. . .] you set forth a very personal conception of poetry, a poetic system. The formulation of this system began to take shape in a series of prose fragments included in your book of poems *La fijeza* (1949). What we might classify as theory had its beginnings as poetry." In José Lezama Lima, *Selections*, ed. Ernesto Livon-Grosman (Berkeley: University of California Press, 2005): 125.

92. Stevens, *Collected Poetry and Prose*, 910.

93. See especially Jorge Mañach, "El arcano de cierta poesía nueva: Carta abierta al poeta José Lezama Lima," *Bohemia* (Sept. 25, 1949), and José Lezama Lima, "Respuesta y nuevas interrogantes: Carta abierta a Jorge Mañach," *Bohemia* (Oct. 2, 1949).

94. José Lezama Lima, *El espacio gnóstico americano: Archivo de José Lezama Lima*, ed. Iván González Cruz (Valencia: Universidad Politécnica de Valencia, 2001).

95. Lezama, *Órbita*, 51.

96. José Lezama Lima, *Poesía Completa* (Havana: Editorial Letras Cubanas, 1985): 139–141.

97. Lezama, *Órbita*, 52–53.

98. Cintio Vitier, *Lo cubano en la poesía* (Havana: Instituto del libro, 1970): 436.

99. Vitier, *Lo cubano*, 438.

100. Ben A. Heller, "Landscape, Femininity, and Caribbean Discourse," *MLN* 111.2 (1996): 391–416; Antonio Benítez-Rojo, *The Repeating Island: The Caribbean and the Postmodern Perspective* (Durham: Duke University Press, 1997): 1–22.

101. Lezama, *Órbita*, 55–56.

102. Lezama, *Poesía Completa*, 151; José Lezama Lima, "Thoughts in Havana," tr. James Irby, *Sulfur* 31 (1993): 70.

103. T. S. Eliot, *Collected Poetry, 1909–1962* (New York: Harcourt Brace, 1963): 184.

104. Lezama, *Poesía Completa*, 151.

105. Lezama, "Thoughts in Havana," tr. Irby.

106. Gregory and Zaturenska, *American Poetry*, 327.

107. Lezama, *Poesia Completa*, 152.

108. De Man glosses "hypogram" as a "sub-text" or "infra-text." Paul de Man, "Hypogram and Inscription: Michael Riffaterre's Poetics of Reading," *Diacritics* 11.4 (1981): 17–35.

109. Ben A. Heller, *Assimilation, Generation, Resurrection: Contrapuntal Readings in the Poetry of José Lezama Lima* (Lewisburg, PA: Bucknell University Press, 1997).

110. Juan Ramón Jiménez, *El modernismo: Notas de un curso*, ed. Ricardo Gullon and Eugenio Fernandez Mendez (Madrid: Aguilar, 1962).

111. Lezama, *Poesía Completa*, 152–153.

112. Fernando Ortiz, *Contrapunteo cubano del tabaco y el azúcar* (Havana: Jesús Montero, 1940).

113. Lezama, *Selections*, 131.

114. Lezama, *Selections*, 133.

115. Billitteri describes "primary Cratylism" as a property of a Whitmanian legacy in US poetry. Genette calls Cratylism a symbolist discourse in modern poetry. Mayhew locates secondary Cratylism in works of Jorge Guillén and Claudio Rodríguez. See Carla Billitteri, *Language and the Renewal of Society in Walt Whitman, Laura Riding Jackson, and Charles Olson: The American Cratylus* (New York: Macmillan, 2009); Gérard Genette, *Mimologiques: Voyage en Cratylie* (Paris: Editions du Seuil, 1976); and Jonathan Mayhew, "Jorge Guillén and the Insufficiency of Poetic Language," *PMLA* 106.5 (1991): 1146–1155.

116. Lezama, *Selections*, 94–97.

117. Sylvia Molloy, "Lost in Translation: Borges, the Western Tradition and Fictions of Latin America," in *Borges and Europe Revisited*, ed. Evelyn Fishburn (London: Institute of Latin American Studies, University of London, 1998): 13.

118. Jorge Luis Borges, *The Craft of Verse* (Cambridge: Harvard University Press, 2000): 80–81.

119. See, for example, "The Poet's Creed," his sixth and final Charles Eliot Norton Lecture at Harvard University in 1967–1968. Borges, *The Craft of Verse*, 97–124.

120. Borges, "Autobiographical Notes," 42.

121. Borges, "Autobiographical Notes," 41.

122. Borges, "Autobiographical Notes," 43.

123. Borges, "Autobiographical Notes," 44.

124. Borges, "Autobiographical Notes," 51.

125. Selden Rodman, *Tongues of Fallen Angels* (New York: New Directions, 1974): 14–15.

126. Borges, "Autobiographical Notes," 48.

127. John Updike, "The Author as Librarian," *The New Yorker* (Oct. 30, 1965): 234; Robert Alter, "Borges and Stevens: A Note on Post-Symbolist Writing," *TriQuarterly* 25 (1972): 323–333.

128. Alfred Kazin, "Meeting Borges," *New York Times* (May 2, 1971).

129. Borges, "Autobiographical Notes," 74.

130. Ronald Christ, *The Narrow Act: Borges' Art of Illusion* (New York: New York University Press, 1969): 44; Maria Mudrovic, "Borges y el Congreso por la Libertad de la Cultura," *Variaciones Borges* 36 (2013): 77–104.

131. Stewart challenges this timeline. See Susan Stewart, "Mirror, Mask, Labyrinth," *The Nation* (June 30, 2010).

132. On Borges's relationship with di Giovanni, see Matthew Howard, "Stranger than Ficción," *Lingua Franca* (June–July 1997).

133. Jorge Luis Borges, *Textos recobrados (1931–1955)*, eds. Sara Luisa del Carril and Mercedes Rubio de Zocchi (Buenos Aires: Emecé, 2001): 235. See also Borges, *Craft of Verse*, 89–90.

134. Jorge Luis Borges, *Historia de la eternidad* (Buenos Aires: F.A. Columbo, 1936).

135. Balderston has discovered a manuscript of a third English poem written contemporaneously. Daniel Balderston, "Borges's Only Writing in English: Three English Poems," Lecture, "Text as Process: Genetic and Textual Criticism in the Digital Age," Conference at the University of Pittsburgh (April 6, 2016).

136. Jorge Luis Borges, *Obra poética, 1923–1976* (Buenos Aires: Emecé, 1977): 179.

137. Jorge Luis Borges, *El informe de Brodie: Historia universal de la infamia* (Esplugas de Llobregat: Ediciones G. P., 1970).

138. Jorge Luis Borges, *Textos recobrados*, 185.

139. "La inocencia de Layamón," *Sur* 197 (1951): 18–21.

140. Williamson, *Borges: A Life*, 342.

141. Borges's own account of learning Anglo-Saxon is in "Autobiographical Notes," 93–94.

142. Borges, *Obra poética*, 155.

143. Alaisdair Reid's "Embarking on the Study of Anglo-Saxon Grammar" is the template for my translation, but I depart from it in several places. See Jorge Luis Borges, *Selected Poems 1923–1967*, ed. Norman Thomas di Giovanni (New York: Delacorte, 1972): 139.

144. Robert Harrison, *The Dominion of the Dead* (Chicago: University of Chicago Press, 2003): 85–86.

Chapter 3

1. Waldo Frank to Pablo Neruda (Dec. 16, 1953), FPN.

2. Delpar, *Looking South*, 129, 184; See also Fox, *Making Art Panamerican*, 13.

3. Roberto Fernández Retamar, "Intercomunicación y nueva literatura," in César Fernández Moreno, *América Latina en su literatura* (Mexico City: Siglo Veintiuno, 1972). Partially translated by Mary C. Berg as *Latin America in Its Literature* (New York: Holmes & Meier, 1980).

4. Cohn, *The Latin American Literary Boom*, 37–64.

5. Barnhisel, *Cold War Modernism*, 93–135.

6. Karl E. Meyer, *The Maya Crisis: A Report on the Pillaging of Maya Sites in Mexico and Guatemala, and a Proposal for a Rescue Fund* (Washington, DC: Privately printed, 1972): 13.

7. Charles Morrow Wilson, "Open Sesame to the Maya," *Bulletin of the Pan American Union* 82.7 (1948): 376–384.

8. Ernesto Cardenal, *Homenaje a los indios americanos* (León: UNAN, 1969): 39.

9. Gordon Brotherston, *The Book of the Fourth World: Reading the Native Americas through Their Literature* (Cambridge: Cambridge University Press, 1995). See also Brotherston, "Indigenous Americas, Poetry of the," in Greene et al., *Princeton Encyclopedia of Poetry and Poetics*, 690–701.

10. Rubén Darío, "Palabras Liminares," in *Prosas profanas y otros poemas* (Buenos Aires: Pablo E. Coni e hijos, 1896).

11. James Clifford, *The Predicament of Culture: Twentieth-Century Ethnography, Literature, and Art* (Cambridge: Harvard University Press, 1989): 117–151.

12. Jeffrey Belnap, "Diego Rivera's Greater America: Pan-American Patronage, Indigenism, and *H.P.*," *Cultural Critique* 63 (2006): 65.

13. Barnett Newman, *Barnett Newman: Selected Writings and Interviews*, eds. John P. O'Neill, Mollie McNickle (1992): 63. On Newman's "Inter-American Consciousness," see also Bill Anthes, *Native Moderns: American Indian Painting, 1940–1960* (Durham: Duke University Press, 2006): 56–86.

14. Joann Phillips, *Los Angeles Art Community: Group Portrait: Emerson Woelffer* (Los Angeles: UCLA, 1977): 64.

15. Some Huston spoils were later revealed to be works of the forger Brígido Lara. See "Mexico: Treasure Traffic," *Time* (March 30, 1959); Lawrence Grobel, *The Hustons* (New York: Cooper Square Press, 1989).

16. On smuggling Mayan artifacts, see Meyer, *The Maya Crisis*. On the stolen art trade in general, see Meyer, *The Plundered Past: The Story of the Illegal International Traffic in Works of Art* (New York: Atheneum, 1973). Charles Portis's *Gringos* (1991) novelizes expatriate US looters in the Yucatán.

17. Morton Dauwen Zabel, "Harriet Monroe: December 23, 1860–September 26, 1936," *Poetry* 49.2 (1936): 93.

18. *The First Inter-American Writers' Conference of the University of Puerto Rico, April 14–23, 1941* (Rio Piedras, PR: The University, 1941): 44.

19. Michael Castro, *Interpreting the Indian: Twentieth-Century Poets and the Native American* (Albuquerque: New Mexico University Press, 1983): 49–50. See also Kenneth Lincoln, *Sing with the Heart of a Bear: Fusions of Native and American Poetry, 1890–1999* (Berkeley: University of California Press, 2000): xvi.

20. Park, *Pan American Imagination*, 20–54.

21. Pablo Neruda, *The Heights of Macchu Picchu*, tr. Nathaniel Tarn (New York: Farrar, Strauss and Giroux, 1966): 27.

22. Charles Olson, *The Collected Poems of Charles Olson*, ed. Geroge F. Butterick (Berkeley: University of California Press, 1987): 93.

23. Allen Ginsberg, *Collected Poems 1947–1997* (New York: Harper Collins, 2006): 109.

24. Charles Olson and Robert Creeley, *The Complete Correspondence*, Vol. 4 (Santa Rosa: Black Sparrow, 1982): 63.

25. Rose Macaulay, *Pleasure of Ruins* (London: Weidenfeld and Nicolson, 1953): xv–xvi.

26. Thomas McFarland, *Romanticism and the Forms of Ruin* (Princeton: Princeton University Press, 1981): 29.

27. Ángel Rama, *Transculturación narrativa en América Latina* (Mexico City: Siglo Veintiuno, 1982).

28. Nick Yablon, *Untimely Ruins: An Archaeology of American Urban Modernity, 1819–1919* (Chicago: University of Chicago Press, 2009).

29. Andreas Huyssen, "Nostalgia for Ruins," *Grey Room* 23 (2006): 6–21.

30. Octavio Paz, "La flor saxífraga: W. C. Williams," in *Excursiones/Incursiones* 2: 300.

31. On site-specificity, see Lytle Shaw, *Fieldworks: From Place to Site in Postwar Poetics* (Tuscaloosa: University of Alabama Press, 2013), 45–88.

32. Charles Olson, *Mayan Letters* (Mallorca: Divers Press, 1953).

33. Ginsberg, *Collected Poems*, 115.

34. See David Ekbladh, *The Great American Mission: Modernization and the Construction of an American World Order* (Princeton: Princeton University Press, 2010).

35. Octavio Paz, *The Bow and the Lyre*, tr. Ruth Simms (Austin: University of Texas Press, 1973): 241.

36. Charles Olson, *Collected Prose*, ed. Donald Allen and Ben Friedlander (Berkeley: University of California Press, 1997): 159–160.

37. Mark Greif, *The Age of the Crisis of Man: Thought and Fiction in America, 1933-1973* (Princeton: Princeton University Press, 2015).

38. Olson, *Selected Writing*, 93.

39. Jorge Coronado, *The Andes Imagined: Indigenismo, Society, and Modernity* (Pittsburgh: University of Pittsburgh Press, 2009).

40. Manuel Luis Martinez, "'With Imperious Eye': Kerouac, Burroughs, and Ginsberg on the Road in South America," *Aztlan* 23.1 (1998): 41.

41. Heriberto Yépez, *The Empire of Neomemory*, tr. Jen Hofer, Christian Nagler, and Brian Whitener (Oakland: ChainLinks, 2013).

42. Octavio Paz, *Early Poems: 1935–1955*, tr. Muriel Rukeyser et al. (New York: New Directions, 1973): 96–97.

43. Octavio Paz, *Selected Poems*, tr. Muriel Rukeyser (Bloomington: Indiana University Press, 1963): 12.

44. Hugo Montes, *Machu Picchu en la poesía* (Santiago: Nueva Universidad, 1972): 9.

45. Montes, *Machu Picchu*, 23.

46. Alejandro Lipschutz, "Pablo Neruda como indigenista," *Revista Pro-Arte* 157 (Sept. 16, 1952).

47. Pablo Neruda, *Alturas de Macchu Picchu* (Santiago: Nascimento, 1954).

48. Santiago del Campo, "Neruda está en Macchu Picchu," *Pro-Arte* 17 (Nov. 4, 1948): 1.

49. See Edmundo Olivares Briones, *Pablo Neruda: Los caminos de América, tras las huellas del poeta itinerante III (1940–1950)* (Santiago: LOM, 2004): 328–344, and John Felstiner, *Translating Neruda: The Way to Macchu Picchu* (Stanford: Stanford University Press, 1980).

50. Pablo Neruda, *Memoirs*, tr. Hardie St. Martin (New York: Farrar, Straus & Giroux, 1976): 165–166.

51. José Uriel García to Pablo Neruda (Feb. 11, 1940), FPN.

52. Uriel García to Neruda, (Feb. 11, 1940), FPN.

53. Critics of the hour debated Neruda's world literary status. In Chile, Parra pronounced him the "Peregrino de cincuenta países," Muñoz granted him an "undisputed Universality," and a university exhibition hailed "Neruda en todos los idiomas." By contrast, U.S.-based liberal critics refuted his global reach. Belitt suggested that "the *Canto General* is specifically a *Canto General de Chile*," and that his "continental sweep and bravura" are inseparable "from the *tierra* of the poet's birth." Milosz wrote: "I am inclined to believe him as long as he speaks about what he knows; I stop believing him when he starts to speak about what I know myself." See Nicanor Parra, "Salutación a Neruda," and Diego Muñoz, "Universalidad de su poesía," *Pro Arte* 157 (1952): 3; Antonio Quintano, "Neruda en la exposición," Universidad de Chile, 1954, FPN; Ben Belitt, "Pablo Neruda and the 'Gigantesque,'" *Poetry* 80.2 (1952): 117; Czeslaw Milosz, *The Captive Mind*, tr. Jane Zielonko (New York: Knopf, 1953): 234.

54. Enrico Mario Santí, *Pablo Neruda: The Poetics of Prophecy* (Ithaca: Cornell University Press, 1982): 112.

55. Filreis and Coyle, *Secretaries of the Moon*, 92.

56. Pablo Neruda, "Reportaje a Neruda," *Pro Arte* 157 (1952): 1.

57. Santiago del Campo, "Neruda está en Macchu Picchu," 1.

58. Tarn, *Embattled Lyric*, 61–67.

59. Tarn, *Embattled Lyric*, 62.

60. Tarn, *Embattled Lyric*, 63.

61. Tarn, *Embattled Lyric*, 65.

62. Emir Rodríguez Monegal, *El viajero inmóvil* (Buenos Aires: Losada, 1966): 106. Rodríguz Monegal may have inflated the 1,000 people reported at the time of this "estrepitoso homenaje de despedida." See *Excelsio* (August 29, 1943): 2.

63. Neruda, *Heights of Macchu Picchu*, ix.

64. Neruda, *Memoirs*, 313.

65. Franco recounts a 1950 reading in Florence, Italy, "before an audience of thousands, and thousands, and thousands of Italian trade unionists." The poems "were rapturously applauded line by line, especially where certain key-words, like *Fascismo*, came up. I, too, found myself applauding madly, particularly at all of the kind of key-words, along with the rest of the people, totally caught up in an electric sort of atmosphere. [. . .] An essential aspect of the poetry reading of Neruda was evident at this meeting: a kind of communion with the audience, an event which he undoubtedly enjoyed more than anything else." Jean Franco, "Orfeo en Utopía: El poeta y la colectividad en el *Canto general*," in *Simposio Pablo Neruda*, eds. Isaac Jack Lévy and Juan Loveluck (Columbia: University of South Carolina Press, 1974): 267.

66. Neruda, *Heights of Macchu Picchu*, 18–19.

67. Neruda, *Heights of Macchu Picchu*, 2–3.

68. Neruda, *Heights of Macchu Picchu*, 38–39. Greene reads *Alturas* as a post-Petrarchan lyric sequence with América as a Petrarchan love object. See Roland Greene, *Post-Petrarchism: Origins and Innovations of the Western Lyric Sequence* (Princeton: Princeton University Press, 1991): 195–229.

69. Neruda, *Heights of Macchu Picchu*, 26–27.

70. Neruda, *Heights of Macchu Picchu*, 46–47.

71. Del Campo, "Neruda está en Macchu Picchu," 1.

72. George Kubler, "Machu Picchu," *Perspecta* 6 (1960): 50.

73. Kubler, "Machu Picchu," 54.

74. Tarn, *Embattled Lyric*, 65.

75. Mary Oppen, *Meaning a Life: An Autobiography* (Santa Rosa: Black Sparrow Press, 1990); Peter Nicholls, *George Oppen and the Fate of Modernism* (Oxford and New York: Oxford University Press, 2007); Rebecca Schreiber, *Cold War Exiles in Mexico: U.S. Dissidents and the Culture of Critical Resistance* (Minneapolis: University of Minnesota Press, 2008).

76. E-mail correspondence with Linda Oppen, October 5, 2013.

77. David Alfaro Siqueiros, *José Venturelli: Galeria de Arte Mexicano del 16 al 31 de octubre de 1950* (Mexico City: Galeria de arte mexicano, [1950]).

78. Robert Pring Mill, Conversations with José Venturelli, Geneva, Switzerland, 1986. Typescript Jan. 24, 1989. Robert Pring-Mill Neruda Collection, Box 9. TLOU.

79. DuPlessis quips that in Mexico he did not so much as sign a check that survives. Rachel Blau DuPlessis, *The Selected Letters of George Oppen* (Durham: Duke University Press, 1990).

80. Walter Lowenfels, "Voyage to Chile," enclosed in a June 10, 1967, letter to Margaret Randall, El Corno Emplumado Collection, HRC.

81. Nuñez earlier argued the same point. See Guy Davenport, "Scholia and Conjectures for Olson's 'The Kingfishers,'" *boundary 2* 2.1/2 (1973/1974): 250–262; Estuardo Nuñez, "Literatura sobre Machu Picchu," *Journal of Inter-American Studies* 5.4 (1963): 461–464.

82. Possibly, Olson read *Alturas* in H. R. Hays' translation in *The Tiger's Eye*. Olson also purchased Flores's translations of *Residence on Earth* (New York: New Directions, 1946) in 1947. In "The Kingfishers," the line "Not one death but many" may quote *Alturas*. However, Olson's source-driven writing has constrained critics to loudly attest or protest direct influences, arguing that "Neruda was not one of his influences" and that in the absence of direct citation, "mere comparisons and general parallels are not enough." See George Butterick, "Charles Olson's 'The Kingfishers' and the Poetics of Change," *American Poetry* 6:2 (1989): 28–69, and Ralph Maud, *What Does Not Change: The Significance of Charles Olson's "The Kingfishers"* (Madison: Fairleigh Dickinson University Press, 1998): 30.

83. Brotherston, *Latin American Poetry*, 27.

84. Jill S. Kuhnheim, *Spanish American Poetry at the End of the Twentieth Century: Textual Disruptions* (Austin: University of Texas Press, 2004): 10.

85. Charles Olson and Robert Creeley, *The Complete Correspondence*, Vol. 5, ed. George Butterick (Santa Barbara: Black Sparrow, 1985): 50.

86. Tyrus Miller, *Time-Images: Alternative Temporalities in Twentieth Century Theory, Literature and Art* (Newcastle: Cambridge Scholars, 2009): 202.

87. Clifford, *The Predicament of Culture*, 117.

88. Edward Dorn, *Hands Up!* (New York: Totem-Corinth, 1963): n.p.

89. Olson, *Collected Prose*, 206–207.

90. James J. Parsons, "'Mr. Sauer' and the Writers," *Geographical Review* 86.1 (1996): 22–41.

91. *Tlalocan* 1 (Sacramento: The House of Tlaloc, 1943).

92. Lawrence Hart, "A Note on Robert Barlow," *Poetry* 78.2 (1951): 115–118.

93. Robert Barlow, *Eyes of the God: The Weird Fiction and Poetry of R. H. Barlow*, ed. S. T. Joshi et al. (New York: Hippocampus, 2002): 192. Other collections include Robert Barlow, *Poems for a Competition* (Sacramento: The Fugitive Press, 1942); Robert Barlow, *View from a Hill* (Azcapotzalco: [Impresora Insurgentes], 1947); and Robert Barlow, *Accent on Barlow: A Commemorative Anthology*, ed. Lawrence Hart (San Rafael: Lawrence Hart, 1962).

94. Brotherston, *Book of the Fourth World*, 311.

95. Michael D. Coe, *Breaking the Maya Code* (New York: Thames and Hudson, 1992).

96. John Lloyd Stephens, *Incidents of Travel in Yucatán* (London: John Murray, 1843).

97. Olson and Creeley, *Complete Correspondence*, Vol. 5, 100.

98. On "spontaneity" in Olson's glyphic writing, see Daniel Belgrad, *The Culture of Spontaneity: Improvisation and the Arts in Postwar America* (Chicago: University of Chicago Press: 1998).

99. Olson, *Collected Poems*, 92–93.

100. Williams, *Spring & All*, 5.

101. Olson, *Collected Poems*, 88.

102. Martin Duberman, *Black Mountain: An Exploration in Community* (New York: E. P. Dutton, 1972): 373.

103. Olson and Creeley, *Complete Correspondence*, Vol. 5, 90.

104. Olson and Creeley, *Complete Correspondence*, Vol. 5, 85.

105. Olson and Creeley, *Complete Correspondence*, Vol. 5, 49.

106. Olson and Creeley, *Complete Correspondence*, Vol. 5, 24.

107. Olson and Creeley, *Complete Correspondence*, Vol. 5, 26.

108. Olson and Creeley, *Complete Correspondence*, Vol. 5, 32.

109. Johannes Fabian, *Time and the Other: How Anthropology Makes Its Object* (New York: Columbia University Press, 2014).

110. "Foreign News: The Pause that Arouses," *Time* (March 13, 1950). See also Reinholdt Wagnleitner, *Coca-Colonization and the Cold War: The Cultural Mission of the United States in Austria after the Second World War* (Chapel Hill: University of North Carolina Press, 1994).

111. Charles Olson, "The Art of the Language of Mayan Glyphs," *Alcheringa* 5 (1973): 100.

112. Olson, "Language of Mayan Glyphs," 96.

113. Olson and Creeley, *Complete Correspondence*, Vol. 5, 100.

114. Olson, *Selected Writings*, 53–54.

115. Olson, *Selected Writings*, 62–63.

116. Antonello Gerbi, *The Dispute of the New World: The History of a Polemic, 1750–1900*, tr. Jeremy Moyle (Pittsburgh: University of Pittsburgh Press, 1973).

117. Olson and Creeley, *Complete Correspondence*, Vol. 4, 127–131.

118. Olson, *Collected Poems*, 214.

119. Olson, *Collected Poems*, 215.

120. Olson, *Collected Poems*, 216.

121. Tom Clark, *Charles Olson: Allegory of the Poet's Life* (New York: Norton, 1991): 241.

122. Allen Ginsberg, *The Letters of Allen Ginsberg*, ed. Bill Morgan (New York: Da Capo, 2008): 202–214.

123. On Ginsberg's old left nostalgia, see Ben Lee, "*Howl and Other Poems*: Is There Old Left in These New Beats?" *American Literature* 76.2 (2004): 367–389.

124. Allen Ginsberg, *Howl and Other Poems* (San Francisco: City Lights, 1956).

125. Lewis Hyde, *On the Poetry of Allen Ginsberg* (Ann Arbor: University of Michigan Press, 1984): 49. Ginsberg named the poem, but once erroneously attributed the title to Kerouac in a dedication. "Several phrases and the title of *Howl* are taken from him." See Ginsberg, *Howl: Original Draft Facsimile*, ed. Barry Miles (New York: Harper and Row, 1986).

126. Ginsberg, *Howl*, 7.

127. Hyde, *Ginsberg*, 26.

128. Charles Olson, *In Adullam's Lair* (Provincetown: To the Lighthouse Press, 1975): 16.

129. Richard Eberhart, "West Coast Rhythms," *New York Times Book Review* (Sept. 2, 1956).

130. Hyde, *Ginsberg*, 29.

131. Hyde, *Ginsberg*, 26.

132. Albert Camus, *The Stranger*, tr. Stuart Gilbert (New York: Knopf, 1946).

133. J. W. Ehrlich, *Howl of the Censor* (San Carlos: Nourse, 1961): 35.

134. The only prior use is a 1943 cowboy doggerel poem: "Bury me out on the prairie/Where the coyotes can howl o'er my grave." Allen Ginsberg, *The Book of Martyrdom and Artifice: First Journals and Poems, 1937–1952*, ed. Bill Morgan (New York: Da Capo Press, 2006): 28.

135. Ginsberg, *Collected Poems*, 100.

136. Allen Ginsberg, *Journals: Early Fifties Early Sixties*, ed. Gordon Ball (New York: Grove Press, 1977): 30–31.

137. William Burroughs, *The Yage Letters Redux*, ed. Oliver Harris (San Francisco: City Lights, 2006).

138. For brief biographical accounts, see Michael Schumacher, *Dharma Lion: A Critical Biography of Allen Ginsberg* (New York: St. Martin's Press, 1994) and Barry Miles, *Allen Ginsberg: A Biography* (New York: Harper Perennial, 1990): 155–165. On Ginsberg's early poems, see Glen Burns, *Great Poets Howl: A Study of Allen Ginsberg's Poetry, 1943–1955* (Frankfurt am Main: Peter Lang, 1983). My account is based on Ginsberg's papers.

139. Nathaniel Tarn, Guatemala Field Notes, Box 106, Nathaniel Tarn Papers, SUL.

140. Alberto Ruz Lhuillier, *Palenque 1947–1958* (Mexico City: Instituto Nacional de Antropología e Historia, 2007).

141. Ginsberg, *Collected Poems*, 44.

142. Ginsberg, *Collected Poems*, 111.

143. Allen Ginsberg to Lucien Carr (Feb. 18, 1954). Allen Ginsberg Collection, SUL.

144. Ginsberg, *Collected Poems*, 100.

145. Allen Ginsberg, *Howl and Other Poems* (San Francisco: City Lights, 1956): 37.

146. Ginsberg to Carr (April 1, 1954), Allen Ginsberg Collection, SUL.

147. Ginsberg, *Collected Poems*, 111.

148. Ginsberg, *Letters*, 202.

149. Ginsberg, *Letters*, 214.

150. Ginsberg, *Collected Poems*, 108.

151. Ginsberg, *Collected Poems*, 6.

152. Ginsberg, *Collected Poems*, 105.

153. Ginsberg, *Collected Poems*, 106.

154. Ginsberg, *Collected Poems*, 106–107.

155. Ginsberg, *Howl and Other Poems*, 10, 12, 18.

156. Ginsberg wrote to Lamantia in the 1980s to request permission to out Lamantia's role in inspiring this line. Allen Ginsberg to Philip Lamantia (Nov. 15, 1985), Philip Lamantia Papers, Carton 1, Folder 14, UCB.

157. John Hoffman and Philip Lamantia, *Tau and Journey to the End*, ed. Garrett Caples (San Francisco: City Lights, 2008).

158. Ginsberg, *Collected Poems*, 114.

159. Ginsberg, *Deliberate Prose*, 442.

160. Philip Lamantia, *The Collected Poems of Philip Lamantia*, eds. Garrett Caples, Andrew Joron, and Nancy Joyce Peters (Berkeley: University of California Press, 2013): 121.

161. Philip Lamantia, Journal of a visit with the Nayeri (April–May, 1955), Philip Lamantia Papers, Carton 5, Folder 28, UCB.

162. Lamantia, *Collected Poems*, 143.
163. Lamantia, *Collected Poems*, 145.
164. Ernesto Cardenal, *Homenaje a los indios americanos* (León: Universidad Autonoma de Nicaragua, 1969): 29.
165. Cardenal, *Homenaje*, 40.
166. Lawrence Ferlinghetti, *Starting Out from San Francisco* (New York: New Directions, 1961): 33.
167. Ferlinghetti, *Starting Out*, 35.
168. Fernando Alegría, "Chileans Shouted 'Bravo' When the Beats Read Poetry," *San Francisco Sunday Chronicle* (Feb. 14, 1960): 16; Fernando Alegría and Lawrence Ferlinghetti interviewed by Dale Miner (Winter 1960). Fernando Alegría Papers, Box 86, Tape 7, SUL.
169. Alegría and Ferlinghetti interviewed by Dale Miner, Fernando Alegría Papers, Box 86, Tape 7, SUL.
170. For example, Louis Armstrong contemporaneously staged himself as an authentic diplomatic alternative in songs such as "Who's The Real Ambassador." See Von Eschen, *Satchmo Blows Up the World*, 87–89.
171. "Que Cristo fue anarquista dice el poeta Ferlinghetti," *La Prensa* (Feb. 4, 1960).
172. Martín Adán, *La mano desasida: Canto a Machu Picchu* (Lima: Juan Mejía Baca, 1964): 17.
173. Adán, *La mano desasida*, 25.
174. Greene, *Post-Petrarchism*, 231; Jim Anchante Arias, *Poesía, ser y quimera: Estudio de La mano desasida de Martín Adán* (Lima: Vicio Perpetuo Vicio Perfecto, 2012): 50.
175. Clayton Eshleman produced an unpublished translation of Hidalgo's *Patria* complete for Rafael Squirru in 1964–1965. Clayton Eshleman Papers, Box 61 Folder 19, UCSD.

Chapter 4

1. Margaret Randall, "Editor's Note," *El Corno Emplumado* 1 (1962): 1.
2. Ernesto Cardenal to Sergio Mondragón, *El Corno Emplumado* 5 (1964): 146.
3. Rafael Squirru to Paul Blackburn (April 3, 1962). Paul Blackburn Papers, Box 44, Folder 13, UCSD.
4. Paul Blackburn, "The International Word," *The Nation* (April 21, 1962): 358.
5. Claudia Gilman, *Entre la pluma y el fusil* (Buenos Aires: Siglo XXI, 2003): 35.
6. Bernstein, "Poetics of the Americas," 1.
7. On anthologies, see Jed Rasula, *The American Poetry Wax Museum: Reality Effects, 1940–1990* (Urbana: National Council of Teachers of English, 1996); on scenes, see Daniel Kane, *All Poets Welcome: The Lower East Side Poetry Scene in the 1960s* (Berkeley: University of California Press, 2003); on sites, see Shaw, *Fieldworks*.
8. Kenneth Rexroth, "Bearded Barbarians or Real Bards?" *New York Times Book Review* (February 12, 1961): 1.
9. See, for example, Eliot Weinberger, *American Poetry since 1950: Innovators & Outsiders* (New York: Marsilio, 1993); Alan Golding, *From Outlaw to Classic: Canons in American Poetry* (Madison: University of Wisconsin Press, 1995); Barrett Watten, *The Constructivist Moment: From Material Text to Cultural Poetics*

(Middletown: Wesleyan University Press, 2003); Gillian White, *Lyric Shame: The "Lyric" Subject of Contemporary American Poetry* (Cambridge: Harvard University Press, 2014).

10. Oren Izenberg, *Being Numerous: Poetry and the Ground of Social Life* (Princeton: Princeton University Press, 2011): 4–12; also Marjorie Perloff, "Whose New American Poetry?: Anthologizing in the Nineties," *Diacritics* 26.3 (1996): 104–123; Stephen Burt, "Is American Poetry Still a Thing?" *ALH* 28.2 (2016): 271–287; and Jahan Ramazani, "Lines and Circles: Transnationalizing American Poetry Studies," *ALH* 28.2 (2016): 308–314.

11. Donna Hollenberg, *A Poet's Revolution: The Life of Denise Levertov* (Berkeley: University of California Press, 2013): 145.

12. On Lamantia in Mexico, see Lamantia, *Collected Poems*, xxiii–lxiv.

13. Donald Allen (ed.), *The New American Poetry: 1945–1960* (New York: Grove Press, 1960): 169.

14. Allen, *The New American Poetry*, 430.

15. Gregory Corso, *Gasoline* (San Francisco: City Lights, 1958): 23.

16. Robert Creeley, *The Selected Letters of Robert Creeley*, ed. Rod Smith et al. (Berkeley: University of California Press, 2014): 182–249.

17. For example, Blackburn wrote to Creeley: "Because of Cuba and one thing and another I've been looking more closely at Central and South America—and I'm wondering how you find Guatemala. Is it really dominated by the United Fruit Co.? I heard it's been very dull since 54–55. I don't know how interested you are in government and politics but I should imagine that one couldn't live there and not have some concern or interest and thoughts on the subject." See Paul Blackburn to Robert Creeley (April 19, 1960). Robert Creeley Papers, Box 11, Folder 34, SUL. See also Ekbert Faas, *Robert Creeley: A Biography* (Hanover: University Press of New England, 2001): 270–271.

18. Robert Creeley, "Statement for the Paterson Society" (Jan. 31, 1961). Robert Creeley Papers, Box 4 Folder 43.1. SUL

19. Robert Creeley, *Collected Poems 1945–1957*, 239.

20. Robert Creeley to Edward Dorn (Oct. 26, 1959). Ed Dorn Papers, UCON.

21. Creeley, "Statement," SUL.

22. Paul Blackburn to Robert Creeley (October 1960). Robert Creeley Papers, SUL.

23. Julio Cortázar, *Cartas 1955–1964* (Buenos Aires: Alfaguara, 2012): 202

24. Clayton Eshleman, *Mexico & North* (Kyoto: Haku-o-do, 1962), n.p.

25. Eliot Weinberger, "Introduction," in *Reversible Monuments: Contemporary Mexican Poetry*, eds. Mónica de la Torre and Michael Wiegers (Port Townsend: Copper Canyon Press, 2002): 14.

26. Louis Simpson, "Death, Death, Death, Death," *The Sixties* 6 (1962): 65–66.

27. Jack Hirschman, *Hip Pocket Poems* 1 (Hanover: Pinwheel Press, 1960).

28. Clayton Eshleman to Margaret Randall (n.d.). El Corno Emplumado Collection, HRC.

29. Robert Creeley, "Olson and Others: Some Orts for the Sports," in *New American Poetry*, 411.

30. Heberto Padilla, "Foreword," tr. Sylvia Carranza, *Cuban Poetry, 1959–1966* (Havana: Book Institute, 1967): 6.

31. Santiago Mathieu, "Sexto Aniversario," *El Corno Emplumado* 15 (1965): 105.

32. Oscar Hurtado, "¿Una Generación Derrotada?," *Lunes de Revolución* (April 18, 1960): 19.

33. Tom Hayden, *Listen, Yankee! Why Cuba Matters* (New York: Seven Stories Press, 2015): xi.

34. Ian Hamilton, *Robert Lowell: A Biography* (New York: Vintage, 1983): 277.

35. Van Gosse, *Where the Boys Are: Cuba, Cold War America, & the Making of a New Left* (London: Verso, 1996): 1.

36. Rafael Rojas, *Fighting Over Fidel: The New York Intellectuals and the Cuban Revolution*, tr. Carl Good (Princeton: Princeton University Press, 2015); Todd Tietchen, *The Cubalogues: Beat Writers in Revolutionary Havana* (Gainesville: University Press of Florida, 2010).

37. Amiri Baraka, *Autobiography of LeRoi Jones*, 161 (see chap. 1, n. 158).

38. Baraka, *Autobiography of LeRoi Jones*, 162.

39. Oscar Hurtado, "Fidel Castro en la poesía norteamericana actual," *Lunes de Revolución* 44 (Jan. 25, 1960): 17.

40. "Los negros en U.S.A." Special issue, *Lunes de Revolución* 44 (July 4, 1960), 36–37.

41. LeRoi Jones, "Cuba Libre," *Evergreen Review* 4.15 (1960): 346–353.

42. Jones reciprocally sparked Shelley's interest in Afro-American jazz and labor. See Shelley, "Occidental Saxo," *El Corno Emplumado* 1: 12.

43. Baraka, *S.O.S.*, 35.

44. LeRoi Jones, "Los libres y los valientes," *Lunes de Revolución* 70 (Aug. 2, 1960): 32.

45. Jones, *S.O.S.*, 38.

46. LeRoi Jones, "How You Sound??" in *The New American Poetry*, 424.

47. Lawrence Ferlinghetti, *Writing Across the Landscape: Travel Journals, 1950–2013* (New York: Liveright, 2015): 40.

48. James Laughlin to Lawrence Ferlinghetti (Nov. 4, 1960). Lawrence Ferlinghetti Papers, Box 34, UCB.

49. Mills depicts U.S. mass media and the fledgling revolutionary news service as a hall of mirrors that mutually distort the two societies, and he attempts to overcome this barrier through acts of journalistic and literary imagination. C. Wright Mills, *Listen, Yankee: The Revolution in Cuba* (New York: Ballantine, 1961): 13.

50. Ferlinghetti to Laughlin (Dec. 13, 1960). Lawrence Ferlinghetti Papers, Box 34, UCB.

51. Ferlinghetti, *Writing Across the Landscape*, 41.

52. Lawrence Ferlinghetti, *The Impeachment of Eisenhower* (Fantasy Records 70004, 1958).

53. Pablo Neruda, "Un minuto cantado para Sierra Maestra," *Lunes de Revolución* 88 (Dec. 26, 1960): 37.

54. Pablo Neruda et al, "'Lunes' conversa con Pablo Neruda," *Lunes de Revolución* 88 (Dec. 26, 1960): 41–42.

55. W. H. Auden, "September 1, 1939," in *Another Time* (London: Faber & Faber, 1940): 112.

56. Lawrence Ferlinghetti, *One Thousand Fearful Words for Fidel Castro* (San Francisco: City Lights, 1961): n.p.

57. *Pa'Lante: Poetry, Polity, Prose of a New World* (New York: The League of Militant Poets, 1962): 5.
58. José Antonio Portuondo, "A New Art for Cuba," in *Pa'Lante*, 48.
59. Michael McClure, "Fidelio," in *Pa'Lante*, 53.
60. Allen Ginsberg, "Prose Contribution to the Cuban Revolution," in *Pa'Lante*, 73.
61. Allen Ginsberg to Robert Creeley (Jan. 4, 1959). Robert Creeley Papers, SUL.
62. Ginsberg, *Collected Poems*, 247.
63. Ginsberg, *Collected Poems*, 247.
64. Jose Mario, "Allen Ginsberg en La Habana," *Mundo Nuevo* (1969): 48–54.
65. Edward Field, *Stand Up, Friend, With Me* (New York: Grove Press, 1963): 66.
66. Field, *Stand Up*, 69.
67. Marc Schleifer, "Juan Pedro Carbo Servia Running Thru the Palace Gate," *El Corno Emplumado* 7 (1963): 60.
68. Blackburn, "The International Word," 358.
69. Kathleen Woodward, *Paul Blackburn: A Checklist* (San Diego: Archive for New Poetry, University of California, 1980).
70. The major exception is Venuti, who offers an excellent account of Blackburn's apprenticeship with Ezra Pound as a modernist poet-translator and describes the subsequent composition of *Proensa*, before touching briefly on Blackburn's relation to Cortázar. See Lawrence Venuti, *The Translator's Invisibility: A History of Translation* Second Edition (Routledge, 2008): 200–231.
71. Paul Blackburn to John Dimoff (April 28, 1966) and Keith Botsford to Paul Blackburn (June 13, 1966). Paul Blackburn Papers, UCSD.
72. Julio Cortázar, *Cartas 1955–1964* (Buenos Aires: Alfaguara, 2012): 150.
73. Cortázar, *Cartas*, 180–181.
74. Cortázar, *Cartas*, 244.
75. Cortázar, *Cartas*, 155.
76. Cortázar, *Cartas*, 156.
77. Cortázar, *Cartas*, 181–182.
78. Cortázar, *Cartas*, 182.
79. Cortázar, *Cartas*, 182.
80. Julio Cortázar, *Historias de cronopios y de famas* (Buenos Aires: Minotauro, 1962): 116.
81. Julio Cortázar, *Cronopios and Famas*, tr. Paul Blackburn (New York: Pantheon, 1969): 114.
82. Cortázar, *Cartas*, 247.
83. Paul Blackburn, "The Cronopios in America – 1," *Floating Bear* 20 (1962): 3.
84. Jacob Smith, *Spoken Word: Postwar American Phonograph Cultures* (Berkeley: University of California Press, 2011): 49–79.
85. Blackburn to Cortázar (Jan. 24, 1964), Paul Blackburn Papers, UCSD.
86. "Poems by Others," Philip Lamantia Papers, Carton 5, Folder 30, UCB.
87. Homero Aridjis, *Eyes to See Othwerise*, eds. Betty Ferber and George McWhirter (New York: New Directions, 2001): 2–3.
88. Philip Lamantia, "Crystals" and other poems (Mexico), some translated into Spanish (1957–1961). Philip Lamantia Papers, Carton 5 Folder 11, UCB.

89. Clayton Eshleman, "Coming to Meet: A Note on *The Plumed Horn*" (unpublished typescript, 1966), El Corno Emplumado Collection, HRC.

90. Margaret Randall, *To Change the World: My Years in Cuba* (New Brunswick: Rutgers University Press, 2009).

91. Margaret Randall in conversation with the author, May 14, 2015.

92. *El Corno Emplumado* 1 (1962): 5.

93. Margaret Randall, "Remembering *El Corno Emplumado*," *Open Door Archive* (Summer 2015), available at http://opendoor.northwestern.edu/archive/exhibits/ show/el-corno-emplumado-hemispheric (accessed Feb. 28, 2017).

94. Margaret Randall to James Merrill (Nov. 5, 1961). El Corno Emplumado Collection, HRC.

95. Bruce Connor, Untitled Assemblage, *El Corno Emplumado* 2 (1962). See also "Photos by Bruce Connor," (handwritten titles on matted prints). Philip Lamantia Collection, UCB.

96. Cecilia Vicuña in conversation with the author, June 2015.

97. *El Corno Emplumado* 5 (1963): 151.

98. Robert Bly to Margaret Randall (April 24, 1962). El Corno Emplumado Collection, HRC.

99. Octavio Paz, *Alternating Current*, tr. Helen Lane (New York: Viking Press, 1973): 33–34

100. Octavio Paz to Charles Tomlinson (May 4, 1969). Charles Tomlinson Papers, HRC.

101. Robert Kelly, "Enstasy: Poem for *El Corno Emplumado* at the Tenth Issue," *El Corno Emplumado* 13 (1965): 37.

102. Margaret Randall to the Bollingen Foundation (April 20, 1964). El Corno Emplumado Collection, HRC.

103. Rolando Peña to Margaret Randall and Sergio Mondragón (December 1964). El Corno Emplumado Collection, HRC.

104. Ernesto Cardenal, "Cartas," in *El Corno Emplumado* 5 (1963): 146.

105. Fox, *Making Art Panamerican*, 41–88.

106. Denise Levertov to Margaret Randall (n.d.). El Corno Emplumado Collection, HRC.

107. Miguel Grinberg, Letter of March 15, 1963, *El Corno Emplumado* 7 (1963): 173.

108. *El Corno Emplumado* 10 (1964): 6; 112–116.

109. Squirru to Blackburn (n.d.). Paul Blackburn Papers, UCSD.

110. Cortázar, *Cartas*, 485.

111. *El Corno Emplumado* 7 (1963): 5.

112. Jerome Rothenberg "Pre-Face," in Steven Clay and Rodney Philips, *A Secret Location on the Lower East Side: Adventures in Writing, 1960–1980* (New York: Granary, 1998): 8–12.

113. Blackburn to Randall (n.d.). El Corno Emplumado Collection, HRC.

114. Rafael Squirru, Letter of June 24, 1963, *El Corno Emplumado* 9 (1964): 144.

115. See Margaret Randall, *Cuban Women Now* (Toronto: The Women's Press, 1974).

116. González Echevarría argues that Lorca's death inspired a unified collective anger among a global confederation of poets, turning the poetry of the Spanish Civil War into a theater of committed action poetry written—in terms borrowed from Auden—by "young poets exploding like bombs." Roberto González Echevarría,

"Prólogo," in Pablo Neruda y Nancy Cunard, *Los poetas del mundo defienden al pueblo español* (Seville: Renacimiento, 2002): 14–15.

117. César Caballero, *Javier Heraud y las voces panegíricas* (Ancash, Peru: Huarí, 1964).

118. Javier Heraud, *El Río* (Lima: Cuadernos del Hontanar, 1960).

119. Paul Blackburn, *Proensa: An Anthology of Troubadour Poetry*, ed. George Economou (Berkeley: University of California Press, 1978).

120. Edward Dorn and Gordon Brotherston, *Our Word: Guerilla Poems from Latin America* (London: Cape Goliard, 1968): n.p.

121. Otto Rene Castillo, *Let's Go!*, tr. Margaret Randall (London: Cape Goliard, 1971): n.p.

122. Dorn and Brotherston, *Our Word*, n.p.

123. Dorn and Brotherston, *Our Word*, n.p.

124. Dorn and Brotherston, *Our Word*, n.p.

125. Che Guevara, *La guerra de guerrillas* (Havana: Departamento de instrucción del MINFAR, 1960); Regis Debray, *Revolution in the Revolution?* (New York: Monthly Review Press, 1968).

126. Caballero, *Javier Heraud*, 45–56.

127. Caballero, *Javier Heraud*, 45–56.

128. "Biography of a Lost Poet," *Time* (May 31, 1963).

129. Clayton Eshleman, *On Mules Sent from Chavin* (Swansea: Galloping Dog Press, 1977): 7.

130. Eshleman to Randall (Sept. 12, 1962). El Corno Emplumado Collection, HRC.

131. Clayton Eshleman, "The Book of Yorunomado," *Poetry* 106.4 (1965): 257–269.

132. Clayton Eshleman in conversation with the author, June 25, 2015.

133. Clayton Eshleman, "Explorations in the Apolitical," *The Nation* (Sept. 26, 1966): 285.

134. Clayton Eshleman in conversation with the author, June 25, 2015.

135. Castillo, *Let's Go!*, n.p.

136. Eshleman, "Explorations in the Apolitical," 286.

137. Clayton Eshleman, *Walks* (New York: Caterpillar Books, 1967): 5.

138. Clayton Eshleman, *Hotel Cro-Magnon* (Santa Barbara: Black Sparrow Press, 1989): 92.

139. Washington Delgado, "The Death of Javier Heraud," tr. Clayton Eshleman, MS. Clayton Eshleman Papers, UCSD.

140. Eshleman, "Explorations in the Apolitical," 287.

141. Clayton Eshleman, Paul Blackburn, Theodore Enslin, and Cid Corman, *Poetas norteamericanos* (Cuzco: Edicones Sunda, 1966).

142. For rich and conflictual accounts, see Eshleman, *On Mules*, 7–20; Eshleman to Ahern, Clayton Eshleman Papers, UCSD; and Georgette de Vallejo, "Sobre la 'traducción' al inglés de Poemas Humanos," *Homenaje Internacional a César Vallejo*, eds. Washington Delgado and Carlos Milla Batres (Lima: Visión del Peru, 1969): 326–330.

143. Eshleman, *Walks*, 15. For more on Kinsey's work with the museum, see Rafael Larco Hoyle, *Checan: Essay on Erotic Elements in Peruvian Art* (Geneva: Nagel, 1965), 71.

144. Eshleman, *Walks*, 15.

145. Eshleman, *Walks*, 46.

146. Williams, *Collected Poems* Vol. II, 358.

147. Elizabeth Bishop to Robert Lowell, in *Words in Air: The Complete Correspondence Between Elizabeth Bishop and Robert Lowell*, eds. Thomas Travisano with Saskia Hamilton (New York: Farrar Straus and Giroux, 2008): 406.

148. Robert Bly, "A Wrong Turning in American Poetry," in *American Poetry: Wildness and Domesticity* (New York: Harper & Row, 1990): 7.

149. Bly, "A Wrong Turning," 8.

150. Marjorie Perloff, "Pound/Stevens: Whose Era?" *New Literary History* 13.3 (1982): 485–514.

151. Bly, "A Wrong Turning," 14.

152. Cohn gives the best account of Neruda's appearance in New York, though her focus is especially on his relation to PEN, and to Latin American writers such as Fuentes and Vargas Llosa. My discussion of Neruda's relations with US poets complements her account. See Cohn, *The Latin American Literary Boom*, 65–94.

153. Belitt to Neruda (June 1, 1966), FPN.

154. Belitt to Neruda (May 11, 1966), FPN.

155. Clayton Eshleman in conversation with the author, June 25, 2015.

156. Ginsberg to Creeley (1959). Robert Creeley Papers, SUL.

157. James Laughlin to Angel Flores (1955). Angel Flores Papers, HRC.

158. Alegría to Neruda (April 20, 1959), FPN; Neruda to Alegría (April 28, 1959), FPN.

159. Rothenberg to Neruda (June 3, 1959), FPN.

160. Eshleman to Neruda (September 1959), FPN.

161. For a cheerier portrait of Belitt's hemispherism, see Loren Glass, *Counterculture Colophon: Grove Press, the* Evergreen Review, *and the Incorporation of the Avant-Garde* (Stanford: Stanford University Press, 2013): 58–61.

162. Richard Seaver to Clayton Eshleman (Dec. 7, 1961). Clayton Eshleman Papers, UCSD; Eshleman to Neruda, (Feb. 2, 1962), FPN.

163. W.S. Merwin to Pablo Neruda (August 1962), FPN.

164. Clayton Eshleman, "Clinkers and Causes," *The Nation* (Sept. 15, 1962).

165. Eshleman to Neruda (Sept. 9, 1962), FPN.

166. Eshleman to Neruda (Sept. 9, 1962), FPN.

167. Pablo Neruda, *Obras Completas* I (Barcelona: Galaxia Gútenberg, 1999): 285.

168. Pablo Neruda, *Selected Poems*, tr. Ben Belitt, 65.

169. Clayton Eshleman, "Lone Gentleman," as read at the Poetry Center (June 11, 1966), in "Pablo Neruda's First Reading in the U.S.," available at https://soundcloud.com/92y/pablo-neruda-1966 (accessed Feb. 28, 2017).

170. Nathaniel Tarn to Pablo Neruda (Oct. 3, 1965). Nathaniel Tarn Papers, SUL.

171. Belitt to Neruda (n.d. [1966]), FPN.

172. José Yglesias, "Pablo Neruda: The Poet in New York," *The Nation* (July 11, 1966): 54.

173. "LBJ's Foreign Policy Successes," *Life Magazine* (June 24, 1966).

174. Blackburn to Creeley (Oct. 24, 1960). Robert Creeley Papers, SUL.

175. Archibald MacLeish, "Introduction by Mr. MacLeish," The Poetry Center (June 11, 1966). Unpublished transcription. FPN.

176. Elena Poniatowska, "Pablo Neruda en Mexico," *Siempre* (July 13, 1966).

177. "Carta abierta a Pablo Neruda," *Punto Final* 10 (1966): 20–22, also *Casa de las Américas* 38 (1966): 131–135.

178. "Responde Neruda," *Punto Final* 10 (1966): 23.

179. Michael Wood, "The Poetry of Neruda," *New York Review of Books* (Oct. 3, 1974).

180. Neruda, *Obras Completas*, 308.

181. Shaw, *O'Hara*, 4–5.

182. Frank O'Hara, *Lunch Poems* (San Francisco: City Lights, 1964): 17.

183. O'Hara, *Lunch Poems*, 15–16.

184. Similarly, Davidson brilliantly critiques the "un-naming" of African and African-American artists in "The Day Lady Died." See Davidson, *Guys Like Us: Citing Masculinity in Cold War Poetics* (Chicago: University of Chicago Press, 2004): 124–126.

185. Paul Blackburn, *The Collected Poems of Paul Blackburn*, ed. Edith Jarolim (New York: Persea, 1985): 127.

186. Blackburn, *Collected Poems*, 128.

187. Corso, *Gasoline*, 26.

188. Frank Lima, *Incidents of Travel in Poetry*, eds. Garrett Caples and Julien Poirier (San Francisco: City Lights, 2015): 9. Caples's introduction contains the most significant portrait of Lima to date.

189. Urayoán Noel's key reading of Lima locates him at a cautious distance from easy identifications with either Nuyorican poetry or the New York School, finding in him a "politics of experience." Noel describes the young Lima as a "cataloger of experiences both transcendent and mundane," whereas I would emphasize his twinned experiences of pyschosexual and social disgust. See Noel, *In Visible Movement*, 5–7.

190. Mario Benedetti, *Poemas del hoyporhoy* (Montevideo: Alfa, 1961); also "Cumpleaños en Manhattan," *El Corno Emplumado* 3 (1962): 112–119.

191. Alcides Iznaga, "Estamos solos en Manhattan," in *La roca y la espuma: Poemas* (Havana: Editora Universitaria, Universidad Central de las Villas, 1965): 197–200.

192. Iznaga, "Estamos solos en Manhattan," 199.

193. Mark Weiss (ed.), *The Whole Island: Six Decades of Cuban Poetry* (Berkeley: University of California Press, 2009): 51.

194. Bruce King, *Derek Walcott: A Caribbean Life* (Oxford: Oxford University Press, 2004): 151.

195. Derek Walcott, *Collected Poems, 1948–1984* (New York: Farrar, Straus & Giroux): 79.

196. Derek Walcott, "Young Trinidadian Poets," *Sunday Guardian* (June 19, 1966), quoted in Gordon Collier, *Derek Walcott, The Journeyman Years* (Amsterdam: Rodopi, 2013): 207.

Chapter 5

1. Thomas Travisano with Saskia Hamilton (eds.), *Words in Air: The Complete Correspondence Between Elizabeth Bishop and Robert Lowell* (New York: Farrar, Straus and Giroux, 2008): ii.

2. Derek Walcott, *What the Twilight Says* (New York: Farrar, Straus and Giroux, 1998): 92.

3. Saunders, *The Cultural Cold War*, 357.

4. Arthur M. Schlesinger, *The Vital Center: The Politics of Freedom* (Boston: Houghton Mifflin, 1949): 56.

5. Foley argues that the "legacy of anti-Communism," taking "different forms over . . . five decades," reshaped 1930s radical discourses. Kohlmann and Taunton call anti-communism "one of the twentieth century's most influential and under-theorised political orientations," linking the disparity between its influence and its under-theorization to its gathering of aesthetically diverse writers from divergent political coordinates. Due to anticommunism's protean program, it sustained a "creative and artistic potential" influencing "literary agendas at a thematic and at a formal level." See Barbara Foley, *Radical Representations: Politics and Form in U.S. Proletarian Fiction, 1929–1941* (Durham: Duke University Press, 1993): 7; Benjamin Kohlmann and Matthew Taunton, "Introduction: Literatures of Anti-Communism," *Literature & History* 24.1 (2015): 5–10.

6. Aside from Franco's important study, few inquiries into literary anticommunism relate to the poetry of the Americas. Nelson stresses how Cold War anticommunism excluded 1930s traditions of committed and experimental verse; Filreis shows how anti-modernist, right-wing literary critics bolstered a wave of quietist academic poetry; Rubin argues that Third World resistance discourses were muffled as a broad-gauged "communist menace." See Franco, *Decline and Fall*; Nelson, *Repression and Recovery*; Alan Filreis, *Counter-Revolution of the Word: The Conservative Attack on Modern Poetry, 1945–1960* (Chapel Hill: University of North Carolina Press, 2008); Rubin, *Archives of Authority*, 34.

7. See John Palattella, "'That Sense of Constant Re-Adjustment': The Great Depression and the Provisional Politics of Elizabeth Bishop's 'North & South,'" *Contemporary Literature* 34.1 (1993): 18–43; James Longenbach, "Elizabeth Bishop's Social Conscience," *ELH* 62 (1995), 467–486; Betsy Erkkilä, "Elizabeth Bishop, Modernism, and the Left," *American Literary History* 8.2 (1996): 284–310; and John Lowney, *History, Memory and the Literary Left: Modern American Poetry, 1935–1968* (Iowa City: University of Iowa Press, 2006): 67–98.

8. Adrienne Rich, "The Eye of the Outsider: The Poetry of Elizabeth Bishop," *Boston Review* 8 (1983): 15–17; Randall Jarrell, "The Poet and His Public," *Partisan Review* 13.4 (1946): 488–500.

9. Camille Roman, *Elizabeth Bishop's World War II–Cold War View* (New York: Palgrave, 2001).

10. Saunders, *The Cultural Cold War*, 13.

11. Caetano Veloso, *Tropical Truth: A Story of Music and Revolution in Brazil*, tr. Barbara Einzig (New York: Knopf, 2002): 6.

12. See, for example, Ramazani's "Traveling Poetry" in *A Transnational Poetics*, 66–68; Jacqueline Vaught Brogan and Cordelia Candelaria, *Women Poets of the Americas: Toward a Pan-American Gathering* (South Bend: Notre Dame University Press, 1999): 176.

13. Robert von Hallberg, *American Poetry and Culture, 1945–1980* (Cambridge: Harvard University Press, 1985): 68–70.

14. Elizabeth Bishop, *One Art: The Selected Letters* (New York: Random House, 1994): 384. Poetic assimilation of Brazilian norms also marks *Questions of Travel*'s dedication to Lota and Camões epigraph: "*O dar-vos quanto tenho e quanto posso/ Que quanto mais vos pago, mais vos devo.*"

15. Just before this book went into production, Hicok published the most comprehensive discussion to date of Bishop's years in Brazil. While continuing to emphasize tropes of travel, translation, and outsiderhood, Hicok attends keenly to class relations in her chapter "Samambaia and the Architecture of Class," where she reads poems including "Squatter's Children" and "Manuelzinho" as fine-tuned, realist class observations amid a larger orbit of writing on Brazilian architecture. In "Bishop's Brazilian Politics," she further takes up Bishop's views on Lacerda, national politics, and the founding of Brasilia. Whereas Hicok exculpates Bishop by locating her at a critical remove from the anticommunism and class politics of Lota and Carlos Lacerda, I argue that her poems are active and expressive agents of a politics she shares with them. See Bethany Hicok, *Elizabeth Bishop's Brazil* (Charlottesville: University of Virginia Press, 2016): 26–31; 64–97.

16. Michel Foucault, *Power/Knowledge: Selected Interviews and Other Writings, 1972–1977*, ed. Colin Gordon (New York: Vintage, 1980): 194.

17. Bishop to Lowell (June 15, 1961), in *Words in Air*, 362.

18. John Dos Passos, *Brazil on the Move* (New York: Doubleday, 1963): 139; Elizabeth Bishop to Morton Dauwen Zabel. Morton Dauwen Zabel Papers, Box 2, Folder 45, NLC; Elizabeth Bishop and the Editors of Life, *Life World Library: Brazil* (New York: Time Inc., 1962): 139.

19. Caroline Elkins, *Imperial Reckoning: The Untold Story of Britain's Gulag in Kenya* (New York: Henry Holt, 2005): 25–28.

20. Derek Walcott, *In A Green Night* (London: J. Cape, 1962): 18.

21. Derek Walcott, "Guggenheim Reading Introduction," 1964, Robert Lowell Papers (MS Am 1905). HU.

22. Elizabeth Bishop, *Questions of Travel* (New York: Farrar, Straus and Giroux, 1965): 35.

23. Jay Prosser, *Light in the Dark Room: Photography and Loss* (Minneapolis: University of Minnesota Press, 2005).

24. Bishop, *Questions of Travel*, 11.

25. Susan Stewart, "Rhyme and Freedom," in Marjorie Perloff and Craig Dworkin (eds.), *The Sound of Poetry/The Poetry of Sound* (Chicago: University of Chicago Press, 2009): 30.

26. Bishop, *Questions of Travel*, 11.

27. Millier, *Elizabeth Bishop*, 271.

28. Bishop, *One Art*, 315.

29. Bishop, *Questions of Travel*, 13.

30. Bishop to Lowell (June 15, 1961), in *Words in Air*, 362.

31. Jean-Paul Sartre, *What is Literature?* (New York: Philosophical Library, 1949): 19–21.

32. Morton Zabel to Elizabeth Bishop (Feb. 2, 1962). Morton Dauwen Zabel Papers, Box 2, Folder 45, NLC.

33. Elizabeth Bishop to Morton Zabel (Jan. 24, 1962). Morton Dauwen Zabel Papers, Box 2, Folder 45, NLC.

34. Keith Botsford to Elizabeth Bishop (April 7, 1962). Keith Botsford Papers, Box 10, YALE.

35. Bishop, *Brazil*, 140.

36. Bishop, *Brazil*, 142.

37. Stephen G. Rabe, *The Most Dangerous Area in the World: John F. Kennedy Confronts Communist Revolution in Latin America* (Chapel Hill: University of North Carolina Press, 1999): 170–171.

38. Bishop to Lowell (May 5, 1959), in *Words in Air*, 302.

39. Juan José Arévalo, *Anti-Kommunism in Latin America: An X-Ray of the Process Leading to a New Colonialism*, tr. Carleton Beals (New York: L. Stuart, 1963): 168.

40. See Harilaos Stecopoulos, *Telling America's Story to the World: Postwar Literature and Cultural Diplomacy* (forthcoming).

41. Arthur Schlesinger, Jr. *A Thousand Days: John F. Kennedy in the White House* (New York: Houghton Mifflin, 1965): 3 and 731.

42. Robert Lowell to Edmund Wilson (May 31, 1962), in *The Letters of Robert Lowell*, ed. Saskia Hamilton (New York: Macmillan, 2007): 409. See also Lowell to Bishop (May 15, 1962), in *Words in Air*, 416.

43. Robert Lowell, *Life Studies* (New York: Farrar, Straus & Giroux, 1959).

44. John McCormick, "The United Snopes Information Service," *Kenyon Review* 24 (1962): 330–350.

45. Bishop to Lowell (May 5, 1959), in *Words in Air*, 300.

46. Bishop to Lowell (Apr. 26, 1962), in *Words in Air*, 410.

47. Botsford to Lowell (March 14, 1962). Keith Botsford Papers, Box 10, YALE.

48. Botsford to Lowell (May 5, 1962). Keith Botsford Papers, Box 10, YALE.

49. Lowell to Botsford (April 23, 1962). Keith Botsford Papers, Box 10, YALE.

50. Botsford to Lowell (May 5, 1962). Keith Botsford Papers, Box 10, YALE.

51. Hardwick to Botsford (May 21, 1962). Keith Botsford Papers, Box 10, YALE.

52. Gilberto Freyre, "Misconceptions of Brazil," *Foreign Affairs* 40.3 (1962): 462.

53. Gilberto Freyre, "Saudando um poeta," *Diário de Pernambuco* (July 1, 1962). Deposited in the Keith Botsford Papers, Box 10, YALE.

54. Saunders, *The Cultural Cold War*, 289–293; Patrick Iber, *Neither Peace Nor Freedom: The Cultural Cold War in Latin America* (Cambridge: Harvard University Press, 2015): 182.

55. Adolfo Bioy Casares, *Borges* (Buenos Aires: Destino, 2006): 808.

56. Ian Hamilton, *Robert Lowell*, 302.

57. Lowell to Alfred (September 1962). Keith Botsford Papers, Box 10, YALE.

58. Mariani, *Lost Puritan: A Life of Robert Lowell* (New York: Norton, 1996): 306–310.

59. Lowell to Botsford (n.d.). Keith Botsford Papers, Box 10, YALE.

60. Robert Lowell, *Collected Poems*, eds. Frank Bidart and David Gewanter (New York: Farrar, Straus and Giroux): 366.

61. Lowell, *Collected Poems*, 366.

62. Lowell, *Collected Poems*, 366.

63. Nicanor Parra, *Artefactos* (Santiago: Ediciones Nueva Universidad, 1972).

64. "I was overwhelmed by da Cunha, as good in its way as Melville." Lowell to Bishop (May 15, 1962), in *Words in Air*, 416.

65. Lowell, *Collected Poems*, 377.

66. Lowell, *Collected Poems*, 367.

67. Lowell, *Collected Poems*, 367.

68. Borges, "La Recoleta," in *Obra poética*, 19.

69. Lowell, *Collected Poems*, 367.

70. Saint-John Perse, *On Poetry: Speech of Acceptance Upon the Award of the Novel Prize for Literature* (Princeton, NJ: Bollingen Foundation, 1961): 12.

71. Lowell, *Collected Poems*, 368.

72. Robert Lowell, "Buenos Aires," *New York Review of Books* (Feb. 1, 1963).

73. Lowell, *Collected Poems*, 369.

74. Lowell to Botsford (Jan. 25, 1963). Keith Botsford Papers, Box 10, YALE.

75. Lowell, *Letters*, 371.

76. *The Old Glory* (New York: Farrar, Straus and Giroux, 1965): 119.

77. Patricia Ismond, *Abandoning Dead Metaphors: The Caribbean Phase of Derek Walcott's Poetry* (Mona: University of West Indies, 2001): 43.

78. Handley, *New World Poetics*, 279–317.

79. Walcott often memorialized Lowell's influence on him following Lowell's 1977 death. Terada's account of Walcott's strategies of influence and mimicry remains the best. Kalliney and Pollard describe the influence of Anglo-modernist poetics from the British metropole on other commonwealth poets such as Brathwaite. See Edward Hirsch, "The Art of Poetry No. 37: Derek Walcott," *Paris Review* 101 (1986): 196–230; Rei Terada, *Derek Walcott's Poetry: American Mimicry* (Boston: Northeastern University Press, 1992): 43–82; Pollard, *New World Modernisms*, 2–10; Kalliney, *Commonwealth of Letters*, 75–115.

80. Walcott, *What the Twilight Says*, 81 and 93.

81. Cary Fraser, *Ambivalent Anti-Colonialism: The United States and the Genesis of West Indian Independence, 1940–1964* (Westport: Greenwood Press, 1994).

82. Walcott also admired West Indian travel fiction with anticommunist overtones, particularly Jan Carew's *Moscow Is Not My Mecca* (London: Secker & Warburg, 1964) and V. S. Reid's *The Leopard* (London: Heinemann,1958).

83. Derek Walcott, "A Self-Interview Raises Questions of Identity: It's All One Gooey Pap," *Trinidad Guardian* (Oct. 16, 1966): 7; Derek Walcott, "The Ban," *Trinidad Guardian* (Oct. 25, 1967): 10. Qtd in Gordon Collier, *Derek Walcott, The Journeyman Years* (Amsterdam: Rodopi, 2013): 42, 81.

84. Breslin's otherwise excellent study pays little attention to *The Gulf*. See Paul Breslin, *Nobody's Nation: Reading Derek Walcott* (Chicago: University of Chicago Press, 2001), and Ismond, *Abandoning Dead Metaphors*, 43–139.

85. Lowell to Bishop (June 13, 1962), in *Words in Air*, 417.

86. Botsford to Lowell (May 26, 1962), Keith Botsford Papers, Box 10, YALE.

87. Derek Walcott, "Poet from the Land of the Bean and the Cod," Trinidad *Guardian* (June 10, 1962): 9. Qtd in Collier, 362–363. See also Hardwick to Botsford (June 1962). Keith Botsford Papers, Box 10, YALE.

88. Hardwick to Botsford (June 1962). Keith Botsford Papers, Box 10, YALE.

89. Walcott, *What the Twilight Said*, 80.

90. Hirsch, "The Art of Poetry No. 37: Derek Walcott," 196–230.

91. Hardwick to Botsford (Sept. 29, 1963). Keith Botsford Papers, Box 10, YALE.

92. Derek and Margaret Walcott to Robert Lowell and Elizabeth Hardwick (Oct. 28, 1963). Robert Lowell Papers (MS Am 1905), 1413, HU.

93. Derek and Margaret Walcott to Robert Lowell and Elizabeth Hardwick (Oct. 28, 1963). Robert Lowell Papers (MS Am 1905), 1413, HU.

94. Derek and Margaret Walcott to Robert Lowell and Elizabeth Hardwick (Oct. 28, 1963). Robert Lowell Papers (MS Am 1905), 1413, HU.

95. On the questionnaire, see King, *Derek Walcott*, 224–225.

96. Derek Walcott, *The Gulf* (New York: Farrar, Straus and Giroux, 1970): 12.

97. Derek Walcott, "Artists Need Some Assistance" *Sunday Guardian* (April 3, 1960): 7. Qtd in Collier, 61.

98. Derek Walcott, "Spreading Our Culture Abroad," *Sunday Guardian* (Nov. 8, 1964): 18. Qtd in Collier, 32.

99. Walcott, *The Gulf*, 12.

100. Roman Jakobson and Linda R. Waugh, *The Sound Shape of Language* (New York: Mouton de Gruyter, 2002): 181–191.

101. Walcott, *The Gulf*, 13.

102. Walcott, *The Gulf*, 13.

103. Walcott, *The Gulf*, 15.

104. Saunders, *The Cultural Cold War*, 357.

105. King, *A Caribbean Life*, 190.

106. Robert Lowell, "Robert Lowell Introduces Derek Walcott at the Solomon R. Guggenheim Museum, October 15, 1964." *Envoy* 46 (1985): 2–3.

107. Derek Walcott, "The Finest Thing Is Its Rhythm," *Trinidad Guardian* (Apr. 15, 1964): 5. Qtd in Collier, 523–524.

108. Walcott, "The Finest Thing Is Its Rhythm," *Trinidad Guardian* (Apr. 15, 1964): 5. Qtd in Collier, 523–524.

109. Derek Walcott, "Berlin: The ABC of Negritude," *Sunday Guardian* (Oct. 18, 1964): 11. Qtd in Collier, 52.

110. Walcott, "Berlin: The ABC of Negritude," *Sunday Guardian* (Oct. 18, 1964): 11. Qtd in Collier, 54.

111. Walcott, "Chapter of History Written in Guyana," *Trinidad Guardian* (June 2, 1966): 5. Qtd in Collier, 40.

112. Walcott, "Chapter of History Written in Guyana," *Trinidad Guardian* (June 2, 1966): 5. Qtd in Collier, 41.

113. Walcott, *The Gulf*, 75.

114. Walcott, *The Gulf*, 27.

115. Walcott, *The Gulf*, 5.

116. On Harrison, see August Frugé, *A Skeptic Among Scholars: August Frugé on University Publishing* (Berkeley: University of California Press, 1993): 110–123; John Watson Foster Dulles, "Focus on the Forty Acres," *Alcalde* 51.2 (1962): 18–19.

117. Walcott, *The Gulf*, 58–59.

118. Walcott, *The Gulf*, 58.
119. Walcott, *The Gulf*, 106.
120. Elizabeth Hardwick, "Grub Street: New York," *New York Review of Books* (Feb. 1, 1963).
121. Based on his interest in Thomas Wolfe later in the passage, the portrait is likely of poet and literature professor Cassiano Nunes Botica. See *Latin American Language and Area Program Newsletter* 1–4 (University of Florida, 1963): 9 and Luiz Carlos Guimarães da Costa, *História da literature brasiliense* (Brasilia: Thesaurus, 2005): 340–346.
122. Lowell, "Robert Lowell Introduces Derek Walcott," 2–3.
123. Walcott, *The Gulf*, 46.
124. Margaret Randall, *Che on My Mind* (Durham: Duke University Press, 2013): 1.
125. Walcott, *The Gulf*, 63.
126. Derek Walcott, "Crossroads of Sensibility," *Sunday Guardian* (Jan. 1, 1967): 8–9. Qtd in Collier, 136.
127. Walcott, *The Gulf*, 39.
128. Walcott, *The Gulf*, 40.
129. Derek Walcott, "Some Jamaican Poets–2," *Public Opinion* (Aug. 10, 1957): 7. Qtd in Collier, 191.
130. Derek Walcott, "Too Much of the Wrong Subject," *Sunday Guardian* (June 14, 1964): 6. Qtd in Collier, 200.
131. Rabe, *U.S. Intervention in British Guiana: A Cold War Story* (Chapel Hill: University of North Carolina Press, 2005): 76.
132. Rabe, *Intervention in British Guiana*, 115.
133. Derek Walcott, "Art in Guyana: Beware of Love Vines: Derek Walcott Takes a Look at the World's Newest Nation," *Sunday Guardian* (May 29, 1966): 9. Qtd in Collier, 37–39.
134. Heberto Padilla, "Se puede ser poeta en Cuba: Intervención de Heberto Padilla en la U.N.E.A.C.," in *Poesia y politica: Poemas escogidos de Heberto Padilla* (Georgetown: Georgetown University, 1974): 125–126.
135. Padilla, "Se puede," 110; 126–127.
136. Heberto Padilla, *Self-Portrait of the Other: A Memoir*, tr. Alexander Coleman (New York: Farrar, Straus and Giroux, 1990): 79.
137. Lillian Guerra, *Visions of Power in Cuba: Revolution, Redemption, and Resistance, 1959–1971* (Chapel Hill: University of North Carolina Press, 2014): 2–3; also 353.
138. See José Yglesias, "The Case of Heberto Padilla," *New York Review of Books* (July 3, 1971); Claudia Gilman, *Entre la pluma y el fusil*; and Jorge Fornet, *El 71*.
139. Clare Cavanagh, *Lyric Poetry and Modern Politics: Russia, Poland, and the West* (New Haven: Yale University Press, 2010).
140. Guillermo Cabrera Infante, "La confundida lengua del poeta," *Primera Plana* 316 (Jan. 14, 1969): 64.
141. Robert Lowell, *Collected Poems*, 189.
142. Rafael Rojas, *Fighting Over Fidel*, 15. See also Alan Wald, *The New York Intellectuals: The Rise and Decline of the Anti-Stalinist Left from the 1930s to the 1980s* (Chapel Hill: University of North Carolina Press, 1987): 267–311.

143. Heberto Padilla and Carlos Verdecia, *La mala memoria* (Argentina: Kosmos, 1992): 32–33.
144. James J. Wilhelm, *Ezra Pound: The Tragic Years, 1925–1972* (State College: Penn State University Press, 1994).
145. Padilla, *Self-Portrait*, 9.
146. Heberto Padilla, "Habla Waldo Frank," *Lunes de Revolución* 30 (Oct. 12, 1959): 3–4.
147. Heberto Padilla, "La poesía en su lugar," *Lunes de Revolución* 38 (Dec. 7, 1959): 5–6.
148. Padilla, "La poesía en su lugar," 6. Lezama remained generous to Padilla, who later expressed affection for Lezama's intellectual commitment and humane support of younger writers amid Cuba's treacherous literary institutional politics. See Padilla, *Self-Portrait*, 167–171.
149. Virgilio Piñera, "Cada cosa en su lugar," *Lunes de Revolución* 39 (Dec. 14, 1959): 11.
150. Padilla, *Fuera del Juego*, 23.
151. Padilla, *Fuera del Juego*, 29.
152. Padilla, "Un dia de reafirmación revolucionaria," *Lunes de Revolución* 89 (Jan. 4, 1961): 31; Padilla, "3 Experiencias de Ernesto Fernandez," *Lunes de Revolución* 104–105 (1961): 12; Padilla, "Así combatió la Marina de Guerra Revolucionaria," *Lunes de Revolución* 106 (May 16, 1961): 10–14.
153. Heberto Padilla, *El justo tiempo humano* (Havana: UNEAC, 1962): 121. On the tradition of civilian war poetry Padilla draws on here, see Rachel Galvin, *News of War: Civilian Poetry, 1936–1945* (New York: Oxford University Press, 2017).
154. Roberto Fernández Retamar, "El otro," in *En su lugar, la poesía* (La Habana: Librería La Tertulia, 1961); Randall Jarrell, "The Survivor among Graves," in *Selected Poems* (New York: Knopf, 1955): 199.
155. Roque Dalton, "El justo tiempo humano," *Casa de las Américas*, 2.13–14 (1962): 58.
156. Virgilio Piñera, "Apuntes sobre la poesía de Heberto Padilla," *La Gaceta de Cuba* 1.6–7 (1962): 14.
157. Carlos Franqui, *Family Portrait with Fidel* (New York: Random House, 1984): 129–130.
158. See Rebecca Gordon-Nesbitt, "*PM* and Its Aftermath (May–June 1961)," in *To Defend the Revolution Is to Defend Culture: The Cultural Policy of the Cuban Revolution* (Chicago: PM Press, 2015).
159. Padilla, *Self-Portrait*, 52–55.
160. Padilla, *Self-Portrait*, 123.
161. Irving Louis Horowitz, "The Political Sociology of Cuban Communism," in *Revolutionary Change in Cuba*, ed. Carmelo Mesa-Lago (Pittsburgh: University of Pittsburgh Press, 1972): 127–129. For a welcome and spirited corrective that outlines the Tricontinental's links to contemporary discourses of the Global South, see Anne Garland Mahler, "The Global South in the Belly of the Beast: Viewing African American Civil Rights through a Tricontinental Lens," *Latin American Research Review* 50.1 (2015): 95–116.
162. Heberto Padilla, "Foreword," tr. Sylvia Carranza, in *Cuban Poetry 1959–1966* (Havana: Book Institute, 1967): 1–2.
163. Padilla, *Self-Portrait*, 130.
164. Padilla, *Fuera del Juego*, 85.

165. Padilla, *La mala memoria*, 68.
166. Heberto Padilla, "En tiempos difíciles," *Casa de las Américas* 7.42 (1967): 114.
167. Padilla, *Fuera del Juego*, 6.
168. Padilla, *Fuera del Juego*, 89.
169. Padilla, *Self-Portrait*, 157–158.
170. Padilla, *Fuera del juego*, 109.
171. Padilla, *Sent off the Field: A Selection from the Poetry of Heberto Padilla* (London: Deutsch, 1972): 102.
172. Pablo Neruda et al., "'Lunes' conversa con Pablo Neruda" *Lunes de Revolución* 88 (Dec. 26, 1960): 38–43.
173. Padilla, *Fuera del Juego*, 8.
174. Padilla, *Fuera del Juego*, 14.
175. Padilla, *Fuera del Juego*, 88–89.
176. Ávila was either Lieutenant Luis Pavón Tamayo or Marxist literary critic José Antonio Portuondo, or perhaps Félix Pita Rodríguez.
177. Leopoldo Ávila, "Las Respuestas de Caín," *Verde Olivo* 9.44 (Nov. 3, 1968): 17–18.
178. Leopoldo Ávila, "Las provocaciones de Padilla," *Verde Olivo* 9.45 (Nov. 10, 1968): 17–18.
179. Heberto Padilla, "Two Poems by Heberto Padilla," tr. Paul Blackburn, *New York Review of Books* (June 3, 1971).
180. Padilla, "Two Poems by Heberto Padilla."
181. Padilla, *Self-Portrait*, 181.
182. Octavio Paz, "Las 'confesiones' de Heberto Padilla," in *Obras completas*, Vol. 9 (Mexico City: Fondo de Cultura Economica, 1993): 171–172.
183. Julio Cortázar, "Policrítica en la hora de los chacales," *Casa de las Américas* 67 (1971): 157–161.
184. Padilla, *Self-Portrait*, 211.
185. Guerra, *Visions of Power*, 22.
186. Bishop, *Questions of Travel*, 86.
187. Lowell, *Collected Poems*, 378.
188. Walcott, *The Gulf*, 39.
189. Walcott, *The Gulf*, 37.
190. Derek Walcott, "Down by the Old Gas Pump," *Trinidad Guardian* (May 12, 1965): 5. Qtd in Collier, 33.
191. Derek Walcott, "March 31 Deadline for BP's Novel Competition," *Trinidad Guardian* (Jan. 20, 1964): 3. Qtd in Collier, 60.
192. Padilla, *Fuera del juego*, 48.
193. Padilla, *Sent off the Field*, 57.

Chapter 6

1. Octavio Paz, *The Siren and the Seashell and Other Essays on Poets and Poetry*, tr. Lysander Kemp and Margaret Sayers Peden (Austin: University of Texas Press, 1976): 173.
2. Octavio Paz, Jacques Roubaud, Edoardo Sanguineti, and Charles Tomlinson, *Renga: A Chain of Poems* (New York: George Braziller, 1972): 24.

3. Donald Davie, *Trying to Explain* (Ann Arbor: University of Michigan Press, 1979): 49.

4. Ted Hughes, *Poetry International 1967* (London: Poetry Book Society, 1967).

5. T. S. Eliot, *Selected Prose of T. S. Eliot*, ed. Frank Kermode (New York: Houghton Mifflin Harcourt, 1975): 111.

6. "Alfred Läutner" appears to be a pseudonym, possibly the "grotesque in-joke" of Charles Osborne, who offered funds to Poetry International in his role as Literature Director of the Arts Council of Great Britain. See Alfred Läutner, "The Nine Lives of *Poetry International*," *The New Review* 1.5 (1974): 35–42 and John Stathatos, "Round the Moulting Mulberry Bush," *Oasis* 12 (1974): 73.

7. Donald Davie, "The Translatability of Poetry," *Listener* (December 28, 1967).

8. Nathaniel Tarn, "The World Wide Open: The Work Laid Out Before Us in This Disunited Kingdom," *International Times* (June 28–July 11, 1968): 34.

9. Lawrence Ferlinghetti, *Starting Out from San Francisco*, 2nd ed. (New York: New Directions, 1967): 64.

10. Tom Raworth to Margaret Randall (June 15, 1965), El Corno Emplumado Collection, HRC.

11. Allen Ginsberg to Pablo Neruda (June 5, 1965), FPN.

12. Peter Whitehead, *Wholly Communion* (New York: Grove Press, 1965): 7. Also, *Peter Whitehead and the Sixties* (London: British Film Institute, 2007), DVD.

13. Octavio Paz to Charles Tomlinson (Nov. 24, 1966). Charles Tomlinson Collection, HRC.

14. Creeley recalled that of all the poets at Poetry International, only "Kavanagh and Ungaretti" impressed Charles Olson for their "simple, wondrous music" amid "the usual welter of professional and/or political maneuvering." Patrick Kavanagh, ed., *Patrick Kavanagh: Man and Poet* (Orono, ME: National Poetry Foundation, 1986). Quoted in Robert Creeley, *Collected Essays* (Berkeley: University of California Press, 1989): 350.

15. Christopher Lasch, "The Cultural Cold War," *The Nation* (Sept. 11, 1967).

16. Lasch traces this view to the late 1930s *Partisan Review*, while identifying the mass "defection" with the immediate postwar period. Christopher Lasch, *The Agony of the American Left* (New York: Random House, 1969): viii.

17. Pheng Cheah and Bruce Robbins, *Cosmopolitics: Thinking and Feeling Beyond the Nation* (Minneapolis: University of Minnesota Press, 1998): 24.

18. Bruce Robbins, *Perpetual War: Cosmopolitanism from the Viewpoint of Violence* (Durham: Duke University Press, 2012): 10.

19. Malcolm Cowley, "The Cultural Cold War: Comments," *The Nation* (Oct. 9, 1967): 341.

20. Jameson, *A Singular Modernity*, 168.

21. See, for example, Ernest Fenollosa, *The Chinese Character as a Medium for Poetry: A Critical Edition*, eds. Haun Saussy, Jonathan Stalling, and Lucas Klein (New York: Fordham University Press, 2008); Jonathan Mayhew, *Apocryphal Lorca: Translation, Parody, Kitsch* (Chicago: University of Chicago Press, 2009); and Ramazani, *A Transnational Poetics*.

22. Odd Arne Westad, *The Global Cold War: Third World Interventions and the Making of Our Times* (Cambridge: Cambridge University Press, 2005).

23. Rebecca Walkowitz, *Cosmopolitan Style: Modernism Beyond the Nation* (New York: Columbia University Press, 2006).

24. Paz to Tomlinson (July 12, 1966). Charles Tomlinson Papers, HRC.

25. Aside from *Renga*, the Paz-Tomlinson friendship established an anti-nativist mythography that buttressed both poets' careers, yielding translations and a collaborative sonnet sequence entitled *Airborn/Hijos del aire* (1981).

26. Tom Lewis, "Renga," *Books Abroad* 46.4 (1972): 636.

27. On the resultant literature about the massacre, see Diana Sorensen, *A Turbulent Decade Remembered: Scenes from the Latin American Sixties* (Stanford: Stanford University Press, 2007): 54–77.

28. Paz to Tomlinson (Oct. 6, 1968), Charles Tomlinson Papers, HRC.

29. Octavio Paz, *The Other Mexico: Critique of the Pyramid*, tr. Lysander Kemp (New York: Grove Press, 1972): 4.

30. Paz to Tomlinson (Oct. 6, 1968). Charles Tomlinson Papers, HRC.

31. Paz to Tomlinson (Feb. 11, 1969). Charles Tomlinson Papers, HRC.

32. Paz to Tomlinson (Feb. 11, 1969). Charles Tomlinson Papers, HRC.

33. Paz et al., *Renga*, 22.

34. Thomas O. Beebee, *The Ideology of Genre: A Comparative Study of Generic Instability* (State College: Pennsylvania State University Press, 1994): 113.

35. Octavio Paz, *The Collected Poems of Octavio Paz: 1957–1987*, ed. Eliot Weinberger (New York: New Directions, 1987): 238.

36. See William Marx (ed.), *Les arrière-gardes au xxᵉ siècle* (Paris: Presses Universitaires de France, 2004).

37. Eliot Weinberger, "Paz in Asia," in *Outside Stories* (New York: New Directions, 1992): 17–45.

38. Paz et al., *Renga*, 11.

39. Kwame Anthony Appiah, *The Ethics of Identity* (Princeton: Princeton University Press, 2005): 213.

40. Paz et al., *Renga*, 35.

41. Paz et al., *Renga*, 94.

42. Paz et al., *Renga*, 80.

43. Paz et al., *Renga*, 24.

44. See also Timothy Clark, "*Renga*: Multi-Lingual Poetry and Questions of Place," *Substances* 21.2.68 (1992): 32–45.

45. See Brotherston, *The Book of the Fourth World*.

46. Olson describes Pound's "beautiful" assumption that history is full of "intelligent men whom he can outtalk." Olson, *Selected Writing*, 82.

47. Marjorie Perloff, "Refiguring the Poundian Ideogram: From Blanco/Branco to the Galáxias." Paper presented at the Stanford University conference "Trans-Poetic Exchange: Around Blanco and 'Campos De Paz.'"

48. On masculinity, see Davidson, *Guys Like Us*.

49. Paz et al., *Renga*, 34.

50. Esperanza Ramirez-Christensen, *Emptiness and Temporality: Buddhism and Medieval Japanese Poetics* (Stanford: Stanford University Press, 2008): 26.

51. Giorgio Agamben, *The End of the Poem: Studies in Poetics* (Stanford: Stanford University Press, 1999): 109–118.

52. Paz et al., *Renga*, 18.

53. Ramirez-Christensen, *Emptiness and Temporality*, 11.

54. Franco, *The Decline and Fall of the Lettered City*, 21–56.

55. Paz et al., *Children of the Mire*, vi.

56. Founding editor Peter Matthiessen revealed in 2007 that the *Paris Review* was partly a cover for Matthiessen's work with the CIA, and as Whitney argues in a slightly sensationalist account, the cultural Cold War clearly haunted the journal's editorial program into the late 1960s. Harry Matthews (the only American associated with Roubaud's Oulipo cohort) captures this air of factitiousness in the novel *My Life in CIA* (Normal, IL: Dalkey Archive, 2005). An American writer in 1960s Paris must convince his milieu he is *not* CIA by posing as an agent. See Joel Whitney, *Finks: How the CIA Tricked the World's Best Writers* (OR Books, 2017). See also Greg Barnhisel, "Finks, Fronts, and Puppets: Revisiting the Cultural Cold War," *Los Angeles Review of Books* (Jan. 8, 2017).

57. The Summer 1969 issue leads off with soon-canonized poems by New American poets like Robert Creeley and John Ashbery (who contributed "Soonest Mended"), then moves to Keith Botsford's fictionalized version of his role in gestating state-sponsored anticommunist cultural diplomacy through his frenzied story "A Member of the Delegation," a portrait of committed writers at a Russian agency called "INTERCULTURE."

58. Bly, "A Wrong Turning," 7.

59. Mayhew, *Apocryphal Lorca*, 143–159. In addition, McHale reads the device nonallusively, as a quintessentially "postmodern" poetics of erasure. See Brian McHale, "Poetry under Erasure," in *Theory into Practice: New Approaches to Poetry*, eds. Eva Müller-Zettelman and Margarete Rubik (Amsterdam and New York: Peter Lang: 2007): 277–301.

60. Eugénio Lisboa with L. C. Taylor (eds.), *A Centenary Pessoa* (Manchester: Carcanet, 1995): 133.

61. Octavio Paz, "Intersecciones y Bifurcaciones: A. O. Barnabooth, Álvara de Campos, Alberto Caeiro," in *Obras Completas: Excursiones/Incursiones*, Vol. 8 (Barcelona: Círculo de Lectores, 1991): 170–188. See also Paz, "Poet Unknown to Himself," in *A Centenary Pessoa*, 1–20.

62. Santí, *Ciphers of History*.

63. Roque Dalton, *Clandestine Poems*, tr. Jack Hirschman (San Francisco: Solidarity Educational Publications, 1986).

64. Margaret Randall, "Roque Dalton: Myth, Man, Martyr, and Poet Who Defined an Era," *Malpais Review* 2.2 (2011): 87.

65. Roland Barthes, "The Death of the Author," *Aspen* 5–6 (1967); "La mort de l'auteur," *Mantéia* 5 (1968).

Index

Note: page numbers followed by "f" and "n" refer to figures and notes, respectively.